T0345079

Measuring and Modeling Health Care Costs

Studies in Income and Wealth
Volume 76

National Bureau of Economic Research
Conference on Research in Income and Wealth

Measuring and Modeling
Health Care Costs

Edited by **Ana Aizcorbe, Colin Baker,
Ernst R. Berndt, and David M. Cutler**

The University of Chicago Press

Chicago and London

The University of Chicago Press, Chicago 60637
The University of Chicago Press, Ltd., London
© 2018 by the National Bureau of Economic Research
Published 2018
Printed in the United States of America

27 26 25 24 23 22 21 20 19 18   1 2 3 4 5

ISBN-13: 978-0-226-53085-7 (cloth)
ISBN-13: 978-0-226-53099-4 (e-book)
DOI: https://doi.org/10.7208/chicago/9780226530994.001.0001

Library of Congress Cataloging-in-Publication Data

Names: Aizcorbe, Ana, editor. | Baker, Colin (Colin Sean), editor. |
    Berndt, Ernst R., editor. | Cutler, David M., editor.
Title: Measuring and modeling health care costs / edited by Ana
    Aizcorbe, Colin Baker, Ernst R. Berndt, and David M. Cutler.
Other titles: Studies in income and wealth ; v. 76.
Description: Chicago ; London : The University of Chicago Press,
    2018. | Series: Studies in income and wealth ; volume 76 | Includes
    bibliographical references and index.
Identifiers: LCCN 2017023350 | ISBN 9780226530857 (cloth : alk.
    paper) | ISBN 9780226530994 (e-book)
Subjects: LCSH: Medical care, Cost of—United States—
    Measurement. | Medical care—United States—Cost control.
Classification: LCC RA410.53 .M387 2018 | DDC
    338.4/336210973—dc23
LC record available at https://lccn.loc.gov/2017023350

Relation of the Directors to the
Work and Publications of the
National Bureau of Economic Research

1. The object of the NBER is to ascertain and present to the economics profession, and to the public more generally, important economic facts and their interpretation in a scientific manner without policy recommendations. The Board of Directors is charged with the responsibility of ensuring that the work of the NBER is carried on in strict conformity with this object.

2. The President shall establish an internal review process to ensure that book manuscripts proposed for publication DO NOT contain policy recommendations. This shall apply both to the proceedings of conferences and to manuscripts by a single author or by one or more co-authors but shall not apply to authors of comments at NBER conferences who are not NBER affiliates.

3. No book manuscript reporting research shall be published by the NBER until the President has sent to each member of the Board a notice that a manuscript is recommended for publication and that in the President's opinion it is suitable for publication in accordance with the above principles of the NBER. Such notification will include a table of contents and an abstract or summary of the manuscript's content, a list of contributors if applicable, and a response form for use by Directors who desire a copy of the manuscript for review. Each manuscript shall contain a summary drawing attention to the nature and treatment of the problem studied and the main conclusions reached.

4. No volume shall be published until forty-five days have elapsed from the above notification of intention to publish it. During this period a copy shall be sent to any Director requesting it, and if any Director objects to publication on the grounds that the manuscript contains policy recommendations, the objection will be presented to the author(s) or editor(s). In case of dispute, all members of the Board shall be notified, and the President shall appoint an ad hoc committee of the Board to decide the matter; thirty days additional shall be granted for this purpose.

5. The President shall present annually to the Board a report describing the internal manuscript review process, any objections made by Directors before publication or by anyone after publication, any disputes about such matters, and how they were handled.

6. Publications of the NBER issued for informational purposes concerning the work of the Bureau, or issued to inform the public of the activities at the Bureau, including but not limited to the NBER Digest and Reporter, shall be consistent with the object stated in paragraph 1. They shall contain a specific disclaimer noting that they have not passed through the review procedures required in this resolution. The Executive Committee of the Board is charged with the review of all such publications from time to time.

7. NBER working papers and manuscripts distributed on the Bureau's web site are not deemed to be publications for the purpose of this resolution, but they shall be consistent with the object stated in paragraph 1. Working papers shall contain a specific disclaimer noting that they have not passed through the review procedures required in this resolution. The NBER's web site shall contain a similar disclaimer. The President shall establish an internal review process to ensure that the working papers and the web site do not contain policy recommendations, and shall report annually to the Board on this process and any concerns raised in connection with it.

8. Unless otherwise determined by the Board or exempted by the terms of paragraphs 6 and 7, a copy of this resolution shall be printed in each NBER publication as described in paragraph 2 above.

Contents

Prefatory Note

This volume contains revised versions of the papers presented at the Conference on Research in Income and Wealth titled "Measuring and Modeling Health Care Costs," held in Washington, DC, on October 18–19, 2013.

We gratefully acknowledge the financial support for this conference provided by the Bureau of Economic Analysis. Support for the general activities of the Conference on Research in Income and Wealth is provided by the following agencies: Bureau of Economic Analysis, Bureau of Labor Statistics, Census Bureau, Board of Governors of the Federal Reserve System, Internal Revenue Service, and Statistics Canada.

We thank Ana Aizcorbe, Colin Baker, Ernst Berndt, and David Cutler, who served as conference organizers and as editors of the volume.

Executive Committee, January 2016

John M. Abowd
Katharine Abraham (chair)
Susanto Basu
Andrew Bernard
Ernst R. Berndt
Carol A. Corrado
Robert C. Feenstra
John C. Haltiwanger
Michael W. Horrigan
Charles R. Hulten

Ronald Jarmin
Barry Johnson
Andre Loranger
Brent Moulton
Brian Moyer
Valerie Ramey
Mark J. Roberts
Daniel Sichel
William Wascher

Introduction

Ana Aizcorbe, Colin Baker, Ernst R. Berndt, and
David M. Cutler

Medical care costs account for nearly 18 percent of gross domestic product (GDP) and 20 percent of government spending. These numbers are so large that it is imperative to understand what we get for that spending.

As a country, we know a lot about where the medical dollar goes. Thirty-eight percent of medical care dollars are paid to hospitals, 31 percent is paid for professional services, 12 percent is for outpatient pharmaceuticals, and so forth. But this is not really what we value. The goal of medical care is not to poke, prod, or take pictures of our insides; rather, it is to improve our well-being. To really understand health care, we need to determine what it is doing for that most precious of commodities—our health.

Health accounting is not easy. Academics and statistical agencies have struggled with it for decades. Questions range from the mundane—how do colonoscopy prices vary across payers?—to the fundamental—to what extent is medical care improving the population's health? With this much uncertainty about the value of medical care, it is incumbent on public and private researchers alike to regularly survey the landscape. What do we know about medical care costs and output? Where can we make improvements in our measurement systems? What areas remain unexplored?

Ana Aizcorbe is senior research economist at the Bureau of Economic Analysis. Colin Baker is social science analyst at the US Department of Health and Human Services, Office of the Assistant Secretary for Planning and Evaluation. Ernst R. Berndt is the Louis E. Seley Professor in Applied Economics at the MIT Sloan School of Management and a research associate of the National Bureau of Economic Research. David M. Cutler is the Otto Eckstein Professor of Applied Economics and Harvard College Professor at Harvard University, and a research associate of the National Bureau of Economic Research.

For acknowledgments, sources of research support, and disclosure of the authors' material financial relationships, if any, please see http://www.nber.org/chapters/c13093.ack.

These issues were the subject of the Conference on Research in Income and Wealth in 2013, and they are the topic of this volume. The chapters in this volume were presented and discussed at the conference. They were then revised, peer refereed, and revised again before this publication.

As if the topic itself were not controversial enough, there was nearly a government shutdown at the time of the conference. Such a shutdown would have prohibited government employees from even attending. Fortunately, the shutdown failed to occur, and government employees were full participants in the conference.

The conference was held and the chapters written at a time when the Affordable Care Act (ACA) was sure to be law for the next several years. As the book went to press, the new Trump administration and Republican Congress were working on plans to repeal it. As the book is read in the future, some of the language surrounding the ACA may be out of date. Fortunately, the themes are not and the empirical analysis will be timely under any set of health care rules.

The Conference staff at the National Bureau of Economic Research, led by Carl Beck, Rob Sherman, and Brett Maranjian, provided flawless logistical and related assistance. Equally fortunate, the chapters were terrific. Befitting the difficulty of the issue, the chapters are organized into several themes. We develop those themes briefly in this introduction, as they appear in the volume.

Methodological Issues in Measuring Health Care Costs and Outcomes

We begin with a survey chapter characterizing the current state of health care cost, outcome, and productivity measurement by Paul Schreyer, Chief Economic Statistician at the Organisation for Economic Co-operation and Development (OECD), and his coauthor, Matilde Mas, from the University of Valencia and Ivie. Schreyer and Mas lay out the type of challenges faced when measuring medical care costs and outcomes and provide a review of how this sector is currently measured in thirty OECD countries. Specifically, they discuss two types of issues that arise. Among the national accounting issues, difficulties in valuing nonmarket activity present challenges for properly measuring the dollar value of health care (nominal output). The second set of issues deals with how to decompose the growth in that value into price and volume measures; that is, decomposing the change in nominal spending into changes attributable to things getting more expensive (inflation) versus changes in the quantity and quality of goods and services provided (growth in real output). In national statistics, this decomposition can be done either indirectly by using price indexes to deflate the growth in nominal output or directly by constructing volume indexes.

Valuing nonmarket activities—such as health care provided for free by the government—is difficult because there are no transaction prices with which to apply the usual methods. Thus, the universal practice in the countries under study is to value these activities at cost—using price indexes to calculate changes in the cost of providing inputs to treatments for conditions. As noted in J. Steven Landefeld's discussion of this chapter (at the time of the conference, Landefeld was Director of the US Bureau of Economic Analysis), valuing these activities at cost implicitly assumes zero productivity gains in providing treatments, which in turn assumes away the possibility that innovations might allow more treatments to be provided at the same cost or the same treatments at a lower cost.

With regard to splitting out changes in spending into price and volume components, several issues arise. First, the authors note that one would, ideally, want to measure *the complete path* of treatments for a medical condition or episode of care. Doing so would properly account for shifts in treatment protocols that affect cost: for example, shifts from talk therapy to (lower cost) drug therapy in the treatment of depression. However, the organization of the available data accounts does not allow one to measure care using this definition. In particular, in the administrative data that is typically available, treatments at different venues (hospital, residential care, etc.) are reported separately and do not allow one to tie all of the spending to specific patients. For that reason, virtually all of the OECD countries use price or volume indexes for the individual treatments. However, as noted by Schreyer and Mas, there is increasing interest in using disease-based price indexes that tie expenditures and activities to specific medical conditions. Construction of such disease-based treatment price indexes is becoming feasible in part because of the increasing availability of government and private-sector medical claims data.

The increasingly available health care claims and outcomes data in electronic format covering millions of lives raises issues of how best to exploit such data statistically. One major problem with many of these observational claims data is that they are not generated from randomization, that is, treatments and nontreatments are not randomly assigned to patients, but instead reflect the decisions of physicians, patients, and payers resulting in data subject to selection biases. This is in contrast to experimental data emanating from randomized controlled trials, or from quasi-randomized data plausibly linked to a quasi-randomized data-generating process. Can one use sophisticated statistical methods, such as propensity score procedures, with observational data to generate reliable estimates of causality that inform cost-effectiveness analyses? That is the focus of the second chapter in this section by Armando Franco of the University of California at Berkeley, Dana Goldman of the University of Southern California, Adam Leive of the University of Pennsylvania, and Daniel McFadden of the University of California at Berkeley.

Franco and colleagues start by noting the broad popularity of comparative effectiveness research. This research, which typically compares one drug to another, is generally based on randomized trials. However, randomized trials are expensive, often underpowered to detect rare outcomes, and typically focused on a homogeneous group of patients. Thus, it is natural to wonder if claims data can substitute for randomized trials.

Franco and colleagues use data from 2006 to 2009 for Medicare Parts A, B, and D to examine these issues. The specific drug class they consider is angiotensin II receptor blockers (ARBs), which are used to treat hypertension. The Food and Drug Administration (FDA) has identified stroke and cancer as possible unintended consequences of using ARBs. They examine whether claims data confirm these results.

Even a cursory examination of claims data highlights the significant difficulties in comparative effectiveness research they entail. Some people discontinue treatment, while others switch from one treatment to another. Neither of these decisions is random. The chapter considers two methods to control for nonrandom selection of people into treatments. First, they assume that physicians have a preferred drug to prescribe, and patients do not choose physicians on the basis of this unobserved propensity. Thus, they compare the outcomes for physicians that prescribe ARBs more frequently compared to physicians that prescribe them less frequently. Second, they instrument for the patient's choice of an ARB using the relative price of ARBs in comparison to other hypertension treatments. If patients do not choose plans on the basis of these price differences, this instrument can serve to randomize treatment to individuals.

Using each of these strategies, the authors find mixed evidence that ARBs lead to higher cancer rates, and some evidence that ARBs lead to higher stroke rates than other antihypertensive medications. However, other signs are troubling. Use of ARBs presumed to be exogenous is associated with greater reports of pain. Since neither ARBs nor other antihypertensive medications would affect pain, these results suggest nonrandom assignment of people to treatments, even with the two methodologies. Overall, their conclusion is cautious in some parts and optimistic in others.

Traditional measures of inflation and productivity published by government statistical agencies aim to provide metrics for the sector as a whole at the macro level. Recently, the arrival of new data sets and development of new methods have allowed further study into the methods underlying the official statistics, how they might be disaggregated from aggregate sectoral to disease-specific treatment metrics, and how those measures might be improved.

The final two chapters in this section provide examples of the kinds of decompositions that can be done using official statistics and discuss the potential frailties in the data and methods. Both chapters exploit patient-centric data that allow them to define the treatment of diseases over the complete course of treatment. Specifically, both sets of authors generate indexes called medical care expenditure indexes (MCEs) that allow one to decompose changes in expenditures into changes in price versus changes in quantity. Notably, because these indexes do not account for changes in the quality of treatment (or patient outcomes), a National Academies Panel recommended using the label "medical care expenditure" indexes instead of price index—and that is what both these chapters do.

The study by Abe Dunn of the Bureau of Economic Analysis, Eli Liebman of Duke, and Adam Hale Shapiro of the Federal Reserve Bank of San Francisco, develops a decomposition of changes in medical care spending and applies that decomposition to a health-claims database for commercially insured patients. Their decomposition first breaks out changes in spending into two components: changes in per capita treated prevalence of disease and changes in the MCE index—that tracks changes in the cost of episodes of care. They then further break out changes in the MCE into changes in procedure prices—by constructing a procedure price index—and changes in utilization of procedures. In their analyses, episodes of care are measured using an episode-grouping algorithm that uses the diagnoses reported in the claims data to allocate spending into individual disease categories. The ability to drill down to the procedure level is made possible by their data set, which is highly granular, and reports spending and diagnosis information for each procedure. As with many papers in the recent literature, given the complexity of the task, no attempt is made to account for changes in quality of care or patient outcomes.

Overall, Dunn, Liebman, and Shapiro report that both prevalence and the cost of treating conditions contributed to the growth in spending from 2003 to 2007. Further breaking out the latter, they find that most of the growth in the MCEs comes from growth in the procedure price index; there is very little change in their index of the utilization of procedures. Given the similarity in their procedure price index and the official price indexes, their finding suggests no obvious bias in the official price indexes for health care spending. Although reassuring, as the authors note, their finding is not definitive owing to differences in the composition of patients in their data—only fee-for-service patients with commercial insurance and drug coverage—and the broader coverage of the official statistics—that include Medicare patients, for example.

Using the five top-spending categories, Dunn, Liebman, and Shapiro show that their finding of little change in the utilization of procedures is the net effect of two shifts that held down costs—shifts from inpatient to outpatient care and a shift from branded drugs to generic drugs—and a shift that works in the other direction—an increase in the utilization of procedures at physicians' offices.

The chapter by Anne E. Hall and Tina Highfill of the Bureau of Economic Analysis also focuses on MCE indexes. In particular, Hall and Highfill study the numerical importance for these indexes of different methods for allocating spending by disease—alternatives to the episode grouper used in Dunn, Liebman, and Shapiro—and different data sets—surveys versus claims. They consider two methods for allocating spending to disease categories: (a) the principal diagnosis method, which allocates all spending from an encounter to the first-listed diagnosis, and (b) a regression method, which scrolls up the encounter-level data to the patient level and uses fixed effects to indicate the conditions for which the patient was treated that year. They apply these methods to two different data sets that contain patient-centric data for Medicare beneficiaries: the Medical Expenditure Panel Survey (MEPS) and the survey and claims components of the Medicare Current Beneficiary Survey (MCBS).

Hall and Highfill find that when the different methods are applied to the same data sets, the primary diagnosis method produces higher average annual aggregate growth rates. They conclude the regression-based method should be employed with caution, given its sensitivity to outliers and propensity for producing volatile indexes. Regarding the different data sets, the MEPS is the only data set with diagnoses attached to drug events, which significantly affects the resulting indexes. On balance, however, the MCBS is probably the preferable data set for Medicare beneficiaries because of its greater sample size and its inclusion of nursing home residents. The optimal index may be a hybrid of the primary diagnosis method applied to Medicare claims and a regression-based index for pharmaceutical spending.

Analyses of Subpopulations and Market Segments

An alternative approach to disease-based measurement aggregated over all providers is to instead focus on costs and outcomes in a particular health care delivery submarket, such as hospitals or physicians. The chapter by Brian Chansky, Corby Garner, and Ronjoy Raichoudhary of the Bureau of Labor Statistics examines different strategies for measuring output and productivity growth in private hospitals in the United States from 1993 to 2010. Specifically, they consider three methods: (a) the course of treatment model, where annual output is the number of inpatient hospital discharges and outpatient visits; (b) the procedures model, which counts individual services separately; and (c) and the revenue model, which measures output using the Producer Price Indexes (PPIs) from the Bureau of Labor Statistics to deflate hospital revenues. They link these utilization and cost measures to the treated conditions using diagnosis-related groups (DRGs) for inpatient care, and sixteen major disease categories reported in the American Hospital Association (AHA) survey for outpatient care.

Chansky, Garner, and Raichoudhary find only minor differences in the resulting output measures and implied labor productivity measures: for 1993–2010, the three methods imply average annual labor productivity growth rates of 0.7 percent, 0.9 percent, and 1.0 percent, with very similar results for the underlying subperiods. Perhaps it is not so surprising that the procedure (1.0 percent) and revenue (0.9 percent) models give very similar results: one uses a volume index based on procedures and the other uses a PPI (essentially a procedure price index) and, thus, obtains an indirect volume index.

The productivity growth implied by the course of treatment model is the slowest (0.7 percent) for the whole period and is surprisingly negative for the 2001–2010 period. This output measure—based on number of discharges by DRG—takes severity into account only imperfectly. The authors argue that the shift from inpatient to outpatient care meant that only the more severe, labor-intensive patients still receive inpatient care, hence reducing output per labor hour in the inpatient setting.

Instead of looking just at costs in the hospital sector, an alternative disaggregation involves examining cost and outcome trends in a distinct subpopulation. The chapter by Allison B. Rosen of the University of Massachusetts, Ana Aizcorbe and Tina Highfill of the BEA, Michael E. Chernew of Harvard, Eli Liebman of Duke, Kaushik Ghosh of the NBER, and David M. Cutler of Harvard looks at decomposition methods using a large commercially insured population.

Rosen and colleagues consider three ways of partitioning medical spending to conditions. The first approach, which is typical in much of the literature, involves assigning each medical care claim to one or more diseases. For example, a visit to a primary care doctor that is coded as being for high cholesterol would be classified as spending for that condition. The difficulty with this approach is that many people have comorbid medical conditions. The claims-based approach requires that physicians adequately solve the comorbidity problem—what factor is really contributing to the patient needing care? In practice, such an attribution is difficult to make, and may not even be possible for patients with particularly complex illnesses. The second approach is a regression approach. In this method, total spending for the year is regressed on the full set of conditions that a patient has. The resulting coefficients are used to back out spending for each condition. In practice, however, the regression approach is only as good as the underlying model of spending, which is itself problematic in a number of ways.

The third approach, which is developed by the authors in the chapter, is to use a propensity score methodology to cost diseases. The idea is to find people with a particular condition and compare their spending to a group of people who are otherwise similar, but without the condition in question. The resulting spending difference is an estimate of the cost of treating that condition.

The data that Rosen and colleagues employ is from the MarketScan database, which has 2.3 million people under age sixty-five with both medical and pharmaceutical coverage. The authors note that the method chosen to allocate spending has a material impact on the findings. Broadly speaking, the claims-based approaches allocate more spending to acute conditions—

a heart attack, for example—while the regression and propensity score approaches attribute some of that spending to comorbid conditions such as musculoskeletal problems and mental illness. In addition, the authors show significant problems with the claims method, where not all spending has a condition associated with it (for example, prescription drugs). Without a gold standard for comparison, the authors do not choose a favorite methodology. They suggest that researchers should be very careful about methodology.

The final chapter in this section by Ralph Bradley of the Bureau of Labor Statistics and Colin Baker, then at the National Institutes of Health and now in the Office of the Assistant Secretary for Planning and Evaluation in the Department of Health and Human Services, focuses on a different subpopulation, namely, the obese. The recent increase in the prevalence of obesity among Americans has received considerable press attention, not only for its possible adverse impact on the prevalence of chronic cardiovascular and metabolic diseases, but also for its impact on health care costs. A number of studies have examined the relationships among obesity and health care costs, with varying findings. Bradley and Baker begin by noting that most of the empirical studies examining obesity and health care cost relationships treat obesity, and for that matter, health insurance coverage, as exogenous variables. Unlike public campaigns to curb smoking that have been substantially successful, even with mounting evidence concerning the adverse health effects of obesity, obesity rates in the United States have continued to increase. The principal contribution of the Bradley-Baker chapter is the construction, interpretation, and empirical estimation of a microeconomic model where an individual's body mass index (BMI) is the outcome of a rational utility-maximizing, decision-making process, that is, BMI is endogenous rather than exogenous.

In their two-period ex ante, ex post micromodel, Bradley and Baker specify that individuals trade off the disutility (psychic cost) of weight reduction (reduction in BMI) with the increased utility coming from better health. More specifically, both insurance status and BMI are simultaneously set ex ante, each depending both on observed and unobserved latent variables. After a draw of a random health status variable in the ex post period, the consumer chooses whether to visit a health service provider. If the consumer visits a health service provider, then based on the consumer's health status, the health service provider and the consumer jointly select a treatment intensity. Hence, as suggested by the chapter title, in the Bradley-Baker framework obesity, insurance choice, and medical visit choice are endogenous, and together they simultaneously affect health care costs. The model predicts that ex ante moral hazard can occur as the presence of health insurance affects the BMI choice, and that adverse selection can occur where those with greater propensity to have higher BMIs will more likely purchase health insurance.

Although the logic of the Bradley-Baker micromodel is relatively straightforward, measurement and econometric specification issues complicate the empirical implementation. In the ex ante period, the consumer makes expectations on her health status and medical spending in the ex post period. Based on these expectations, consumer i decides her insurance status I_i and her BMI level BMI_i. If individual i buys insurance, $I_i = 1$, else it is zero. Cost sharing, respectively, under insurance and no insurance is $c_{I,i}$ and $c_{N,i}$, with $c_{I,i} < c_{N,i}$. Although the ideal BMI does not vary across the i individuals, there is a "natural" BMI, denoted $B_{N,I}$, that occurs when the individual eats to satiation and pursues no other activity to manage weight. Hence, $B_{N,I}$ varies by individual. The lower the individual's ideal BMI goes below the satiated BMI, $B_{N,I}$, there is an increasing marginal disutility (i.e., hunger) of nonsatiation. The econometrician cannot observe $B_{N,I}$. When the ex post period begins, the consumer draws an unpredictable shock ε_i. After the draw of ε_i, the individual decides whether to visit a health service provider. Hence, in the ex ante period the consumer simultaneously selects her BMI and insurance status (each of which depends on unobserved latent variables) to maximize her expected utility in the ex post period. Since $B_{N,I}$ is private, asymmetric information that only the individual knows, her health insurance premium cannot be risk adjusted for this private information, thereby generating adverse selection. The ex ante moral hazard occurs because the insured individual bears a smaller financial risk for her BMI decisions, and the BMI choice cannot be written into a health insurance contract. In the resulting Bradley-Baker Tobit cost equation, there are two selection effects—the insurance decision and the provider insurance effect, which is estimated as a multiple-selection Heckman procedure. Notably, BMI decisions affect costs both directly and through health insurance decisions. To correct for the endogeneity of BMI, Bradley-Baker employ a control variable approach where a reduced-form equation is estimated.

To implement the model empirically, Bradley-Baker use 2002–2010 annual data from the Medical Expenditure Panel Survey (MEPS). Between 2002 and 2010, the US obesity prevalence rate increased from about 17.5 percent to 21.5 percent, with the mass BMI range migrating from the 21 to 26 range in 2002 to the 30 to 45 range in 2010, and with both distributions right skewed. To avoid a possible nonresponse bias, Bradley-Baker estimate a probit model for the probability of the respondent providing information on his/her BMI. Males and those with more education are more likely to respond, while the older and unemployed individuals are less likely to respond. Since corn syrup is an intermediate product for foods considered the major culprit behind obesity, Bradley-Baker construct a relative food price index as the Producer Price Index for corn syrup divided by the all-items Consumer Price Index; its coefficient in the estimated ex ante BMI equation is negative, but not statistically significant. In the ex ante insurance choice equation, the coefficient estimate on the BMI variable is positive and significant, indicating that there is adverse selection with BMI. Young men have a lower propensity to purchase insurance, while individuals with children who are not beneficiaries from the State Children's Health Insurance Program and where both spouses work in technical, professional, or government occupations have a much higher propensity to purchase insurance. Within the structural BMI equation where private insurance is treated as an endogenous variable, the coefficient on the private insurance indicator variable is positive and significant, indicating the presence of ex ante moral hazard.

In summary, in the ex ante period, both insurance status and BMI are determined. If the individual purchases insurance, the financial consequences of illness are less severe, and the policyholder is not compensated by the plan for the savings generated by suffering additional disutility to get the BMI nearer to an ideal level—thereby generating ex ante moral hazard. Likewise, employer-sponsored insurance premiums do not appear to be risk adjusted for increases in BMI. As BMI increases, so does the risk of severe disease. This increases the expected utility of having health insurance, yielding adverse selection.

After having estimated the ex post cost equation, Bradley-Baker undertake several simulations. Of particular interest is a simulation of a 10 percent BMI reduction for all obese persons on costs. Bradley-Baker report a $45 per capita annual cost reduction were all obese people to reduce their BMI by 10 percent—a rather modest amount. They conclude that while high BMI does increase costs, policies that are successful in reducing BMI will not generate the large cost savings previously estimated by other researchers. They conjecture that current intervention programs to reduce obesity may underestimate the marginal disutility that obese individuals experience when they reduce an additional BMI.

Prescription Pharmaceutical Markets

Pharmaceutical markets present an important case for measuring and modeling health spending. Pharmaceuticals themselves account for more than 10 percent of medical spending. In addition, though, there are changes in the form of delivery and producer of the good (e.g., branded v. generic) that need to be accounted for. Indeed, the classic example of health price index adjustments that are thought to be essential is the lower price that results from substituting generic medications for branded ones. Despite the importance of pharmaceuticals in understanding medical care costs and prices, there has been relatively little work taking a close look at the pharmaceutical sector. The next section of this volume remedies this deficiency.

The first chapter, by Murray L. Aitken of the IMS Institute for Healthcare Informatics, Ernst R. Berndt of MIT, Barry Bosworth of Brookings, Iain M. Cockburn of Boston University, Richard Frank of Harvard Medical School, Michael Kleinrock of IMS, and Bradley T. Shapiro of MIT, examines pricing and utilization trends around the time of patent expiration. The data they use are from IMS, one of the leading companies tracking pharmaceutical quantities and prices over time. Their analysis focuses on data from six molecules that lost patent exclusivity between June 2009 and May 2013, and which were among the fifty most prescribed medications in May 2013. Because the trends may differ across population groups, they divide the population by payer (Medicaid, Medicare Part D, commercial and other third-party payers [TPPs], and cash customers) and age (above and below sixty-five).

Their analysis reaches several conclusions. First, the major trends that occur with loss of exclusivity are on the price side. Many patients switch to generic versions of medications. This switch, at relative constant prices, lowers spending significantly. Because generics are less expensive than branded drugs, the total quantity of drugs consumed rises. Second, offsetting some of the lower spending from substitution is the fact that branded drug prices continue to raise prices after generics enter. The authors rationalize this as a result of an increasingly inelastic purchasing pool when price-sensitive consumers have shifted to generic formulations, leaving brand-loyal consumers vulnerable to brand price increases.

Generic penetration rates differ across patient groups. They are generally highest for third-party payers and lowest for Medicaid. Correspondingly, cash payers and seniors generally pay the highest prices for brands and generics, while third-party payers (and those under age sixty-five) pay the lowest prices. It is likely that third-party payers can steer more patients to less expensive formulations, and they use this power to extract lower prices from pharmaceutical companies.

Finally, they explore the impact of an "authorized generic" during the 180-day exclusivity period—a molecule that has been authorized as an official generic version, and has a 180-day exclusivity period as a generic drug. They find that having an authorized generic has a significant impact on prices and volume of prescriptions, but this varies across molecules. In two of the cases studied, the brand and its licensee collectively retained almost two-thirds share of the market by volume, and in the others they captured less than half. Price discounts off the brand prevailing during the "triopoly" period (the period with a branded medication and two authorized generic medications) also showed substantial variation. In some cases, the price of the authorized generic product was between the brand and the independent generic, in others it was significantly below the independent generic. All told, these dynamics have important implications for price and quantity of pharmaceuticals.

A particularly important pharmaceutical market is for so-called specialty drugs—drugs that are administered by physicians to patients through a nonoral route (e.g., injected, infused, or inhaled) or taken directly by patients after requiring very exacting production processes. Many drugs with prices exceeding $10,000 per annual treatment are specialty drugs, whose prices have become controversial. Insulin is a classic example of a specialty drug. On the supply side, because of the difficulty of production, there are often few suppliers of any particular medication. As a result, shortages can (and do) occur.

Rena M. Conti of the University of Chicago and Ernst R. Berndt of MIT examine how the loss of patent exclusivity affects the prices and utilization of specialty drugs. To do this, they utilize a unique set of information on drug prices and sales from IMS health. They focus on cancer medications because specialty drugs are particularly important for the treatment of cancer and the side effects associated with their use.

Loss of patent exclusivity allows generic firms to enter a market; Conti and Berndt show that they do so. After a patent expires, between two and five generic firms enter the market. However, true competition is somewhat lower than this, since many of the drugs are made by the same company and marketed by different intermediaries. Thus, the manufacturer likely has more market power than it appears.

Even so, loss of exclusivity results in significant generic price declines. Conti and Berndt estimate that generic drug prices fall by 25–50 percent after exclusivity is lost. The prices of specialty drugs administered by physicians through infusion or injection fall by more than the price of orally formulated drugs, but each declines greatly. Prices of the branded product increase, however, a result consistent with prior studies. For people who continue taking the branded drug, even when a generic drug is available, there is little reason for the brand manufacturer not to increase the price substantially. The combined volume of the generic plus brand medications taken rises after loss of exclusivity; it is clear that some patients and physicians are put off by the high cost of the patented medication.

Welfare results are difficult in any market, particularly one for lifesaving goods. But Conti and Berndt note one summary to the welfare analysis. With generic entry, there are effectively two prices for cancer medications: the (now higher) branded price, and the lower generic price. There is also greater use of the medications after patent expiry. Greater price dispersion and higher overall utilization are hallmarks of increased consumer welfare. Thus, Conti and Berndt tentatively conclude that loss of patent protection is associated with increases in consumer welfare.

In contrast to the Conti-Berndt chapter that focuses attention on high-profile generic injectable drugs that have experienced drug shortages, the analysis of Christopher Stomberg of Bates White Economic Consulting reveals that shortages of injectable and noninjectable drugs have very similar time trends: the correlation between the number of ongoing injectable and noninjectable drug shortages is 0.94, while the average length of ongoing drug shortages for injectable and noninjectable drugs is also highly correlated at 0.89. This suggests that whatever are the factors explaining drug shortages, they apply equally and with roughly the same timing in both the injectable and noninjectable markets. It also suggests that shortage theories relying on distinguishing features of injectable drugs (e.g., changing reimbursement of Medicare Part B drugs) are incomplete, and that broader causes such as changes in competition, market structure, and quality monitoring—affecting both markets—merit further scrutiny. Stomberg examines each of these three broader potential causes.

Although there may be no single "cause" of drug shortages, Stomberg notes that the overwhelming majority of shortages affect generic drugs. A key difference between brand and generic drugs is the low margin available to manufacturers on generic drugs, particularly for those drugs that have been on the market for some time. Given the US Food and Drug Administration's AB rating of generic drugs, generic versions are not only essentially perfectly substitutable with the same-molecule brand, but also with each other. While both quality/purity of product and reliability of supply are costly attributes for the manufacturer to provide, they are generally invisible to buyers and patients. In nonpharmaceutical markets where the quality/purity and reliability of supply attributes are observable, a premium is paid for them. An important consequence of this institutionalized substitutability among generic drugs is that when competition takes the form of near-Bertrand auctions, where suppliers are asked to meet or beat the price of the competition to win a supply contract, the firms surviving the intense price competition with any sort of profit margin will need to implement relentless cost cutting. Given that many dominant modern generic manufacturers are multiproduct firms with dozens if not hundreds of products on the market at any one time, once price competition has had its relentless effect on prices for more mature generic products, revenues and profits for individual products may not make a large contribution to the bottom line of the company. As a result, when faced with supply disruptions of any magnitude on older, mature low-margin products, generic manufacturers may not find it worthwhile to address manufacturing quality issues, instead reducing their investments in maintenance and product quality. The nature of market competition in US generic pharmaceutical markets thus leads to a "race to the bottom" in both price and quality. If the current costs of plant maintenance and product-quality investment exceed the discounted expected value of lost profits due to a shutdown, then the investments are not worth undertaking. Note that this market competition affects both injectable and noninjectable drugs.

Regulatory actions regarding quality/purity monitoring are a second potential broad cause of shortages. In particular, in a market where product quality is not generally observable but the actions of the regulator are, the FDA's actions may play an important role in setting expectations for both buyers and sellers. The profit-maximizing decisions of producers may be to undertake only those expenses required to pass the FDA's threshold and no more—leading to a generally consistent low level of quality. Were product quality an observable attribute, manufacturers might find it optimal to differentiate themselves by optimizing around different levels of observable quality. Manufacturers facing the uncertainty of whether they will be subject to an FDA inspection may well pick a level of quality that is below the public regulatory threshold if the probability of future inspection is less than one. Manufacturers may assign different probabilities to the possibility of detection, and/or may be risk averse to varying degrees, which could lead them to choose heterogeneous levels of quality. To the extent such heterogeneity exists and it translates into differences in marginal production costs, an adverse selection problem could arise. With Bertrand-like competition, the producers most likely to survive in the market are those that are most willing to take a risk with low spending on quality, giving them a low marginal cost and an advantage in price competition. Moreover, even if the relatively risk-loving, low-cost firms were eventually inspected and shut down, the consequences could be long lasting if they have already edged out high-quality competition, leaving no alternative higher-quality supply available. Thus, in Stomberg's scenarios, a key ingredient is the FDA's setting clear expectations and time-consistent quality-monitoring policies. If the FDA sets expectations both about the probability of inspection and the quality threshold in one time period, but then changes one or the other of these subsequently, it could potentially cause either disruption or time-inconsistent issues. Stomberg conjectures that altered FDA inspection rates, to the extent they reflect exogenous regime changes, are a plausible factor that could contribute to increased shortage rates (at least in the short run), and this would be an effect likely to cut across both injectable and noninjectable drugs. Later in the chapter, Stomberg analyzes this possibility empirically.

The third broad possible cause of shortages put forward by Stomberg is limited price responsiveness on both the demand and supply side, at least in the short run. For suppliers, short-run price inelasticity generally stems from FDA regulatory requirements for approval of new manufacturing facilities and/or abbreviated new drug applications required to market generic drugs in the United States, as well as technological obstacles to adding new capacity. On the demand side, patients' medical necessity for prescription drugs and the fact that neither they, nor their physicians, generally pay market prices for generic drugs argues for low responsiveness of demand to changes in price. Absent price responsiveness in the market, endogenous incentives for manufacturers to address supply issues are likely to be attenuated.

Stomberg then implements an empirical analysis of one of the three possible broad factors causing shortages—changes in the FDA's regulatory activity. Using FDA data on the number of inspections of manufacturing facilities and the number of citations issued, separately for US and ex-US manufacturing sites, Stomberg regresses the number of monthly shortages (both newly reported and ongoing) on current and lagged values of the inspection and citation measures. He identifies a consistent and statistically significant predictive relationship between FDA regulatory activity in drug-quality inspections and citations and the incidence of new drug shortages, with the relationship being similar across both injectable and noninjectable drugs. He concludes that changes in regulatory activity may be one of the cross-cutting factors contributing to the ongoing wave of drug shortages, and that supply interruptions resulting from changes in regulatory activity can be viewed as a necessary step on the road to a different quality equilibrium. He cautions, however, that the predictive power of his empirical model is modest, leaving a substantial amount of variation in new drug shortage starts remaining unexplained by the regulatory activity factor. Pricing and market structure (such as changes in the number of generic manufacturers for a molecule due to mergers and acquisitions) could be additional important factors to consider in future research on drug shortages.

Issues in Industrial Organization and Market Design

Many of the previous chapters refer to issues of how the industrial organization (IO) of medical care affects costs and outcomes. Several of the chapters address this topic directly. Laurence C. Baker and M. Kate Bundorf of Stanford University, along with Anne Royalty of Indiana University, start with a central issue in physician markets: how to measure the concentration of physician ownership.

As Baker, Bundorf, and Royalty note, measuring concentration is important for several reasons. In the hospital industry, hospitals with greater market shares have higher prices for both inpatient and outpatient care. Some data suggest that this is true for physicians as well, although measures of physician concentration are scarce. Concentration may also influence quality, with some authors suggesting that more concentrated markets have higher quality and others suggesting lower quality.

Measuring physician concentration is difficult because ownership patterns are difficult to follow. A small physician practice may be owned by a larger group, which itself might be owned by a big health system. Is the physician practice small, or part of a large system? Baker, Bundorf, and Royalty propose to use Medicare data to measure concentration. Specifically, they investigate the use of Tax Identification Numbers (TINs) to measure physician firms. The TIN is the organization that receives the payment from Medicare for physician services. For a measure of financial integration (their aim), this is a natural measure of concentration.

Baker, Bundorf, and Royalty use the TINs to characterize physician practices in the period 1998–2010. They reach several conclusions. First, they conclude that TINs provide a reasonable way to group practices. They tend to be consistent over time and identify groups of physicians that are known to be large. Second, many physician markets are highly concentrated. For many specialties in many areas, physician Herfindahl-Hirschman Indexes (HHIs) are well above 2,500, the standard measure that triggers antitrust worry. Third, these concentration measures have been increasing over time. The increase is particularly pronounced in areas such as surgeries, while concentration has fallen over time in some medical specialties. Fourth, they do not find a large advantage to incorporating data on ownership of physicians by hospitals or other systems. Most physicians still practice independent of institutional providers. Finally, they note that other data will need to be added to Medicare claims, since data on pediatricians, obstetricians, and some other specialists are not always prevalent in Medicare data. Even still, they conclude that they have identified a promising way to measure market concentration.

A particularly important market in which to analyze competition is the health insurance market. Many countries rely on insurance market competition to promote high-quality, low-cost access to medical care. For example, the Affordable Care Act in the United States provides subsidies to individuals to purchase insurance in state-based insurance exchanges. Medicare also has a private insurance option, as do national health care systems in the Netherlands, Germany, Switzerland, and other countries.

Competition in health insurance is different from competition in other markets, however. In most markets, the cost of serving people is independent of who buys the product; the cost of producing a pill, for example, depends only on manufacturing and distribution costs, not how sick the patient is. In health insurance, that is not the case. Insurers that attract less healthy enrollees will have higher costs than those that attract healthier enrollees, even with the same coverage network and prices paid.

For this reason, payments to health plans in choice-based system are often "risk adjusted." The goal behind risk adjustment is to pay more for less healthy enrollees, so that such individuals do not raise the price to all enrollees. Typical risk-adjustment formulae base payments on demographics, along with clinical conditions.

Jacob Glazer of Tel Aviv, along with Thomas G. McGuire and Julie Shi of Harvard University explore optimal risk adjustment in their chapter. Glazer, McGuire, and Shi begin by noting a fundamental anomaly with risk adjustment based on conditions. The procedures used for risk adjustment make the weights used a function of the data on enrollees, but the enrollees are a function of the risk-adjustment formula. Thus, the formula builds in adverse selection.

The question that Glazer, McGuire, and Shi ask is how to account for this adverse selection in designing risk-adjustment formulae. Their analysis has both a theoretical and an empirical component. Theoretically, they design the optimal second-best risk-adjustment formula—second best because there is always sorting based on the risk-adjustment formula itself. They show that optimal risk adjustment can be determined by constrained regression, where the constraints (on the risk-adjustment weights) require that risk adjustment transfer sufficient funds to the premium group to achieve the desired subsidy in equilibrium. Intuitively, the second-best risk adjustment trades off several features, including the degree of adverse selection, which itself is based on peoples' (possibly incorrect) forecasts of their own future spending.

Empirically, they use data from seven years of the Medical Expenditure Panel Study (MEPS) to estimate the optimal risk-adjustment formula. The sample is selected to be representative of people in the insurance exchanges. They consider choices between a typical Gold and Silver plan, using data on spending to sort people to plans. Not surprisingly, the market fares poorly when there is no risk adjustment; the Gold plan attracts sick people, and the Silver plan enrolls healthy people. Conventional risk adjustment improves the situation significantly. But the optimal risk adjustment is even better. Glazer, McGuire, and Shi show that the optimal risk-adjustment formula has significantly lower welfare cost than the conventional risk adjustment. They also show how to incorporate other constraints on pricing that may be desired, for example, limiting cost differentials between older and younger people.

Rather than focusing on risk-adjustment characteristics of aspects of the Affordable Care Act (ACA) as in Glazer, McGuire, and Shi, Pinar Karaca-Mandic, Jean M. Abraham, and Roger Feldman of the University of Minnesota, along with Kosali Simon of Indiana University, attempt to establish a pre-ACA implementation baseline of data from which to compare post-ACA changes. The Affordable Care Act (ACA) of 2010 is likely the most significant new health care legislation passed by the US Congress during the Obama administration. One important provision of the ACA is that all low-income Americans above the poverty line who lack access to affordable employer-sponsored insurance will be eligible for subsidies to purchase individual insurance in state-based or federally operated insurance exchanges. Since in 2012 only about 5 percent of the nonelderly population had coverage in the individual market and by 2016 this proportion is projected to increase to about 17 percent, this provision of the ACA may greatly expand the size and importance of the individual market. Another provision in the original ACA legislation sought to simplify the health insurance shopping experience for small employers with fifty or fewer full-time equivalent employees, and allow their employees to choose among options in an analogous Health Insurance Exchange, though without similar access to exchange tax credits; in 2012, only 35.2 percent of private-sector establishments with fewer than fifty employees offered health insurance to their employees, compared with 95.9 percent of establishments with fifty or more employees. Other important provisions of the ACA legislation seek to control insurance premium increases through rate review regulation, and by regulating insurers' medical loss ratios (MLRs—which generally represents the proportion of health insurance premium revenues that are paid out by the insurer in medical claims).

What will be the effects of these and other provisions of the ACA legislation? To answer such important questions (and undoubtedly, there will be differences of opinion), it will be necessary to establish a pre-ACA, or at least a pre-ACA implementation baseline of data, from which to compare post-ACA changes. In this chapter, Karaca-Mandic and her coauthors discuss challenges in describing and measuring the size, structure, and performance of the individual and small group markets. Along the way they discuss improvements in data availability beginning in 2010 that could, in principle, address some of these issues. Finally, using data from the National Association of Insurance Commissioners (NAIC), they evaluate insurance market structure and performance during the 2010–2012 immediate post-ACA time period, focusing on enrollment, the number of participating insurers, premiums, claims spending, MLR, and administrative expenses.

Regarding the size of the individual market, earlier work by one of the coauthors and collaborators found that federal survey estimates of the individual market varied widely, from 9.5 million nonelderly in the Medical Expenditure Panel Survey Household Component, to 25 million in the American Community Survey; they attributed the wide range to variability in the precision of the survey questions, as well as differences in the reference period of the insurance questions (a particular point in time vs. any time during the previous calendar year), which generate significant measurement issues since enrollment patterns in the individual market are typically dynamic throughout a given year. Using their best judgment to narrow the range of individuals with health insurance coverage, the current authors still find a 2-to-1 ratio, from 8 to 16 million. This is disappointing, for it suggests we may never know to what to compare the post-ACA individual enrollment. Since most household surveys do not ask working individuals about the size of their employer, obtaining baseline enrollment data for the small group market may be even more elusive, although estimates based on employer surveys linked to administrative data appear more reliable.

Regarding the structure of the individual and small group markets for health insurance, an obvious issue is whether these markets are "competitive" and how market structure interacts with premiums/prices. In this context, the authors document very substantial heterogeneity in market competition across states and regions. Counting the number of competitors in a state is not a trivial issue, for health insurance is sold by life insurance firms, fraternal, and property/casualty insurers, as well as by health insurance firms. The authors report on data from "credible" firms, defined as having a minimum number of member years (e.g., at least 1,000 in 2010 and 2011). The authors compute Herfindahl-Hirschman Indexes (HHIs) for the individual and small group markets in 2010 and 2012. Fourteen states had an individual market HHI less than 2,500 (a minimum threshold for highly concentrated) in both years, while in the small group market the number of states with an HHI < 2,500 was relatively stable at eighteen in 2010 and twenty in 2012. However, in 2012 thirteen states had an HHI > 5,000 in the individual market (indicating very highly concentrated), while only six states had that large an HHI in the small group market. Not only is the individual market highly concentrated in many states, but the average HHI in all states increased from 3,680 in 2010 to 3,920 in 2012. Overall, the small group market was slightly less concentrated relative to the individual market; the average HHI across all states was 3,252 in 2010 and 3,353 in 2012.

In terms of new regulations, the MLR regulations were among the first ACA provisions to be implemented. Beginning January 2011, insurers in the individual and small group markets must spend at least 80 percent of their premium revenue on medical care and quality-improvement activities, while insurers in the large group have a minimum threshold of 85 percent, with those insurers not meeting those thresholds being required to provide equivalent rebates to their policyholders beginning in 2012.

Since 2010 passage of the ACA, the National Association of Insurance Commissioners (NAIC) has actively collaborated with the US Department of Health and Human Services to design standard measures, definitions, and methodologies related to the regulatory targets such as MLR. Although this may make pre- and post-ACA comparisons problematic, in principle it allows for evaluation of post-ACA trends. However, one study by three of the current coauthors examining NAIC 2001–2009 data found that markets with only one credible insurer (defined as having at least 1,000 member years of enrollment) have lower MLRs, controlling for insurer characteristics, health-care-provider market structure and other market attributes, and population-level demographics and health status. Although a number of definitional changes for measurement of MLRs took place in 2009–2012, the current authors report on a previous study examining 2010 and 2011 NAIC Supplemental Health Care Exhibit filings, which found that the average MLR increased from 80.8 percent to 84.1 percent in the individual market, while it remained unchanged at 83.6 percent in the small group market. Distinguishing for-profit from not-for-profit insurers, they also report that nonprofit insurers already had high MLRs in 2010 relative to for-profit insurers (88.1 percent vs. 71.8).

In terms of early responses to the MLR regulation, in a study by three of the four current coauthors, it is found that individual market insurers with 2010 MLRs that are more than 10 percentage points under the 80 percent threshold experienced a 10.94 percentage point increase in MLR from 2010 to 2011 (controlling for a wide variety of factors), while those within 5 points under the threshold experienced only a 2.91 percentage point increase in MLR. Individual market insurers with MLRs more than 10 points above the threshold in 2010 reported a decrease, on average, relative to insurers that were only slightly above the 80 percent threshold. A similar pattern of changes in insurers' MLRs was found in the small group market.

In summary, while there is some post-2010 data available on various performance metrics of insurers in the individual, small group, and larger employer insurance markets indicating potential improvements in meeting MLR targets, the authors conclude that even after various plausible data-curating procedures are implemented, federal household surveys give widely different estimates of how many individuals were covered in the individual market prior to passage of the ACA. Hence, it may be difficult to track changes in enrollment and to conduct studies based on a pre-/post-ACA design using federal household surveys because of the limitations in properly estimating the size of the individual market at the baseline. However, unlike in the individual market, the authors conclude that better estimates of the small group market enrollment can be obtained from the Insurance Component of the Medical Expenditure Panel Survey. Moreover, since major improvements were made in the NAIC's Supplemental Health Care Exhibit filings in 2010, at least some empirical evaluations on certain regulatory developments such as those involving MLRs, can be reasonably assessed for the single pre-ACA year (2010) and for early post-ACA years beginning in 2011.

Potpourri

The two final chapters in this volume deal with somewhat different topics than those presented by the author conference participants. Nonetheless, they are equally important in addressing these issues. Didem Bernard and Thomas Selden of the Agency for Health Care Research and Quality (AHRQ), and Yuriy Pylypchuk of Social and Scientific Systems, Inc., examine the total amount of public spending on medical care and its "benefit incidence" in 2010. That year was important, in part, because it laid the foundation for modeling of the Affordable Care Act. And the effort here is particularly important in supporting the modeling that AHRQ and other agencies do to understand the likely impact of health care reforms.

The data that are used are primarily from the Medical Expenditure Panel Study. However, the MEPS is known to understate certain categories of spending and certain categories of people (for example, high spenders). Thus, the first challenge for the research is to adjust MEPS spending to national totals. The authors follow previous methodology that they and others developed to do this. In addition, the authors use data from the NBER's TAXSIM model to attribute tax expenditures to relevant groups.

The results show large amounts of government spending for medical care, directed primarily at the elderly. For example, total government spending on medical care is approximately three times higher for the elderly than the adult population, and five times higher for the elderly than for children.

Much of this spending is for the very poor, but not all of it. Medicaid benefits are predominately for the poor, but tax expenditures for employer-provided health insurance reach much higher up in the income distribution—both because higher-income people are more likely to have employer-provided insurance and because the value of the tax exclusion is higher at higher incomes. Because medical costs have increased over time, the value of this spending has risen as well.

One of the fundamental issues in the measurement of health costs is determining how such costs relate to health benefits. Nominal prices count only what is spent. Real prices—and corresponding real output—require a quality adjustment. Frank R. Lichtenberg of Columbia University explores a novel way to measure the health benefits of medical innovation. Lichtenberg's methodology is to measure how much medical knowledge is learned about diseases, measured as the number of publications referring to the disease. He then relates this to mortality reductions for the disease.

The clinical setting Lichtenberg considers is cancer. Cancer is natural to study because there are about forty-five well-identified sites; the National Cancer Institute calculates consistent incidence and mortality data by cancer site since 1975, and research innovation can be measured through Medline searches. For each cancer site, Lichtenberg calculates the number of articles published pre-1975 and the number of articles published between 1975 and various later years.

Lichtenberg shows a clear relationship between recent research findings and mortality declines. The number of articles published in the last five to ten years has a large and significant effect in lowering mortality. The effects are such that many cancers with declining mortality would have increasing mortality were it not for new research findings.

Taken together, the chapters in this volume present a compelling case that we have made significant advances in understanding the cost of medical care, and that we can continue to make such improvements in the future. Current and future analyses will have much to learn from the studies reported here.

I

Methodological Issues in Measuring Health Care Costs and Outcomes

Measuring Health Services in the National Accounts
An International Perspective

Paul Schreyer and Matilde Mas

1.1 Introduction

In 2011, domestic demand for health services accounted for an average of 11 percent of gross domestic product (GDP) in Organisation for Economic Co-operation and Development (OECD) countries, as an item of household demand second only to housing. At the same time, variations between countries are significant, ranging from a modest 4 percent in Luxembourg to a sizable 15 percent in the United States. Such differences within a fairly homogeneous set of countries immediately raise a number of questions: Are we comparing like with like? And if so, are differences in the value of health services due to differences in prices or to differences in the volume of health services provided? A similar question arises when comparing the evolution of health expenditure within a country over time: How much of an increase in expenditure has occurred because of more services delivered and how much has occurred because of services having become more expensive? This chapter aims at exploring the issue of measuring health services and the breakdown of expenditures between prices and volumes from an international perspective. It will ask whether health services are defined in

Paul Schreyer is deputy chief statistician at the Organisation for Economic Co-operation and Development (OECD). Matilde Mas is professor of economic analysis at the University of Valencia and director of international projects at the Valencian Institute of Economic Research (IVIE).

Chapter prepared for the NBER/CRIW Conference on Evaluating Health Care Spending: Progress and Gaps in the Health Care Statistical Infrastructure on October 18 and 19, 2013, in Washington, DC. We thank participants at the conference and Steve Landefeld for helpful comments. This chapter reflects the view of the authors and not necessarily those of the OECD or its member countries. For acknowledgments, sources of research support, and disclosure of the authors' material financial relationships, if any, please see http://www.nber.org/chapters/c13116.ack.

the same way across countries and whether statistical offices apply similar methods to undertake a price-volume split when nominal expenditures are tracked over time. The chapter will also present new intercountry comparisons of the volume of health services consumed, based on an approach recently put in place by the OECD and Eurostat.

Figure 1.1 is more complex to construct than meets the eye. Indeed, its construction reflects a number of measurement issues that are specific to health services. The first specificity is that unlike, say, a haircut, health services are not necessarily the object of transactions between two parties. Most countries' health systems operate under a private or public insurance system and the price for the service is often negotiated between the insurer and the health care provider rather than between the patient and the health care provider. Payments or reimbursements by health insurers are counted as consumer expenditures in the national accounts, and so require an imputation. A second specificity is that government may provide health services directly to individuals with only a nominal fee or no fee involved at all. Such social transfers in kind do not figure among consumer expenditures. International comparisons of health expenditures are thus best based on a measure of individual health services that sums up expenditures by patients and the value of the in-kind services provided by government. Such in-kind services need to be identified and valued. Figure 1.1 reflects such a valuation and shows total health expenditures whether incurred by patients (or their insurance companies) or whether provided by government. The third specificity is that health-care-providing units[1] are more often nonmarket producers than in other industries. This distinction entails a different accounting treatment, at least in the way the value of health services at current prices is measured: whereas the value of sales constitutes output for market producers, the value of output for nonmarket producers is measured as the sum of production costs.[2] The distinction between market and nonmarket producers is also important from the perspective of assessing efficiency in the provision of health services: market and nonmarket producers may take their decision on the quantities (and prices charged) following different objective functions. Differences in health care productivity performance may be associated with the share of nonmarket versus market producers and provide useful insights from international comparisons. Finally, the measurement of the volume of health services (as opposed to health expenditure) is tricky: rapid progress in medical technology and complex services bring out many of the measure-

1. Statistical information on health providers can be found in Section Q, Division 86, of the *International Standard Industrial Classification of All Economic Activities* (ISIC) Rev. 4, which includes hospital services, medical and dental practices, and other human health services providers.
2. As will be discussed below, the costs recognized by the SNA are incomplete as only depreciation is recognized as capital costs.

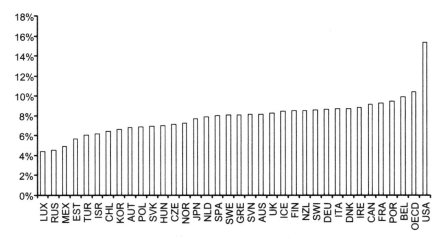

Fig. 1.1   Domestic health expenditure as a percentage of GDP, current prices (2011)
Source: Derived from OECD *Annual National Accounts* (2013).

ment challenges that statisticians face when developing price indices and volume measures in the national accounts.

The discussion about the measurement of health and education services is by no means new. Nearly forty years ago, Peter Hill (1975) developed a set of principles and guidance for measuring health, education, and collective government services. More recently, the debate has resurfaced. Eurostat (2001) stated the desirability of applying output-based measures to nonmarket services. In the United Kingdom, the topic was taken up by the widely discussed *Atkinson Review* (Atkinson 2005). The measurement of services output and productivity has also been a longstanding topic of interest in the United States, with a series of publications including Triplett (2001), Cutler and Berndt (2001), Triplett and Bosworth (2004), Abraham and Mackie (2006), and National Research Council (2010). Health services in particular have been the subject of research on cost-effectiveness and productivity (Cutler, Rosen, and Vijan 2006; Rosen and Cutler 2007). Much data development is also ongoing with the construction of health accounts for the United States, so as to be better able to track the flow of health-related funds through the economy. A recent overview of concepts and quality adjustments of measures of health and education services can be found in Schreyer (2010, 2012).

This chapter will only provide partial answers to these issues. Its aim is to provide an international perspective on the measurement of health care in the national accounts. Section 1.2 takes a look at the international accounting conventions for health services, as spelled out in the 2008 System of National Accounts (SNA 2008). Section 1.3 reviews relevant national accounts practices in a broad selection of OECD countries. Section 1.4 turns from intertemporal to interspatial comparisons and reports on recent efforts by the OECD to construct internationally comparable measures of the price levels and volumes of health care services. Section 1.5 concludes by summing up the key measurement tasks ahead.

1.2   What the SNA Has to Say about Measuring Health Services

1.2.1   Current Price Measures

The national accountant's task of measuring production begins with identifying the units that produce health services and distinguishing between market and nonmarket producers. Market producers sell their output at prices that are economically significant. Thus, for market health services, the value of output in current prices can be measured by the value of sales of these services. However, health provision is among the most common examples of services provided by government free of charge or at prices that are not economically significant and thus constitute nonmarket output. A price that is not economically significant is deliberately fixed well below the equilibrium price that would clear the market. The SNA defines it as a price that has little or no influence over how much the producer is willing to supply and that has only a marginal influence on the quantities demanded.

There are differences in country practices to identify the economic significance of prices. For instance, the European System of Accounts (ESA 1995) considers, for practical reasons, that a price is not economically significant if it covers less than half of the costs of producing the service. Neither the 2008 SNA nor its predecessor, the 1993 SNA have specified a particular level of cost coverage that complicates international comparisons of market and nonmarket provision. Whatever the exact rule, valuation of output is based on adding the costs incurred in production; namely, the sum of:

- intermediate consumption (the goods and services used up in producing the service);
- compensation of employees (costs of doctors, nurses, etc.);
- consumption of fixed capital (depreciation of hospital buildings, of medical equipment etc.); and
- other taxes, less subsidies, on production.

Note that, according to the 2008 SNA, capital costs for nonmarket producers are solely measured as the value of depreciation, thus ignoring that part of costs of capital services that reflect the opportunity costs of capital and revaluation. The main reason for this convention lies in the fact that any such imputation directly affects GDP and national income and that there is a broad spectrum of possible imputations. That said, Jorgenson and Landefeld (2006), Jorgenson and Yun (2001), and OECD (2009) show alternatives for dealing with this complication. From the perspective of productivity measurement, the asymmetric treatment of assets used in market

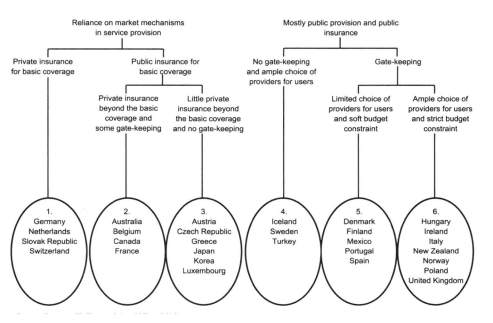

Fig. 1.2   Institutions in health care provision in OECD countries
Source: Joumard et al. (2010).

and in nonmarket production results in an incomplete estimate of capital inputs and in an asymmetric treatment of the same asset, depending on the sector affiliation of the asset owner (Jorgenson and Schreyer 2013). For analytical applications it may therefore be considered useful to deviate from the national accounts convention. An example for such an application is Mas, Pérez, and Uriel (2006), who examine the contribution of infrastructure capital, largely held by government entities, to economic growth in Spain and who apply a complete user cost expression to public capital. We conclude that a breakdown between market and nonmarket production in the publication of national accounts data would be of significant interest to analysts.

A further complication arises in health provision measurement due to the existence of insurance schemes of different scopes and variations. Unlike other services that are directly transacted between the supplier and the consumer, health service transactions often occur between three parties: the health service supplier, the consumer, and the public or private insurance schemes. The consequence is that transacted payments between the supplier and the consumer are not necessarily indicative of the price of the health service. Institutions vary greatly between countries, as shown in figure 1.2. Any international comparison of health care expenditures, say, in proportion to GDP, needs therefore to be based on measures reflecting full costs in health care provision, whether they accrue to patients, private providers, or government. This is indeed the approach pursued by the OECD-Eurostat Programme on Purchasing Power Parities (Koechlin, Lorenzoni, and Schreyer 2010), where the value of actual individual consumption of health care is deflated with international price indices to arrive at volume comparisons of per capita consumption of health services between countries.

1.2.2   Volumes

Market and Nonmarket Producers

The current value of health services, if provided by nonmarket producers, is always valued at cost in the national accounts. Thus, the value of inputs equals the value of outputs. At the same time, this does not mean that the volume of outputs cannot be distinguished from the inputs used to produce it. Changes in productivity may occur in all fields of production, including the production of nonmarket services.[3] Volume measurement is thus inherently different from the measurement of values, also in the case of nonmarket producers. However, volume measurement of the services provided by nonmarket producers is not inherently different from volume measurement of the services provided by market producers. This was first pointed out by Hill (1975, 19):

> It is proposed as a matter of principle that the basic methodology used to measure changes in the volume of real output should always be the same irrespective of whether a service is provided on a market or on a non-market basis. This is not to say that the actual numerical measures would not be affected by whether the service is market or non-market, because different weighting systems would be involved, but at least the methods of measurement should be conceptually similar.

Schreyer (2010) confirms this principle, but points out that in practice there has been a tendency to create separate volume indices for market and nonmarket production.[4] Traditionally, volume output measures for nonmarket producers have been based on volume measures of inputs with the implication of assuming zero productivity change and the risk of inadequately capturing changes in living standards and macroeconomic productivity. A number of possibilities exist for deriving output-based volume measures of health services.

In a market-based health system where there is information on market prices, expenditure on the treatment of a disease can be deflated by a

3. See SNA (2008, paragraph 15.116).
4. Perhaps slightly confusing, the 2008 SNA (2008, paragraph 15.118) recommends a "volume output method" for volume measurement of health services, but anchors this recommendation in a discussion on nonmarket output. This may create the impression that the volume output method is specific to nonmarket producers, which it is not.

disease-specific price index to arrive at a volume output measure of the disease. For example, Berndt et al. (2000) have estimated a price index for heart attacks and this index can be used to deflate disease-specific expenditures. This is similar to what happens in other market sectors in the economy where volume output measurement is accomplished by dividing data on revenues or sales by a price index.

In some countries, hospitals and other providers of medical services are considered market producers because they receive economically significant revenues from reimbursement schemes that, on average, cover their costs. In such cases, a "quasi-price" index consists of average revenues per treatment. One notes, however, that reimbursement schemes are themselves based on cost so that the differentiation between costs and revenues is blurred. Also, the fact that there are revenues does not imply that there is a competitive market where prices necessarily carry signals about consumer preferences.

In some instances, it may also be possible to draw on market price information for purposes of deflating values of nonmarket production. A potential candidate is the medical services part of the Consumer Price Index. However, care has to be exerted to make sure that the CPI is representative for the deflation of the nonmarket production. In particular, (a) the services supplied by the market provider have to be sufficiently similar to those supplied by the nonmarket provider, and (b) the scope of the CPI has to match the scope of nonmarket production. This may not be the case when the CPI is designed to reflect prices for out-of-pocket expenditures and when consumers only pay part of the full price for the medical good or service. In this case, the CPI is not an appropriate tool for deflation of nonmarket production, which relies on a concept of measuring production at its full cost.

Alternatively, direct volume indices can be constructed. A direct volume index is the weighted average of the volume indices of different types of treatments, where the cost share of each type of treatment constitutes the weight. Berndt et al. (2000, 173) suggest that "real output of medical care could be formed from cost of disease accounts by counting quantities of medical procedures (the number of heart bypass operations, say, or of appendectomies, or of influenza shots), and weighing each procedure by its cost." Although there are some differences between a direct volume index and a volume index derived at by deflation (such as index number formulae, timeliness of data), the basic idea remains the same—volume measures of outputs are sought, as opposed to volume measures of inputs.

Outputs and Outcomes

A key distinction in this context is between inputs, outputs, and outcomes. The 2008 SNA makes this distinction as follows:

> Taking health services as an example, input is defined as the labour input of medical and non-medical staff, the drugs, the electricity and other

inputs purchased [. . .] These resources are used in the activity of primary care and in hospital activities, such as a general practitioner making an examination, the carrying out of a heart operation and other activities designed to benefit the individual patient. The benefits to the patient constitute the output associated with these activities. Finally, there is the health outcome, which may depend on a number of factors apart from the output of health care, such as whether or not the person gives up smoking. (SNA 2008, paragraph 15.120)

From a national accounts perspective, the target measure for the production of health services is outputs, not outcomes. This distinction is more difficult than meets the eye, however. First, the SNA reference to output as "benefits to the patient" is best understood as the marginal contribution of health care activities to health outcomes, controlling for all other factors influencing outcomes. This means that the notion of outputs does not exist independently of outcomes. A similar conclusion (Schreyer 2012) arises in the context of quality adjustment (see below). Berndt et al. (1998) distinguish between medical care ("output" in our terminology), the state of health ("outcome" in our terminology), and utility. They envisage a relationship whereby utility depends, among other variables, on the state of health and where the state of health is itself dependent on health care services, on the environment, lifestyle, and so forth. Thus, a health care activity with a higher composite quality than another health care activity could be identified as such if it contributes more to health outcome than the alternative activity.[5]

In practice, output of health service providers in the national accounts is increasingly operationalized via disease-based measures of health service provision, more or less in line with the OECD guidance on the matter: "In the case of diseases, our central notion in defining health care services is the *treatment of a disease or medical services to prevent a disease*. Volume measures of output are then disease-based measures. Ideally, in the case of a treatment, the unit of output would capture *complete treatments*, and would take into account quality change in the provision of treatments. This measurement of health care output would then be able to differentiate among price, quantity and quality changes." (Schreyer 2010, 73). When disease-based measures are introduced, they tend to be applied to both market and nonmarket producers of health services. This does not apply to those general government institutions that are part of the health sector at

---

5. Things are further complicated in practice. First, as Berndt et al. (1998) point out, there is an issue of lags: the state of health may be affected by medical care and by other factors with a lag so that utility derived from the state of health occurs at a different date from when medical services are provided. Second, there may also be a trade-off between immediate utility derived from consumption (say, a fatty diet) and long-term disutility from reduced health status. This complicates formalization of consumer behavior, but is secondary to the issue at hand, namely, the measurement of health services.

large (such as Ministries of Health), but not part of the providing industry. Nearly universally, the volume of general government output is measured via the volume of its inputs.

Weights

Another conceptual question concerns the choice of weights to aggregate across different types of outputs. For nonmarket production, prices, if they exist, are not a meaningful tool to aggregate. However, measurement can be based on *unit costs or quasi prices*. They are those (unobserved) "prices" that emulate a competitive situation where prices equal average costs per product. Unit costs are observable and can be treated *as if they were prices*. Diewert (2011, 2012) and Schreyer (2012) discuss the question of weights extensively, but for the purpose at hand it suffices to remind us that unit cost weights are a legitimate way of aggregating across nonmarket services that can subsequently be applied to obtain productivity measures.

Consider the treatment of disease i that is characterized by a unit cost function $c_i^t(\mathbf{w}^t)$ where $\mathbf{w}^t$ is a vector of input prices such as doctors' wages or user costs of hospital equipment. As c_i^t is a cost function, it represents minimum costs necessary to carry out the treatment at hand. Quasi prices are then simply defined to equal unit costs:

$$(1) \qquad\qquad p_i^t \equiv c_i^t(\mathbf{w}^t).$$

If minimum costs equal actual costs one has $c_i^t(\mathbf{w}^t)y_i^t = \mathbf{w}^t \cdot \mathbf{x}_i^t$, where y_i^t is the number of treatments of type i, and $\mathbf{x}_i^t$ is the quantity vector of inputs that corresponds to $\mathbf{w}^t$:

$$(2) \qquad\qquad p_i^t y_i^t \equiv c_i^t(\mathbf{w}^t)y_i^t = \mathbf{w}^t \cdot \mathbf{x}_i^t.$$

Expression (2) states the obvious; namely, that with quasi prices, the value output of product i equals the value of inputs used in production of product i. This is the way nonmarket output is valued in the *System of National Accounts*.[6] However, as pointed out earlier, equality of inputs and outputs in value does *not* imply equality of inputs and outputs in volume or quantity.

The main difference between cost-based prices of outputs (quasi prices) and prices of inputs is that the former correspond to *costs per unit of output* (such as the costs for one treatment of a heart attack), whereas the latter correspond to the *costs per unit of input* (such as wages per hour of a nurse).

Diewert (2011) shows formally how a cost-based volume index of output can be defined. He defines the Laspeyres version of a cost-based output quantity index as the (hypothetical) total cost $C^0(\mathbf{y}^1, \mathbf{w}^0)$ of producing the output vector $\mathbf{y}^1$ of period 1 under the conditions of period 0 technology

---

6. For a genesis of the treatment of nonmarket production in the national accounts and the many issues associated with it, see Vanoli (2002).

and input prices, divided by the actual costs of period 0, $C^0(y^0, w^0)$. Similarly, he defines a Paasche version of a cost-based output quantity index as the actual costs of period 1, $C^1(y^1, w^1)$, divided by the hypothetical costs $C^1(y^0, w^1)$ that would have been incurred, had the products of period 0 been produced in period 1, under the technological constraints of period 1 and given period 1 input prices:

(3) $$Q_L = C^0(y^1, w^0)/ C^0(y^0, w^0) = \Sigma_i^N c_i^0 y_i^1 / \Sigma_i^N c_i^0 y_i^0$$

$$Q_P = C^1(y^1, w^1)/C^1(y^0, w^1) = \Sigma_i^N c_i^1 y_i^1 / \Sigma_i^N c_i^1 y_i^0$$

$$Q_F = [Q_L Q_P]^{1/2}.$$

The same reasoning can be applied to quasi prices and an *indirect index of quasi prices* constructed by dividing total costs by the volume index of output:

(4) $$P_L = [C^1(y^1, w^1)/C^0(y^0, w^0)]/Q_P = \Sigma_i^N c_i^1 y_i^0 / \Sigma_i^N c_i^0 y_i^0$$

$$P_P = [C^1(y^1, w^1)/C^0(y^0, w^0)]/Q_L = \Sigma_i^N c_i^1 y_i^1 / \Sigma_i^N c_i^0 y_i^1$$

$$P_F = [P_L P_P]^{1/2}.$$

Although these indexes are constructed using input prices, the indexes do take into account productivity gains in providing medical care. To see this, insert the theoretical expression for Q_P into the first line of (4) and rewrite the Laspeyres expression (4) as the product of two terms:

(5) $$P_L = [C^1(y^1, w^1)/C^0(y^0, w^0)]/Q_P$$

$$= [C^1(y^1, w^1)/C^0(y^0, w^0)]/[C^1(y^1, w^1)/C^1(y^0, w^1)]$$

$$= [C^1(y^0, w^1)/C^0(y^0, w^0)]$$

$$= [C^1(y^0, w^1)/C^1(y^0, w^0)][C^1(y^0, w^0)/C^0(y^0, w^0)].$$

The first term in the last line of expression (5) is an economic index of input prices: costs are compared between two situations, with technology and the level of output held fixed, but input prices are allowed to vary. The second term in the same line is an inverted productivity index: for a given reference output and input prices, changes in minimum costs between the periods are compared. Similar transformations could be applied to P_P and then combined with P_L to yield a decomposition of P_F, but there is no need to present them here. The main point can easily be explained with the decomposition of P_L only: in a market situation, a productivity index equals an input price index divided by an (output) price index: if output prices rise less rapidly than input prices, this implies productivity improvements. In the nonmarket case, the quasi-price index for outputs plays a similar role as the output price index in a market situation. If quasi prices (unit costs) rise less rapidly than input prices, there has been productivity change.

The measurement of productivity as a shift in the cost function is a well-established methodology[7] and we conclude that the cost-weighted measure of outputs is a fully valid measure output that also qualifies for productivity comparisons. Despite the fact that much of the discussion about nonmarket producers has been by way of costs, we *are* lending an output perspective to our calculations: unit costs or quasi prices are productivity-adjusted input prices and the productivity adjustment marks the movement from an input perspective toward an output perspective in measuring nonmarket activity. This is not always well understood because costs are rightly seen as input-related variables. The above makes it clear that considering costs per unit *of output* differentiates an output perspective from considering costs per unit *of input*, that is, the input perspective. However, the cost-based measures of output remain incomplete insofar as they invoke no direct element of consumer valuation—unit costs are not a product of the interplay between producers and consumers as in the market case. Unit costs are only reflective of the supply side.

Quality Change

An unrealistic assumption in the model above is the unchanged set of products between two periods. In reality, the quality of products changes over time, certain products disappear from the market and new products emerge. These changes constitute not only a major practical challenge for statisticians, they also have consequences for theoretical considerations about output and utility. The distinction between new products and quality change[8] will be ignored here, but a few general points about quality adjustment[9] of prices or quantities will be noted.

One technique to deal with quality change in products is to group them such that only products of the same specification are compared over time or in space. Such grouping or matching ensures that only prices or quantities of products of the same or very similar quality are compared. The idea is that products of different quality are treated as different products. Examples for such grouping are medical services provided by hospitals with different levels of nonmedical services. Also, when the nature of the service changes due to certain consumer characteristics, grouping may be necessary. For example, an elderly patient suffering from the same disease as a young patient may need more care due to longer time to recover. This may result in higher expenditures for the group of older patients. Note that capturing quality differences through grouping and matching the groups over time

---

7. Balk (1998, 58) provides a full treatment of the various productivity measures. In his terminology, our measure of technical change would be labeled a "dual input based technical change index." Diewert and Nakamura (2007) also discuss dual, cost-based measures of productivity change.

8. For a discussion see, for example, ILO et al. (2004).

9. For an in-depth treatment of quality adjustment in price measurement, see Triplett (2006).

relies on an important assumption: the price or quantity movements of those products that are matched have to be a good indicator of the price or quantity movements of those products that are not matched—in particular, products that are newly entering the market. Also, all other price or quantity changes that arise outside the sample of matched products are ignored.

A more sophisticated way of grouping is with hedonic regression techniques[10] that help controlling for characteristics of treatments and patients. For instance, Berndt et al. (2001) use patient characteristics, information on different types of depression, variables on medication and the like, to estimate a hedonic price model for the treatment of depression; the idea being to isolate those price changes that are due to changes in characteristics from those price changes that constitute "inflation." However, in situations of nonmarket production, the applicability of hedonic techniques is more limited or at least more complex (Schreyer 2012).

Yet another way to tackle quality change in medical care is to start from the observation that consumers attach utility to a good or to a service because it affects outcome, that is, a particular state that they value and that can be measured. One could also say that outcome is an intermediate step between consumption and utility, and this is indeed the way it has been treated in the literature. Thus, one possibility to deal with quality adjustment and aggregation is to subsume several characteristics into a single indicator that reflects the *contribution of the product to outcome*. For example, in the case of price indices for health care, Triplett (2003) suggests quality-adjusted life years (QALYs) as a single dimensional measure that could be used for the quality adjustment of different treatments within a product group. The point is to derive a single indicator that serves as a reasonable summary of a true, multidimensional set of quality characteristics valued by consumers when purchasing health services. Careful judgment needs to be applied in the choice of such a measure. In particular, it should not be affected by any other factors that influence consumer outcome (e.g., socioeconomic background of students or lifestyle of patients).

While quality adjustment is a tricky task, there should be no reason to recommend against it. Oddly, the latest Eurostat *Handbook on Price and Volume Measures* in the National Accounts (Eurostat, forthcoming), expressly advises against explicit quality adjustment of health output measures. At the same time, this recommendation only seems to apply to nonmarket production of health services. For market production, the use of a producer price index is recommended. As good practice for producer prices includes adequate quality adjustment, the Eurostat recommendation also entails an asymmetry between market and nonmarket production (see box 1.1).

---

10. See Triplett (2006) for a comprehensive discussion.

Box 1.1 The Meanings of "Outcome"

Outcome has been used in different ways in the relevant literature on health services. Two usages are common:

In the health care literature, "outcome" is typically defined as the resulting change in health status that is directly attributable to the health care received. Triplett (2001) indicates this usage in the cost-effectiveness literature and quotes Gold et al. (1996), who define a health outcome as the end result of a medical intervention, or the change in health status associated with the intervention over some evaluation period or over the patient's lifetime. Employed in this sense, some authors suggest that the "output" of the health care industry be measured by outcome.

Among national accountants, outcome is typically used to describe a state that consumers value; for example, the health status without necessarily relating the change in this state to the medical intervention. For example, Eurostat (2001) gives as examples of "outcome indicators" the level of education of the population, life expectancy, or the level of crime. Atkinson (2005) has the same usage of the word. Understood in this sense, outcome in itself cannot be a useful way to measure output or the effectiveness of the health or education system. In terms of national accounts semantics, the "marginal contribution of the health care industry to outcome" is the equivalent to the notion of outcome as used in the health care literature.

As long as a particular definition is used consistently, the substance of the argument is, of course, unaffected and the only question is the usefulness of one definition or the other. As the note follows in the line of Eurostat (2001) and the *Atkinson Review* (Atkinson 2005), it also employs the term "outcome" in the sense of the national accounts literature.

1.3   Overview of Country Practices—Comparisons in Time

In this section, we take an international perspective and address the issue of how health services are measured in countries' national accounts in practice. Schreyer (2010, table 4.4) provided an overview for thirty OECD countries, plus a more detailed analysis for six European countries: Austria, Denmark, Germany, Netherlands, Norway, and the United Kingdom. The first task addressed in this section is updating the information for the set of countries. Table 1.1 reflects a few updates, but a more extensive process of updating is presently being launched through the OECD's Working Party

Table 1.1 Overview of country practices in the volume measurement of health services

Country	Status	Hospital activities			Medical and dental practice activities		Other human health activities
		Acute hospitals	Mental health and substance abuse hospitals; specialized hospitals	Residential care activities	Doctor services	Dental services	
Austria	Implemented, data since 2001	Deflation with index based on unit costs per treatment by DRGs, cost weights	Deflation with index based on unit costs per treatment by DRGs, cost weights	Number of occupant days, weighted by revenues, no quality adjustment	Number of treatments weighted by revenues, no quality adjustments	Sixty-four indices based on fees per single service item paid by the social security, weighted by revenues	Deflation by HCPI
Australia	Implemented	Direct volume index based on DRGs, cost weights	n/a	Number of cases by level of care weighted by subsidy rates	Number of services weighted by fees charged	Number of services weighted by cost	n/a
Belgium	Implemented in 2009, data available since 1995	All hospitals are market producers; direct volume index, based on DRGs, cost weights	Number of occupant days by level of care, weighted by income by category of hospital services	Number of occupant days by level of care, weighted by income by category of hospital services	Number of consultations, use of regulated price of services	Number of consultations, use of regulated price of services	Number of consultations, use of regulated price of services
Canada	Implemented	Deflation with input price index	n/a	n/a	n/a	n/a	n/a
	Planned	Exploratory work (Gu and Morin 2014)					
Czech Republic	Implemented	Deflation with index based on daily rates for hospital			Number of treatments	Number of treatments	CPI component
Denmark	Implemented	Deflation with index based on unit costs per treatment by DRGs, cost weights	Deflation with index based on unit costs per discharge by diagnostic group, cost weights	Deflation with index based on unit cost per type of patient by type of care, cost weights	Deflation—CPI component	Deflation with index based on unit cost per patient by two types of care, cost weights	n/a
Finland	Implemented, data available since 2000	Volume index based on DRGs, cost weights	Number of day care days	Number of day care days	Number of consultations by type of consultation (17)	Number of consultations by type of consultation (3)	n/a

Country							
France	Implemented, data available since 1998	Volume index based on DRGs, cost weights	Volume index based on DRGs, cost weights	Volume index based on DRGs, cost weights	Deflation—CPI component	Deflation—CPI component	Deflation—CPI component
Germany	Implemented, data available since 2006	All hospitals are market producers; deflation with index based on unit costs per inpatient treatment by groups of DRGs, cost weights + explicit quality adjustment	Number of day care days or number of treatments, cost weights	Number of persons at the end of the year, cost weights by care level	Deflation—unit value for medical/dental services (statutory) and CPI component (private)	Deflation—CPI component	Deflation—CPI component
Greece	Implemented	Number of day care days	Number of day care days	Number of day care days	Deflation—CPI component	Deflation—CPI component	Deflation—CPI component
Hungary	Implemented, data available since 2001	Volume indices based on DRGs weighted by quasi-prices	Volume indices based on DRGs weighted by quasi-prices	Number of visits	Number of consultations	Number of scores	Number of treatments on basis of services provided
Iceland	Implemented	Deflation with input price index	n/a	n/a	n/a	n/a	n/a
	Planned	n/a	n/a	n/a	n/a	n/a	n/a
Ireland	Implemented	Deflation with input price index	n/a	n/a	n/a	n/a	n/a
	Planned	n/a	n/a	n/a	n/a	n/a	n/a
Italy	Implemented, data available since 2000	Volume indices based on DRGs, weighted by costs	Volume indices based on DRGs, weighted by costs	Volume indices based on DRGs, weighted by costs	Number of prescriptions	Deflation—CPI component	Deflation—CPI component
Japan	Implemented	Market—CPI component	Market—CPI component	Market—CPI component	Market—CPI component	Market—CPI component	Market—CPI component
Korea	Implemented	Market—CPI component	Market—CPI component	Market—CPI component	Market—CPI component	Market—CPI component	Market—CPI component

(continued)

Table 1.1 (continued)

| Country | Status | Hospital activities | | Residential care activities | Medical and dental practice activities | | Other human health activities |
		Acute hospitals	Mental health and substance abuse hospitals; specialized hospitals		Doctor services	Dental services	
Luxembourg	Implemented, data available since 2000	Deflation—CPI component	Deflation—CPI component	Number of day care days or number of cases by level of care for nonmarket (cost weighted, no quality adjustments); deflation—CPI component for market	Number of consultations or treatments for nonmarket (cost weighted, no quality adjustments); deflation—CPI component for market		
Netherlands	Implemented	Direct volume index based on ICDs by age and discharge numbers + share in day care days as weight	Direct volume indicators based on days of treatments, days of hospitalization, and hours of delivered care	Deflation—CPI component (CTG tariff)	Deflation—CPI component (CTG tariff)	Deflation—CPI component (CTG tariff)	
New Zealand	Implemented	Government (nonmarket) hospitals: composite volume index based on DRGs, cost weighted; patient discharge and bed-night numbers. Private market: deflation—CPI component	Combined with acute hospitals	Number of employee hours worked	Deflation—CPI component	Deflation—CPI component	Deflation—CPI component

Country			Number of day care days by levels of care	Number of day care days	Deflation—CPI component	Deflation—CPI component	Deflation—CPI component
Norway	Implemented	Direct volume index based on DRGs, cost weighted	Direct volume index based on DRGs; use of regulated price by DRGs (quasi-price)	n/a	Direct volume index based on number of consultations, use of regulated price (quasi-price)	n/a	Number of consultations or treatments
Portugal	Implemented	Direct volume index based on DRGs; use of regulated price by DRGs (quasi-price)	Direct volume index based on DRGs; use of regulated price by DRGs (quasi-price)	n/a	Direct volume index based on number of consultations, use of regulated price (quasi-price)	n/a	n/a
Sweden	Implemented, data available since 2003	Direct volume index based on DRGs, cost weights	Direct volume index based on number of days of care by level of care	Direct volume index based on number of days of care by level of care	Direct volume index based on number of consultations, cost weighted	Direct volume index based on number of consultations, cost weighted	Number of consultations or treatments
Switzerland	Implemented	Deflation with input price index	n/a	n/a	n/a	n/a	n/a
United Kingdom	Implemented, data from 1995. England and Northern Ireland	Direct volume index based on HRGs, cost weights	Direct volume index based on HRGs, cost weights	Proxied by growth in hospital activities (only includes health-related residential care activities)	Direct volume index based on number of consultations, cost weighted	1995–2006: Direct volume index based on number of treatments, cost weighted. From 2006: proxied by growth in hospital activities	Proxied by growth in hospital activities
United States	Implemented	Deflation using DRG-based indexes from BLS for inpatient care and the BLS PPI for outpatient care	Deflation—use of relevant component of CPI/PPI	Deflation—use of relevant component of CPI/PPI	Deflation—use of relevant component of CPI/PPI	Deflation—use of relevant component of CPI/PPI	Deflation—use of relevant component of CPI/PPI
	Planned	Direct volume index based on DRGs, cost weights; further development of price indexes	n/a	n/a	n/a	n/a	n/a

Source: Adapted from Schreyer (2010).

on National Accounts in 2014. Consequently, for the time being, we mainly rely on existing information from Schreyer (2010) and some more recent and specific examples for Germany, Spain, Hungary, and the United Kingdom that have been investigated as part of the European Union's INDESCER project (Goerlich et al. 2012; Hüttl et al. 2011; Hüttl et al., forthcoming), as well as a research project by Statistics Canada (Gu and Morin 2014).

Pathway through Institutions. Another issue, potentially important, is whether treatments can be observed throughout the pathways of health care institutions. For instance, a treatment may start as an inpatient treatment in a hospital and continue as outpatient treatment. In most countries, tracking treatments in this way is not possible. As a consequence, the effects of shifts between inpatient and outpatient treatments on volume measures of health care may be lost or obscured.

Residential Care. Note important differences between areas of health care. The above, conceptual, discussion was framed with "a treatment" in mind and led to endorsing a disease-based approach toward measuring health care services. While the disease-based approach is no doubt useful for hospital services, it may be less evident when it comes to the broader set of health care institutions. In particular, residential care activities are different in nature from hospital and medical practice activities and account for sizable shares of overall health expenditure. It is difficult to conceptualize the correct measure of output of residential care and, typically, one will be led back to a measure of inputs or number of days in residential care, possibly differentiated by intensity of care. Certainly in practice, these are the measures most frequently found.

Table 1.1 calls for several observations:

- There are still significant differences in the methods used to measure the volume of hospital services. For instance, to date, the United States, Canada, Mexico, Chile, Japan, and Korea are employing input-based volume measures; Australia, New Zealand, and many EU countries use output-based measures. At the same time, there are many shadings to the output-based measures and, indeed, it is not always clear whether certain methods do qualify as input based or output based, for example, the number of hospital days.[11] More information is also required to pass a judgement on the nature of those output measurements that are based on relevant CPI or Producer Price Index (PPI) components. Do these components reflect full prices? How have they been valued?
- Where output-based methods for hospital care have been chosen, these tend to rely on diagnosis-related groups (DRGs) or hospital discharge information, and thus share the characteristic of a disease-based mea-

11. This is the case of Greece that has been placed under the "deflation with input price index" heading in table 1.1.

sure. For reasons mentioned earlier, there is also great similarity in countries' approaches toward measuring residential care activities.

• It is tremendously difficult to make a statement about the degree of international comparability of measures of hospital services based on table 1.1. While it is obvious that methods vary between countries, this does not necessarily imply significant problems of comparability of results. Comparability is often quoted as one of the advantages of traditional, input-based measures for health services. However, as there is no reason to believe that the bias induced by input-based methods (instead of output-based measures) is the same across countries, reverting to input-based computations would not really solve the problem of comparability. One avenue to gain insight into the comparability of output-based measures is currently pursued by the OECD: as standardized data for spatial comparisons of health prices is progressively collected (see Koechlin, Lorenzoni, and Schreyer 2010), it may be possible to use this information to also construct temporal indices of health care services that would then serve as a counterfact to national methods.

Quality Adjustment in Practice. Of the various methods to quality-adjust volume or price indices of health care, the vast majority of OECD countries has relied on stratification and matching. A good example is Finland, whose approach toward quality adjustment is clearly rooted in stratification. Statistics Finland aims at capturing quality change by classifying medical services into strictly homogeneous quality groups of products. Statistics Finland considers that outcome is not a concept in national accounts, and correcting for changes in outcome introduces a normative element that is not in line with the positive approach of national accounts. From a practical angle, Statistics Finland considers that outcome-based quality corrections might offer too little and arrive too late for decision makers. Experimental work with explicit quality adjustment has been pursued by the UK Office of National Statistics (see box 1.2), but is scarce otherwise. Eurostat, the Statistical Office of the European Union, has even advised against the use of explicit quality-adjustment procedures on the grounds that if explicit methods are used by some EU countries but not by others or if the quality-adjustment methods used are very different, this would undermine comparability of volume measures of health care in the European national accounts.

1.4   Price Levels and Volumes of Health Services—Comparisons in Space

While the measurement of the evolution of health services in a particular country is of considerable interest, so is the comparison of the level of health services in different countries at a particular point in time. For example, figure 1.1 showed levels of health expenditure as a share of GDP across countries with marked differences. What policymakers and analysts would

Box 1.2 Explicit Quality Adjustments—United Kingdom

The UK Office for National Statistics (ONS) is the statistical office among OECD countries that has gone furthest in investigating and advancing the measurement of volume health services, and government services more generally. One of the triggers for this activity was the *Atkinson Review* (Atkinson 2005) commissioned by the British government and work carried out for the UK Department of Health by the University of York and the National Institute of Economics and Social Research ([NIESR]; Dawson et al. 2005). However, at present, the quality adjustments remain exploratory and have not been reflected in the UK National Accounts. The explicit quality-adjustment procedure is developed by the Centre for Health Economics (CHE) at York University (CHE 2005) and the Department of Health (DH 2005, 2007). The method was implemented using data for England, and an assumption is made that the rest of the United Kingdom follows the same trend. The quality adjustments take account of some aspects of quality that are not readily captured by disease-

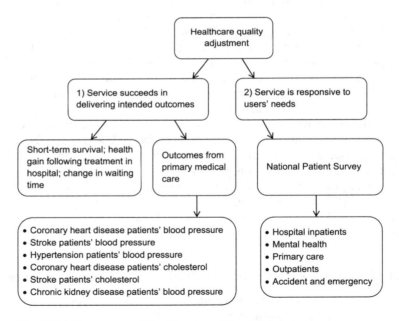

Fig. 1B2.1 Components of healthcare quality adjustment
Source: ONS (2011, 12).

Box 1.2   (continued)

based activity measures. The adjustments reflect two dimensions of quality (see figure 1B2.1): (a) the extent to which the service succeeds in delivering its intended outcomes, and (b) the extent to which the service is responsive to users' needs.

In practice, the first dimension accounts for at least 99.5 percent of total quality adjustment. It consists of two composite measures: (a) short-term survival rates, health gain following treatment in hospital and change in waiting times; and (b) outcomes from primary medical care. According to the ONS (2011), in 2009 quality-adjusted output was 7.1 percent greater than quantity (unadjusted output). From 2001 to 2009, quality adjustments added an average of 0.5 percentage points (pp) a year to output growth. The main contribution to quality change came from survival, health gain, and waiting times, which improved by an annual average of 0.66 pp from 2001–02 to 2008–09. Smaller contributions come from primary care and responsiveness to users' needs, with an annual coverage improvement of 0.07 pp and 0.01 pp, respectively, over the same period. Finally, quality change rose from 0.4 pp in 2007–08 to 1.11 pp in 2008–09. This came almost entirely from an improvement in thirty-day survival rates following treatment, and a reduction in waiting times was the main reason for an increase in quality in 2009.

like to understand is whether these differences in expenditure reflect more or less health services or higher or lower prices for these services in the various countries. This requires a spatial price index of health services that permits breaking down nominal expenditures into a price and volume component. The spatial price index comes in the form of a health-specific purchasing power parity (PPP).

The PPPs are regularly measured for all components of GDP.[12] Despite a long tradition of work in the area, the task remains challenging. Three main problems have to be addressed in the measurement of PPPs. The first is to identify products that are comparable across countries. This can be complicated because products are not identical, because there are differences in quality, or because products simply do not exist in all countries. The second issue is to ensure representativeness of products: whatever price

---

12. For a full description of the methods used, the reader is referred to Eurostat-OECD (2006, 2013).

is compared, it has to be the price of a product that is widely and typically purchased in each country. The third issue arises when there is a product, but no meaningful market price for comparison. Issues one and two arise in the comparison of all prices, issue three arises in the comparison of products that are produced and delivered outside markets. In many countries, health services count among these products.

When goods or services are supplied by a nonmarket producer, the prices charged to consumers are significantly below the price that a market producer would charge. In some cases, the price may even be zero. It would make no sense to compare such prices charged to patients or consumers across countries, as they reflect administrative decisions and not the value of products. A recent pilot study by the OECD (Koechlin, Lorenzoni, and Schreyer 2010) compares *quasi prices* across countries. In direct analogy to the temporal indices of quasi prices (see above), this deals with the issue of absent market prices in health provision. In what follows we briefly report on these results, pointing out that work is progressing in the area to move from a pilot stage to full, period implementation and to a broader scope than hospital services.

The Products: Case Types. For the study at hand, products were defined through *case types*. These refer to classes of hospital services that are similar from a clinical perspective. For instance, "heart failure" constitutes one case type. Each case type is further specified so as to compare similar occurrences of diseases. In the case of heart failure, the indication is given that "no operating room procedure is performed." This leads to greater homogeneity of case types also in terms of their consumption of resources. Twenty-nine inpatient[13] case types were identified[14] based on the following criteria. The case types should:

- represent common procedures or diagnoses;
- account for a significant percentage of hospital expenditures;
- represent procedures that are likely to be the principal procedure within one hospitalization (for surgical-case types); and
- represent well-identified conditions (for medical-case types).

The Valuation: Quasi Prices. It is rare that case types can be directly valued through freestanding costing studies and clinical trials. A more promising avenue is to use secondary data sets available through health administrations

13. Akin to temporal price and volume indices, we note that the explicit distinction between inpatient and outpatient case types implies that inpatient and outpatient services are considered different products. While plausible in some ways, this also means that the methodology is not able to capture price differences that are due to the fact that an inpatient treatment has been substituted by an outpatient treatment or vice versa. At this point it is not possible to quantify the extent of this possible bias.

14. See Koechlin, Lorenzoni, and Schreyer (2010) for a full list. The selection was based on a list of inpatient case vignettes (Huber 2007), on a proposal by the OECD Expert group on procedures under the Hospital Data Project (Smedby 2007), and on the list that is currently used at the OECD for Health Data collection (OECD 2011).

and national insurance funds for purposes of reimbursement and health financing. The administrative data sets provide quasi prices, encompassing both negotiated prices and administered prices. The former are established through independent negotiations between purchasers/third-party payers and providers, and are not necessarily directly tied to the cost of care. While there may be differences between negotiated and administered regimes (Castelli 2007; Triplett 2003), the general principle for compilation of quasi prices is that at a minimum they are reflective of the full set of costs, compatible with costs as defined in the national accounts (see above).

Results. One key result of a comparison of hospital quasi prices is an index of comparative price levels for medical services. By way of example, table 1.2 shows results from the OECD pilot study for different types of inpatient hospital services.

Results were compiled for twelve countries. They are expressed as indices, with the average for the group of countries set to equal 100. The PPPs were computed so as to be invariant to the choice of the base country. Computation started with the United States as reference country, then comparative price levels (CPLs) were derived by dividing PPPs by market exchange rates, and the average of the group was calculated as the geometric mean of the CPLs of the different countries. This average was then set to equal 100 and each country's CPL expressed in relation to it. The CPLs provide a measure of the difference in price levels between countries by indicating—for a given category or aggregate—the number of units of the common currency needed to buy the same volume of the category or aggregate. In our example there is no common currency as such, and results should be interpreted looking at the relativities between countries rather than looking at absolute levels. For example, the figures in the table should be read as follows: in 2007, price levels for total inpatient hospital services in the United States stood at 163 percent of the average price level of the group of countries, and were therefore nearly 44 percent (163 compared to 113) higher than in Canada.

Main findings, generally in line with evidence from other sources, include: (a) hospital services in the United States are significantly more costly than in the other countries considered in this study, in particular, price levels in Korea and Israel are only around 60 percent of the average of all countries; and (b) for the twelve countries under consideration, price-level differences cannot be explained by differences in the average length of stay—rather, high-priced countries also exhibit high prices per day of hospitalization.

The above results are a first step toward more systematic and broad-based measurement of spatial price and volume indices for health services. The methodology needs further refinement, and a second-best approach for countries where the available data does not allow following the standard approach. Also, the methodology has to be expanded to cover PPPs for the services of mental health and specialty hospitals, nursing, and residential care facilities. The objective is to translate PPP results into volume measures

Table 1.2   Comparative price levels for hospital services and GDP (2007)

	AUS	CAN	FIN	FRA	ITA	ISR	KOR	POR	SLV	SWE	USA	Group
Inpatient medical services	122	125	91	140	158	60	37	90	65	112	173	100
Inpatient surgical services	124	113	99	114	132	65	66	81	56	116	163	100
Total inpatient hospital services	123	113	98	121	140	62	57	85	59	114	164	100
GDP	104	101	118	112	103	120	73	83	79	121	90	100
Reference: Per capita real GDP	115	118	108	99	95	82	81	69	81	113	142	100

Source: Koechlin, Lorenzoni, and Schreyer (2010).

of health services. This requires a set of expenditure data from the national accounts that are consistent with the present framework for health PPPs. Such consistency (for example, with regard to classifications) is important; otherwise, deflating health expenditure with health PPPs will give rise to biased measures of the volumes of health services across countries. These and other developments are presently undertaken by the OECD and Eurostat.

1.5   Conclusions

This chapter provided a national accounts perspective to the measurement of health service provision. It spelled out some of the key concepts and looked at practices in a number of OECD countries. A new approach toward cross-country comparisons of price and volume measures of health services was also presented. Key messages and conclusions are:

- While the measurement of the *value* of production of nonmarket producers is necessarily different from the measurement of the value of production of market producers (sum of costs for the former, revenues for the latter), the measurement of the *volume* of production may, and indeed should, follow the same method. There is increasing recognition that for many purposes, a disease-based approach toward output measurement is the right way forward.
- Information on the precise treatment in national accounts of institutional units involved in health care provision is scattered and incomplete. In particular, there are gaps in the information on market versus nonmarket producers, although this constitutes an analytically relevant distinction. It is not always clear whether methodologies for volume-output figures differ between market and nonmarket producers (and, among nonmarket producers between general government and nonprofit institutions serving households).
- It is tremendously difficult to make a statement about the degree of international comparability of measures of hospital services. While methods vary between countries, this does not necessarily imply significant problems of comparability of results. Comparability is often quoted as one of the advantages of traditional, input-based measures for health services. However, as there is no reason to believe that the bias induced by input-based methods (instead of output-based measures) is the same across countries, reverting to input-based computations would not really solve the problem of comparability.
- A new approach toward comparing volumes of health services internationally has been developed in the context of the Eurostat-OECD Purchasing Power Parity Programme. As evidence from this approach accumulates over several years, it is planned to construct time series of health service provision, which will provide a new point of comparison

with the existing national accounts data and advance the discussion on future developments in the measurement of health services nationally and internationally.

References

Abraham, K. G., and C. Mackie. 2006. "A Framework for Nonmarket Accounting." In *A New Architecture for the US National Account*, edited by Dale Jorgenson, J. Steven Landefeld, and William D. Nordhaus. Chicago: University of Chicago Press.

Atkinson, A. 2005. *The Atkinson Review: Final Report. Measurement of Government Output and Productivity for the National Accounts.* Basingstoke, UK: Palgrave Macmillan.

Balk, B. 1998. *Industrial Price, Quantity, and Productivity Indices: The Micro-Economic Theory and an Application.* Kluwer Academic Publishers.

Berndt, E. R., D. M. Cutler, R. G. Frank, Z. Griliches, J. P. Newhouse, and J. E. Triplett. 1998. "Price Indexes for Medical Care Goods and Services: An Overview of Measurement Issues." NBER Working Paper no. 6817, Cambridge, MA.

———. 2000. "Medical Care Price and Output." In *Handbook in Health Economics*, vol. 1a, edited by A. J. Culyer and J. P. Newhouse. Amsterdam: Elsevier.

———. 2001. "Price Indexes for Medical Goods and Services: An Overview of Measurement Issues." In *Medical Care Output and Productivity*, edited by D. M. Cutler and E. R. Berndt. Chicago: University of Chicago Press.

Castelli, A., D. Dawson, H. Gravelle, and A. Street. 2007. "Improving the Measurement of Health Systems Output Growth." *Health Economics* 16 (10): 1091–107.

CHE. 2005. "Developing New Approaches to Measuring Health Care Output and Productivity." CHE Technical Paper Series no. 31, York University and National Institute of Economics and Social Research.

Cutler, D. M., and E. R. Berndt, eds. 2001. *Medical Care Output and Productivity.* NBER Studies in Income and Wealth, vol. 62. Chicago: University of Chicago Press.

Cutler, D. M., A. B. Rosen, and S. Vijan. 2006. "The Value of Medical Spending in the United States, 1960–2000." *New England Journal of Medicine* 355:920–27.

Dawson, D., H. Gravelle, M. O'Mahony, A. Street, M. Weale, A. Castelli, R. Jacobs, P. Kind, P. Loveridge, S. Martin, P. Stevens, and L. Stokes. 2005. "Developing New Approaches to Measuring NHS Outputs and Productivity." Final Report to the Department of Health, Centre for Health Economics (York), and National Institute of Economic and Social Research.

Diewert, W. E. 2011. "Measuring Productivity in the Public Sector: Some Conceptual Problems." *Journal of Productivity Analysis* 36:177–91.

———. 2012. "The Measurement of Productivity in the Nonmarket Sector." *Journal of Productivity Analysis* 37:217–29.

Diewert, W. E., and A. Nakamura. 2007. "The Measurement of Aggregate Total Factor Productivity Growth." In *Handbook of Econometrics*, vol. 6A, edited by J. Heckman and E. Leamer. Amsterdam: North-Holland.

European System of Accounts (ESA). 1995. *European System of Accounts 1995.* Brussels-Luxembourg: Eurostat.

Eurostat. 2001. *Handbook on Price and Volume Measures in National Accounts.* Luxembourg: European Communities.

———. Forthcoming. *Handbook on Price and Volume Measures in National Accounts, revised version.* Luxembourg: European Communities.

Eurostat-OECD. 2006. *Methodological Manual on Purchasing Power Parities.* Paris: OECD.

———. 2013. *Methodological Manual on Purchasing Power Parities.* Paris: OECD.

Goerlich, F., J. Peréz, A. Hüttl, M. O'Mahony, E. Schulz, and L. Stokes. 2012. "Health Capital: An Application for Germany, Hungary, Spain and the UK." http://indicser.com/images/dp26_goerlich_et_al.pdf.

Gold, M. R., J. E. Siegel, L. B. Russel, and M. C. Weinstein, eds. 1996. *Cost Effectiveness in Health and Medicine.* New York: Oxford University Press.

Gu, W., and S. Morin. 2014. "Experimental Measures of Output and Productivity in the Canadian Hospital Sector, 2002 to 2010." In *Measuring Economic Sustainability and Progress*, edited by Dale W. Jorgenson, J. Steve Landefeld, and Paul Schreyer. Chicago: University of Chicago Press.

Hill, T. P. 1975. *Price and Volume Measures for Non-Market Services.* Report to the Statistical Office of the European Communities, Brussels.

Huber, M. 2007. "International Comparison of Prices and Volumes in Health Care among OECD Countries." European Center for Social Welfare Policy and Research. Paper presented at the first meeting of the Task Force for the Development of Health-Specific Purchasing Power Parities, Paris, June 8.

Hüttl, A., M. Mas, A. Nagy, G. Okem, M. O'Mahony, E. Schulz, and L. Stokes. 2011. "Measuring the Productivity of the Healthcare Sector: Theory and Implementation." http://indicser.com/images/RP5_Huttl_etal.pdf.

Hüttl, A., M. Mas, A. Nagy, M. O'Mahony, E. Schulz, and L. Stokes. Forthcoming. *Output and Productivity Growth in the Healthcare Sector: A Study of Four European Countries.*

International Labour Office (ILO), IMF, OECD, UN-ECE, World Bank. 2004. *Consumer Price Index Manual: Theory and Practice.* Washington, DC: International Monetary Fund.

Jorgenson, D. W., and J. S. Landefeld. 2006. "Blueprint for Expanded and Integrated US Accounts: Review, Assessment, and Next Steps." In *A New Architecture for the US National Accounts*, edited by Jorgenson, Landefeld, and Nordhaus, 13–112. Chicago: University of Chicago Press.

Jorgenson, D. W., and P. Schreyer. 2013. "Industry-Level Productivity Measurement and the 2008 System of National Accounts." *Review of Income and Wealth* 59 (2): 185–211.

Jorgenson, D. W., and K.-Y. Yun. 2001. *Lifting the Burden: Tax Reform, the Cost of Capital, and US Economic Growth.* Cambridge, MA: MIT Press.

Joumard, I., P. Hoeller, C. André, and C. Nicq. 2010. *Health Care Systems: Efficiency and Policy Settings.* Paris: OECD Publishing.

Koechlin, F., L. Lorenzoni, and P. Schreyer. 2010. "Comparing Price Levels of Hospital Services across Countries: Results of a Pilot Study." OECD Health Working Paper no. 53, Organisation for Economic Co-operation and Development.

Mas, M., F. Pérez, and E. Uriel. 2006. "Capital Stock in Spain, 1964–2002. New Estimates." In *Growth, Capital and New Technologies*, edited by M. Mas and P. Schreyer. Madrid: Fundación BBVA.

National Research Council. 2010. "Accounting for Health and Health Care: Approaches to Measuring the Sources and Costs of Their Improvement." Washington, DC: The National Academies Press. http://www.nap.edu/catalog.php?record_id=12938.

Office for National Statistics (ONS). 2011. "Public Service Output, Inputs and Productivity: Healthcare. Correction Notice." London: Office for National Statistics, April 7.

Organisation for Economic Co-Operation and Development (OECD). 2009. *Measuring Capital: Revised Manual.* Paris.

———. 2011. *Health at a Glance 2011: OECD Indicators.* Paris.

Rosen, A. B., and D. Cutler. 2007. "Measuring Medical Care Productivity: A Proposal for US National Health Accounts." *Survey of Current Business* June:54–58.

Schreyer, P. 2010. "Towards Measuring the Volume Output of Education and Health Services: A Handbook." OECD Statistics Working Paper no. 2010/02, Paris.

———. 2012. "Output, Outcome and Quality Adjustment in Measuring Health and Education Services." *Review of Income and Wealth* 58 (2): 257–78.

Smedby, B. 2007. "A Selected List of Hospital Procedures for International Comparison." Report on the Work of the Expert Group on Procedures under the HDP2 Project. Presentation at the OECD Health Data National Correspondents meeting, Paris, October 9–10.

System of National Accounts (SNA). 2008. *System of National Accounts 2008.* Washington, DC: International Monetary Fund.

Triplett, J. E. 2001. "What's Different about Health? Human Repair and Car Repair in National Accounts and in National Health Accounts." In *Medical Care Output and Productivity,* NBER Studies in Income and Wealth, vol. 62, edited by D. M. Cutler and E. R. Berndt, 15–96. Chicago: University of Chicago Press.

———. 2003. "Integrating Cost-of-Disease Studies into Purchasing Power Parities." In *A Disease-Based Comparison of Health Systems.* Paris: OECD.

———. 2006. *Handbook on Hedonic Indexes and Quality Adjustment in Price Indexes: Special Application to Information Technology Products.* Paris: OECD.

Triplett, J. E., and B. P. Bosworth. 2004. *Productivity in the US Services Sector: New Sources of Economic Growth.* Washington, DC: The Brookings Institution.

UK Department of Health (DH). 2005. *Healthcare Output and Productivity: Accounting for Quality Change.* December.

———. 2007. *Review of Data Sources and Methodology for the Calculations of Hospital Output in the NHS.*

Vanoli, A. 2002. *Une Histoire de la Comptabilité Nationale.* Paris: La Découverte.

Comment   J. Steven Landefeld

This chapter by Schreyer and Mas, "Measuring Health Services in the National Accounts: An International Perspective," is an important step in efforts to improve the consistency and relevance of health data used for public policy. Cross-country comparisons of health care spending and outcomes are common reference points in debates on the efficacy of alternative

J. Steven Landefeld was director of the Bureau of Economic Analysis when this comment was written and is currently a visiting professor at the United States Naval Academy and a consultant to the United Nations.

For acknowledgments, sources of research support, and disclosure of the author's material financial relationships, if any, please see http://www.nber.org/chapters/c13117.ack.

health care debates. Discussions of the US health care system, for example, often start by noting that the United States spends more on health care (per capita and as a share of GDP) than any other nation, yet it ranks last in the quality of health among major developed economies. Although, in broad terms these cross-country "facts" may be correct, for purposes of public policy, more nuanced, consistent, and relevant measures on health care spending, the distribution of that spending across the population, the drivers of cost by type of provider and disease, and the productivity (or quality-adjusted real output) of spending are needed.

One example of an important difference across countries, pointed out by Mas and Schreyer, is the inconsistent treatment under international accounting rules—the System of National Accounts (SNA)—of the costs of private relative to those of publicly provided and nonprofit health care institutions. The SNA counts all the costs for private for-profit hospitals, including their capital costs, but only counts the depreciation component of capital costs and excludes the interest component for government and nonprofit institutions. The result is to lower heath care costs in countries with a higher share of publicly provided services relative to countries with higher privately owned and operated share. One might also expect that there are problems in decomposing the administrative costs of governmentally run health systems between health-care and non-health-care costs relative to systems more reliant on private (for profit and nonprofit) institutions.

As Schreyer and Mas point out, other differences in measuring nominal health care expenditures are the inclusion of medical research and development and training and education expenditures by a number of countries. According to the SNA, such costs should be excluded from health care costs (and included in other GDP categories), but are included in health care costs for the majority of European countries covered by the authors' survey of metadata.

In addition to differences across countries in the measurement of nominal spending, there are large differences in the measurement of real output. Some countries use input-based output measures and others use output-based measures. Input-based measures of costs give no indication of the value of one medical outcome as compared to another and produce zero measured productivity growth in medical care as real inputs grow at the same rate as real output. As a result, output-based measures are essential to comparing the efficacy and productivity of medical care spending across countries.

Fortunately, as Mas and Schreyer observe, there is increasing use of disease-based price indexes that price out the cost of treating an episode of illness by disease categories. This method captures the impact on the total cost of treating an illness by the switch from one mode of treatment to another mode, for example, from high-cost talk therapy in the treatment of mental illness to lower-cost drug therapy, from expensive bypass surgery to drug therapy, or from inpatient to outpatient treatment. The impact of such switches from high to low cost (or low to high) are difficult to capture in conventional medical care price indexes, which tend to produce a weighted average of inflation rates for the various bundle of medical services used to treat a disease.

An interesting example of this work on pricing the cost of disease at the individual country level, using administrative claims microdata for the United States, is the work by Aizcorbe et al., described in chapter 6 of this volume. The cross-country results reported by Schreyer and Mas, using administrative data for representative and comparable hospital procedures for comparable diagnosis, are an important first step in applying this approach to comparisons of the costs and efficacy of medical services across countries.

Such disease-based indexes, using commercial and administrative "big" data, are likely to be essential to international health care debates. When combined with consistent reporting within and across countries, such data will be important in going beyond top-down projections of health care costs and case studies of efficacy by enabling a consistent breakdown of the drivers of costs at the national level by disease, by type of treatment, and by regions.

Despite progress in better measuring of medical care prices, considerable work remains in measuring the quality of care, or quality-adjusted price indexes. While one can envision adding measures of the indirect costs of health, such as work loss days, or adding such measures as quality-adjusted life years, overall methods for developing quality-adjusted price indexes are, as Schreyer and Mass note, "still in the research domain." Hopefully, the research on such adjustments can be accelerated. While the introduction of disease-based price indexes offers the potential for significant progress in measuring and controlling health care costs, further progress will require consistent valuation of the quality and quantity of health care outcomes produced by alternative modes of treatment.

2

A Cautionary Tale in Comparative Effectiveness Research
Pitfalls and Perils of Observational Data Analysis

Armando Franco, Dana P. Goldman, Adam Leive, and Daniel McFadden

2.1 Introduction

Comparative effectiveness research (CER) has become increasingly important for payers and policymakers as health care costs continue to grow rapidly. Such research is usually based on the results of randomized controlled trials (RCTs). However, determining whether the "blue pill" or the "red pill" is more effective (and for whom) can be time consuming, challenging, and expensive. Serious but rare side effects may be missed by an underpowered RCT, making surveillance important. Moreover, there may be interest in comparing the benefits and costs of competing drug treatments outside of a clinical trials setting; the populations studied in trials are almost certainly not representative of all patients who will ultimately consume the drug, and trial participants may also behave differently than people "in the real world."

Armando Franco is a health care data scientist at the University of California, Berkeley. Dana P. Goldman is the Leonard D. Schaeffer Chair and Distinguished Professor at the University of Southern California and a research associate of the National Bureau of Economic Research. Adam Leive is assistant professor of public policy and economics at the University of Virginia. Daniel McFadden is a professor of the graduate school at the University of California, Berkeley, the Presidential Professor of Health Economics at the University of Southern California, and a research associate of the National Bureau of Economic Research.

This research was supported by the Behavioral and Social Research program of the National Institute on Aging (grants P01AG033559 and RC4AG039036), with additional support from the E. Morris Cox Fund at the University of California, Berkeley. We are grateful to David Meltzer and participants at the 2013 NBER/CRIW Conference on Measuring and Modeling Health Care Costs for helpful comments. We thank Patricia St. Clair for her support of the data construction effort and Florian Heiss and Joachim Winter for helpful comments and discussions on an earlier draft. For acknowledgments, sources of research support, and disclosure of the authors' material financial relationships, if any, please see http://www.nber.org/chapters/c13104.ack.

Conducting CER using observational data presents a potential solution to some of these problems. Perhaps the most promising source of observational data comes from insurance claims. Claims data generally include large sample sizes that allow for more precise estimates of treatment effects than those possible through RCTs. The greater statistical power of claims data may also permit the detection of rare events not possible with RCTs, such as side effects or interactions with other drugs. Moreover, some side effects may occur after the conclusion of an RCT evaluation. The longer time frame of some claims data is thus another reason why claims data may be particularly well suited to identify drug risks. In addition, RCTs are very expensive compared to accessing observational data.

The Food and Drug Administration (FDA)'s Mini-Sentinel Project is perhaps the most prominent example of pharmacovigilance. Using insurance data on roughly 100 million patients and 2.9 billion prescription drug fills, the project seeks rapid dissemination of safety issues associated with drugs and adverse-reported events. Of course, the lack of randomization is the trade-off for the greater statistical power and detailed information on past medical histories and drug consumption patterns available with claims data. Accordingly, making valid inferences between treatments becomes much harder and there is a greater need for empirical methods to focus on causality.

The purpose of this chapter is to discuss some of the key methodological issues involved in using claims data to conduct CER. Using Medicare claims data from Parts A, B, and D between 2006 and 2009, we discuss the inherent challenges in using claims data and illustrate these issues by analyzing angiotensin II receptor blockers (ARBs) drugs for hypertension. We first document sample contamination observed in the claims—substantial crossover between therapies and discontinuation of hypertension treatment. We then discuss the implications of such sample contamination for CER. We employ two methods to deal with the nonrandom treatment assignment. First, we assume that physicians may have underlying propensities to prescribe ARBs, conditional on observed patient characteristics, and we examine the relationship between ARB prescription propensity and our outcomes at the physician level. Our rationale is that if physicians have underlying propensities to prescribe certain hypertension drugs but patients cannot observe such propensities, then we may view the initial prescription as random. Our second approach is to instrument for individual treatment choice using relative price differences between ARBs and substitute hypertension drugs.

Our evaluation of drug treatment effectiveness focuses on two outcomes: stroke and cancer. Stroke can result from uncontrolled high blood pressure. In general, RCTs have found little evidence of any difference in strokes between ARB users and users of other hypertension drugs, with some indication of fewer strokes among certain groups of ARB users (Wang, Franklin, and Safar 2007; Dahlof et al., 2002; Strauss and Hall 2009). Our second outcome is cancer, which was flagged by the FDA in 2010 as a potential adverse effect of ARBs. Despite the FDA later determining no link between cancer and ARBs, the safety of ARBs is still debated internally within the FDA (Burton 2013). A key objective of our study is to use observational data to investigate potential side effects or rare events not easily detected in RCTs, especially when consensus of such effects is lacking. We examine strokes in an attempt to validate our methods to assess the relationship between ARBs and cancer. In particular, if we can replicate the results of RCTs for strokes, we would be more confident that the association between ARBs and cancer can be interpreted as causal. This approach is similar to how RCTs are sometimes used in the policy evaluation literature to test the out-of-sample validity of structural econometric models (Todd and Wolpin 2006).

Using these strategies to identify treatment effects, we find mixed evidence that ARBs lead to higher cancer rates and some evidence that ARBs lead to higher stroke rates compared to other hypertension drugs. The increase in strokes associated with ARBs is contrary to evidence from RCTs that demonstrate, if anything, a modest reduction in strokes. As an additional falsification test, we rerun our analysis with a diagnosis of pain as the dependent variable—under the assumption that there should be no relationship between pain and choice of antihypertensive. However, we find that ARBs are associated with more pain diagnoses and the magnitudes of the effects are often larger than those for our main outcomes, possibly due to omitted variable bias from individual-level socioeconomic factors. Combined, these results suggest the relationship between ARBs and cancer should not be interpreted as causal.

The news is not all bad, though. While we document some pitfalls in using observational data to conduct CER, our results also suggest value to using relative price as an instrument for drug treatments, given how well our relative price measure predicts drug use. The remainder of the chapter is organized as follows. Section 2.2 provides background on ARBs and their possible link with cancer. Section 2.3 discusses sample selection and sample contamination, which occurs when people either discontinue treatment or switch treatments. Selection into treatment is discussed in section 2.4. Two robustness checks are presented in section 2.5. Section 2.6 compares our findings with those of RCTs. We briefly conclude in section 2.7.

2.2 Background on Hypertension, ARBs, and Cancer Risk

Hypertension is clinically defined as having either high levels of systolic blood pressure (above 140 millimeters of mercury) or diastolic blood pressure (over 90 millimeters of mercury). There is no single cause for hypertension; blood pressure levels are affected by the levels of water, salt, and hormones in the body as well as the condition of the kidneys, nervous system, and blood vessels. As people age, their blood vessels become stiffer, which increases blood pressure. Other risk factors include obesity, diabetes, smoking, and being an African American.[1] The major health consequences of hypertension are stroke and heart disease.

There are a variety of drugs used to treat hypertension. In this chapter, we compare ARBs to other common classes of treatment. In some models, we compare ARBs to angiotensin-converting enzyme (ACE) inhibitors alone, since these drugs represent the closest substitutes, with both operating through the effect of angiotensin (a peptide hormone, angiotensin causes vasoconstriction and also releases aldosterone, both of which lead to an increase in blood pressure). Drug classes we analyze and the mechanism by which they affect blood pressure are summarized below:

- Angiotensin-II Receptor Blockers (ARBs): relaxes blood vessels by blocking the action of angiotensin II.
- ACE inhibitors: prevents the formation of angiotensin II.
- Beta blockers: blocks the effects of the hormone epinephrine, leading the heart to beat more slowly.
- Diuretics: removes salt and water from the body by inducing the kidneys to put more salt into urine, thereby decreasing pressures on artery walls.
- Calcium channel blockers: widens and relaxes blood vessels through influencing the muscle cells in the walls of arteries.
- Other antihypertensives (e.g., vasodilators): opens blood vessels by preventing muscles from tightening and by stopping the walls in the arteries from narrowing.

In July 2010, the FDA issued a safety alert in response to a meta-analysis by Sipahi et al. (2010) suggesting a possible risk of cancer associated with use of ARBs (Food and Drug Administration 2010). The meta-analysis used data on 60,000 patients and found a small but statistically significant increase in new cancer cases among ARB users: 7.2 percent compared to 6.0 percent.[2] The authors considered breast, prostate, and lung cancers and grouped all remaining cancers together. Over the next year, the FDA pursued further analysis based on 156,000 patients enrolled in RCTs. In June 2011, the FDA released its finding that ARBs do not pose a greater risk of cancer relative to other hypertension drugs (Food and Drug Administration 2011).

---

1. For more background information on risk factors, see http://www.nhlbi.nih.gov/health/health-topics/topics/hbp/.

2. Cancer was not a prespecified endpoint in several of the trials analyzed by Sipahi et al. (2010). This suggests the difference in cancer deaths observed may have resulted from differential effects of drug use on cancer detection. In particular, ARBs may cause more side effects that prompt a diagnostic workup, which ultimately reveal the presence of cancer, even though there is no causal biological mechanism between ARBs and cancer. We investigated this possibility by calculating prevalence rates of major diagnostic cancer tests among people taking different drugs. To keep the comparison as clean as possible, we also only examined one-year incident cases—people who did not take any hypertension drug in 2006 and began taking one in 2007—for those on monotherapy (i.e., treatment with a single drug). We did not find evidence of higher rates of diagnostic cancer exams among ARB users compared to other classes of drugs, adjusting for differences in age and sex across drug classes.

However, by some accounts, the debate remains unresolved. In May 2013, the *Wall Street Journal* reported on dissent within the FDA, where a senior FDA regulator conducted additional analysis with individual-level trial data that estimated an increased cancer risk of over 20 percent among patients taking ARBs (Burton 2013). The research was rebuked by top officials within the FDA, but this rare internal dispute illustrates the lack of consensus on the side effects of ARBs.

The presence of many alternative drug options to treat hypertension increases the value of understanding side effects related to ARBs. If there were no other viable treatments, then rational patients should be willing to accept more risk of potential side effects. But with a plethora of alternative therapy choices, the (expected) benefits of ARBs may not be worth the risk of cancer or other side effects. Although data is currently unavailable to determine how the FDA's 2010 warning affected drug use, it seems likely that determining within a shorter time frame that ARBs do not cause cancer would generate important benefits to patients. The following sections of the chapter describe our attempts to analyze these issues using observational data.

2.3   Sample Selection and Contamination

Our sample is constructed from individual claims data from Medicare parts A, B, and D between 2006 and 2009. We examine enrollees in stand-alone prescription drug plans (PDPs) only because complete Medicare claims for enrollees in Part C are unavailable. Hypertension cases are classified by use of at least one drug commonly used to treat high blood pressure. Patients taking hypertension drugs for less than thirty days are excluded from our sample. We use the word "treatment" to refer to prescription drugs, but recognize there are other forms of treatment for hypertension, such as exercise and dieting. Ignoring unobservable activities like exercise will only be problematic for our results to the extent that these activities vary differentially across drug classes. One way such differential variation could occur is if certain drugs, due to higher prices, are consumed mainly by patients with higher incomes or education levels and such patients also exercise more often. The inability to control for individual-level socioeconomic factors is an important limitation of our study and an issue to which we return in the discussion.

2.3.1   Sample Selection (Left Censoring)

It is common for patients to take hypertension drugs before age sixty-five, when most beneficiaries become eligible for Medicare. We refer to those already on hypertension drugs when they are first observed in claims as "prevalent cases." For these patients, claims data do not permit the researcher to observe the duration of current treatment or patterns of past treatments prior to age sixty-five. Clearly, this unobservability is problematic for classifying the presence and intensity of drug consumption. An alternative to this left-censoring problem is to restrict the sample to patients enrolled in 2006 who initiate hypertension treatment in 2007. We refer to this group as "incident cases" with a "one-year window." Since hypertension is a chronic condition, incident cases provide a cleaner comparison between ARBs and other drug classes because patients are likely first-time drug users.

Left censoring is a serious analytical problem for evaluating drug treatments, although not necessarily a serious empirical problem. With left censoring, a beneficiary's prior history in terms of both drug consumption and health outcomes is unobserved. Using external information on incident cases that can be linked to Medicare claims, such as the Health and Retirement Study (HRS), to impute "back-dated" information for prevalent cases is not an attractive option, because the real analytical danger is the unobservability of switching between drug classes, to be discussed below. To the extent this unobserved switching is correlated with unobserved health status, using prevalent cases creates analytic problems for researchers that are difficult to surmount. Nevertheless, left censoring should not be an empirical problem because the number of incident cases will grow over time with additional waves of data.

2.3.2   Contamination Bias

An RCT has a very powerful instrument (randomization) that has a strong effect on treatment assignment. Even in RCTs, however, patients often change treatment as their diseases get managed in the trial. In an observational study, the goal is to classify patients based on patterns of drug consumption, and to group patients with similar histories of drug consumption together into pseudotreatment and control arms. For reasons of interpretability and statistical power, it would be ideal to have a small number of treatment and control groups. However, there are several challenges to a precise assignment of such groups. If there were only two competing therapies, classification would be relatively simple with only three possible combinations: drug 1 alone, drug 2 alone, or both drug 1 and drug 2. However, dimensionality problems quickly arise when more than a few drugs can be taken possibly in combination. Moreover, the order in which drugs are taken further complicates analysis. Some drugs may generally be taken as first-line therapy, while others are prescribed as therapies of "last resort." Indeed, this is the case with hypertension; diuretics are often prescribed first, in line with the Joint National Committee's recommendation, and ARBs are more often prescribed after the patient has tried other drug therapies. By including more therapy groups, we trade off ease of interpretation and greater statistical power against contamination bias resulting from heterogeneity within any single group.

How serious is this problem? We find that most patients discontinue their initial drug treatment within the first year. Table 2.1 illustrates that over two-thirds of patients stop their initial treatment within one year for both prevalent and incident cases—where discontinuation is defined as having a

Table 2.1   **Adherence of initial treatment by drug class**

Therapy	Initial treatment	On treatment through one year	Percent of initial users	On treatment through two years	Percent of initial users
		Prevalent cases, 2006–2009			
ACE inhibitors	608,641	78,932	13	51,973	9
ARBs	300,583	32,357	11	20,193	7
Diuretics	809,900	130,917	16	98,432	12
Calcium channel blockers	474,429	63,824	13	41,692	9
Beta blockers	1,010,950	219,443	22	179,434	18
Other antihypertensives	48,119	7,809	16	5,327	11
		Incident cases, 2007			
ACE inhibitors	152,561	40,033	26	36,814	24
ARBs	56,005	11,111	20	9,903	18
Diuretics	181,630	54,289	30	50,413	28
Calcium channel blockers	91,490	23,144	25	20,849	23
Beta blockers	264,639	84,836	32	78,407	30
Other antihypertensives	9,216	2,423	26	2,144	23

gap in prescription coverage of more than thirty days. However, conditional on maintaining treatment through the first year, most continue through the second year. This pattern suggests that side effects for a subset of patients or heterogeneity in treatment response may drive adherence patterns. It also suggests that the (selected) groups of patients who have maintained initial therapy for one year might make for adequate treatment and control groups.

However, polytherapy also poses a problem. Table 2.2 documents that conditional on not discontinuing initial treatment in the first year, between 14 and 26 percent of patients take at least one other hypertension drug at some point. Between 9 and 15 percent of such patients take at least two other drugs. So not only do people often discontinue their initial treatments, but those who adhere often take multiple treatments concurrently.

Roughly one-third of incident cases are on the same, single monotherapy throughout the sample period (results not shown). The majority of these patients are on either beta blockers or ACE inhibitors. Among combinations of drugs, beta blockers with diuretics are the most common. However, the mix of drugs taken varies widely. We find rates of polytherapy are similar to those cited in the 2003 JNC report, which documents more than two-thirds of patients require at least two drugs to control hypertension.

Other studies find greater rates of adherence than we document in table 2.1, however. A meta-analysis by Matchar et al. (2008) finds one-year adherence rates for ARBs and ACE inhibitors range between 40 and 60 percent. Relaxing our restriction that patients must not discontinue treatment for more than thirty days to be considered adhering to ninety days brings our

Table 2.2   Combination therapy by drug class

Total number of therapies ever taken, incident cases 2007–2008	On initial treatment through one year	On one plus other drugs during first year	Percent of one-year users	On two plus other drugs during first year	Percent of one-year users
ACE inhibitors	78,932	17,692	22	11,033	14
ARBs	32,357	6,060	19	4,912	15
Diuretics	130,917	34,060	26	16,810	13
Calcium channel blockers	63,824	10,360	16	5,596	9
Beta blockers	219,443	51,699	24	26,947	12
Other antihypertensives	7,809	1,088	14	765	10

estimates closer to other studies, but they are still at least 10 percentage points lower across drug classes. We suspect that the main driver behind our higher rates of discontinuation is the greater cost sharing under Part D. Simple preliminary analysis reveals that hypertension use decreases in the "doughnut hole," and this is consistent with more general work on drug consumption in Part D plans by Joyce, Zissimopolous, and Goldman (2013).

As an example of how various drugs are used in sequence, figure 2.1 displays the usage rates of drug treatments among people who ever take an ARB. Over 40 percent of ARB users take another drug before starting ARBs, with most taking either diuretics or beta blockers. The figure clearly reveals that ACE inhibitors substitute for ARBs, as is clinically indicated. There is also evidence that diuretics tend to complement ARB use. Finally, many patients who discontinue ARB use subsequently take another drug.

The multitude and timing of drug consumption patterns issues raise the question of how to measure drug consumption in empirical models. We follow two different approaches. The simplest is to classify patients as using a drug if they have ever had at least two fills of the drug, even if they have previously taken other antihypertensives. We term this group "ever users." The second way is to classify patients based on the initial drug therapy prescribed. This represents an intent-to-treat approach. In both of these approaches, treatment is measured as an indicator function.[3] One might be tempted to restrict attention to incident cases who maintain monotherapy for at least twelve months. Doing so, however, would imply throwing away 71 percent of the observed incident cases and 84 percent of all cases (including prevalent hypertension), and this case deletion obviously occurs in a nonrandom way.

---

3. A third approach is to model the cumulative exposure to the drug, using a function with an exponential rate of decay. We experimented with this approach by running a series of survival models measuring duration until cancer or stroke instead of using linear IV regressions. The results were qualitatively similar.

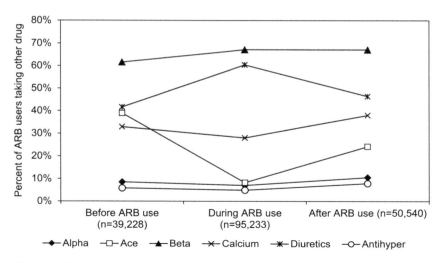

Fig. 2.1   Empirical sequencing of drug use for ARB users

Some of this can be seen in tables 2.3 and 2.4, which present descriptive statistics among "ever users" for prevalent and incident cases, respectively. These unconditional means reveal important differences by drug class. Cancer rates are lowest among ARB and ACE users. The fact that there is much less variation in cancer rates by class among incident users suggests that past history may be very important to determining outcomes. For example, the difference between the highest and lowest cancer rates among incident cases is 33.4 per 10,000, but is 81.8 per 10,000 among prevalent cases. Death rates are considerably lower for ARB users in both prevalent and incident cases.

2.4   Selection into Treatment

One of the fundamental challenges to using observational data for CER is that treatment assignment is not random. Instead, drug treatment is a decision made between the physician and patient. The decision is likely based on many characteristics of the patient, some of which may be unobserved and may also affect cancer risk. We pursue two approaches to deal with selection into treatment: (a) examine how physician propensities to prescribe ARBs are correlated with health outcomes, and (b) estimate linear instrumental variables (IV) regressions using relative price to predict treatment choice. These approaches differ conceptually in the power they ascribe to each side of the physician-patient relationship; the first approach implicitly assumes the physician has control over which drug the patient takes and has latent preferences for prescribing certain drugs. By using the out-of-pocket (OOP) cost the patient pays for drugs as an instrument, the second approach implicitly treats the patient as the decision maker and price as the key factor

Table 2.3   Descriptive statistics, prevalent cases

Therapy		Age	Sex (1 = female, 0 = male)	Cancer (per 10,000)	Stroke (per 10,000)	Death (per 10,000)	Avg. no. chronic conditions
ARBs	mean	77.5	0.722	182.0	1,818.4	526.7	4.99
(N = 184,067)	s.d.	7.4	0.448	1,336.9	3,857.1	2,233.7	2.30
ACE inhibitors	mean	77.5	0.647	187.2	1,907.1	736.1	4.78
(N = 406,100)	s.d.	7.6	0.478	1,355.5	3,928.6	2,611.3	2.33
Beta blockers	mean	78.1	0.677	251.0	1,947.2	920.8	5.03
(N = 648,429)	s.d.	7.6	0.468	1,564.3	3,959.9	2,891.4	2.27
Calcium channel blockers	mean	78.2	0.725	251.6	1,981.9	840.4	4.93
(N = 496,334)	s.d.	7.7	0.447	1,566.1	3,986.4	2,774.5	2.31
Other antihypertensives	mean	78.7	0.759	263.8	2,897.2	1,084.8	5.59
(N = 85,437)	s.d.	7.7	0.428	1,602.6	4,536.4	3,109.9	2.34
Diuretics	mean	78.4	0.722	272.2	1,821.3	1,392.4	4.94
(N = 909,615)	s.d.	7.9	0.448	1,627.3	3,859.5	3,461.9	2.34

Table 2.4   Descriptive statistics, incident cases

Therapy		Age	Sex (1 = female, 0 = male)	Cancer (per 10,000)	Stroke (per 10,000)	Death (per 10,000)	Avg. no. chronic conditions
ARBs	mean	77.4	0.669	119.7	1,509.6	315.0	4.33
(N = 23,143)	s.d.	7.3	0.470	1,087.4	3,580.2	1,746.6	2.29
ACE inhibitors	mean	77.4	0.587	124.5	1,613.5	452.3	4.19
(N = 63,763)	s.d.	7.4	0.492	1,108.9	3,678.5	2,078.0	2.29
Beta blockers	mean	78.3	0.615	144.2	1,705.1	620.5	4.61
(N = 104,901)	s.d.	7.5	0.487	1,192.2	3,760.8	2,412.5	2.26
Calcium channel blockers	mean	78.4	0.660	153.1	1,773.3	543.0	4.43
(N = 64,267)	s.d.	7.6	0.474	1,227.8	3,819.5	2,266.1	2.31
Other antihypertensives	mean	79.2	0.680	148.9	2748.4	842.4	5.06
(N = 9,268)	s.d.	7.8	0.467	1,211.0	4,464.6	2,777.6	2.36
Diuretics	mean	78.7	0.663	148.6	1,567.7	932.3	4.45
(N = 130,572)	s.d.	7.9	0.473	1210.1	3635.9	2907.5	2.36

influencing her decision. These approaches thus attempt to identify the effect of ARBs on health outcomes along different margins.

2.4.1   Physician Propensity to Prescribe ARBs

The rationale behind our first approach using physician propensities is to view the initial physician-patient match as random. More precisely, if physicians have underlying propensities to prescribe certain hypertension drugs, conditional on patient characteristics, but patients cannot observe such propensities and thus do not choose physicians based on them, then we may view the initial prescription as random. In this sense, physicians with a greater propensity to prescribe ARBs are analogous to the randomly assigned treatment group of an RCT. (We fully recognize that many patients may shop for doctors in certain clinical circumstances, thereby violating this assumption. However, in the case of antihypertensive prescribing, such an assumption seems more plausible.)

To examine physician-prescribing decisions, we limit our sample to include only initial therapy choice and do not allow for switching or adding therapies. To fully capture a physician's prescribing tendencies, the sample is restricted to physicians with at least thirty patients on hypertension drugs. Our final data set for this analysis is composed of 1,176,311 patients and 25,477 physicians, with the average physician treating forty-six patients for hypertension.

Following the theoretical model derived by Chandra and Staiger (2011), we model physician's propensity θ to prescribe ARBs based on the fact that some physicians might have an underlying tendency to prescribe ARBs. We regress whether a patient receives ARBs against her chronic conditions, basic demographics, and the physician's propensity effect. Here θ is assumed to be a normally distributed random effect with mean μ and σ^2. The functional form of $F(.)$ is taken to be logistic. We estimate the mixed-effects model and recover estimates of both μ and σ and use them to construct a posterior distribution of the estimated θ for each physician, which we then use to regress against death and cancer rates.

2.4.2   Results

Figure 2.2 plots the cancer rate for each physician's set of hypertension patients against the physician's propensity to prescribe ARBs. Our measure of cancer includes breast, prostate, lung, colorectal, and endometrial cancers, which account for the large majority of cancer deaths. Here, the diameter of each circle represents the number of patients with at least one claim to that particular physician. There appears to be a slight positive relationship between ARB use and cancer, which is statistically significant at the 1 percent level based on the large sample size. Perhaps more interestingly, figure 2.3 displays a stronger negative relationship between death rates and

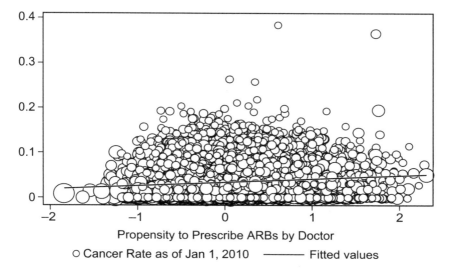

Fig. 2.2 **Unconditional relationship between cancer rate and propensity to prescribe ARBs**

Note: For 25,000 prescribers with 30–500 patients: events from 2006 to 2008. Beta = .007 and significant at the 1 percent level.

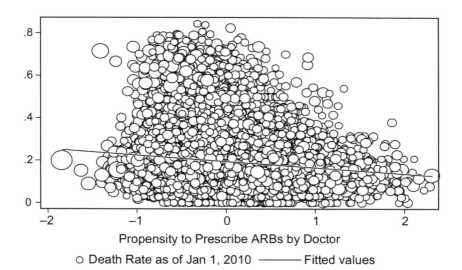

Fig. 2.3 **Unconditional relationship between death rate and propensity to prescribe ARBs**

Note: For 25,000 prescribers with 30–500 patients: events from 2006 to 2008. Beta = −.03 and significant at the 1 percent level.

Table 2.5   Simulations of reducing prescriber propensity

Cancer	No. predicted cancer cases	Percent of total	Decreased no. of cancer cases	Percent of cancer cases
No restrictions	39,530	3.36	n/a	n/a
Restrict those with propensity in the top 75% to 25%	35,822	3.05	3,708	10.35
Restrict those with propensity greater than 2 std. dev.	39,455	3.35	75	0.19
Restrict those with propensity greater than 1 std. dev.	39,096	3.32	434	1.10

Death	No. predicted deaths	Percent of total	Increased no. of deaths	Percent of deaths
No restrictions	227,415	19.33	n/a	n/a
Restrict those with propensity in the top 75% to 25%	242,489	20.61	15,074	6.22
Restrict those with propensity greater than 2 std. dev.	227,718	19.36	303	0.13
Restrict those with propensity greater than 1 std. dev.	229,179	19.48	1,764	0.77

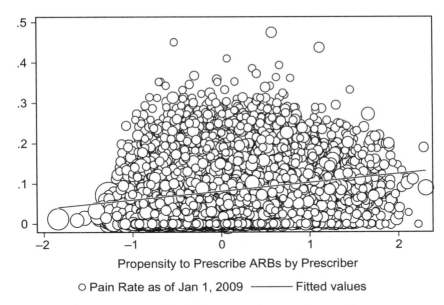

Fig. 2.4   Unconditional relationship between pain rate and propensity to prescribe ARBs

Note: For 25,000 prescribers with 30–500 patients: events from 2006 to 2008. Beta = .022 and significant at the 1 percent level.

the propensity to prescribe ARBs. This may be due to an omitted variable, or it may be explained by competing risks; ARBs may increase cancer rates but reduce overall death rates due to fewer occurrences of some other disease(s).

Taking these estimates as "true" causal estimates, the natural question is how many cancer cases and deaths would be avoided (or incurred) if physicians lowered their ARB-prescribing tendencies. As an illustration, table 2.5 displays the results of several simulations. If only the physicians in the right tail of the distribution were to reduce their prescribing rates to two standard deviations above the mean, the changes in outcomes are modest. If physicians above the 25th percentile reduced their prescribing rates to those of the 25th percentile, the implications are, not surprisingly, more dramatic. Doing so would decrease cancer rates by more than 10 percent and increase death rates by 6 percent. These are sizable numbers: saving 3,700 cancer cases through less ARB prescribing involves sacrificing 15,000 lives—hardly an attractive trade-off.

We do not, however, believe these are causal. When we replicate these scatterplots using pain as the dependent variable in the regressions—an outcome we assume is clinically independent of ARB prescribing—we actually find a stronger relationship between pain and ARB use than that for cancer (figure 2.4).

This finding unfortunately raises questions about the validity of using physician treatment propensities to identify CER models, at least in the case of antihypertensives.

2.4.3   Linear IV Models

Our second approach follows more standard, economic techniques to deal with causality using observational data: instrumental variables regressions. We use the ratio of the average OOP cost of ARBs to the average OOP cost of ACE inhibitors at the regional level using cost-sharing information at the plan level. In particular, we calculate the average OOP based on the copayment or the coinsurance rate of the plan multiplied by the average total cost of ARBs and ACE inhibitors at the regional level. We choose to examine ARBs with ACE inhibitors alone for a cleaner comparison since these two drugs represent the closest substitutes for one another. There is little reason to believe that the price difference between ARBs and ACE inhibitors at the regional level should be correlated with health outcomes.

The ARBs are nearly always more expensive than ACE inhibitors. In fact, only 10 of 10,087 county-years have cheaper ARBs. On average, ARBs are over 4.5 times as expensive as ACE inhibitors, and the standard deviation for this ratio is 1.5. As will be shown in the first-stage regressions below, there is still enough variation for price to serve as a good predictor of ARB use.[4]

Our first-stage regression is a probit of treatment on relative price, a vector of chronic conditions (diabetes, heart disease, heart failure, depression, Alzheimer's disease, glaucoma, ischemic heart disease, chronic obstructive pulmonary disease, pelvic/hip fracture, osteoporosis, rheumatoid arthritis/osteoarthritis, cataracts, and chronic kidney disease), age, sex, county-level socioeconomic factors (percent home ownership, education levels, percent African American, average income, percent below poverty line, unemployment rate, percent married, and percent foreign born, all among adults), and state fixed effects. The second stage is a linear probability model where the dependent variable is an indicator of the health outcome in the two years following the first hypertension prescription. The first hypertension prescription is calculated as the first ARB fill among ARB users or the first fill for another drug class among non-ARB users. We adjust standard errors in all regressions by clustering at the county level.

Our rationale for examining the incidence of outcomes up to two years posttreatment is to adjust the duration of exposure for the sequencing of drug classes. As described earlier, some treatments, such as ARBs, are often initiated after trying other therapies first. This mechanically reduces the amount of time spent on ARBs compared to other drugs over the time

---

4. Other percentiles of the distribution of relative price are as follows: 1st percentile—2.1; 25th percentile—3.7; 75th percentile—5.5; and 99th percentile—9.6.

Table 2.6   **First-stage IV regressions**

	Prevalent cases		Incident cases	
	All drug users (1)	ACE or ARB monotherapy only (2)	All drug users (3)	ACE or ARB monotherapy only (4)
	Treatment definition: Patient ever used drug			
Price	−0.039	−0.035	−0.024	−0.039
	(−60.77)	(−16.83)	(−12.36)	(−7.51)
F-stat	520.99	31.35	55.09	7.75
N	1,406,463	95,386	153,904	19,466
	Treatment definition: Intent to treat			
Price	−0.018	−0.035	−0.020	−0.039
	(−33.02)	(−16.83)	(−11.87)	(−7.51)
F-stat	271.5	31.55	40.35	7.75
N	1,406,469	95,386	153,904	19,466

Notes: Cluster-adjusted robust *T*-statistics in parentheses. Regressions also include indicators for age, sex, diabetes, heart disease, heart failure, depression, Alzheimer's disease, glaucoma, ischemic heart disease, chronic obstructive pulmonary disease, pelvic/hip fracture, osteoporosis, rheumatoid arthritis/osteoarthritis, cataracts, and chronic kidney disease, state fixed effects, and the following county-level variables: percent home ownership, percent with high school degree, percent with some college or two-year degree, percent with four-year college degree or beyond, percent African American, average income, percent below poverty line, unemployment rate, percent married, and percent foreign born, all among adults.

period we observe, and so there is also less time to be diagnosed with cancer or stroke.[5] We only examine patients with a full two-year window after they begin antihypertensives. Since our data extends to December 31, 2009, we exclude anyone beginning hypertension treatment in 2008 or later. By imposing a standard level of follow-up across all drug classes, this improves the comparability of different drugs even when some are routinely prescribed first.

The first-stage regressions in table 2.6 show that price is a strong predictor of ARB use. For both definitions of treatment, we run four sets of regressions that divide the population based on drug use. The first column includes all patients who are prevalent cases, representing the largest number of beneficiaries. The second column includes prevalent cases who either only take ARBs or only take ACE inhibitors. This dramatically reduces sample size, given the popularity of combination therapy. The third column includes all incident cases, comprising slightly more than 10 percent of prevalent cases.

5. We ran regressions with the number of days without the outcome as the dependent variable along the lines of Basu et al. (2007), but this does not get around the issue of drug therapy sequencing that is prevalent in our data. As part of this alternative analysis, we classified incident hypertension cases using shorter time windows to test whether later initiation of ARBs drove our findings, but we did not find support for this hypothesis.

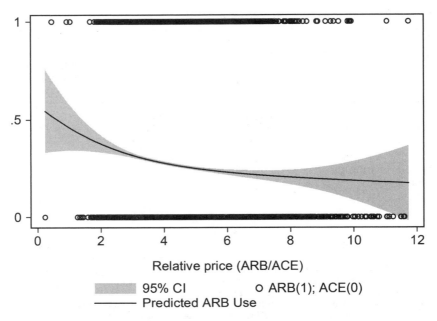

Fig. 2.5   Unconditional relationship between ARB use and relative price

The fourth column is the smallest sample and includes only incident ARB or ACE monotherapy users. The comparisons between ARB users and the control group thus become progressively "cleaner" moving from left to right. The second and fourth columns are the same between the two treatment definitions, because the ACE monotherapy group is restricted to never be on ARBs.

Figure 2.5 graphically displays the results of the first-stage regressions for incident cases. The binary indicator for treatment (0 or 1) for each patient is plotted against the relative price of ARBs to ACE inhibitors. The downward sloping curve reveals that as ARBs become more expensive, more patients take ACE inhibitors.

There appears to be little evidence that ARBs lead to cancer based on the second-stage regressions. Table 2.7 presents the results using the "ever use" treatment definition. The point estimate on predicted treatment is negative and statistically significant among all prevalent cases (column [1]), with ever using ARBs decreasing the probability of cancer within two years by 1.2 percent. However, the estimate becomes positive and statistically significant among monotherapy users (column [2]), increasing the probability of cancer by 2.8 percent. Among incident cases, the point estimates on predicted treatment are positive, but not statistically significant. So as the sample becomes "cleaner," the evidence that ARBs are associated with cancer becomes weaker. Using the intent-to-treat definition as shown in table 2.8, the evidence on a link between ARB use and cancer remains weak. Under both treatment definitions, there is

Table 2.7   **Second-stage IV regressions: Ever-user treatment definition**

	Prevalent cases		Incident cases	
	All drug users (1)	ACE or ARB monotherapy only (2)	All drug users (3)	ACE or ARB monotherapy only (4)
	Cancer			
ARB treatment	−0.012	0.0288	0.0057	0.0273
	(−1.90)	(2.97)	(0.43)	(1.73)
N	1,406,463	95,386	153,904	19,466
	Stroke			
ARB treatment	0.0154	0.0268	0.0234	0.0501
	(1.65)	(2.46)	(1.47)	(2.71)
N	1,406,469	95,386	153,904	19,466

Notes: Cluster-adjusted robust *T*-statistics in parentheses. Regressions also include indicators for age, sex, diabetes, heart disease, heart failure, depression, Alzheimer's disease, glaucoma, ischemic heart disease, chronic obstructive pulmonary disease, pelvic/hip fracture, osteoporosis, rheumatoid arthritis/osteoarthritis, cataracts, and chronic kidney disease, state fixed effects, and the following county-level variables: percent home ownership, percent with high school degree, percent with some college or two-year degree, percent with four-year college degree or beyond, percent African American, average income, percent below poverty line, unemployment rate, percent married, and percent foreign born, all among adults.

more consistent evidence that ARB users have more strokes, although it is fair to question whether a 5 percent significance level is an appropriate threshold given the large sample size. Nonetheless, we should expect fewer or no difference in the number of strokes based on the results of RCTs, and our opposite finding casts further doubt on the validity of our IV methods.

2.5   Robustness Checks

2.5.1   Subsample Analysis: Healthy Patients

Healthy patients serve as a first robustness check. Such patients arguably represent cleaner treatment and control groups than the full sample that includes people with a variety of health conditions, since healthy patients likely also have fewer unobserved conditions that may be correlated with both ARB use and the outcomes. We classify healthy patients as beneficiaries without any of the thirteen Chronic Conditions Data Warehouse (CCW) chronic conditions measured, which comprises 28 percent of the full sample.

Price is still statistically significant in the first-stage IV regressions as shown in appendix table 2A.1. However, the *F*-statistic is lower than in the baseline regressions and below ten in three of the four specifications. This may be due to the smaller sample size or suggest that chronic conditions are important to explain treatment patterns. In the second-stage regressions, the

Table 2.8 **Second-stage IV regressions: Intent-to-treat treatment definition**

Cancer	Prevalent cases		Incident cases	
	All drug users (1)	ACE or ARB monotherapy only (2)	All drug users (3)	ACE or ARB monotherapy only (4)
ARB treatment	−0.0139	0.0288	−0.002	0.0273
	(−1.26)	(2.97)	(−0.13)	(1.73)
N	1,406,469	95,386	153,904	19,466

Stroke	Prevalent cases		Incident cases	
	All drug users (1)	ACE and ARB users only (2)	All drug users (3)	ACE and ARB users only (4)
Treatment	0.041	0.0268	0.0249	0.0501
	(2.40)	(2.46)	(1.32)	(2.71)
N	1,406,469	95,386	153,904	19,466

Notes: Cluster-adjusted robust *T*-statistics in parentheses. Regressions also include indicators for age, sex, diabetes, heart disease, heart failure, depression, Alzheimer's disease, glaucoma, ischemic heart disease, chronic obstructive pulmonary disease, pelvic/hip fracture, osteoporosis, rheumatoid arthritis/osteoarthritis, cataracts, and chronic kidney disease, state fixed effects, and the following county-level variables: percent home ownership, percent with high school degree, percent with some college or two-year degree, percent with four-year college degree or beyond, percent African American, average income, percent below poverty line, unemployment rate, percent married, and percent foreign born, all among adults.

estimates on predicted treatment are lower than in the baseline regressions and very imprecise. To the extent that the healthy subsample produces more similar control and treatment groups, the IV regressions in appendix tables 2A.2 and 2A.3 suggest that there is little meaningful or statistically significant difference between ARBs and other hypertension drugs.

2.5.2   Falsification Test: Pain

As another falsification check, we rerun our IV regressions with a diagnosis of pain within one year of starting hypertension treatment as the dependent variable. Since hypertension drugs should have little impact on the diagnosis of pain, the magnitude of any association between ARBs and pain should be lower if the effects with cancer and stroke are real. We consider ICD-9 codes for sprains and strains (excluding ankle and back) and open wounds (excluding head wounds) in diagnosing pain. The ARBs are associated with less pain as shown in appendix table 2A.4, but the magnitude of the coefficient estimates are similar to the results for cancer and stroke, and in some cases larger.[6]

6. In case pain followed or preceded a stroke, we also recoded any diagnosis of pain to 0 within a one-month window of a stroke diagnosis. The results were similar as reported in table 2.8.

As the samples become cleaner, the estimates become smaller in magnitude and less precise. We find a similar pattern if we use the subsample of healthy patients to estimate the incidence of pain (results not shown). Perhaps these results are due to the omitted variable bias, such as individual-level socioeconomic factors, which may drive both treatment choice and the number of office visits (and thus diagnoses) of a patient. Since ARBs are more expensive than other antihypertensives (there are no generic ARBs), one might speculate that higher-income patients are more likely to take ARBs. There is also evidence that higher-income, white Medicare beneficiaries have fewer hospital discharges than lower-income beneficiaries (Gornick et al. 1996; Gornick 2003). So if higher-income patients are also less likely to receive a pain diagnosis due to fewer hospital admissions, then the omission of individual income biases our estimates downward. Overall, our falsification test fails, casting doubt on the validity of the IV regressions of cancer and stroke.

2.6   Comparison with Randomized Controlled Trials

The results of RCTs and IV regressions are both relevant for policy, but measure different quantities. The RCTs measure the average treatment effect (ATE), while IV regressions measure the local average treatment effect (LATE). Importantly, the parameter in IV regressions is identified only by the subgroup of observations affected by changes in the instrument (price in our example). This implies that IV regressions are only useful for drawing inferences to people who are affected by price changes. For example, the LATE tells us nothing about people who would never consider changing drug treatments because of side effects. From the perspective of evaluating drug safety, the ATE is arguably the more relevant quantity than the LATE, since policymakers are interested in the effect of ARBs on all individuals. It is hard to envision many cases where the LATE is more informative for policy than the ATE. Given that the population in RCTs can sometimes be narrowly defined, the ATE estimate may only apply to a group with select covariates, whereas the LATE calculated from observational data on a wider population may be more informative about treatment effects among individuals with different levels of covariates (e.g., age, sex, medical history, etc.). However, that is a shortcoming in the construction of small, tightly defined RCTs, not with the ATE per se, and calls for expanding the population of RCTs or conducting numerous RCTs on different subpopulations.

Although RCTs are viewed (rightly) as the gold standard in evaluation, there may still be unobserved behavioral changes between treatment and control groups that bias results. In RCTs, for example, individuals may not always comply with the therapy assigned to them. In comparing the treatment and control groups, assuring that both groups comply at the same rates is critical to obtaining unbiased estimates (Hamilton 2001). The implication for using observational data is that researchers should also compare groups that are most likely to comply with the therapy prescribed. Additionally, compliance may also depend on whether an individual believes to be assigned to the treatment or control arms of an RCT. Malani (2006) builds a model demonstrating the importance of placebo effects, where individuals believing to be assigned to the treatment arm are more likely to comply. Using data on the probabilities of assignment to the treatment group of various RCTs, he finds empirical support for this model. So behavior changes within RCTs may be just as important as behavioral patterns in observational data. Furthermore, even when a study includes both randomized and self-selected observational data for the same population, economic and statistical models using self-selected data may fail to replicate the results of RCTs (Goldman, Leibowitz, and Buchanan 1998).

2.7   Conclusion

This chapter highlights some of the perils and pitfalls of using observational data for CER. We document that not only is the lack of randomization a problem, but the existence of competing therapies and prevalence of polytherapy also poses challenges to researchers. To deal with sample selection problems, we restrict our sample to monotherapy users and incident hypertension cases. While this allows us to sidestep the unobservability of prior drug use, it comes at the price of a sample that is not only small, but also not representative of all drug users. This partly defeats one of the key assets of observational data, which is the potential for greater representativeness than RCTs.

Our empirical approaches to tackle nonrandom treatment assignment are strong conceptually, albeit unsuccessful. Our first approach of using physician propensities is an innovative solution to initial therapy choice, but does not pass our falsification test using pain. Our second approach using conventional IV methods finds price to be a strong predictor of treatment, but our results are often sensitive to the sample analyzed. Overall, we find little evidence from our IV regressions that ARBs are associated with cancer and weak evidence that ARBs are positively related to strokes. The latter result contradicts the findings from RCTs, and thus indicates our empirical approach is likely not valid. In addition, the fact that estimates from our pain regressions are often larger than estimates for cancer or stroke also suggest our IV estimates are not causal.

One might argue with the exogeneity of both our instrument and physician-prescribing propensities in purging selection bias. For example, perhaps unobserved patient attributes affect plan choice and thus ARB prices through copayments. And copayments (for non-ARB utilization) may affect cancer detection through moral hazard. As evidence of this pattern, Meeker et al. (2011) find first-dollar coverage increases utilization of common cancer screens—lipid screens, Pap smears, mammograms, and fecal occult blood tests—relative to plans with cost sharing. So even if patients do not choose a plan based on ARB copayments, correlation between ARB copayments and copayments for other services would make prices endogenous to cancer rates. Our use of regional ARB prices attempts to deal with such issues, but correlation between regional costs and cancer would still bias our results. In terms of physician propensities, unobserved patient attributes might affect the choice of physician and also be correlated with attributes of other patients in the region, which in turn affects physician propensities. In short, selection could contaminate our results if patients are neither randomly assigned to physicians with high propensity to prescribe ARBs nor randomly assigned to insurance with a low price for ARBs. And despite our best efforts to use observational data for causal inference, we certainly cannot rule out the possibility of such bias.

While claims data, in principle, offer several advantages to evaluating drug treatments over RCTs, researchers must be careful to deal with left-censoring, contamination bias, and selection into treatment. By illustrating these pitfalls with the case of ARBs for hypertension, our chapter provides a cautionary tale for researchers interested in using claims data for CER.

Appendix

Table 2A.1   **First-stage regressions: Healthy subpopulation**

	Prevalent cases		Incident cases	
	All drug users (1)	ACE or ARB monotherapy only (2)	All drug users (3)	ACE or ARB monotherapy only (4)
Treatment definition: Patient ever used drug				
Price	−0.038	−0.019	−0.032	−0.038
	(−21.47)	(−3.95)	(−6.53)	(−3.03)
F-stat	60.11	6.69	9.26	2.22
N	175,346	14,667	22,057	3,259
Treatment definition: Intent to treat				
Price	−0.014	−0.019	−0.023	−0.038
	(−9.69)	(−3.95)	(−5.51)	(−3.03)
F-stat	44.43	6.69	7.01	2.22
N	175,348	14,667	22,057	3,259

Notes: Cluster-adjusted robust *T*-statistics in parentheses. Regressions also include indicators for age and sex, state fixed effects, and the following county-level variables: percent home ownership, percent with high school degree, percent with some college or two-year degree, percent with four-year college degree or beyond, percent African American, average income, percent below poverty line, unemployment rate, percent married, and percent foreign born, all among adults.

Table 2A.2 **Second-stage IV regressions: Ever-user treatment definition, healthy subpopulation**

	Prevalent cases		Incident cases	
Cancer	All drug users (1)	ACE or ARB monotherapy only (2)	All drug users (3)	ACE or ARB monotherapy only (4)
Treatment	−0.0209	0.0071	0.0068	0.0399
	(−4.00)	(0.51)	(0.41)	(1.27)
N	175,346	14,667	22,057	3,259

	Prevalent cases		Incident cases	
Stroke	All drug users (1)	ACE and ARB users only (2)	All drug users (3)	ACE and ARB users only (4)
Treatment	−0.0067	−0.0006	−0.0022	0.0054
	(−1.88)	(−0.09)	(−0.17)	(0.32)
N	175,346	14,667	22,057	3,259

Notes: Cluster-adjusted robust T-statistics in parentheses. Regressions also include indicators for age and sex, state fixed effects, and the following county-level variables: percent home ownership, percent with high school degree, percent with some college or two-year degree, percent with four-year college degree or beyond, percent African American, average income, percent below poverty line, unemployment rate, percent married, and percent foreign born, all among adults.

Table 2A.3 **Second-stage IV regressions: Intent-to-treat treatment definition, healthy subpopulation**

	Prevalent cases		Incident cases	
Cancer	All drug users (1)	ACE or ARB monotherapy only (2)	All drug users (3)	ACE or ARB monotherapy only (4)
Treatment	−0.0076	0.0071	0.0134	0.0399
	(−0.90)	(0.51)	(0.71)	(1.27)
N	175,348	14,667	22,057	3,259

	Prevalent cases		Incident cases	
Stroke	All drug users (1)	ACE and ARB users only (2)	All drug users (3)	ACE and ARB users only (4)
Treatment	0.0068	−0.0006	0.0028	0.0054
	(1.08)	(−0.09)	(0.18)	(0.32)
N	175,348	14,667	22,057	3,259

Notes: Cluster-adjusted robust T-statistics in parentheses. Regressions also include indicators for age and sex, state fixed effects, and the following county-level variables: percent home ownership, percent with high school degree, percent with some college or two-year degree, percent with four-year college degree or beyond, percent African American, average income, percent below poverty line, unemployment rate, percent married, and percent foreign born, all among adults.

Table 2A.4   **Falsification test: Second-stage regressions for pain**

	Prevalent cases		Incident cases	
	All drug users (1)	ACE and ARB users only (2)	All drug users (3)	ACE and ARB users only (4)
	Ever users			
Treatment	−0.0511	−0.0255	−0.0249	−0.0248
	(−5.11)	(−1.95)	(−1.65)	(−1.19)
N	1,406,469	95,386	153,904	19,466
	Intent to treat			
Treatment	−0.0718	−0.0255	−0.0329	−0.0248
	(−4.42)	(−1.95)	(−1.73)	(−1.19)
N	1,406,469	95,386	153,904	19,466

Notes: Cluster-adjusted robust T-statistics in parentheses. Regressions also include indicators for age, sex, diabetes, heart disease, heart failure, depression, Alzheimer's disease, glaucoma, ischemic heart disease, chronic obstructive pulmonary disease, pelvic/hip fracture, osteoporosis, rheumatoid arthritis/osteoarthritis, cataracts, and chronic kidney disease, state fixed effects, and the following county-level variables: percent home ownership, percent with high school degree, percent with some college or two-year degree, percent with four-year college degree or beyond, percent African American, average income, percent below poverty line, unemployment rate, percent married, and percent foreign born, all among adults.

References

Basu, A., J. Heckman, N. L. Salvador, and S. Urzua. 2007. "Use of Instrumental Variables in the Presence of Heterogeneity and Self-Selection: An Application to the Treatments of Breast Cancer Patients." *Health Economics* 16 (11): 1133–57.

Burton, Thomas. 2013. "Dispute Flares inside FDA over Safety of Popular Blood-Pressure Drugs." *Wall Street Journal*, May 30.

Chandra, A., and D. O. Staiger. 2011. "Expertise, Underuse, and Overuse in Healthcare." Unpublished Manuscript, March.

Dahlof, B., R. Devereux, S. Kjeldsen, S. Julius, G. Beevers, U. de Faire, F. Fyhrquist, et al. 2002. "Cardiovascular Morbidity and Mortality in the Losartan Intervention for Endpoint Reduction in Hypertension Study (LIFE): A Randomized Trial against Atenolol." *Lancet* 359:995–1003.

Food and Drug Administration (FDA). 2010. "FDA Drug Safety Communication: Ongoing Safety Review of the Angiotensin Receptor Blockers and Cancer." July 15. www.fda.gov/Drugs/DrugSafety/PostmarketDrugSafetyInformationforPatients andProviders/ucm218845.htm.

———. 2011. "FDA Drug Safety Communication: No Increase in Risk of Cancer with Certain Blood Pressure Drugs—Angiotensin Receptor Blockers (ARBs)." June 2. www.fda.gov/Drugs/DrugSafety/ucm257516.htm.

Goldman, D., A. Leibowitz, and J. Buchanan. 1998. "Cost-Containment and Adverse Selection in Medicaid HMOs." *Journal of the American Statistical Association* 93 (441): 54–62.

Gornick, M. 2003. "A Decade of Research on Disparities in Medicare Utilization: Lessons for the Health and Health Care of Vulnerable Men." *American Journal of Public Health* 93 (5): 753–59.

Gornick, M., P. Eggers, T. Reilly, R. Mentnech, L. Fitterman, L. Kucken, and B. Vladeck. 1996. "Effects of Race and Income on Mortality and Use of Services among Medicare Beneficiaries." *New England Journal of Medicine* 335:791–99.

Hamilton, B. 2001. "Estimating Treatment Effects in Randomized Clinical Trials with Non-Compliance: The Impact of Maternal Smoking on Birthweight." *Health Economics* 10:399–410.

Joyce, G., J. Zissimopolous, and D. Goldman. 2013. "Digesting the Doughnut Hole." *Journal of Health Economics* 32 (6): 1345–55.

Malani, A. 2006. "Identifying Placebo Effects with Data from Clinical Trials." *Journal of Political Economy* 114 (2): 236–56.

Matchar, D., D. McCrory, L. Orlando, M. Patel, P. Uptal, M. Patwardhan, B. Powers, G. Samsa, and R. Gray. 2008. "Systematic Review: Comparative Effectiveness of Angiotensin-Converting Enzyme Inhibitors and Angiotensin II Receptor Blockers for Treating Essential Hypertension." *Annals of Internal Medicine* 148 (1): 16–29.

Meeker, D., J. Joyce, J. Malkin, S. Teutsch, A. Haddix, and D. Goldman. 2011. "Coverage and Preventive Screening." *Health Services Research* 46 (1): 173–84.

Sipahi, I., S. M. Debanne, D. Y. Rowland, D. I. Simon, and J. C. Fang. 2010. "Angiotensin-Receptor Blockade and Risk of Cancer: Meta-Analysis of Randomised Controlled Trials." *Lancet Oncology* 11 (7): 627–36.

Strauss, M., and H. Hall. 2009. "Angiotensin Receptor Blockers Should Be Regarded as First-Line Drugs for Stroke Prevention in Both Primary and Secondary Prevention Settings: No." *Stroke* 40:3161–62.

Todd, P., and K. Wolpin. 2006. "Assessing the Impact of a School Subsidy Program in Mexico Using Experimental Data to Validate a Dynamic Behavioral Model of Child Schooling." *American Economic Review* 96 (5): 1384–417.

Wang, J., Y. Li, S. Franklin, and M. Safar. 2007. "Prevention of Stroke and Myocardial Infarction by Amlodipine and Angiotensin Receptor Blockers: A Quantitative Overview." *Hypertension* 2007 (50): 181–88.

3

Decomposing Medical Care Expenditure Growth

Abe Dunn, Eli Liebman, and Adam Hale Shapiro

3.1 Introduction

Medical care expenditures per capita in the United States is larger and rising faster relative to other developed countries (see Chernew and Newhouse 2012; Chandra and Skinner 2012). In 2012, health care accounted for more than 17 percent of US gross domestic product (GDP), which was nearly double the average of other Organisation for Economic Co-operation and Development (OECD) countries. Despite the substantial expenditures on medical care in the United States, many gaps remain in our understanding of the sources of expenditure growth. Current national statistics that track spending by service category (for example, physicians, hospitals, and prescription drugs) do not convey information about spending for specific disease categories. To fill this void, academics and policymakers have advocated for more detailed statistics on health care expenditures centered around a key target of health spending: disease treatment (see Berndt et al. 2000; National Research Council 2010). Additional information on disease spending may provide greater insight into how to contain and efficiently manage health care expenditure growth.

Abe Dunn is an economist at the Bureau of Economic Analysis. Eli Liebman is an economist at the Bureau of Economic Analysis. Adam Hale Shapiro is a research advisor at the Federal Reserve Bank of San Francisco.

We would like to thank Ana Aizcorbe, Ernie Berndt, Michael Chernew, David Cutler, Bill Marder, Joe Newhouse, Allison Rosen, and Jack Triplett. We would also like to thank the participants at the NBER/CRIW Conference on Measuring and Modeling Health Care Costs and 2013 iHEA 9th World Congress. The views expressed in this chapter are solely those of the authors and do not necessarily reflect the views of the Bureau of Economic Analysis, the Federal Reserve Bank of San Francisco, or the Board of Governors of the Federal Reserve System. For acknowledgments, sources of research support, and disclosure of the authors' material financial relationships, if any, please see http://www.nber.org/chapters/c13112.ack.

We analyze health care expenditures in the commercial sector over the period 2003 to 2007. The commercial health care market is economically important, accounting for 60 percent more expenditures than Medicare in 2012. Over this period of study, commercial medical care expenditures per commercially insured person grew by 26 percent, surpassing the 20 percent growth in nominal GDP per capita.[1] Prior research studies have examined several factors driving the growth in medical care expenditures, but each of these studies leaves out pieces of the puzzle. For instance, Roehrig and Rousseau (2011), Starr, Dominiak, and Aizcorbe (2013), and Thorpe, Florence, and Joski (2004) look at the cost of disease and the prevalence of disease, but do not analyze changes in service prices or service utilization (that is, the quantity of services per episode of care); Aizcorbe and Nestoriak (2011) and Dunn et al. (2012) look at cost of disease treatment used as a measure of disease price growth, but do not assess disease prevalence. Statistical agencies such as the Bureau of Labor Statistics (BLS) and Bureau of Economic Analysis (BEA), as well as research by Bundorf, Royalty, and Baker (2009) report changes in service prices for precisely defined services, but do not focus on the cost of disease treatment or disease prevalence. None of the prior literature has analyzed all these factors in one setting, which can leave policymakers without context for the different results and without understanding about where these studies disagree. This is important, since we find that broad generalizations for why spending changes often overlook important trends that are disease specific.

The aim of this study is to more comprehensively assess the sources of medical care expenditure growth. We do so by decomposing expenditure growth into four distinct components: service-price growth, service-utilization growth, prevalence-of-treated-disease growth, and demographic shift. We track and dissect these key components of medical care expenditure growth for the years 2003 to 2007 for the commercial sector using a rich claims database from MarketScan that contains millions of enrollees. The framework presented in this chapter breaks expenditures into various components applying a similar methodology to that developed in Dunn, Shapiro, and Liebman (2014). First, using demographic population weights assessed in Dunn, Liebman, and Shapiro (2014), we extract expenditure growth attributable to demographic shifts—primarily, an aging population. Second, as advocated by most health experts, we allocate expenditures into disease-level categories. This allows protocols, technologies, and prices relevant for treating specific diseases to vary uniquely over time. Third, we break expenditures down into expenditures per treatment and treated prevalence

---

1. Commercial medical care expenditure growth is calculated from the National Health Expenditure Accounts. Overall inflation as reported by the BEA PCE deflator grew by 11.5 percent over the period of study. Commercial premiums also grew faster than inflation with a growth rate of around 32 percent according to estimates from the Kaiser Employee Health Benefit Survey.

of a disease. For example, in the case of hypertension, we track the number of episodes of treatment for hypertension per capita as well as the expenditures per episode of treating hypertension. Finally, expenditures per episode of treatment is split into service price and service utilization. Service price represents the payment for a specific service, for example, a fifteen-minute office visit. Service utilization represents the quantity, or intensity, of services performed during an episode of treatment. For example, in our methodology, a thirty-minute doctor office visit will be a higher quantity of services than a fifteen-minute office visit.

Analyzing each of these factors within a single framework allows for a simple and tractable way of comparing the various contributors to medical care expenditure growth. Foremost, determining whether expenditures are rising from disease prevalence, service utilization, service prices, or demographic reasons is informative to policymakers attempting to hold back the rising cost of health care. The methodology also provides a more precise mapping between BLS methods (which track price per service) and the types of price indexes that health economists have advocated (expenditures per episode for a specific disease, often referred to as a disease price).

We find that, between 2003 and 2007, rising medical care expenditures per capita (that is, per commercially enrolled person) came from two primary sources: an increase in the prevalence of treated diseases (accounting for around one-third of the increase in expenditure growth) and an increase in service prices (accounting for around half of the increase in expenditure growth). The remaining increase is attributable to demographic shifts, in particular, a slightly aging commercially insured population. Interestingly, there is no aggregate growth in expenditures due to service utilization per episode. In fact, service utilization may be falling slightly for some conditions and increasing for others. While service-price growth is a large contributor to expenditure growth, it is important to highlight that price growth does not greatly exceed inflation. After deflating price-growth measures by the national personal consumption expenditure (PCE) deflator, we find that growth in prevalence accounts for 60 percent of expenditure growth in our sample. Around 27 percent is attributable to real service price growth and 18 percent to demographic shift. Service utilization has no impact on growth.

The three largest contributors to expenditure growth are the medical practice categories of orthopedics, gastroenterology, and endocrinology. These practice categories represented 33 percent of expenditures in 2003, but made up 40 percent of expenditure growth between 2003 and 2007. Each of these practice categories had large growth in service prices and the prevalence of treated disease. The major practice category with the largest expenditure growth was preventive and administrative services, which grew 64 percent over the sample period, although this category accounted for only 2.4 percent of spending in 2003. On the flip side, cardiology made up 12 percent of 2003 expenditures but accounted for less than 8 percent of the share in expenditure growth. This relatively slow rise in expenditures per capita for cardiology services is attributable to a decline in the prevalence of heart disease but also to a decrease in service utilization. Our decomposition for the cardiology condition category shows that the decline in service utilization was driven by a shift from inpatient to outpatient services and from brand to generic drugs. These shifts may be indicative of greater efficiency, since fewer resources are necessary to treat each episode. The shifts are reflected in lower disease price growth relative to the service price index, which holds utilization constant. This finding is consistent with the work of Cutler et al. (1998), who find that a price index that allows for greater substitution across services leads to lower price growth for the case of heart attack treatments.

Digging deeper into the specific disease categories reveals some interesting patterns. Within cardiology and endocrinology services, there has been a large increase in the prevalence of early stage contributors to heart disease such as hypertension, diabetes, obesity, and hyperlipidemia. However, there has been a decline in the prevalence of ischemic heart disease. This pattern may indicate that people are simply seeking treatment for heart disease at an earlier stage of illness. Indeed, there has been a large increase in spending on preventive services across the entire sample. For example, two of the largest contributors to growth in spending for gastroenterology were attributable to preventive services. Specifically, there was a 41 percent increase in expenditures per capita on "gastroenterology signs and symptoms" (a large portion of which includes colonoscopy) and a 34 percent increase in expenditures per capita for patients with "nonmalignant neoplasm of intestines" (e.g., benign polyps). Our decomposition shows that the majority of this growth is attributable to an increase in the prevalence of treatment and demographic shifts.

Our decomposition also sheds light on the factors that contribute to the rapid rise in the treatment cost of cancer. Over the five-year sample period, expenditures per capita rose twice as fast for malignant neoplasms (48 percent growth in expenditures per capita) than nonmalignant neoplasms (24 percent growth in expenditures per capita). A large reason for the discrepancy is the difference in growth in the costs of treatment (that is, expenditures per episode of care). Service prices for malignant neoplasms grew over twice as fast as service prices for nonmalignant neoplasms. This may indicate that more expensive and innovative services are playing a role in cancer-spending growth.

This chapter finds results in the aggregate that are consistent with Bundorf, Royalty, and Baker (2009) that use a similar data and time period. Specifically, after accounting for overall inflation, they show that the growth in the health sector is mostly driven by nonprice factors. Our chapter adds to their findings by providing a more nuanced picture of the factors leading to more health care utilization and higher prices. In particular, we find that overall utilization growth is rising because of a higher treated prevalence growth for many conditions, while for other condition categories, such as cardiology, it appears that demographics play a more important role. We also find that service prices do not rise uniformly and that price growth for the treatment of malignant neoplasms is growing particularly fast. Several other disease-specific findings are highlighted throughout the text.

One limitation of our study is that it looks at a shorter time period and only a subset of the population (i.e., the commercial population) compared to some of the previous studies that apply survey data, such as Roehrig and Rousseau (2011) and Starr, Dominiak, and Aizcorbe (2013), so a direct comparison with our chapter is not possible. Indeed, the use of large claims data is especially important for accurately measuring factors driving expenditure growth for precisely defined disease categories, to account for underreporting in survey data, and to study patterns in relatively rare but economically important health conditions (see Zuvekas and Olin 2009; Aizcorbe et al. 2012).

This chapter focuses on the economic analysis of the components of medical care expenditure growth and trends. However, there are several methodological issues that arise when studying the components of expenditure growth that are not covered in this chapter. Some of these topics are explored in companion pieces to this work: (a) Dunn et al. (2015) examine different approaches for assigning medical services to disease categories and the effect of these assignments on the components of spending growth; (b) Dunn, Liebman, and Shapiro (2015) examine alternative strategies for separating utilization and price, which offer some implications for medical care price indexes; (c) Dunn, Liebman, and Shapiro (2014) examine the representativeness of the data used in our study and the effects of analyzing different samples and applying alternative weights; and (d) Dunn, Shapiro, and Liebman (2014) study the geographic differences in expenditure levels across Metropolitan Statistical Areas (MSAs).

3.2   Methodology of Index Construction

The methodology of this chapter borrows heavily from the Dunn, Shapiro, and Liebman (2014) study of geographic variation in disease expenditures. However, instead of focusing on differences across regions, we examine differences over time. To begin, we measure expenditures per capita for disease d for time period t, $C_{d,t}^*$, which is simply total expenditures for disease d in period t divided by the total commercial-insured population in period t. To create a measure of medical care expenditure growth, we form the following expenditure-per-capita index (ECI):

$$(1) \qquad ECI_{d,t} = \frac{C_{d,t}^*}{C_{d,0}^*}$$

where $C_{d,0}^*$ is expenditures per capita for disease d in the base period, 0. Next, we create a demographically fixed ECI, or $DECI$, by applying age, geographic location, and gender weights to our selected commercially insured population, so that the age and sex distribution is identical across regions and time periods.[2] A measure of demographically fixed medical care expenditure growth from period 0 (the base period) to t is then:

$$(2) \qquad DECI_{d,t} = \frac{C_{d,t}}{C_{d,0}}$$

where $C_{d,t}$ is expenditures per capita after fixing the demographic distribution to the base period. Note that any difference between the ECI and $DECI$ will be attributable to demographic shifts in the commercially insured population. We label this the "demographic residual" (Dem):

$$(3) \qquad Dem_{d,t} = ECI_{d,t} - DECI_{d,t} + 1.$$

Since the denominator of the $C_{d,t}$ term is the full population, this measure of expenditure growth does not take into account the health of the population. For instance, if expenditures per capita are higher in the second period because more individuals develop ischemic heart disease (i.e., a rise in the prevalence of ischemic heart disease), the expenditure measure $C_{d,t}$ will grow, even if the expenditures per episode of heart disease does not change. Alternatively, $C_{d,t}$ may grow if the expenditures per heart disease episode increases, even if prevalence remains unchanged. In the following section we will decompose the growth in population expenditures into the prevalence of the condition and the expenditures per episode of the condition.

3.2.1   Decomposing Expenditure per Capita into Expenditure per Episode and Prevalence of Treated Disease

We divide demographically fixed expenditures per capita, $C_{d,t}$, into two components. One component is the prevalence of treated disease index, $PREV_{d,t}$, which we define as growth in the demographically fixed prevalence of treated disease, $prev_{d,t}$:

$$(4) \qquad PREV_{d,t} = \frac{prev_{d,t}}{prev_{d,0}}$$

where $prev_{d,t}$ is the number of episodes treated in the population divided by the commercially insured population, holding fixed the demographic distribution. Note that $prev_{d,t}$ includes only those who are aware of their condition

2. Age, sex, and major census region counts of those with private health insurance were accessed for each year from http://www.census.gov/cps/data/cpstablecreator.html. The age categories were: birth (babies only), one to seventeen, eighteen to twenty-four, twenty-five to thirty-four, thirty-five to forty-four, forty-five to fifty-four, and fifty-five to sixty-four. This left us with forty-two buckets (seven age buckets × two gender buckets × four regions). Then, using those counts we weighted up the number of enrollees in each of those forty-two buckets to match the population counts from the CPS. For the ECI we weighted to the CPS population for each year, to compute the DECI we weight each year of our sample to the 2007 CPS population (see Dunn, Liebman, and Shapiro 2014).

and seek some medical attention, and excludes those individuals who are unaware of their condition or are aware of their condition and choose not to be treated.[3] Note that the definition of treated prevalence in this chapter denotes the number of episodes per capita rather than the number of individuals treated per capita within a year, which is a measure that is often reported in the literature.[4] However, work by Dunn et al. (2015) finds little differences in the treated prevalence growth or growth in cost per case when using this alternative definition of treated prevalence and cost per case.

The second component of $C_{d,t}$ is the expenditures per episode d, $c_{d,t}$. This is sometimes referred to as cost per case or treatment cost in the literature. The value $c_{d,t}$ may be calculated by dividing total expenditures of disease d by the number of episodes of disease d in period t, holding fixed the demographic distribution to the base period. It follows that the medical care expenditure index, or MCE index, is a measure of the medical care expenditures for the treatment of an episode of care for a certain disease, and is defined as the dollar amount of medical care used until treatment is completed.[5] Denoting $c_{d,0}$ as the average expenditures per episode in the base period, $t = 0$, the MCE index for disease d is the ratio of the two measures:

$$(5) \qquad MCE_{d,t} = \frac{c_{d,t}}{c_{d,0}}.$$

Since this index controls for the health of the individual, it may be viewed as measuring the cost of treatment. Thus, if the $MCE_{d,t}$ is larger than one, it signifies that the expenditure for treating disease d is larger than the base period and if the index is less than one it signifies that the expenditure is less than the base.

Using these equations it follows that $C_{d,t} = c_{d,t} \cdot prev_{d,t}$. From this we can see that the $DECI_{d,t}$ may be decomposed into its two components, which include the episode-based index, $MCE_{d,t}$ and the prevalence of treated disease index, $PREV_{d,t}$:[6]

$$(6) \quad DECI_{d,t} = MCE_{d,t} + PREV_{d,t} + \frac{(prev_{d,t} - prev_{d,0})(c_{d,t} - c_{d,0})}{prev_{d,0}c_{d,0}} - 1.$$

3. Those individuals who have a condition but are unaware that they have a condition or do not seek medical attention for their condition would be considered in measuring the population's prevalence, but are not included in the treated prevalence figure.

4. For cases of conditions that appear multiple times in a year, episodes of care per population is likely a more accurate measure of the probability that the disease is treated in the population. For example, comparing a population where the flu appears twice a year per person, to a population where the flu appears a single time per year, the episode-based statistic will reflect the higher probability of observing the flu in the first population. In practice, Dunn et al. (2015) find this difference to be unimportant when measuring changes in treated prevalence or cost per case.

5. For example, for an individual with a broken foot, the episode of treatment will be defined by the dollars of medical services used to treat that condition from the first visit to a provider until the foot is healed. For medical conditions that are chronic, we interpret an episode as expenditure for services used to treat the chronic condition over a one-year period.

6. A decomposition using logs is: $\log(DECI_{d,t}) = \log(MCE_{d,t}) + \log(PREV_{d,t})$.

This equation makes it clear that the *DECI* will rise if there is either an increase in the $PREV_{d,t}$ or an increase in the $MCE_{d,t}$. These two components of expenditure capture distinct elements of cost growth. Changes in the prevalence of a condition capture the changing health of the population, such as the growth in diabetes due to obesity. It may also reflect a growing awareness of a condition, such as the increase in awareness and diagnosis of high cholesterol. The second component of care may be viewed as the price for treating the disease, which includes the prices of those services and also the mix of those services provided. Assuming that the quality of the underlying treatment mix remains constant, this treatment price reflects the productivity in the health sector for the treatment of disease d.

The indexes presented here are directly related to a simple and often reported figure, total medical care expenditures per capita. To see this, we can create aggregate disease-specific indexes from the population-based measure, $ECI_{d,t}$. When $ECI_{d,t}$ is weighted by the national expenditure share for each disease in the base period, this becomes a measure of medical care expenditures per capita relative to the base period's medical care expenditures per capita:

$$ECI_t = \sum_D ECI_{d,t} \cdot (\text{ExpenditureShare}_0)$$

$$= \sum_D \frac{C_{d,t}}{C_{d,0}} \cdot \left(\frac{C_{d,0}}{\Sigma_D C_{d,0}} \right) = \frac{\Sigma_D C_{d,t}}{\Sigma_D C_{d,0}}$$

$$= \frac{\text{ExpendituresPerPerson}_t}{\text{ExpendituresPerPerson}_0}.$$

3.2.2   Expenditure per Episode Decomposition: Service Price and Service Utilization

A Motivating Example

To help motivate our methodology for decomposing service price and service utilization, we start with a simple example. Consider a time period t where people are treated for hypertension (h) (i.e., high blood pressure) where there exists only one type of treatment available—a fifteen-minute office visit. Let

$N_{h,t}$ = number of treated hypertension episodes,
$c_{h,t}$ = average expenditure for hypertension per episode,[7]
$q_{h,t}$ = number of fifteen-minute office visits per episode, and
$p_{h,t}$ = price per fifteen-minute office visit (i.e., $c_{h,t} / q_{h,t}$).

---

7. That is, (total out-of-pocket expenditures plus expenditures paid by the insurer) / $N_{h,t}$.

Also suppose there is a comparison or base time period, $t = 0$, where the price for a fifteen-minute office visit for hypertension is $p_{h,0}$. In this simple case, the relative price level of t to 0 is simply $p_{h,t} / p_{h,0}$. Clearly, this ratio reflects only differences in the contracted prices, not the number of fifteen-minute office visits. Similarly, the relative utilization level is $q_{h,t} / q_{h,0}$, which depends only on the number of fifteen-minute office visits performed per episode. It follows that the relative expenditures per episode between t and 0 may be expressed as:

$$(7) \qquad MCE_{h,t} = \frac{c_{h,t}}{c_{h,0}} = \left(\frac{p_{h,t} \cdot q_{h,0}}{p_{h,0} \cdot q_{h,0}} \right) \cdot \left(\frac{p_{h,t} \cdot q_{h,t}}{p_{h,t} \cdot q_{h,0}} \right).$$

The first term in equation (7) is a price index, and the second term is a utilization index. Expanding on this example, now suppose that hypertension may be treated with two types of services, prescription drugs and physician office services, where the service categories correspond to the subscripts (D) and (O). That is, $q_{h,t,O}$ and $p_{h,t,O}$ are the utilization and price for the physician office visits, and $q_{h,t,D}$ and $p_{h,t,D}$ are the utilization and price for prescription drugs. Continuing with the index decomposition that is parallel to equation (7), but with two services, the decomposition becomes:

$$(8) \qquad \frac{c_{h,t}}{c_{h,0}} = \frac{p_{h,t,O} \cdot q_{h,t,O} + p_{h,t,D} \cdot q_{h,t,D}}{p_{h,0,O} \cdot q_{h,0,O} + p_{h,0,D} \cdot q_{h,0,D}}$$

$$(9) \qquad = \left(\frac{p_{h,t,O} \cdot q_{h,0,O} + p_{h,t,D} \cdot q_{h,0,D}}{p_{h,0,O} \cdot q_{h,0,O} + p_{h,0,D} \cdot q_{h,0,D}} \right) \cdot \left(\frac{p_{h,t,O} \cdot q_{h,t,O} + p_{h,t,D} \cdot q_{h,t,D}}{p_{h,t,O} \cdot q_{h,0,O} + p_{h,t,D} \cdot q_{h,0,D}} \right).$$

Again the first term corresponds to the price index and the second term corresponds to the utilization index.

The General Case

In the general case, we define the medical care expenditure for the treatment of an episode of a disease (that is, a specific condition) as the total dollar amount of medical care used until treatment is completed, including *all* service categories.[8] To demonstrate how to decompose the MCE in the general case, it is useful to start by showing that the average expenditure is calculated by totaling dollars spent on all services to treat the condition and dividing those dollars by the number of episodes: $c_{d,t} = \Sigma_s p_{d,t,s} Q_{d,t,s} / N_{d,t}$, where $Q_{d,t,s}$ is the quantity of services for service type, s; $p_{d,t,s}$ is the service price for service type s; and $N_{d,t}$ is the number of episodes treated. To simplify, let $q_{d,t}$ be a vector of services utilized for the typical treatment of diseases at time t, $q_{d,t} = Q_{d,t} / N_{d,t}$, where the component of the utilization vector for service type s is $q_{d,t,s} = Q_{d,t,s} / N_{d,t}$. Similarly, let $p_{d,rt}$ be a vector of service

---

8. For medical diseases that are chronic, we interpret a. n episode as the total expenditure for services used to treat the chronic disease over a one-year period.

prices, where the price for a particular service type and disease can be calculated by dividing its average expenditure by the average quantity of services provided: $p_{d,t,s} = c_{d,t,s} / q_{d,t,s}$ where $c_{d,t,s}$ is the average episode expenditure for disease d for service type s at time t. This decomposition allows us to create a service price and service utilization index. The service price index (SPI) is then calculated as

$$SPI_{d,t} = \frac{p_{d,t} \cdot q_{d,0}}{c_{d,0}},$$

which holds the utilization of services fixed at a base-period level. The SPI measures the compensation necessary to purchase a fixed utilization of medical goods when going from the base period to time t. The service utilization index (SUI) may be defined as:

$$SUI_{d,t} = \frac{p_{d,0} \cdot q_{d,t}}{c_{d,0}},$$

which holds the price of services fixed while allowing the utilization of services to vary. The SUI measures the compensation necessary to purchase medical goods in the time period t to the amount of compensation necessary in the base period. We choose to apply Laspeyres indexes for price and quantity, so that the estimates may be compared to a base period: essentially answering the question, how much are disease expenditures different than the base period due to price differences or due to utilization differences? With these indexes the decomposition that relates these three indexes is additive, rather than multiplicative.[9] The relationship between these three indexes is described by the following decomposition:

$$MCE_{d,t} = SPI_{d,t} + SUI_{d,t} + \frac{(q_{d,t} - q_{d,0})(p_{d,t} - p_{d,0})}{c_{d,0}} - \frac{p_{d,0} \cdot q_{d,0}}{c_{d,0}}.$$

Here the MCE index is equal to the service price index, $SPI_{d,t}$, plus the service utilization index, $SUI_{d,t}$, plus a cross term, $(q_{d,t} - q_{d,0})(p_{d,t} - p_{d,0}) / c_{d,0}$, and subtracting $(p_{d,0} \cdot q_{d,0}) / c_{d,0}$ (which is close to 1). The cross term accounts for joint changes in both price vectors and utilization vectors and, in practice, the term is near zero. In the case where there are very few changes in utilization over time, $SUI_{d,t}$ is fixed near 1, then the $MCE_{d,t}$ will entirely be determined by service prices. Similarly, if there are very few changes in service prices over time, $SPI_{d,t}$, is near 1, and the $MCE_{d,t}$ will entirely be determined by utilization.

---

9. This approach follows others in the health literature that also apply additive decompositions (e.g., Roehrig and Rousseau 2011), which leaves a cross term. As another possibility, we could have used a Laspeyres index for the price index and a Paasche index for the quantity index, which provides an exact decomposition (e.g., $SUI^{Laspeyres} \cdot SPI^{Paasche} = MCE$).

3.3 Data

We use retrospective claims data for a sample of commercially insured patients from the MarketScan Research Databases from Truven Health. The specific claims data used is the Commercial Claims and Encounters Database, which contains data from the employer and health plan sources containing medical and drug data for several million commercially insured individuals, including employees, their spouses, and dependents. Each observation in the data corresponds to a line item in an "explanation of benefits" form in a medical claim. Each claim can consist of many records, and each encounter can consist of many claims.

We use a sample of enrollees that are not in capitated plans from the MarketScan database for the years 2003 to 2007. We also limit our sample to enrollees with drug benefits because drug purchases will not be observed for individuals without drug coverage. The MarketScan database tracks claims from all providers using a nationwide convenience sample of enrollees. Each enrollee has a unique identifier and includes age, sex, and region information that may be used when calculating patient weights. All claims have been paid and adjudicated.[10]

The claims data were processed using the Symmetry grouper from Optum. The grouper assigns each claim to a particular episode treatment group (ETG) disease and severity category. Thus each disease category d represents a type of disease (e.g., hypertension), as well as the severity of the disease classified into up to four severity bins. A higher severity number indicates a more serious medical condition. In this manner, "hypertension 3" is a distinct disease with a higher severity relative to "hypertension 1."

The grouper uses a proprietary algorithm, based on clinical knowledge, that is applied to the claims data to assign each record to a clinically homogeneous episode. The episode grouper allocates all spending from individual claim records to a distinct condition; the grouper also uses other information on the claim (e.g., procedures) and information from the patient's history to allocate the spending. For instance, for claims submitted by a physician, the grouper uses the ICD-9 code to allocate spending. If there are procedure codes present, they can be used to decide which ICD-9 code is most applicable to that claim.

An advantage of using the grouper is that it can use patients' medical history to assign diseases to drug claims, which typically do not provide a diagnosis. For example, each claim is grouped to one distinct episode that consists of one disease grouping (ETG). The grouper works in chronological fashion, but can update old episodes as it gathers more information, so an early diagnosis of chest pain can be updated to heart disease as further

---

10. Additional details about the data and the grouper used in this chapter are in Dunn et al. (2012).

ICD-9 codes arrive. This is in contrast to the primary diagnosis method, which would imply that a person had both chest pain and heart disease. Furthermore, severity operates the same way: when someone is grouped to hypertension 3, their previous claims, which were grouped to hypertension 2, get updated to hypertension 3.

Another advantage of the grouper over the primary diagnosis method is that it uses a patient's history to assign diseases to drug claims, which typically do not provide a diagnosis and account for a lot of spending. For instance, the grouper examines which episodes the patient has, then matches their drug claims to an episode based on the NDC code on the drug claim and the timing of the episodes.[11]

However, one downside of using these algorithms is that they are also considered a "black box" in the sense that they rely entirely on the grouper software developer's expertise. The ETG Symmetry grouper is applied to one calendar year of data at a time. Although this limits the amount of information used for each person (since we often observe multiple years), it also avoids potential biases that may occur if the grouper is not applied symmetrically across all years.[12]

Finally, it is important to note that while the ETG groupings are based mostly on ICD-9 disease codes, we aggregate the ETGs to Major Practice Categories, as is done in Aizcorbe and Nestoriak. However, this is solely for presentation purposes, and the practice category of the physician on the claim has little bearing into which ETG the claim is assigned. Rather, we group entire episodes to practice categories after the ETGs have been assigned to each claim.

For all measures but the *ECI*, demographic weights are applied to each individual to adjust for differences in age, sex, and region across populations, so the expenditure estimates may be comparable across years. Specifically, enrollees in each year are assigned weights so the weighted population has an age and sex distribution that is identical to that of the US commercially insured population in 2007.[13] To look at the growth in expenditure due to

---

11. See Rosen et al. (2012) and Dunn et al. (2015) for more detailed information about how the grouper works and for information about how the ETG grouper relates to other groupers. For instance, Dunn et al. (2015) compares the robustness of their results using the ETG to other grouping methods, including the CCS codes used by Roehrig and Rousseau.

12. The ETG grouper allocates each record into one of over 500 disease groups. To symmetrically process the data, we apply the ETG episode grouper on the claims data one year at a time. Applying the grouper one year at a time can split episodes into two, which may lead to an overstatement of the count of episodes and an understatement to the average price of an episode. However, applying the grouper across years leads the grouper to incorporate more information in later years, introducing an artificial time trend to the results. We explore the robustness of the estimates to various grouping methodologies in Dunn et al. (2015).

13. We use 2007 as the base to look at a population of individuals and their diseases that is more similar to our current population distribution. Similar results are found if we use the 2003 population as the base.

population growth and shifts, we also calculate total weighted spending over this period in a way that allows populations to vary.

3.3.1 Service Price, Utilization, and Episodes

The number of episodes is a simple count of the total number of episodes of a medical disease that end in the sample period. Total episode expenditures are measured as the total dollar amount received by all providers for the services used to treat an episode of a specific disease (including both out-of-pocket payments and amounts paid by insurance firms).

Service utilization measures are created for each type of service based on the definition of a service within that service type. The service-type categories are inpatient hospital, outpatient hospital, physician, prescription drug, and other. Measuring service utilization is not a straightforward task since the definition of "service" is a bit ambiguous and there are a variety of ways that one could define it across various service types. Ideally, we would like the definition of a specific service to depend on how the price of that service is typically set and paid. For example, for physician services, individuals pay a unique price for each procedure done to them (that is, the insurer and the patient together pay this amount), whereas the prices paid to facilities are often set based on the treated disease. Next we describe how the quantity of services is measured for each service type.

Measuring the Quantity of Service by Service Type

For each claim line in the data, we first categorize it by place of service, which determines the service-type category. For each category, the following steps describe how the amount is determined for each visit, where a visit is defined by the enrollee, and the date of service or admission:

Physician office. Physician visits are priced based on procedures performed in a physician's office. Since not all procedures are equivalent, each procedure is weighted to reflect the intensity of the service. For the Medicare payment system, Relative Value Units (RVUs) define reimbursement rates and are intended to capture the intensity of the services provided. In that spirit, we proxy for the intensity of service by using the average prices for each Current Procedural Terminology (CPT-4) code and modifier code. The total quantity of services performed in an office is then computed by summing over these RVU amounts. More precisely, the total amount of services from a physician office visit is computed as $q_{office} = \Sigma_{cpt \in Visit} \overline{p}_{cpt,office}$, where $cpt \in Visit$ is a complete list of CPT procedures performed during the visit in an office setting and $\overline{p}_{cpt,office}$ is the base price for procedure code, cpt. The base group price, $\overline{p}_{cpt,office}$, is computed as the average price in the data for that procedure code and modifier code across all time periods. Since most insurers set prices from a base price schedule (e.g., 10 percent above Medicare rates), one can think of the price of a cpt code at time t as the base price multiplied by a scalar price, α_t, where $p^t_{cpt} = \alpha_t \overline{p}_{cpt}$. For instance, if a CPT code that equals 99213 indicating a fifteen-minute established patient office visit has an average price of $100, its value will be 100 RVUs (i.e., p_{99213} = 100). It should be clear that the RVU amount is a measure of utilization and not price. To see this, if the fee on a fifteen-minute office visit is $120 at time t (p_{99213}^t = $120), then the price of the service will be calculated as $120/100RVU = 1.2$ $/RVU (i.e., $\alpha_t = p_{cpt}^t / \overline{p}_{cpt}$).[14]

Hospital inpatient. Inpatient hospital stays not only consist of facility fees paid to the hospital, but also fees paid to the physician. A variable in the claims data distinguishes these two types of payments. For the portion of fees paid to the hospital, the amount of services is measured as the average dollar amount for an inpatient stay for the observed disease. For the portion of fees paid to the physician, we assign an RVU in the same way that we calculate an RVU in an office setting. The total amount of services performed in an inpatient setting is calculated by adding the physician and facility amounts. Specifically, $q_{inpatient} = \overline{p}_{d,inpatient} + \Sigma_{cpt \in Visit} \overline{p}_{cpt,inpatient}$ where $\overline{p}_{d,inpatient}$ is the base price for inpatient facility claims for disease d, where the base price is the average price in the data across all time periods for a visit to an inpatient facility for treating disease d. The term $\Sigma_{cpt \in Visit} \overline{p}_{cpt,inpatient}$ is the amount calculated for the physician portion of the bill and is computed in a manner identical to the physician office category, but is based on only physician claims in an inpatient setting.

Hospital outpatient. Outpatient hospital visits are calculated in an identical fashion to the inpatient hospital visits. That is, the facility amount is calculated based on the average outpatient visit for that disease, and the doctor's portion of the total amount is calculated based on the average payment for the procedure codes in an outpatient setting.

Prescription drugs. The amount of the prescription drug varies based on the molecule, the number of pills in the bottle, the strength of the drug, and the manufacturer. An eleven-digit National Drug Code (NDC) uniquely identifies the manufacturer, the strength, dosage, formulation, package size, and type of package. To capture these differences, we calculate the average price for each NDC code. This means we treat branded and generic products that contain the same active molecule as distinct drugs. The average price for each NDC code represents the amount of the service used. Specifically, the amount of drug services used is $q_{drug} = \Sigma_{NDC \in Visit} \overline{p}_{NDC}$, where $NDC \in Visit$ is a complete list of NDC codes purchased from a visit to a pharmacy and $\overline{p}_{NDC}$ is the base price for a specific NDC code. The base price for each NDC is computed as the average price in the data.

All other. The other category primarily includes ambulatory care, independent labs, and emergency room visits. For these services, if no procedure code is available, the amount of each category is measured as the average cost for a visit to that particular place of service for treating a particular disease

14. This methodology for calculating utilization for physician services is identical to that conducted by Dunn and Shapiro (2014).

(for example, the average cost of an ambulatory care visit to treat ischemic heart disease). For cases where procedure codes are available, we use the average cost of that procedure code for that place of service.

Our decomposition relies on the institutional feature that insurers and providers typically negotiate from a percentage of a base fee schedule (for example, 10 percent above Medicare rates).[15] As our measure of service price can be intuited as the expenditures from a visit divided by a proxy for a "RVU," it can also be thought of as a percentage amount from a base (or average) payment—a measure close to how prices are actually set. For this reason, these measures of service quantity subsequently allow us to create service prices that correspond well with how fees are negotiated in the marketplace. In other words, our approach attempts to construct a unit value index that reflects the heterogeneity in how goods and services are actually priced.[16] It can also be shown that if pricing is set based on a percentage of a set fee schedule, then our index is equivalent to an index that prices specific procedures. See Dunn, Shapiro, and Liebman (2014) and the associated appendix for additional details.

3.3.2   Summary Statistics

Table 3.1 provides some basic descriptive statistics for the selected commercially insured population of the MarketScan data. Each enrollee is assigned a population weight based on age, gender, and location so that the number of enrollees represents the actual number of commercially insured enrollees measured by the Current Population Survey (CPS). Note that this table reports figures where weights are applied, so that the population changes and grows with the actual commercially insured population.[17] As described above, when calculating the *DECI* and subsequent decomposition indexes, we hold fixed the age, gender, and location. There are 455 ETG disease categories in the sample,[18] representing $454.4 billion for 180.5 million

---

15. In a survey of twenty health plans conducted by Dyckman & Associates, all twenty health plan fee schedules were influenced by the Medicare fee schedule. That is, a resource-based relative value scale (RBRVS), essentially adopting Medicare's base fee schedule.

16. Note that our approach differs from Bundorf, Royalty, and Baker (2009), which also studied individual service prices over time, though not at the disease level. Since they do not calculate disease-level prices, they are able to separately price each individual CPT code and NDC code. In contrast, this is not possible in a disease-based framework because not all CPT codes and NDC codes are observed for every disease across all years. It should also be noted that there are alternative methods for pricing medical services that may not be reflected in the methods applied here. For instance, for Medicare patients, outpatient hospital facility services are often priced based on the Ambulatory Payment Classification system and this method is also used by many commercial insurers.

17. Our weights were constructed using data from http://www.census.gov/cps/data/cpstablecreator.html.

18. Severity adjustment increases the number of disease categories to 682. About 19 percent of expenditures are not assigned to any ETG disease category. Ungrouped claims include screening for diseases and other records that cannot be assigned a category. The ungrouped claims are removed from our analysis. If we do not adjust for severity, then the ungrouped share falls to 13 percent, but the results stay the same.

Table 3.1   Summary statistics

	2003	2007
Expenditure (billions)	$454.39	$589.35
Enrollees (millions)	180.58	182.53
Expenditure per capita (enrollee)	$2,516	$3,229
Episodes per capita (enrollee)	2.71	2.96
Expenditure per episode	$929	$1,092
Percent male	49.5	49.6
Average age	32.3	32.9
< Age 18 (%)	27.3	26.3
Age 18–age 24 (%)	9.6	9.6
Age 25–age 34 (%)	14.5	14.7
Age 35–age 54 (%)	36.3	35.6
> Age 55	12.2	13.8

enrollees in 2003, growing to $589.4 billion and 182.5 million enrollees in 2007. This growth is accompanied by a growth in the number of episodes from 2.7 per enrollee in 2003 to 3.0 per enrollee in 2007. The average age grew slightly from 32.3 to 32.9 over the sample period. The table shows that this growth is primarily from an increased percentage of enrollees over the age of fifty-five.

3.4   Results

3.4.1   Aggregated Indexes

We begin our analysis by examining aggregated time-specific indexes, which provide information about the entire commercial health care market for a given year. Specifically, we create ECI_t, $DECI_t$, $PREV_t$, MCE_t, SPI_t, SUI_t, and Dem_t by weighting each disease-specific index by the expenditure share of that disease in the base period. The top panel of figure 3.1 displays the aggregated expenditures per capita index (ECI_t) along with its decomposition between the demographic residual (Dem_t) and the demographically fixed expenditures per capita index ($DECI_t$). The ECI grew 6.4 percent per year from 2003 to 2007—a total of 28 percent over the four years. Demographic factors accounted for about a tenth of this growth, as the demographic residual grew by only 3 percent over the four years and the $DECI$ grew by 25 percent.

The second panel displays the $DECI_t$ along with its decomposition between the MCE_t and $PREV_t$. Growth in MCE_t represents about 56 percent of the total growth in the $DECI$ while growth in the prevalence index accounted for about 41 percent. Specifically, the MCE_t grew by 3.3 percent per year while the $PREV_t$ grew by 2.5 percent. Note that the growth in the

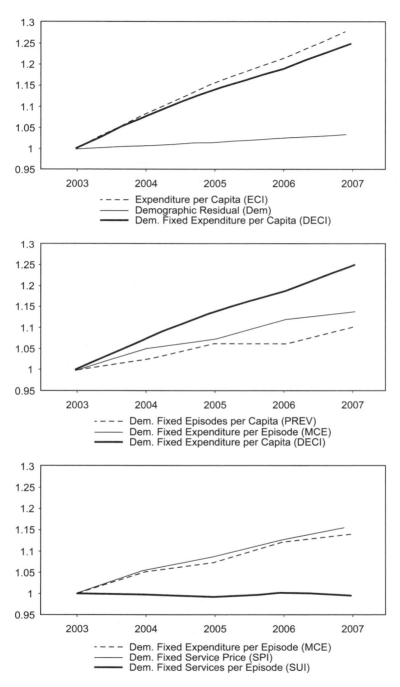

Fig. 3.1 Aggregated indexes

aggregate $PREV_t$ may reflect either an increase in treated prevalence or a shift toward more expensive diseases. Finally, the third panel decomposes the MCE_t between service prices (SPI_t) and service utilization (SUI_t). These aggregate indexes show that the cost of treatment growth is entirely due to changes in the underlying prices of the services and not the quantity of services being provided per episode. To be more precise, the SPI_t grew by 3.8 percent per year (15.9 percent over the sample period) while the SUI_t fell just 0.4 percent over the sample period.

All spending is calculated in nominal terms, but because health care has taken up an increasing share of GDP, it is interesting to investigate the contributing factors to growth after accounting for national inflation figures. Previous researchers also accounted for inflation, including Roehrig and Rousseau (2011) and Bundorf, Royalty, and Baker (2009), two papers that have looked at decomposing expenditure growth into components of price and utilization. After accounting for inflation by the PCE deflator (which grew by 11.5 percentage points between 2003 and 2007), we find that real service prices grew by 1 percent per year—about 4 percent from 2003 to 2007. This is consistent with the finding in Bundorf, Royalty, and Baker (2009), who also look at commercial markets and find very little service price growth relative to inflation over the 2001–2006 time period for the commercial sector. Another way of stating this is that, of the 28 percent expenditures per capita (ECI_t) growth from 2003 to 2007, 15.1 percentage points were attributable to things other than PCE inflation. Two-thirds of those 15.1 percentage points are attributable to increasing prevalence of treated diseases[19] and one-fifth was attributable to demographic shifts.[20]

3.4.2   Major Practice Categories

The aggregated indexes discussed above suggest that expenditure growth is occurring for two primary reasons: (a) growth in service prices, and

---

19. This was calculated as $(1 - PREV_{2007}) / (1 - ECI_{2007} / PCE_{2007})$, where PCE_{2007} is one plus the percentage growth in the PCE deflator between 2003 and 2007.

20. At first glance, a one-year increase in the average age seems too small to lead to a 3 percent increase in expenditures, but a more careful look at the data highlights the considerable differences in costs for those in different age groups. For example, the composition of the population shifts so that those over age fifty-five account for 1.6 percent more of the population. Likewise, those under age eighteen account for 1 percent less of the share of the population. This can make a significant impact since those over fifty-five are more than four times as expensive as those under eighteen, on average. Back-of-the-envelope calculations seem to suggest that these small changes in the composition of the population are sufficient to cause a 3 percent increase in the expenditure growth. The results presented here are quite distinct from the results of Roehrig and Rousseau (2011), who use the Medical Expenditure Panel Survey data and find that, even after accounting for inflation, expenditure per capita growth is primarily driven by expenditures per episode (i.e., MCE) and not prevalence, with the growth in the expenditure per episode accounting for 75 percent of expenditure growth. We find that expenditure per episode accounts for only about 20 percent of inflation-adjusted growth in the commercial sector. The study of a distinct time period may be a key factor causing these different findings. These differences warrant future investigation.

(b) growth in the prevalence of treated diseases. As treatments and changes in treatments are unique to each disease,[21] we next show indexes specific to twenty-two Major Practice Categories (MPC), the ETG aggregate categories provided by Optum for the Symmetry ETG grouper.[22] Each category is calculated as a weighted average of the many underlying disease-severity specific indexes in that category, where the weights are the proportions of expenditure shares in 2003.[23] These broader categories give some sense of where expenditure growth is occurring.

We report MPCs ordered according to the size of their expenditure share in table 3.2. The largest category is orthopedics and rheumatology, which accounted for 16.6 percent of spending in 2003. Spending in this category grew from $418 per capita in 2003 to $558 per capita in 2007—an increase of 33 percent as indicated by the 2007 *ECI* of 1.33. Orthopedics' share of expenditure growth (19.6 percent) exceeded its share of 2003 expenditure (16.6 percent), which is attributable to the fact that this diagnostic category grew faster than average. We can assess the sources of this growth by examining the 2007 indexes. For instance, demographic shift accounted for 3 points of the 33-percentage-point increase in expenditures per capita, treated prevalence accounted for another 12 percentage points, service prices accounted for 15 percentage points, service utilization 3 percentage points, and the cross term is zero.

One striking feature of table 3.2 is the substantial growth in preventive health services. This category represented only 2.4 percent of 2003 expenditures, but 5.3 percent of expenditure growth between 2003 and 2007. This category appears to be growing out of proportion for two reasons: increased prevalence of treatment (29 percent growth), as well as a large increase in service utilization (11 percent growth). Looking more deeply at this category, it appears that expenditures are driven primarily by more individuals receiving routine exams. One question raised is whether the greater prevalence and utilization of preventive services ultimately leads to lower overall health expenditures and better health outcomes. This is especially important given that the recent health care reform passed in the Patient Protection and Affordable Care Act encourages the use of preventive care services. Although more preventive care services are likely to lead to expenditures increasing in the short term, it is unclear what the long-term effects may be on both future health and expenditures.

21. This has been demonstrated in prior work by Thorpe, Florence, and Joski (2004), Roehrig and Rousseau (2011), Aizcorbe and Nestoriak (2011), Dunn et al. (2012), and Dunn, Shapiro, and Liebman (2014).

22. These categories align with specialties, but they have no bearing on how the grouper processed the data. A visit to a general practitioner would be treated as identical to a visit to a specialist, if the same diagnoses and procedures were performed.

23. For instance, the aggregated *ECI* for cardiology was calculated as $ECI_{Card,t} = \Sigma_{d \in Card} \omega_d \cdot ECI_{d,t}$ where $\omega_d = C_{d,0} / \Sigma_{d \in Card} C_{d,0}$ and *Card* is the set of diseases in the Major Practice Category: Cardiology.

Table 3.2 Major practice category

Major practice category	2003 Expenditure per capita ($)	2007 Expenditure per capita ($)	2003 Share of total expenditure (%)	Share of expenditure growth (%)	2007 Indexes						
					ECI	DEM	DECI	PREV	MCE	SPI	SUI
Orthopedics and rheumatology	418	558	16.6	19.6	1.33	1.03	1.30	1.12	1.17	1.15	1.03
Cardiology	296	348	11.8	7.3	1.18	1.07	1.11	1.04	1.06	1.16	0.93
Gastroenterology	228	304	9.1	10.6	1.33	1.04	1.29	1.11	1.17	1.17	1.01
Gynecology	181	222	7.2	5.9	1.23	1.02	1.22	1.01	1.20	1.19	1.01
Endocrinology	169	236	6.7	9.4	1.40	1.05	1.34	1.27	1.07	1.17	0.93
Otolaryngology	163	186	6.5	3.2	1.14	1.00	1.14	1.03	1.11	1.13	1.00
Neurology	147	195	5.8	6.7	1.33	1.03	1.30	1.10	1.19	1.21	0.99
Pulmonology	119	143	4.7	3.4	1.20	1.04	1.16	1.01	1.16	1.20	0.97
Psychiatry	119	150	4.7	4.3	1.26	1.00	1.26	1.13	1.12	1.15	1.01
Dermatology	115	149	4.6	4.7	1.29	1.02	1.28	1.08	1.18	1.16	1.03
Obstetrics	112	139	4.4	3.9	1.25	0.99	1.26	1.08	1.17	1.15	1.02
Urology	91	116	3.6	3.5	1.27	1.05	1.22	1.12	1.11	1.14	0.98
Hematology	62	82	2.5	2.8	1.32	1.04	1.28	1.11	1.15	1.22	0.96
Preventive & administrative	59	97	2.4	5.3	1.64	1.02	1.62	1.29	1.26	1.14	1.11
Hepatology	59	68	2.3	1.2	1.15	1.03	1.12	0.99	1.12	1.17	0.96
Ophthalmology	40	50	1.6	1.4	1.25	1.06	1.19	1.13	1.05	1.09	0.98
Infectious diseases	34	48	1.3	1.9	1.41	1.03	1.38	1.15	1.18	1.12	1.06
Nephrology	34	47	1.3	1.9	1.39	1.06	1.33	1.49	0.90	0.91	1.00
Neonatology	25	36	1.0	1.5	1.43	1.12	1.32	1.14	1.17	1.13	1.03
Isolated signs & symptoms	19	21	0.7	0.3	1.12	1.01	1.11	1.00	1.11	1.10	1.02
Late effects, environmental trauma	14	18	0.6	0.6	1.30	1.02	1.27	0.96	1.34	1.29	1.04
Chemical dependency	12	18	0.5	0.7	1.42	1.00	1.41	1.38	1.06	1.10	0.99
Total	2,516	3,229	100.00	100.0	1.28	1.03	1.25	1.10	1.14	1.16	1.00

It is especially interesting to note that many of the other diagnostic categories do not grow in proportion to their expenditure share. For example, cardiology diseases accounted for around 12 percent of spending in 2003, but only 7.3 percent of the expenditure growth between 2003 and 2007. Although service prices in this area are growing at a similar pace with other disease categories (around 16 percent), expenditure growth is kept in check by slower-than-average growth in prevalence as well as *declining* service utilization. Endocrinological diseases, many of which are major contributors to cardiovascular diseases, also show a decline in service utilization, however, they show much faster growth in treated disease prevalence. For this reason, expenditures per capita rose twice as fast for endocrinological diseases than for cardiology diseases.

For many disease conditions, we see important differences between the disease price (MCE) and the prices of the underlying services (SPI). These differences may be of significant economic importance. For instance, if the SPI growth exceeds the MCE, this indicates that the price of disease treatment is growing slower than the rate implied by traditional inflation measures. To better understand the difference between SPI and MCE indexes, we apply an additional decomposition that reports the difference between the SPI and MCE indexes by service type, s.[24] The decomposition equation is

$$(10) \quad MCE_{d,t} = SPI_{d,t} + (MCE_{d,t} - SPI_{d,t})$$

$$= SPI_{d,t} + \sum_s (MCE_{d,t,s} - SPI_{d,t,s})(\text{Exp.Share}_{d,0,s})$$

$$= SPI_{d,t} + \sum_s \frac{(MCE_{d,t,s} - SPI_{d,t,s})q_{d,0,s} \cdot p_{d,0,s}}{\sum_s q_{d,0,s} \cdot p_{d,0,s}}.$$

The term $(MCE_{d,t,s} - SPI_{d,t,s})(\text{Exp.Share}_{d,0,s})$ represents service category s's contribution to the difference between the MCE and SPI indexes. To gain some additional intuition for this equation, we take the decomposition from equation (10), but remove the cross term, which gives the approximate relationship $MCE_{d,t} \approx SPI_{d,t} + SUI_{d,t} - 1$. Applying this approximation, we substitute $SUI - 1$ for $MCE - SPI$ into equation (10); then the decomposition by service category is $MCE_{d,t} \approx SPI_{d,t} + \sum_s (SUI_{d,t,s} - 1)(\text{Exp.Share}_{d,0,s})$. From this approximate decomposition, one can see that the difference between the two indexes will primarily depend on the change in utilization of the different services and the corresponding expenditure share of the service category.

Table 3.3 shows the contribution of each service type, s, to the difference between the MCE and SPI (applying the exact decomposition 10). Table 3.3 shows several clear patterns across services for the top five spending diseases.[25] First, nearly every disease category shifts away from spending

---

24. This same decomposition is applied in Dunn, Liebman, and Shapiro (2015). The only difference is that here we apply it to the full sample of diseases, while Dunn, Liebman, and Shapiro (2015) looked only at disease conditions with more than 10,000 episodes.
25. See Dunn, Shapiro, and Liebman (2014) for a more complete discussion of this topic.

Table 3.3   Comparison of MCE and SPI and sources of differences, 2003–2007

		Contribution to MCE-SPI difference					
	MCE-SPI	Inpatient hospital	Outpatient hospital	Physician office	Other	Brand drugs	Generic drugs
Orthopedics and rheumatology	0.017	−0.026	0.001	0.038	0.021	−0.036	0.019
Cardiology	−0.097	−0.101	−0.005	0.017	−0.001	−0.028	0.021
Gastroenterology	−0.003	−0.035	−0.008	0.014	0.041	−0.029	0.015
Gynecology	0.010	−0.044	0.029	0.030	0.002	−0.016	0.009
Endocrinology	−0.092	−0.090	0.000	−0.001	0.008	−0.055	0.047

on inpatient services, which is especially large for cardiology and endocrinology conditions. This savings from reduced utilization on inpatient services is partly offset by an increase in the utilization of physician services for most disease categories. For drug services, we observe a shifting away from branded drugs, leading to a relative decline in the MCE, and we see an increase in generic drugs, contributing to an increase in the MCE. Combined, the shifting away from branded drugs toward generics causes a net decline in the MCE relative to the SPI for these top five diseases.[26]

3.4.3   Disease-Specific Indexes

Our methodology for decomposing expenditure growth may be used to drill down even further to the specific disease-severity level. Due to the large number of diseases, there are numerous dimensions in which we could look at the growth in expenditures. In the following section, we demonstrate how the methodology may be applied to a few areas of spending. Specifically, we focus on those diseases that are included in some of the larger MPCs and on the treatment of neoplasms (that is, benign and malignant tumors).

Cardiology and Endocrinology

Table 3.4 reports the expenditure decomposition for the ten largest diseases by spending in the two major practice categories of cardiology and endocrinology. The number that appears after each disease description is the severity level, ranging between 1 and 4 for many diseases, with a higher number indicating a greater severity. The table shows there have been large increases in the prevalence of treated hypertension, hyperlipidemia, diabetes, and obesity. This may correspond to changing lifestyles or eating habits of the commercially insured population. However, these four diseases are also major contributors to ischemic heart disease, which has strikingly shown a decline in treated prevalence.[27] This may indicate that people are seeking treatment earlier, *before* ischemic heart disease arises, perhaps reflecting a growing awareness of this medical condition. Indeed, evidence from the National Health and Nutrition Examination Survey shows very rapid growth in treated prevalence for diabetes, hyperlipidemia, and hypertension, even though the underlying clinical prevalence has remained relatively flat for these conditions.[28]

---

26. Although generics are considerably cheaper than branded drugs, the total difference may not be reflected in the tables. Generic drugs tend to be cheaper, pulling down the cost of treatment, but the lower cost of generics may also imply that consumers are purchasing more generic prescription drugs.

27. The decline in treated prevalence may be seen by averaging over the different severities of ischemic heart disease based on expenditures per capita. A study by the Centers for Disease Control and Prevention has also reported a decline in the prevalence of ischemic heart disease for the 2006 to 2010 period based on the Behavioral Risk Factor Surveillance System surveys (http://www.cdc.gov/mmwr/preview/mmwrhtml/mm6040a1.htm).

28. Specific values of these trends from the National Health and Nutrition Examination Survey are reported in Roehrig and Rousseau (2011).

Table 3.4   Cardiology and endocrinology

	2003 Expenditure per capita ($)	2007 Expenditure per capita ($)	2007 Indexes						
			ECI	DEM	DECI	PREV	MCE	SPI	SUI
Ischemic heart disease 1	55	54	0.98	1.07	0.91	0.95	0.96	1.14	0.86
Hypertension 1	48	64	1.33	1.06	1.27	1.14	1.11	1.13	1.01
Diabetes 1	43	68	1.58	1.09	1.48	1.28	1.16	1.17	1.01
Ischemic heart disease 2	30	32	1.07	1.08	0.99	1.09	0.91	1.09	0.84
Hyperlipidemia, other 1	26	37	1.43	1.08	1.35	1.29	1.05	1.16	0.95
Ischemic heart disease 3	24	24	1.01	1.07	0.94	0.88	1.07	1.20	0.90
Ischemic heart disease 4	22	23	1.05	1.07	0.98	0.91	1.08	1.20	0.90
Obesity 2	17	15	0.89	1.00	0.88	1.55	0.57	1.04	0.54
Cardiovascular diseases signs and symptoms 1	16	18	1.13	1.02	1.11	1.02	1.09	1.11	1.00
Diabetes 4	13	17	1.27	1.03	1.23	1.04	1.19	1.20	1.00

Also of note is that spending for low-severity ischemic heart disease has been declining over the sample period. In fact, were it not for an aging commercial population, spending per capita would have fallen by almost 10 percent between 2003 and 2007. This decline in spending is mostly attributable to the large decline in service utilization. This finding is also consistent with the work of Cutler et al. (1998), who find the quality-adjusted prices for treating heart attacks to be declining. As discussed in the previous section, this shift in utilization is attributable to the shift from inpatient to outpatient services in the treatment of heart disease.

Gastroenterology

Similar to cardiological and endocrinological diseases, gastroenterological diseases saw a shift in prevalence to earlier stage-of-illness treatment. Table 3.5 shows that prevalence in "gastroenterology signs and symptoms 1" and "nonmalignant neoplasm of intestines and abdomen 1" (e.g., benign polyps) both saw 16 percent growth in prevalence over the sample period. These two diseases represented one-fifth of gastroenterological expenditures in 2003 and grew by 41 and 34 percent, respectively, over the sample period. Endoscopic procedures (mainly colonoscopy) represented the largest share of spending (16.4 percent of spending) for "gastroenterology signs and symptoms 1," indicating that this disease category likely represents a large amount of preventive treatment. By contrast, "malignant neoplasm of the rectum or anus" saw a decline in prevalence. Similar to cardiology services, there seems to be shift in prevalence from later-stage severe illnesses to preventive care. This growth in prevalence of preventive treatment may be attributable to the new screening guidelines instituted by the Committee of the American College of Gastroenterology (ACG) in 2000.[29] Note that, although prevalence declined for rectal cancer, expenditures per capita rose significantly over the sample period. Our decomposition shows that this was mainly attributable to the large growth in the cost of treatment (the *MCE* index grew by approximately 50 percent). As we discuss in the section on neoplasms, many other types of cancer also reported large growth in treatment costs over the sample period.

Gynecology

As shown in table 3.2, gynecology was the fourth largest diagnostic category in 2003 but the fifth largest in 2007, falling behind endocrinology. This was attributable to the slightly lower-than-average growth in *ECI* (23 percent) for this diagnostic category. Table 3.6 reports the ten largest gynecological diseases in terms of expenditures per capita. These ten diseases made

---

29. The ACG recommends colonoscopy every ten years, beginning at age fifty, as the preferred strategy. This is in contrast to a menu of options strategy endorsed by the American Cancer Society.

Table 3.5   **Gastroenterology**

	2003 Expenditure per capita ($)	2007 Expenditure per capita ($)	2007 Indexes							
			ECI	DEM	DECI	PREV	MCE	SPI	SUI
Inflammation of esophagus 1	27	29	1.09	1.02	1.07	1.06	1.01	1.12	0.92
Gastroenterology diseases signs and symptoms 1	23	33	1.41	1.03	1.39	1.16	1.20	1.15	1.05
Nonmalignant neoplasm of intestines and abdomen 1	20	27	1.34	1.08	1.26	1.16	1.08	1.08	1.02
Hernias, except hiatal 1	10	12	1.19	1.03	1.16	1.02	1.14	1.19	0.96
Appendicitis 1	9	12	1.41	0.99	1.42	1.15	1.24	1.20	1.02
Inflammatory bowel disease 3	7	11	1.51	0.99	1.52	1.28	1.19	1.18	1.03
Malignant neoplasm of rectum or anus 2	6	9	1.45	1.08	1.37	0.93	1.47	1.41	1.05
Inflammation of esophagus 2	5	6	1.12	1.06	1.06	1.12	0.95	1.12	0.86
Bowel obstruction 1	5	7	1.26	1.05	1.22	1.04	1.16	1.13	1.03
Malignant neoplasm of rectum or anus 3	5	8	1.55	1.10	1.45	0.95	1.54	1.49	1.04

up about three-quarters of 2003 gynecological spending. The results show that the lower-than-average spending was mainly attributable to "nonmalignant neoplasm of the genital tract 3 and 1," "nonmalignant neoplasm of the breast 1," and "conditions associated with menstruation 1." Expenditures for these diseases all grew less than 10 percent over the 2003 to 2007 sample period. Our decomposition shows that cost of treatment (MCE) growth was about average for these diseases, however, they had low growth in prevalence and had negligible growth due to demographic factors. By contrast, the highest spending gynecological disease, breast cancer, had large growth in the cost of treatment—40 percent growth in MCE for severity 1 and 36 percent growth in MCE for severity 2.

Neoplasms

To more comprehensively assess expenditure growth for cancer treatment, we group neoplasm conditions in table 3.7. Specifically, we display the five most expensive neoplasm conditions (in terms of expenditures per capita), both malignant neoplasms and nonmalignant neoplasms, separately. For ease of display, we aggregated severity types into one disease category (e.g., neoplasm of breast 1, 2, and 3 were aggregated into "neoplasm of breast"). Note that neoplasms are not a MPC; rather, we pull neoplasms from across different MPCs to compare them for table 3.7. At the bottom of the table we also report aggregated indexes of all malignant and nonmalignant neoplasms, along with aggregated indexes of all conditions but neoplasms.[30]

The first result to note is that "nonmalignant neoplasms" look very similar to "all other diseases." Specifically, the MCE for nonmalignant neoplasm treatment grew by 11 percent over the sample period, slightly below the 13 percent growth in all other diseases. By contrast, the cost of treatment for malignant neoplasms grew much more rapidly, with an MCE growth of 30 percent. Faster growth for malignant neoplasms is attributable to both service prices, which grew by 25 percent, and service utilization, which grew by 5 percent. A plausible reason for this discrepancy between malignant neoplasms and the rest of the sample is the distinct and likely innovative technologies that are used to treat malignant neoplasms. Note that in our framework, when a procedure is first introduced into the market (i.e., an innovation), it will show up as an increase in utilization if this new procedure is measured to have a large quantity of RVUs. Furthermore, its price may subsequently increase as the new procedure diffuses and demand rises.

---

30. For instance, the aggregated ECI for nonmalignant neoplasms was calculated as $ECI_{Non,t} = \Sigma_{d \in Non} \omega_d \cdot ECI_{d,t}$ where $\omega_d = C_{d,0} / \Sigma_{d \in Non} C_{d,0}$ and *Non* are the set of nonmalignant diseases.

Table 3.6   Gynecology

	2003 Expenditure per capita ($)	2007 Expenditure per capita ($)	2007 Indexes						
			ECI	DEM	DECI	PREV	MCE	SPI	SUI
Malignant neoplasm of breast 1	26	41	1.60	1.10	1.50	1.07	1.40	1.27	1.10
Nonmalignant neoplasm of female genital tract 3	19	21	1.09	0.99	1.09	1.02	1.07	1.16	0.92
Malignant neoplasm of breast 2	17	25	1.52	1.03	1.49	1.10	1.36	1.28	1.06
Conditions associated with menstruation 1	15	14	0.99	1.01	0.99	0.87	1.14	1.13	1.03
Nonmalignant neoplasm of female genital tract 1	12	15	1.18	0.99	1.19	0.94	1.26	1.19	1.06
Nonmalignant neoplasm of breast 1	11	11	1.03	1.01	1.02	0.85	1.20	1.18	1.02
Endometriosis 1	9	8	0.89	0.98	0.90	0.82	1.10	1.14	0.97
Conditions associated with menstruation 2	9	13	1.43	0.99	1.43	1.11	1.29	1.21	1.07
Other diseases of female genital tract 1	9	9	1.08	1.03	1.05	1.04	1.01	1.17	0.86
Malignant neoplasm of breast 3	8	10	1.33	1.02	1.31	1.07	1.23	1.26	0.98

Table 3.7   Neoplasms

	2003 Expenditure per capita ($)	2007 Expenditure per capita ($)	2007 Indexes						
			ECI	DEM	DECI	PREV	MCE	SPI	SUI
Neoplasm of breast									
Malignant	50	77	1.53	1.06	1.47	1.07	1.37	1.27	1.33
Nonmalignant	11	12	1.04	1.01	1.03	0.85	1.21	1.18	1.03
Neoplasm of pulmonary system									
Malignant	16	21	1.27	1.09	1.17	0.95	1.23	1.28	1.40
Nonmalignant	1	1	1.12	1.03	1.09	1.04	1.05	0.97	1.08
Neoplasm of rectum or anus									
Malignant	13	21	1.55	1.09	1.46	0.97	1.51	1.45	0.99
Nonmalignant	2	3	1.73	1.09	1.64	1.52	1.08	1.06	1.04
Neoplasm of prostate									
Malignant	13	20	1.55	1.15	1.40	1.09	1.29	1.17	1.07
Nonmalignant	4	6	1.56	1.13	1.43	1.06	1.35	1.15	1.19
Neoplasm of skin, major									
Malignant	10	14	1.35	1.08	1.28	1.08	1.18	1.11	1.04
Nonmalignant	15	19	1.27	1.03	1.25	1.13	1.10	1.11	1.00
All neoplasms									
Malignant	162	240	1.48	1.08	1.40	1.08	1.30	1.25	1.05
Nonmalignant	107	133	1.24	1.03	1.21	1.11	1.11	1.15	0.98
All other diseases	2,247	2,856	1.27	1.03	1.24	1.10	1.13	1.15	0.99

3.5   Conclusion

This chapter presents a descriptive picture of the various sources of health care expenditure growth. Our decomposition shows that growth in both service prices and prevalence of treated disease are responsible for the large increase in nominal medical care expenditure growth. Other factors, such as changes in the demographics of the population or changes in service utilization, have a limited impact on expenditures.

Perhaps equally important to the descriptive findings of this study are the avenues for future research that it reveals. For instance, our analysis shows that there has been tremendous growth in preventive service expenditures. Future research may decipher whether these preventive services ultimately lead to lower expenditures in the future, better health outcomes, or both. Second, although utilization has been declining for some diseases due to a shift from inpatient to outpatient services, some areas such as the treatment for malignant neoplasms have seen a growth in both service utilization and service prices. We hypothesize that this growth in the cost of treatment is attributable to the large degree of innovation for cancer treatment. However, a more comprehensive study specific to cancer treatment will likely lead to a better understanding of this cost of treatment growth. Third, future research may uncover if the shift in treated prevalence toward diseases that lead to ischemic heart failure (e.g., hypertension and hyperlipidemia) and away from ischemic failure is due to a worsening health status of the population or if it is attributable to better awareness of these types of conditions or more individuals with a condition seeking treatment. If the growth is attributable to an earlier awareness of a health condition, this may translate into lower expenditure growth or better health outcomes in the future.

References

Aizcorbe, Ana, Eli Liebman, Sarah Pack, David Cutler, Michael Chernew, and Allison Rosen. 2012. "Measuring Health Care Costs of Individuals with Employer-Sponsored Health Insurance in the US: A Comparison of Survey and Claims Data." *Statistical Journal of the International Association for Official Statistics* 28 (1–2): 43–51.

Aizcorbe, Ana, and Nicole Nestoriak. 2011. "Changing Mix of Medical Care Services: Stylized Facts and Implications for Price Indexes." *Journal of Health Economics* 30 (3): 568–74.

Berndt, Ernst, David Cutler, Richard Frank, Zvi Griliches, Joseph Newhouse, and Jack Triplett. 2000. "Medical Care Prices and Output." In *Handbook of Health Economics*, vol. 1, part A, edited by A. J. Culyer and J. P. Newhouse, 119–80. Amsterdam: Elsevier.

Bundorf, Kate, Anne Royalty, and Laurence Baker. 2009. "Health Care Cost Growth among the Privately Insured." *Health Affairs* 28:1294–304.

Chandra, Amitabh, and Jonathan Skinner. 2012. "Technology Growth and Expenditure Growth in Health Care." *Journal of Economic Literature* 50 (3): 645–80.

Chernew, Michael, and Joseph Newhouse. 2012. "Health Care Spending Growth." In *Handbook of Health Economics*, vol. 2, edited by M. V. Pauly, T. G. McGuire, and P. P. Barros, 1–43. Amsterdam: Elsevier.

Cutler, David M., Mark McClellan, Joseph P. Newhouse, and Dahlia Remler. 1998. "Are Medical Prices Declining? Evidence from Heart Attack Treatments." *Quarterly Journal of Economics* 113:991–1024.

Dunn, Abe, Eli Liebman, Sarah Pack, and Adam Shapiro. 2012. "Medical Care Price Indexes for Patients with Employer-Provided Insurance: Nationally Representative Estimates from MarketScan Data." *Health Services Research* 48 (3): 1173–90.

Dunn, Abe, Eli Liebman, Lindsey Rittmueller, and Adam Shapiro. 2015. "Implications of Utilization Shifts on Medical-Care Price Measurement." *Health Economics* 24 (5): 539–57.

Dunn, Abe, Eli Liebman, and Adam Shapiro. 2014. "Developing a Framework for Decomposing Medical-Care Expenditure Growth: Exploring Issues of Representativeness." In *Measuring Economic Sustainability and Progress*, edited by Dale W. Jorgenson, J. Steven Landefeld, and Paul Schreyer. Chicago: University of Chicago Press.

———. 2015. "Implications of Utilization Shifts on Medical-Care Price Measurement." *Health Economics* 24 (5): 539–57.

Dunn, Abe, and Adam Shapiro. 2014. "Do Physicians Possess Market Power?" *Journal of Law and Economics* 57 (1): 159–93.

Dunn, Abe, Adam Shapiro, and Eli Liebman. 2014. "Geographic Variation in Commercial Medical-Care Expenditures: A Framework for Decomposing Price and Utilization." *Journal of Health Economics* 32 (6): 1153–65.

National Research Council. 2010. *Accounting for Health and Health Care: Approaches to Measuring the Sources and Costs of Their Improvement*. Washington, DC: The National Academies Press.

Roehrig, Charles, and David Rousseau. 2011. "The Growth in Cost Per Case Explains Far More of US Health Spending Increases Than Rising Disease Prevalence." *Health Affairs* 30 (9): 1657–63.

Rosen, Allison, Eli Liebman, Ana Aizcorbe, and David Cutler. 2012. "Comparing Commercial Systems for Characterizing Episodes of Care." Working Paper, Bureau of Economic Analysis.

Starr, Martha, Laura Dominiak, and Ana Aizcorbe. 2013. "Decomposing Growth in Spending Finds Annual Cost of Treatment Contributed Most to Spending Growth, 1980–2006." *Health Affairs* 33 (5): 1657–63.

Thorpe, Kenneth, Curtis Florence, and Peter Joski. 2004. "Which Medical Conditions Account for the Rise in Health Care Spending?" *Health Affairs* Web Exclusive. August. http://content.healthaffairs.org/content/early/2004/08/25/hlthaff.w4.437.citation.

Zuvekas, Samuel, and Gary Olin. 2009. "Accuracy of Medicare Expenditures in the Medical Expenditure Panel Survey." *Inquiry* 46:92–108.

4

Calculating Disease-Based Medical Care Expenditure Indexes for Medicare Beneficiaries
A Comparison of Method and Data Choices

Anne E. Hall and Tina Highfill

4.1 Introduction

Inflation in the health care sector is usually measured by tracking the costs of patient goods and services and how these costs change over time. Indexes to measure the cost of services are the indexes used by the Bureau of Labor Statistics in the Consumer and Producer Price Indexes for services such as doctor visits and goods such as prescription drugs. The Committee on National Statistics of the National Research Council, however, has recommended that government statistical agencies investigate methods and data for measuring inflation in health care by measuring the costs of treating medical conditions on the grounds that measurement in this way will better capture changes in productivity in the health care sector. Papers such as Aizcorbe and Nestoriak (2011), Dunn et al. (2013), and our previous work (Hall and Highfill 2013) followed these recommendations and found average annual growth rates for health care inflation that ranged from 2.9 percent to 6.9 percent. However, the papers used different data sets on different populations and employed different methods for splitting up health care expenditure by condition, making it difficult to analyze why the results varied so much.

Anne E. Hall is an economist at the US Treasury. This work was completed while she was an employee of the US Bureau of Economic Analysis. Tina Highfill is an economist at the Bureau of Economic Analysis.

We would like to thank Ana Aizcorbe, Abe Dunn, Richard Frank, Virginia Henriksen, participants in the NBER/CRIW conference on modeling health care costs, Tom Selden, and other staff at the Agency for Healthcare Research and Quality, and an anonymous reviewer for helpful comments and advice. The views expressed in this chapter are solely those of the authors and do not necessarily reflect the views of the Bureau of Economic Analysis. For acknowledgments, sources of research support, and disclosure of the authors' material financial relationships, if any, please see http://www.nber.org/chapters/c13106.ack.

In this chapter, we are following up on our previous work by comparing medical expenditure indexes for the Medicare population calculated from different data sets and using different methods. The Medicare program plays a very large role in the US health care system, in the federal budget, and in the US economy. In calendar year 2012, the program covered 50.8 million people (42.2 million aged and 8.6 million disabled). Medicare spending comprised about one-fifth of national health care spending in the 2012 National Health Expenditure Accounts (Center for Medicare and Medicaid Services). According to the Congressional Budget Office (CBO), outlays on Medicare were 17 percent of total federal outlays in 2013 and the CBO expects the aging of the population and rising health care costs, through their effect on Medicare spending, to be major factors in the projected increase in the deficit later this decade (CBO 2013, 2014). Finally, outlays on Medicare were 3.5 percent of US gross domestic product in 2013 (CBO 2014). Accurately measuring inflation in the spending of Medicare beneficiaries is therefore important both for more precise measurement of the economy and for better understanding of the value of a large fraction of public spending.

Several Medicare program data sets are available, each with unique characteristics that present measurement challenges. In this chapter, we compare two major data sources on Medicare beneficiaries: the Medicare Current Beneficiary Survey (MCBS) and the Household Component of the Medical Expenditure Panel Survey (MEPS). Both surveys are conducted by the Department of Health and Human Services. The MCBS surveys Medicare beneficiaries exclusively, while the MEPS Household Component surveys US residents living in the community (that is, not in institutions such as nursing homes) about their health care and spending.

By necessity, our comparison focuses on the potential indexes for Medicare beneficiaries enrolled in fee-for-service (FFS) Medicare, for whom the most complete data exists. Medicare private plan enrollees are, however, making up an increasing share of Medicare enrollment, but the data for them is much less comprehensive. In the MCBS the only source for their spending, diagnoses, and medical events is the in-person survey, but as we shall see, the survey asks about a limited set of diagnoses and some important ones would be omitted if we based their expenditure index on the MCBS survey. However, the Medicare private plan sample in the MEPS is quite small, only about 300 to 400 beneficiaries per year.

Using the MCBS and MEPS, we compare two methods for calculating medical expenditure indexes: the primary diagnosis method and a regression-based approach. The primary diagnosis method simply assigns spending to the illness associated with the diagnosis code (or first diagnosis code in the case of multiple diagnosis codes) of each claim or survey-collected medical event. The regression-based approach regresses individual annual health care spending on dummy variables for a beneficiary's diagnosed medical conditions, and divides up each beneficiary's health care spending on that basis.

The chapter is organized as follows. Section 4.2 gives background on the concept of a disease-based medical care expenditure index. Section 4.3 introduces the various methods available for producing medical care expenditure indexes. Section 4.4 introduces the data sets available for Medicare beneficiaries. Section 4.5 introduces our full matrix of comparisons, compares the methods, and draws some conclusions about the methods. Section 4.6 compares the data sets and draws some conclusions about the data sets. Section 4.7 concludes.

4.2   Medical Care Expenditure Indexes

Medical care expenditure indexes (MCE indexes) measure inflation in health care spending by measuring the changes in the costs of treating individual illnesses. This approach contrasts with that of the official health care price indexes, such as the Consumer Price Index (CPI) and the Producer Price Index (PPI), which measure the change in price over time of specific health care services, such as doctor's visits. Early papers that used MCE indexes, such as Cutler et al. (1998), Shapiro, Shapiro, and Wilcox (2001), and Berndt et al. (2002), argued that measuring health care inflation with MCE indexes was more meaningful since it took into account shifts in utilization from one service category to another as the technology of treating a particular disease improves and becomes more efficient. Examples include shifting from psychotherapy to prescription drugs in the treatment of psychiatric illnesses and shifting surgeries from inpatient to outpatient procedures. Health care inflation, when measured in this way, often turns out to be lower than inflation as measured by service price indexes (SPI) such as the CPI or PPI. For example, Cutler et al. found that the measured price change of treating a heart attack was lower than an SPI by 3 percentage points annually. For more on these issues, see Berndt et al. (2000) and National Research Council (2002).

Cutler et al. and Berndt et al. constructed quality-adjusted expenditure indexes for individual conditions (heart attacks and major depression, respectively). Quality adjustment of expenditure indexes in the health care context entails connecting shifts in treatments with changes in health outcomes. This adjustment requires high-quality data on individual treatments and outcomes, and papers such as Aizcorbe and Nestoriak (2011) and Dunn et al. (2013) that constructed expenditure indexes for a broad set of illnesses did not adjust for changes in health outcomes when comparing MCE indexes to SPIs like the CPI. Both papers found that health care inflation was lower when measured by MCE indexes than by SPIs even though the MCE indexes were not quality adjusted. In this chapter, we will only present MCE indexes that are not quality adjusted.

4.3   Methods

Individuals seeking medical care are often diagnosed with more than one disease; a central problem in the creation of MCEs is how to divide expenditures among multiple diagnoses. Several different methods have been proposed and used in prior papers. It should be noted that economic theory is no guide on methodology in this area and there is no true way of validating any of the methods. Brief descriptions of the methods available to us follow here and the results of the previous papers are summarized in table 4.1.

4.3.1   Regression-Based Method

This method models total individual annual health care spending as a function of each individual's diagnoses during that year and uses the parameter values to divide the individual's health care spending among his or her diagnoses. Then individual spending on conditions is averaged to give mean expenditures, which are the inputs to an MCE index. Health care spending has certain characteristics that make it challenging to model econometrically: spending is nonnegative, there are a large number of observations with zero spending, and the distribution of spending is typically skewed with a long right-hand tail. Modeling health care spending is the subject of an extensive literature (Duan 1983; Manning 1998; Jones 2000; Manning and Mullahy 2001; Buntin and Zaslavsky 2004). The consensus is that health care spending should be transformed (with a log or square root transformation) to accommodate its skewness. Either a one-part or two-part model, where the probability of having spending at all is modeled in a separate step, may be used. The parameters may be estimated with either ordinary least squares (OLS) or a generalized linear model (GLM). Buntin and Zaslavsky (2004) investigate the modeling of the spending of Medicare beneficiaries in particular. Their recommendation is to estimate with GLM the mean-variance relationship established with a Park test (Park 1966). Following the results of a Park test, we estimate the following equation with a one-step GLM, with a log link, and the standard deviation proportional to the mean (a gamma distribution):

$$\ln(y_i) = \beta_0 + \sum_{j=1}^{J} \beta_j D_{ij} + E_i.$$

In this equation, i indexes the individual beneficiary, j indexes the conditions, y_i is each beneficiary's annual health care spending, and D_{ij} is an indicator variable for whether individual i has condition j.

Since we are fitting log spending, we cannot use the resulting coefficients to directly find the average spending on each condition. Instead, we use a method for using parameter estimates from a model of the log of health care spending to assign spending to conditions originally proposed by Trogdon,

Table 4.1   Previous papers calculating medical care expenditure indexes

Paper	Data set	Population	Years	Method	Results (AAGR of price index in percentage points)
Aizcorbe and Nestoriak 2011	Pharmetrics, Inc. (medical claims from private employer-sponsored health insurance plans)	Beneficiaries of private employer-sponsored insurance	2003–2005	Commercial grouper (Symmetry)	3.7
Dunn et al. 2013	MarketScan (medical claims from private employer-sponsored health insurance plans)	Beneficiaries of private employer-sponsored insurance	2003–2007	Commercial grouper (Symmetry)	3.6
Aizcorbe et al. 2011	Medical Expenditure Panel Survey (MEPS)	US noninstitutionalized civilian residents	2001–2005	Primary diagnosis, proportional diagnosis, commercial grouper (Truven Health Analytics)	6.9, 6.6, 6.8
Hall and Highfill 2013	Medicare Current Beneficiary Survey	Medicare beneficiaries	2001–2005	Regression based	5.8

Finkelstein, and Hoerger (2008). In this method, each individual's spending is divided up into their diagnosed conditions in proportion to the regression coefficients. A share of spending is calculated for each beneficiary-illness combination as follows:

$$S_{ij} = \frac{[\exp(\beta_j) - 1] * D_{ij}}{\Sigma_{j=1}^J\{[\exp(\beta_j) - 1] * D_{ij}\}}.$$

The shares are then applied to each individual's spending to give that individual's spending on each condition with which he or she is diagnosed. Then the average expenditure for each condition is calculated across individuals. These average expenditures are analogous to prices in a price index and are the inputs to the MCE indexes. We combine them with the diagnosed prevalences for each condition (which are analogous to quantities in a price index) and calculate the MCE indexes as Fisher indexes in the usual manner.

The regression-based method has the advantage that it does not make huge demands of the data compared to the other methods discussed here: it only requires individual annual medical spending and dummy variables for whether or not the individual was diagnosed with a certain condition that year. The primary disadvantage is that the method of assignment of spending to particular diagnoses is not based on any theory or model that relates health care spending to conditions diagnosed.

4.3.2   Primary Diagnosis

This method is used in Aizcorbe et al. (2011). With this method, the spending attached to a claim or medical event is assigned to the diagnosis or the first diagnosis, if there are multiple diagnoses, attached to that claim or event. In some sense, the primary diagnosis method is preferable to all others because the connection between spending and diagnosis is transparent and not dependent on an econometric model of health care spending. This method requires, however, that every claim or event have a diagnosis attached to it. Other than the MEPS, the data sets being considered for the Medicare population do not have a diagnosis attached to every claim or event; the survey events collected by the Medicare Current Beneficiary Survey that are not in the Medicare claims (such as drug events and all medical events for Medicare private plan enrollees) do not have diagnoses attached to them and the Medicare Part D claims do not have diagnoses attached to them, either.

A further difference between the two methods to keep in mind is that they measure slightly different costs. The regression-based method measures the net cost of a condition; that is, the average difference in spending between a beneficiary with the condition and one without. The net cost of a condition can be negative and we found in Hall and Highfill (2013) that several conditions from the MCBS in-person survey, such as Alzheimer's disease, had negative coefficients in the regression and were therefore assigned negative costs. With the primary diagnosis method, all conditions have positive costs. If there are more beneficiaries with, for example, Alzheimer's disease, the per-patient expenditures of other conditions that are comorbid with Alzheimer's disease will be lower in the primary diagnosis while they would, in theory, be unaffected in the regression-based method. This is another reason for preferring the primary diagnosis method since price indexes in other sectors generally do not allow goods or services with negative prices.

4.3.3   Commercial Grouper

Several private companies have developed commercial software for grouping medical spending by episode of illness based on clinical knowledge. These packages are used in Aizcorbe and Nestoriak (2011), Dunn et al. (2013), and Aizcorbe et al. (2011) to create expenditure indexes for medical care. Aizcorbe and Nestoriak (2011) use one on medical claims data from private employer-sponsored health insurance plans collected by Pharmetrics, Inc., and Dunn et al. (2013) use one on the MarketScan database, a similar data set of medical claims collected by Truven Health Analytics. Aizcorbe et al. (2011) use a commercial grouper on the MEPS data. The main advantage of these packages over the primary diagnosis method is that they are able to assign spending associated with claims, such as drug claims, that do not have a diagnosis attached directly to them. In addition, unlike the annual regression-based method, they are able to separate out multiple episodes of the same illness occurring in one year. Depending on the package, they are also able to assign a severity level to the illness. However, their methods are proprietary and therefore completely opaque to the economist using them. We will not be considering groupers in our comparisons in this chapter, but may study them in future work.

4.4   Data Sets

Table 4.2 summarizes the features of data sets available for calculating medical care expenditure indexes for Medicare beneficiaries. In general, to create a medical care expenditure index, we need variables for total spending and for diagnoses at least at an annual level.

Medicare Current Beneficiary Survey (MCBS). The MCBS is a survey of the demographics, diagnosed conditions, health status, and total medical spending of a representative sample of Medicare beneficiaries. It is conducted by the Center for Medicare and Medicaid Services, the agency that operates Medicare. As it samples from the universe of Medicare beneficiaries, it includes both FFS Medicare beneficiaries and those enrolled in Medicare private plans, and both beneficiaries residing in the community and in institutions such as nursing homes. The medical conditions portion

Table 4.2   **Summary of data sets covering Medicare beneficiaries**

Data set	Coverage	Annual sample size of Medicare beneficiaries	Data available for FFS beneficiaries	Data available for private plan enrollees
Medicare Current Beneficiary Survey (MCBS)	All Medicare beneficiaries	12,000	Annual demographic and conditions survey, all medical events and spending, Medicare Part A (hospital) and Part B (physician) claims	Annual demographic and conditions survey, all medical events and spending
Medicare claims	FFS Medicare beneficiaries	~2 million	Part A and Part B claims; Part D (pharmaceutical) claims for about 50–60% of 5% sample	n/a
Medical Expenditure Panel Survey (MEPS)	Noninstitutionalized Medicare beneficiaries	4,600	All medical events and spending, with diagnoses attached (collected by survey)	All medical events and spending, with diagnoses attached (collected by survey)

of the survey takes place once a year, toward the end of the year, and in it, the respondent is asked whether they have been told by a doctor if they have each of about thirty conditions. Health care spending and medical events are also collected directly from the respondent on a regular basis. For FFS beneficiaries, the Part A and Part B claims with dollar amounts and diagnosis codes are also attached to the survey so there are two sources of diagnoses and spending for these beneficiaries. The MCBS reconciles the orally reported events and the claims so that spending and events are not duplicated in the final version of the data set. For private plan enrollees, the only source of information is the spending, events, and diagnoses reported in the in-person survey.

Medicare claims. Part A (hospital) and Part B (doctor) claims are available for a 5 percent random sample of Medicare beneficiaries from CMS for research purposes. In addition, starting in 2006, a sample of Part D claims are available for those 50–60 percent of FFS beneficiaries in the 5 percent who are on Part D. In this chapter, rather than showing calculations from the full 5 percent sample, we will evaluate Medicare claims data by using the Medicare claims data tied to the MCBS.

Medical Expenditure Panel Survey (MEPS). The MEPS is a nationally representative survey of health care coverage, utilization, and expenditures for the civilian noninstitutionalized US population. It is conducted by the Department of Health and Human Services' Agency for Healthcare Research and Quality (AHRQ). The survey sample is drawn from the respondents of the prior year's National Health Interview Survey (NHIS) and includes both fee-for-service and private plan Medicare beneficiaries living in the community (that is, not in a nursing home or other institution). Using an overlapping panel design, each household is surveyed over the course of two years in five rounds of interviews. The family member most knowledgeable about the entire household's health and health care use is interviewed. Observations are collected and reported for every medical event and may contain up to four diagnoses each. The MEPS also collects data from a sample of respondents' providers to verify use of services, charges, and sources of payments and diagnoses.

Table 4.3 compares the spending of all Medicare FFS beneficiaries in the MCBS, Medicare FFS beneficiaries in the MCBS who are living in the community, and Medicare FFS beneficiaries in the MEPS (who all reside in the community). As it shows, mean spending by Medicare beneficiaries in the MEPS is quite a bit lower than that of similar Medicare beneficiaries in the MCBS. Zuvekas and Olin (2009) conduct a detailed comparison of full-year Medicare beneficiaries residing in the community in the MEPS, those same beneficiaries' Medicare claims, and similar beneficiaries in the MCBS in the years 2002–2003. They find that the ratio of mean spending of beneficiaries in the MEPS to that of similar beneficiaries in the MCBS to be 0.81. We find a similar result; as table 4.3 shows, the ratio of the spending

Table 4.3   Comparison of spending of Medicare beneficiaries in the MCBS and in the MEPS

	Mean spending				Skewness coefficient		Maximum	
	MCBS full-year FFS beneficiaries		MEPS full-year FFS Medicare beneficiaries ($)	Ratio of mean spending of MEPS beneficiaries to MCBS community beneficiaries	MCBS full-year FFS beneficiaries residing in community	MEPS full-year FFS Medicare beneficiaries	MCBS full-year FFS beneficiaries residing in community ($)	MEPS full-year FFS Medicare beneficiaries ($)
	All ($)	Residing in community ($)						
2001	8,698	7,701	5,846	0.76	10.1	7.3	389,580	219,759
2002	9,237	8,309	6,676	0.80	6.5	5.5	459,811	204,382
2003	10,027	8,902	7,138	0.80	13.9	4.8	358,672	122,983
2004	10,759	9,741	7,688	0.79	18.1	5.7	356,998	222,006
2005	11,737	10,638	8,001	0.75	10.3	7.8	545,486	234,373
2006	12,168	10,938	7,899	0.72	14.3	11.3	678,642	521,209
2007	12,671	11,433	8,566	0.75	12.0	5.2	682,065	303,650
2008	13,371	12,034	8,335	0.69	14.3	4.3	755,329	170,687
2009	13,198	11,855	9,089	0.77	5.2	5.6	354,089	217,142

of full-year Medicare beneficiaries living in the community in our analytic sample from the MEPS to that of similar beneficiaries in our sample from the MCBS ranges between 0.69 and 0.80 over the period studied. Our MCBS sample includes claims by separately billing labs, which that of Zuvekas and Olin does not, which may explain the slightly lower ratio. Zuvekas and Olin find that about half of the gap is due to underreporting of spending by respondents to the MEPS, and about half is due to the absence of higher-expenditure cases in the MEPS. We also find an absence of higher-expenditure cases in the MEPS as compared to the MCBS; as table 4.3 shows, both the skewness coefficient for the distribution of spending and the value of the maximum observation are generally much higher in the MCBS, implying a longer tail in that distribution. Unfortunately, we have no way of adjusting for underreporting and the absence of more expensive cases in the MEPS, but simply note that they may be factors in any differences we observe between the MEPS and the MCBS.

4.4.1   Prevalence

In this section, we discuss issues relating to how treated prevalence of medical conditions is measured in the data sets we are using since it has important implications for the resulting expenditure index. To see this, consider that total health care spending in a population can be expressed as a sum over conditions:

$$\text{Total healthcare spending} = \sum_{j=1}^{J} \overline{p}_j N_j,$$

where j indexes conditions, P_j is the average amount spent to treat condition j, and N_j is the number of people treated for condition j; N_j divided by the total population is the treated prevalence for that condition.

The object of concern when we are calculating an expenditure index is P_j; however, the data we use have total spending and N_j as given, and we must infer P_j with one of the various methods that will be discussed further down. In addition, as is standard in a Fisher index formula, treated prevalences are used to weight the indexes for the individual conditions when they are aggregated into an expenditure index for medical care as a whole. Differences in methods for collecting conditions from respondents will therefore lead to different results in the resulting expenditure indexes.

Treated Prevalence in the Medicare Current Beneficiary Survey

The first issue we note is the differences in the MCBS between survey-based prevalences and claims-based prevalences. The survey-based prevalences in the MCBS are based on the annual survey administered to all respondents. In this survey, respondents who live in the community are asked if they have been told by a doctor in the past year if they have each of about thirty conditions. For respondents who are residing in nursing homes, the

MCBS has a nursing home staff member fill out a questionnaire about conditions based on the respondent's nursing home and medical records. The claims-based prevalences are based on the respondent's Part A (hospital) and Part B (physician) Medicare claims. The claims are only available for respondents who are enrolled in fee-for-service (FFS) Medicare and not for respondents enrolled in Medicare private plans.

For the FFS beneficiaries in the MCBS, therefore, we have both sets of diagnoses for the same beneficiaries and can examine the degree of agreement between them. Table 4.4 reports prevalences in 2001 from the MCBS survey and from the MCBS claims, as well as the percent of beneficiaries who are indicated as having an illness in both the survey and the claims.[1] First, note that in general claims-based prevalence is higher than survey-based prevalence. There is also quite a bit of disagreement between the two sources of diagnoses, and the agreement rate is often less than half of either the survey-based prevalence or the claims-based prevalence. When weighted by prevalence, the overlap rate divided by the claims-based prevalence averages about 40 percent and the overlap rate divided by the survey-based prevalence averages about 62 percent. One possible cause of disagreement in prevalence between the survey and the claims may come from the lack of drug-related diagnoses in the claims data. As mentioned above, the claims data attached to the MCBS only include doctor and hospital claims. There are no prescription drug claims, even for beneficiaries enrolled in Medicare Part D after 2006 and, in any case, prescription drug claims generally do not include diagnoses. Beneficiaries may therefore have chronic illnesses for which they are taking prescription drugs regularly and that they report on the survey, but either they did not have a nondrug event related to the condition during the survey year or these conditions are not recorded by their health care providers. However, some of the highest rates of agreement between survey and claims are in illnesses for which this issue would most be of concern. There are five chronic illnesses for which the share of spending on pharmaceuticals is over 50 percent of total spending on the illness: diabetes, mental/psychiatric disorder, Alzheimer's/dementia, osteoporosis, and hypertension. Agreement rates between survey-based and claims-based prevalence are in fact noticeably higher for this group: the overlap rate divided by the claims-based prevalence has a weighted average of 63 percent and the overlap rate divided by the survey-based prevalence has a weighted average of 72 percent. It seems possible, therefore, that the act of taking a daily drug for an illness may actually improve survey respondents' knowledge and memory of what diagnoses they have.

There are multiple other potential causes of the discrepancies between survey-based and claims-based prevalence. The reasons that a condition

---

1. For how the survey diagnoses were translated into ICD-9 codes for purposes of comparison with the claims, see appendix table 1 in Hall and Highfill (2013).

Table 4.4   Prevalence in survey portion and claims portion of MCBS in 2001

Condition	Survey prevalence (%)	Claims prevalence (%)	Overlap prevalence (%)
Hardening of arteries/arteriosclerotic heart disease	10.9	20.4	5.1
Myocardial infarction/heart attack	2.6	2.1	0.8
Angina/CHD	3.8	15.6	2.4
Other heart conditions and valve problems	5.6	22.1	3.2
Congestive heart failure	3.3	12.5	2.4
Heart rhythm problem	7.5	19.3	4.7
Stroke/transient ischemic attack (TIA)	3.5	8.1	2.1
Skin cancer	4.9	5.0	2.5
Lung cancer	0.2	0.9	0.2
Colon cancer	0.4	1.5	0.3
Breast cancer	0.6	2.4	0.4
Prostate cancer	0.6	3.5	0.5
Other cancer	1.2	13.6	0.8
Diabetes	19.3	22.6	16.9
Arthritis	23.1	24.8	9.1
Mental/psychiatric disorder (excl. Alzheimer's/dementia)	12.2	16.2	7.0
Alzheimer's/dementia	5.0	6.9	3.3
Osteoporosis	17.5	11.1	6.8
Hypertension	44.4	56.2	37.2
Broken hip	1.0	1.4	0.5
Parkinson's	1.6	1.4	1.0
Emphysema/asthma/chronic obstructive pulmonary disease (COPD)	15.5	19.5	9.5
Paralysis in past year	1.8	1.7	0.5
Mental retardation (excl. Alzheimer's/dementia)	3.1	0.9	0.7
Renal failure	0.8	4.0	0.8

Notes: Refer to appendix table 1 in Hall and Highfill (2013) to see how illnesses from the MCBS survey were translated into ICD-9 codes to compare with the claims data. Prevalences are weighted by the MCBS survey weights.

might be reported in the survey but not in the claims include beneficiary errors in the existence of illnesses, beneficiary errors in the timing of illnesses, providers omitting to code a condition, and that the condition was treated but the treatment was not paid for by Medicare. The reasons that a condition might be reported in the claims but not in the survey include, again, beneficiary or provider error and the provider upcoding a diagnosis. Given that claims-based prevalence is generally higher than survey-based prevalence and that the disagreement is noticeably lower for conditions for which beneficiaries are taking a prescription drug on a regular basis, it seems likely that beneficiary error is the largest source of disagreement. Claims-based prevalence may therefore be a more reliable measure of treated prevalence in the MCBS. However, as noted above, there is a notable disadvantage to relying solely on claims data as the source data for Medicare beneficiaries when constructing an MCE index, namely, that we do not have claims for the enrollees in Medicare private plans.

Treated Prevalence in the Medical Expenditure Panel Survey

The second problem with measuring treated prevalence in the data sets we are examining relates to a change in the household component of the MEPS in 2007 in its method for relating health care events and spending to medical conditions. In the MEPS, medical conditions are collected up front from respondents in their initial survey. Before 2007, in the initial interview, conditions were only reported if the respondent volunteered them in response to a general question about medical conditions. In 2007, MEPS introduced the Priority Conditions Enumeration section of the survey, in which respondents were asked whether they had certain priority conditions. (This method is similar to how conditions are collected in the MCBS throughout the entire period.) When medical events are later collected, the respondent is prompted to relate these events to conditions that had been reported in the initial survey.

The treated prevalences from the MEPS that we use to calculate an MCE are calculated from the medical events files and not from the conditions survey because we are primarily interested in conditions as they relate directly to health care expenditure. However, the methodology change in 2007 resulted in a dramatic increase in the event-based treated prevalences of certain conditions. Table 4.5 shows the treated prevalences of the priority conditions in the Priority Conditions Enumeration file from the MEPS by year from 2001 to 2009. The total prevalence in 2007 is the top number of the three reported for each condition for that year. As it shows, there are increases in nearly all the conditions between 2006 and 2008. There are particularly dramatic rises in the prevalences of heart disease, arthritis, heart attacks, and stroke, which are clearly unrelated to any preexisting trend in treated prevalence.

The Priority Conditions Enumeration section was phased in with the introduction of Panel 12 of the MEPS.[2] Table 4.5 also shows treated prevalence by condition in 2007 split out by panel. Treated prevalence in Panel 11 in 2007 for most conditions is comparable to treated prevalence in 2006, while treated prevalence of most conditions in Panel 12 in 2007 is more similar to treated prevalence as measured in 2008, reflecting the methodology change that affected Panel 12 but not Panel 11. The differences between Panels 11 and 12 in treated prevalence are especially noticeable for the conditions mentioned above that have the greatest increases in treated prevalence. For example, the treated prevalence of heart disease is more than four times higher in Panel 12 than in Panel 11, and that of arthritis is more than five times higher. Similarly, the treated prevalence of myocardial infarction

---

2. We are grateful to Tom Selden of AHRQ for this information and for proposing the solution that follows.

Table 4.5   Prevalence by year in the MEPS

Condition	2001	2002	2003	2004	2005	2006	2007: Total Panel 11 Panel 12	2008	2009
Hypertension	44.82	47.38	49.1	51.98	54.52	55.44	59.93 57.59 63.18	62.88	64.85
High cholesterol	19.88	22.14	23.3	28.24	31.25	34.61	42.93 38.85 48.6	49.94	49.87
Heart disease	3.86	4.45	4.41	4.49	4.37	4.33	10.41 4.5 18.61	18.37	18.09
Myocardial infarction/heart attack	1.53	1.72	1.88	1.91	1.79	1.51	4.11 1.73 7.42	6.81	7.97
Stroke/transient ischemic attack (TIA)	2.96	3.49	3.37	3.03	2.96	2.75	4.06 3.66 4.62	4.95	5.06
Cancer	11.37	11.27	11.41	12.34	12.38	12	13.57 11.57 16.33	15.86	14.65

(continued)

Table 4.5 (continued)

Condition	2001	2002	2003	2004	2005	2006	2007: Total Panel 11 Panel 12	2008	2009
Diabetes	17.87	19.5	20.68	21.67	22.31	23.41	25.25 24.7 26.02	25.39	25.7
Arthritis	3.38	3.1	3.6	3.67	3.41	3.75	9.86 3.28 19	16.46	16.86
Emphysema/COPD	6.95	7.48	6.53	6.47	7.64	7.06	7.68 6.51 9.3	9.22	9.74
Asthma	5.34	5.46	5.75	5.63	5.67	6.57	6.89 6.94 6.83	7.78	8.04

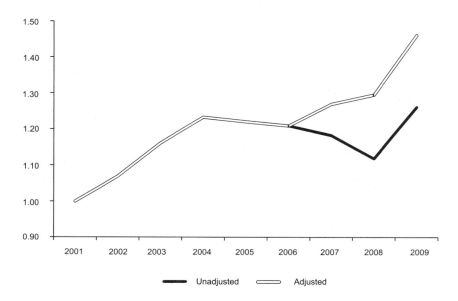

Fig. 4.1   Effect of adjustment to growth rates on MEPS-based MCE index for all Medicare beneficiaries

is more than four times higher in Panel 12 than Panel 11. The methodology change also helps explain part of the increases in treated prevalence of hypertension and hypercholesterolemia, two conditions with treated prevalence that are both high and trending up over this period. Panel 12 has a treated prevalence of hypertension in 2007 that is over 5 percentage points higher than that of Panel 11, and for hypercholesterolemia the difference is just over 10 percentage points.

In our MEPS-based MCE indexes, in order to have growth rates that are at least measured over consistent samples, we use the growth rate calculated from Panel 11 alone for the change from 2006 to 2007, and the growth rate calculated from Panel 12 alone for the change from 2007 to 2008. The expenditure indexes based on the MEPS are therefore not strictly comparable before and after 2007, but this solution is the best we can do with the data available. The effect of implementing this change on one of the MCE indexes we calculate is shown in figure 4.1. This MCE index is calculated from the MEPS on all Medicare beneficiaries using the primary diagnosis method. (See below for a discussion of this method for calculating MCE indexes.) As the figure shows, using the growth rate from Panel 11 for the change from 2006 to 2007 and the growth rate from Panel 12 for the change from 2007 to 2008 removes an unusual drop in the MCE index in 2007 that is out of line with the underlying trend.

4.5   Comparisons of Different Methods for Calculating Medical Care Expenditure Indexes

As was shown in the previous two sections, we have a choice of methods and data sets available to us to calculate medical expenditure indexes for the Medicare population, although not every method will work with every data set. Table 4.6 lays out the possible combinations of methods and data sets and shows the average annual growth rates of Fisher medical care expenditure indexes calculated from those methods and data sets for the years 2001–2009. The columns represent different combinations of samples (FFS and private plan, FFS only), data sets (MCBS or MEPS), and sets of illnesses, and the rows of the table represent different methods (regression based or primary diagnosis, with or without drug spending). The illnesses used are either the twenty-seven illnesses from the MCBS survey (see Hall and Highfill [2013] for a list and detailed discussion) or the 260 categories from the Clinical Classifications System (CCS), a system devised by the AHRQ for classifying the 10,000 or so ICD-9 diagnosis codes used in claims data sets into medical conditions. In one column, we use twenty-seven CCS diagnoses that correspond to the MCBS survey diagnoses; see appendix table 1 in Hall and Highfill (2013) for a crosswalk that translates survey diagnoses into claims diagnoses. For ease of comparison across years, when creating the FFS- only sample, we restricted the sample to beneficiaries enrolled in Medicare for the full calendar year. The downside of this approach is that we lose beneficiaries who pass away during the year and who are responsible for a good part of total Medicare spending.

The cells in the table are labeled with letters for ease of reference. As described above in section 4.3, the regression-based indexes are based on a GLM model of the log of health care spending as a function of diagnoses. For most of the regression-based indexes, a beneficiary is coded as having a condition if the associated diagnosis code appears in any diagnosis variable but for the indexes whose references end in 2 (H2, I2, and M2), the diagnosis codes were only counted if they appeared as a primary diagnosis in order to make those indexes more comparable to the primary diagnosis analyses. As described in section 4.4, the growth rates of the MEPS indexes from 2006 to 2007 are only calculated from Panel 11 while those of the MEPS indexes from 2007 to 2008 are only calculated from Panel 12, in order to adjust for the methodology change in collecting conditions from respondents in the MEPS in 2007.

As table 4.6 shows, the MCE indexes show a range of average annual growth rates, from 1.4 percent to 6.4 percent per year. In general, average annual growth rates are higher in the indexes based on the MEPS than in those based on the MCBS, and are higher when calculated with the primary diagnosis method than with a regression-based method. The growth rates in the indexes based on the MCBS are lower when drug spending is omitted, but those in indexes based on the MEPS are higher when drug spending is omitted; we will discuss this result further below.

Table 4.6   Average annual growth rates of aggregate medical care expenditure indexes for full-year Medicare beneficiaries 2001–2009

	MCBS				MEPS	
	FFS and private plan beneficiaries	FFS beneficiaries			FFS beneficiaries	FFS and private plan beneficiaries
	27 survey diagnoses	27 survey diagnoses	27 claims diagnoses (CCS categories)	260 CCS claims diagnoses	260 CCS claims diagnoses	260 CCS claims diagnoses
Trogdon regressions with drug spending	3.3 (A)	4.5 (B)	2.2 (C)	2.1 (D)	2.8 (F)	2.7 (G)
Trogdon regressions with drug spending, dropping MEPS events with no diagnosis					3.2 (H) 3.6 (H2)	3.2 (I) 3.8 (I2)
Trogdon regressions without drug spending	2.8 (J)	3.7 (K)	1.6 (L)	1.4 (M) 2.0 (M2)	4.8 (N)	4.7 (O)
Trogdon regressions without drug spending, dropping MEPS events with no diagnosis					3.8 (V)	3.9 (W)
Primary diagnosis with drug spending					5.0 (P)	5.0 (Q)
Primary diagnosis without drug spending			2.5 (R)	2.8 (S)	6.4 (T)	6.2 (U)

Notes: The growth rates for the expenditure indexes based on the MEPS for 2006–2007 were calculated solely from Panel 11, and those for 2007–2008 were calculated solely from Panel 12. In most of the regression-based indexes, a beneficiary was counted as having a condition if the condition appeared in any diagnosis variable in the claims. In the indexes ending in 2 (M2, H2, and I2), a diagnosis was only counted if it was the primary diagnosis in order to make the indexes more comparable to the primary diagnosis analyses.

Table 4.7 shows the growth rates of some selected indexes by year. There is a significant amount of volatility in the growth rates from year to year. In addition, there is surprisingly little correlation in yearly movements between the data sets with the exception that all indexes have strongly positive growth rates in 2003. There is some correlation in yearly movements between the two indexes constructed from the MCBS claims as the two indexes always move in the same direction, but little correlation among the indexes constructed from the MEPS.

The first step in our comparisons is to compare the price indexes obtained using the regression-based method with the primary diagnosis method when we use them on the same samples and the same illnesses. As noted above, the primary diagnosis method is probably preferable but can only be used when the data meet its stringent requirements. The main purpose of this comparison, therefore, is to see if the regression-based method gives similar or very different results from the primary diagnosis method and if it is an adequate substitute for the primary diagnosis method when the data do not have a diagnosis attached to each event or claim.

There are three pairs of analyses to compare, as summarized in table 4.8, which shows their average annual growth rates from 2001 to 2009 as reported in table 4.6. As the table shows, the primary diagnosis method produces higher growth rates for the MCE indexes. The difference is over a percentage point for the indexes based on the MEPS, and almost a percentage point for the index based on the MCBS.

Table 4.9 examines the similarity of the two methods in measuring the per-patient expenditures of individual conditions. It shows the correlations in per-patient expenditure assigned to conditions by the two methods, both in their level (averaged over 2001 and 2009) and in their annualized growth rates from 2001 to 2009. As the table shows, the correlations between the levels of per-patient expenditures are strongly positive. They are especially high in the two MEPS comparisons, at over 80 percent, but slightly lower for the MCBS comparison where the correlation is about 68 percent. The correlations between the growth rates in per-patient expenditures are much lower. They are still positive in the two MEPS comparisons, but are essentially zero for the MCBS comparison.

Table 4.10 shows the annualized net growth rates of per-patient expenditures from 2001 to 2009 for a selection of individual conditions. The conditions shown are the union of the sets of the top ten conditions by per capita spending in 2001 and 2009 for each data set and method combination shown. As suggested by the results in table 4.9, there is little similarity in growth rates across methods applied to the same data. The table shows that, in general, the regression-based method produces more extreme growth rates, both positive and negative, than the primary diagnosis method. The regression-based method can produce particularly extreme growth rates when combined with the MCBS claims data, as in the case of "deficiency and other anemia,"

Table 4.7   Annual growth rates of selected indexes

Year	MCBS survey Regression based (A) (%)	MCBS claims (omitting drug spending) Regression based (M2) (%)	MCBS claims (omitting drug spending) Primary diagnosis (S) (%)	MEPS (FFS only) Regression based (H2) (%)	MEPS (FFS only) Primary diagnosis (P) (%)	MEPS (FFS and private plan) Regression based (I2) (%)	MEPS (FFS and private plan) Primary diagnosis (Q) (%)
2001–2002	8.5	3.3	3.1	3.8	5.7	5.1	6.9
2002–2003	4.7	5.8	7.1	16.7	7.7	17.3	8.6
2003–2004	1.0	3.3	2.3	–0.4	7.1	–2.6	6.2
2004–2005	7.1	2.5	10.0	–2.2	0.8	–1.9	–1.0
2005–2006	2.0	–0.8	–3.4	4.0	–2.5	4.4	–0.9
2006–2007	5.1	3.3	0.5	1.0	6.5	1.5	5.0
2007–2008	2.2	3.8	3.1	1.4	1.7	–13.1	2.1
2008–2009	–4.4	–5.6	–0.4	4.4	12.9	20.0	12.8
Average annual growth rate	3.3	2.0	2.8	3.6	5.0	3.8	5.0

Note: The growth rate for the expenditure indexes based on the MEPS for 2006–2007 was calculated solely from Panel 11, and that for 2007–2008 was calculated solely from Panel 12.

Table 4.8   Average annual growth rates for selected medical expenditure indexes
                   2001–2009

Data	Regression based	Primary diagnosis
MEPS FFS beneficiaries	3.6 (H2)	5.0 (P)
MEPS FFS and private plan beneficiaries	3.8 (I2)	5.0 (Q)
Medicare claims (omits drug spending)	2.0 (M2)	2.8 (S)

Table 4.9   Correlations in per-patient expenditures across conditions and between
                   regression-based indexes and primary diagnosis indexes

Data	Levels, averaged between 2001 and 2009 (%)	Growth rates from 2001 to 2009 (%)
MEPS FFS beneficiaries (H2 and P)	83.4	11.1
MEPS FFS and HMO beneficiaries (I2 and Q)	82.9	26.5
MCBS FFS claims, omitting drug spending (M2 and S)	68.4	0.3

Note: Correlations are weighted by disease prevalence.

"aortic and peripheral arterial embolism or thrombosis," and "other disorders of stomach and duodenum." In addition, as we noted above, table 4.9 shows that the correlation in results between the two methods is noticeably smaller for the MCBS claims data than for the MEPS data. These results are probably due to the greater sensitivity of the regression-based method to outliers combined with the greater presence of outliers in the MCBS claims data as shown above in table 4.3. As we discussed in the introduction to the methods section, there is no reason to use the regression-based method with data where it is possible to use the primary diagnosis method, and the evidence in this table supports that claim. In situations where it is necessary to use the regression-based method, the individual and aggregate growth rates of the MCE indexes should be interpreted with caution.

It is unclear why the primary diagnosis method consistently produces higher growth rates than the regression-based method. There is no reason to expect it a priori to do so. The difference is widespread across conditions; as table 4.10 shows, the primary diagnosis method produces higher growth rates for just over half of the thirty conditions, and the relationship holds for both chronic and acute conditions. Of the full set of conditions, about half have a higher growth rate in their MCEs when estimated with the primary diagnosis method.

In conclusion, it seems that the regression-based method should be employed with caution, given its sensitivity to outliers and propensity for producing volatile indexes. In addition, as we discussed above, the regression-based method has the undesirable feature that it can assign negative costs

Table 4.10 Annualized growth rates of indexes for selected individual conditions 2001–2009

Conditions[a]	MCBS claims		MEPS (FFS only)		MEPS (FFS and private plan)	
	Regression based (M2) (%)	Primary diagnosis (S) (%)	Regression based (H2) (%)	Primary diagnosis (P) (%)	Regression based (12) (%)	Primary diagnosis (Q) (%)
Medical examination/evaluation	9.0	4.2	−14.6	−2.1	−15.8	−2.1
Other lower respiratory disease	1.6	4.1	−11.8	−0.9	−9.7	−1.1
Other connective tissue disease	18.3	5.7	−0.4	1.3	4.1	1.8
Nonspecific chest pain	5.1	6.2	36.5	9.9	52.9	10.2
Other aftercare	7.1	7.3	12.8	7.1	5.9	7.2
Chronic renal failure	−9.7	−4.6	1.4	−1.5	−0.7	−1.3
Complication of device, implant, or graft	5.2	−1.4	−14.0	24.3	−13.8	25.8
Deficiency and other anemia	102.9	8.9	7.9	−4.0	9.5	−3.6
Coronary atherosclerosis and other heart disease	−0.3	0.1	5.4	4.1	6.1	3.5
Spondylosis, intervertebral disc disorders, other back problems	9.4	9.4	2.4	7.9	1.2	7.2
Residual codes, unclassified	20.1	9.1	6.9	11.8	6.3	9.6
Diabetes mellitus without complication	4.5	1.9	2.8	0.7	2.3	0.9
Pneumonia (except that caused by tuberculosis or sexually transmitted disease)	3.9	6.6	6.7	6.4	5.2	6.3
Cardiac dysrhythmias	−4.2	2.8	7.0	−6.2	7.2	−5.3
Chronic obstructive pulmonary disease and bronchiectasis	−3.5	2.6	−5.1	5.1	−4.8	5.3
Acute myocardial infarction	3.1	3.5	−8.0	−6.8	−8.5	−7.4
Congestive heart failure, nonhypertensive	14.3	9.0	−2.4	2.4	−3.8	3.0
Osteoarthritis	3.0	4.0	−7.9	−7.1	−8.6	−6.8
Cataract	−0.5	3.7	−1.6	5.1	−2.0	4.5

(continued)

Table 4.10 (continued)

Conditions[a]	MCBS claims		MEPS (FFS only)		MEPS (FFS and private plan)	
	Regression based (M2) (%)	Primary diagnosis (S) (%)	Regression based (H2) (%)	Primary diagnosis (P) (%)	Regression based (I2) (%)	Primary diagnosis (Q) (%)
Rehabilitation care, fitting of prostheses, and adjustment of devices	−2.4	3.2	−6.5	−1.1	106.1	−1.3
Other nontraumatic joint disorders	−7.2	8.0	17.4	14.2	14.7	12.3
Mood disorders	−7.6	−1.0	−9.6	−8.5	−9.4	−8.3
Acute cerebrovascular disease	−4.8	−3.6	−2.9	0.6	−2.6	1.1
Other and ill-defined heart disease	−7.6	1.2	9.3	2.5	9.9	2.9
Essential hypertension	−10.3	4.0	6.2	2.9	4.6	3.2
Anxiety and personality disorders	28.7	7.5	47.3	−3.0	31.1	−3.8
Aortic and peripheral arterial embolism or thrombosis	915.7	37.8	11.0	−4.8	12.0	−3.9
Acute and unspecified renal failure	12.7	3.7	1.6	5.5	−0.5	4.3
Other disorders of stomach and duodenum	−129.0	2.0	−9.0	2.3	−6.6	3.6
Disorders of lipid metabolism	3.4	6.8	−2.3	1.2	0.3	1.4

[a] Ranked by 2009 per capita spending in M2.

Table 4.11   **Average annual growth rates for selected MCE indexes 2001–2009**

Method	MCBS	MEPS
Regression based including drug spending	2.1 (D)	2.8 (F)
Regression based omitting drug spending	1.4 (M)	4.8 (N)
Primary diagnosis omitting drug spending	2.8 (S)	6.4 (T)

to some conditions. However, it may be necessary to use it with data where events are not assigned diagnoses individually. It should be noted that, while we presented one regression-based approach, there is a considerable amount of discretion in how this approach can be applied, both in the modeling of spending as a function of diagnoses and in how the coefficients are used to divide up individuals' health care spending. One potential approach going forward, therefore, may be to adjust the regression-based approach until the results match the primary diagnosis method within a certain level of tolerance in the MEPS data, and then apply that adjusted approach to the larger sample and larger targeted population of the MCBS. Another approach may be to combine the two methods: use the primary diagnosis method on the Medicare Part A and B claims in the MCBS, but use a regression-based method on the drug spending from the survey portion of the MCBS.

4.6   Comparison of Medical Care Expenditure Indexes Calculated from Different Data Sets

As table 4.6 shows, we also calculated price indexes with the same methods and on comparable populations from the MCBS and the MEPS, for the purposes of comparing the results. In general, the MCBS or the Medicare claims are preferable data sets for analyzing the Medicare population to the MEPS since they have larger samples, also include the nursing home population, and do not seem to have the same underreporting issues as the MEPS. However, comparing the data sets offers a useful check on the MEPS, which has been used on other populations in the medical care expenditure index literature.

Table 4.11 shows the pairs of cells from table 4.6 that directly compare data sets with the same method and comparable populations. The population in both cases is FFS Medicare beneficiaries who are enrolled in Medicare for the full calendar year. In the MCBS sample, we use claims for diagnoses so as to be able to compare on a condition-by-condition basis with the MEPS, in which conditions are coded in ICD-9 diagnosis codes. As the table shows, when drug spending is included and we use a regression-based method, the MCE index based on the MEPS is slightly higher, by about 0.8 percentage point, than that based on the MCBS. When drug spending is omitted, however, the difference is over 3 percentage points, whether a regression-based method or the primary diagnosis method is used.

Table 4.12   **Correlations in per-patient expenditures across conditions and between the MCBS and the MEPS**

Method	Levels, averaged between 2001 and 2009 (%)	Growth rates from 2001 to 2009 (%)
Regression based (with drugs) (D & F)	31.9	1.2
Regression based (without drugs) (M & N)	40.0	−1.2
Primary diagnosis without drug spending (S & T)	56.8	7.9

Note: Correlations are weighted by disease prevalence.

Table 4.12 shows the correlations in per-patient expenditures across conditions between the expenditure indexes calculated from the MCBS and the MEPS with the same methods. The first column shows the correlations in the level of per-patient expenditure averaged across 2001 and 2009; as they show, the correlations are positive but not overwhelmingly strong. The correlations are strongest for the two indexes calculated using a primary diagnosis method without drug spending, which is the pair with the largest difference between their annual average growth rates. It is important to keep in mind, therefore, that the same method, similar data, and similar results can still produce substantively different average annual growth rates for an MCE index. The next column shows the correlations in the growth rates of the expenditure indexes for individual conditions from 2001 and 2009 across the two data sets; these are much lower and often close to zero.

Returning to table 4.11, we see that omitting spending and events related to pharmaceuticals from the MCE indexes has the opposite effect on the indexes from the two data sets. The growth rates of MCE indexes without pharmaceuticals are lower than those with pharmaceuticals when they are calculated from the MCBS, but omitting pharmaceuticals raises the growth rates of MCE indexes based on the MEPS considerably. The difference arises from the way pharmaceutical events are recorded in the two surveys. Pharmaceutical events are recorded together with a diagnosis in the MEPS, while in the MCBS pharmaceutical events are collected in the oral survey portion and are not associated with a diagnosis. In the MEPS dropping the pharmaceutical events can, therefore, change the treated prevalence of conditions since some conditions are only reported in pharmaceutical events. As discussed above in the section on prevalence, a change in the growth rate of treated prevalence can affect the growth rate of an MCE index, all other things equal, both because the per-patient expenditure will change and because the aggregation weights in the Fisher index will change.

When we compare an unweighted average of treated prevalences across conditions based on drug events and the same average based on nondrug events in the MEPS, we find that the former grows considerably faster over the period studied. Treated prevalence based on drug events has an average annual growth rate between 2001 and 2009 of 4.8 percent, while that based on nondrug events has an average annual growth rate of 2.8 percent. Omitting drug events would therefore tend to lower the growth rate of prevalence and raise the growth rate of the MCE index, all other things equal. The other main factor affecting the difference between MCE indexes with and without pharmaceutical spending and events is pharmaceutical spending itself. Omitting pharmaceutical spending but not the associated diagnoses would tend to lower the growth rate of the MCE index since pharmaceutical spending generally grows more quickly than other categories of medical spending. In the case of these indexes based on the MEPS, however, it appears that the changes in prevalence resulting from removing the pharmaceutical events more than offset the change to the index resulting from removing pharmaceutical spending.

From these comparisons we may conclude that the inclusion of pharmaceutical events in the treated prevalence in the data can have a substantive effect on an MCE index based upon that data; this has repercussions for the use of the MCBS as a data source for Medicare beneficiaries. As the MCBS lacks diagnoses related to pharmaceutical events, it will omit some conditions that beneficiaries are diagnosed with entirely and a regression-based index will misattribute their pharmaceutical spending to other conditions.

4.7   Conclusion

We have compared medical care expenditure indexes calculated from different data sets and using different methods. Our belief going into this research was that the primary diagnosis method was the best method for dividing up health care expenditure by disease, but that the Medicare Current Beneficiary Survey was the best data set for analyzing Medicare beneficiaries, as it has the widest coverage and the most information on them. However, the primary diagnosis method cannot be used with the drug spending and events in the MCBS. We therefore compared the primary diagnosis method with a regression-based method for estimating expenditures by disease and found that, when they are used to calculate MCE indexes on the same data sets, the primary diagnosis method produces higher average annual aggregate growth rates. The difference is relatively small for the analyses with the MCBS claims and much larger with the analyses using the MEPS. The annual indexes show some correlation between methods in yearly movements with the MCBS data but little correlation across the MEPS analyses, possibly because of the smaller sample size of the MEPS. There is strongly positive correlation in the levels of per-patient expenditures across conditions and between the two methods, but almost no correlations in the growth rates of the individual condition indexes. The regression-based method produces much more volatile individual indexes when applied to the MCBS claims data, probably because its results are more sensitive to outliers and there are more outliers in the MCBS claims data. Therefore, the regression-based method should be employed with caution and only when necessary.

We also compared medical care expenditure indexes for Medicare beneficiaries produced from the MCBS and the MEPS. As noted above, the MCBS has greater coverage and a larger sample size and the MEPS appears to have some problems with underreporting and underwent a methodology change in collecting diagnoses during the time period we are studying. When drug spending is included, however, the two data sets produce MCE indexes with very similar average annual growth rates, the one from the MEPS being a bit higher. When drug spending is omitted, however, the indexes from the MEPS have much higher growth rates, by more than 3 percentage points. As we discuss, the difference probably comes from the fact that when drug events are dropped from the analyses, the measurement of prevalence is affected in the MEPS but not in the MCBS, since the MCBS lacks diagnoses for its drug events. That the omission of drug-related diagnoses affects the MCE indexes for Medicare beneficiaries to such a degree is an argument in favor of using the MEPS, which attaches diagnoses to individual drug events. On balance, however, the MCBS is probably the preferable data set for Medicare beneficiaries because of its greater sample size and its inclusion of nursing home residents.

The best solution for FFS Medicare beneficiaries, in the end, may be a hybrid index: one that combines the primary diagnosis method applied to the Part A and Part B claims in the MCBS with a regression-based index for pharmaceutical spending. For private plan beneficiaries, however, the solution is not as clear. For this population, our choices are between a regression-based method run on the MCBS with only the twenty-seven diagnoses included in the MCBS survey, or the primary diagnosis or regression-based method run on the small group (about 300–400 a year) of Medicare private plan enrollees in the MEPS. Exploring these options will probably be the subject of some of our future work.

While we believe this comparison has covered the most important methods and data sets, it is not comprehensive. In particular, we did not cover the use of commercial groupers and we did not explore the larger sample of Medicare claims that are available for research (including the Part D pharmaceutical claims). We hope to address these gaps in future work.

References

Aizcorbe, A., R. Bradley, R. Greenaway-McGrevy, B. Herauf, R. Kane, E. Liebman, S. Pack, and L. Rozental. 2011. "Alternative Price Indexes for Medical Care: Evidence from the MEPS Survey." Working Paper, Bureau of Economic Analysis.

Aizcorbe, A., and N. Nestoriak. 2011. "Changing Mix of Medical Care Services: Stylized Facts and Implications for Price Indexes." *Journal of Health Economics* 30:568–74.

Berndt, E. R., A. Bir, S. H. Busch, R. G. Frank, and S. T. Normande. 2002. "The Medical Treatment of Depression, 1991–1996: Productive Inefficiency, Expected Outcome Variations, and Price Indexes." *Journal of Health Economics* 21:373–96.

Berndt, E. R., D. Cutler, R. Frank, Z. Griliches, J. Newhouse, and J. Triplett. 2000. "Medical Care Prices and Output." In *Handbook of Health Economics*, vol. 1., edited by A. J. Culyer and J. P. Newhouse. Amsterdam: Elsevier.

Buntin, M. B., and A. M. Zaslavsky. 2004. "Too Much Ado about Two-Part Models and Transformation? Comparing Methods of Modeling Medicare Expenditures." *Journal of Health Economics* 23:525–42.

Center for Medicare and Medicaid Services, National Health Expenditure Data. http://www.cms.gov/Research-Statistics-Data-and-Systems/Statistics-Trends-and -Reports/NationalHealthExpendData/NationalHealthAccountsHistorical.html.

Congressional Budget Office. 2013. "The Budget and Economic Outlook: Fiscal Years 2013 to 2023." February 13. http://www.cbo.gov/publication/43861.

———. 2014. "Updated Budget Projections: 2014 to 2024." April. http://www.cbo .gov/publication/45229.

Cutler, D. M., M. McClellan, J. P. Newhouse, and D. Remler. 1998. "Are Medical Prices Declining? Evidence from Heart Attack Treatments." *Quarterly Journal of Economics* 113:991–1024.

Duan, N. 1983. "Smearing Estimate: A Nonparametric Retransformation Method." *Journal of the American Statistical Association* 78:605–10.

Dunn, A., E. Liebman, S. Pack, and A. Shapiro. 2013. "Medical Care Price Indexes for Patients with Employer-Provided Insurance: Nationally-Representative Estimates from MarketScan Data." *Health Services Research* 48 (3): 1173–90.

Hall, A., and T. Highfill. 2013. "A Regression-Based Medical Care Expenditure Index for Medicare Beneficiaries." Working Paper, Bureau of Economic Analysis. http://www.bea.gov/papers/pdf/a_regression_base_medical_care_expenditure _index_for_medicare.pdf.

Jones, A. M. 2000. "Chapter Six: Health Econometrics." In *Handbook of Health Economics*, vol. 1, edited by A. J. Culyer and J. P. Newhouse. Amsterdam: Elsevier.

Manning, W. G. 1998. "The Logged Dependent Variable, Heteroscedasticity, and the Retransformation Problem." *Journal of Health Economics* 17:283–95.

Manning, W. G., and J. Mullahy. 2001. "Estimating Log Models: To Transform or Not to Transform?" *Journal of Health Economics* 20:461–94.

National Research Council. 2002. *At What Price? Conceptualizing and Measuring Cost-of-Living and Price Indexes.* Panel on Conceptual, Measurement, and Other Statistical Issues in Developing Cost-of-Living Indexes, edited by C. L. Schultze and C. Mackie. Committee on National Statistics, Division of Behavioral and Social Sciences and Education. Washington, DC: National Academy Press.

Park, R. 1966. "Estimation with Heteroscedastic Errors." *Econometrica* 34:888.

Shapiro, I., M. D. Shapiro, and D. W. Wilcox. 2001. "Measuring the Value of Cataract Surgery." In *Medical Care Output and Productivity*, edited by D. M. Cutler and E. R. Berndt. Chicago: University of Chicago Press.

Trogdon, J., E. A. Finkelstein, and T. J. Hoerger. 2008. "Use of Econometric Models to Estimate Expenditure Shares." *Health Services Research* 43 (4): 1442–52.

Zuvekas, S. H., and G. L. Olin. 2009. "Accuracy of Medicare Expenditures in the Medical Expenditure Panel Survey." *Inquiry* 46 (Spring): 92–108.

II

Analyses of Subpopulations and Market Segments

5

Measuring Output and Productivity in Private Hospitals

Brian Chansky, Corby Garner, and Ronjoy Raichoudhary

5.1 Introduction

Health care is one of the largest and most important sectors in the US economy. This sector accounted for 7.6 percent of gross domestic product (GDP)[1] and 12.6 percent of all nonfarm workers[2] in 2010 and continues to grow. The Bureau of Labor Statistics (BLS) projects health care and social assistance industries to generate 5.6 million new jobs by 2020,[3] partially in response to the growth in the population of the elderly (Henderson 2012). Within this sector, hospitals made up 28.6 percent of all employees in 2010.[4] Hospitals and nursing and residential care facilities accounted for 46 percent of gross output within the health care and social assistance sector in 2010.[5]

Brian Chansky, Corby Garner, and Ronjoy Raichoudhary are economists in the Office of Productivity and Technology at the US Bureau of Labor Statistics.

The authors wish to thank the Agency for Healthcare Research and Quality (AHRQ) and the Centers for Medicare & Medicaid Services (CMS) for providing data used in this article. The views expressed here are those of the authors and do not necessarily reflect the views of the US Department of Labor or the Bureau of Labor Statistics. For acknowledgments, sources of research support, and disclosure of the authors' material financial relationships, if any, please see http://www.nber.org/chapters/c13096.ack.

1. Source: BEA, Gross-Domestic-Product-(GDP)-by-Industry Data, Value Added by Industry, Value Added as a Percentage of Gross Domestic Product (Percent); http://www.bea .gov/industry/gdpbyind_data.htm.

2. Source: Based on data from BLS, Current Employment Statistics survey; http://www.bls .gov/ces/.

3. Source: BLS, Employment Projections: Employment by Major Industry Sector; http:// www.bls.gov/emp/ep_table_201.htm.

4. Source: Based on data from BLS, Current Employment Statistics survey; http://www.bls .gov/ces/.

5. Source: Based on data from BEA, Gross-Domestic-Product-(GDP)-by-Industry Data, Gross Output by Industry, Gross Output (Millions of dollars); http://www.bea.gov/industry/ gdpbyind_data.htm.

Over the last two decades, hospitals have experienced dramatic operational changes. Hospitals are constantly incorporating new and improved scientific advancements and technologies in an effort to improve medical care. The scale and dynamic nature of hospitals underscore the importance of measuring how efficiently hospitals are utilizing the growing labor force to provide health services.

In the United States, the concept of "health care" may be spread across many different types of activities and involve transactions in the marketplace as well as actions taken by groups and individuals. In order to study trends in the efficiency with which health services are provided, it is helpful to define the sphere where that activity takes place. A useful organization of that sphere of activity is the industry.[6] Employment and hours of workers classified by industry are readily available, and by organizing economic activity along the definitions of detailed industries, the efficiency with which health services are provided by specific enterprises and distinct labor pools can be analyzed. The BLS uses this approach to produce official labor productivity measures for detailed industries.[7]

This chapter will analyze labor productivity specifically for private hospitals. Private hospitals comprise the nongovernment portions of two North American Industry Classification System (NAICS) industries: General Medical and Surgical Hospitals (NAICS 6221) and Specialty (except psychiatric and substance abuse) Hospitals (NAICS 6223). These hospitals employed approximately 4.6 million workers in 2010.[8]

Industry-specific measures of labor hours and output are required to calculate labor productivity. Measurement of labor hours for private hospitals is relatively straightforward. However, measuring output is more difficult because of the complex array of services hospitals produce. This chapter develops three models to define and measure the services provided by hospitals, and then presents the labor productivity indexes created using each model.

5.2   What Is Hospital Output and How Can We Measure It?

To create an output index for the hospital industry, we first must *define* the services provided. Next, we *measure* those services. Finally, we *aggregate* the individual services into an overall measure of output for the industry.

6. Federal data by industry is classified according to the North American Industry Classification System (NAICS). Data for this study reflect the NAICS 2007 industry definitions.
7. Bureau of Labor Statistics productivity information and data can be accessed at www.bls .gov/lpc (for labor productivity) and at www.bls.gov/mfp (for multifactor productivity).
8. Source: Based on data from the BLS, Current Employment Statistics survey; http://www .bls.gov/ces/.

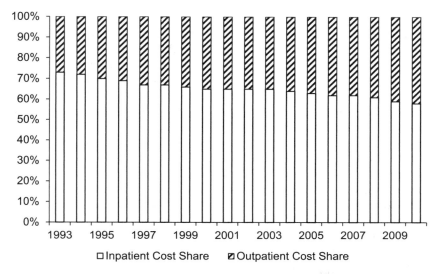

Fig. 5.1   Revenue cost shares for community hospitals, 1993–2010

We classify hospital services into two general categories, *outpatient services* and *inpatient services*. Outpatient services are those that do not require an overnight stay and can include things such as diagnostic tests or simple surgical procedures. The consumer purchases a service from the hospital, and each outpatient service can be counted as a discrete unit of output. According to the American Hospital Association (AHA), outpatient services accounted for 42 percent of total hospital revenue in 2010, up from 27 percent in 1993 (see figure 5.1).[9]

Inpatient services are those that require an overnight stay for extended treatment over a period of one or more days. An inpatient service requires the patient to be admitted to the hospital at the start of treatment and then to be discharged upon completion of the treatment. The course of treatment may include several different services such as diagnostic tests, surgical procedures, recuperation time, meals, and so forth. The inpatient course of treatment is designed to address a primary pathology, or reason for admission. However, secondary pathologies, often called "comorbidities," may also be treated during an inpatient stay.

The complex nature of inpatient services allows for multiple definitions of this component of output. One way to define output is as the entire bundle

9. Source: AHA, Trendwatch *Chartbook* 2012: Supplementary Data Table, Trends in Hospital Financing, Table 4.2: Distribution of Inpatient vs. Outpatient Revenues, 1990–2010; http://www.aha.org/research/reports/tw/chartbook/2012/appendix4.pdf.

of services delivered over the course of treatment during an inpatient stay (National Research Council 2010). In essence, the total course of treatment is counted as a single unit of output. This will be referred to as the *course of treatment model*. When a patient is admitted to a hospital, he or she is purchasing the course of treatment, which is ultimately carried out at the discretion of the hospital. In this model, the annual output of the hospital industry is based on the total number of inpatient hospital discharges and outpatient hospital visits in a given year.

Another way to define inpatient services is to disaggregate the bundle of services that comprise a course of treatment, whereby each individual service provided is counted separately. We refer to this as the *procedures model*. This method of defining output may be more precise, as each course of treatment may require more or less component services. Outpatient visits are treated the same under this model as the course of treatment model.

There is another aspect to defining hospital services, which is the *outcome* of the treatment itself. Presumably, a patient seeking treatment in a hospital wishes to have his or her pathology cured, or at least alleviated. Therefore, treatments that are unsuccessful are different in a fundamental way from those that result in a cure or alleviation. Positive outcomes of hospital treatment are the most direct indicator of the quality of service, followed by expediency and comfort.

An ideal measure of hospital output would include complete information on all of the aspects listed above. In a "perfect world" where all data were available, output would be calculated as the total number of treatments, adjusted by the number of procedures that improve outcomes. The basic service of a hospital is the course of treatment that the patient receives, so the quantity of these treatments would be defined as output. To account for the quality of the services provided, the quantity of treatments would be adjusted based upon how successful they were. However, to ensure that the outcome of the treatment was attributable to the quality of hospital care, each individual procedure would be evaluated to determine how much utility was provided.

Unfortunately, the measurement of treatment outcomes is not feasible, mainly due to a lack of data availability. Currently, the only available patient-level statistic related to outcomes is whether an inpatient died during the course of treatment. However, this mortality statistic does not provide a complete story, since the health status of patients that did not die is unknown. Even if data were available on the exact number of patients that were not cured, a true measure of outcomes would require knowledge of the role the hospital's care plays in these outcomes. This is a difficult task due to the many exogenous factors that can play a role in the recovery of a patient. Factors such as diet, lifestyle, genetics, and even random chance can affect the success of specific treatments. Therefore, due to the complexities involved in the measurement of outcomes, the measures of hospital output presented in this chapter do not account for the outcome of treatments.[10]

Two primary methods to measure industry output are physical quantity and deflated value. Both the course of treatment and procedures models of hospital output are based on physical quantities of inpatient and outpatient services. The deflated value method measures output based on revenues that have been adjusted with one or more price indexes to remove the effect of price change. With this method, an industry's deflated revenue serves as a proxy for the quantity of output. We refer to this approach as the *revenue model*.

Like most service industries, the hospital industry provides many different types of services. We combine these services into a single index of output using weights based on the value of each service relative to the total value of output. Thus, the effect of each individual service on the change in total output is proportional to the amount of resources required to provide that service.[11]

5.3   Data Sources

To create the three models of hospital output and subsequent indexes of labor productivity, we use the following data sources:

BLS Industry Employment and Hours Data. The measure of labor hours used to calculate labor productivity come from the BLS industry productivity program's comprehensive database of employment and hours.[12] This labor index represents the sum of hours of all workers in private hospitals each year. This measure is based primarily on data from the BLS Current Employment Statistics program, supplemented with data from the Current Population Survey. Annual hours are estimated separately for General Medical & Surgical Hospitals (NAICS 6221) and Specialty Hospitals (NAICS 6223) and then summed.

Nationwide Inpatient Sample (NIS). Our measures of inpatient services are based on patient discharge data from the NIS. The NIS is the largest all-payer inpatient care database publicly available in the United States,

---

10. A number of other countries' statistical agencies have investigated methods and developed measures for quality change to adjust their health statistics. As of the publication of this chapter, no single method of measuring quality change has been widely adopted internationally. For a discussion of potential quality-change measurements, see Douglas (2006, 13). For a discussion of the reasons quality-change metrics were not ultimately included, see Statistics New Zealand (2013, 8).

11. The Industry Productivity Program releases labor productivity measures that incorporate annual chain-weighted indexes for measuring changes in industry output. The Tornqvist index aggregates the growth rates of various industry outputs with annual weights based on the products' shares in total value of industry production. For a more detailed look at Tornqvist aggregation, see the BLS *Handbook of Methods*, chapter 11: "Industry Productivity Measures."

12. Bureau of Labor Statistics, Labor Productivity and Costs, Industry Employment and Hours Data Tables; http://www.bls.gov/lpc/iprhoursdata.htm.

providing information on health care utilization and costs. The unit of observation is an inpatient stay record. The NIS contains discharge-level records, rather than patient-level records. Therefore, individual patients who are hospitalized more than once in one year may be present in the NIS multiple times. We use the NIS to count all inpatient discharges and procedures in private hospitals for each year from 1993 to 2010.[13] Each discharge is assigned a diagnosis-related group (DRG) that corresponds to both the primary pathology being treated as well as the associated bundle of procedures and services used during treatment. A single charge is reported for the complete stay.

American Hospital Association (AHA) Annual Survey. Data for the quantity of outpatient visits comes from the AHA Annual Survey. An outpatient visit is defined as a:

> Visit by a patient not lodged in the hospital while receiving medical, dental, or other services. Each visit an outpatient makes to a discrete unit constitutes one visit regardless of the number of diagnostic and/or therapeutic treatments that the patient receives. Total outpatient visits should include all clinic visits, referred visits, observation services, outpatient surgeries, and emergency room visits.[14]

National Hospital Ambulatory Medical Care Survey (NHAMCS). While the AHA Annual Survey includes extensive data on the quantity of outpatient visits, the survey does not provide detail regarding diagnosis. The NHAMCS, however, does provide a measure of outpatient visits separated into major disease categories.[15] The ratios of each major disease category are applied to total AHA outpatient visits.

CMS Statistical Supplement. The Medicare and Medicaid Statistical Supplement provides comprehensive annual data about Medicare, Medicaid, and other CMS programs. The CMS compiles billing data for hospital outpatient visits that are covered by Medicare and Medicaid, including the total number of outpatient visits and the associated charges for each of the 900-plus ICD-9-CM[16] categories. The total visits and charges for individual ICD-9-CM categories are aggregated to the level of sixteen major disease category groupings.

13. The NIS is built from data provided by state health agencies. Prior to 1993, only a small number of states were sampled. Thus, based primarily on the addition of states to the NIS data set over time, HHS recommends that time series analyses on these data begin with 1993.

14. Source: AHA, Trendwatch *Chartbook* 2009: Trends Affecting Hospitals and Health Systems, Glossary; http://www.aha.org/research/reports/tw/chartbook/2009/glossary.pdf.

15. The scope of the AHA data set is greater than that of the NHAMCS. The AHA collects data from 98 percent of community hospitals, making it the preferred source of outpatient data.

16. The International Classification of Diseases, Ninth Revision, Clinical Modification (ICD-9-CM) is the official system of assigning codes to diagnoses and procedures associated with hospital utilization in the United States; http://www.cdc.gov/nchs/icd/icd9cm.htm.

Table 5.1	Data sources for output	
Data source	Provider	Element
	Course of treatment and procedures models: Inpatient	
NIS	HCUP	Number of discharges per DRG
		Number of procedures per DRG
		Cost per DRG discharge
	Course of treatment and procedures models: Outpatient	
AHA Annual Survey	AHA	Total number of outpatient visits
		Inpatient and outpatient revenue shares
	Revenue model	
SAS	Census	Total revenue for community hospitals
PPI	BLS	Industry price deflators

Service Annual Survey (SAS). The primary source for revenue data is the SAS from the Census Bureau, which publishes total hospital revenue by industry for General Medical and Surgical Hospitals (NAICS 6221) and for Specialty (except psychiatric and substance abuse) Hospitals (NAICS 6223). The aggregate value includes revenues for inpatient and outpatient services, plus miscellaneous services such as food and parking revenue.

Producer Price Index (PPI). Total revenue for each industry is deflated using appropriate BLS PPIs.[17] The PPIs for general and specialty hospitals define output as a bundle of services provided for the treatment of a medical condition, not as the individual services rendered such as x-rays, drugs, and medical supplies (Catron and Murphy 1996).

Table 5.1 provides a brief summary of the data sources used in each model of output. More information about these data sources can be found in appendix A.

5.4   Three Models of Output

5.4.1   The Course of Treatment Model of Output

The course of treatment model defines hospital output as the full course of treatment received by a patient admitted to a hospital. This model is based on the "direct quantity index" approach suggested by Triplett (2012). The final output index is an aggregation of inpatient and outpatient services.

Inpatient Stays

The physical quantity measure of output for inpatient stays is a weighted aggregation of patient discharge data from the NIS. The total number of

---

17. NAICS 6221 is deflated using PPI 622110622110 G, and NAICS 6223 is deflated using PPI 6223106223106 G.

inpatient discharges in each DRG category are combined into a single quantity index of inpatient output with weights based on each DRG's share of total cost. Equation (1):

(1)
$$\frac{Q_t}{Q_{t-1}} = \exp\left[\sum_{i=1}^{n} w_{i,t}\left(\ln\left(\frac{q_{i,t}}{q_{i,t-1}}\right)\right)\right],$$

where

Q_t / Q_{t-1} = the ratio of inpatient output in the current year (t) to the previous year ($t - 1$),

n = the number of DRGs,

$\ln(q_{i,t} / q_{i,t-1})$ = the natural logarithm of the ratio of the quantity of **inpatient stays** for DRG i in the current year to the quantity in the previous year, and

$w_{i,t}$ = the average value share weight for DRG i_t and DRG i_{t-1}.

Total inpatient values are calculated by multiplying the quantity of inpatient treatments for each DRG category by their associated average cost or average charge. Relative weights based on these values are derived by dividing the total value for each DRG category in a given year by the sum of values for all DRGs in that year.

We use average cost data for 2001 forward. Cost is defined as the dollar amount incurred by a hospital to provide services. Prior to 2001, cost data are unavailable, so we use average charge data for that period. Charge is defined as the final amount on a patient's bill.

Costs are a more accurate measure of the value of an inpatient stay because they are not subject to exogenous price factors. In those years where cost data are unavailable, the charge data are an acceptable proxy because the primary factor that determines the relative charge for inpatient services is the value of hospital resources used in the provision of such services.

Outpatient Services

We use the number of outpatient visits from the AHA *Chartbook* as the basis of our physical quantity measure of outpatient services.[18] To obtain a more accurate representation of outpatient output, we disaggregate the yearly outpatient totals from AHA into sixteen major disease categories using data from the NHAMCS.

We match the number of visits for each major disease category with corresponding charge data from CMS. The total charges are divided by the number of visits for each respective major disease category to obtain an average charge per outpatient visit. We then multiply average charges by the quantity of outpatient visits that are calculated using data from AHA

---

18. American Hospital Association statistics do not separate private from government hospitals. The NIS data is used to calculate a percentage of hospitals that are privately owned in the United States. This ratio is applied to the AHA data to remove government-owned hospitals.

and CDC. The resulting values are used to derive weights for combining the quantities of various outpatient visits.[19]

A variation of equation (1) is used to calculate outpatient index growth, where

Q_t / Q_{t-1} = the ratio of outpatient output in the current year (t) to the previous year ($t-1$),

n = the number of major disease categories,

$\ln(q_{i,t} / q_{i,t-1})$ = the natural logarithm of the ratio of the quantity of **outpatient visits** for major disease category i in the current year to the quantity in the previous year, and

$w_{i,t}$ = the average value share weight for MDC i_t and MDC i_{t-1}.

It is possible that the use of Medicare and Medicaid charges may introduce some bias to the outpatient measure, as these charges are drawn from only a subset of the population. However, as with the charge data used to weight the inpatient services, the value of hospital resources used in order to provide the outpatient services is thought to be the primary factor affecting these charges. Therefore, we expect shares for each major disease category calculated from the CMS data to be similar to corresponding shares for the general population. The various quantities of outpatient visits are combined into a single outpatient index using their associated share of the total nationwide value as weights.

An alternative data source for outpatient visits and charges is the Medical Expenditure Panel Survey (MEPS). See appendix B for an outpatient index created using these data.

Output Index

We combine the independently constructed indexes of inpatient services and outpatient services to create an output index for private hospitals using the course of treatment model. Percentages of inpatient and outpatient gross revenue from AHA's *Trendwatch* report[20] are used to calculate the average share weights for inpatient and outpatient services. Equation (2):

$$(2) \qquad \ln\left(\frac{A_t}{A_{t-1}}\right) = w_i\left(\ln\frac{I_t}{I_{t-1}}\right) + w_o\left(\ln\frac{O_t}{O_{t-1}}\right),$$

where

A = output index for community hospitals,
I = Inpatient input,

19. The CMS data are only available from 2004 to the present. Therefore, all average charge data are held constant from 1993 to 2003, using the 2004 values.

20. American Hospital Association, Trendwatch *Chartbook* 2012: Supplementary Data Table, Trends in Hospital Financing, Table 4.2: Distribution of Inpatient vs. Outpatient Revenues, 1990–2010; http://www.aha.org/research/reports/tw/chartbook/2012/appendix4.pdf.

O = Outpatient input, and
w_i, w_o = value share weights.

5.4.2   Review of the Course of Treatment Model

The course of treatment model has several strengths. The data on inpatient discharges and outpatient visits are comprehensive and reliable. A wealth of information about the activity of hospitals in the United States has accumulated over time from a number of sources including NIS, NHAMCS, AHA, and CMS. These data sources can be used to calculate the total number of courses of treatment and their associated charges/costs for the entirety of US private hospitals. Also, the course of treatment model of output is sensible from a demand perspective. Whether a patient goes to a hospital for a few hours or a few days, the objective is the same: to have a particular health problem treated. The idea that hospital output should be defined as a course of treatment has been advocated by a number of health economists (Triplett 2012).

The simplicity of a course of treatment measure of output may also be the model's primary weakness, however. As opposed to the ideal "perfect world" scenario described earlier in this chapter, the course of treatment measure lacks the robustness of data that could be provided by including procedure and outcome data. A count of hospital discharges does not provide as much information about the quantity of individual health services delivered over time as does a count of the actual procedures provided during the hospital stay. Instead, in the course of treatment model different output intensities related to each DRG are implicitly accounted for in the average value share weights used to combine the various DRG categories of a hospital stay.

A measure of output based on courses of treatment also does not address issues relating to variable outcomes and changes in the quality of treatment over time. When treatments improve over time, ideally they should be counted as an increase in output. A disadvantage of a physical quantity measure of output is that it cannot directly account for quality change. Instead, all courses of treatment are counted equally, regardless of the result. While it can be argued that unsuccessful treatments should not be counted as equal output, the data to accommodate this distinction are not currently available. Although there are numerous sources that measure some aspects of variable outcomes and quality change in the health services sector, there is no broad agreement on how to apply this type of data to nationwide statistics.[21] Until a consensus is reached on this topic, a measure free of these complicating factors is a more sensible approach for the measurement of hospitals' output.[22] Given the current data limitations, the simplicity and directness of the course

21. We incorporate a mortality data element into the course of treatment inpatient model to create a survival-adjusted series (see appendix C).

22. The output measures for service-providing industries currently maintained by DIPS are not adjusted for variable outcomes, although this issue may be present to a lesser degree. Furthermore, when a physical-quantity approach is used, quality changes are not accounted for.

of treatments model may actually be an advantage. By using only data that are highly reliable, the resulting output index can be assumed trustworthy.

Comorbidities, which are defined as one or more disorders that are present in addition to a primary pathology, also pose an obstacle to the accurate measurement of hospital services. Ideally, when a patient is treated for multiple disorders, each pathology should be accounted for individually. Unfortunately, the level of data needed to separate each comorbidity into its own category of treatment is not available. The DRG system has recognized this problem, however, and many diagnosis groups have been split to account for cases where there are serious complications or comorbidities. Presumably these DRGs, which include complications and comorbidities, have higher average charges/costs and thus contribute more weight to the overall inpatient index. By organizing hospital discharges according to the DRG system, the course of treatment model of output indirectly accounts for the presence of comorbidities in private hospitals.

5.4.3   The Procedures Model of Output

As discussed previously, hospital output can be defined as a procedure rather than a course of treatment. The NIS provides some data that can be used to measure these detailed services. Specifically, for each hospital inpatient stay the NIS records the number and types of procedures performed. A procedure is defined as a medical intervention that was performed during a hospital stay. Procedures are classified into one of four broad categories: minor diagnostic, minor therapeutic, major diagnostic, and major therapeutic. Examples of common procedures include blood transfusions, cesarean sections, vaccinations, and kidney dialysis. According to the Agency for Healthcare Research and Quality (AHRQ), in 2007 approximately 70 percent of hospital inpatient stays included at least one procedure (Stranges, Russo, and Friedman 2009). We use a physical quantity approach based on the number of procedures per DRG to develop an alternative measure of inpatient output of the hospital industry.

While charge or cost data are available for total inpatient stays, values for individual procedures are not available in the NIS. This precludes an accurate valuation of procedures across different DRGs. A reasonable alternative is to count the total yearly number of procedures within each DRG, and then weight them together using the associated DRG charge/cost data. This method uses the number of procedures as the unit of output within the context of the DRG classification system. Equation (3):

$$(3) \qquad \frac{Q_t}{Q_{t-1}} = \exp\left[\sum_{i=1}^{n} w_{i,t}\left(\ln\left(\frac{q_{i,t}}{q_{i,t-1}}\right)\right)\right],$$

where

Q_t / Q_{t-1} = the ratio of inpatient output in the current year (t) to the previous year ($t-1$),

n = the number of DRGs

$\ln(q_{i,t} / q_{i,t-1})$ = the natural logarithm of the ratio of the quantity of **procedures** in DRG i in the current year to the quantity in the previous year, and

$w_{i,t}$ = the average value share weight for DRG i_t and DRG i_{t-1}.

As with the course of treatment model, the procedures index of inpatient output is combined with an index of outpatient services. The outpatient index for the procedures model is identical to that of the course of treatment model (see equation [2]). Because an outpatient visit is defined as a single encounter in a hospital rather than a bundle of services, the count of procedures and treatments is the same. The purpose of an outpatient visit can be considered as either a single procedure or a single treatment.

5.4.4   Review of the Procedures Model

A procedures model provides more detail about actual health services provided during inpatient stays than does a simple count of admissions or discharges. In this model, increases in the average number of procedures performed per inpatient stay will lead to growth in the output index. When output of a hospital is defined as individual services performed, a procedures model of output may be preferable. Additional procedures may result in improved diagnosis or treatment of pathologies that benefit the patient. This benefit would be missed with other methods such as the courses of treatment measure of output. However, it is not clear that all procedures that are undertaken are necessary or that an increase in the number of procedures necessarily leads to better treatment of a pathology. While the procedures model may be attractive from the hospital's viewpoint, to define procedures as the hospital's unit of output can create a conflict with the needs of the patient. Data currently available are not sufficient to construct a direct link between the number of procedures provided by hospitals and the outcomes of treatments. Patients seek to have their pathology addressed, and yet the precise type and number of procedures is generally left to the hospital's discretion. From the point of view of the consumer, additional procedures do not necessarily represent an increase or improvement in the health service received.

Other than a mortality variable (whether the patient was discharged alive or dead), there are no data elements currently available that provide information on the efficacy of the course of treatment. And even if such data were available, it would be difficult to ascertain whether the increased number of procedures were the cause of improved outcomes, or if the improvements were due to factors outside the hospital's control. One could conceive of situations where an increase in the number of procedures even has a negative effect on a patient's health, such as a misdiagnosis or treating an infection acquired during a hospital stay. More accurate data on the link between procedures and treatment outcomes would be useful. There are other problems with the procedures approach for an inpatient index. Some hospital inpatient stays do not require any procedures as classified by ICD-9-CM. For example, inpatient stays for the sole purposes of bed rest or observation fall into this category. The DRGs in which these types of stays are common would likely be underrepresented in a procedures inpatient index. Also, the lack of charge/cost data for different procedures prevents the use of weights that would accurately adjust the inpatient index based on changes in the mix of procedures over time.

5.4.5   Output Derived from Revenue

The majority of industry productivity measures produced by the BLS use a deflated value concept of output measurement. In these industries, deflated revenues serve as a proxy for quantities of goods and services produced. Deflated value methodology is used because in most cases, industry revenue data are more available than physical quantity data. Ideally, revenue data should be as detailed as possible to account for the variety of different services provided by hospitals and each revenue category should be deflated with a price deflator specific to that category. The SAS reports total hospital revenue; however, it is not disaggregated into detailed services provided. Instead, total revenue for each industry is deflated using the BLS PPIs for the industry.[23] The final output index produced with this model is an aggregation of the deflated revenues for NAICS 6221 and NAICS 6223. Due to a lack of data availability, inpatient and outpatient services are not calculated independently under the revenue model, as is the case with the course of treatment and procedures models.

5.4.6   Review of the Revenue Model

An important benefit of a revenue model is the potential to account for quality change through the use of price deflators. Price deflators that are adjusted for quality change ensure that revenue increases that are driven by inflation are removed from the output series, while those that are driven by quality improvements are not. To the extent that quality adjustments are made to the price indexes, a deflated value measure of output allows for an increase in the actual services rendered by a hospital to be counted (Aizcorbe and Nestoriak 2008). The general medical and surgical hospital PPI currently accounts for quality change by incorporating quality indicators for three DRGs: heart attack, heart failure, and pneumonia (Hospital Quality Valuation Team 2008).

Some health economists have cautioned that current price indexes may not adequately respond to changing treatments. For example, Aizcorbe and Nestoriak (2011) suggest that use of a standard fixed-basket index inflates price growth. They suggest a medical care expenditure index to address this

---

23. NAICS 6221 is deflated using PPI 622110622110 G, and NAICS 6223 is deflated using PPI 6223106223106 G.

concern. These types of price indexes "track the overall cost of care (all expenditures), not the cost of the individual services." At present, medical care expenditure indexes specific to hospitals are not available. However, the BLS has recently developed hospital PPIs on a disease basis. Beginning in 2008, PPIs are available for major diagnostic categories (MDC) within General Medical and Surgical Hospitals. These indexes represent price change for all hospital services and are grouped according to the system of the body being treated (e.g., circulatory system, digestive system, etc.). All payer types (e.g., Medicare, Medicaid, private insurance, etc.) are covered by these price deflators.[24]

The quinquennial Economic Census of 2007 is the first to report detailed hospital revenue based on both MDCs as well as ancillary hospital services. If this detailed data continues with the 2012 Economic Census, it could potentially be combined with the BLS MDC-based PPI to create an improved deflated-value measure of output.

There are several characteristics of the hospital industry that present challenges to measuring output based on revenues and prices. First, there are a variety of types of payers for hospital services, and hospital prices are not uniform for all customers. Different patients pay different amounts for the same hospital services based on whether payment is out of pocket, through private insurance, or Medicare/Medicaid. Because prices are negotiated between insurers and hospitals, the amount of revenue received for hospital services varies from patient to patient. The assumption that prices reflect marginal costs does not necessarily hold in the hospital industry because prices are administered rather than reached through open competition. Cylus and Dickensheets (2007, 61) recognize that "it can be argued that deriving outputs using nominal payments and the hospital PPI results in a distorted measure."

Another unique characteristic of the hospital industry is that the provider (e.g., physician) often chooses the services provided. This is because the consumer may be a minor, unconscious, lacking knowledge of medical procedures, or simply apathetic because the payments are made by third-party insurance plans. Rosen and Cutler (2007, 54) point out that "In medical care, however, the link between purchase and value is not clear . . . [Thus], most health care analysts do not assume that purchase decisions will reflect the true value of the good." In addition, different hospitals may choose to treat the same pathologies in different ways, and the revenue they receive from these courses of treatment will reflect such choices. Thus, the revenue from any given course of treatment differs from hospital to hospital, based on decisions made by the hospitals themselves.

---

24. The MDC-based PPIs are actually available going back to 1992. However, these older PPIs only cover private insurance patients. They do not account for bills paid with Medicare, Medicaid, or other public sources, which combined in 1997 for 62 percent of all hospital gross patient revenues (Lane 2001).

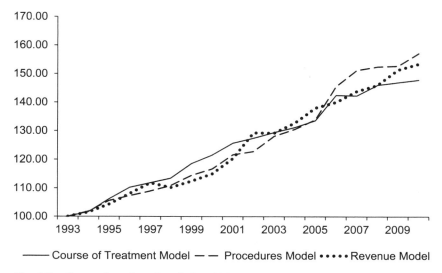

Fig. 5.2   **Output for private hospitals, 1993–2010**

Deflated values serve as a proxy for quantity, and are of interest in assessing trends in hospital output. However, in the hospital industry, the data sources for physical quantity are more accurate and more comprehensive than those for revenue. Furthermore, there are industry-specific factors, such as the complex structures of payments, which can cause revenues to move differently than services. For these reasons, we prefer physical quantities to deflated revenues.

5.5   Results

Over the last two decades, hospitals have experienced dramatic changes in the way they operate. As with any industry that experiences significant technological change, labor productivity is expected to increase. All three models of output show positive growth for output and labor productivity for 1993–2010. However, labor productivity varies in the selected subperiods (see figures 5.2 and 5.3).

5.5.1   Course of Treatment Model

With the course of treatment model of output, real output of private hospitals exhibits average annual growth of 2.3 percent from 1993 to 2010 and shows positive year-to-year growth every year except in 2007. The indexes of inpatient and outpatient services posted yearly average growth rates of 1.7 and 3.5 percent, respectively, from 1993 to 2010 (see figure 5.4). The hospital industry experienced long-term average annual labor productivity growth of 0.7 percent from 1993 to 2010 (see table 5.2).

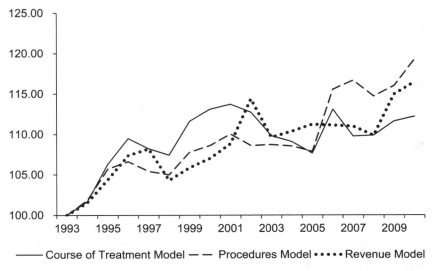

Fig. 5.3   Labor productivity for private hospitals, 1993–2010

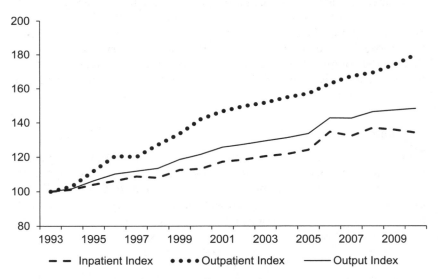

Fig. 5.4   Indexes of inpatient services, outpatient services, and combined output for community hospitals, course of treatment model: 1993–2010

Table 5.2   **Average annual percent change in labor productivity for private hospitals**

Time period	Course of treatment model (%)	Procedures model (%)	Revenue model (%)
1993–2010	0.7	1.0	0.9
1993–2001	1.6	1.2	1.1
2001–2010	−0.2	0.9	0.8

Table 5.3   **Average annual percent change in labor productivity and related series for private hospitals using a course of treatment model of output, 1993–2010 and selected subperiods**

	1993–2010 (%)	1993–2001 (%)	2001–2010 (%)
Output index	2.3	2.9	1.8
Inpatient index	1.7	2.0	1.5
Outpatient index	3.5	4.9	2.3
Hours index	1.6	1.3	2.0
Labor productivity	0.7	1.6	−0.2

Labor productivity grew on average by 1.6 percent per year for the years 1993–2001. In contrast, growth in labor hours outpaced that of output from 2001 through 2010, leading to an average annual decline in labor productivity of 0.2 percent for the time period (see table 5.3).

The decrease in productivity for the years 2001–2010 may seem to contradict conventional wisdom, but is not totally unexpected. As technology in the medical field advances, procedures that once required an inpatient stay can now be performed on an outpatient basis inside or outside the hospital. As a result, the remaining inpatient cases being treated by hospitals have become increasingly difficult and complex. These types of treatments would likely require more staff attention, and thus more hours. This is one explanation for the greater growth in labor hours relative to output for 2001–2010.

5.5.2   Procedures Model

With the procedures model, output experienced long-term average growth of 2.7 percent per year for the period 1993–2010. As figure 5.5 shows, the outpatient index grows at a faster rate than the inpatient index. As with the course of treatment model, however, the final output index is influenced more heavily by the change in the inpatient index because the inpatient services require more resources and therefore have a larger weight. Labor productivity rose at a long-term annual rate of 1 percent for the period 1993–2010 (see table 5.2).

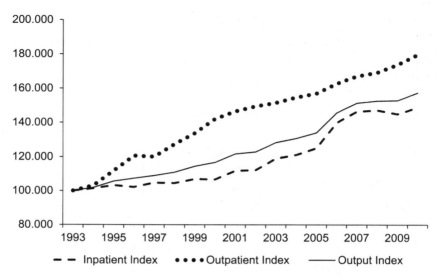

Fig. 5.5   Indexes of inpatient services, outpatient services, and output for community hospitals, procedures model: 1993–2010

5.5.3   Revenue Model

The long-term yearly average growth of output under the revenue model is 2.6 percent for the period 1993–2010. The same labor index from the previous two models is used, leading to a 0.9 percent average annual gain in labor productivity during the period.

5.6   Conclusion

Each of the three output models discussed in this chapter has strengths and weaknesses. For a model to be broadly accepted there are two concerns to be addressed: the data must be accurate and the definition of output must be compelling. The revenue model presented in this chapter is weak in both the availability of the data and the definition of output. Revenue and price data are not yet detailed enough to achieve in-depth coverage of the hospital industry. Additionally, the weak link between consumer choices, services rendered, and compensation received implies a tenuous relationship between revenue and actual output. The promise of the deflated value method is the ability to more easily incorporate quality change through prices. More research into these issues would be needed for a revenue model to be considered.

Of the two physical quantity models, the course of treatment model has the advantage of more precise data. Inpatient treatments are categorized by DRG, a common practice in the hospital industry, and each inpatient treatment is weighted using matching charge/cost data. This is more reliable than the procedures model, where the data are lacking to organize and value the different types of procedures. Although the course of treatment model does not explicitly account for hospital quality change, a non-quality-adjusted measure can be beneficial as a baseline against which to judge future work in this field.

The ultimate question of how to define output in the hospital industry is subjective and open to debate. However, in our opinion, the most natural way to define the output of an industry is to answer the question: What services are being demanded? For hospitals, the consumer is purchasing the service of treatment for a specific health problem. We believe counting the full courses of treatments has the advantage of data availability, and is the most direct way to determine industry output.

Appendix A
Data Sources in Depth

Befitting such a vast and complex part of the economy, there are a number of different government agencies and private organizations that measure the activity of the health care sector. The US Department of Health and Human Services (HHS) administers a wide variety of data-collection programs covering the nation's health care infrastructure. These include the Nationwide Inpatient Sample (NIS) and the National Hospital Discharge Survey (NHDS), which collect information on hospital inpatient care. Data on physicians' offices and emergency departments are provided by the National Ambulatory Medical Care Survey (NAMCS) and the Nationwide Emergency Department Sample (NEDS), respectively. The Medical Expenditure Panel Survey (MEPS) provides data on the cost and use of health care and health insurance coverage. Additionally, the Centers for Medicare and Medicaid Services (CMS) collects a wealth of data relating to government-sponsored health insurance programs.

Outside of HHS, the Census Bureau collects revenue data for the health care sector in its Services Annual Survey (SAS) and the quinquennial Economic Census, while the Bureau of Economic Analysis (BEA) measures the economic activity of the health care sector in its National Income Product Accounts (NIPAs). In the private sector, the American Hospital Association (AHA) collects a wealth of data on its members, which number over 6,500 hospitals.

We use the following data sources to create our models of hospital output:
Nationwide Inpatient Sample (NIS). Our measures of inpatient services are based on patient discharge data from the NIS. Sponsored by the Agency for Healthcare Research and Quality (AHRQ), the NIS is the largest all-payer inpatient care database publicly available in the United States, providing

information on health care utilization and charge data, with annual data starting in 1988. As part of the Healthcare Cost and Utilization Project (HCUP), the NIS is drawn from those states participating in HCUP; for 2010, these states comprise over 96 percent of the US population. The 2010 database contains information on approximately eight million hospital stays from 1,051 hospitals in forty-five states sampled to approximate a 20 percent stratified sample of US community hospitals. The NIS is a stratified probability sample of hospitals in the frame, with sampling probabilities proportional to the number of US community hospitals in each stratum. The universe of US community hospitals is divided into strata using five hospital characteristics: ownership/control, bed size, teaching status, urban/rural location, and US region.

The unit of observation is an inpatient stay record. Inpatient stay records in the NIS include clinical and resource use information typically available from discharge abstracts. It includes more than 100 data elements for each hospital stay, including primary and secondary diagnoses, admission and discharge status, hospital characteristics, expected payment source, primary and secondary procedures, length of stay, patient demographics, and total costs/charges.[25] The NIS is the only national hospital database with charge information on all patients, regardless of payer, including persons covered by Medicare, Medicaid, private insurance, and the uninsured.[26] The NIS contains discharge-level records, rather than patient-level records. Therefore, individual patients who are hospitalized more than once in one year may be present in the NIS multiple times.

We use the NIS to count all inpatient discharges in private hospitals for each year from 1993 to 2010.[27] Each discharge is assigned a diagnosis-related group (DRG) that corresponds to both the primary pathology being treated as well as the associated bundle of procedures and services used during treatment. These treatment bundles correspond to differing amounts of hospital resource utilization. The DRG classification system was developed and is used by the Centers for Medicare and Medicaid Services (CMS) to create a uniform payment system for Medicare and Medicaid patients across the United States.[28] The DRGs are the primary means by which

25. Healthcare Cost and Utilization Project, Overview of the Nationwide Inpatient Sample (NIS); http://www.hcup-us.ahrq.gov/nisoverview.jsp.

26. Healthcare Cost and Utilization Project, Introduction to the HCUP Nationwide Inpatient Sample (NIS) 2009, Abstract; http://www.hcup-us.ahrq.gov/db/nation/nis/NIS_2009 _INTRODUCTION.pdf.

27. The NIS is built from data provided by state health agencies. Prior to 1993, only a small number of states were sampled. Thus, based primarily on the addition of states to the NIS data set over time, HHS recommends that time series analyses on these data begin with 1993.

28. The DRGs are derived from the *International Classification of Diseases, Ninth Revision, Clinical Modification* (ICD-9-CM) (US Department of Health and Human Services, Centers for Medicare and Medicaid Services). Official version: International Classification of Diseases, Ninth Revision, Clinical Modification, Sixth Edition. DHHS Pub No. (PHS) 06-1260.

hospital discharges are categorized nationwide. They constitute a reasonable way to categorize inpatient services for the purpose of constructing an inpatient index because each patient is assigned a single DRG (as opposed to a set of multiple procedures or diagnoses) with one corresponding charge. The classification of diagnoses in the DRG system are updated annually to include more specific types of ailments as well as differing levels of severity. New DRGs are also assigned for substantially new methods of treatment.[29]

For the purposes of this study, we remove state and local government hospitals from the original NIS data set, leaving only the privately owned nonprofit and for-profit hospitals. We do this to ensure consistency between the output measure and the BLS labor input series that is used in the final labor productivity calculations.[30] The sample of discharge records is made into a nationwide measure by applying weights to each inpatient discharge and its associated charge. Patient-level data are weighted with respect to the type of hospital where the service takes place.[31] The nationwide discharge data are then summed with respect to each DRG.

American Hospital Association (AHA) Annual Survey. A data source commonly used in conjunction with the NIS is the AHA Annual Survey. The AHA has conducted the Annual Survey of hospitals since 1946 to construct a comprehensive health care provider database. Administered by Health Forum, the AHA Annual Survey contains hospital-specific data items on more than 6,500 US hospitals, including more than 1,000 data fields covering organizational structure, personnel, hospital facilities, services, and financial performance.[32] One data element particularly beneficial in the creation of an output measure is the physical quantity measure of outpatient visits. Outpatient visits in community hospital data begins in 1988 and is available from AHA's web-based publication *Chartbook*.

This definition of the outpatient visit parallels that of the inpatient stay, because a patient's visit encompasses their course of medical service for one specific health issue. However, unlike an inpatient stay, a single person can record multiple outpatient visits on the same day, provided that each visit occurs at a different unit of the hospital.

National Hospital Ambulatory Medical Care Survey (NHAMCS). The NHAMCS provides a measure of outpatient visits separated into major

29. We are able to create time series of inpatient services by using DRG Versions 10, 18, and 24. The NIS provides yearly discharge data using these versions of the DRG system for time series analysis.

30. According to the NIS, government hospitals accounted for 21 percent of all United States hospitals in 2010.

31. These weights take into account geographic region, urban/rural location, teaching status, bed size, and ownership control; http://www.hcup-us.ahrq.gov/db/nation/nis/NIS_Introduction _2009.jsp.

32. American Hospital Association, AHA Annual Survey Database Fiscal Year 2011; http:// www.ahadataviewer.com/book-cd-products/AHA-Survey/.

disease categories.[33] The NHAMCS is produced by the Centers for Disease Control and Prevention's (CDC) National Center for Health Statistics (NCHS). It began in 1991 and is the principal federal source of information on the utilization of hospital emergency departments, outpatient departments, and hospital-based ambulatory surgery centers.[34] It provides nationally representative estimates on the demographic characteristics of outpatients, diagnoses, diagnostic services, medication therapy, and the patterns of use of emergency and outpatient services in hospitals which differ in size, location, and ownership.[35]

The NHAMCS collects data from both hospital outpatient and emergency departments. An outpatient department is defined as a hospital facility where nonurgent ambulatory medical care is provided under the supervision of a physician. Outpatient clinics are included if ambulatory medical care is provided under the supervision of a physician and under the auspices of the hospital. Clinics where only ancillary services are provided or other settings in which physician services are not typically provided are not included.[36]

Emergency departments are sampled separately from outpatient departments. Statistics for each type of ambulatory care are calculated and published independently. Outpatient visits are the sum of both outpatient and emergency department visits.

As with the NIS data, we remove outpatient visits to government hospitals from the NHAMCS data set. The NIS includes emergency department patients who are admitted to the hospital, so we remove them from the NHAMCS to avoid double counting. While the number of outpatient visits is obtainable from the AHA Annual Survey and NHAMCS, neither of these sources provides cost or charge information.

CMS Statistical Supplement. The Medicare and Medicaid Statistical Supplement provides comprehensive annual data about Medicare, Medicaid, and other CMS programs. The supplement shows health expenditures for the entire US population, characteristics of the covered populations, use of services, and expenditures under these programs.[37] The supplement includes

---

33. The scope of the AHA data set is greater than that of the NHAMCS. The AHA collects data from 98 percent of community hospitals, making it the preferred source of outpatient data.

34. Hospital-based ambulatory surgery centers were first added to this study in 2009, and freestanding ambulatory surgery centers were added in 2010.

35. Centers for Disease Control, Ambulatory Health Care Data, about the Ambulatory Health Care Surveys, National Hospital Ambulatory Medical Care Survey; http://www.cdc.gov/nchs/ahcd/about_ahcd.htm.

36. Centers for Disease Control, 2010 NHAMCS Micro-Data File Documentation; ftp://ftp.cdc.gov/pub/Health_statistics/NCHs/Dataset_Documentation/NHAMCS/doc2010.pdf.

37. Centers for Medicare and Medicaid Services, Research, Statistics, Data and Systems, Medicare & Medicaid Statistical Supplement; https://www.cms.gov/Research-Statistics-Data-and-Systems/Statistics-Trends-and-Reports/MedicareMedicaidStatSupp/index.html.

a subsection for Hospital Outpatient Bills, Covered Charges, and Program Payments for various calendar years.[38]

Producer Price Index (PPI). Total revenue for each industry is deflated using the appropriate BLS PPI.[39] The PPIs for general and specialty hospitals define output as a bundle of services provided for the treatment of a medical condition, not as the individual services rendered such as x-rays, drugs, and medical supplies (Catron and Murphy 1996). The PPIs for both types of hospitals account for all services provided, including inpatient, outpatient, food services, and so forth, capturing the substitution effects of replacing costly inpatient treatments with more efficient outpatient procedures (Smith 2009). The general PPIs for each of the two types of hospitals measure actual payment to the hospital, not charges. Hospital bills are used to determine a price via the payments made by patients and third-party payers (Fixler and Ginsburg 2001).

BLS Industry Employment and Hours Data. Total annual hours are based primarily on data from the Current Employment Statistics (CES) survey, a monthly establishment survey conducted by BLS, and supplemented with data from the Current Population Survey (CPS), a monthly household survey conducted by the US Census Bureau for BLS. Employment and average weekly hours are measured separately for supervisory and nonsupervisory workers. The hours are treated as homogeneous and are directly aggregated. No adjustment was made to account for changes in labor composition.

Appendix B

Using the Medical Expenditure Panel Survey (MEPS) to Construct an Outpatient Index

The Medical Expenditure Panel Survey (MEPS) is an alternative data source that can be used to create an outpatient index in lieu of using CMS and NHAMCS data. This appendix will examine the MEPS and create an outpatient index using its data, while leaving the methodology unchanged from the original CMS and NHAMCS-based outpatient index.

Sponsored by the Agency for Healthcare Research and Quality (AHRQ), the MEPS is a series of nationally representative surveys of families and

---

38. Centers for Medicare and Medicaid Services, Research, Statistics, Data and Systems, Medicare & Medicaid Statistical Supplement, 2011 Edition, Chapter 10: Medicare Hospital Outpatient Services, Table 10.4—Hospital Outpatient Bills, Covered Charges, and Program Payments Under Medicare, by Selected Reasons for the Visit: Calendar Year 2010; https://www.cms.gov/Research-Statistics-Data-and-Systems/Statistics-Trends-and-Reports/MedicareMedicaidStatSupp/2011.html.

39. NAICS 6221 is deflated using PPI 622110622110 G, and NAICS 6223 is deflated using PPI 6223106223106 G.

individuals, medical providers, and employers. The MEPS provides data on health services, health care utilization, and health expenditures in the United States. The Household Component (HC) of the MEPS surveys approximately 15,000 households each year and collects detailed information for each person in the household on health service type, frequency of use, and health conditions, as well as data on health insurance. In the Medical Provider Component (MPC), a sample of medical providers are contacted to acquire data that household respondents may not be able to accurately supply, such as information on visit dates, diagnosis and procedure codes, charges, and payments. The MEPS data are available starting in 1996 and can be analyzed at either the person or event level and weights are provided to produce national estimates. The number of outpatient visits and expenditures are reported on an ICD-9-CM basis.

As with the outpatient measure used in the main body of this chapter, the American Hospital Association total outpatient visits for each year is used as the baseline for the MEPS outpatient index. Detailed ICD-9-CM visits from the MEPS are aggregated to the major disease category level and are used to disaggregate the quantity of total visits as reported by the AHA. The ICD-9-CM charge data from the MEPS is also aggregated to the major disease category level and combined with major disease category-level visits to create an outpatient index. The MEPS charge values and the proportions of MEPS visits for each major disease category to total MEPS visits are held constant from 1993 to 1996. The following equation is used to create the outpatient index based on MEPS data. Equation (B.1):

$$(B.1) \qquad \frac{Q_t}{Q_{t-1}} = \exp\left[\sum_{i=1}^{n} w_{i,t}\left(\ln\left(\frac{q_{i,t}}{q_{i,t-1}} \right) \right) \right],$$

where

Q_t / Q_{t-1} = the ratio of outpatient output in the current year (t) to the previous year ($t - 1$),

n = the number of major disease categories

$\ln(q_{i,t} / q_{i,t-1})$ = the natural logarithm of the ratio of the quantity of **outpatient visits** for major disease category i in the current year to the quantity in the previous year, and

$w_{i,t}$ = the average value share weight for major disease category i.

Critique of the MEPS

While the CMS and NHAMCS-based outpatient index relies upon visit and charge data from separate sources, the MEPS-based index uses a single source for this data. This provides a level of consistency not found in the original outpatient measure. In addition, while CMS data account for only Medicare and Medicaid populations, the MEPS does not focus on any subset of the US population as it is a nationally representative survey of the US

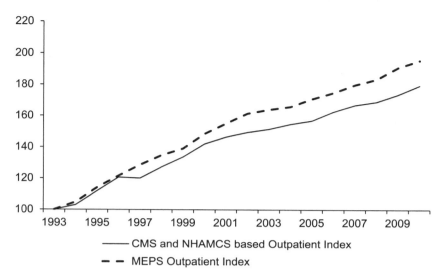

Fig. 5B.1   Index of outpatient services using MEPS 1993–2010

civilian noninstitutionalized population. Emergency room visit data from the MEPS are available; however, these figures have not been incorporated into this measure. Further research into this topic has the potential to augment the outpatient index.

The MEPS definition of an outpatient department encompasses not only outpatient centers within hospitals, but also those that are affiliated with hospitals.[40] The hospital-affiliated outpatient departments may cross NAICS industry borders, creating inconsistency with the labor input measure. Additionally, each MEPS outpatient visit has up to four condition codes that are sequenced in the data files in the order reported by the household respondent and not in order of importance or severity.[41] The lack of condition-specific charge data for respondents with multiple condition codes prevents accounting for multiple condition codes in the MEPS measure.

Results

The outpatient services index for community hospitals created with MEPS data shows positive growth for 1993–2010. As figure 5B.1 demonstrates, the

40. The AHRQ, MEPS, Medical Expenditure Panel Survey Household Component Main Study, Glossary, Outpatient Department; http://meps.ahrq.gov/survey_comp/hc_ques_glossary .shtml.
41. The AHRQ, MEPS, MEPS HC-135F: 2010 Outpatient Department Visits, 2.5.4 Conditions and Procedures Codes; http://meps.ahrq.gov/mepsweb/data_stats/download_data/pufs/ h135f/h135fdoc.shtml.

output index is closely aligned with the output index based on CMS charges and NHAMCS visits.

The positive trend of both outpatient measures shows that using either the MEPS data or the combination of CMS and NHAMCS data are both viable options. The choice of data source for the outpatient index thus depends on which survey is more reliable and how well it aligns with the AHA and BLS definitions of community hospitals.

Appendix C
Adjusting the Inpatient Index for Survival Rates

The NIS data set that is used to create the inpatient index includes information regarding whether the patient was discharged alive or dead. From this information, we can calculate survival rates for each year and each DRG. The survival rate is defined as the number of patients who were discharged alive divided by the total number of patients.

It has been suggested that incorporating the year-to-year change in survival rates into the output index may be an indirect way to measure the quality change in hospital treatments. For each DRG, yearly survival rates are calculated. The change in survival rate from year $t - 1$ to year t is then multiplied by the number of discharges in year t. In effect, the quantity of discharges for each year is adjusted upward for gains in the survival rate or downward for decreases in the survival rate.

The effects of this adjustment are surprisingly negligent. Figure 5C.1 shows both the survival-adjusted inpatient index and the unadjusted index. The two lines are virtually indistinguishable.

For most years and most DRGs, the change in survival rates is very small. There are also a significant number of DRGs where the survival rate remains unchanged or decreases. Table 5C.1 shows the ratio of survival rate changes by year.

In most (but not all) years, the number of DRGs where the survival rate increased outnumbered those where the survival rate decreased. However, the trend is not so overwhelming so as to actually affect the output index in a significant manner.

There are other possible aspects that could be included in creating a survival-adjusted inpatient measure. For example, the adjustment could be made only upon those DRGs that have a high rate of mortality in the first place ("high" being defined in any number of ways). The concept in this case is that some DRGs have inherently very low mortality rates. In those cases where patients do die, the hospital was likely not responsible, and thus any change in mortality rates for these DRGs are not indicative of hospital quality.

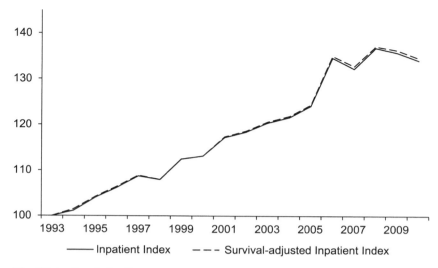

Fig. 5C.1   Survival-adjusted inpatient index

Table 5C.1 Percent of DRGs where the survival rate

Year	Increased (%)	Decreased (%)	Stayed the same (%)
1994	59	31	10
1995	54	34	12
1996	51	35	14
1997	52	35	14
1998	39	49	12
1999	38	50	12
2000	47	41	12
2001	47	40	12
2002	52	35	13
2003	50	35	15
2004	49	35	15
2005	50	35	15
2006	46	38	16
2007	52	32	16
2008	41	45	14
2009	51	34	15
2010	50	33	17

The question of how to link survival rates with actual hospital actions is crucial. It only makes sense to include a survival adjustment if the change in survival rates is directly attributable to the quality of hospital services. But mortality rates can be affected by numerous outside forces, such as public health trends, the patient's adherence to treatment, and random chance. A subtle factor that influences survival rates are choices made by gravely ill patients. If a patient chooses risky treatment in a hospital versus palliative care in a hospice, that influences the hospital's survival rate.

At this time, it is not practical to incorporate a survival adjustment into the inpatient index. However, as a potential method for incorporating quality data into a physical quantity output measure, this type of adjustment may be worth further study.

References

Aizcorbe, Ana, and Nicole Nestoriak. 2008. "The Importance of Pricing the Bundle of Treatments." Working Paper, Bureau of Economic Analysis, July.
———. 2011. "Changing Mix of Medical Care Services: Stylized Facts and Implications for Price Indexes." *Journal of Health Economics* 30 (3): 568–74.
Catron, Brian, and Bonnie Murphy. 1996. "Hospital Price Inflation: What Does the New PPI Tell Us?" *Monthly Labor Review* July:24–31.
Cylus, Jonathan, and Bridget Dickensheets. 2007. "Hospital Multifactor Productivity: A Presentation and Analysis of Two Methodologies." *Health Care Financing Review* 29 (2): 49–64.
Douglas, James. 2006. "Measurement of Public Sector Output and Productivity." New Zealand Treasury Policy Perspectives Paper, November.
Fixler, Dennis, and Mitchell Ginsburg. 2001. "Health Care Output and Prices in the Producer Price Index." *Medical Care Output and Productivity* January:221–70.
Henderson, Richard. 2012. "Industry Employment and Output Projections to 2020." *Monthly Labor Review* January:65–83.
Hospital Quality Valuation Team. 2008. "Proposal for Adjusting the General Hospital Producer Price Index for Quality Change." Paper presented at the National Bureau of Economic Research Summer Institute Conference on Research in Income and Wealth, July 14.
Lane, Sarah Gunther. 2001. *A Community Leader's Guide to Hospital Finance: Evaluating How a Hospital Gets and Spends its Money.* Boston: The Access Project.
National Research Council. 2010. "Accounting for Health and Health Care: Approaches to Measuring the Sources and Costs of their Improvement." Panel to Advance a Research Program on the Design of National Health Accounts, Committee on National Statistics.
Rosen, Allison B., and David M. Cutler. 2007. "Measuring Medical Care Productivity: A Proposal for US National Health Accounts." *Survey of Current Business* June:54–88.
Smith, Shelly. 2009. "A New Approach to Price Measures for Health Care." *Survey of Current Business* February:17–20.
Stranges, Elizabeth, C. Allison Russo, and Bernard Friedman. 2009. "Procedures with the Most Rapidly Increasing Hospital Costs, 2004–2007." HCUP Statistical Brief no. 82, Healthcare Cost and Utilization Project, December.
Statistics New Zealand. 2013. "Education and Health Industry Productivity 1996–2011." http://www.stats.govt.nz/.
Triplett, Jack. 2012. "Health System Productivity." *Oxford Handbook of Health Economics*, edited by Sherry Glied and Peter C. Smith. DOI: 10.1093/oxfordhb/9780199238828.013.0030.

6

Attribution of Health Care Costs to Diseases
Does the Method Matter?

Allison B. Rosen, Ana Aizcorbe, Tina Highfill,
Michael E. Chernew, Eli Liebman, Kaushik Ghosh,
and David M. Cutler

While health care cost growth in the United States has slowed in the past few years (Hartman et al. 2015), health costs are projected to grow faster than the economy over the next decade (Cutler and Sahni 2013; Sisko et al. 2014; Keehan et al. 2015) and are one of the biggest fiscal challenges to the nation. As such, policymakers and analysts regularly try to better understand the value of this spending, so as to target cost containment efforts to curb excess—rather than essential—spending.

Unfortunately, there is often a mismatch between the data that are available and what policymakers need. Current National Health Expenditure Accounts measure medical spending at the level of the payers (Medicare, Medicaid, private insurance, etc.) and recipient of funds (hospital, physicians' office, pharmaceutical company, etc.). However, measuring the value of medical spending requires relating expenditures to the health outcomes

Allison B. Rosen is an associate professor in the Division of Biostatistics and Health Services Research, Department of Quantitative Health Sciences, at the University of Massachusetts Medical School and a faculty research fellow of the National Bureau of Economic Research. Ana Aizcorbe is a senior research economist at the Bureau of Economic Analysis. Tina Highfill is an economist at the Bureau of Economic Analysis. Michael E. Chernew is the Leonard D. Schaeffer Professor of Health Care Policy and the director of the Healthcare Markets and Regulation (HMR) Lab in the Department of Health Care Policy at Harvard Medical School and a research associate of the National Bureau of Economic Research. Eli Liebman is an economist at the Bureau of Economic Analysis. Kaushik Ghosh is a research specialist at the National Bureau of Economic Research. David M. Cutler is the Otto Eckstein Professor of Applied Economics and Harvard College Professor at Harvard University and a research associate of the National Bureau of Economic Research.

We are grateful to Arlene Ash for comments, and to the National Institute of Aging (P01 AG031098 and R37AG047312) and the National Center for Research Resources (UL1 RR000161) for research support. For acknowledgments, sources of research support, and disclosure of the authors' material financial relationships, if any, please see http://www.nber.org/chapters/c13110.ack.

they produce. This is most readily done at the disease level. For example, the value of spending more on physicians may be reflected in outcomes of hospitalization, or in hospitalizations avoided. This will only be picked up by looking at treatment for particular conditions. Thus, accurate cost-of-illness (COI) studies that allocate national health expenditures to a comprehensive set of diseases are an essential part of health policy.

Despite the importance of COI studies for health policy, no methodological standards for such studies exist and, to date, no side-by-side comparisons of estimates formed using different methods have been published. We address this gap in this chapter.

Cost-of-illness studies come in two broad flavors. Most COI studies are *disease based*, working from the bottom up to allocate costs to a single or limited number of diseases; absent constraints on collective spending, substantial double counting may—and often does—result (Koopmanschap 1998; Bloom et al. 2001; Rosen and Cutler 2009). In contrast, *general* COI studies start with a population's total health care spending (often total health sector spending) and allocate some fraction of the sector's expenditures to each disease in a comprehensive, mutually exclusive set (Rosen and Cutler 2007, 2009). By constraining spending to national totals and applying consistent methods across diseases, *general* COI estimates are conceptually more meaningful for policy purposes and are, therefore, the focus of ongoing federal efforts to understand the diseases driving heath care cost growth (Aizcorbe, Retus, and Smith 2008; Aizcorbe and Nestoriak 2011; Aizcorbe, Liebman, Cutler, et al. 2012; Aizcorbe, Liebman, Pack, et al. 2012; Aizcorbe 2013; Bradley et al. 2010; Bradley 2013; Dunn et al. 2013; Dunn, Shapiro, and Liebman 2013; Dunn, Liebman, and Shapiro 2014; Dunn, Rittmueller, and Whitmire 2015; National Research Council 2005, 2008, 2010; Song et al. 2009). This chapter focuses on the methods used to obtain these *general* COI estimates.

General COI studies date back to the 1960s (Scitovsky 1964, 1967; Rice 1967; Rice and Horowitz 1967) and have increased in volume over time (see, e.g., Cooper and Rice 1976; Berk, Paringer, and Mushkin 1978; Rice, Hodgson, and Kopstein 1985; Hoffman, Rice, and Sung 1996; Hodgson and Cohen 1999; Druss et al. 2001, 2002; Thorpe, Florence, and Joski 2004; Thorpe et al. 2004, 2005; Thorpe and Howard 2006; Thorpe, Howard, and Galactionova 2007; Thorpe, Ogden, and Galactionova 2010; Thorpe 2013; Roehrig et al. 2009; Roehrig and Rousseau 2011; Starr, Dominiak, and Aizcorbe 2014). As these general COI studies have proliferated, so have the methods used to generate their cost estimates.

Historically, most general COI studies have allocated claims to particular diseases at the *encounter level*, assigning spending based on the diagnoses coded on each encounter's claim (Rosen and Cutler 2009; National Research Council 2010). The ease with which costs are attributed to diseases is a major advantage of this approach—it is essentially an accounting exercise.

However, encounter-level costing is fairly limited in its capacity to handle comorbidities and downstream complications. If a person with diabetes and hypertension is prescribed an ACE inhibitor (which can treat either condition), to which disease should the visit's costs and the medication cost be attributed? If this patient has a heart attack several years later, is the subsequent spending a result of the diabetes, the hypertension, or the heart attack? Another disadvantage of encounter-level costing is that it cannot allocate spending for which there are no valid claims or diagnosis codes. How will the ACE inhibitor cost get allocated if the pharmacy claim has no diagnosis—and most pharmacy claims do not? Perhaps the biggest disadvantage of encounter-level cost-of-illness estimates is that they are not readily compared to health outcomes, which are measured at the *person level*.

As such, interest has increased in using econometric models to recast cost-of-illness estimates at the *person level*. This approach uses regression analysis to allocate an individual's total annual spending to their complete set of medical conditions (as indicated on their medical claims from that year). As such, person-level costing may produce more valid estimates in patients with multiple chronic diseases, as expenditures for comorbidities and complications are better captured. Person-level costing also allows spending for which there are no valid claims or diagnosis codes to be allocated. But, person-level analysis may be sensitive to choosing appropriate time windows in measuring disease prevalence (current year vs. previous year), and subject to bias if unobservables (e.g., socioeconomic status, or SES) are correlated with disease and spending.

However, these advantages come at the cost of added complexity. There is no single-best econometric approach for modeling health care costs, leaving the analyst to test and decide between different model specifications. Further, the regression assumes that comorbidities have an independent effect on spending unless appropriate interaction terms are included in the models. Identifying the appropriate groups of co-occurring diseases is an empirical issue that requires clinical expertise. Despite these limitations, person-level costing is quite appealing conceptually, as it allows for more meaningful comparisons between health care spending and health outcomes (such as mortality and quality of life), thereby providing the critical link between spending and health needed to more systematically measure value.

While both encounter- and person-level COI allocation methods are increasing in use, there have been no side-by-side comparisons of estimates from the different approaches to date. In this chapter, we apply three different allocation methods—two encounter-level approaches common in the literature and a person-level approach—to allocate a population's annual medical expenditures to a common comprehensive set of diseases, and to investigate the impact of method choice on the mix of spending across diseases and, for individual diseases, the treated prevalence, cost per case, and overall disease spending.

Our data are from the 2006 MarketScan commercial claims and encounters database. We have randomly selected 2.3 million individuals under the age of sixty-five with commercial insurance and prescription drug coverage in 2006. Using these data, we attribute annual spending to diseases using three different COI allocation approaches used in the literature: (a) the *primary-encounter* approach identifies all health care encounters and attributes spending to the principal diagnosis coded on the corresponding claim, (b) the *all-encounter* approach assigns each encounter's spending to a combination of all (not just the principal) diagnoses coded on the corresponding claim, and (c) the *person* approach identifies all of a person's health conditions and, using regression analysis, allocates total spending to the diseases they experienced.

We compare outputs of the three approaches on several criteria, including the portion of spending allocated, the mix of spending across diseases, and, for individual diseases, treated disease prevalence, cost per case, and overall disease spending. For each approach, we explore in more detail the ten conditions contributing the most to total spending.

The three approaches vary both in how much and how spending was allocated. The two encounter approaches allocate 77.7 percent of overall spending to diseases, while the person approach allocated 94.9 percent of spending to diseases. Further, the mix of spending across diseases differs substantially by method. Spending was concentrated in a small number of conditions; the ten most expensive diseases accounted for 40.4 percent of total spending with the person approach and 18.1 percent and 18.3 percent of spending with the principal-diagnosis and all-diagnoses-encounter approaches, respectively. These differences are sufficiently big that they warrant very careful attention to the choice of method in any cost allocation study.

This chapter is structured as follows. Section 6.1 provides a review of the literature on different techniques used in measuring health care spending. In section 6.2, we discuss the different methodologies used in this study. In section 6.3, we explain our results. Section 6.4 discusses our findings and concludes.

6.1   Literature Review

In this section, we describe the methods that have been used to allocate total spending to diseases. We do so in parts.

6.1.1   Primary-Encounter Approach

The cost of illness studies dates back to the sixties. A seminal study by Rice (1967) presented single-year estimates of health expenditures by type of disease for the year 1963. This study categorized diseases using International Classification of Diseases, Adapted (ICDA). The total National Health expenditure in 1963 was estimated to be around $22.5 billion. The diseases with highest spending were: the diseases of the digestive system (18.5 percent); mental, psychoneurotic and personality disorders (10.7 percent); and the diseases of the circulatory system (10.1 percent).

This study and the subsequent "cost-of-illness" literature in the 1960s, 1970s, and 1980s measured the total costs of illness in two dimensions: direct cost—which includes spending for different services including hospital, nursing home, physicians, medical professional services, drugs, medical supplies, research, training, and other nonpersonal—and indirect costs on morbidity and mortality, which account for economic losses arising from illness, disability, and death. Our focus in this chapter is on direct costs.

Cooper and Rice (1976) estimated that in 1972, the total cost of illness was $188 billion, out of which $75 billion was direct cost, and for indirect cost $42 billion for morbidity and $71 billion for mortality. Berk, Paringer, and Mushkin (1978) estimated that the direct and indirect cost continued to increase, reaching $264 billion dollars in 1975, with the diseases of digestive system, the diseases of circulatory system, and mental disorders being the most expensive disease categories. Rice, Hodgson, and Kopstein (1985) estimated the total economic cost of illness were $455 billion in 1980. Other major studies in the 1970s and 1980s include Scitovsky (1985) and Hoffman, Rice, and Sung (1996).

But the biggest challenge in the 1960s and 1970s in measuring the cost of illness by disease was the lack of comprehensive and quality data on medical diagnoses and detailed spending breakdowns. Also, sophisticated econometric and statistical methods commonly used now to measure health care spending were not readily available. Most studies attempting to measure disease-based health care spending relied on the principal diagnosis on medical claims to assign spending to disease categories. These estimates were often overestimated or underestimated due to the presence of comorbid conditions. Starting in the mid- to late 1990s, as more detailed data became available, researchers have been able to disaggregate spending more comprehensively.

One such study using the newer data sets in the late 1990s was by Hodgson and Cohen (1999). Hodgson and Cohen (1999) allocated 87 percent of personal health care expenditures as reported by the former Health Care Financing Administration (now the Centers for Medicare and Medicaid Services [CMS]) by age, sex, diagnosis, and health-service type using additional data from sources such as the National Medical Expenditure Survey. The diseases were classified using International Classification of Diseases, Ninth Revision (ICD-9) codes. Further disaggregation included home health care and hospital care by type of hospital. The diseases of the circulatory system (including, for example, heart disease and hypertension) were the most expensive conditions, accounting for 17 percent of total personal health care expenditure. The diseases of the digestive system were the second most expensive conditions, totaling 11 percent. The other major categories were injuries and poisoning, nervous system and sense organ diseases, and respiratory diseases. The top six categories contributed to 66 percent of Personal Health Care spending. Table 6.1 gives a detailed review of the literature on studies that used a primary-encounter approach.

Table 6.1　　Major cost of illness studies: Primary encounter (*principal diagnosis*) method

Study	Study period	Medical conditions/behavioral factors	Findings
Scitovsky (1967)	1951–1965	Otitis media in children, fracture of the forearm, acute cystitis, treated hypertension, pneumonia proved by x-ray, duodenal ulcer, coronary occlusion, maternity care, acute appendicitis, and cancer of the breast.	From 1951–52 to 1964–65, the costs of treatment of diseases covered by this study increased more than the US Bureau of Labor Statistics medical care price index.
Rice (1967)	1963	Categorized according to the International Classification of Diseases, Adapted (ICDA).	Total National Health expenditure in 1963 was estimated to be $22.5 billion. Out of that: neoplasm (5.7 percent), mental, psychoneurotic and personality disorders (10.7 percent), diseases of nervous and sense organs (6.3 percent), diseases of circulatory system (10.1 percent), diseases of respiratory system (7 percent), diseases of digestive system(18.5 percent), diseases of bones and organs of movement (7.6 percent), and "all others" (28 percent). The diseases of digestive system were the biggest contributor.
Cooper and Rice (1976)	1972	Classified by International Classification of Diseases, Ninth Revision (ICD-9) codes.	The estimated total cost of illness in 1972 was $188 billion, $75 billion for direct costs. The top three were: the diseases of digestive system ($11 billion), diseases of circulatory system ($10.9 billion), and mental disorders ($7 billion). Also, $42 billion for morbidity and $71 billion for mortality. The diseases of circulatory system were the most costly, representing about 20 percent of all costs of illness.
Berk, Paringer, and Mushkin (1978)	1975	Classified by International Classification of Diseases, Ninth Revision (ICD-9) codes.	Estimation of the direct and indirect costs of illness showed that the upward trend into total costs continued, reaching $264 billion in 1975. The direct cost was $118.5 billion and indirect cost was $145.8 billion—$57.8 billion on morbidity and $87.9 billion on mortality. In direct cost, the top three were the diseases of circulatory system ($16 billion), diseases of digestive system ($14 billion), and mental disorders ($9.4 billion).
Rice, Hodgson, and Kopstein (1985)	1980	Classified by International Classification of Diseases, Ninth Revision (ICD-9) codes.	In 1980, the estimated total economic cost of illness was $455 billion: $211 billion for direct costs, $68 billion for morbidity, and $176 billion for mortality. Diseases of the circulatory system and injuries and poisonings were the most expensive. There were variations in the diagnostic distributions among the three types of costs and by age and sex. In direct cost, the top three were the diseases of circulatory system ($32.4 billion), diseases of digestive system ($30.9 billion), and mental disorders ($19.8 billion).

Scitovsky (1985)	1971 and 1981	Otitis media, forearm fractures, pneumonia, duodenal ulcer, complete physical examination, appendicitis, maternity care, myocardial infarction, breast cancer.	The earlier study by the author, covering the periods 1951–1964 and 1964–1971, showed that cost increased due to change in relatively low-cost ancillary services, such as laboratory tests and x-rays ("little-ticket" technologies). This study showed that in the period 1971–1981, the use of these technologies barely changed, but the use of a number of new and expensive technologies ("big-ticket" technologies) came into use, which raised health care costs significantly.
Hoffman, Rice, and Sung (1996)	1987	Classified by International Classification of Diseases, Ninth Revision (ICD-9) codes.	The study estimated about 90 million Americans in 1987 were living with chronic conditions; 39 million of whom were living with more than one chronic condition. In the noninstitutionalized population, over 45 percent had one or more chronic conditions. The direct health care costs account for 75 percent of the US health care expenditures. For people with chronic conditions, total costs projected to 1990 amounted to $659 billion—$425 billion in direct health care costs and $234 billion in indirect costs.
Hodgson and Cohen (1999)	1995	Classified by International Classification of Diseases, Ninth Revision (ICD-9) codes.	This comprehensive study estimated that the diseases of the circulatory system were the most expensive category, costing $127.8 billion and accounting for 17 percent of all personal health care expenditure (PHCE). Diseases of the digestive system cost $86.7 billion, accounting for 11 percent of aggregate PHCE. The other six most costly disease categories in descending order were mental disorders ($71.4 billion and 9 percent), injuries and poisonings ($69.0 billion and 8 percent), nervous system and sense organ diseases ($63.3 billion and 8 percent), and respiratory diseases ($59.3 billion and 8 percent). Together, these six disease groups accounted for almost 66 percent of all PHCE. Neoplasm, including all cancers, represents only about 5 percent of total PHCE.

6.1.2   All-Encounter Approach

Beginning early in the first decade of the twenty-first century, there has been a trend in identifying the sources of changes in health care spending, focusing on medical conditions that make up a disproportionate amount of spending on health care and spending growth (e.g., see Druss et al. 2001, 2002; Thorpe, Florence, and Joski 2004; Thorpe et al. 2004; Roehrig et al. 2009; Roehrig and Rousseau 2011). The studies by Thorpe and Roehrig were especially important as they looked at all diseases and their estimates were based on "all encounters" and not just the principal diagnosis coded on claims (i.e., "primary encounter").

Thorpe, Florence, and Joski (2004) used ICD-9 codes (truncated to three digits before inclusion in public-use national survey data sets) and subsequently coded them to 259 clinically relevant medical condition groupings using the Clinical Classification Software (CCS) developed by the US Department of Health and Human Services (HHS). The authors started by pointing out that by using only the principal diagnosis, spending for some conditions will be understated. For example, diseases like hypertension, hyperlipidemia, and diabetes will likely be underestimated using only the primary diagnosis as they are major comorbid conditions for acute events like heart attack, stroke, and renal failure.

To avoid such biases, Thorpe, Florence, and Joski (2004) proposed an estimation technique that has maximum (upper) and minimum (lower) bounds on cost estimates, and also proposed a novel estimation technique called "best guess." Their upper-bound estimate attributed total spending to *each* health care event for which a given condition is listed. Since many medical conditions (up to fourteen) can be reported for each event, this will obviously include some double counting. As a lower bound, they summed spending from each medical event for which only a single condition is reported. Although the total spending calculated from this approach obviously does not account for all spending associated with a given condition, it does not include any double counting.

Finally, they developed a "best-guess" estimate of condition-attributable spending using the following approach. They tabulated spending per event for those reporting a single medical condition. They then tabulated spending per event for those reporting two or more medical conditions associated with the event. They calculated the ratio of these two spending totals from single-diagnosis claims and used this to determine how much of the spending for claims with multiple conditions should be attributed to each individual condition.

Roehrig et al. (2009), in a similar and more comprehensive effort, provided health expenditure estimates from the National Health Expenditure Accounts (NHEA) distributed across medical conditions. The study allocated spending to medical conditions using the nationally representative

Medical Expenditure Panel Survey (MEPS) for the community population from 1996 to 2005. In addition, it provides guidance in identifying data and methods that cover the full range of expenditures in the National Health Expenditure Accounts (NHEA). Roehrig and colleagues found that the diseases of the circulatory system had the highest spending, accounting for 17 percent of total spending in 2005.

Roehrig and Rousseau (2011) found that between 1996 and 2006, 75 percent of the increase in real per capita health care spending was attributable to growth in cost per case, while treated disease prevalence accounted for 25 percent of spending growth. Table 6.2 gives more detail on studies using an "all-encounter" approach to attribute health care costs to diseases.

Although the "best-guess" approach addresses many of the concerns of the "primary-encounter" method, it still has some limitations. First, it lacks a solid statistical or econometric framework. Second, it is heavily dependent on finding claims with a single diagnosis for all medical conditions. At times, it is hard to satisfy this criterion for major claims like hospital visits and nursing home stays (which are often associated with multiple comorbid conditions). Finally, it is very difficult to assign prescription dollars to a medical condition, as prescription drugs claims do not include diagnosis codes. Next, we discuss a variant of encounter-based cost, referred to as an episode-based approach, which can address these issues and has been getting more popular in recent studies.

6.1.3   Episode-Based Approach

Increasingly, analysts are estimating disease costs using episode groupers—software programs with algorithms that organize claims from different sources (hospitals, nursing homes, physicians, hospital outpatient, home health, hospice, durable medical equipment and other medical services) for a given period of time (usually six months to a year) into distinct episodes of care that are clinically meaningful. Episodes are natural to examine because they group related claims regardless of where the service was provided; if a person is hospitalized for heart attack and stayed at a nursing home and then seen in follow-up at a physician's office, all costs are included in the episode of heart attack care.

The most recent research at the Bureau of Economic Analysis (Dunn et al. 2013; Dunn, Shapiro, and Liebman 2013; Dunn, Liebman, and Shapiro 2014; Dunn et al. 2014; Dunn, Rittmueller, and Whitmire 2015; Aizcorbe, Retus, and Smith 2008; Aizcorbe and Nestoriak 2011; Aizcorbe et al. 2011; Aizcorbe, Liebman, Cutler, et al. 2012; Aizcorbe, Liebman, Pack, et al. 2012; Aizcorbe 2013) uses this alternative method for measuring spending by disease. These so-called episode groupers use computer algorithms that sift through medical claims data and allocate spending to over 500 types of distinct disease episodes. There are a few groupers available in the market. One popular grouper is Optum Symmetry Episode Treatment Group (ETG). It is

Table 6.2   **Major cost of illness studies: All-encounter or proportional method**

Study	Study period	Medical conditional/behavioral factors	Findings
Druss et al. (2001)	1996	Mood disorders (depressive and manic depressive disorders), diabetes, heart disease, hypertension, and asthma.	Direct per capita health costs for treatment of condition (mean per capita costs of health services that a person identified as resulting from the specific condition) was mood disorder ($1,122), diabetes ($1,097), heart disease ($6,463), hypertension ($569), and asthma ($663). Mean per capita health costs for persons with condition (all costs borne by persons with the particular condition, including both direct costs and costs for comorbid conditions): mood disorder ($4,328), diabetes($5,646), heart disease ($10,823), hypertension($4,073), and asthma ($2,779). Estimated total health costs (billions) for persons with condition: mood disorder ($54.9), diabetes ($54.2), heart disease ($38.5), hypertension ($110.3), and asthma ($27.7).
Druss et al. (2002)	1996	Classified diseases based on slightly modified Global Burden of Disease categories.	Spending for the fifteen highest-cost conditions accounted for 44.2 percent of total US health care spending in 1996. The top fifteen conditions in billions of dollars were: ischemic heart disease ($21.5), motor vehicle accidents ($21.2), acute respiratory infection ($17.9), arthropathies ($15.9), hypertension ($14.8), back problems ($12.2), mood disorders ($10.2), diabetes ($10.1), cerebrovascular disease ($8.3), cardiac dysrythmias ($7.2), peripheral vascular disorders ($6.8), COPD ($6.4), asthma ($5.7), congestive heart failure ($5.2), and respiratory malignancies ($5.0).
Thorpe, Florence, and Joski (2004)	1987 and 2000	The ICD-9 codes are collapsed to three-digit codes and subsequently coded into 259 clinically relevant medical conditions using the Clinical Classification System (CCS) developed by the US Department of Health and Human Services (HHS).	Estimates included upper bound, lower bound, and best guess estimates . The top fifteen conditions accounted for 56 percent spending growth, with a lower bound of 43 percent and upper bound of 61 percent. The top fifteen conditions in descending order were heart disease (8.06 percent), pulmonary disease (5.63 percent), mental disorders (7.40 percent), cancer (5.36 percent), hypertension (4.24 percent), trauma (4.64 percent), cerebrovascular disease (3.52 percent), arthritis (3.27 percent), diabetes (2.37 percent), back problems (2.99 percent), skin disorders (2.26 percent), pneumonia (2.26 percent), infectious disease (1.35 percent), endocrine disease (1.18 percent), and kidney disease (1.03 percent).

Study	Period	Methods	Findings
Thorpe et al. (2004)	1987–2001	The ICD-9 codes were collapsed to three-digit codes and subsequently coded into 259 clinically relevant medical conditions using the Clinical Classification System (CCS) developed by the US Department of Health and Human Services (HHS).	Obesity-attributable health care spending increased between 1987 and 2001. Increases in obesity prevalence alone account for about one-tenth of the growth in health spending. The study estimated that the increases in the share of and spending on obese individuals relative to individuals of normal weight account for one-third of the rise in inflation-adjusted per capita spending between 1987 and 2001. Out of that: spending for diabetes, 38 percent; spending for hyperlipidemia, 22 percent; and spending for heart disease, 41 percent.
Roehrig et al. (2009)	1996–2005	ICD-9 codes mapped into CCS categories. Additional categories for prevention/exams (general checkups, well-child visits, immunizations, eye exams, and disease-specific screening procedures) and dental care were added.	This study provided health expenditures from the National Health Expenditure Accounts (NHEA) distributed across medical conditions. It provided annual estimates from 1996 to 2005 for about thirty or so medical conditions combined into thirteen all-inclusive diagnostic categories. Circulatory system spending was highest, accounting for 17 percent of spending in 2005. The most costly conditions were mental disorders and heart conditions. Spending growth rates were lowest for lung cancer, chronic obstructive pulmonary disease, pneumonia, coronary heart disease, and stroke. The slow growth in these diseases was attributed to benefits of preventive care.
Roehrig and Rousseau (2011)	1996 and 2006	The distribution of spending by condition was made using the Clinical Classification System software—developed by the Agency for Healthcare Research and Quality (AHRQ)—which maps detailed diseases onto an all-inclusive set of 260 medical conditions.	The authors examined treated prevalence, clinical prevalence—the number of people with a given disease, treated or not—and cost per case across all medical conditions between 1996 and 2006. Over this period, 75 percent of the increase in real per capita health spending was attributable to growth in cost per case, while treated prevalence accounted for about 25 percent of spending growth.

an episode grouper for medical and pharmacy claims. It provides a condition classification methodology that combines related services into medically relevant and distinct units describing complete and severity-adjusted episodes of care and associated costs. Table 6.3 gives a detailed account of the studies by the US Bureau of Economic Analysis (BEA) that assign spending to medical conditions using the ETG grouper.

Episode-based cost estimates have their own challenges. Identifying the start and end points of an episode of treatment is not straightforward, and it often takes many iterations to identify the optimum window. Comorbidities and their joint costs pose challenges as well, just as with the encounter approach. Other limitations include lack of clear guidelines on how to handle episodes related to the care of chronic diseases (should the episode be one year or two years?), handling complications of treatment, and a few medical treatments that clearly do not fall under a specific episode of care (screenings, etc.).

Finally, while a number of different commercial episode groupers are already widely in use, they have received little scientific evaluation to date (McGlynn 2008), and the small but growing body of research by CMS and others points to real differences in the output of different vendors' groupers (MaCurdy et al. 2008; MaCurdy, Kerwin, and Theobald 2009; Rosen et al. 2012).

6.1.4   Person-Based Approach

The final approach to cost estimation regresses a person's total annual health care spending on indicators for the set of medical conditions that person had during the calendar year. The results of this estimation can then be used to infer the cost of different conditions.

The most common estimation method is ordinary least square (OLS). The dependent variable in these regressions is total health care spending for each person. The independent variables usually are dummy variables indicating the presence (or absence) of various medical conditions. Other control variables generally include age, sex, gender, race, and so forth. The coefficients on disease dummy variables are the ones of interest. The regression coefficient on a disease dummy variable is the incremental additional cost of that condition, controlling for the other conditions the person has.

Because of the regression framework, a person-based approach is likely to produce more reliable estimates for patients with multiple chronic conditions, as it better accounts for spending related to comorbidities and complications. Further, prescription drug spending is naturally included, given that costs are not assigned to the specific condition on that claim.

That said, a regression specification may be sensitive to how comorbidities are entered. A standard linear regression may not be right since it imposes additivity of joint conditions. If having one condition increases (or decreases) the costs of another, an adjustment is needed to ensure that condition-specific spending does not sum to more (or less) than the total. Another empirical issue is what interaction terms to include. For the most

Table 6.3   **Major cost of illness studies: Episode grouper method**

Study	Study period	Medical conditions/behavioral factors	Findings
Dunn et al. (2013)	2003 to 2007	Classified disease spending using a commercial algorithm called a grouper; specifically, the authors use the ETG grouper from Symmetry. The ETG grouper allocates each record into one of over 500 disease groups called "episode treatment groups" (ETGs).	Service Price Index (SPI) grew 0.7 percentage points faster than the preferred MCE (Medical Care Expenditure) index.
Aizcorbe, Liebman, Pack, et al. (2012)	2005	All conditions.	Both total spending and the distribution of annual per-person spending differed across the two data sources, with MEPS estimates 10 percent lower on average than estimates from MarketScan. These differences appeared to be a function of both.
Dunn et al. (2014)	2003 to 2007	Classified disease spending using a commercial algorithm called a grouper; specifically, the authors use the ETG grouper from Symmetry. The ETG grouper allocates each record into one of over 500 disease groups called "episode treatment groups" (ETGs).	The goal of this paper was to better obtain nationally representative estimates of the various components of expenditure growth. Using a multitude of weighting strategies, including weighted and unweighted estimates, the authors found similar qualitative results with higher prevalence and increases in medical care service prices being the key drivers of spending growth.
Dunn, Rittmueller, and Whitmire (2015)	2015	In this study, the MEPS account was constructed using data from the MEPS. Each encounter in the data includes expenditure information and a primary ICD-9 diagnosis code. Each diagnosis code was mapped into one of 263 possible CCS categories. In MarketScan data, the authors apply a person-based approach to allocate expenditures across CCS disease categories (Dunn et al. 2014)	The main focus of this study was creation of "The Blended Account" to comprehensive account spending by medical conditions. The Blended Account was to substitute pieces of the Medical Expenditure Panel Survey for certain populations (with inadequate or no data) with corresponding big data. The two data sets that they incorporate into the blended account are the Medicare and MarketScan data. The results show significant improvement in measurements adding this big data.

part, clinical expertise is needed to identify the appropriate group(s) of co-occurring diseases, which may represent a limitation for policy purposes. Table 6.4 reviews some of the literature that used such a regression approach. Importantly, as yet, no published studies have used a regression approach to allocate health care spending to a *comprehensive* set of conditions; rather, published studies focus on one or a limited number of conditions of interest.

6.1.5 Estimation Techniques in the Person-Based Approach

Medical spending data has very specific characteristics that create challenges in efficiently estimating health care spending using the regression approach. A few common data issues are heteroscedasticity, heavy tails, and zero spenders. Several studies have proposed more efficient estimation techniques to handle these data problems (Manning 1998; Manning and Mullahy 2001; Manning, Basu, and Mullahy 2005; Buntin and Zaslavsky 2004; Basu and Manning 2009).

Manning (1998) showed that the possibility of heteroscedasticity raises issues about the efficiency of the ordinary least squares estimates. In such cases, they recommended using generalized linear squares estimators to obtain efficient estimates of the coefficients and to further make accurate inference statistics for the standard error of such coefficients. Also, in case of log transformed or any other transformed dependent variable, the authors suggest that the researchers need to check if the error term is heteroscedastic across treatment groups or depends on some combination of independent variables. They also recommend that if the error terms is heteroscedastic, then the researchers should try to determine the form of the heteroscedasticity and use that information to obtain an unbiased estimate of the retransformation factor in order to estimate the overall expected level of spending to the independent variables (e.g., medical condition dummies).

Manning and Mullahy (2001) examined how well the alternative estimators behave econometrically in terms of estimation bias and accuracy when the health spending data are skewed or have other common health expenditure data problems (zero spenders, heteroscedasticity, heavy tails, etc.). They could not clearly identify any single alternative that best suits all conditions examined. They present a simple algorithm for choosing among the alternative estimators. Selecting the right estimator is important for most accurate estimation. Their recommendation is to begin with both the raw-scale and log-scale residuals from one of the consistent generalized liner model (GLM) estimators.

Manning, Basu, and Mullahy (2005) found that there are two broad classes of models that can be commonly used to address the econometric problems caused by skewness in the health spending data. In the person-level analysis, often times researchers encounter common data issues like zero spenders, heteroscedasticity, and heavy tails. The two common solutions proposed by the authors to deal with such data problem are: (a) transformation to deal with skewness (e.g., ordinary least square [OLS] on ln[spending]), and

Table 6.4 Major cost of illness studies: Person-based allocations

Study	Study period	Medical conditions/ behavioral factors	Method	Findings
Sturm (2002)	1997–1998	Smoking, drinking, obesity	Regression approach	Regression analysis showed that obese adults incurred annual medical expenditures that were $395 (36 percent) higher than those of normal weight incur.
Finkelstein, Fiebelkorn, and Wang (2003)	1996–1998	Overweight and obesity	Regression approach	Used regression approach and national data in 1998 to calculate aggregate overweight- and obesity-attributable medical spending for the United States and by select payers. Expenditures for this group accounted for 9.1 percent of total annual medical expenditures. Medicare and Medicaid paid about 50 percent of these costs.
Finkelstein et al. (2005)	1998 and 1999	Fall-related injuries	The case-control design using regression and case-crossover approach.	On average, the estimates of the costs of fall injuries from the case-control design were between 6 percent and 17 percent greater than those from the case-crossover approach.
Trogdon, Finkelstein, and Hoerger (2008)	2000–2003	Other MH/SA, hypertension, diabetes, arthritis, dyslipidemia, heart disease, asthma, skin disorders, depression, and HIV	Per-person expenditures (generalized linear model), attributable fraction (percent) generalized linear model	The authors stated that "incremental effects of conditions on expenditures, expressed as a fraction of total expenditures, cannot generally be interpreted as shares. When the presence of one condition increases treatment costs for another condition, summing condition-specific shares leads to double-counting of expenditures. Condition-specific shares generated from multiplicative models should not be summed." The authors provide an algorithm that allows estimates based on these models to be interpreted as shares and summed across conditions.
Honeycutt et al. (2009)	1998–2003	Diabetes	Regression-based approach, attributable fraction approach	The RB approach produced higher estimates of diabetes-attributable medical spending ($52.9 billion in 2004 dollars) than the AF approach ($37.1 billion in 2004 dollars).

(b) different weighting approaches based on exponential conditional models (ECM) and generalized linear model (GLM) approaches. In this paper, they discuss these two classes of models using the three-parameter generalized gamma (GGM) distribution, which includes OLS with a normal error, OLS for the log-normal, the standard gamma and exponential with log link, and the Weibull. The GGM also provides a potentially more robust alternative estimator to the standard alternatives.

Buntin and Zaslavsky (2004) compare the performance of eight alternative estimators, including OLS and GLM estimators and one- and two-part models, in predicting Medicare costs. They found that four of the alternatives produce very similar results in practice. They then suggest an efficient method for researchers to use when selecting estimators of health care costs. They recommended that researchers considering alternative models where the probability of use per se is not of interest would do well to start with the one-part GLM models.

Basu and Manning (2009) find that zero spenders and skewed positive expenditure data can be best handled by one-part or two-part generalized linear model (GLM) with a gamma distribution and a log link. In the two-part model, they use a logit model to predict the probability of having any medical spending and then use a GLM model with a gamma distribution and a log link to estimate the level of expenditures, given positive spending. Table 6.5 gives a detailed review of the literature on studies addressing different techniques to estimate health care spending under a regression framework.

6.2   Methods

In the United States, most people (54 percent) were covered by a health insurance plan related to employment for some or all of 2006 (State Health Facts Online, The Henry J. Kaiser Family Foundation). About 26 percent were covered by government health programs, including Medicare, Medicaid, and other public programs. About 16 percent of the population was uninsured. Figure 6.1 shows the population distribution by insurance coverage in 2006. For our analysis, we focus on the population covered under employer-sponsored insurance.

6.2.1   Data and Study Sample

Study data were drawn from the 2006 MarketScan Commercial Claims and Encounters Database from Truven Health, which included enrollment and claims data for approximately 31 million individuals with employer-sponsored health insurance, provided largely by very large employers. MarketScan Commercial Claims and Encounters Database consists of employer- and health-plan-sourced data containing medical and drug data for several million individuals annually.

Table 6.5   Major cost of illness studies: Person-based allocations, methodological issues

Study	Study period	Method	Findings
Manning (1998)	1998	OLS and GLS	Manning (1998) showed that the possibility of heteroscedasticity could raise major issues about the efficiency of the ordinary least squares estimates. In such cases, they recommended using generalized linear squares estimators to obtain efficient estimates of the coefficients, and to further make accurate inference statistics for the standard error of such coefficients. Also, in case of log transformed or any other transformed dependent variable, the authors suggested that the researchers need to check if the error term is heteroscedastic across treatment groups or depends on some combination of independent variables. They also recommend that if the error term is heteroscedastic, then the researchers should try to determine the form of the heteroscedasticity and use that information to obtain an unbiased estimate of the retransformation factor in order to estimate the overall expected level of spending to the independent variables (e.g., medical condition dummies).
Manning and Mullahy (2001)	2001	OLS, GLM	Manning and Mullahy (2001) examined how well the alternative estimators behave econometrically in terms of estimation bias and accuracy when the health spending data are skewed or have other most common data problems (zero spenders, heteroscedasticity, heavy tails, etc.). They could not clearly identify any single alternative that best suits all conditions examined. Although, they present a simple algorithm for choosing among the alternative estimators. Selecting the right estimator is important for most accurate estimation. Their recommendation is to begin with both the raw-scale and log-scale residuals from one of the consistent generalized linear model (GLM) estimators.

(continued)

Table 6.5 (continued)

Study	Study period	Method	Findings
Manning, Basu, and Mullahy (2005)	2005	Ordinary least squares (OLS), exponential conditional models (ECM), generalized linear model (GLM)	Manning, Basu, and Mullahy (2005) found that there are two broad classes of models that can be commonly used to address the econometric problems caused by skewness in the health spending data. In the person-level analysis, often times researchers encounter common data issues like zero spenders, heteroscedasticity, and heavy tails. The two common solutions proposed by the authors to deal with such data problem are: (a) transformation to deal with skewness (e.g., ordinary least squares [OLS] on ln[spending]), and (b) different weighting approaches based on exponential conditional models (ECM) and generalized linear model (GLM) approaches. In this paper, they also discussed these two classes of models using the three-parameter generalized gamma (GGM) distribution, which includes OLS with a normal error, OLS for the log-normal, the standard gamma and exponential with a log link, and the Weibull. The GGM also provides a potentially more robust alternative estimator to the standard alternatives.
Buntin and Zaslavsky (2004)	2004	OLS, GLM	Buntin and Zaslavsky (2004) compare the performance of eight alternative estimators, including OLS and GLM estimators and one- and two-part models, in predicting Medicare costs. They find that four of the alternatives produce very similar results in practice. They then suggest an efficient method for researchers to use when selecting estimators of health care costs. Researchers considering alternative models where the probability of use per se is not of interest would do well to start with the one-part GLM models.
Basu and Manning (2009)	2009	Single-equation models: OLS regression for logarithmic or MLE estimation from Box-Cox transformations. Sophisticated single equation: One part generalized linear model (GLM) with a gamma distribution and a log link. Two-part models: Two-part generalized linear model (GLM) with a gamma distribution and a log link.	Given zero spenders and skewed positive expenditures data can be best handled by one-part or two-part generalized linear models (GLM) with a gamma distribution and a log link. In two-part models, use a logit model to predict the probability of having any medical spending and then use a GLM model with a gamma distribution and a log link to estimate the level of expenditures, given positive spending.

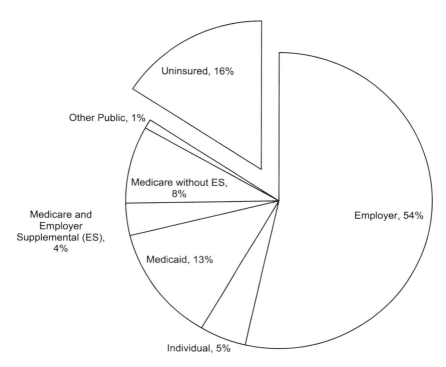

Fig. 6.1   Population distribution by insurance coverage, 2006
Source: State Health Facts Online, The Henry J. Kaiser Foundation.
Note: US residents—296 million.

Enrollees include employees, their spouses, and dependents who are covered by the policy. Health care for these individuals is provided under a variety of fee-for-service (FFS), fully capitated, and partially capitated health plans, including preferred and exclusive provider organizations (PPOs and EPOs), point-of-service plans, indemnity plans, and health maintenance organizations (HMOs). Medical claims are linked to outpatient prescription drug claims and person-level enrollment information. Figure 6.2 provides a schematic diagram of the Truven Health MarketScan claims data.

The enrollment files provide patient demographics, enrollment periods, types of coverage, and presence of medication coverage. The claims files provide inpatient, outpatient, and prescription drug claims, and include dates and types of services, diagnosis (ICD-9-CM) codes, and costs of services. The maximum number of diagnoses recorded varies by claim type. Hospitalization claims include up to fifteen diagnoses, outpatient claims up to two diagnoses, and prescription drug claims do not contain diagnosis codes. Table 6.6 gives an account of the relevant variables in the MarketScan data.

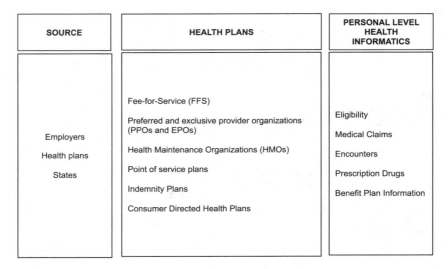

Fig. 6.2   MarketScan claims structure
Source: Truven Health Analytics.

We restricted our analysis by randomly selecting approximately three million individuals under the age of sixty-five with commercial insurance and prescription drug coverage in 2006. We excluded 0.58 million individuals with capitated insurance plans and dropped those with negative spending. The final analytic sample included 2.3 million individuals with 71.7 million claims totaling $8.89 billion in annual spending (in 2006 US dollars).

Classification of Diseases

Our goal was to use each method to allocate the samples' total health care spending in 2006 to a common set of mutually exclusive diseases. For our common core set of diseases, we used the 2012 version of AHRQ's Clinical Classification Software (CCS) (Elixhauser, Steiner, and Palmer 2012). The CCS software maps the approximately 14,000+ ICD-9-CM diagnosis codes into 283 mutually exclusive, clinically meaningful groups; the 283 single-level groups can then be aggregated up to eighteen multilevel CCS chapters.

Methods for Allocation of Spending to Diseases

We allocated spending to the 283 CCS groups using three different approaches, as described in the previous section. Each approach is characterized by its methodological choices across three domains: the unit of observation (encounter versus person), the method of allocating costs to diseases (accounting versus econometric), and the handling of comorbidities (using all diagnoses versus principal diagnosis only).

Table 6.6   Relevant variables in MarketScan data

Demographic variables	Enrollment data	Health plan features	Inpatient claims and outpatients claims	Drug claims	Payment information
Enrollee identification	Date of enrollment	Plan type	Enrollee identification	Enrollee identification	Total payments
Age of patient			Date of admission	National Drug Code	
Patient birth year	Member days	Deductible amount	Date of discharge	Pharmacy ID	Net payments
Gender of patient			Length of stay	Date service incurred	
Relationship of patient to employee	Date of disenrollment	Copayment amount	Diagnosis-related group	Therapeutic group	Payments to physicians
			Principal diagnosis code	Refill number	
Employment status		Coordination of benefits amount	Secondary diagnosis codes (up to fourteen)	Therapeutic class	Payments to hospitals
			Principal procedure code	Average wholesale price	
Employment classification			Secondary procedure codes (up to fourteen)	Coinsurance/copayment	Payments total admission
Industry			Place of service		
			Type of admission	Number of days supply	
			Provider ID	Deductible	
Geographic location (state, ZIP Code)			Quality of services	Generic product identification	

Source: Truven Health Analytics.

6.2.2   Encounter-Based Allocations

We examine two different encounter-based allocation approaches; both use basic accounting to allocate each medical claim's costs into the 283 CCS disease groups. Following the methodology of Rice (1967), Cooper and Rice (1976), and Hodgson and Cohen (1999), our first approach (which we refer to as *primary encounter*) assigns all of the spending on a single medical encounter to the principal diagnosis coded on its claim. While this approach is straightforward, it does not take into account the contribution of comorbidities to costs.

Our second approach follows more recent peer-reviewed literature (Thorpe, Florence, and Joski 2004; Roehrig et al. 2009; Roehrig and Rousseau 2011) allocating a portion of each encounter's spending to each (not just the principal) diagnosis coded on its claim. For claims with multiple diagnosis codes, the claims' spending is assigned to the coded diagnoses in proportion to the ratio of spending reported on claims with only one diagnosis (for more detail, see appendix to Thorpe, Florence, and Joski [2004]). This approach, which we refer to as *all encounter*, attempts to better address the contribution of comorbidities to costs.

6.2.3   Person-Based Allocation

To implement the *person* approach, we regress each individual's total annual health care spending on indicators for the presence of diseases, as identified by diagnosis codes in the concurrent year's claims. In the simplest ordinary least squares (OLS) specification, the coefficient on each condition represents the incremental additional spending for a person with that condition relative to someone without it. To deal with the right-skewed data, we used OLS regressions on log total expenditures; prior to log transformation, we added $1 to each person's spending to ensure inclusion of individuals with no spending in 2006. Results were retransformed into their natural units using a smearing estimator (Duan 1983), and $1 was subtracted from each person's spending prior to final reporting. In the case of two conditions (d_1 and d_2), the regression is: $\ln(1 + y) = \beta_0 + \beta_1 d_1 + \beta_2 d_2 + \varepsilon$.

The log specification implicitly assumes that spending caused by any disease is multiplicative relative to spending without that disease. Because the underlying equation is nonlinear, however, this approach will not lead to total spending matching population totals. To address this issue, we followed a methodology described by Trogdon et al. (2007) and Trogdon, Finkelstein, and Hoerger (2008), which estimates expenditures associated with co-occurring diseases and reallocates these expenditures to individual diseases. In this method, the estimated coefficients from the log regression are first used to separate out the portion of patients' spending that can be attributed to the conditions coded in their medical claims. The "attributable spending" for a patient is calculated as his observed spending less what his spending would have been if he had no conditions divided by observed spending:

$$AF_j = (E[y|d_j] - e[Y|d_j = 0]) / E[y|d_j].$$

The attributable spending for each individual is then allocated to conditions using shares calculated from the estimated coefficients. In the case of two conditions, the share of expenditures that are allocated to condition 1, for example, is:

$$S_1 = [\exp(\beta_1 - 1) / \{[\exp(\beta_1 - 1)] + [\exp(\beta_2 - 1)]\}].$$

This method ensures that (a) all shares sum to one (i.e., all attributable spending is allocated), (b) conditions with the larger coefficient are attributed a greater share of spending, and (c) the only spending allocated to the patient are for conditions that the patient has.

6.2.4 Analyses

Analyses were restricted to the actual amounts paid for care for all claims completed during calendar year 2006. Charges are often reported on claims, but we do not use them. Because the encounter and the person-allocation approaches are at different units of analysis—the individual claim and the person-year, respectively—we aggregated disease-spending estimates output by the two encounter approaches to the person-year to allow comparisons between the person and encounter estimates on a level playing field.

We started by comparing the proportion of total spending that each method was able to allocate to conditions. We then examined how each of the three methods distributed spending across CCS chapters. Then, for each CCS chapter, we examined differences in the number of patients with disease (*treated disease prevalence*), the average annual disease cost per patient with disease (*cost per case*), and the overall annual disease spending output by each allocation method. Finally, we examined in more detail the ten conditions accounting for the greatest share of total spending with each of the allocation method. All estimates are reported in 2006 dollars.

6.3 Results

Table 6.7 presents descriptive statistics for our study sample and their encounters (or claims). The study sample included 2.3 million commercially insured individuals with a mean age of thirty-four; 51.3 percent are female. In 2006, the sample filed 71.7 million claims totaling $8.89 billion in annual spending. This translated to a mean annual per-person spending of $3,788 (median $1,640). The majority of claims (66.5 percent) were for outpatient services, with another 33.3 percent for pharmacy services. Inpatient claims are a very small part of this sample. The average number of recorded

Table 6.7   **Summary statistics for sample persons and their encounters/claims, 2006**

Characteristic	N	Percent
Total claims	71,665,728	
Number of claims by type		
Inpatient	137,628	0.2
Outpatient	47,641,979	66.5
Drug	23,886,121	33.3
Mean (median) cost per claim by type		
Inpatient	$14,134 ($8,076)	
Outpatient	$104 ($37)	
Drug	$83 ($41)	
Total persons	2,346,934	
Age		
< 18	607,937	25.9
18–34	459,470	19.6
35–44	406,129	17.3
45–54	486,100	20.7
55–64	387,298	16.5
Female gender	1,204,089	51.3
Region		
Northeast	280,951	12
North central	619,047	26.4
South	1,070,411	45.6
West	357,558	15.2
Unknown	18,967	0.9
Mean (median) annual per-person cost		
Total	$3,788 ($1,640)	
Inpatient	$829 ($474)	
Outpatient	$2,118 ($753)	
Drug	$841 ($414)	

Notes: We restricted our analysis by randomly selecting approximately three million individuals in MarketScan data under the age of sixty-five with commercial insurance and prescription drug coverage in 2006. We excluded 0.58 million individuals with capitated insurance plans and dropped those with negative spending. The final analytic sample included 2.3 million individuals with 71.7 million claims totaling $8.89 billion in annual spending (in 2006 US dollars).

diagnoses varied by claim type: one for outpatient services, five for inpatient services, and zero for pharmacy claims.

The three methods differed in the portion of overall spending that could (and could not) be allocated to diseases, with far more spending allocated by the person method than by the encounter methods (see first line in table 6.8). Both encounter approaches had unallocated spending of $1.98 billion (22.3 percent of total). In contrast, the person approach had unallocated spending of $450.0 million (5.1 percent of total). Over 99 percent of the unallocated encounter spending ($1.97 billion) was for drug claims, which do not have diagnosis codes. In the person approach, unallocated spending is a result of unallocated constant.

Table 6.8   Disease-spending estimates by method of allocation

Condition category	Encounter-level allocations						Person-level allocations		
	Principal diagnosis only			All coded diagnoses					
	Treated prevalence (%)	Cost per patient ($)	Total cost (millions $)	Treated prevalence (%)	Cost per patient ($)	Total cost (millions $)	Treated prevalence (%)	Cost per patient ($)	Total cost (millions $)
Unattributable spending			*1,981.1*			*1,981.1*			*450.0*
Infectious and parasitic diseases	18.1	239	101.7	19.2	200	90.4	19.2	450	203.1
Neoplasms	10.4	3,315	809.5	10.9	3,019	774.6	10.9	1,690	433.7
Endocrine/nutritional/metabolic diseases and immunity disorders	21.2	533	264.8	23.0	526	284.6	23.0	1,353	731.8
Diseases of the blood and blood-forming organs	2.8	1,077	71.8	3.4	1,176	92.5	3.4	195	15.4
Mental illness	8.6	997	201.9	10.1	950	225.7	10.1	1,403	333.3
Diseases of the nervous system and sense organs	24.6	714	411.8	25.8	728	439.9	25.8	803	485.5
Diseases of the circulatory system	20.3	1,806	859.3	21.6	1,705	863.6	21.6	1,873	949.0
Diseases of the respiratory system	35.2	523	432.3	36.2	560	475.8	36.2	956	813.3
Diseases of the digestive system	14.0	1,644	539.3	15.1	1,524	540.6	15.1	929	329.6
Diseases of the genitourinary system	20.7	1,127	547.4	21.6	1,075	544.5	21.6	660	334.2
Complications of pregnancy, childbirth, puerperium	3.2	3,865	292.4	3.4	3,365	269.8	3.4	2,645	212.1
Diseases of the skin and subcutaneous tissue	13.8	348	112.6	14.4	314	105.9	14.4	721	243.3
Diseases of the musculoskeletal system & connective tissue	25.8	1,554	941.8	26.8	1,399	878.9	26.8	1,258	790.5
Congenital anomalies	1.4	1,666	56.2	1.6	1,462	55.5	1.6	1,090	41.4
Certain conditions originating in perinatal period	0.2	1,271	6.9	0.4	1,429	12.1	0.4	513	4.3
Injury and poisoning	17.3	1,454	590.0	17.8	1,289	538.3	17.8	1,182	493.8
Symptoms, signs, ill-defined conditions/ factors influencing health	51.1	459	551.5	52.5	448	552.0	52.5	1,502	1,849.3
Residual codes; unclassified; all E codes	7.8	641	117.4	10.5	668	163.8	10.5	719	176.3
Total			8,889.79			8,889.79			8,889.79

The remaining rows of table 6.8 present, for each method, the treated disease prevalence, cost per case, and overall annual disease spending at the CCS chapter level. For all conditions, the treated disease prevalence is lower with the *primary-encounter* than with the *all-encounter* (or *person*) allocations. This is not surprising, as 10.7 percent of claims had more than one diagnosis coded. In contrast, the cost-per-case estimates from the two encounter methods were much closer than the estimates from the person approach. Diseases of the respiratory system provide an illustrative example: treated disease prevalence was 36.2 percent with the *person* and *all-encounter* allocations, and 35.2 percent with the *primary-encounter* allocation; the cost per case was $523, $560, and $956 from the *primary-encounter*, *all-encounter*, and *person* allocation methods, respectively.

For any given disease, the overall disease spending estimated using the person approach often differed substantially from the estimates from either encounter approach, largely due to differences in the cost-per-case estimates. From our example above, total spending on diseases of the respiratory system was much higher with the person approach ($813 million) than with the primary-encounter or the all-encounter approaches ($432 and $476 million, respectively). The mental health expenditures were higher with the person approach than with either encounter approach ($333.3 million vs. $225.7 and $201.9 million), perhaps indicating that comorbid conditions are better handled by regression approach. Total annual spending on neoplasms, on the other hand, was far higher with the primary- and all-encounter approaches ($810 million and $775 million, respectively) than with the person approach ($434 million).

Figure 6.3 shows a radar plot of spending attributed to eighteen broad ICD-9 disease categories by the all-encounter approach and the person-based approach. The biggest difference in attributable spending between the two methods is for "symptoms, signs, ill-defined conditions/factors influencing health." There is a big unattributable spending under claims-based all-encounter approach.

Spending was concentrated in a small number of conditions. Table 6.9 shows, for each allocation method, the ten diseases (out of 283 CCS groups) accounting for the greatest total spending—and the spending on those conditions estimated by each of the other methods. The ten most expensive diseases output by the person method accounted for 40.4 percent of total spending. In contrast, the ten most expensive diseases output by the encounter methods accounted for 18.1 percent of spending when based on primary diagnosis alone, and 18.3 percent of spending when all diagnoses were used.

The top ten most expensive diseases differed by method (table 6.9 notes their ranking with each method). Both the primary- and all-encounter approaches identified "spondylosis, intervertebral disc and other back prob-

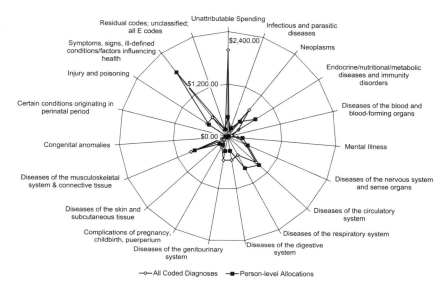

Fig. 6.3   Total cost (millions)

Notes: We have attributed $8.89 billion spending among eighteen broad ICD-9 disease categories. The biggest difference in attributable spending by the two methods is for "symptoms, signs, ill-defined conditions/factors influencing health."

lems" as the most expensive condition with overall spending of $390 and $358 million, respectively (versus $304 million by person approach), and "coronary atherosclerosis and other heart disease" as the second-most expensive with overall spending of $197 and $182 million, respectively (compared to $124 million by the person approach). In contrast, the person approach attributed the most spending to the medical examination/evaluation bucket, with overall spending of $941 million (compared to $108 million from both encounter approaches). Essential hypertension was the second-most expensive disease from the person approach with overall spending of $521 million; neither the primary- nor all-encounter approaches ranked hypertension among its ten most expensive conditions (overall hypertension spending of $56 and $80 million, respectively). Several of the other top ten most expensive conditions with the person approach were not among the ten most expensive from either of the encounter approaches, including lipid disorders, uncomplicated diabetes mellitus, other upper-respiratory infections, and screening for conditions. In contrast, the two encounter approaches had nonspecific chest pain and breast cancer among their ten most expensive diseases, while the person approach ranked them as the thirteenth and sixteenth most expensive, respectively.

Table 6.9 Spending on ten most expensive diseases by method

Disease	Primary-encounter		Overall costs ($) by method			
			All-encounter		Person	
	Rank	Dollars	Rank	Dollars	Rank	Dollars
Spondylosis, intervertebral disc and other back problems	1	389,715,873	1	357,920,863	5	304,271,176
Coronary atherosclerosis and other heart disease	2	196,579,627	2	182,455,430		124,485,308
Other connective tissue disease	3	150,535,660	3	166,567,806	7	200,708,175
Nonspecific chest pain	4	143,561,929	4	155,836,027		121,940,108
Osteoarthritis	5	133,035,281		96,306,494		18,174,807
Other and unspecified benign neoplasm	6	126,971,601	7	126,254,146		112,859,389
Cancer of breast	7	124,172,316	8	124,645,215		46,350,248
Abdominal pain	8	117,988,870	6	134,284,641	10	164,797,269
Residual codes; unclassified	9	117,230,458	5	153,625,332	9	170,533,590
Medical examination/evaluation	10	107,973,591		107,561,624	1	971,356,981
Other nontraumatic joint disorders		101,100,976	9	114,490,237		157,060,353
Other upper-respiratory infections		99,226,131		96,231,728	3	399,125,448
Other screening for conditions (not mental or infectious)		92,026,348		85,270,130	6	289,369,276
Other lower-respiratory disease		72,178,215	10	113,797,598		96,880,125
Essential hypertension		55,994,716		80,485,942	2	520,802,516
Disorders of lipid metabolism		41,044,961		47,001,777	4	379,037,069
Diabetes mellitus without complication		35,194,998		44,886,469	8	195,275,011
Overall spending on:						
Top ten conditions with method		1,607,765,205		1,629,877,294		3,595,276,513
All seventeen conditions in table (includes all top tens)		2,104,531,550		2,187,621,458		4,273,026,852

6.4 Discussion

Proposals for fundamental change both in the financing and delivery of health care and in the measurement of health sector productivity has stimulated interest by payers, policymakers, and statistical agencies in allocating national spending across a comprehensive set of diseases (National Research Council 2005, 2008, 2010; Rosen and Cutler 2007, 2009; Aizcorbe, Retus, and Smith 2008; Aizcorbe and Nestoriak 2011; Aizcorbe, Liebman, Cutler, et al. 2012; Aizcorbe, Liebman, Pack, et al. 2012; Aizcorbe 2013; Song et al. 2009; Bradley et al. 2010; Bradley 2013; Dunn et al. 2013; Dunn, Shapiro, and Liebman 2013; Dunn, Liebman, and Shapiro 2014; Dunn, Rittmueller, and Whitmire 2015). However, there are no methodological gold standards guiding the performance of these COI studies. Applying three different COI methods to the same data, we found that choice of method affected both how much spending could be allocated to diseases and how that spending was allocated. The distribution of spending across diseases differed by method. In turn, for individual diseases, treated disease prevalence, cost per case, and overall disease spending varied depending on the method used. Results were close for some diseases, but quite disparate for others.

Past studies comparing person-level and encounter-level cost-of-illness approaches demonstrate that COI *for a given disease* can vary widely depending on the choice of method (Lipscomb et al. 1998; Honeycutt et al. 2009; Ward et al. 2000; Akobundu et al. 2006; Yabroff et al. 2009); importantly, these studies have largely been restricted to individual diseases (i.e., they are effectively disease-specific COIs). However, as the policy import of general COI studies grows (National Research Council 2005, 2008, 2010; Rosen and Cutler 2007, 2009; Aizcorbe, Retus, and Smith 2008; Aizcorbe and Nestoriak 2011; Aizcorbe, Liebman, Cutler, et al. 2012; Aizcorbe, Liebman, Pack, et al. 2012; Aizcorbe 2013; Song et al. 2009; Bradley et al. 2010; Bradley 2013; Dunn et al. 2013; Dunn, Shapiro, and Liebman 2013; Dunn, Liebman, and Shapiro 2014; Dunn, Rittmueller, and Whitmire 2015), so does the critical need for studies comparing the different cost-allocation methods employed specifically in this context.

While the research comparing different cost-allocation methods in the context of general COI studies is in its infancy, a number of ongoing studies are under way. Several working papers report that the allocation of spending to diseases and, in turn, the price indexes that rely on these disease-spending estimates, may be sensitive to the method employed (see, e.g., Aizcorbe et al. 2011; Rosen et al. 2012; Hall and Highfill 2013; Dunn et al. 2014). Indeed, in the recent release of the Bureau of Economic Analysis's new experimental Health Care Satellite Account, Dunn, Rittmueller, and Whitmire (2015) comment on the importance of such comparisons moving forward (this first account employed a primary-encounter approach).

In the current study, we saw large differences both in the distribution of spending across diseases and in the within-disease spending totals between the person-level and encounter-level methods. For example, mental health expenditures were much higher with the person approach than with either encounter approach, perhaps indicating that mental health is picking up the costs of common comorbid conditions. This would be consistent with literature demonstrating that depression raises the costs of treating a number of different chronic conditions (Welch et al. 2009). In contrast, spending on cancers was far higher with both encounter approaches than with the person approach, perhaps reflecting physician coding practices (diagnoses of cancer tend to get carried over from the initial claim to all subsequent claims).

The major advantage of the encounter approaches is the ease with which costs are attributed to diseases. Disadvantages include unclear handling of comorbidities, unallocated spending (i.e., claims without diagnoses), and inability to meaningfully link costs to health outcomes. The person approach is conceptually more appealing because it addresses the disadvantages of the encounter approach; most importantly, it allows for meaningful comparisons between health care spending and health outcomes. However, this comes with the price of additional complexity. There is no single-best econometric approach for modeling health care costs, leaving the analyst to test and decide between a number of different model specifications. That said, there is a rich economics literature that can help guide the choice of model and its implementation (Manning et al. 1998, 2001, 2005; Buntin and Zaslavsky 2004; Basu and Manning 2009; Mullahy 2009).

Despite their apparent strengths and weaknesses, there are no standard metrics with which to compare encounter- and person-level methods. Therefore, the best approach may depend on the question on hand, data available, and the needs of the target audience, among other things. For example, if the goal is to compare costs and health effects within a given disease, as is done in cost-effectiveness analyses, a person-based approach may be best. In contrast, if price index construction is the goal, federal agencies may find an encounter-based approach more meaningful initially, until they are ready to make quality adjustments. In the long term, more empirical work is needed on what approaches work best in which situations.

While our study has many strengths, it also has some limitations. While this study has demonstrated clear differences between the three COI allocation methods, it cannot provide definitive guidance on the choice of a "best" or "most appropriate" method for any given purpose. Rather, payers and policymakers must weigh the pros, cons, and potentially conflicting information provided by each method, making value judgments as to which will best suit their needs. Second, while other COI allocation methods exist, we can only speak to those examined in the current study. One notable method—the use of episode groupers to allocate spending to diseases—is not used herein. Finally, our study compared the three methods at a point in time (i.e., cross-sectionally) and cannot be used to further inform efforts to understand the impact of method choice on price indices or other inherently longitudinal questions.

In summary, as the need to demonstrate the value of our health care spending increases, interest in allocating economy-wide spending to a comprehensive set of diseases is likely to increase. This chapter demonstrates that the choice of method may have very real implications for both how much and how that spending gets allocated. Additional empirical work developing these methodological tools and conceptual work exploring their ideal use will maximize their policy relevance and use.

Appendix

CCS Categories and ICD-9-CM Codes for All Seventeen Conditions in Table 6.9

205 Spondylosis; Intervertebral Disc Disorders; Other Back Problems

7201, 7202, 72081, 72089, 7209, 7210, 7211, 7212, 7213, 72141, 72142, 7215, 7216, 7217, 7218, 72190, 72191, 7220, 72210, 72211, 7222, 72230, 72231, 72232, 72239, 7224, 72251, 72252, 7226, 72270, 72271, 72272, 72273, 72280, 72281, 72282, 72283, 72290, 72291, 72292, 72293, 7230, 7231, 7232, 7233, 7234, 7235, 7236, 7237, 7238, 7239, 72400, 72401, 72402, 72403, 72409, 7241, 7242, 7243, 7244, 7245, 7246, 72470, 72471, 72479, 7248, 7249

101 Coronary Atherosclerosis and Other Heart Disease

4110, 4111, 4118, 41181, 41189, 412, 4130, 4131, 4139, 4140, 41400, 41401, 41406, 4142, 4143, 4144, 4148, 4149, V4581, V4582

211 Other Connective Tissue Disease

32752, 56731, 7105, 725, 7260, 72610, 72611, 72612, 72613, 72619, 7262, 72630, 72631, 72632, 72633, 72639, 7264, 7265, 72660, 72661, 72662, 72663, 72664, 72665, 72669, 72670, 72671, 72672, 72673, 72679, 7268, 72690, 72691, 72700, 72701, 72702, 72703, 72704, 72705, 72706, 72709, 7272, 7273, 72740, 72741, 72742, 72743, 72749, 72750, 72751, 72759, 72760, 72761, 72762, 72763, 72764, 72765, 72766, 72767, 72768, 72769, 72781, 72782, 72783, 72789, 7279, 7280, 72810, 72811, 72812, 72813, 72819, 7282, 7283, 7284, 7285, 7286, 72871, 72879, 72881, 72882, 72883, 72884, 72885, 72886, 72887, 72888, 72889, 7289, 7290, 7291, 7292, 72930, 72931, 72939, 7294, 7295, 7296, 72971, 72972, 72973, 72979, 72981, 72982, 72989, 7299, 72990, 72991, 72992, 72999, 7819, 78191, 78192, 78194, 78199, 7937, V135, V1359, V436, V4360, V4361, V4362, V4363, V4364, V4365, V4366, V4369, V437, V454,

V481, V482, V483, V490, V491, V492, V495, V4960, V4961, V4962, V4963, V4964, V4965, V4966, V4967, V4970, V4971, V4972, V4973, V4974, V4975, V4976, V4977, V537

102 Nonspecific Chest Pain

78650, 78651, 78659

203 Osteoarthritis

71500, 71504, 71509, 71510, 71511, 71512, 71513, 71514, 71515, 71516, 71517, 71518, 71520, 71521, 71522, 71523, 71524, 71525, 71526, 71527, 71528, 71530, 71531, 71532, 71533, 71534, 71535, 71536, 71537, 71538, 71580, 71589, 71590, 71591, 71592, 71593, 71594, 71595, 71596, 71597, 71598, V134

47 Other and Unspecified Benign Neoplasm

20940, 20941, 20942, 20943, 20950, 20951, 20952, 20953, 20954, 20955, 20956, 20957, 20960, 20961, 20962, 20963, 20964, 20965, 20966, 20967, 20969, 2100, 2101, 2102, 2103, 2104, 2105, 2106, 2107, 2108, 2109, 2110, 2111, 2112, 2113, 2114, 2115, 2116, 2117, 2118, 2119, 2120, 2121, 2122, 2123, 2124, 2125, 2126, 2127, 2128, 2129, 2130, 2131, 2132, 2133, 2134, 2135, 2136, 2137, 2138, 2139, 2140, 2141, 2142, 2143, 2144, 2148, 2149, 2150, 2152, 2153, 2154, 2155, 2156, 2157, 2158, 2159, 2160, 2161, 2162, 2163, 2164, 2165, 2166, 2167, 2168, 2169, 217, 220, 2210, 2211, 2212, 2218, 2219, 2220, 2221, 2222, 2223, 2224, 2228, 2229, 2230, 2231, 2232, 2233, 22381, 22389, 2239, 2240, 2241, 2242, 2243, 2244, 2245, 2246, 2247, 2248, 2249, 2250, 2251, 2252, 2253, 2254, 2258, 2259, 226, 2270, 2271, 2273, 2274, 2275, 2276, 2278, 2279, 22800, 22801, 22802, 22803, 22804, 22809, 2281, 2290, 2298, 2299, V1272

24 Cancer of Breast

1740, 1741, 1742, 1743, 1744, 1745, 1746, 1748, 1749, 1750, 1759, 2330, V103

251 Abdominal Pain

7890, 78900, 78901, 78902, 78903, 78904, 78905, 78906, 78907, 78909, 78960, 78961, 78962, 78963, 78964, 78965, 78966, 78967, 78969

259 Residual Codes; Unclassified

3020, 32700, 32701, 32709, 32710, 32711, 32712, 32713, 32714, 32719, 32720, 32721, 32722, 32723, 32724, 32725, 32726, 32727, 32729, 32740, 32741, 32742, 32743, 32744, 32749, 32751, 32759, 3278, 78002, 7801, 78050, 78051, 78052, 78053, 78054, 78055, 78056, 78057, 78058, 78059, 78064, 78065, 7809, 78093, 78094, 78095, 78096, 78097, 78099, 7815, 7816, 7823, 78261, 78262, 7828, 7829, 7830, 7836, 7842, 7901, 7906, 7909, 79091, 79092, 79093, 79094, 79095, 79099, 7932, 7939, 79399, 7949, 79581, 79582, 79589, 7963, 7964, 7965, 7966, 7969, 7980, 7981, 7982, 7989, 7992, 79921, 79922,

79923, 79924, 79925, 79929, 7993, 7998, 79981, 79982, 79989, 7999, V070, V072, V073, V0731, V0739, V0751, V0752, V0759, V078, V079, V131, V138, V1389, V139, V152, V1521, V1522, V1529, V153, V1581, V1584, V1585, V1586, V1587, V1589, V159, V160, V161, V162, V163, V164, V1640, V1641, V1642, V1643, V1649, V165, V1651, V1652, V1659, V166, V167, V168, V169, V170, V171, V172, V173, V174, V1741, V1749, V175, V176, V177, V178, V1781, V1789, V180, V181, V1811, V1819, V182, V183, V184, V185, V1851, V1859, V186, V1861, V1869, V187, V188, V189, V190, V191, V1911, V1919, V192, V193, V194, V195, V196, V197, V198, V210, V211, V21 218, V219, V418, V419, V428, V4281, V4282, V4283, V4284, V4289, V429, V438, V4381, V4382, V4383, V4389, V447, V448, V449, V4571, V4572, V4573, V4574, V4575, V4576, V4577, V4578, V4579, V4583, V4584, V4586, V4587, V4588, V4589, V460, V463, V468, V469, V470, V471, V472, V479, V480, V488, V489, V498, V4981, V4982, V4983, V4984, V4986, V4987, V4989, V499, V500, V501, V503, V5041, V5042, V5049, V508, V509, V590, V5901, V5902, V5909, V591, V592, V593, V594, V595, V596, V5970, V5971, V5972, V5973, V5974, V598, V599, V640, V6400, V6401, V6402, V6403, V6404, V6405, V6406, V6407, V6408, V6409, V641, V642, V643, V644, V6441, V6442, V6443, V690, V691, V692, V693, V694, V695, V698, V699, V8301, V8302, V8381, V8389, V8401, V8402, V8403, V8404, V8409, V848, V8481, V8489, V851, V8552, V860, V861, V8701, V8702, V8709, V8711, V8712, V8719, V872, V8731, V8732, V8739, V8741, V8742, V8743, V8744, V8745, V8746, V8749, V8801, V8802, V8803, V8811, V8812, V8901, V8902, V8903, V8904, V8905, V8909

256 Medical Examination/Evaluation

V290, V291, V292, V293, V298, V299, V6801, V6809, V700, V703, V704, V705, V706, V707, V708, V709, V718, V719, V7231, V7232, V725, V726, V7260, V7261, V7262, V7263, V7269, V728, V7281, V7282, V7283, V7284, V7285, V7286, V729

204 Other Nontraumatic Joint Disorders

7130, 7131, 7132, 7133, 7134, 7135, 7136, 7137, 7138, 71600, 71601, 71602, 71603, 71604, 71605, 71606, 71607, 71608, 71609, 71620, 71621, 71622, 71623, 71624, 71625, 71626, 71627, 71628, 71629, 71630, 71631, 71632, 71633, 71634, 71635, 71636, 71637, 71638, 71639, 71640, 71641, 71642, 71643, 71644, 71645, 71646, 71647, 71648, 71649, 71650, 71651, 71652, 71653, 71654, 71655, 71656, 71657, 71658, 71659, 71660, 71661, 71662, 71663, 71664, 71665, 71666, 71667, 71668, 71680, 71681, 71682, 71683, 71684, 71685, 71686, 71687, 71688, 71689, 71690, 71691, 71692, 71693, 71694, 71695, 71696, 71697, 71698, 71699, 71810, 71811, 71812, 71813, 71814, 71815, 71817, 71818, 71819, 71820, 71821, 71822, 71823, 71824, 71825, 71826, 71827, 71828, 71829, 71850, 71851, 71852, 71853, 71854, 71855, 71856, 71857, 71858, 71859, 71860, 71865, 71870, 71871, 71872,

71873, 71874, 71875, 71876, 71877, 71878, 71879, 71880, 71881, 71882, 71883, 71884, 71885, 71886, 71887, 71888, 71889, 71890, 71891, 71892, 71893, 71894, 71895, 71897, 71898, 71899, 71900, 71901, 71902, 71903, 71904, 71905, 71906, 71907, 71908, 71909, 71910, 71911, 71912, 71913, 71914, 71915, 71916, 71917, 71918, 71919, 71920, 71921, 71922, 72923, 71924, 71925, 71926, 71927, 71928, 71929, 71930, 71931, 71932, 71933, 71934, 71935, 71936, 71937, 71938, 71939, 71940, 71941, 71942, 71943, 71944, 71945, 71946, 71947, 71948, 71949, 71950, 71951, 71952, 71953, 71954, 71955, 71956, 71957, 71958, 71959, 71960, 71961, 71962, 71963, 71964, 71965, 71966, 71967, 71968, 71969, 7197, 71970, 71975, 71976, 71977, 71978, 71979, 71980, 71981, 71982, 71983, 71984, 71985, 71986, 71987, 71988, 71989, 71990, 71991, 71992, 71993, 71994, 71995, 71996, 71997, 71998, 71999

126 Other Upper Respiratory Infections

0320, 0321, 0322, 0323, 0340, 460, 4610, 4611, 4612, 4613, 4618, 4619, 462, 4640, 46400, 46401, 46410, 46411, 46420, 46421, 46430, 46431, 4644, 46450, 46451, 4650, 4658, 4659, 4730, 4731, 4732, 4733, 4738, 4739, 78491

10 Immunizations and Screening for Infectious Disease

7955, 79551, 79552, 7956, V010, V011, V012, V013, V014, V015, V016, V017, V0171, V0179, V018, V0181, V0182, V0183, V0184, V0189, V019, V020, V021, V022, V023, V024, V025, V0251, V0252, V0253, V0254, V0259, V026, V0260, V0261, V0262, V0269, V027, V028, V029, V030, V031, V032, V033, V034, V035, V036, V037, V038, V0381, V0382, V0389, V039, V040, V041, V042, V043, V044, V045, V046, V047, V048, V0481, V0482, V0489, V050, V051, V052, V053, V054, V058, V059, V060, V061, V062, V063, V064, V065, V066, V068, V069, V286, V712, V7182, V7183, V730, V731, V732, V733, V734, V735, V736, V738, V7381, V7388, V7389, V739, V7398, V7399, V740, V741, V742, V743, V744, V745, V746, V748, V749, V750, V751, V752, V753, V754, V755, V756, V757, V758, V759, 79579

133 Other Lower Respiratory Disease

5131, 514, 515, 5160, 5161, 5162, 5163, 51630, 51631, 51632, 51633, 51634, 51635, 51636, 51637, 5164, 5165, 51661, 51662, 51663, 51664, 51669, 5168, 5169, 5172, 5178, 5183, 5184, 51889, 5194, 5198, 5199, 7825, 78600, 78601, 78602, 78603, 78604, 78605, 78606, 78607, 78609, 7862, 7863, 78630, 78631, 78639, 7864, 78652, 7866, 7867, 7868, 7869, 7931, 79311, 79319, 7942, V126, V1260, V1261, V1269, V426

98 Essential Hypertension

4011, 4019

53 Disorders of Lipid Metabolism

2720, 2721, 2722, 2723, 2724

49 Diabetes Mellitus without Complication

24900, 25000, 25001, 7902, 79021, 79022, 79029, 7915, 7916, V4585, V5391, V6546

References

Aizcorbe, A. M. 2013. "Recent Research on Disease-Based Price Indexes: Where Do We Stand?" *Survey of Current Business* 93:9–13.

Aizcorbe, A. M., R. Bradley, R. Greenaway-McGrevy, B. Herauf, R. Kane, E. Liebman, S. Pack, and L. Rozental. 2011. "Alternative Price Indexes for Medical Care: Evidence from the MEPS Survey." BEA Working Paper no. WP2011-01, Washington, DC, Bureau of Economic Analysis.

Aizcorbe, A. M., E. Liebman, D. M. Cutler, and A. B. Rosen. 2012. "Household Consumption Expenditures for Medical Care: An Alternate Presentation." *Survey of Current Business* 92 (6): 34–48.

Aizcorbe, A. M., E. Liebman, S. Pack, D. M. Cutler, M. E. Chernew, and A. B. Rosen. 2012. "Measuring Health Care Costs of Individuals with Employer-Sponsored Health Insurance in the US: Comparison of Survey and Claims Data." *Statistical Journal of the International Association for Official Statistics* 28 (1): 43–51.

Aizcorbe, A. M., and N. Nestoriak. 2011. "Changing Mix of Medical Care Services: Stylized Facts and Implications for Price Indexes." *Journal of Health Economics* 30 (3): 568–74.

Aizcorbe, A. M., B. A. Retus, and S. Smith. 2008. "Toward a Health Care Satellite Account." *Survey of Current Business* 88:24–30.

Akobundu, E., J. Ju, L. Blatt, and C. D. Mullins. 2006. "Cost-of-Illness Studies: A Review of Current Methods." *PharmacoEconomics* 24:869–90.

Basu, A., and W. G. Manning. 2009. "Issues for the Next Generation of Health Care Cost Analyses." *Medical Care* 47 (suppl. 7): S109–14.

Berk, A., L. Paringer, and S. J. Mushkin. 1978. "The Economic Cost of Illness: Fiscal 1975." *Medical Care* 16 (9): 785–90.

Bloom, B. S., D. J. Bruno, D. Y. Maman, and R. Jayadevappa. 2001. "Usefulness of US Cost-of-Illness Studies in Healthcare Decision Making." *PharmacoEconomics* 19 (2): 207–13.

Bradley, R. 2013. "Feasible Methods to Estimate Disease-Based Price Indexes." *Journal of Health Economics* 32 (3): 504–14.

Bradley, R., E. Cardenas, D. H. Ginsburg, L. Rozental, and F. Velez. 2010. "Producing Disease-Based Price Indexes." *Monthly Labor Review* 133:20–28.

Buntin, M. B., and A. M. Zaslavsky. 2004. "Too Much Ado about Two-Part Models and Transformation? Comparing Methods of Modeling Medicare Expenditures." *Journal of Health Economics* 23:525–42.

Cooper, B. S., and D. P. Rice. 1976. "The Economic Cost of Illness Revisited." *Social Security Bulletin* 39:21–36.

Cutler, D. M., and N. R. Sahni. 2013. "If Slow Rate of Health Care Spending Growth Persists, Projections May be Off by $770 Billion." *Health Affairs* 32 (5): 841–50.

Druss, B. G., S. C. Marcus, M. Olfson, and H. A. Pincus. 2002. "The Most Expensive Medical Conditions in America." *Health Affairs* 21 (4): 105–11.

Druss, B. G., S. C. Marcus, M. Olfson, T. Tanielian, L. Elinson, and H. A. Pincus. 2001. "Comparing the National Economic Burden of Five Chronic Conditions." *Health Affairs* 20 (6): 233–41.

Duan, N. 1983. "Smearing Estimate: A Nonparametric Retransformation Method." *Journal of the American Statistical Association* 78 (383): 605–10.

Dunn, A., E. B. Liebman, S. Pack, and A. Shapiro. 2013. "Medical Care Price Indexes for Patients with Employer-Provided Insurance: Nationally Representative Estimates from MarketScan Data." *Health Services Research* 48 (3): 1173–90.

Dunn, A., E. B. Liebman, L. Rittmueller, and A. Shapiro. 2014. "Defining Disease Episodes and the Effects on the Components of Expenditure Growth." BEA Working Paper no. WP2014-4, Washington, DC, Bureau of Economic Analysis.

Dunn, A., E. B. Liebman, and A. Shapiro. 2014. "Developing a Framework for Decomposing Medical-Care Expenditure Growth: Exploring Issues of Representativeness." In *Measuring Economic Sustainability and Progress*, edited by Dale W. Jorgenson, J. Steven Landefeld, and Paul Schreyer. Chicago: University of Chicago Press.

Dunn, A., L. Rittmueller, and B. Whitmire. 2015. "Introducing the New BEA Health Care Satellite Account." *Survey of Current Business* 95:1–21.

Dunn, A., A. Shapiro, and E. Liebman. 2013. "Geographic Variation in Commercial Medical-Care Expenditures: A Framework for Decomposing Price and Utilization." *Journal of Health Economics* 32:1153–65.

Elixhauser, A., C. Steiner, and L. Palmer. 2012. Clinical Classifications Software (CCS). US Agency for Healthcare Research and Quality. http://www.hcup-us.ahrq .gov/toolssoftware/ccs/ccs.jsp.

Finkelstein, E. A., H. Chen, T. R. Miller, P. S. Corso, and J. A. Stevens. 2005. "A Comparison of the Case-Control and Case-Crossover Designs for Estimating Medical Costs of Nonfatal Fall-Related Injuries among Older Americans." *Medical Care* 43 (11): 1087–91.

Finkelstein, E. A., I. C. Fiebelkorn, and G. Wang. 2003. "National Medical Spending Attributable to Overweight and Obesity: How Much, and Who's Paying?" *Health Affairs* W3:219–26.

Hall, A. E., and T. Highfill. 2013. "A Regression-Based Medical Care Expenditure Index for Medicare Beneficiaries." BEA Working Paper no. WP2013-4, Washington, DC, Bureau of Economic Analysis.

Hartman, M., A. B. Martin, D. Lassman, A. Catlin, and the National Health Expenditure Accounts Team. 2015. "National Health Spending in 2013: Growth Slows, Remains in Step with the Overall Economy." *Health Affairs* 34 (1): 150–60.

Hodgson, T. A., and A. J. Cohen. 1999. "Medical Expenditures for Major Diseases." *Health Care Financing Review* 21 (2): 119–64.

Hoffman, C., D. Rice, and H. Y. Sung. 1996. "Persons with Chronic Condition: Their Prevalence and Costs." *Journal of the American Medical Association* 276 (18): 1473–79.

Honeycutt, A. A., J. E. Segel, T. J. Hoerger, and E. A. Finkelstein. 2009. "Comparing Cost-of-Illness Estimates from Alternative Approaches: An Application to Diabetes." *Health Services Research* 44 (1): 303–20.

Koopmanschap, M. A. 1998. "Cost-of-Illness Studies, Useful for Health Policy?" *PharmacoEconomics* 14 (2): 143–48.

Keehan, S. P., G. A. Cuckler, A. M. Sisko, A. J. Madison, S. D. Smith, D. A. Stone, J. A. Poisal, C. J. Wolfe, and J. M. Lizonitz. 2015. "National Health Expenditure Projections, 2014–24: Spending Growth Faster than Recent Trends." *Health Affairs* 34 (8): 1407–17.

Lipscomb, J., M. Ancukiewicz, G. Parmigiani, V. Hasselblad, G. Samsa, and D. B. Matchar. 1998. "Predicting the Cost of Illness: A Comparison of Alternative Models Applied to Stroke." *Medical Decision Making* 18:S39–56.

MaCurdy, T., J. Kerwin, J. Gibbs, E. Lin, C. Cotterman, M. O'Brien-Strain, and N. Theobald. 2008. *Evaluating the Functionality of the Symmetry ETG and Medstat MEG Software in Forming Episodes of Care Using Medicare Data.* Burlingame, CA: Acumen, LLC. www.cms.gov/Reports/downloads/MaCurdy.pdf.

MaCurdy, T., J. Kerwin, and N. Theobald. 2009. "Need for Risk Adjustment in Adapting Episode Grouping Software to Medicare Data." *Health Care Financing Review* 30 (4): 33–46.

Manning, W. G. 1998. "The Logged Dependent Variable, Heteroscedasticity, and the Retransformation Problem." *Journal of Health Economics* 17 (3): 283–95.

Manning, W. G., A. Basu, and J. Mullahy. 2005. "Generalized Modeling Approaches to Risk Adjustment of Skewed Outcomes Data." *Journal of Health Economics* 24:465–88.

Manning, W. G., and J. Mullahy. 2001. "Estimating LogModels: To Transform or not to Transform?" *Journal of Health Economics* 21:461–94.

McGlynn, Elizabeth A. 2008. "Identifying, Categorizing, and Evaluating Health Care Efficiency Measures: Final Report." AHRQ Publication no. 08-0030, Agency for Healthcare Research and Quality, Rockville, MD. April. https://archive.ahrq .gov/research/findings/final-reports/efficiency/efficiency.pdf.

Mullahy, J. 2009. "Econometric Modeling of Health Care Costs and Expenditures." *Medical Care* 47 (suppl. 7): S104–8.

National Research Council. 2005. *Beyond the Market: Designing Nonmarket Accounts for the United States.* Washington, DC: The National Academies Press.

———. 2008. *Strategies for a BEA Satellite Health Care Account: Summary of a Workshop.* Washington, DC: The National Academies Press.

———. 2010. *Accounting for Health and Health Care: Approaches to Measuring the Sources and Costs of Their Improvement.* Washington, DC: The National Academies Press.

Rice, D. P. 1967. "Estimating the Cost of Illness." *American Journal of Public Health* 57 (3): 424–40.

Rice, D. P., T. A. Hodgson, and A. N. Kopstein. 1985. "The Economic Costs of Illness: A Replication and Update." *Health Care Financing Review* 6 (1): 61–80.

Rice, D. P., and L. A. Horowitz. 1967. "Trends in Medical Care Prices." *Social Security Bulletin* 30:13–28.

Roehrig, C., G. Miller, C. Lake, and J. Bryant. 2009. "National Health Spending by Medical Condition, 1996–2005." *Health Affairs* 28:w358–67.

Roehrig, C. S., and D. M. Rousseau. 2011. "The Growth in Cost Per Case Explains Far More of US Health Spending Increases Than Rising Disease Prevalence." Health Affairs 30 (9): 1657–63.

Rosen, A. B., and D. M. Cutler. 2007. "Measuring Medical Care Productivity: A Proposal for US National Health Accounts." *Survey of Current Business* 87 (6): 54–58.

———. 2009. "Challenges in Building Disease-Based National Health Accounts." *Medical Care* 47 (suppl. 7): S7–13.

Rosen, A. B., E. Liebman, A. M. Aizcorbe, and D. M. Cutler. 2012. "Comparing Commercial Systems for Characterizing Episodes of Care." BEA Working Paper no. WP2012-7, Washington, DC, Bureau of Economic Analysis.

Scitovsky, A. A. 1964. "An Index of the Cost of Medical Care—A Proposed New Approach." In *The Economics of Health and Medical Care,* edited by S. J. Axelrod, 128–42. Ann Arbor: University of Michigan, Bureau of Public Health Economics.

———. 1967. "Changes in the Costs of Treatment of Selected Illnesses, 1951–65." *American Economic Review* 57 (5): 1182–95.

————. 1985. "Changes in the Costs of Treatment of Selected Illnesses, 1971–1981." *Medical Care* 23 (12): 1345–57.

Sisko, A. M., S. P. Keehan, G. A. Cuckler, A. J. Madison, S. D. Smith, C. J. Wolfe, D. A. Stone, J. M. Lizonitz, and J. A. Poisal. 2014. "National Health Expenditure Projections, 2013–23: Faster Growth Expected with Expanded Coverage and Improving Economy." *Health Affairs* 33 (10): 1841–50.

Song, X., W. D. Marder, R. Houchens, J. E. Conklin, and R. Bradley. 2009. "Can a Disease-Based Price Index Improve the Estimation of the Medical Consumer Price Index?" In *Price Index Concepts and Measurements*, edited by W. E. Diewert, John S. Greenlees, and Charles R. Hulten. Chicago: University of Chicago Press.

Starr, M., L. Dominiak, and A. Aizcorbe. 2014. "Decomposing Growth in Spending Finds Annual Cost of Treatment Contributed Most to Spending Growth, 1980–2006." *Health Affairs* 33:823–31.

State Health Facts Online. 2006. The Henry J. Kaiser Family Foundation. www.statehealthfacts.org.

Sturm, R. 2002. "The Effects of Obesity, Smoking, and Drinking on Medical Problems and Costs." *Health Affairs* 21 (2): 245–53.

Thorpe, K. E. 2013. "Treated Disease Prevalence and Spending per Treated Case Drove Most of the Growth in Health Care Spending in 1987–2009." *Health Affairs* 32 (5): 851–58.

Thorpe, K. E., C. S. Florence, D. H. Howard, and P. Joski. 2004. "The Impact of Obesity on Rising Medical Spending." *Health Affairs* 24:w480–86.

————. 2005. "The Rising Prevalence of Treated Disease: Effects on Private Health Insurance Spending." *Health Affairs* 24:w317–25.

Thorpe, K. E., C. S. Florence, and P. Joski. 2004. "Which Medical Conditions Account for the Rise in Health Care Spending?" *Health Affairs* 23:w437–45.

Thorpe, K. E., and D. H. Howard. 2006. "The Rise in Spending among Medicare Beneficiaries: The Role of Chronic Disease Prevalence and Changes in Treatment Intensity." *Health Affairs* 25:w378–88.

Thorpe, K. E., D. H. Howard, and K. Galactionova. 2007. "Differences in Disease Prevalence as a Source of the US-European Health Care Spending Gap." *Health Affairs* 26:w678–86.

Thorpe, K. E., L. L. Ogden, and K. Galactionova. 2010. "Chronic Conditions Account for Rise in Medicare Spending from 1987 to 2006." *Health Affairs* 29 (4): 718–24.

Trogdon, J. G., E. A. Finkelstein, and T. J. Hoerger. 2008. "Use of Econometric Models to Estimate Expenditure Shares." *Health Services Research* 43 (4): 1442–52.

Trogdon, J. G., E. A. Finkelstein, I. A. Nwaise, F. K. Tangka, and D. Orenstein. 2007. "The Economic Burden of Chronic Cardiovascular Disease for Major Insurers." *Health Promotion Practice* 8 (3): 234–42.

Ward, M. M., H. S. Javitz, W. F. Smith, and A. Bakst. 2000. "A Comparison of Three Approaches for Attributing Hospitalizations to Specific Diseases in Cost Analyses." *International Journal of Technology Assessment in Health Care* 16 (1): 125–36.

Welch, C. A., D. Czerwinski, B. Ghimire, and D. Bertsimas. 2009. "Depression and Costs of Health Care." *Psychosomatics* 50 (4): 392–401.

Yabroff, K. R., J. L. Warren, D. Schrag, A. Mariotto, A. Meekins, M. Topor, and M. L. Brown. 2009. "Comparison of Approaches for Estimating Incidence Costs of Care for Colorectal Cancer Patients." *Medical Care* 47 (suppl. 7): S56–63.

The Simultaneous Effects of Obesity, Insurance Choice, and Medical Visit Choice on Health Care Costs

Ralph Bradley and Colin Baker

7.1 Introduction

Several studies suggest that obesity increases health risk and health care spending. A publication from the National Institute of Health (1999) cites over 600 medical studies showing that obesity increases the risk of various diseases such as diabetes, stroke, and heart disease. Three examples of studies concluding that obesity increases health care costs are Cawley and Meyerhoefer (2012), who conclude "that obesity raises medical costs by $2,741"; Thorpe, Florence, and Joski (2004); and Finkelstein, Fiebelkorn, and Wang (2003).

Most studies of the effect of obesity on health care costs treat obesity and body mass index (BMI) as exogenous.[1] However, Cawley and Meyerhoefer (2012) recognize that BMI could be an endogenous right-side regressor, and use instrumental variable estimation. Their instrument is the BMI of biological children, and thus their study is limited to adults with biological children. In addition, they estimate a two-part model for medical expenditures. In the first part the probability of a nonzero medical expenditure is estimated, and in the second part a gamma regression with a log link function is estimated. Insurance status is treated as exogenous.

Other studies estimate the dollar-equivalent cost to the obese from life-expectancy loss. Others attempt to investigate the incidence of obesity costs

Ralph Bradley is division chief of Price and Index Number Research at the Bureau of Labor Statistics. Colin Baker is social science analyst at the US Department of Health and Human Services, Office of the Assistant Secretary for Planning and Evaluation.

For acknowledgments, sources of research support, and disclosure of the authors' material financial relationships, if any, please see http://www.nber.org/chapters/c13118.ack.

1. Body Mass Index is derived as (Weight in Pounds/[Height in inches]^2)703. The obesity threshhold is a BMI over 30.

(i.e., who bears the cost—the obese individual or the obese individual's employer). See Bhattacharya and Sood (2011) for a review of this literature. Like Cawley and Meyerhoefer (2012), we focus on annual per capita costs.

Despite all the evidence of obesity's adverse health effects and numerous public and private efforts, obesity rates continue to rise. This contrasts with the substantial success at reducing US smoking rates. It is difficult to find reasons that obesity rates continue to climb even though it increases the risk of many diseases. We try to do this with a simple micromodel of BMI choice. It has latent variables observable only to the individual that influences preferences when BMI, insurance, and medical visit choices are set. The model predicts that the individual will take into account the BMI choice when making the insurance choice, and conversely, when making the BMI choice, will consider the insurance choice. The endogeneity coming from the latent variables and simultaneously determined choices creates inconsistent estimates unless this endogeneity is properly treated.

Several studies explain the obesity problem through the use of behavioral economics. Ruhm (2012) models weight choice as an interaction between a deliberative (rational) system and an affective system where the weighting of the two systems is a function of an exogenous endowment of "self-control." Cutler, Glaeser, and Shapiro (2003) suggest that obesity can occur from nonrational discounting of the future benefits of dieting. These behavioral economic models are appealing because they are consistent with a neuroscience-based explanation. The difficulty with such models is that there are so many latent variables, such as self-control and the irrational discount rate, that they are hard to verify empirically. We argue in this study that disutility occurs when reducing BMI and the marginal disutility per unit of BMI reduction is randomly distributed across the population. This disutility could easily be a function of an individual's neurotransmitter system, metabolism, access to healthy food, and income/leisure resources to access gyms and weight clubs. While Cawley and Meyerhoefer (2102) emphasize genetics, we argue that genetics is at best only a part of the cause of obesity. Body mass index is still the result of choices. We use a simple micromodel to show that an unhealthy BMI could be a rational maximizing choice where the individual trades off the increased disutility of weight reduction with the increased utility coming from better health. Such a model is still consistent with the behavioral economic approach, and it provides a better guide for econometric specification of structure because it shows where and how the endogeneity occurs.[2]

In this study, instead of always using instruments to correct for endogeneity of BMI, we use control variables as outlined in Newey, Powell, and

---

2. Our micromodel is consistent with the explanation given by the Centers for Disease Control and Prevention. Their website says, "Body weight is the result of genes, metabolism, behavior, environment, culture, and socioeconomic status." See http://www.cdc.gov/obesity/adult/causes/index.html.

Vella (1999). Unlike Cawley and Meyerhoefer (2102), we do not use a two-part model, but instead estimate a multiple-selection tobit-type model that allows for the possibility that when consumers set their BMI and insurance status, and decide whether to visit a provider, latent variables are common to all these choices. If this is true, then the two-part model with exogenous insurance does not provide consistent estimates. Our methods are based on a two-period (ex ante and ex post) microeconomic model adapted from Dragone and Savorelli (2012). Their model recognizes that getting one's BMI (through consuming calories below the level of satiation) nearer to an ideal level invokes disutility, and when setting BMI, the consumer must trade off the marginal utility of additional health with the marginal disutility of feeling increasingly unsatiated.[3] In our model, both insurance status and BMI are simultaneously set ex ante. After a draw of a random health status variable in the ex post period, the consumer chooses whether or not to visit a service provider. If the consumer visits a provider, then based on the consumer's health status, the provider selects a treatment intensity.

This study uses data from the Medical Expenditure Panel Survey (MEPS). One limitation of MEPS data is that if individuals visit a provider such as an emergency room and the provider receives no payment, then the expenditure is recorded as a zero even though the treatment had an actual cost. Unlike previous studies, this study adjusts for uncompensated care. Another challenge is that not all MEPS respondents answer the height and weight questions, introducing possible bias if BMI is a consideration in not responding.

We use eight years of MEPS data from 2002 to 2010. This is a very interesting period to study obesity. During this period, MEPS shows that the national obesity rate continues to climb despite a rise in food prices in 2008 and despite little or no change in food-processing technology as during the period of the Cutler, Glaeser, and Shapiro (2003) study. Additionally, during this period, the adverse health effects of obesity were well known. Not only is obesity rising during this period, but the diseases arising from obesity such as diabetes, hypertension, and hyperlipidemia are also rising.

We start this study with a simple micromodel that shows that unhealthy BMIs can be a result of an optimizing decision. This model predicts that there can be ex ante moral hazard from having health insurance when making BMI choices, and there can be adverse selection where those with greater propensity to have higher BMIs will more likely purchase health insurance.[4] In the simple micromodel, the individual has unobserved characteristics that influence the BMI, the insurance decision, the decision to visit a medical

---

3. Their focus is on anorexia nervosa, but their micromodel can be easily adapted to obesity.
4. If wages adjust for the expected ex post costs of obesity for all employer plans, and if individual-plan premiums adjust for expected ex post costs, then there is no ex ante moral hazard or adverse selection.

provider, and the level of medical expenditures. When these conditions exist, the two-part model will not generate consistent estimates.

Since we wish to test the ex ante moral hazard and adverse-selection predictions of the model, we can only do this when individuals have a health insurance status choice. We therefore limit our analysis to adults who are not eligible for any public insurance program and are free to choose whether or not to be insured.

When we run simulations to estimate the impact of an exogenous reduction in BMI on costs, we use our model first to estimate the effects of BMI change on propensity to insure and propensity to visit a provider. Our final estimate on cost is the sum of the cost impacts due to changes in propensity to insure, medical visitation propensity, and the direct effects on costs. The Cawley and Meyerhoefer (2012) estimates only incorporate the visitation-propensity effect and the direct effects on costs.

Unlike previous studies, we account for the endogeneity of BMI by explicitly modeling and estimating BMI choice.[5] Other previous studies have not been concerned with the individual's trade-off between the health benefits of a lower BMI with the increased disutility of making the effort to reduce BMI.[6] Since this disutility of effort or BMI outcome cannot be written into an employer-sponsored insurance contract (noncontractible) nor can employer-sponsored plans risk-adjust premiums for the marginal actuarial cost of a marginal increase in BMI, we cannot get a "first-best" allocation of this disutility. (This is the reason for the ex ante moral hazard).[7] If genetics is the key factor behind BMI determination, and individuals do not choose their own BMI, then there is no ex ante moral hazard.

We get many interesting empirical results. First, we find evidence that the nonignorable response for the MEPS weight question is most likely for individuals with BMIs between 27 and 30. They are not fully obese, but there is a possibility that it is difficult to assess their weight by appearance. The obese are more likely to report their weight. Second, we find that food prices have no statistically significant effect on BMI choice. Third, we find that an increase in

5. There are other studies in other areas of obesity that also do not account for the endogeneity of obesity. Bhattacharya and Bundorf (2009) estimate the incidence of obesity by running an ordinary least squares (OLS) equation with wage as the dependent and obesity dummies as an exogenous regressor. They get unexpected results, such as a positive parameter estimate for the employer-sponsored insurance dummy. Many of their obesity parameter estimates are negative, but not statistically significant.

6. We focus on the disutility of BMI reduction because possibly intervention programs misestimate this disutility and make weight reduction sound easier than it is. When participants find that BMI reduction is not as easy as they were led to believe, they might get discouraged and drop out.

7. Bhattacharya and Sood (2006) focus entirely on this source of ex ante moral hazard, but they do use these words. Instead, they use the words "obesity externality." Even for individual plans, a marginal BMI addition to premiums can be problematic. Bhattacharya and Bundorf (2009) find that wages for employees with employer-sponsored plans do adjust for BMI effects. In this case, there is no ex ante moral hazard or adverse selection.

BMI will increase the propensity to purchase health insurance (adverse selection) and the presence of insurance has a positive effect on BMI choice (ex ante moral hazard). This confirms the predictions of our micromodel. Fourth, there is evidence that there are common latent variables that the researcher cannot observe when individuals make the medical utilization and insurance choices. Thus, correct modeling requires either the use of instrumental or control variables. The fifth finding is not directly related to the effect of obesity on costs and is counterintuitive. Those who have a high propensity not to visit providers, on average, create more cost because when they are induced to see a provider their illness has become far more severe, and this severity could have been prevented had they seen a provider earlier. Since a higher BMI increases this visit propensity, obesity's effect on this propensity generates a small cost savings. We argue that the Cawley and Meyerhoefer focus on the cost of obesity is the wrong focus. However, we find that obesity only increases costs by $430.33 compared to their $2,741. If each obese individual reduces BMI by 10 percent, on average there will only be a $45.28 reduction in medical costs. The cost elasticity of obesity is only .0115 percent.

Section 7.2 establishes the microfoundations for the econometric model in this study. Section 7.3 describes the data and estimation methods, and section 7.4 describes the results.

7.2 A Simple Micromodel

Several microeconomic studies employ behavioral economics to explain the presence of obesity. Such studies are Ruhm (2012) and Cutler, Glaeser, and Shapiro (2003). In this study, we argue that obesity can be the result of a rational utility-maximizing process. Our micromodel is borrowed from Dragone and Savorelli (2012). While their concern is with anorexia nervosa, it is still useful here because it accounts for the disutility of consuming calories below (or above) a level of satiation. Since body weight is a monotonic function of calories consumed, choosing a calorie consumption is equivalent to choosing a BMI. Therefore, unlike Dragone and Savorelli, we focus solely on the BMI choice.

There are two periods—ex ante and ex post. In the ex ante period, the consumer makes expectations on her health status and medical spending in the ex post period. Based on these expectations the consumer decides her insurance status (denoted as I_i where i indexes consumers), and her BMI (denoted as B_i). If the individual decides to buy insurance then $I_i = 1$, otherwise it is 0. Cost sharing, respectively, under insurance and no insurance is $c_{I,i}$ and $c_{N,i}(c_{I,i} < c_{N,i})$.[8] The ideal BMI (denoted as B_I) does not vary. However, there is a "natural" BMI (denoted as $B_{N,i}$), which occurs when the individual eats to

---

8. $c_{N,i}$ can be less than one. Often an uninsured individual can visit a provider and pay nothing for the service. This is particularly true of emergency room visits.

satiation and pursues no other activity to manage weight; $B_{N,i}$ varies by individual. The lower the individual's B_i goes below the satiated BMI, $B_{N,i}$, there is an increasing marginal disutility of nonsatiation. The econometrician cannot observe $B_{N,i}$. When forming expectations, there are characteristics observable by the econometrician (denoted as X_i) and other unobservable characteristics (denoted as ξ_i) that help predict the ex post health status (denoted as S_i).[9] When the ex post period begins, the consumer draws an unpredictable shock, ε_i, and the log of the health status variable is determined by[10]

(1) $$\ln(S_i) = \beta_0 + X_i\beta_1 + (|B_i - B_I|)\beta_2 + \xi_i + \varepsilon_i.$$

The severity of the ex post illness is measured by S_i. A higher S_i indicates a higher illness severity. After the draw of ε_i, the individual decides whether or not to visit a service provider. If the individual does visit the provider, the total cost (C_i) is determined as:

(2) $$C_i = Ac_i^\alpha S_i, \; c_i \in c_{I,i}, c_{N,i}, -1 < \alpha < 0.$$

In other words, after making the discrete choice of visiting the provider, total medical cost is set to equation (2). The individual's out-of-pocket cost is $c_i C_i$. The parameter α accounts for any ex post moral hazard. The effect on utility from S_i is

(3) $$U(S_i) = -BS_i^\Gamma, \; \text{No provider visit}$$

$$= -BS_i^\Gamma C_i^\theta, \; \text{With a visit}, \Gamma > 2, -1 < \theta < 0.$$

Medical spending helps lessen the disutility of illness, but not fully. To ensure this, the parameter A in equation (2) is less than B in equation (3).

The individual visits the provider if the income loss, the nonmonetary cost (t_i), and the disutility of illness after treatment is greater than the disutility of getting no treatment or[11]

(4) $$-t_i - c_iC_i - BS_i^\Gamma C_i^\theta > -BS_i^\Gamma, \text{or}$$

$$-t_i - c_iAc_i^\alpha S_i - BS_i^\Gamma(Ac_i^\alpha S_i)^\theta > -BS_i^\Gamma$$

$$-t_i - c_iAc_i^\alpha S_i - BS_i^{\Gamma+\theta}(Ac_i^\alpha)^\theta + BS_i^\Gamma > 0$$

$$H(S_i, t_i, c_i) > 0.$$

The second line is derived by substituting for C_i using equation (2). At $S_i = 0$, there is no visit since the inequality is not satisfied. However, given the restrictions $\partial H(S_i) / \partial S_i > 0$, as S_i increases there will be a threshold

---

9. ξ_i is unobservable to the econometrician, but observable to individual i.

10. ε_i is completely unpredictable by the individual, and thus is independent of X_i and ξ_i. Since S_i is a function of unobserved variables, it too is unobservable.

11. t_i incorporates time costs, anxiety costs, and all other nonobserved nonmonetary costs of seeing a provider.

$\bar{S}_i(c_i, t_i)$ where the consumer will be indifferent between visiting and not visiting the provider. If $S_i > \bar{S}_i(c_i, t_i)$, the consumer visits the provider. Obviously $\bar{S}_i(c_{I,i}, t_i) < \bar{S}_i(c_{N,i}, t_i)$.

In the ex ante period the consumer chooses her B_i and I_i by forming expectations about S_i and the choice to visit the provider in the ex post period. She will simultaneously select her BMI and insurance status to maximize the expected utility in the ex post period. In terms of the variables known by the consumer, the expected utility conditional on all variables observable to the consumer can be characterized by

(5) $$ U = U(\pi_i, c_i, X_i, B_i - B_I, B_i - B_{N,i}, \xi_i). $$

The insurance premium is π_i and is zero if the individual chooses not to buy insurance; c_i is the cost-sharing variable and can take on the values $c_{I,i}$ or $c_{N,i}$ depending on the insurance choice. The fourth argument measures the impact on expected utility from deviating from the ideal BMI, B_I. As equation (1) shows, a greater deviation from the ideal BMI increases expected illness severity.[12] The fifth argument measures the disutility of deviating away from the individual's natural BMI, $B_{N,i}$. It accounts for the increasing disutility of nonsatiation (and discomfort of physical activity) as the consumer moves further away from her natural BMI. Let U_j and U_{jk} be, respectively, the first derivative with respect to the jth argument and the second derivative with the jth and k^{th} argument. Suppose that $B_{N,i} > B_I$, and B_i is any value between $B_{N,i}$ and B_I, and the following holds[13]

(6) $$ B_i > B_I \Rightarrow U_4 < 0, U_{44} < 0 $$
$$ B_i = B_I \Rightarrow U_4 = 0, U_{44} < 0 $$
$$ B_i < B_{Ni} \Rightarrow U_5 > 0, U_{55} < 0 $$
$$ B_i = B_{Ni} \Rightarrow U_5 = 0, U_{55} < 0 $$
$$ U_1 < 0 $$
$$ U_2 < 0, U_{24} < 0. $$

The fourth argument of equation (5) is maximized when $B_i = B_I$ for any fixed values of the other arguments The fifth argument is maximized when $B_i = B_{Ni}$ for any fixed values of the other arguments. Since $B_{N,i} > B_I$, if the consumer reduces B_i there is marginal increase in utility from the fourth argument,

12. An increase of B_i away from B_I increases S_i. Equation (3) gives the reduction in utility from this additional severity, and equation (4) gives the income loss from increased medical expenditures. There could be other sources of utility loss such as reduced income from productivity losses and nonmonetary costs of increased social disapproval. Bhattacharya and Sood (2006) give more detail than this study on the results of income loss from productivity loss.

13. $U_{24} < 0$ occur because as c increases, the ex post financial impact of a higher level from illness resulting from the increased BMI increases. If wages adjust for the actuarial cost of increased BMI, then $U_{2,4} = 0$.

but a marginal decrease in the fifth argument. For a fixed insurance status, when the consumer selects B_i and $B_{N,i} > B_I$, there is a trade-off between all the benefits coming from improving health and suffering the disutility of deviating from the natural BMI.

Given the conditions in equation (6), it is easy to see that if $B_{N,i} > B_I$, then optimal B_i choice will be in the strict interior of the interval, $[B_I, B_{N,i}]$. To see this, for any π_i, c_i, X_i, ξ_i, the first-order conditions for the optimal B_i are $U_4 + U_5 = 0$. If B_i equals either B_I or $B_{N,i}$, the first-order conditions fail. If $B_i = B_I$, then individual i can increase expected utility by increasing B_i.[14]

The optimal B_i is also increasing in $B_{N,i}$. A total differentiation of the first-order conditions with respect to B_i and $B_{N,i}$ gets

(7) $(U_{44} + U_{55} + 2U_{54})dB_i - U_{55}dB_{N,i} = 0$

$$\frac{dB_i}{dB_{N,i}} = \frac{U_{55}}{U_{44} + U_{55} + 2U_{54}} > 0.$$

This result shows that $B_{N,i}$ can be high enough that obesity is a rational and optimal choice.

If the consumer decides to purchase health insurance, then the first-order conditions for the optimal choice of B_i is $U_4(\pi_i, c_{I,i}, X_i, B_i - B_I, B_i - B_{N,i}, \xi_i) + U_5(\pi_i, c_{I,i}, X_i, B_i - B_I, B_i - B_{N,i}, \xi_i) = 0$, and if the consumer decides not to buy insurance, the first-order conditions are $U_4(0, c_{N,i}, X_i, B_i - B_I, B_i - B_{N,i}, \xi_i) + U_5(0, c_{N,i}, X_i, B_i - B_I, B_i - B_{N,i}, \xi_i) = 0$. Letting B_i^{I*} and B_i^{N*} be, respectively, the optimal choices for BMI for being insured and uninsured, the consumer chooses to be insured if

(8) $U(\pi_i, c_{I,i}, X_i, B_i^{I*} - B_I, B_i^{I*} - B_{N,i}, \xi_i) >$

$$U(0, c_{N,i}, X_i, B_i^{N*} - B_I, B_i^{N*} - B_{N,i}, \xi_i).$$

Given the conditions in equation (6), we show in the first section of the appendix that $B_i^{I*} > B_i^{N*}$. Thus, insurance can generate ex ante moral hazard when it comes to BMI choices.[15]

In the second section of the appendix we show that there is also adverse selection, or equivalently, that an increase in $B_{N,i}$ increases the propensity to purchase health insurance.

---

14. The second-order condition is $U_{44} + U_{55} + 2U_{54} < 0$.

15. There are two types of moral hazard, ex post and ex ante. Ex post moral hazard occurs from the ex post overconsumption of medical services because the consumer does not pay the full marginal costs. Ex ante moral hazard occurs because efforts to prevent diseases are non-contractible in an insurance policy or premiums can't adjust for BMI choices and consumers are not compensated for the effects that their efforts at prevention have on expected benefits. Additionally, they get a lower return on their preventive efforts because they are only paying a fraction of the full costs of getting ill. In this study, the effort is the disutility of nonsatiation when setting the BMI below the natural BMI. See Bradley (2005) or Bhattacharya and Sood (2006) on a fuller depiction of ex ante moral hazard and Pauly (1968) on ex post moral hazard.

This simple model predicts both ex ante moral hazard and adverse selection. The empirical section of this study will test the predictions of this simple micromodel. The intuition here is that $B_{N,i}$ is private, asymmetric information that only the individual knows. The premium, π_i, cannot be risk adjusted for this private information. Since the optimal B_i^* choice monotonically increases with $B_{N,i}$, we can use B_i^* as an endogenous proxy when econometrically testing for adverse selection. The ex ante moral hazard occurs because the insured individual bears a smaller financial burden for her BMI decisions, and the BMI choice cannot be written into a health insurance contract.

In this framework, insurance choice, BMI choice, provider visits, and medical costs are influenced by variables $B_{N,i}$ and ξ_i that are not observable to the econometrician. Simply modeling medical cost (or C_i in equation [2]) by using insurance and B_i as an exogenous regressors, and not accounting for the provider-visit decision, will lead to endogeneit bias. Obviously, we cannot estimate equation (2) directly because we cannot observe S_i. When we substitute equation (1) to equation (2) and take logs, the estimating cost equation is

(9) $$\ln C_i = a + \alpha \ln(c_i) + X_i \beta_1 + (|B_i - B_I|)\beta_2 + \xi_i + \varepsilon_i.$$

The coefficient of interest is β_2. However, we cannot observe ξ_i. Yet, it influences both insurance and BMI choice. Suppose both $C_i > 0$ and $I_i = 1$, then both conditions (4) and (8) hold where $H(S_i(X_i, \xi_i), t_i, c_i) > 0$, and $U(\pi_i, c_{I,i}, X_i, B_i^{I*} - B_I, B_i^{I*} - B_{N,i}, \xi_i) > U(0, c_{N,i}, X_i, B_i^{N*} - B_I, B_i - B_{N,i}, \xi_i)$. The right-side regressors of equation (9) are correlated with

(10) $$\lambda(\pi_i, c_i, t_i X_i) = E(\xi_i \mid \{H(S_i(X_i, \xi_i), t_i, c_i) > 0\}$$

$$\cap \{U(\pi_i, c_{I,i}, X_i, B_i^{I*} - B_I, B_i^{I*} - B_{N,i}, \xi_i) >$$

$$U(0, c_{N,i}, X_i, B_i^{N*} - B_I, B_i - B_{N,i}, \xi_i)\}).$$

We rewrite equation (9) as:

(11) $$\ln C_i = a + \alpha \ln(c_i) + X_i \beta_1$$
$$+ (|B_i - B_I|)\beta_2 + \lambda(\pi_i, c_i, t_i X_i)$$
$$+ v_i + \varepsilon_i,$$

$$\xi_i = \lambda(\pi_i, c_i, t_i X_i) + v_i.$$

Here equation (11) is a tobit model with two selection effects, the insurance decision and the provider insurance effects. Models such as these are rarely covered in the econometrics literature. Maddala (1983, 278–83) briefly covers models with multiple selectivity, and without proof provides the estimating procedure for extending the Heckit model for two-selection effects.

The microfoundations in this section lead me to a different estimation strategy than Cawley and Meyerhoefer (2012), who emphasize evidence that genetic factors are the major determinant of weight. They do not model BMI determination as the result of decisions based on unobserved conditions. However, our micromodel predicts that ex post medical costs are a function of the simultaneous ex ante insurance and BMI decisions. The BMI decisions will affect costs both directly and through health insurance decisions. This is a feature that the Cawley and Meyerhoefer (2012) model misses. In our model, the natural BMI, $B_{N,i}$ is a condition that could easily be influenced by genetic factors, but in the end, individual i's BMI, B_i, is the result of a decision-making process. To correct for the endogeneity of BMI, we use a control variable approach where we estimate a reduced-form equation for B_i. To test the result, $B_i^{I*} > B_i^{N*}$ or that insurance induces the increase in BMI, we estimate a structural form for B_i where private insurance is endogenous.

This study's biggest departure from Cawley and Meyerhoefer (2012) is that they use a two-part model where in the first part the provider-visit decision is estimated with a logit model, and in the second part the cost equation conditional on nonzero medical expenditures is estimated independently as a gamma regression with a log link. They do not mention how they treat insurance choice, and they do not even report insurance status as a summary statistic. Their methods will only provide consistent estimates as long as the multiple-selection effects, $\lambda(\pi_i, c_i, t_i, X_i)$ in equation (11), are zero everywhere. We find that the multiple-selection effects are statistically significant.[16]

7.3   Data and Estimating Equations

7.3.1   Data

The Medical Expenditure Panel Survey (MEPS) is a stratified random sample of households in the United States in which each household remains in the sample for two years. Each year new households are sampled, and for a given year a household was either in the sample in the previous year or it was not. The survey collects for each household individual her medical expenditures, her diagnosed diseases, her perceived health status, her insurance status, her employment, and her demographic variables. While each household is interviewed five times, medical expenditures are only reported annually. This survey also surveys the medical providers and pharmacies used by the households in order to obtain more accurate expenditure data.

The MEPS household file has each individual as a unique observation and lists the total annual medical expenditure along with the economic, demographic, and BMI information. The conditions file has a diagnosed

---

16. There is a debate between the relative merits of the two-part model and the Heckit model. Dow and Norton (2003) argue that the Heckit model is often misused and t-tests for the null hypothesis, $\lambda(\pi_i, c_i, t_i, X_i) = 0$, perform poorly.

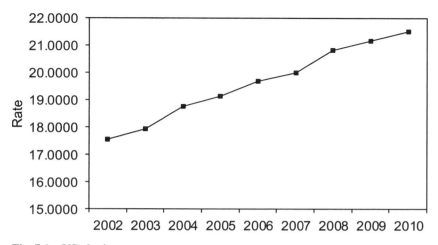

Fig. 7.1   US obesity rate
Source: Medical Expenditures Panel Survey.

condition as the unique observation, and a new record is created with each newly reported treated disease. The event files has a separate record for each office, outpatient, emergency room, and hospital visit. There is also a separate record for each pharmaceutical refill.[17]

Since 2002, MEPS has collected individual BMIs. Thus, the sample in this study starts in 2002 and ends in the last year available, 2010.

Figure 7.1 shows how the obesity rate has climbed from 2002 to 2010. Figure 7.2 compares the kernel densities for BMI for 2002 and 2010. The 2010 distribution is "flatter" and mass migrated from the 21 to 26 range in 2002 to the 30 to 45 range in 2010. Figure 7.3 compares the kernel densities for nominal per-person medical expenditures. Both the 2002 and 2010 distributions are skewed to the left. Again, the 2010 distribution is flatter and there are larger outliers. Figure 7.4 compares individual medical expenditures in 2002 dollars.[18] While there is a slight increase in the average, the densities have not changed greatly.

Table 7.1 lists selected summary statistics for the beginning year and ending year of this study.[19] Of note, the national obesity rate has climbed from 17.5 percent in 2002 to 21.5 percent in 2010. The fraction of individuals with no medical visits and cost ($C_i = 0$) rose from 14.8 percent in 2002 to 15.4

17. Since MEPS is a stratified sample, consistent variance estimation requires accounting for the clustering of the primary-sampling units and strata.
18. To get real medical expenditures, we deflate by the medical CPI so that all medical expenditures can be expressed in 2002 dollars.
19. The standard errors of the mean are in parentheses. Since MEPS is a stratified random sample, variance estimation needs to account for the stratification. In this study, we use the Taylor Series (linearization) method.

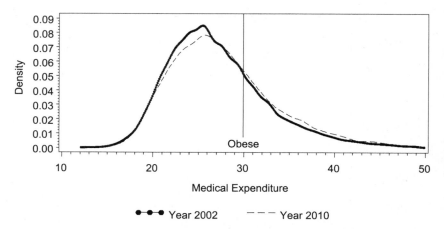

Fig. 7.2   A comparison of BMI densities between 2002 and 2010
Source: Medical Expenditures Panel Survey 2002 and 2010.

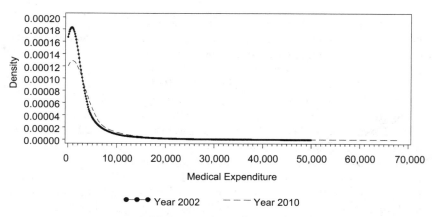

Fig. 7.3   Per-person nominal medical expenditure densities between 2002 and 2010
Source: Medical Expenditures Panel Survey 2002 and 2010.

percent in 2010. The MEPS attempts to record actual household expenditures. If an individual visits, say, an emergency room, and this visit is not reimbursed, then the event file will record a zero expenditure for this visit. In 2002, 14.7 percent of all individuals had at least one fully unreimbursed visit and this rose to 15.3 percent in 2010. This can present challenges when attempting to measure the effect of obesity on costs. Even though a visit goes unreimbursed, this does not mean that the cost of the visit is zero. This table also shows that in 2010 a smaller fraction of the population had access to a primary care physician and were covered by private health insurance.

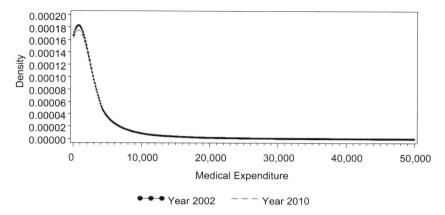

Fig. 7.4   Per-person real medical expenditure densities between 2002 and 2010
Source: Medical Expenditures Panel Survey 2002 and 2010.

Table 7.1   **Summary statistics from the Medical Expenditures Panel Survey**

Variable	Mean 2002 (Standard deviation)	Mean 2010 (Standard deviation)
Have a usual primary provider (%)	79.72	78.02
	(0.44)	(0.49)
At least one zero-cost visit (%)	14.75	15.33
	(0.32)	(0.34)
Do not see any provider (%)	14.81	15.38
	(0.32)	(0.34)
Black (%)	12.32	12.49
	(0.56)	(0.72)
Excellent perceived health	31.72	33.73
	(0.46)	(0.53)
Male (%)	48.86	49.12
	(0.26)	(0.28)
Obese (%)	17.54	21.53
	(0.24)	(0.37)
Poor perceived health (%)	2.86	2.78
	(0.13)	(0.12)
Have private insurance (%)	71.19	65.00
	(0.62)	(0.77)
Have public insurance (%)	17.05	21.89
	(0.49)	(0.59)
Uninsured (%)	11.75	13.10
	(0.33)	(0.41)
Has diabetes (%)	4.84	6.81
	(0.16)	(0.18)
Married (%)	41.63	40.19
	(0.41)	(0.49)
		(continued)

Table 7.1   (continued)

Variable	Mean 2002 (Standard deviation)	Mean 2010 (Standard deviation)
Student or employed (%)	52.78	51.72
	(0.38)	(0.47)
Other nonblack race (%)	6.64	7.71
	(0.37)	(0.58)
No children (%)	48.11	50.92
	(0.52)	(0.66)
One child (%)	17.78	17.39
	(0.38)	(0.46)
Two or more children (%)	34.11	31.69
	(0.41)	(0.39)
Age	35.75	36.83
	(0.23)	(0.26)
BMI	26.99	27.75
	(0.05)	(0.06)
Years of education	10.17	10.63
	(0.05)	(0.06)
Household size	2.73	2.64
	(0.02)	(0.03)
Individual income	22,166.50	25,711.01
	(270.38)	(365.05)
Per capita expenditure in 2002 dollars	2,813.24	3,010.42
	(59.12)	(68.26)
Imputed per capita expenditure in 2002 dollars	3,406.23	3,498.54
	(74.39)	(79.33)
Nominal per capita expenditure	2,813.24	4,094.38
	(59.12)	(92.84)
Imputed nominal per capita expenditure	3,406.23	4,758.25
	74.39	107.89
Nominal per capita out of pocket payments	538.59	581.55
	(10.20)	(13.43)
Sample size	37,418	31,228

Nominal medical spending per capita increases from \$2,813 to \$4,094, while medical spending in 2002 dollars rises only to \$3,010 in 2010.

We impute a cost for unreimbursed visits by a using an average with a shock for reimbursed expenditures. While there are controversies behind this approach, we do it to get an alternative per capita cost. Table 7.1 shows that the imputation in 2002 adds \$600 to the per capita costs.

7.3.2   Estimating Equations

Ex Ante Period

To simplify exposition, we change notation slightly in this subsection. Now X represents all the observable right-side covariates, and ξ represents all unobservables, including $B_{N,i}$ and t_i. Different models will have different right-side covariates and there is an additional subscript to distinguish the different covariates among the different models.

We model the ex ante period first where BMI and insurance choices are made. We want to verify that there is both ex ante moral hazard and adverse selection as the simple micromodel predicts.

We start with the reduced-form BMI (B_i) equation. We first need to control for the effects of responding to the weight question, as not all MEPS respondents responded. We estimate a probit model for responding to the weight question in MEPS. Let $X_{i,R}$ be the observable characteristics that govern the response to the weight question in MEPS. The individual responds if

$$(12) \qquad X_{i,R}\beta_R + u_{i,R} > 0$$

where $u_{i,R} \sim N(0, 1)$ and contains the effects of ξ_i. (From here on, all residuals, u, contain the effects of ξ_i; so for equation [12] $u_{i,R} = \gamma_R\xi_i + v_{R,i}$ where $v_{R,i}$ is an unobservable residual that effects the response decision, but not the ex post variable S_i.) Let $\hat{\beta}_R$ be the parameter estimate. We can next estimate the reduced-form equation for BMI (B_i) as

$$(13) \qquad B_i = X_{i,B}\beta_B + \lambda(X_{i,R}\hat{\beta}_R) + u_{i,B}$$

where $u_{i,B}$ is a mean zero residual and $X_{i,B}$ are exogenous covariates; $\lambda(X_{i,R}\hat{\beta}_R)$ is the inverse Mills ratio using the parameter estimate from equation (12). The estimated residual, $\hat{u}_{i,B}$, is the control variable that corrects for the endogeneity of B_i in the other models.

We estimate a structural health insurance choice model using the control variable to correct for the endogeneity of BMI choice. Let $X_{i,I}$ represent both the observable endogenous and exogenous covariate influencing insurance choice. Then

$$I_i = 1 \Rightarrow X_{i,I}\beta_I + u_{i,I} > 0$$

$$I_i = 0 \Rightarrow X_{i,I}\beta_I + u_{i,I} \leq 0.$$

In this model the coefficient for BMI is the coefficient of interest. If it is positive and significant, this gives evidence that there is adverse selection.

Next, we add private insurance status to $X_{i,B}$ in equation (12) and account for its endogeneity. When we reestimate this BMI model, interest is on the private insurance coefficient. The coefficient of interest is the private insurance effect. If it is positive and significant, then there is evidence of ex ante moral hazard.

Ex Post Period

In the ex post period, the individual decides whether or not to visit a provider, and if there is a visit then medical expenditures are set. As discussed in the section in the micromodel, the BMI, insurance, and provider visit decisions are a function of unobserved individual characteristics, ξ_i. The residuals, $u_{i,B}$ and $u_{i,P}$, from the ex ante models are functions of ξ_i as they were in the ex ante subsection.

The decision to visit a medical provider and the resulting medical expenditure from a visit are also functions of ξ_i. Therefore, BMI is an endogenous right-side regressor where a control variable is used to correct for its endogeneity. The ex ante choice of insurance status and the ex post decision to visit a provider generate a multiselection effect. The individual decision to visit a provider is specified as

(14)
$$C_i > 0 \Rightarrow X_i^C \beta_C + u_{i,C} > 0$$

$$C_i = 0 \Rightarrow X_i^C \beta_C + u_{i,C} \leq 0.$$

Finally, if $C_i > 0$, then medical expenditures estimated as a gamma regression with mean μ_i and a log link function

$$\ln \mu_i = X_i^{C>0} \beta_{C>0}$$

$$+ \text{ multiple selection effects.}$$

Notice that $X_i^C \beta_C$ in the visit choice equation (14) is not the same as $X_i^{C>0} \beta_{C>0}$ in the medical cost equation since it is the individual that is solely involved in the visit decision, but the physician is involved in the setting of medical expenditures. In the third section of the appendix, we detail how we first estimate the multivariate probit for the joint event of being insured and visiting a provider or

$$\Pr(\{X_i^C \beta_C + u_{i,C} > 0\} \cap \{X_i^I \beta_I + u_{i,I} > 0\}),$$

and then use this estimation to compute the multiple-selection effects.

7.4   Results

7.4.1   Models for the Ex Ante Period

Table 7.2 lists the parameter estimates of the probit model in equation (12) for responding to the MEPS weight questionnaire. Males are more likely to respond than females. Response improves with education. Most of the year dummies do not produce significant results. Unemployed individuals are less likely to respond. As one ages, one is less likely to respond.

Table 7.3 lists the results for the reduced-form BMI equation in (13). We used the Producer Price Index (PPI) for corn syrup divided by the all items Consumer Price Index (CPI) as a proxy for the relative price for the food. Corn syrup is an intermediate product for foods considered the major culprit behind obesity. The parameter estimate is negative but not significant. Income is excluded for endogeneity reasons, but we include a regressor label

Table 7.2   **Estimates for BMI response model**

Variable	Estimate
Intercept	1.549**
	(0.095)
Male	0.327**
	(0.019)
Age	−0.004**
	(0.001)
Black	−0.014
	(0.032)
Employed or student	0.099**
	(0.027)
Number of children	0.090*
	(0.038)
Years of education	0.026**
	(0.006)
Other race	0.112**
	(0.042)
Household size	−0.085*
	(0.036)
Dummy for 2002	0.080*
	(0.035)
Dummy for 2003	0.086*
	(0.038)
Dummy for 2004	0.004
	(0.037)
Dummy for 2005	0.026
	(0.037)
Dummy for 2006	0.021
	(0.041)
Dummy for 2007	−0.033
	(0.037)
Dummy for 2008	0.076*
	0.033
Married	−0.051
	(0.040)
Household income	0.000
	(0.000)
Individual income	0.000
	(0.000)
Sum of household's years of education	0.008*
	(0.004)
Number of high occupations	−0.017
	(0.020)

**Significant at the 1 percent level.
*Significant at the 5 percent level.

Table 7.3	Control equation for BMI	
	Variable	Estimate
	Intercept	20.109**
		(0.803)
	Age	0.009**
		(0.003)
	Years of education	0.106**
		(0.021)
	Have a provider	1.015**
		(0.039)
	Price of corn syrup	−0.887
		(0.491)
	Has arthritis	−0.646**
		(0.026)
	Black	1.673**
		(0.054)
	Spouse's income	0.000**
		(0.000)
	Employed or student	0.928**
		(0.077)
	Household size	−0.106**
		(0.045)
	Male	3.464**
		(0.186)
	Number of high occupations	−0.146**
		(0.030)
	Number of children	0.334**
		(0.054)
	Other race	−0.974**
		(0.085)
	Dummy for 2002	−0.508**
		(0.151)
	Dummy for 2003	−0.384**
		(0.137)
	Dummy for 2004	−0.826**
		(0.137)
	Dummy for 2005	−0.609**
		(0.143)
	Dummy for 2006	−0.478**
		(0.117)
	Dummy for 2007	−0.742**
		(0.078)
	Dummy for 2008	0.432**
		(0.072)
	Inverse Mills	103.333**
		(7.416)
	Inverse Mills sq.	−275.670**
		(22.837)

**Significant at the 1 percent level.
*Significant at the 5 percent level.

"number of high occupations." This is the total number of people in the individual's household who are either in a professional, technical, or government occupation. It proxies one's ability to access resources that can help control weight such as gyms and better food. We exclude the individual's own income because of possible income discrimination against obese individuals. We include spouse's income, and set to 0 for single individuals. While the coefficient on the number of high occupations is significantly negative, the coefficient for the spouse's income is positive and significant although it is small in magnitude. The most interesting result is that if one does a simple Heckit, the coefficient on the inverse Mills ratio is negative. We then add the square of the inverse Mills ratio. The parameter estimate for the squared term is negative, while it is positive for the regular inverse Mills ratio. It seems that the BMIs where the sum of these two terms peak is in the 26 to 28 BMI range. This is the range where it is perhaps most possible to hide one's true weight.

Table 7.4 shows the parameter estimates for the ex ante insurance choice in equation (14). The coefficient of interests is for the BMI (B_i) and it is significantly positive. This leads to the conclusion that there is adverse selection with BMI. Individuals with higher BMI are more likely to purchase insurance. The other results are not surprising. Young men have a lower propensity to purchase insurance, where as individuals with children who do not benefit from the State Children's Health Insurance Program (SCHIP) where both spouses work in technical, professional, or government occupations have a much higher propensity to purchase insurance.

Table 7.5 lists the parameter estimates from a structural BMI equation where private insurance is treated as an endogenous variable. The coefficient of interest is the dummy variable for being privately insured. This provides evidence of ex ante moral hazard.

In the ex ante period, both insurance status and BMI are determined. If the individual purchases insurance, the financial consequences of illness are less severe, and the policyholder is not compensated by the plan for the savings generated by suffering additional disutility to get the BMI nearer to an ideal level. This is ex ante moral hazard.

Likewise, employer-sponsored insurance premiums do not seem to be risk adjusted for increases in BMI. As BMI increases, so does the risk of severe diseases. This increases the expected utility of holding health insurance. This is adverse selection.

7.4.2   Models for the Ex Post Period

The goal is to estimate a cost equation. Yet, the choice to visit a provider in the ex post period and the ex ante choice of insurance status are statistically dependent decisions (because of ξ_i), and will influence medical spending if and when the individual decides to visit a provider.

We estimate a multiple-selection model where the estimation methods is detailed in the third section of the appendix. In this method, we first estimate

Table 7.4   **Insurance selection with BMI as endogenous**

Variable	Estimate
Intercept	−2.46112**
	(0.1131)
Age	−0.00009
	(0.0016)
EDUCYR	0.11093**
	0.00488
BMI	0.00510**
	(0.0012)
Male	−0.39402**
	(0.0803)
Age * male	0.00464**
	(0.0018)
Household size	0.21084**
	(0.0375)
Individual income	0.00002**
	(0.0000)
Total household income	0.00001**
	(0.0000)
Number of high occupations	0.58573**
	(0.0319)
Black	0.10209*
	(0.0401)
Perceived poor health	−0.23748**
	(0.0556)
SCHIP children	−0.86159**
	(0.0300)
Perceived excellent health	0.06659*
	(0.0286)
Number of children	0.00612
	(0.0517)
Have a primary provider	1.21294**
	(0.0273)
Dummy for 2002	0.37017**
	(0.0493)
Dummy for 2003	0.29947**
	(0.0489)
Dummy for 2004	0.26344**
	(0.0497)
Dummy for 2005	0.18161**
	(0.0499)
Dummy for 2006	0.09834*
	(0.0466)
Dummy for 2007	0.09592*
	(0.0452)
Dummy for 2008	0.02465
	(0.0365)

**Significant at the 1 percent level.
*Significant at the 5 percent level.

Table 7.5   **BMI choice with insurance as endogenous**

Variable	Estimate
Intercept	19.333**
	(0.380)
Age	0.015**
	(0.002)
Years of education	0.106**
	(0.013)
Individual income	0.000**
	(0.000)
Privately insured	1.528**
	(0.075)
Male	2.805**
	(0.110)
Number of children	0.631**
	(0.045)
Black	1.661**
	(0.048)
Other race	−1.322**
	(0.069)
Household size	−0.390**
	(0.036)
Employed or student	0.711**
	(0.055)
Response Mills	87.090**
	(4.326)
Response Mills sq.	−206.489**
	14.540
Insurance Mills	−1.314**
	(0.072)

**Significant at the 1 percent level.
*Significant at the 5 percent level.

a bivariate normal probit for insurance choice ($I_i = 1$ or 0) and for provider choice ($C_i > 0$ or $C_i = 0$). The results of this model are detailed in table 7.6. The income variables have been scaled where they are divided by \$100,000. The estimated parameters have signs that are expected except for the "poor perceived health" coefficient, which is negative in the insurance-choice equation. Perhaps, most who have poor perceived health find that medical treatments are not effective at mitigating their illness, and this gives them less propensity to insure. The coefficient ρ that measures the statistical dependence between the two decisions is positive and significant.

It should be noted that the corner solution tobit effects for ($C_i > 0$) are not as simple as the standard tobit model (type 1) as depicted in section 10.2 of Amemiya (1985). It better conforms to the type 2 definition as defined

Table 7.6 **Parameter estimates of multivariate probit model**

Insurance propensity	Estimate	Propensity to visit provider	Estimate
Intercept	−1.545**	Intercept	−3.240**
	(0.037)		(0.277)
Age	0.002**	Male	−0.539**
	(0.001)		(0.013)
Years of education	0.064**	Age	0.010**
	(0.002)		(0.001)
BMI	0.002**	Black	−0.327**
	(0.000)		(0.022)
Male	−0.106**	Poor perceived health	0.710**
	(0.036)		(0.040)
Age * male	0.001	BMI	0.090**
	(0.001)		(0.010)
Household size	0.100**	Employed or student	−0.063**
	(0.011)		(0.013)
Individual income	0.873**	Number of children	0.052**
	(0.034)		(0.018)
Sum of family income	0.644**	Years education	0.054**
	(0.026)		(0.003)
Number in high occupations	0.346**	Other race	−0.067**
	(0.009)		(0.024)
Black	0.112**	Household size	−0.127**
	(0.013)		(0.017)
Poor perceived health	−0.133**	2002 dummy	0.174**
	(0.027)		(0.018)
SCHIP household	−0.438**	2003 dummy	0.174**
	(0.007)		(0.019)
Perceived excellent health	0.081**	2004 dummy	0.106**
	(0.011)		(0.017)
Number of children	0.028*	2005 dummy	0.125**
	(0.013)		(0.017)
Have primary provider	0.710**	2006 dummy	0.096**
	(0.010)		(0.017)
2002 dummy	0.223**	2007 dummy	0.111**
	(0.016)		(0.017)
2003 dummy	0.163**	2008 dummy	0.047**
	(0.017)		(0.016)
2004 dummy	0.139**	Married	0.009
	(0.017)		(0.019)
2005 dummy	0.096**	All income	0.284**
	(0.017)		(0.025)
2006 dummy	0.062**	Individual income	0.206**
	(0.017)		(0.031)
2007 dummy	0.067**	Sum of household's	0.012**
	(0.017)	education years	(0.002)

Table 7.6   (continued)

Insurance propensity	Estimate	Propensity to visit provider	Estimate
2008 dummy	0.034*	Number in high	0.149**
	(0.017)	occupations	(0.009)
		Have primary	0.816**
		provider	(0.014)
		ρ	0.310**
			(0.006)

**Significant at the 1 percent level.
*Significant at the 5 percent level.

in section 10.7 of Amemiya (1985), where the covariates of the selection effect of choosing to visit can be different from the covariates in the medical expenditure equation. The visiting decision is made solely by the individual, whereas the physician has final authority over the medical expenditure decision.

The parameter estimates for the gamma medical expenditure regression with a log link function are listed in table 7.7. We estimated one regression without imputing the zero costs for unreimbursed payment and another with the imputed costs. All the coefficients have the expected sign except for the visit selection effect, $E_{i,2}$ as defined in equation (A.7) in the third section of the appendix. The result here says that those with a very low propensity to visit a provider do end up generating higher costs when they do see a provider. In our micromodel in equation (4), the individual's underlying illness severity, S_i is not the only variable influencing the decision to visit the provider. There is also the nonmonetary cost variable, t_i (as depicted in equation [4]), that is randomly distributed throughout the population. This variable will have a large absolute value if individual i has a phobia against visiting providers. Suppose that individuals i and j have the same observable covariates, X, but if i has a phobia against visiting physicians but j does not, then $t_i > t_j$. This implies that threshold sickness level of i to visit a provider is greater than j's threshold level. Since they have the same observable variables, it must be that when i does visit a provider, the expected value of ξ_i is greater than the expected value of ξ_j. This implies that given that both i and j have decided to visit a provider, the expected value of i's expenditure will be greater than j's expected expenditure. For example, suppose both individuals have colon cancer. Individual j goes to the provider when this cancer is in its early stages, and individual i waits until the cancer is extreme and has spread throughout his body.

The other coefficients have their expected signs. The insurance effect is positive and significant as expected. The BMI coefficient is significant and positive.

Table 7.7   **Parameter estimates for cost equation**

Variable	Cost not imputed	Cost imputed
Intercept	7.706**	7.606**
	(0.039)	(0.040)
BMI	0.003**	0.003**
	(0.001)	(0.001)
Male	−0.117**	−0.184**
	(0.011)	(0.011)
Perceived poor health	1.002**	1.114**
	(0.030)	(0.031)
Have a primary provider	0.071**	0.211**
	(0.020)	(0.020)
Perceived excellent health	−0.421**	−0.444**
	(0.010)	(0.011)
Black	−0.001	0.020
	(0.016)	(0.016)
Age	0.018**	0.019**
	(0.000)	(0.000)
Employed or student	−0.300**	−0.298**
	(0.013)	(0.013)
Other race	−0.042*	−0.112**
	(0.018)	(0.019)
2002 dummy	−0.146**	−0.112**
	(0.017)	(0.017)
2003 dummy	0.006	0.027
	(0.017)	(0.017)
2004 dummy	−0.007	0.013
	(0.017)	(0.017)
2005 dummy	−0.015	0.023
	(0.016)	(0.017)
2006 dummy	−0.061**	−0.030
	(0.016)	(0.017)
2007 dummy	0.009	−0.003
	(0.016)	(0.017)
2008 dummy	−0.058**	−0.033
	0.016	0.017
E1	0.227**	0.191**
	(0.009)	(0.010)
E2	−0.928**	−0.372**
	(0.040)	(0.041)

**Significant at the 1 percent level.
*Significant at the 5 percent level.

7.4.3   Simulations

We run three separate simulations. The first one estimates the cost of obesity on a per-person basis. This is the same estimation as the $2,741 estimate made by Cawley and Meyerhoefer (2012). The second one estimates the effect of a 10 percent BMI reduction for all obese persons. The last estimates the obesity elasticity of cost.

Table 7.8   **Impact of obesity on medical cost**

Cost of obesity	Estimate ($)
Average direct cost of obesity	430.52
Cost from additional propensity to insure	3.83
Cost reduction from increase propensity to visit provider	−4.02
Cumulative effects	430.33

Average effect of a 10 percent reduction in BMI	Estimate ($)
Average direct effect	−45.44
Effect from reduced propensity to insure	−0.63
Effect from reduced propensity to visit provider	0.79
Cumulative effects	−45.28

Percent reduction in cost from a 1 percent reduction in BMI	Estimate (%)
Direct	0.0115
Effect from insurance propensity	0.0002
Effect from visiting propensity	−0.0003
Cumulative effects	0.0115

The results of the simulation are listed in table 7.8; our counterpart estimate to Cawley and Meyerhoefer (2012) is $430. We break down the components of this effect into the effects coming from insurance change and change-in-visit propensity, as well as the direct effect. Notice that the increased-visiting propensity actually reduces costs by $4. Our result represents 14 percent of real per-person expenditures in 2010. My results are 84 percent lower than Cawley and Meyerhoefer (2012).

Obesity has always been with us and it will not go away. Therefore, we do not believe that the correct question is the cost of obesity. It might be more instructive to determine the impact of an exogenous 10 percent in BMI for all obese persons. Table 7.8 reports a $45 reduction if all obese persons reduce their BMI by 10 percent. There are many reasons that our results might differ from the Cawley and Meyerhoefer (2012) results. Our estimation uses all adults who are not eligible for public insurance, while they use only adults with biological children. Our estimation methods are vastly different. We use a control variable method to account for the endogeneity of BMI in a cost estimation; they instrument with the BMI of biological children. We also model and estimate how individuals make their BMI decisions and this influences our parameter estimates, but do not influence Cawley and Meyerhoefer's (2012) estimates. We also account for the endogeneity of insurance.

Finally, we find the percent reduction in costs for every 1 percent decrease in BMI for obese persons. Here the elasticity is only .0115 percent.

High BMI does increase costs, but a policy that is successful in reducing BMI will not generate the cost savings that were previously thought.

7.5 Conclusions

While we do find that obesity does have a positive impact on health care costs, its magnitude is lower than that of Thorpe, Florence, and Joski (2004), and especially Cawley and Meyerhoefer (2012). It conforms more closely to results from Baker and Duchnovny (2010). They found that "if the distribution of adults by weight between 1987 and 2007 had changed only to reflect demographic changes, then health care spending per adult in 2007 would have been roughly 3 percent below the actual 2007 amount." Unlike Cawley and Meyerhoefer (2012), we do not limit our attention to adults with biological children.

Nonetheless, obesity is a national problem and it continues to increase. While we have found that moral hazard plays a role in setting BMI choices, and likewise BMI is a consideration in health insurance choices, we have not been able to answer the questions, "Why is obesity increasing when we know its adverse health effects?" and "Why haven't past private and public interventions worked?" The answers to these questions, perhaps, require the coordinated research of many disciplines—biology, epidemiology, statistics, and maybe even economics. Yet, our micromodel might provide an initial clue. Perhaps current intervention programs underestimate the marginal disutility that obese individuals face when reducing an additional BMI. People enter these interventions with a false notion of the required effort, and this leads most to fail.

One major problem of modeling and estimating health care costs is that the observable covariates such as age, gender, race, and so forth, explain very little of the variation of health care costs. This gives evidence that the unobserved characteristics that we denote as ξ_i in this study play a larger role in cost determination than the observable characteristics.

We have findings that are unrelated to obesity, but they are important. A higher propensity to visit a provider reduces expected health costs because diseases can be treated at an earlier stage. Important in this decision to visit a provider is the access to a primary provider. The MEPS survey shows that from 2002 to 2010 the percentage of individuals with a primary provider has dropped from 79.7 percent to 78.0 percent. This trend could have negative effects on both future costs and health outcomes.

Appendix

Proof $B_i^{I*} > B_i^{N*}$

This is the proof that $B_i^{I*} > B_i^{N*}$. Differentiating $U_4(0, c_{N,i}, X_i, B_i - B_I, B_i - B_{N,i}, \xi_i) + U_5(0, c_{N,i}, X_i, B_i - B_I, B_i - B_{N,i}, \xi_i) = 0$ with respect to both B_i and c_i gets

$$U_{42}dc_i + (U_{44} + U_{55} + 2U_{54})dB_i = 0.$$

The second-order condition of the optimization for B_i is $U_{44} + U_{55} + 2U_{54} < 0$. Thus

$$\frac{dB_i}{dc_i} = -\frac{U_{42}}{U_{44} + U_{55} + 2U_{54}} < 0.$$

Since $c_{I,i} < c_{N,i}$, the result holds.

Proof of Increases in $B_{N,i}$ Increases Propensity to Insure

The individual insures if

$$U^I = U(\pi_i, c_{I,i}, X_i, B_i^{I*} - B_I, B_i^{I*} - B_{N,i}, \xi_i) >$$

$$U(0, c_{N,i}, X_i, B_i^{N*} - B_I, B_i - B_{N,i}, \xi_i) = U^N.$$

An increase in $B_{N,i}$ will increase the propensity to insure if

$$U_4^I \frac{dB_i^{I*}}{dB_{N,i}} + U_5^I \left(\frac{dB_i^{I*}}{dB_{N,i}} - 1\right) -$$

$$U_4^N \frac{dB_i^{N*}}{dB_{N,i}} + U_5^N \left(\frac{dB_i^{N*}}{dB_{N,i}} - 1\right) > 0.$$

From the Envelope Theorem,

$$U_4^I \frac{dB_i^{I*}}{dB_{N,i}} + U_5^I \frac{dB_i^{I*}}{dB_{N,i}} = U_4^N \frac{dB_i^{N*}}{dB_{N,i}} + U_5^N \frac{dB_i^{N*}}{dB_{N,i}} = 0.$$

Thus, I need only show that $U_5^N > U_5^I$. This result holds because from the first appendix section, $B_i^{I*} > B_i^{N*}$.

Derivation of Multiselection Effects

Let X_i^I and X_i^C be, respectively, the observed variables that influence the decision to insure and the decision to visit a medical provider. The individual will insure if

(A.1) $$X_i^I \beta_I + u_{i,I} > 0,$$

and will visit a provider if

(A.2) $$X_i^C \beta_C + u_{i,C} > 0.$$

If the individual visits a provider, then medical expenditures C_i has a gamma distribution with mean μ_i. I posit a log link function where

(A.3) $\ln\mu_i = X_i^{C>0}\beta_{C>0} + E(\xi_i \mid \{X_i^C\beta_C + u_{i,C} > 0\}\cap\{X_i^I\beta_I + u_{i,I} > 0\}$

for insured patients, and for uninsured patients

(A.4) $\ln\mu_i = X_i^{C>0}\beta_{C>0} + E(\xi_i \mid \{X_i^C\beta_C + u_{i,C} > 0\}\cap\{X_i^I\beta_I + u_{i,I} \leq 0\}$.

I then posit

(A.5)
$$\begin{bmatrix} u_{i,I} \\ u_{i,C} \\ \xi_i \end{bmatrix} \sim N(0, \Sigma).$$

Let $\Sigma_{i,j}$ be the (i, j) element of Σ; $\Sigma_{1,1} = \Sigma_{2,2} = 1$ and $\Sigma_{1,2} = \rho$. Then, from Manjunath and Stephan (2012)

(A.6) $E(\xi_i \mid \{a_1 < u_{i,I} < b_1\}\cap\{a_2 < u_{i,C} < b_2\}) = \Sigma_{1,3}E_{1,i} + \Sigma_{2,3}E_{2,i}$

and

(A.7) $E_{1,i} = E(u_{i,I} \mid \{a_1 < u_{i,I} < b_1\}\cap\{a_2 < u_{i,C} < b_2\})$

$E_{2,i} = E(u_{i,C} \mid \{a_1 < u_{i,I} < b_1\}\cap\{a_2 < u_{i,C} < b_2\})$.

More specifically, let $c = 1 / \sqrt{1 - \rho^2}$

(A.8) $E(u_{i,I} \mid \{a_1 < u_{i,I} < b_1\}\cap\{a_2 < u_{i,C} < b_2\})$

$= \phi(a_1)[\Phi((b_2 - \rho a_1)c) - \Phi((a_2 - \rho a_1)c)]$

$- \phi(b_1)[\Phi((b_2 - \rho b_1)c) - \Phi((a_2 - \rho b_1)c)]$

$+ \rho\phi(a_2)[\Phi((b_1 - \rho a_2)c) - \Phi((a_1 - \rho a_2)c)]$

$- \rho\phi(b_2)[\Phi((b_1 - \rho b_2)c) - \Phi((a_1 - \rho b_2)c)]$.

Likewise, let $p = \Pr\{a_1 < u_{i,I} < b_1\}\cap\{a_2 < u_{i,C} < b_2\}$, then

(A.9) $pE(u_{i,C} \mid \{a_1 < u_{i,I} < b_1\}\cap\{a_2 < u_{i,C} < b_2\})$

$= \phi(a_2)[\Phi((b_1 - \rho a_2)c) - \Phi((a_1 - \rho a_2)c)]$

$- \phi(b_2)[\Phi((b_1 - \rho b_2)c) - \Phi((a_1 - \rho b_2)c)]$

$+ \rho\phi(a_1)[\Phi((b_2 - \rho a_1)c) - \Phi((a_2 - \rho a_1)c)]$

$- \rho\phi(b_1)[\Phi((b_2 - \rho b_1)c) - \Phi((a_2 - \rho b_1)c)]$.

To estimate the selection effects, $\Sigma_{1,3}E_{1,i} + \Sigma_{2,3}E_{2,i}$, I start with a bivariate probit estimation of $I_i = 1$ and $C_i > 0$, or

(A.10) $\Pr(X_i'\beta_I + u_{i,I} > 0, X_i^C\beta_C + u_{i,C} > 0) = \Pr(-u_{i,I} < X_i'\beta_I, -u_{i,C} < X_i'\beta_I)$

$$= \Phi(X_i'\beta_I, X_i^C\beta_C, \rho)$$

where $\Phi(.,.,.)$ is a standard bivariate normal distribution. Let $\hat{\beta}_I, \hat{\beta}_C, \hat{\rho}$ be the parameter estimates from this bivariate probit estimation. Then if $I_i = 0$ and $C_i = 0$, I compute equations (A.9) and (A.10) by setting $a_1 = -\infty, b_1 = -X_i'\hat{\beta}_I, a_2 = -\infty, \beta_2 = -X_i^C\hat{\beta}_C$, and $\rho = \hat{\rho}$. Likewise if $I_i = 0$ and $C_i > 0$, then $X_i'\beta_I + u_{i,I} \le 0$ or $u_{i,I} \le -X_i'\beta_I$ and $X_i^C\beta_C > -u_{i,C}$. I compute equations (A.9) and (A.10) by setting $a_1 = -\infty, b_1 = -X_i'\hat{\beta}_I, a_2 = -\infty$, $\beta_2 = X_i^C\hat{\beta}_C$, and $\rho = -\hat{\rho}$. I do similar calculations for ($I_i = 1$ and $C_i = 0$) and ($I_i = 1$ and $C_i > 0$).

The parameters $\Sigma_{1,3}$ and $\Sigma_{2,3}$ are estimated as coefficients in the gamma regression of cost equation. Apparently, there is a negative coefficient for $\Sigma_{2,3}$. This is evidence that individuals with a high unobserved propensity not to see a provider (i.e., a highly negative $u_{i,C}$) will generate higher medical costs if they do see a provider because they have usually waited too long to see a provider and are sicker than they would have been if they had seen a provider sooner.

References

Amemiya, T. 1985. *Advanced Econometrics*. Cambridge, MA: Harvard University Press.

Baker, C., and N. Duchnovny. 2010. "How Does Obesity in Adults Affect Spending on Health Care?" *Economic and Budget Issue Brief*, Sept. 8. Congressional Budget Office.

Bhattacharya, J., and M. K. Bundorf. 2009. "The Incidence of the Healthcare Cost of Obesity." *Journal of Health Economics* 28:649–58.

Bhattacharya, J., and N. Sood. 2006. "Health Insurance and the Obesity Externality." In *Advances in Health Economics and Health Services Research*, vol. 17, edited by K. Bolin and J. Cawley, 279–318. Bingley, UK: Emerald Group Publishing Limited.

———. 2011. "Who Pays for Obesity?" *Journal of Economic Perspectives* 25 (1): 139–58.

Bradley, R. 2005. "A Semi-Parametric Model For Asymmetric Information In Health Plan Markets." *Economic Inquiry* 43:812–22.

Cawley, J., and C. Meyerhoefer. 2012. "The Medical Care Costs of Obesity: An Instrumental Variables Approach." *Journal of Health Economics* 31 (1): 219–30.

Cutler, D. M., E. M. Glaeser, and J. M. Shapiro. 2003. "Why Have Americans Become More Obese?" *Journal of Economic Perspectives* 17 (3): 93–118.

Dow, W. H., and E. C. Norton. 2003. "Choosing between and Interpreting the Heckit and Two-Part Models for Corner Solutions." *Health Services and Outcomes Research Methodology* 4:5–18.

Dragone, D., and L. Savorelli. 2012. "Thinness and Obesity: A Model of Food Consumption, Health Concerns, and Social Pressure." *Journal of Health Economics* 31 (1): 243–56.

Finkelstein, E. A., I. C. Fiebelkorn, and G. Wang. 2003. "National Medical Spending Attributable to Overweight and Obesity: How Much and Who is Paying?" *Health Affairs* W3:219–26.

Maddala, G. S. 1983. *Limited Dependent and Qualitative Variables in Econometrics.* New York: Cambridge University Press.

Manjunath, B. G., and W. Stephan. 2012. "Moments Calculations for the Doubly Truncated Multivariate Normal Density." Working Paper, University of Portugal.

National Institute of Health. 1999. "NHLBI Obesity Education Initiative. Clinical Guidelines on the Identification, Evaluation, and Treatment of Overweight and Obesity in Adults." Publication no. 98-4083, National Institute of Health and National Heart, Blood, and Lung Institute.

Newey, W. K., J. L. Powell, and F. Vella. 1999. "Nonparametric Estimation of Triangular Simultaneous Equations Models." *Econometrica* 67 (3): 565–603.

Pauly, M. V. 1968. "The Economics of Moral Hazard: Comment." *American Economic Review* 58 (3, part 1): 531–37.

Ruhm, C. J. 2012. "Understanding Overeating and Obesity." *Journal of Health Economics* 31 (6): 781–98.

Thorpe, K. E., C. S. Florence, and P. Joski. 2004. "Which Medical Conditions Account for the Rise in Health Care Spending?" *Health Affairs* 23: W437–45.

III

Prescription Pharmaceutical Markets

8

The Regulation of Prescription Drug Competition and Market Responses
Patterns in Prices and Sales following Loss of Exclusivity

Murray L. Aitken, Ernst R. Berndt, Barry Bosworth, Iain M. Cockburn, Richard Frank, Michael Kleinrock, and Bradley T. Shapiro

8.1 Introduction and Background

Since early in the first decade of the twenty-first century, large numbers of brand name prescription drugs have lost the exclusive right to sell their products due to patent expiration and challenges. This loss of exclusivity (LOE) resulted in substantially lower prices for payers and consumers and reduced revenues for brand name prescription drug manufacturers. Com-

Murray L. Aitken is senior vice president and executive director of QuintilesIMS. Ernst R. Berndt is the Louis E. Seley Professor in Applied Economics at the MIT Sloan School of Management, and a research associate of the National Bureau of Economic Research. Barry Bosworth is a senior fellow in the economic studies program, the Robert V. Roosa Chair in International Economics, at the Brookings Institution. Iain M. Cockburn is the Richard C. Shipley Professor of Management at Boston University and a research associate of the National Bureau of Economic Research. Richard Frank is the Margaret T. Morris Professor of Health Economics at Harvard Medical School and a research associate of the National Bureau of Economic Research. Michael Kleinrock is research director at QuintilesIMS. Bradley T. Shapiro is assistant professor of marketing and Beatrice Foods Co. Faculty Scholar at the University of Chicago Booth School of Business.
This research was supported by the National Institute of Aging of the National Institutes of Health under grant number R01 AG043560 to the National Bureau of Economic Research. In addition, Mr. Shapiro's research was supported in part by a Health and Aging Fellowship from the National Institute of Aging via the National Bureau of Economic Research, grant number T32-AG000186. The statements, findings, conclusions, views, and opinions contained and expressed herein are based in part on data provided under license from IMS Health Incorporated Information Services: National Prescription Audit (June 2009–May 2013), IMS Health Incorporated. All rights reserved. The statements, findings, conclusions, views, and opinions contained and expressed herein are solely the responsibility of the authors and do not necessarily represent the official views of the National Institutes of Health, IMS Health Incorporated, any of its affiliated or subsidiary entities, the National Bureau of Economic Research, or the institutions with whom the authors are affiliated. For acknowledgments, sources of research support, and disclosure of the authors' material financial relationships, if any, please see http://www.nber.org/chapters/c13094.ack.

pared with the 1980s and 1990s, the speed with which generics have gained market share from brands following LOE has accelerated.[1] Research has investigated market responses to LOE by examining generic entry, focusing on the rate at which generics are substituted for brands,[2] the path of prices (generic, brand, and molecule) paid,[3] total (brand plus generic) molecule utilization following LOE,[4] the relationship between the number of generic manufacturers entering markets and prices, and trends in the duration of market exclusivity prior to initial LOE,[5] among other issues.[6]

In recent years, the policy debate related to LOE in the United States has centered on provisions in the Hatch-Waxman Act that govern entry of generics. Most recently these provisions have figured prominently in the 2013 Supreme Court ruling on "pay for delay." Under the Hatch-Waxman framework, generic drug companies have increased the rate at which they file so-called Paragraph IV challenges to the patent position of originator companies, either contesting the validity of the patents that protect brand name products or claiming that their version of the drug does not infringe them. The substantial number of these challenges is in large measure due to the strong incentives created by the provision of the Hatch-Waxman Act that grants a 180-day period during which the successful challenger is the exclusive seller of the generic. In these circumstances, the generic may be able to win substantial market share from the brand with only a modest discount off the brand price, though it is important to note that the substantial profits that can accrue to the generic during this period may be reduced by additional competition from the brand that has the right to contract with a generic manufacturer to market a so-called authorized generic product.[7] In fact, launching an authorized generic in the face of challenges from a generic

1. See, for example, Aitken, Berndt, and Cutler (2008), Aitken and Berndt (2011), Berndt and Aitken (2011), and Generic Pharmaceutical Association (2012, 2013).

2. Berndt, Cockburn, and Griliches (1996), Caves, Whinston, and Hurwitz (1991), Cook (1998), Ellison et al. (1997), Ellison and Ellison (2011), Frank and Salkever (1992, 1997), Grabowski and Kyle (2007), Grabowski et al. (2011), Grabowski, Long, and Mortimer (2011, 2013), Grabowski and Vernon (1992, 1996), Griliches and Cockburn (1994), Hurwitz and Caves (1998), Reiffen and Ward (2005), Saha et al. (2006), Scott Morton (1999, 2000), and Wiggins and Maness (2004).

3. Cook (1998), Frank and Salkever (1992, 1997), Regan (2008), and Wiggins and Maness (2004).

4. Aitken, Berndt, and Cutler (2008) and Caves, Whinston, and Hurwitz (1991).

5. Grabowski et al. (2011), Grabowski and Kyle (2007), and Hemphill and Sampat (2012).

6. Other aspects studied include factors determining the extent and composition of generic manufacturer entry (Scott Morton 1999, 2000), characteristics of molecules that impede or accelerate generic penetration (Grabowski, Long, and Mortimer 2011, 2013), differential therapeutic class composition between retail and mail order generic-drug dispensing (Wosinska and Huckman 2004), and variation among states with large public-funded programs such as Medicaid in exploiting cost-savings opportunities following the brand's LOE (Avalere Health LLC 2010; Brill 2010; Kelton, Chang, and Kreling 2013).

7. Appelt (2013), Berndt et al. (2007), Branstetter, Chatterjee, and Higgins (2011), Federal Trade Commission (2002, 2009, 2011), Grabowski et al. (2011), Hemphill and Sampat (2012), Olson and Wendling (2013), Panattoni (2011), and Wang (2012).

manufacturer has become a widespread industry practice.[8] Following the 180-day limited competition (duopoly with brand and exclusive generic, or triopoly with an additional authorized generic entrant), unfettered competition emerges, typically characterized by extensive generic entry and sharp price declines. In such situations the generic penetration and price reductions during the first 180 days following LOE can differ substantially from subsequent generic price and quantity movements when generic entry is unfettered.[9]

We extend and expand upon this literature by comparing the magnitude of quantity movements with the size of price reductions during and after the 180-day exclusivity period. We do so by carefully examining six molecules facing initial LOE between June 2009 and May 2013 that were among the fifty most prescribed molecules in the United States in May 2013. We focus on retail rather than wholesale prices, and are able to disaggregate buyers in the overall retail market and separately examine the relative price and quantity movements before and following LOE for four distinct payers: Medicaid, Medicare Part D, commercial and other third-party payers (TPPs), and cash customers. Relatively little is known about retail price and quantity movements during the 180-day exclusivity period,[10] or about the magnitude of any differences by payer type in prices paid, and in the speed and extent of shifts from brand to generic. Finally, since information is available on the age of customers receiving medications, we examine relative prices and generic substitution rates for those under age sixty-five with those age sixty-five and older. We are not aware of any published research that examines these brand and generic price and quantity movements following LOE by payer type and patient age.

Our analyses yield the following main findings. First, quantity substitutions away from the brand are much larger proportionately and more rapid than average molecule price reductions during the first six months following LOE. Second, brands continue to raise prices after generics enter. Third, expansion of total molecule sales (brand plus generic) following LOE is an increasingly common phenomenon compared with prior observations. Fourth, generic penetration rates are generally highest for third-party payers and lowest for Medicaid. Fifth, cash (and seniors over age sixty-five) generally pay the highest prices for brands and generics, third-party payers (and those under age sixty-five) pay the lowest prices, with Medicaid and Medicare Part D prices being in between those of cash and third-party payers. Sixth, the presence of an authorized generic during the 180-day exclusivity

8. Federal Trade Commission (2011).

9. Appelt (2013), Berndt et al. (2007), Olson and Wendling (2013), and Reiffen and Ward (2007). For a discussion of the implications of Paragraph IV challenges on consumers' and producers' welfare, see Branstetter, Chatterjee, and Higgins (2011).

10. See, however, Federal Trade Commission (2011, ch. 3) and Alpert, Duggan, and Hellerstein (2013).

period has a significant impact on prices and volume of prescriptions, but this varies across molecules. In two of the cases studied, the brand and its licensee collectively retained almost two-thirds share of the market by volume, in the others they captured less than half. Price discounts off the brand prevailing during the "triopoly" period also showed substantial variation. In some cases, the price of the authorized generic product was between the brand and the independent generic, in others it was significantly below the independent generic.

8.2 Data and Methods

The IMS Health Incorporated National Prescription Audit (NPA) database tracks prescriptions dispensed at a nationally representative sample of retail, mail order, and long-term care pharmacies and is projected to an estimate of total national prescriptions dispensed through these pharmacies on a monthly basis. We limit our analysis to prescriptions dispensed at retail pharmacies, and focus on the fifty most prescribed molecules (measured by number of prescriptions dispensed during May 2013). For each of these molecules, data are available on the distribution by payer type: Medicaid, Medicare Part D, commercial, or other third-party payer, and cash; for about half the transactions, information is also available on the age of the patient dispensed the prescription: sixty-five and over, or under age sixty-five.

These NPA data reflect the perspective of the retail pharmacy, and prices measured at this point in the distribution chain correspond to the retail prices that the US Bureau of Labor Statistics attempts to measure in constructing its monthly Consumer Price Index for Prescription Drugs.[11] The total revenue received by the dispensing pharmacy is the sum of the customer's copayment or coinsurance contribution, plus the amount (if any) reimbursed the dispensing pharmacy by the third-party payer—Medicare Part D insurer, Medicaid, or commercial or other third-party payer. This pharmacy price therefore includes reimbursement for the active pharmaceutical ingredient, a dispensing fee, and any customer copayment or coinsurance contribution. If the customer presents the pharmacy with a coupon, the value of that coupon is attributed to the patient copayment or coinsurance contribution; how well the NPA is able to capture coupon transactions is not publicly known. For our purposes, however, it is important to note that this pharmacy price already includes margins realized by wholesalers, pharmacies, and any other distributors, and is therefore generally larger than the price (net of rebates and discounts) received by the brand and generic manufacturers. These rebates and discounts can be substantial, in some cases larger than the amount that consumers actually pay.[12]

11. Berndt et al. (2000) and US Department of Labor, Bureau of Labor Statistics (2011).
12. Federal Trade Commission (2011) and Centers for Medicare & Medicaid Services (2012).

Starting from the fifty most prescribed molecules in May 2013 we used information from the Food and Drug Administration (FDA)'s Orange Book to identify the six of these molecules that faced initial LOE during the June 2009–May 2013 time period.[13] For each of the six molecules, we identified NDC codes of the brand's strengths/formulations, monthly number of prescriptions dispensed by payer type (Medicare Part D, Medicaid, third-party commercial payer, and cash customer), customer age (number under age sixty-five, age sixty-five and over, and age unknown), average customer copayment/coinsurance contributions, and mean reimbursement to the pharmacy by third-party payer. Similar monthly data were obtained for generic and authorized generic versions of the strengths/formulations of the molecule. The National Drug Codes (NDCs) of authorized generics were identified and were alternatively treated separately or combined with NDC codes of abbreviated new drug application (ANDA) holders. Data on the mean number of extended units ([EUs]; e.g., tablets, capsules) per prescription along with recommended daily dosing data from the Drugs@ FDA website were used to convert average price per prescription to average price per day of therapy (only Augmentin XR differed from once-daily dosing, with its recommended dosing being twice daily for seven to ten days). These NDC-specific average data were then aggregated up to the molecule level separately for brands, generics and authorized generics, and by payer type and customer age, using relative number of prescriptions by NDC code as weights.

8.3   Findings: Characteristics of Six Initial Generic Launches, June 2009–May 2013

The most salient characteristics of the six molecules are summarized in table 8.1, in chronological order by date of LOE from left to right. When originally approved by the FDA as New Drug Applications (NDAs), three of the six were new molecular entities, whereas the other three were new formulations of a previously approved molecular entity. Four of the six were designated standard review by the FDA, and two were tagged for

---

13. One brand product, Plavix (generic name clopidogrel), faced an at-risk launch by Apotex in August 2006; later that month, Bristol-Myers Squibb (the firm marketing Plavix in the United States) obtained an injunction preventing further production and distribution by Apotex and subsequently won a patent infringement case against Apotex. As the single non-brand entrant in the market for the three-week period, Apotex charged about 87 percent of the brand's price, but stuffed inventory channels with massive sales. Although Apotex had been awarded tentative Paragraph IV exclusivity, this exclusivity was forfeited by Apotex. By late 2007, Apotex's clopidogrel inventory had essentially disappeared from the US retail marketplace. We therefore treat the May 2012 launch of generic clopidogrel as the initial LOE for Plavix, and not the August 2006 at-risk launch by Apotex. Additional details are given in Berndt and Aitken (2011); for a journalist's account of the Plavix—clopidogrel episode, see Smith (2007).

priority review. The six molecules are in six different therapeutic classes, and represent five different original NDA holders (Sanofi Aventis is the only multiple NDA holder at two). Effective market exclusivity (time between initial NDA approval and first ANDA entry) varies substantially among the six molecules—from about 5.5 years for Ambien CR to about 15.0 years for both Cozaar and Lipitor. Although all six derive from the fifty most prescribed molecules, because several are new formulations of an older molecule, the market size (measured by total number of monthly prescriptions) varies dramatically. Specifically, for the three months prior to initial LOE, the market size ("mean TRX before LOE" in table 8.1) varied from largest (Lipitor—atorvastatin) to smallest (Augmentin XR—amoxicillin/clavulanate potassium) by a factor of 1251:1; market size of the second largest (Plavix—clopidogrel) relative to second smallest (Ambien CR—zolpidem tartrate) varied by a factor of 4.66:1, while the market size of the third largest (Lexapro—escitalopram oxalate) relative to the third smallest (Cozaar—losartan) was 2.33:1. Hence, even though the sample of six molecules is small and comes entirely from among the fifty most prescribed molecules, the variation in market size of the molecular formulations in our sample is large.

All six brands faced successful Paragraph IV challengers, although because of its infringing prepatent expiration entry, Apotex forfeited its 180-day exclusivity for Plavix (clopidogrel). As a result, Plavix was the only brand to face unrestricted generic entry at the time of its LOE. Of the remaining five molecules, following LOE four of the brands (Cozaar, Ambien CR, Lipitor, and Lexapro) launched authorized generics thereby creating a triopoly market for 180 days, while the remaining brand (Augmentin XR) did not launch an authorized generic and thereby faced duopoly competition between brand and generic for 180 days. By seven (twelve) months after initial generic entry, the molecule with the smallest prepatent expiration market size that also involved complex manufacturing processes (Augmentin XR) had just two (two) competitors, a reformulated extended release molecule with modest prepatent expiration market size (Ambien CR) had four (five) competitors, while the molecule with the largest prepatent expiration market size (Lipitor) had only six (seven) competitors. Three other molecules (Cozaar, Lexapro, and Plavix) each had thirteen or fourteen competitors at both seven and twelve months following initial ANDA entry.

A more detailed discussion of each of the six molecules, in chronological order of initial ANDA launch, is provided in the appendix.

8.4   Results

We now discuss results, in separate subsections for generic penetration rates by payer type and age; quantities post-LOE relative to pre-LOE;

Table 8.1   Characteristics of six initial generic launches, June 2009–May 2013 (in chronological order—ANDA entry date, left to right)

Trade name, generic name	Cozaar losartan	Augmentin XR amoxicillin/ clavulanate potassium	Ambien CR zolpidem tartrate	Lipitor atorvastatin	Lexapro escitalopramoxalate	Plavix clopidogrel
NDA approval	4/14/1995	9/25/2002	4/2/2005	11/17/1996	8/14/02	11/17/97
NME or new formulation	NME	NF	NF	NME	NF	NME
Review status	Standard	Standard	Standard	Priority	Standard	Priority
Therapeutic class	AIIRA antihypertensive	Aminopenicillin antibiotic	Insomnia	Antihyperlipidemic	SSRI antidepressant	Antiplatelet aggregation inhibitor
NDA sponsor	Merck	Dr. Reddys Labs	Sanofi Aventis US	Pfizer	Forest	Sanofi Aventis US
Mean TRX before LOE	634,846	2,281	371,580	2,854,162	1,485,203	1,730,464
Paragraph IV challenger	Teva	Sandoz	Actavis Elizabeth	Ranbaxy	Ivax	Apotex (forfeited)
Initial ANDA entry date	4/6/2010	4/21/2010	10/13/2010	11/30/2011	3/14/2012	5/17/2012
Authorized generic	Sandoz	Winthrop	None	Watson	Mylan	None
Max. no. mfrs. during 1–6 months	2	2	2	3	3	12
No. mfrs. at 7 months	14	2	4	6	14	13
No. mfrs. at 12 months	14	2	5	7	14	13

Notes: NF is new formulation; AIIRA is Angiotensin II Receptor Antagonists; SSRI is selective serotonin reuptake inhibitor; NDA sponsor is patent holder at time of patent expiration; and mean TRX before LOE is the mean monthly number of prescriptions dispensed in the three full months preceding loss of exclusivity.

number extended units per prescription; prices by payer type pre-LOE, during any 180-day exclusivity periods, and post-180-day exclusivity; as well as prescription shares and prices for brands, Paragraph IV challengers, and authorized generics (AGs) during the 180-day exclusivity period.

8.4.1   Generic Penetration Rates, Overall and by Payer Type and Age

We compute the generic penetration rate as the proportion of all prescriptions for a given molecule dispensed as generics (or authorized generic). With six molecules, five payer types, and two age groups, the number of quantitative findings is voluminous. As an overview we first ask, how long in number of months does it take for a molecule to reach certain specified generic penetration thresholds? Results for 60 percent and 90 percent generic penetration thresholds are presented in table 8.2. A number of findings are striking.

First, looking at the six molecules over all payer types, we observe that for all six drugs, the time required to reach a 60 percent generic penetration threshold is three months or less. A 60 percent generic penetration threshold was reached in one month or less by Lexapro, Plavix, Cozaar, and Lipitor (< 1 month is interpreted as the average generic penetration in the first month of entry exceeding 0.6); for the two smallest market drugs, Augmentin XR and Ambien CR, the 60 percent threshold over all payer types was two and three months, respectively. The 90 percent threshold for all payer types is attained within two months for Plavix (that faced unfettered generic entry throughout), four months for Cozaar and Augmentin XR, six months for Lexapro, and nine months for Lipitor; only for Ambien CR is the 90 percent threshold more than a year (thirteen months). This very rapid shift from brand to generic following LOE is much greater than has been reported in earlier US studies.[14]

A second set of findings in table 8.2 reflects difference in the speed of generic penetration by payer type. Looking at the four payer types and over all payers within each molecule (the top row in each panel), we see that for all six molecules, third-party payer (TPP) is always the most (or tied for most) rapid in reaching the 60 percent generic penetration threshold, whereas Medicaid is the slowest. To reach the 90 percent generic penetration threshold, in all cases but one (Lipitor, Medicare), TPPs take the shortest amount of time, followed by Medicare, cash customers, and finally, Medicaid. The relative speed with which TPPs reached high generic penetration thresholds could reflect in part aggressive formulary management by

---

14. See, for example, Grabowski and Vernon (1992, 1996), Griliches and Cockburn (1994), Ellison et al. (1997), Cook (1998), Aitken, Berndt, and Cutler (2008), and Berndt and Newhouse (2012).

Table 8.2   **Months to generic penetration rate thresholds, June 2009–May 2013 (in chronological order—ANDA entry date, top to bottom)**

Trade name, generic name	Buyer type	Threshold all buyers 60%	90%	Threshold under 65 60%	90%	Threshold over 65 60%	90%
Cozaar, losartan	All	1	4	1	5	1	3
	TPP	1	2	1	2	1	3
	Medicare	1	3	1	2	1	3
	Cash	1	9	1	7	1	9
	Medicaid	8	21	8	17	8	24
Augmentin XR,	All	2	4	2	4	2	4
amoxicillin/clavulanate	TPP	2	3	2	3	2	4
potassium	Medicare	2	3	2	3	2	3
	Cash	2	9	2	9	4	5
	Medicaid	5	9	5	9	4	4
Ambien CR, zolpidem	All	3	13	3	12	3	17
tartrate	TPP	3	10	3	10	3	14
	Medicare	3	20	3	20	3	23
	Cash	3	22	3	22	3	—
	Medicaid	10	—	10	31	16	27
Lipitor, atorvastatin	All	1	9	1	9	1	8
	TPP	1	9	1	9	1	8
	Medicare	2	8	2	8	2	8
	Cash	1	10	1	10	1	11
	Medicaid	8	11	8	12	8	11
Lexapro, escitalopram	All	<1	6	<1	6	<1	5
oxalate	TPP	<1	4	<1	4	<1	4
	Medicare	<1	4	<1	3	<1	5
	Cash	<1	8	<1	8	1	9
	Medicaid	7	11	7	11	7	13
Plavix, clopidogrel	All	1	2	1	2	1	2
	TPP	1	1	1	1	1	1
	Medicare	1	2	1	2	1	2
	Cash	1	3	1	2	1	3
	Medicaid	1	4	1	4	1	3

pharmaceutical benefit managers (PBMs) working on behalf of TPPs and Medicare Part D prescription drug plans. Other researchers have noted the relatively slow generic take-up by Medicaid and have leveled criticism at the program for failing to exploit available cost savings (e.g., Brill 2010). It is worth noting, however, that manufacturer rebates to Medicaid from brands are several times larger than those from generic manufacturers (currently, on average about 30+ percent for brands having recent price increases vs.

13 percent for generics),[15] and during the first few months following LOE in which there is only limited competition (say, at the beginning of the 180-day exclusivity period), it is possible that net of rebates, prices to Medicaid may be lower for brands than generics, thereby rationalizing a slower speed of generic substitution by the Medicaid programs. Recall that the prices we measure here are the total consumer plus third-party payer payments to retail pharmacies, not prices net of rebates paid by payers or received by generic manufacturers. The lower brand than generic price net of rebates to Medicaid is not just a theoretical possibility. In their evaluation of state Medicaid program responses to Prozac's (fluoxetine) LOE in August 2001, Kelton, Chang, and Kreling (2013, 1207) report that during 2001:Q3—the first full quarter in which generic fluoxetine was available—net of estimated Medicaid rebates, the average price of a 20 mg tablet/capsule of branded Prozac at $1.91 was slightly less than the average price of a 20 mg tablet/capsule of generic fluoxetine at $1.95.

A third set of results in table 8.2 is a negative finding: Evaluated at either the time required to reach a 60 percent or 90 percent generic penetration threshold, over all payer types those under age sixty-five take on average about the same length of time to reach the 60 percent generic penetration as do senior citizens age sixty-five and over; for the 90 percent threshold over all payers, for three of the six drugs seniors substitute more rapidly, and for one more slowly, than do those under age sixty-five; for the other two drugs the switching speed is the same. Moreover, when one examines time to reach thresholds across payer types, there does not appear to be any dominant pattern for seniors versus those under age sixty-five.

The patterns observed in table 8.2 suggest that consumers take FDA judgments about interchangeability at face value, and benefits managers to make polices independent of clinical or demographic circumstances. We note in passing because TPPs often manage prescription drug benefits for both employees and retirees age sixty-five and over, and because Medicare beneficiaries include some individuals under age sixty-five (e.g., end-stage renal disease beneficiaries and most dually eligible beneficiaries), there is a considerable overlap between prescriptions paid for by Medicare and those dispensed to customers age sixty-five and over.

Finally, the extent and speed of generic penetration in the single case with 180-day exclusivity but no authorized generic—Augmentin XR—appear

---

15. For the purpose of calculating average manufacturer price (AMP) and best prices that trigger Medicaid rebates, since 2007 the prices of authorized generics have been treated as brand prices, not generic (Federal Trade Commission 2011, 13 and appendix J). For brands, in addition to the statutory 23.1 percent rebate, the extent to which the brand's current quarter AMP has exceeded growth in the Consumer Price Index-Urban since product launch is applied to the rebate, implying that for many brands, the total Medicaid rebate is above 30 percent. For noninnovator multisource drugs (independent generics), the rebate is 13 percent of AMP, with no adjustment for excess price inflation. (See Medicaid Drug Rebate Program 2013.)

to be a bit less aggressive and rapid than for Cozaar, Lexapro, and Lipitor (but not for Ambien CR), each of which had an authorized generic during its 180-day exclusivity period; Cozaar, Lexapro, and Lipitor reached the 60 percent threshold in one month or less, whereas Augmentin XR and Ambien CR needed two to three months. With no 180-day exclusivity and unfettered generic entry at patent expiry, Plavix reached the 90 percent generic penetration threshold in the shortest amount of time—two months.

8.4.2   Quantities Post-LOE Relative to Pre-LOE

For quite some time it has been conventional wisdom that total brand plus generic utilization of a molecule declines following patent expiration.[16] This is in large part because brands reduce their marketing as the date of patent expiration and initial loss of exclusivity (LOE) approaches. They then tend to terminate almost all marketing efforts immediately following LOE. As reported by Aitken, Berndt, and Cutler (2008), however, this is not always the case. When the statin Zocor went off patent in 2006, payers and PBMs aggressively switched individuals taking the relatively costly statin brand drug Lipitor (still under patent protection) to generic versions of Zocor (simvastatin), and also initiated new patients on simvastatin instead of Lipitor. We now examine whether the Zocor experience is unique or has become more common. Results are presented in table 8.3 for average utilization six to nine months post-LOE relative to the three months pre-LOE, and for ten to twelve months post-LOE relative to the three months pre-LOE, over all payer (buyer) types and both age groups. A number of results are worth noting.

First, for four of the six molecules, over all payer types, the total molecule utilization at both six to nine and ten to twelve months post-LOE is greater than during the three complete months prior to LOE. For one of the molecules (Plavix—clopidogrel) total molecule utilization is essentially flat, whereas for one other molecule (Ambien CR—zolpidem tartrate) there is a very slight reduction in total molecule utilization post-LOE across all payer types. The reason for post-LOE total molecule utilization being so large for Augmentin XR is unclear to us, but we note from table 8.1 that the number of monthly prescriptions in the three complete months pre-LOE was very small for Augmentin XR.[17]

Second, considerable variation occurs among payer types. Notably, in the four cases when post-LOE total molecule utilization increases, the increase is driven primarily by TPP payers (although for Lipitor, cash and Medicare customers are also large drivers of increased molecule utilization). This is

16. See, for example, Berndt, Cockburn, and Griliches (1996), Caves, Whinston, and Hurwitz (1991), Cook (1998), Ellison and Ellison (2011), Grabowski and Vernon (1996), Hurwitz and Caves (1988), Huskamp et al. (2008), and Regan (2008).
17. The number of Augmentin XR prescriptions in the three months pre-LOE displayed no growth pattern; the increase post-LOE represents a break in trend (results not shown).

Table 8.3   Quantities post-LOE six to nine months and post-LOE ten to twelve months, relative to pre-LOE quantities, June 2009–May 2013 (in chronological order—ANDA entry date, top to bottom)

Trade name, generic name	Buyer type	All buyers		Under 65		Over 65	
		Post/pre 6–9	Post/pre 10–12	Post/pre 6–9	Post/pre 10–12	Post/pre 6–9	Post/pre 10–12
Cozaar, losartan	All	1.60	1.86	1.67	1.89	1.54	1.81
	TPP	1.61	1.84	1.72	1.97	1.43	1.58
	Medicare	1.30	1.68	1.78	1.91	1.66	2.04
	Cash	1.40	1.59	1.57	1.80	1.23	1.37
	Medicaid	1.11	1.20	1.13	1.22	1.03	1.09
Augmentin XR, amoxicillin/ clavulanate potassium	All	4.52	4.68	4.50	4.55	4.59	5.17
	TPP	5.76	5.93	5.87	5.95	4.85	5.25
	Medicare	4.83	5.46	4.46	4.53	5.03	5.99
	Cash	2.82	2.94	3.09	3.09	1.78	2.06
	Medicaid	0.64	0.61	0.64	0.62	0.43	0.41
Ambien CR, zolpidem tartrate	All	0.96	0.96	0.97	0.97	0.92	0.89
	TPP	1.00	1.00	1.00	1.00	1.00	0.97
	Medicare	0.77	0.78	0.85	0.87	0.71	0.70
	Cash	0.86	0.84	0.80	0.80	1.12	1.04
	Medicaid	0.80	0.73	0.81	0.74	0.62	0.52
Lipitor, atorvastatin	All	1.24	1.31	1.25	1.35	1.22	1.24
	TPP	1.24	1.29	1.29	1.37	1.11	1.10
	Medicare	1.29	1.36	1.23	1.38	1.31	1.35
	Cash	1.40	1.89	1.34	1.88	1.49	1.90
	Medicaid	0.63	0.75	0.63	0.75	0.63	0.73
Lexapro, escitalopram xalate	All	1.09	1.14	1.11	1.15	1.01	1.08
	TPP	1.13	1.18	1.15	1.20	0.94	0.97
	Medicare	1.07	1.10	1.07	1.02	1.06	1.15
	Cash	0.92	1.12	0.93	1.12	0.90	1.16
	Medicaid	0.83	0.81	0.83	0.81	0.70	0.72
Plavix, clopidogrel	All	1.00	0.98	1.05	0.99	0.98	0.97
	TPP	1.00	0.95	1.05	1.00	0.93	0.88
	Medicare	1.00	1.00	1.08	0.97	0.99	1.00
	Cash	1.60	1.45	1.62	1.56	1.56	1.35
	Medicaid	0.86	0.80	0.85	0.78	0.96	0.92

consistent with the large shift to generics and the substantial reduction in average molecule price that results. The smallest utilization increase or largest decrease occurs for Medicaid payers. In the one case where total molecule utilization decreases slightly post-LOE (Ambien CR), it is Medicare and Medicaid prescriptions that decline most post-LOE. Since we observed that Medicaid is generally the slowest payer to switch from brand to generic, the relatively large reductions post-LOE by Medicaid payers suggests they are not staying with the brand, but rather are either discontinuing treatment with that molecule altogether or are instead switching to another molecule, either brand or generic. This issue merits further examination.

Table 8.3 shows that in all four cases in which ten to twelve months post-LOE total molecule utilization increased, total molecule utilization by cash customers increased. Note that because certain retail chains such as Walmart and Target introduced $4 prescriptions for thirty days and $9.99 prescriptions for ninety days, customer out-of-pocket cash payments for these prescriptions were likely less than the typical copayment or coinsurance customer contribution to the pharmacy for a first-tier generic drug under a private or public insurance plan formulary arrangement. While this shift to box merchandiser pharmacies might explain some of the growth in cash payer total molecule utilization, because Medicaid beneficiaries typically have very low if any copayment for first-tier generic drugs, the shift to box merchandiser pharmacies is unlikely to be the source of the post-LOE decline in Medicaid total molecule utilization. Alternatively, price declines to the uninsured may generate more demand response for the molecule than do price declines to an insured population. The extent to which the increase in utilization can be decomposed into increased demand from existing patients (through better compliance) versus demand from new patients, for example those that switch in to a newly genericized molecule from another branded molecule, is unclear and also merits further analysis.

Third, there is considerable heterogeneity among the five molecules having a 180-day exclusivity period. For Augmentin XR having no authorized generic entry, and for Ambien CR—both extended release reformulations—the post-LOE utilization experiences are dramatically different, with Augmentin XR showing a very substantial increase and Ambien CR a slight decline. While the other three molecules having an authorized generic present during the 180-day exclusivity each experienced a post-LOE total molecule utilization increase, the extent of this increased utilization varied considerably—being largest for Cozaar, followed by Lipitor and then Lexapro.

Finally, regarding total molecule utilization post- versus pre-LOE by age group, as seen in the final columns of table 8.3, there is no striking pattern. In most, but certainly not all cases, those under age sixty-five increase more or decrease less in their total molecule utilization than do those age sixty-five and over six to nine months after LOE, but even this modest trend is mitigated at ten to twelve months after LOE.

8.4.3 Number Extended Units per Prescription

One of the strategies employed by PBMs has been to encourage beneficiaries to switch from obtaining thirty-day prescriptions at brick-and-mortar retail pharmacies to ordering ninety-day prescriptions via mail order. Such a switch has been accomplished in part by ninety-day copayments being only twice as large as thirty-day copayments, thereby reducing beneficiaries' per diem copayment amount. This strategy has been particularly attractive for maintenance medications that treat chronic diseases (i.e., taken each day indefinitely), but obviously is less practical for medicines needed immediately to treat acute conditions or episodes.[18] In response to seeing reduced foot traffic in their brick-and-mortar stores from this shift to ninety-day mail-order prescriptions, several retail pharmacy chains have begun offering copayment incentive schemes similar to those by the PBM mail-order firms.[19]

One implication of this shift from thirty- to ninety-day prescriptions is that the number of extended units ([EUs]; e.g., tablets, capsules) per prescription is likely to have increased somewhat during our forty-eight-month sample time period (June 2009–May 2013). Since our data are limited to retail-pharmacy dispensing and excludes mail order, we expect this increase in number of EUs per prescription (Rx) to be modest. However, we also expect that the extent to which prescriptions contain more EUs per prescription will vary among the six molecules in our sample since they are in six distinct therapeutic classes of medicines. A consequence is that the average price per prescription not taking into account shifts in the number of EUs per Rx could give a misleading picture of prescription drug per diem price changes over time. Therefore, before presenting results on price differences among payer types and age groups, we digress and first examine trends among our six molecules on number of EUs per Rx.

Due to space limitations, we do not present detailed results on EUs per Rx here; detailed figures can be accessed at the IMS Institute for Healthcare Informatics website. Our principal findings on number of EUs per Rx can be summarized as follows. For all molecules except Augmentin XR, the number of EUs per Rx increased over time, with the largest increase being from about thirty-nine to forty-five for Cozaar. For Augmentin XR with twice-daily dosing recommended for seven to ten days, while the number of EUs per Rx for the branded version increased from about thirty-two to thirty-eight (sixteen to nineteen days' supply), for the generic version it declined from thirty-six to thirty-two (eighteen to sixteen days' supply). The smallest number of EUs per Rx occurred with Ambien CR prescriptions, for whom the increase during the sample time period was from almost twenty-nine to just under thirty-one EUs per Rx. We conclude that while there is heterogeneity in EUs per Rx across the six molecules, the additional variability over time implies that it is preferable to measure trends in price per day of therapy rather than price per prescription.

8.4.4   Price per Day of Therapy by Payer Type

Price per day of therapy by payer type for the six molecules over the June 2009–May 2013 time period are graphed in the six panels of figure 8.1; the

---

18. Wosinska and Huckman (2004) discuss variations in the therapeutic class composition between prescriptions dispensed by retail versus mail order.

19. Trends in mail order versus retail prescription copayment levels and coinsurance rates are discussed in Berndt and Newhouse (2012, 241–48).

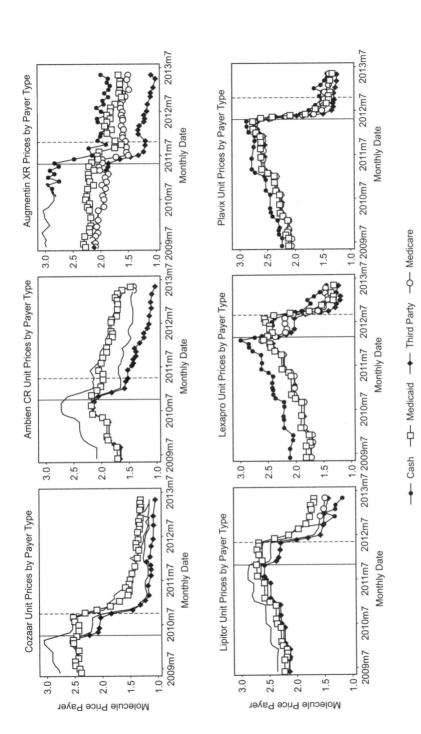

Fig. 8.1 Price per day of therapy

solid vertical line denotes the date of initial LOE, while the dotted vertical line represents 180 days later, corresponding with the expiry of any 180-day exclusivity (except for Plavix). Several results in figure 8.1 merit special attention.

First, although the decline in average molecule price per day of therapy at the time of initial LOE is evident for all molecules, the price drop is most dramatic for Plavix (clopidogrel), for which generic entry at the time of LOE was unfettered, resulting in price per day of therapy falling from about $6.50 to about $3.50 (46 percent) within a month after initial LOE.

Second, we see important differences in prices across different classes of payers. We treat these cautiously, given the potential for differences in the level of unobserved rebates received by different classes of payers. (Recall that our price measure is from the perspective of average revenue per Rx received by the pharmacy, which does not include manufacturers' rebates to Medicaid and other payers; net of such rebates, Medicaid price premiums might be much smaller and perhaps may even be nonexistent.) Nonetheless, it is interesting to note that both pre-LOE and during the 180-day exclusivity window, cash payers paid the highest prices, TPPs the lowest price, with Medicaid and then Medicare Part D in between. Price differences among payer types generally tended to decline over time, and by the end of the sample time period (May 2013) cash payers paid the highest prices for four of the six molecules (Ambien CR, Augmentin XR, Lexapro, and Plavix), while Medicaid paid the highest prices for Cozaar and Lipitor. For Lipitor, the average price per day of therapy for Medicaid at just under $3 was about twice that paid by TPPs.

Third, an intriguing phenomenon we observe in figure 8.1 is that while at the time of initial LOE there is a noticeable immediate price decline for Cozaar, Ambien CR, Lipitor, and Lexapro—each of which was in a tri-opoly market structure, including an authorized generic during the 180-day exclusivity period—the average price per day of therapy is relatively flat during the remainder of the 180-day exclusivity window, and then (except for Ambien CR) falls sharply immediately following expiry of the exclusivity window. Somewhat counterintuitively, the post-LOE price decline is larger and more sustained for Augmentin XR—in a duopoly market structure with no authorized generic entrant during the 180-day window. Why a three-competitor market structure generates higher and more stable prices than does a duopoly runs counter to basic economic intuition and merits further analysis.[20] In particular, future research might focus on the role played by the brand and its authorized generic agent in creating price discipline during the 180-day exclusivity window.

---

20. For a preliminary theoretical analysis and empirical implementation based on data from the 1980s and 1990s, see Reiffen and Ward (2007).

Table 8.4   **Prices and prescription shares during the 180-day exclusivity period for branded, generic, and authorized generic molecules**

Variable/molecule	Cozaar	Ambien CR	Lipitor	Lexapro
Mean (s.d.) branded price	2.55 (0.06)	6.27 (0.04)	5.13 (0.12)	4.49 (0.20)
Mean (s.d.) generic price	2.19 (0.07)	5.15 (0.35)	3.82 (0.44)	3.06 (0.14)
Mean (s.d.) authorized generic price	1.86 (0.10)	4.46 (0.07)	4.46 (0.20)	3.99 (0.10)
Mean (s.d.) branded share	0.16 (0.14)	0.44 (0.36)	0.40 (0.27)	0.15 (0.07)
Mean (s.d.) generic share	0.50 (0.09)	0.32 (0.23)	0.36 (0.18)	0.48 (0.14)
Mean (s.d.) authorized generic share	0.34 (0.05)	0.24 (0.16)	0.24 (0.12)	0.37 (0.07)

Finally, although we do not present price trends per day of therapy separately for those under age sixty-five and age sixty-five and over, we find there do not appear to be systematic differences paid per day of therapy by age group, and that any differences are relatively small in magnitude.

What is clear, however, in comparing quantity data in tables 8.2 and 8.3 with price trends in figure 8.1 is that even though the price reductions in the 180 days immediately following initial LOE are significant, they are much smaller and slower than the very dramatic increases in generic penetration rates, that is, for these prescription drugs, following LOE quantities move much more quickly and proportionately than do prices.

8.4.5   Prices and Prescription Shares during the 180-Day Triopoly

In table 8.4 we present means (and standard deviations) of price per day of therapy and prescription shares during the four 180-day triopolies we observe in our data set (Cozaar, Ambien CR, Lipitor, and Lexapro) in which not only does the brand face a successful Paragraph IV challenger, but it also launches an authorized generic (AG) that both competes with and contributes revenues to the branded franchise. Although our sample size is but four molecules, and any results should therefore be viewed as tentative requiring confirmation with a larger data set, several preliminary results are worth noting.

First, in terms of maintaining market share in the face of LOE, Sanofi's experience with Ambien CR and Pfizer's experience with Lipitor stand out. As seen in the bottom three panels of table 8.4, while for both Cozaar and Lexapro the mean brand share during the triopoly falls to about 15 percent, at 44 percent, and 40 percent, respectively, the Ambien CR and Lipitor brand shares were much larger; in addition, while the AG share for both Cozaar and Lexapro was about 35 percent, for Ambien CR and Lipitor it was just under 25 percent. An implication is that when one sums the prescription share for the brand plus that of its authorized generic, for both Cozaar and Lexapro this comes to about 50 percent, whereas for Ambien

CR and Lipitor it soars to 65–68 percent.[21] For the successful Paragraph IV challenger, therefore, while being able to capture approximately 50 percent of prescriptions during the triopolies involving Cozaar and Lexapro, during Ambien CR's and Lipitor's 180-day exclusivity period, Actavis Elizabeth and Ranbaxy—the independent nonauthorized generic entrants—only garnered about 35 percent of prescriptions. Industry analysts have suggested that Pfizer was able to secure this substantial share by giving payers, mail-order firms, and pharmaceutical benefit managers (PBMs) large rebates, aggressively marketing $4 copay coupons in print media, and maintaining and perhaps even increasing direct-to-consumer marketing efforts before LOE and during the 180-day exclusivity period.[22] We have no information regarding whether Sanofi undertook similar actions to protect its brand and authorized generic shares during the Ambien CR exclusivity period. Whether the more recent Lipitor experience remains historically unique or instead ushers in a new form of triopoly competition remains to be seen; the only other major brand facing initial LOE since the 2011–2012 Lipitor LOE was Plavix, but as noted earlier, because Apotex forfeited its Paragraph IV exclusivity, Plavix faced unfettered generic entry at the time of its initial LOE later in 2012 rather than a triopoly market structure.

A second set of findings (in the top panels of table 8.4) involves revenues or average prices (any patient copayment plus third-party-payer reimbursements) received by retail pharmacies. Here the outlier drugs are Cozaar and Ambien CR, not Lipitor. For both Lipitor and Lexapro, the AG average price is in between that of the brand and the generic (the successful Paragraph IV challenger), whereas for Ambien CR and Cozaar the AG average price is even lower than that of the generic; this latter phenomenon of AG retail prices being lowest was reported by the Federal Trade Commission (2011, ch. 3), but our finding based on more recent data of the independent generic average price being the lowest is novel. In all four cases, however, the brand has the highest price, being 25–30 percent higher than the generic except in the cases of Ambien CR and Cozaar, where the brand-generic premium ranges between about 15–22 percent. It is worth emphasizing again that the prices measured here are those recouped by the retail pharmacy, and not the prices at which they acquire drugs from generic manufacturers (which are typically much lower).[23]

---

21. When the authorized generic is launched by the subsidiary of the brand (e.g., Winthrop for Sanofi Aventis), the brand franchise captures all nonindependent generic sales dollars. However, when the brand licenses out authorized generic marketing rights to an independent generic manufacturer, the brand franchise still benefits from royalties it receives from the independent generic manufacturer. In recent years, according to the Federal Trade Commission (2011, 85), this royalty rate has been 90 percent and above.

22. See, for example, Drug Channels (2012).

23. Drug Channels (2012). Also see Federal Trade Commission (2011, chs. 3 and 6) and Olson and Wendling (2013).

8.4.6   Cash versus Full Sample Average Price Levels and Growth Rates

Our final set of analyses involves examining relative price levels and growth rates of prescriptions paid for by cash in comparison to the full sample of retail-dispensed prescriptions. Several outcomes are plausible. One line of reasoning is that because cash customers must pay the full price of the drug, cash purchasers must value the prescription at a relatively high level, and knowing this, pharmacies can exploit this fact by charging cash customers higher prescription prices. A related view is that cash customers are less informed and cannot move market share across products, whereas benefit managers for third-party payer insurers are more knowledgeable concerning alternative treatments for various conditions, and can use this knowledge and bargaining power to obtain lower prescription prices from pharmacies. An alternative view is that cash customers will be on average more price sensitive, and therefore will seek out those pharmacies advertising discounted prescriptions, such as the mass merchandiser pharmacies, thereby paying lower prices than those with insurance. While these views have diverse predictions for relative price levels paid by insured versus the uninsured, without additional assumptions they make no predictions on relative growth rates of prescription prices for cash versus insured customers.

To measure mean price-growth rates, for each molecule we compute the average of log $[P(t) / P(t - 1)]$ over the selected time interval, which for relatively small price changes such as that observed with our monthly data, yield results that can be interpreted as the mean percent growth rate in price.

In the top row of each of the six drug molecule panels in table 8.5, we present mean cash/full-sample prices (standard deviations in parentheses) over the full forty-eight-month June 2009–May 2013 sample time period, and then for three subperiods: pre-LOE, during the 180-day exclusivity, and post-180-day exclusivity. In the case of Plavix, there was no 180-day exclusivity and we therefore present relative cash/full-sample prices for only the pre-LOE and post-LOE time periods where generic entry is unfettered by any exclusivity. Several results are worth highlighting.

First, for all six molecules prices paid by cash customers are generally greater than those for the full sample. Over the entire forty-eight-month time period and six molecules, the average cash-price premium is about 17 percent, ranging from 11 percent for Lipitor to 24 percent for Augmentin XR. In the pre-LOE time periods, cash prices for brands are on average about 16 percent greater than for the full sample, and this cash-price premium grows slightly to about 18 percent during and following 180-day exclusivity. There is remarkably little variability in the cash-price premium during the 180-day exclusivity window (small standard deviation), and generally (except for Augmentin XR) considerably more variability following unfettered generic entry in the post-180-day time frame.

Table 8.5   Cash versus full sample price levels and growth rates (standard deviations in parentheses)

Trade name, generic name	Measure	Full 48 months	Pre-LOE	During 180 day	Post 180 day
Cozaar, losartan	Mean cash/full	1.19	1.17	1.20	1.20
		(0.107)	(0.014)	(0.005)	(0.133)
	Log[$P(t) / P(t-1)$] full	−0.017	0.007	−0.031	−0.011
		(0.046)	(0.013)	(0.039)	(0.026)
	Log[$P(t) / P(t-1)$] cash	−0.019	0.010	−0.032	−0.018
		(0.048)	(0.011)	(0.043)	(0.047)
Augmentin XR, amoxicillin/ clavulanate potassium	Mean cash/full	1.24	1.23	1.25	1.23
		(0.027)	(0.015)	(0.035)	(0.034)
	Log[$P(t) / P(t-1)$] full	−0.006	−0.002	−0.035	−0.003
		(0.019)	(0.007)	(0.039)	(0.010)
	Log[$P(t) / P(t-1)$] cash	−0.005	−0.002	−0.031	−0.0002
		(0.029)	(0.019)	(0.056)	(0.026)
Ambien CR, zolpidem tartrate	Mean cash/full	1.21	1.16	1.18	1.24
		(0.041)	(0.013)	(0.021)	(0.022)
	Log[$P(t) / P(t-1)$] full	−0.005	0.011	−0.033	−0.008
		(0.022)	(0.021)	(0.035)	(0.010)
	Log[$P(t) / P(t-1)$] cash	−0.003	0.012	−0.026	−0.008
		(0.020)	(0.018)	(0.031)	(0.010)
Lipitor, atorvastatin	Mean cash/full	1.11	1.15	1.14	1.02
		(0.157)	(0.009)	(0.011)	(0.303)
	Log[$P(t) / P(t-1)$] full	−0.013	0.009	−0.023	−0.039
		(0.061)	(0.021)	(0.041)	(0.064)
	Log[$P(t) / P(t-1)$] cash	−0.024	0.009	−0.019	−0.093
		(0.092)	(0.024)	(0.032)	(0.156)
Lexapro, escitalopram oxalate	Mean cash/full	1.16	1.16	1.13	1.21
		(0.039)	(0.007)	(0.012)	(0.078)
	Log[$P(t) / P(t-1)$] full	−0.005	0.010	−0.025	−0.016
		(0.044)	(0.020)	(0.034)	(0.031)
	Log[$P(t) / P(t-1)$] cash	−0.007	0.010	−0.026	−0.032
		(0.036)	(0.018)	(0.032)	(0.028)
Plavix, clopidogrel	Mean cash/full	1.11	1.09	—	1.17
		(0.053)	(0.013)		(0.078)
	Log[$P(t) / P(t-1)$] full	−0.012	0.009	—	−0.060
		(0.079)	(0.019)		(0.140)
	Log [$P(t) / P(t-1)$ cash	−0.012	0.008	—	−0.056
		(0.063)	(0.017)		(0.010)

While results on relative price levels are quite robust and unambiguous, for relative growth rates our findings are more nuanced. Looking at the pre-LOE column in table 8.5, when we compare the mean log $[P(t) / P(t-1)]$ over the six molecules, we observe that cash prices increase on average about 0.0078 percent per month, very slightly greater than the full-sample prices that increase on average 0.0073 percent monthly, which when accumulated over twelve months, results in cash prices annually growing at 0.6 percent more rapidly than full-sample prices. During any 180-day exclusivity period, on average cash prices fall slightly less rapidly (−0.0268 vs. −0.0294) than do full-sample prices, but this inequality is reversed following any 180-day exclusivity or when unfettered generic entry occurs, during which time cash prices fall about 1.2 percent more rapidly (−0.0345 vs. −0.0228) than do full-sample prices. This last result is consistent with the pricing strategies of the mass merchandisers such as Walmart that offer $4 thirty-day or $9.99 ninety-day prescriptions to their customers once unfettered generic entry occurs, typically lower prices than those available from chain and independent retail pharmacies. Finally, averaged over all six molecules and the entire forty-eight-month time period, cash prices fall very slightly more rapidly (−0.0117 vs. −0.0097, a difference of −0.0020 per month, or about 2.4 percent annually) than do full-sample prices. Hence, cash versus full-sample differences in price levels are quite substantial though stable over time, but differences in the growth rates vary during exclusivity and LOE subperiods, although in general these growth-rate differences are relatively small, that is, the cash-price-level premiums are proportionately stable over time.

8.5 Summary and Concluding Remarks

The extent and rate at which generic drugs capture market share in US retail drug markets as brands lose market exclusivity has increased sharply over the last decade. This heightened generic penetration has been particularly evident for third-party payers (TPPs), and likely reflects the increased bargaining power derived from formulary design by pharmaceutical benefit management (PBM) firms serving TPPs' drug benefit plans. One implication of this phenomenon is that to the extent "reverse payment" or "pay-for-delay" settlements result in delayed generic entry, consumers are harmed immediately by not gaining access to lower-cost medicines. The relatively large number of top-selling drugs facing initial loss of exclusivity (LOE) in the United States in 2012 and 2013 has been unprecedented, with the resulting patent cliff revenue losses for brands in 2012 alone approaching $29 billion and contributing to an overall 1 percent decline in US nominal pharmaceutical spending,[24] but providing a temporary windfall for the profit margins of wholesalers, retail, and mail-order pharmacies. Whether these recent impacts on pharmaceutical spending will be repeated is unclear, particularly since the total dollar revenues of brand drugs facing initial LOE in the next few years is expected to be considerably smaller than in 2012 and 2013.[25]

For four of the six molecules experiencing initial LOE in our 2009–2013 time frame, total monthly molecule utilization post-LOE exceeded that

---

24. IMS Institute for Healthcare Informatics (2013, 8, 12); FiercePharma (2012).
25. Drug Channels (2011, 2012).

prior to patent expiration, reflecting the combined effects of cross-molecule substitution, new patients gaining access to lower-cost medicines, and non-adherent patients resuming drug treatment. This post-LOE increase in molecule utilization runs counter to prior understanding of this market, and also likely reflects the increased formulary design policies by PBMs. An implication is that not only do patent-protected brands need to worry about their own patents expiring, but their brand's revenues can also be adversely affected if a competitive brand faces initial generic entry, for the newly competitive generic molecule can steal market share. More generally, these post-LOE utilization increases are creating novel complexities in defining drug markets for antitrust and other litigation-related damage assessments.

Our data also document that the probability of a brand's patent being challenged by a potential generic entrant is now very high, continuing an aggressive litigation trend reported by the Federal Trade Commission (2011) that often results in the Paragraph IV first-filer being awarded 180 days of exclusivity. With their expected revenues being threatened, brands have responded by launching their authorized generic (AG), thereby creating a 180-day triopoly calm before the patent cliff storm, with competition among the brand, its authorized generic, and the successful Paragraph IV challenger. In spite of only modest average molecule price reductions during this 180-day exclusivity period (much less than after it expires), the substitution of prescription quantities away from the brand is already very large. Since through its combined sales of the brand and its AG the brand franchise can moderate the revenue loss from LOE, the financial lure of generics being awarded 180-day exclusivity is decreased. However, the evidence we find, as has the Federal Trade Commission (2011, ch. 7), suggests that the existence of an AG during the 180-day exclusivity period does not dampen the extent of generic entry postexclusivity: on the 181st day following initial LOE, the number of generics competing with the brand and with each other tends consistently to be large, in our sample between seven and fourteen. Whether Pfizer's relatively successful defense of Lipitor during the 180-day exclusivity period through the use of coupons, rebates, and other discounts is a historical quirk or instead is a harbinger of future more aggressive attempts by brands to protect brand revenues as patents expire remains to be seen.

A novel set of findings we have reported here involves identifying separate retail prices by payer type—cash, Medicare Part D, Medicaid, and other commercial TPP. Our results suggest that declines in retail prices follow the incentives to each payer to pursue policies that result in price declines. In particular, the slower decline in Medicaid prices following LOE may be more rational than previously thought. Three caveats are worth noting, however. First, the prices we calculate represent the average total revenue received by a retail pharmacy for a dispensed prescription, converted to price per day of therapy. This average revenue is the sum of any reimbursement the pharmacy receives from a private or public payer for a dispensed prescription, plus any copayment or coinsurance amount contributed directly by the patient at the point of sale. This average revenue, viewed from the perspective of the retail pharmacy, differs from and is likely considerably larger than the average acquisition cost of the drug the retail pharmacy pays wholesalers or manufacturers.[26] It also differs from the average revenue net of rebates and other discounts that is received by the manufacturer selling to wholesalers or providers, and the average amount per prescription contracted among payers, PBMs, and manufacturers—in both these latter cases, rebates from the manufacturer to payers and PBMs make it likely that these other prices are lower than the average total revenue received by the retail pharmacy. Second, because the retail pharmacy average revenue price is not directly affected by rebates from manufacturers to public and private payers, the relative brand-generic prices that payers provide retail pharmacies might differ considerably once rebates from manufacturers to payers are taken into account. In particular, as noted earlier, provisions of the Affordable Care Act of 2010 mandate that Medicaid receive a rebate of 13 percent off the average manufacturer price (AMP) for a generic, and on average approximately 30+ percent discount off AMP for a branded patent-protected drug. Third, our sample is very small—six molecules each for forty-eight months, and thus these small sample findings cannot at this point be generalized to the entire US retail pharmaceutical market (a similar analysis of a much larger sample is on our research agenda).

With these caveats regarding rebates and small sample size in mind, we find that in general the price levels paid retail pharmacies per day of therapy are highest for cash and Medicaid payers and are lowest for other TPPs, with the cash-price premium over TPP prices being on average just under 20 percent. In terms of growth rates, however, cash prices of patent-protected molecules grow at virtually the same rate as overall market prices (the annualized difference being +0.06 percent), during 180-day exclusivity the cash prices fall slightly less rapidly than overall market prices, and post any exclusivity cash prices fall about 1 percent more rapidly per month than do overall market prices. Averaged over all six molecules and all forty-eight months, cash prices fall slightly more rapidly (about 2.4 percent annually) than do overall market prices. An implication of this is that if for administrative and logistical reasons statistical agencies such as the US Bureau of Labor Statistics find themselves disproportionately reliant on cash-transaction price quotes, the potential consequences for price mismeasurement are likely to be relatively minor. Establishing this last conclusion will be the focus of our immediate future research program.

---

26. For details, see Centers for Medicare & Medicaid Services (2012); also see Drug Channels (2011, 2012).

Appendix

Brief Description of the Six Molecules in the Data Sample

Cozaar (losartan)

Two weeks after Cozaar, an antihypertensive, was approved by the FDA, Merck obtained FDA approval for Hyzaar, a combination product that contained Cozaar (losartan potassium) as one component and a very old off-patent beta blocker called hydrochlorothiazide as the other component. Teva successfully challenged a Merck patent underlying both Cozaar and Hyzaar, and was granted 180-day exclusivity effective April 5, 2010, and launched its product one day later. Merck contracted with Sandoz to launch an authorized generic version of Cozaar coinciding with the launch of Teva's generic Cozaar. On October 6, 2010, when the 180-day exclusivity expired, massive generic entry occurred at all three Cozaar dosages, with twelve new ANDAs entering.

Augmentin XR (amoxicillin/clavulanate potassium)

Although GlaxoSmithKline (GSK) was the original NDA holder for Augmentin XR, a combination antibiotic product with amoxicillin (an old penicillin) and clavulanate potassium as components, at the time of patent expiration in 2010 the NDA holder was Dr. Reddy's Labs Inc., a manufacturer best known as a generic manufacturer. According to Drugs@FDA, Sandoz is the only FDA-recognized ANDA entrant. Currently there are only two manufacturers (Dr. Reddy's Labs Inc. and Sandoz). This may be explained by the relatively small market size (2,281 mean monthly prescriptions) and the complexity of manufacturing processes of the extended-release version. Notably, the recommended use of this antibiotic is a twice-daily dosing for seven to ten days,[27] implying that the recommended number of extended units in a typical single-episode prescription (fourteen to twenty) is smaller than for thirty- or ninety-day prescriptions of once-daily maintenance medications (in effect, an even smaller market than is implied by the prescription count).

Ambien CR (zolpidem tartrate)

Ambien CR is an extended-release version of Ambien immediate release (Ambien CR has a pharmacokinetic activity that provides an immediate dose release to facilitate getting to sleep, but then provides a sustained release that facilitates a longer duration of sleeping). Sanofi Aventis US obtained FDA approval for Ambien CR about eighteen months before the Ambien immediate release patent expiry. Actavis was granted 180-day exclusivity for the 6.25 mg formulation on October 13, 2010, while Anchen was awarded

27. Drug Facts and Comparisons (2011, 2088).

exclusivity for the 12.5 mg formulation on December 3, 2010. Winthrop, a subsidiary of Sanofi Aventis US, launched an authorized generic for each of the dosage forms within days of each exclusivity taking effect. Sublingual (under the tongue) and oral spray formulations at varying dosages are also available having different brand names, Edluar, Intermezzo, and Zolpimist, but they are not rated as therapeutic equivalents to Ambien CR by the FDA.

Lipitor (atorvastatin)

Perhaps the most highly publicized patent expiry in the last decade was that for Pfizer's Lipitor (atorvastatin), a drug controlling cholesterol lipids. Patents on all formulations were successfully challenged by Ranbaxy, who was awarded 180-day exclusivity on its ANDA on November 30, 2011, that expired May 28, 2012. However, Pfizer contracted with Watson (later Actavis)[28] to market an authorized generic version of all dosages, and also initiated an aggressive coupon program that reduced considerably the customer copayment typically required for branded drugs on the second or higher tier of a formulary.[29] During the exclusivity period, therefore, there were three competitors (Pfizer's brand, its authorized generic through Watson, and Ranbaxy) and on the day exclusivity expired, three additional ANDA holders entered at all four dosages (Apotex, Mylan, and Sandoz). A notable feature of the Lipitor-atorvastatin patent expiry is that even though it had the largest pre-LOE market size, more than a year after the May 2012 unfettered ANDA entry, there are only five ANDA holders competing at each dosage strength; as seen in table 8.1, for other molecules the number of ANDA-holder entrants is much larger, at twelve to fifteen entrants. The small number of competitors in this market is curious—it may reflect the fact that the small number of approved ANDA holders is each known to have substantial manufacturing capacity, or that Pfizer's highly publicized aggressive protection of its brand reduced the perceived payoff to entry by generic manufacturers.[30]

Lexapro

Lexapro (escitalopram oxalate) is an antidepressant marketed in the United States by Forest Labs; its NDA was approved as a new formulation (it is an isomer of the earlier Forest antidepressant drug Celexa—citalopram—both of which were licensed into Forest after being on the European market

28. Pfizer entered into an authorized generic arrangement with a generic challenger (Arrow) on a separate patent dispute, and Arrow was subsequently acquired by Watson, which merged with Actavis.

29. The coupon program was only available to cash or third-party patients in states that did not preclude use of coupons. Though highly visible and heavily promoted in mass media, the number of patients that participated in the program appears to have been quite small, likely well below 10 percent of those eligible.

30. On the market's perception of the reputation of Pfizer and its generic subsidiary, Greenstone, see Federal Trade Commission (2011, 82).

for a number of years). Ivax was awarded 180-day exclusivity effective March 14, 2012, for all three tablet versions. On the day after exclusivity expiration—September 11, 2012—a total of nine additional generic entrants came to market, each offering tablets at all three dosages, and the next day two additional entrants were launched, for a total of twelve generic manufacturers of escitalopram immediately following the exclusivity period.

Plavix

The launch of Plavix (clopidogrel) represented the culmination of contentious legal skirmishes among Sanofi, Bristol-Myers Squibb (the US marketer of Plavix), Apotex, and various states' attorneys general. Initial proposed settlements between BMS and Apotex allowing Apotex to have several months of exclusivity were rejected by the attorneys general, and eventually Apotex acceded to forfeiting any rights to exclusivity. The Plavix patent finally expired on May 17, 2012, on which date with unfettered generic entry seven ANDAs launched at 75 mg and four at 300 mg; as of June 10, 2013, there appear to be thirteen ANDA entrants at the 75 mg formulation, and six at the 300 mg dosage.

References

Aitken, Murray L., and Ernst R. Berndt. 2011. "Medicare Part D at Age Five: What Has Happened to Seniors' Prescription Drug Prices?" Report by the IMS Institute for Healthcare Bioinformatics, July.

Aitken, Murray L., Ernst R. Berndt, and David M. Cutler. 2008. "Prescription Drug Spending Trends in the United States: Looking Beyond the Turning Point." *Health Affairs Web Exclusive* 28 (1): W151–60.

Alpert, Abby, Mark Duggan, and Judith K. Hellerstein. 2013. "Perverse Reverse Price Competition: Average Wholesale Prices and Medicaid Pharmaceutical Spending." *Journal of Public Economics* 108 (Dec.): 44–62.

Appelt, Silvia. 2013. "Authorized Generic Entry Prior to Patent Expiry: Reassessing Incentives for Independent Generic Entry." Working Paper, University of Munich, May. Available from the author at silvia.appelt@lrz.uni-muenchen.de.

Avalere Health LLC. 2010. "State Policies Regarding Generic Substitution, 2010." PowerPoint presentation. www.avalerehealth.net/research/docs/Generic_Substitution.pdf.

Berndt, Ernst R., and Murray L. Aitken. 2011. "Brand Loyalty, Generic Entry and Price Competition in Pharmaceuticals in the Quarter Century after the 1984 Waxman-Hatch Legislation." *International Journal of the Economics of Business* 18 (2): 177–201.

Berndt, Ernst R., Iain M. Cockburn, and Zvi Griliches. 1996. "Pharmaceutical Innovation and Market Dynamics: Tracking Effects on Price Indexes for Antidepressant Drugs." *Brookings Papers on Economic Activity: Microeconomics* 1996 (2): 1133–88.

Berndt, Ernst R., David M. Cutler, Richard G. Frank, Zvi Griliches, Joseph P. New-house, and Jack E. Triplett. 2000. "Medical Care Prices and Output." In *Handbook of Health Economics*, vol. 1A, edited by Anthony Culyer and Joseph P. Newhouse, 117–80. Amsterdam: Elsevier Sciences B.V.

Berndt, Ernst R., Richard Mortimer, Ashoke M. Bhattacharjya, Andrew Parece, and Edward Tuttle. 2007. "Authorized Generic Drugs, Price Competition, and Consumers' Welfare." *Health Affairs* 26 (3): 790–99.

Berndt, Ernst R., and Joseph P. Newhouse. 2012. "Pricing and Reimbursement in US Pharmaceutical Markets." In *The Oxford Handbook of the Economics of the Biopharmaceutical Industry*, edited by Patricia M. Danzon and Sean Nicholson, 201–65. New York: Oxford University Press.

Branstetter, Lee G., Chirantan Chatterjee, and Matthew J. Higgins. 2011. "Regulation and Welfare: Evidence from Paragraph IV Generic Entry in the Pharmaceutical Industry." NBER Working Paper no. 17188, Cambridge, MA.

Brill, Alex. 2010. "Overspending on Multi-Source Drugs in Medicaid." AEI Health Policy Studies Working Paper no. 2010-01, Washington, DC, American Enterprise Institute, July 21. http://www.aei.org/paper/100127.

Caves, Richard E., Michael D. Whinston, and Mark A. Hurwitz. 1991. "Patent Expiration, Entry, and Competition in the US Pharmaceutical Industry." *Brookings Papers on Economic Activity: Microeconomics* 1991:1–66.

Centers for Medicare & Medicaid Services. 2012. "Survey of Retail Prices." May 31. http://medicaid.gov/Medicaid-CHIP-Program-Information/By-Topics/Benefits/Prescription-Drugs/Survey-of-Retail-Prices.html.

Cook, Anna. 1998. *How Increased Competition from Generic Drugs Has Affected Prices and Returns in the Pharmaceutical Industry*. Washington, DC: Congress of the United States, Congressional Budget Office. http://www.cbo.gov/.

Drug Channels. 2011. "Ranbaxy Makes Three: The Battle for Generic Lipitor Profits." December 1. http://www.drugchannels.net/2011//12/ranbaxy-makes-three-battle-for-generic.html.

———. 2012. "Pfizer's Lipitor Strategy and the 2012 Generic Monster." March 15. http://www.drugchannels.net/2012/03/pfizers-lipitor-strategy-and-2012.html.

Drug Facts and Comparisons 2011 Edition. 2011. St. Louis, MO: Wolters Kluwer Health, Inc.

Ellison, Glenn, and Sara Fisher Ellison. 2011. "Strategic Entry Deterrence and the Behavior of Pharmaceutical Incumbents Prior to Patent Expiration." *American Economic Journal: Microeconomics* 3 (1): 1–36.

Ellison, Sara Fisher, Iain M. Cockburn, Zvi Griliches, and Jerry A. Hausman. 1997. "Characteristics of Demand for Pharmaceutical Products: An Examination of Four Cephalosporins." *RAND Journal of Economics* 28 (3): 426–46.

Federal Trade Commission. 2002. *Generic Drug Entry Prior to Patent Expiration: An FTC Study*. July. http://www.ftc.gov/os/2002/07/genericdrugstudy.pdf.

———. 2009. *Authorized Generics: An Interim Report of the Federal Trade Commission*. June 24. http://www.ftc.gov/os/2009/06/P062105authorizedgenericsreport.pdf.

———. 2011. *Authorized Generic Drugs: Short-Term Effects and Long-Term Impact*. August. http://www.ftc.gov/opa/2011/08/genericdrugs.shtm.

FiercePharma. 2012. "Top 15 Drug Patent Losses for 2013." November 1. http://www.fiercepharma.com/special-reports/top-15-patent-expirations-2013.

Frank, Richard G., and David S. Salkever. 1992. "Pricing, Patent Loss and the Market for Pharmaceuticals." *Southern Economic Journal* 59:165–79.

———. 1997. "Generic Entry and the Pricing of Pharmaceuticals." *Journal of Economics and Management Strategy* 6 (1): 75–90.

Generic Pharmaceutical Association. 2012. *Generic Drug Savings in the US: Savings $1 Trillion over 10 Years*, 4th annual ed. August 2. www.gphaonline.org.

———. 2013. "Generic Industry by the Numbers." *Generic Pharmaceutical Association 2012 Annual Report*. www.gphaonline.org.

Grabowski, Henry G., and Margaret K. Kyle. 2007. "Generic Competition and Market Exclusivity Periods in Pharmaceuticals." *Managerial Decision and Economics* 28:491–502.

Grabowski, Henry G., Margaret K. Kyle, Richard Mortimer, Genia Long, and Noam Kirson. 2011. "Evolving Brand-Name and Generic Drug Competition May Warrant a Revision of the Hatch-Waxman Act." *Health Affairs* 30 (11): 2157–66.

Grabowski, Henry G., Genia Long, and Richard Mortimer. 2011. "Implementation of the Biosimilar Pathway: Economic and Policy Issues." *Seton Hall Law Review* 41 (2): 511–57.

———. 2013. "Biosimilars." Unpublished manuscript, Duke University, August.

Grabowski, Henry G., and John M. Vernon. 1992. "Brand Loyalty, Entry, and Price Competition in Pharmaceuticals after the 1984 Drug Act." *Journal of Law and Economics* 35:331–50.

———. 1996. "Longer Patents for Increased Generic Competition in the US: The Waxman-Hatch Act after One Decade." *PharmacoEconomics* 10 (suppl. 2): 110–23.

Griliches, Zvi, and Iain M. Cockburn. 1994. "Generics and New Goods in Pharmaceutical Price Indexes." *American Economic Review* 84 (5): 1213–32.

Hemphill, C. Scott, and Bhaven N. Sampat. 2012. "Evergreening, Patent Challenges, and Effective Market Life in Pharmaceuticals." *Journal of Health Economics* 31 (2): 327–39.

Hurwitz, Mark A., and Richard E. Caves. 1988. "Persuasion or Information? Promotion and the Shares of Brand Name and Generic Pharmaceuticals." *Journal of Law and Economics* 31:299–320.

Huskamp, Haiden A., Julie M. Donohue, Catherine Koss, Ernst R. Berndt, and Richard G. Frank. 2008. "Generic Entry, Reformulations, and Promotion of SSRIs." *PharmacoEconomics* 26 (7): 603–16.

IMS Institute for Healthcare Informatics. 2013. *Declining Medicine Use and Costs: For Better or Worse?* May. www.theimsinstitute.org.

Kelton, Christina M. L., Lenisa V. Chang, and David H. Kreling. 2013. "State Medicaid Programs Missed $220 Million in Uncaptured Savings as Generic Fluoxetine Came to Market, 2001–05." *Health Affairs* 32 (7): 1204–11.

Medicaid Drug Rebate Program. 2013. Last updated August 15, 2013. http://www.medicaid.gov.

Olson, Luke M., and Brett W. Wendling. 2013. "The Effect of Generic Drug Competition on Generic Drug Prices during the Hatch-Waxman 180-Day Exclusivity Period." BEA Working Paper no. 317, Washington, DC, Bureau of Economics. April.

Panattoni, Laura E. 2011. "The Effect of Paragraph IV Decisions and Generic Entry before Patent Expiration on Brand Pharmaceutical Firms." *Journal of Health Economics* 30 (1): 126–45.

Regan, Tracy L. 2008. "Generic Entry, Price Competition, and Market Segmentation in the Prescription Drug Market." *International Journal of Industrial Organization* 26 (4): 930–48.

Reiffen, David E., and Michael E. Ward. 2005. "Generic Drug Industry Dynamics." *Review of Economics and Statistics* 87 (1): 37–49.

————. 2007. "'Branded Generics' as a Strategy to Limit Cannibalization of Pharmaceutical Markets." *Managerial and Decision Economics* 28:251–67.

Saha, Atanu, Henry G. Grabowski, Howard M. Birnbaum, Paul E. Greenberg, and Oded Bizan. 2006. "Generic Competition in the US Pharmaceutical Industry." *International Journal of the Economics of Business* 13 (1): 15–38.

Scott Morton, Fiona M. 1999. "Entry Decisions in the Generic Pharmaceutical Industry." *RAND Journal of Economics* 30:421–40.

————. 2000. "Barriers to Entry, Brand Advertising and Generic Entry in the US Pharmaceutical Industry." *International Journal of Industrial Organization* 18 (7): 1085–104.

Smith, Aaron. 2007. "Federal Judge Whacks Generic Plavix." CNN Money.com, June 10. http://money.cnn.com/2007/06/19/news/companies/plavix/index.htm.

US Department of Labor, Bureau of Labor Statistics. 2011. "The Pharmaceutical Industry: An Overview of CPI, PPI, and IPP Methodology." Office of Prices & Living Conditions, October. http://www.bls.gov/ppi/pharmpricescomparison.pdf.

Wang, Xiangnong. 2012. "Understanding Current Trends and Outcomes in Generic Drug Patent Litigation: An Empirical Investigation." Unpublished master's honors thesis, Stanford University, Public Policy Program, May.

Wiggins, Steven N., and Robert Maness. 2004. "Price Competition in Pharmaceuticals: The Case of Anti-Infectives." *Economic Inquiry* 42 (2): 247–63.

Wosinska, Marta, and Robert S. Huckman. 2004. "Generic Dispensing and Substitution in Mail and Retail Pharmacies." *Health Affairs Web Exclusive*, W4:409–16. www.healthaffairs.org.

Specialty Drug Prices and Utilization after Loss of US Patent Exclusivity, 2001–2007

Rena M. Conti and Ernst R. Berndt

9.1 Introduction

We examine the impact of generic entry on the prices and utilization of prescription drugs between 2001 and 2007 in the United States (US). Whereas previous research on the impact of loss of exclusivity (LOE) on entry patterns and use trends following the enactment of the 1984 Drug Price Competition and Patent Term Restoration Act (the "Hatch-Waxman Act") has focused primarily on self-administered oral and tablet/capsule formulations dispensed through the retail pharmacy sector, here we focus on specialty drugs. Although there is no universally accepted definition of specialty drugs, typically they fall into at least one of several categories: they are physician-administered parenterally or self-administered by patients

Rena M. Conti is associate professor of pediatrics and public health sciences at the University of Chicago. Ernst R. Berndt is the Louis E. Seley Professor in Applied Economics at the MIT Sloan School of Management and a research associate of the National Bureau of Economic Research.

The efforts of Conti were funded by a K07 CA138906 award from the National Cancer Institute to the University of Chicago. Berndt's efforts were not sponsored. The funding source had no role in the design and conduct of the study; collection, management, analysis, or interpretation of the data; and preparation, review, or approval of the manuscript for publication. The statements, findings, conclusions, views, and opinions contained and expressed in this chapter are those of the authors and are based in part on National Sales Perspectives data obtained by the National Bureau of Economic Research (NBER) under license from IMS Health (all rights reserved), and are not necessarily those of IMS Health, its affiliates or subsidiaries, or the institutions with whom the authors are affiliated. We thank David Cutler, Judy Hellerstein, Christopher Stromberg, and participants at the October 18–19, 2013, NBER/Conference on Research in Income and Wealth, "Measuring and Modeling Health Care Costs" in Washington, DC, for helpful comments. All errors are our own. For acknowledgments, sources of research support, and disclosure of the authors' material financial relationships, if any, please see http://www.nber.org/chapters/c13100.ack.

through injection, inhalation, or another nonoral method; they require specialized knowledge or manufacturing processes to reliably and reproducibly manufacture; they entail specialty distribution channels rather than retail pharmacies; they are covered under the outpatient medical benefit of public and private insurers; and when patent protected are said to have "high prices." Among those categories, here we limit our empirical cohort to specialty drugs commonly used to treat cancer, and base our analyses on nationally representative data from IMS Health on monthly volume and inflation-adjusted sales revenues. This empirical focus is relevant both to researchers and policymakers. While the market for producing cancer drugs is small compared to that of all prescription drug manufacturing, specialty drug use is an important driver of current national prescription drug spending levels and trends (Aitken, Berndt, and Cutler 2009; GAO 2013). The potential impact on national spending levels and trends among high-price and high-revenue cancer and other specialty drugs expected to undergo LOE is the subject of significant policy interest (US Department of Health and Human Services [OIG] 2011; Conti et al. 2013).

Among pharmaceuticals, LOE opens a drug up to potential competition from multiple manufacturers previously limited to the sole "branded" producer. Price and utilization of drugs post-LOE have been studied extensively among nonspecialty drugs (Caves, Whinston, and Hurwitz 1991; Grabowski and Vernon 1992, 1996; Frank and Salkever 1997; Wiggins and Maness 2004; Reiffen and Ward 2005; Berndt, Kyle, and Ling 2003). Our chapter contributes to this literature by describing the average number of manufacturers entering specialty drugs undergoing LOE in the first year after patent expiration and thereafter, and by comparing raw counts of generic firm entrants to those observed among studies of specialty and nonspecialty drugs in a contemporaneous cohort (Scott Morton 1999, 2000). However, we do not derive welfare implications from these entry count results. Our review of the organization of specialty drug-production literature suggests the substantial presence of time-varying and unobservable contract manufacturing practices seriously complicates and may even obviate the definition of unique "manufacturers" entering this market.

Rather, using pooled cross-sectional and time-series methods, we engage in a three-step examination of whether the neoclassical relationship between presumed price declines upon LOE and volume increases holds among these drugs. First, we examine the extent to which estimated prices of these drugs undergoing LOE fall with generic entry among oral and physician-administered (injected and/or infused) drug formulations. Second, we document raw trends in inflation-adjusted sales revenues and utilization following initial LOE. Third, we estimate reduced-form random effect models of utilization subsequent to LOE, accounting for molecule formulation and therapeutic class and entry patterns (Wiggins and Maness 2004). We discuss second-best welfare consequences of these estimated prices and use results after acknowledging the presence of complications to first-best welfare calculations in this market. Finally, we examine whether molecule characteristics and utilization patterns can help predict drug shortages that occurred in the United States subsequent to our 2001–2007 sample time period.

9.2   Unique Institutions Governing Generic Entry, Manufacturing, and Pricing of Specialty Drugs

In this section, we review unique aspects of the supply and demand for specialty drugs. This discussion is not meant to be exhaustive, but rather is intended to provide sufficient context to motivate our empirical approach and lay the foundation for the interpretation and discussion of our findings.

9.2.1   Branded and Generic Drug Regulatory Approval

The prescription drug market distinguishes two types of drugs. Brand name ("innovator") drugs are approved for use in a given indication by the US Food and Drug Administration (FDA) under New Drug Applications (NDAs) submitted by pioneer manufacturers typically based on the results of one or two phase III randomized controlled clinical trials. Pioneer manufacturers are able to sell their products exclusively while the drug is patent protected. In anticipation of patent expiration and any other loss of exclusivity, other manufacturers (called "sponsors") apply to the FDA to obtain approval to market the "generic" drug under an Abbreviated New Drug Application (ANDA).

The FDA approval of an ANDA does not require its sponsor to repeat clinical or animal research on active ingredients or finished dosage forms already found to be safe and effective. Rather, to gain approval the ANDA sponsor must only establish that the generic contains the same active ingredients; be identical in strength, dosage form, and route of administration; be bioequivalent; and be manufactured under the same strict standards as the brand-name drug. When submitting an ANDA, a sponsor provides evidence either substantiating bioequivalence and compliance with current good manufacturing practices (CGMP) at its own manufacturing sites, or else indicates that portions of the manufacturing (such as production of active pharmaceutical ingredients [APIs] or final fill and finish production) will be outsourced to another supplier or contract manufacturing organization [CMO]). The FDA is responsible for enforcing ANDA requirements and CGMP standards among generic manufacturers both upon entry and via subsequent periodic routine inspections. Production facilities may be inspected and certified postapproval to verify they meet FDA requirements, including in particular specific lines, vats, and batches; typically inspections occur every eighteen to thirty-six months per facility. For oral tablets and capsules, the direct costs of ANDA applications are modest ($1–$5 million) compared to potential profitability (Berndt and Newhouse 2013). Not much is known regarding the direct costs of obtaining ANDA approvals among infused or injected drugs.

9.2.2 Supply Conditions

What is known is that the manufacturing technology involved in the production of infused or injected drugs is highly specialized. Sterility is particularly important for these drugs, providing the primary challenge related to their manufacturing, packaging, and distribution. Sterile production requires keeping human operator intervention to a minimum, which is accomplished by separating or removing highly trained and skilled employees from the aseptic clean air and water environment. Contamination can involve pathogens, fragments of vial rubber stoppers, and broken glass. Because manual steps create opportunities for contamination, automated processes for the filling and finishing of these products are desirable. Unlike most capsules and tablets, liquid active pharmaceutical ingredients (API) are the base materials for production of these drugs. Risk of contamination is also important in the sourcing of API. The API is typically sterilized using filtration, with the sterile product then held in an aseptic storage tank until it is used for final "fill and finish" ANDA production.

Therefore, even though regulatory barriers to entry among manufacturers of these drugs are likely rather modest, the small market size and high fixed and variable production costs of at least some specialty drugs likely results in modest entry post-LOE and production being concentrated among specialized manufacturers. Evidence in support of this market characterization is derived from multiple sources. From industry sources, it is clear manufacturers with noted current commitments to the production of specialized injected or infused drugs for the domestic market include Hospira, Teva Pharmaceuticals and Teva Parenteral ME, and Baxter and Fresenius (APP) (EMD Serono 2013; PBMI 2014). Furthermore, only a handful of injected or infused generic drug manufacturers produce their own liquid or lyophilized API (Teva, Sandoz, and Watson), with the remaining manufacturers acquiring it from nonaffiliated producers. Adding some measure of confidence to our characterization, we note these observations are consistent with previous empirical work on generic entry into these markets, suggesting the mean number of approved ANDA sponsors of injected or infused specialty drugs ranges between two and five, compared to the five to fifteen ANDA sponsors of oral drugs undergoing LOE between 1984 and 1994 in the United States (Scott Morton 1999, 2000; Aitken et al. 2013) and among oral drugs undergoing LOE in Japan between 2004 and 2006 (Iizuka 2009).

Another important characteristic of the market for injected or infused drugs is that a number of prominent manufacturers hold ANDAs for their own drugs and simultaneously act as contract manufacturers for others (e.g., Hospira, Boehringer Ingelheim, Luitpold, Fresenius/APP, West-Ward)

(FDA 2011; Conti 2014). For example, one notable manufacturer of many generic injectable drugs, Ben Venue, was (until very recently) the CMO subsidiary of Boehringer Ingelheim of Germany. There are likely significant cost efficiencies gained from outsourcing the production of injected or infused drugs to established CMOs. To the extent that they are able to exploit economies of scope and scale, CMOs can offer their services at a cost lower than that incurred by self-manufacturing. Moreover, because of scope economies, CMOs face incentives to expand the portfolio of products they produce, but they can also take advantage of scale economies, producing the same injected or infused drug for different ANDA sponsors (Macher and Nickerson 2006). A recent report (FDA 2011) documents more than a doubling of manufacturers relying on CMOs among branded and generic drugs worldwide between 2001 and 2010.

Yet, the FDA does not make public a list of which CMOs manufacture a given drug. As far as we are aware, this information is not made available publicly by any other regulatory agency or private data vendor, either. Thus, the importance of contract manufacturing for drugs supplied to the US market generally (both specialty and nonspecialty), and our sample of drugs specifically, is unobservable by researchers, stakeholders, and regulators. This point fundamentally casts doubt on the validity of simple manufacturer counts, as well as on the interpretation of manufacturing count entry models of any and all generic drugs, and has further implications for policymakers charged with monitoring competition in this market.

9.2.3 Information and Regulatory Timing

The FDA does not publicly reveal when it receives an ANDA, nor the identity of its sponsor. In this sense, the limited information regarding the entry process is symmetric and simultaneous among potential entrants. However, sponsor executives might announce their entry plans to inform their shareholders. Scott Morton (1999) suggests such announcements may be used to deter other competitors from entering the market. Although a firm may announce its intentions to enter the supply of a particular molecule for the domestic market, there is no guarantee that FDA approval will be granted in the time frame anticipated by the applicant. Consequently, an ANDA sponsor cannot generally credibly commit to a market with its application announcement alone.

Supporting this view, a review of recent trends suggests the timing of ANDA approval has become more variable for sponsors between 2001 and 2011 and consequently less predictable among potential entrants (Parexel 2013). While the number of original total ANDA approvals has increased substantially, from 132 in 2001 and 392 in 2007 to 422 in 2011, the number of original injectable ANDA approvals also increased from thirty-two in 2001 (24.2 percent of total) and sixty-four in 2007 (16.3 percent of total) to eighty-eight in 2011 (21 percent of total). Mean (median) FDA ANDA review times initially fell from 21.1 (18.1) months in 2001 to 19.9 (15.7) months in 2004, but then increased to 21.4 (18.9) months in 2007 and 32.9 (29.5) months in 2011. The number of backlogged pending ANDAs under FDA review increased sharply during this period, from 374 in 2001 to 615 in 2004, 1,309 in 2007, and 2,693 in 2011.

9.2.4   Drug Shortages

Since 2006, the United States has experienced a marked increase in prescription drug shortages. Three-quarters of shorted drugs in 2011 were sterile injectable products, such as chemotherapy, anesthesia, and anti-infective agents (US Department of Health and Human Services [ASPE] 2011; Woodcock and Wosinska 2013) and over 80 percent had lost patent protection, experienced generic entry, and consequently were (in theory) multisourced by competing generic drug manufacturers. The majority of generic specialty-drug shortages initially appeared around 2009 and thereafter. These shortages have raised specific alarm since the welfare consequences for pediatric cancers and discontinuation of clinical trials are presumed to be disproportionately high (Gatesman and Smith 2011; Wilson 2012). The University of Utah Drug Information Service tracks the number of shortages at the end of each quarter. Recently, they reported that over the past five quarters the number of shortages was at the highest level since the beginning of 2010. This growth is primarily due to the unusual persistence of existing shortages rather than growth in the number of new shortages (Goldberg 2013).

The proximal causes of most domestic drug shortages are also clear. Beginning around 2009–2011, routine certification inspections performed by the FDA uncovered significant lapses in maintenance of facilities that produce the fill and finished dosage of the drug among many manufacturers (Woodcock and Wosinska 2013). Various inspections investigating suspected lapses in manufacturing practices resulted in the closure of other "fill and finish" facilities (Ben Venue and American Regent in 2010 and Ranbaxy in 2014) and API suppliers (Ranbaxy in 2014). Perhaps as a consequence, policy efforts to mitigate shortages have largely focused on improving the FDA's capabilities to respond to the crises (FDA 2013).

9.2.5   Supply and Demand Side Prices

Among physician-administered injected and infused specialty drugs, the acquisition price of the drug paid by the provider (the price received by the supplying manufacturer—supplier prices) may differ substantially from the insurer reimbursement received by the provider (demand side prices). This divergence is largely due to Medicare and commercial insurers' reimbursement policies that imperfectly reflect the actual acquisition costs of these drugs.

On acquisition prices, NDA and ANDA sponsors (and in some cases, drug catalog publishers) set the wholesale acquisition cost (WAC) of a given drug irrespective of formulation. Wholesalers, retail pharmacies, and other purchasers generally acquire branded drugs from manufacturers at a modest discount off WAC (commonly a 1–2 percent prompt payment discount); generic drugs are typically discounted much more heavily off of WAC. Additional discounts from wholesalers or from manufacturers negotiated by retail pharmacies, by pharmacy benefit managers (PBMs), or by group purchasing organizations (GPOs) on behalf of their members may be directly related to a purchaser's volume or share of a drug within a therapeutic class and also over a bundle of drugs (Frank 2001). The ANDA sponsors of oral drugs can compete intensively on price to win GPO or PBM contracts, which in exchange offers the lowest priced manufacturer preferred formulary and copayment status. Generally, orally formulated anticancer and other selected specialty drugs are less prone than others to formulary based acquisition price negotiations because of the lack of perceived therapeutic substitutes (EMD Serono 2013; PBMI 2014). Physician-administered infused and/or injected drugs may not be prone to acquisition cost discounts related to preferred formulary and/or copayment status arrangements at all, but may be subject to volume-based purchaser discounts. In addition, purchasers of specialty oral and injected/infused drugs can be eligible for federally mandated "best-price" rebates off average manufacturer price (AMP) for Medicaid-insured patients, similar to nonspecialty drugs. The AMP is essentially the average price wholesalers and certain pharmacies pay for drugs distributed to retail community pharmacies (US Department of Health and Human Services [OIG] 2010).

Qualified outpatient hospital-based clinics, affiliated community-based clinics, and contract pharmacies are also able to purchase oral and injected/infused drugs directly from manufacturers or wholesalers (but not via GPOs) at the federally mandated 340B Drug Pricing Program discounted price off AMP. The 340B prices for branded drugs must be at least 23.1 percent discounted off of the AMP, but actual negotiated 340B prices are frequently lower than the 340B ceiling price (GAO 2011). Consequently, discounts through the 340B program have become a prominent part of supplier prices in the specialty and nonspecialty drug market. A recent analysis by Drug Channels (2014) suggests drug purchases under the 340B drug discount program have grown by 800 percent, from $0.8 billion in 2004 to $7.2 billion in 2013. In 2013, hospitals received 340B discounts on at least 25 percent of their drug purchases, compared with only 3 percent in 2004.

Insurers reimburse the use of the specialty drugs in two ways: via the pharmacy benefit (oral specialty drugs, similar to that of nonspecialty oral drugs) or the outpatient medical benefit (all physician-administered injected and infused drugs and a small number of oral drugs). Commercial insurers also provide coverage for Medicare-insured individuals using drugs covered under the pharmacy benefit ("Part D"). Commercial insurers that provide Part D coverage for prescription drugs are required to cover all drugs in six protected classes, one of which is anticancer drugs. This protection requires commercial insurers to offer pharmacy benefits to Medicare beneficiaries that include all available anticancer drugs, with limited supply-side access controls. Reimbursement for pharmacy benefit-covered drugs is generally considered to reflect acquisition costs (albeit imperfectly), other than the discounts obtained through the 340B program (PBMI 2014).

Medicare, the public insurance program providing virtually universal coverage to adults age sixty-five and older, is the most prominent payer for drugs covered under the outpatient medical benefit ("Part B"), followed by commercial insurers, and then state Medicaid agencies (MedPAC 2006). By law, neither Medicare nor Medicaid can consider the cost of drugs or cost effectiveness in coverage decisions (Neumann 2005). Consequently, Medicare and Medicaid cover all newly approved specialty drugs. Indeed, drugs to treat cancer accounted for a majority of outpatient Part B (i.e., largely infused and/or injected specialty) drug spending in 2004. While in theory private payers have more leeway to set coverage policies, de facto coverage (and reimbursement) policy for most specialty drugs follows that of Medicare's policies (Clemens and Gottlieb 2013).

Prior to 2006, Medicare reimbursed providers for purchasing and administering physician-administered specialty drugs as a percentage of the AWP: 95 percent from 1998 to 2003 and 85 percent in 2004. Enacted as part of the 2003 Medicare Drug Improvement and Modernization Act (MMA), Medicare instituted a new average sales price (ASP) payment system intended to more closely reflect actual acquisition prices than AWP, with two notable exceptions: Medicaid best prices and rebates, and 340B discounts. Effective January 2006, Medicare changed reimbursements for Part B drugs to the manufacturers' national ASP two quarters prior plus a 6 percent markup (Jacobson, Alpert, and Duarte 2012). The 2011 Budget Control Act reduced Medicare Part B reimbursement effective April 1, 2013, from ASP plus 6 percent to ASP plus 4.3 percent, where it remains currently. Recent industry reports suggest commercial insurance reimbursement may be more generous than ASP plus 4.3 percent (PBMI 2014).

These policies were responses to the widely recognized fact that reimbursement for many physician-administered specialty drugs covered under outpatient medical insurance benefits had been well in excess of their acquisition prices. Indeed, hospitals, many provider groups, and specialty pharmacy outlets profit from the gap between drugs' acquisition price and reimbursement by insurers and patients, often termed the "spread" (GAO 2004; Barr, Towle, and Jordan 2008; Barr and Towle 2011, 2012; Towle and Barr 2009, 2010; Towle, Barr, and Senese 2012). According to the GAO, prior to 2006 many drugs were available for purchase by provider groups at acquisition prices averaging 13 to 34 percent below their average wholesale price (AWP), while others—particularly generics—were acquired at even significantly lower prices, largely due to PBM and GPO pricing negotiations.

Due to statutory exemptions, the spread can be substantial among drugs purchased under 340B discounts and Medicaid rebates for eligible patients.

By setting the ratio of drug reimbursement to ASP plus 6 percent through 2012 and ASP plus 4.3 percent thereafter, the MMA reform generated the largest reimbursement decline for physician-administered drugs in Medicare's history. For oncology drugs, the policy change represented a marked decline from the weighted average reimbursement-to-cost ratio of 1.22 in 2004, and an even larger decline relative to the years prior to the passage of the MMA when the AWP rather than ASP was used as the benchmark to measure costs (GAO 2004). Jacobson et al. (2010) plot payment rates for drugs commonly used to treat lung and other solid tumor cancers; they observe the payment change due to the MMA to be very dramatic for some drugs. However, the changes were heterogeneous, with some drugs facing no change and others even a slight increase.

Nevertheless, a 2006 survey of oncologists suggests those practicing in selected outpatient settings obtained 70 to 77 percent of their practice revenues from drug payments (Akscin, Barr, and Towle 2007). Later surveys using 2009–2011 data report over 50 percent of outpatient oncology practice revenues continued to be derived from the spread between drug acquisition costs, insurer reimbursements, and patient payments (Towle and Barr 2009, 2010; Towle, Barr, and Senese 2012). Due to these payment incentives, many outpatient specialty physicians, notably oncologists, report that they face financial incentives to administer chemotherapeutics with high "spread" (Malin et al. 2013). In addition, various studies suggest oncologists' drug choices are responsive to profit margins. Conti et al. (2012) found that the use of irinotecan decreased following patent expiration even though the price dropped by more than 80 percent, possibly reflecting declines in the spread between the reimbursement level and oncologists' acquisition cost. Jacobson et al. (2006, 2010) and Jacobson, Earle, and Newhouse (2012) find that oncologists switched away from drugs that lost the most margin after MMA reform implementation and toward expensive drugs favored by the equalized 6 percent markup across all drugs.

9.3   The Model

In this section, we outline our empirical models of ANDA sponsor entry as well as pricing and utilization effects among specialty drugs following LOE, grounding them in theoretical considerations.

9.3.1   Theoretical Considerations and Empirical Findings for Entry Models

Classic economic theory has much to say about firms' short-run decisions to invest in their capability to produce an undifferentiated product in the context of their cost, demand, and marginal revenue curves (Pindyck and Rubinfeld 2013). Notably, when the supply of production inputs is constrained and/or there are substantial fixed costs of entry, entry may be more limited than assumed in classical models (Tirole 1988; Mankiw and Whinston 1986; Bresnahan and Reiss 1988, 1991; Berry 1992). Berry and Reiss (2007) describe reduced-form and structural models where for any given product market, the number of entrant firms is a function of their fixed entry costs that may differ among firms based on their scale and scope, and potential revenues related to the demand elasticity for this product relative to available substitutes and other production opportunities.

In the pharmaceutical market context, a number of empirical studies have relied on this intuition to study firm entry after a drug's LOE. Reiffen and Ward (2005) examined generic entry using data on thirty-one drugs experiencing LOE in the late 1980s and early 1990s. They find that more generic firms enter and enter more quickly into markets when expected profits are greater. Scott Morton (2000) conducted a market-level analysis of eighty-one drugs undergoing LOE between 1986 and 1992, and found that drugs that have higher prepatent expiration revenues and that are used to treat highly prevalent chronic diseases experience greater generic entry. Scott Morton (1999) examined firm characteristics associated with generic entry decisions. Among drugs undergoing patent expiration between 1984 and 1994, she finds a generic firm's previous experience with a given type of drug formulation and therapeutic class increases the probability of similar subsequent generic entry. This work and others (Kyle 2006; Grabowski and Vernon 1992, 1996) suggest drug manufacturing economies of scope may be an important determinant of entry decisions. Outside the United States, Iizuka (2009) examines the relative importance of drug reimbursement policies on the number of generic entrants in Japan between 2004 and 2006. She finds fewer generic manufacturers enter markets when the drug is subject to administrative pricing policies (drugs commonly used in the hospital) compared to those that are not (drugs commonly dispensed in the outpatient setting).

Based on this literature, we implement descriptive reduced-form count models to examine molecule-specific, industry- and firm-level entry determinants in the specialty drug market. The base model we estimate is of the following general form:

(1) $\text{Mancount(entrants}_k) = F(Z_k\delta + X_i\beta),$

where Mancount is the number of firms having an approved ANDA for a given molform, Z_k is a matrix of characteristics of drug market k that affect market size, while X_i is a matrix of firm or molecule characteristics that predict the fixed cost of entry for firm i into market k. Holding all else equal, we expect to observe more firms wanting to enter a market as potential market size increases and less firms entering drug markets where the manufacturing technology needed for production is highly specialized and entails large fixed costs. We assume regulatory cost differences among molecules are small and that we can control adequately for different manufacturing techniques for different product groups (Wiggins and Maness 2004; Caves, Whinston, and Hurwitz 1991; Grabowski and Vernon 1992, 1996). Year and year squared enter the model to help control for changes in regulatory and other fixed cost differences over time.

As discussed in the background section, the 2003 MMA altered reimbursement and benefit policy between 2004 and 2006 for many drugs in our sample, and therefore may have affected specialty market entry patterns (Iizuka 2009). Specifically, provisions of the MMA: (a) lowered Medicare reimbursement for Part B drugs from 95 percent of AWP to 85 percent of AWP effective January 2004 ("MMA1"); (b) provided Medicare coverage to pharmacy dispensed, largely orally formulated drugs in January 2006 (Medicare Part D) ("MMA2"); and (c) instituted the new ASP plus 6 percent payment scheme in January 2006 ("MMA2"). To mark these events, we define two 0–1 indicator variables MMA1 and MMA2 that take on the value of one after January 2004 and January 2006, respectively. We also create interaction variables MMA1 * Part B and MMA2 * Part B defined as the product of the MMA indicator variables and whether the molform was covered by Part B. We include these dummies in our manufacturer count models.

Furthermore, while the MMA1 and MMA2 policies targeted all drugs covered under Part B, the impact of these changes varied across drugs depending on the magnitude of the payment changes. Following Jacobson et al. (2010) and Jacobson, Alpert, and Duarte (2012), for each drug j, we compute the absolute value of the percentage change in reimbursement just before versus after the MMA1 reform, and call the variable "MMA1bite":

$$\text{MMA1bite} = \text{Payment}_{j,04-05}$$

$$= \text{Abs}\left|\text{Log}(\text{Payment}_{j,05}) - \text{Log}(\text{Payment}_{j,04})\right|$$

where $\text{Payment}_{j,05}$ is the Medicare payment in quarter 1 of 2005 (based on ASP) for drug j and $\text{Payment}_{j,04}$ is the Medicare payment in quarter 4 of 2004 (95 percent of AWP); this variable takes on identical nonzero values in 2005:Q1 and thereafter, and is zero before 2005:Q1. We focus on this one-quarter change for the first reform because it is plausibly exogenous to manufacturer supply decisions.

However, as noted earlier, we do not use these measures to derive welfare implications of entry under existing and alternative policy regimes (similar to that pursued by Berry [1992] and Berry and Reiss [2007]) given the host of agency, information, and moral hazard issues plaguing health care markets. Rather, as described in further detail below, we indirectly examine the welfare implications of LOE among these drugs by examining whether the neoclassical relationships among presumed price declines upon LOE and generic entry and volume increases hold.

9.3.2   Theoretical Considerations—Price and Use Models

A number of empirical studies have relied on the framework proposed by Bresnahan and Reiss (1991) among others (Caves, Whinston, and Hurwitz 1991; Grabowski and Vernon 1992, 1996; Frank and Salkever 1997; Wiggins and Maness 2004) to examine the relationship between product prices and the number of suppliers. This framework posits a Cournot quantity-setting model or an entry threshold model (Bresnahan and Reiss 1991), predicting prices should initially fall quickly and then steadily, gradually approaching marginal cost as additional entry occurs. Bresnahan and Reiss (1991) examined prices for dentists, auto repair shops, and the like in geographically isolated county seats. They found prices decline significantly when the supplier count moves from two to three firms, with an even larger price impact observed moving from three to four firms, but smaller price impacts from subsequent entry; thus, they conclude that frequently it requires only three or four entrants to approximate competitive conditions in these markets. They also find a significant difference between price estimates in concentrated county seats and unconcentrated urban markets, suggesting local product market conditions are important in determining price declines. Similarly, Wiggins and Maness (2004) find continuing price declines among drugs undergoing LOE as the number of suppliers becomes large (more than five competitors). Reiffen and Ward (2005) find that generic drug prices fall with increasing number of competitors, but remain above long-run marginal costs until there are eight or more competitors. They also find the size and time paths of generic revenues and the number of firms are greatly affected by expected market size.

Several other authors have reported very small changes in price associated with entry into drug markets after LOE, and even price increases in some drug markets (Caves, Whinston, and Hurwitz 1991; Grabowski and Vernon 1992, 1996). Frank and Salkever (1992) developed a theoretical model to explain the anomaly of rising branded prices in the face of generic competition. Their model posits a segmented market where two consumer segments exist—a quality-conscious, brand-loyal segment that continues to buy the established branded drug after generic entry and a price-conscious segment that is less brand loyal. Frank and Salkever (1997) report that branded prices rise and generic prices fall in response to LOE and generic entry. Ellison et al. (1997) and Griliches and Cockburn (1994) also find that average branded anti-infective prices rise with generic entry; Ellison et al. (1997) and Aitken et al. (2013) report similar findings and also document significant price responsiveness between branded and generic drugs.

We draw on this literature to establish the plausibility of the presumed price drop following LOE among generic specialty drugs. Specifically, we first examine the relationship between supplier prices received by manufacturers (inflation-adjusted monthly total sales revenues/total extended unit use) and the number and nature (branded vs. generic) of firms supplying the market (Caves, Whinston, and Hurwitz 1991; Grabowski and Vernon 1992, 1996; Frank and Salkever 1997; Wiggins and Maness 2004; Reiffen and Ward 2005). We then examine the extent to which supplier prices of the generic drug across manufacturers fall with generic entry, using the following Cournot model:

$$(2) \qquad P * (n) = (a + cN) / (N + 1),$$

in which we assume a roughly linear relationship between price and the inverse of the number of sellers. Like others, here we assume that at any given point in time the number of approved suppliers, N, is exogenously determined reflecting FDA approval and timing uncertainty, and variability in reducing ANDA backlogs (Ellison et al. 1997; Scott Morton 1999, 2000; Wiggens and Maness 2004).

We then estimate reduced-form models of utilization after generic entry as the "dual" of the Cournot model of price competition in equation (2) (Grabowski and Vernon 1992, 1996; Berndt, Kyle, and Ling 2003; Knittel and Huckfeldt 2012) using generalized least squares.[1] We estimate random-effect regression models that quantify the importance of drug-specific demand and cost differences in influencing the use-supplier relationship (Wiggins and Maness 2004) having the following form:

$$(3) \qquad \ln Y_{kt} = \alpha + \beta_t + \kappa Z_k + \theta \text{Post}_{kt} + \varepsilon_{kt},$$

where Y_{kt} is the utilization volume of drug k at month t, α is a constant, β_t are time fixed effects capturing general changes in specialty drug demand, and κZ_k are effects from the characteristics of the molecule formulation ("molform" characteristics). The variable Post_{kt} is an indicator variable denoting generic entry month-year for each molform experiencing post-LOE generic entry in the sample. Positive estimates of θ suggest volume increases post-LOE (presumably, reflecting increased quantity demanded from lower average molecule price post-LOE), whereas negative estimates suggest utilization declines post-LOE.

To interpret the hypothesized result (finding that $\theta < 0$ in equation [3]), we include in one specification whether LOE has an independent and negative effect on usage among physician-administered drugs after LOE, all else equal. In addition, LOE should act to induce institutional consumers to shift their demand away from low-cost generic specialty drugs toward high-priced branded alternatives when the drug is covered under insurers' outpatient medical benefit (where the absolute value of insurer reimbursement would be greater, holding all else constant) (Jacobson et al. 2010; Jacobson, Earle, and Newhouse 2012; Conti et al. 2012). We identify these independent

---

1. Duggan and Scott Morton (2010) and Berndt and Aitken (2011) have found significant volume increases related to policy changes that act to decrease drug prices to consumers.

effects on use by including in the model the variables that capture Medicare coverage in Part B and the MMA reimbursement and coverage changes outlined above.

9.3.3   Theoretical Considerations—Shortage Models

Our monthly data cover the 2001–2007 time period. Widespread drug shortages did not occur in the United States until after 2008. However, consistent with economic theory, our data can be uniquely used to consider two aspects of the market for drugs preceding incident shortage reports. First, among our sample drugs we examine the correlation between shortage reports at the molform level and the number of manufacturers manufacturing these drugs in 2007:Q4. Second, we examine whether 2007:Q4 molecule revenues, and/or Medicare reimbursement and their reforms implemented between 2001 and 2007 are associated with shortage reports among our sample of specialty drugs, reflecting reduced incentives to maintain manufacturing quality standards.

9.4   Data and Descriptive Trends

We obtained national monthly data on the use, volume, and retail and nonretail dollar sales of all specialty drugs by distributor from IMS Health Incorporated's National Sales Perspectives™ (NSP) database covering periods between January 2001 and December 2007. The NSP data have been used in numerous published studies of pharmaceutical revenues and volumes. The NSP data derive from a projected audit describing 100 percent of the national unit volume and dollar sales in every major class of trade and distribution channel for US prescription pharmaceuticals. The NSP sample is based on over 1.5 billion annual transactions from over 100 pharmaceutical manufacturers and more than 700 distribution centers. The NSP provides information on the molecule-specific chemical and branded names, route of administration, strength, and the name of distributing firm(s). Each firm-molecule-formulation-strength (hereafter, "molform strength") is uniquely identified in the data set by its eleven-digit National Drug Code (NDC).

"Dollar sales" measures the amount of funds retail pharmacies, mail pharmacies, nonfederal hospitals, federal facilities, long-term care facilities, clinics, home health care facilities, and miscellaneous facilities spent on a drug acquired from manufacturers and drug wholesalers. The prices reflected in this sales measure are the actual invoice prices outlets (e.g., pharmacies, hospitals, clinics) pay for the products, whether purchased directly from a manufacturer or indirectly via a wholesaler or chain warehouse. Invoice line item discounts are included, but prompt-payment discounts and bottom-line invoice discounts are not included. Rebates, typically paid by the manufacturer directly to a customer, insurer, or PBM are not reflected in these data. Dollar sales are converted into 2012 US dollars using the

Table 9.1   **Count of unique sample NDCs by therapeutic class**

ATC	Count of unique NDCs by anatomic therapeutic class designation						
	2001	2002	2003	2004	2005	2006	2007
A04 antiemetcs + antinauseants	247	240	258	273	259	289	328
L01A alkylating agents	68	70	72	78	80	72	81
L02B antimetabolites	117	114	114	120	125	128	130
L01C vinca alkaloids	55	59	66	67	75	73	67
L01C antineoplas. antibiotics	82	87	83	82	80	90	115
L01X all other antineoplastics	40	42	53	91	107	121	133
L02A cytostatic hormones	63	64	67	73	74	75	74
L02B cyto hormone antagonists	22	29	49	52	54	55	55
L04X other immunosuppressants	0	0	0	0	0	12	12
V03D detox ag a-neoplast. trmt.	58	56	46	46	51	51	49
Grand total	752	761	808	882	905	966	1,044

Consumer Price Index for All Urban Consumers (CPI-U) inflation calculator. "Extended units" measures the number of single items (such as vials, syringes, bottles, or packets of tablets/capsules) contained in a unit or shipping package purchased by providers and pharmacies, and may include varying available doses and strengths.

Our NSP data covers the following ten World Health Organization's four-digit cancer-related anatomic therapeutic classes (ATCs): antiemetics and antinauseants (A04A), alkylating agents (L01A), antimetabolites (L01B), vinca alkaloids (L01C), antineoplastic antibiotics (L02D), all other antineoplastics (L01X), cytostatic hormones (L02A), cytostatic hormone antagonists (L04B), other immune suppressants (L04X), and detox ag a-neoplastic treatments (V03D). This sample frame has the advantage of including branded and generic versions of the same molecule having similar manufacturing requirements, and including drugs that are covered under both insurers' pharmacy and medical benefits. The ATC four-digit and more disaggregated ATC class designations are retained and coded for use in the analysis.

The distribution of NDCs by ATC class is listed in table 9.1. The majority of drugs in the full sample fall into several categories: drugs used to treat cancer (antimetabolites, antineoplastics agents, other antineoplastic treatments—215 of 752 in 2001, 312/1,044 in 2007), supportive therapy (antiemetics and antinauseants, cytostatic hormones, cytostatic hormone antagonists—332/752 in 2001, 457/1,044 in 2007) and other (other immune suppressants, antineoplastic antibiotics—82/752 in 2001, 127/1,044 in 2007).

According to economic theory, pre-LOE differences in fixed costs affect the subsequent number of generic entrants. Therefore, similar to Scott Morton (1999, 2000), Iizuka (2009), and Wiggins and Maness (2004), we code formulations into several categories according to the type of specialized equipment needed to manufacture a drug and the cleanliness standards required in the manufacturing facility (oral solid tablets or capsules; injectable or infusible products; topical preparations; and other formulations, including ocular drugs, patches, and aerosols).

For each molecule, the earliest ANDA approval for each molform was identified using the FDA's comprehensive online listing. This method stratified the full sample (166 molforms) into three groups: (a) forty-one molforms (25 percent of full sample) experiencing initial generic entry between January 2001 and July 2007, (b) fifty molforms (30 percent) experiencing generic entry prior to January 2001, and (c) seventy-five molforms (45 percent) only available as exclusively marketed "brands" between January 2001 and December 2007 (appendix table 9A.1). Because of our focus on the extent and impact of generic entry, we excluded molforms in the (c) category from our analyses (all molforms are listed in appendix table 9A.2).

Among the forty-one molforms experiencing generic entry in our study period, the majority underwent LOE in 2002 and 2004 (appendix table 9A.2). Nine (22 percent) underwent generic entry on or following January 2006. Sixty-one percent (twenty-five out of forty-one molforms) had FDA-approved labels that indicated their use in combination therapy to treat cancer. Among this sample, we observed the following drug formulation pattern: 37 percent oral and 63 percent infused/injected or otherwise physician administered. Our check of Part B Medicare reimbursement schedules revealed 76 percent (thirty-one of our forty-one molforms experiencing initial LOE between 2001 and 2007) were covered by the Medicare Part B benefit (the remainder presumably covered under Part D benefits) (CMS 2014).

Using the FDA's comprehensive online listing we identified whether, for a given molecule, generic entry timing differed by formulation and/or strength. The subsequent entry of differing formulations (and/or strengths) among existing ANDAs may reflect a different underlying demand structure than with novel entrants, with the more commonly utilized formulations/strengths being produced earliest. We found that the majority of molecules undergoing generic entry shared identical entry dates across multiple formulations; yet, a limited number of molforms experienced sequential entry by different strengths. Consequently, in our empirical models we estimate parameters first at the molform level and in sensitivity analyses at the molform-strength level.

The number of "manufacturers" for each molform and molform strength was identified using the NSP and was cross-checked using the FDA's Orange Book. We identified sixty-three manufacturers distributing at least one cancer drug undergoing initial generic entry in our study period. In appendix table 9A.3, we enumerate these manufacturers and the total number of molforms produced by them among all drugs in the parent sample. As expected

Table 9.2   Number of all sample cancer drugs produced by top ANDA sponsors; number of cancer drugs produced by top manufacturers of drugs undergoing LOE

	APP	Bedford Labs	Teva Parenteral Me	Teva Pharmaceuticals
2001		16		9
2002		15		9
2003	12	16		12
2004	16	20	20	14
2005	17	21	19	15
2006	16	23	22	18
2007	20	26	22	19

from our institutional review, we find production of these drugs concentrates in several manufacturers. Branded manufacturers of drugs undergoing LOE in our sample are primarily limited to the following: Abbott, AstraZeneca, Bayer Healthcare, Bristol-Myers Oncology, Genzyme, GSK, Novartis, Pfizer, Roche, and Watson. Among generic manufacturers, APP, Bedford Laboratories, Teva Parenteral Me, and Teva Pharmaceuticals dominate the production of drugs undergoing initial LOE in our sample. We also observe growth in the commitment of these ANDA sponsors to the production of all generic cancer drugs over time, as the number produced is generally larger in 2007 than in earlier years, although year-to-year changes are occasionally negative (table 9.2). We use these branded/generic manufacturer designations for examining pricing trends at the molform-manufacturer level after LOE.

We construct measures of prepatent expiration brand *revenues* and *ln revenues*, adopting a definition of "market" size consisting of sales only by the branded molecule in the four complete quarters prior to LOE (average monthly revenue = 439,000 [standard deviation = 452,000, min. = 0, max. = 1,722]; average ln revenue = 5.6 [standard deviation = 6.2, min. = 0, max. = 13.2]) (Frank and Salkever 1997; Scott Morton 1999; Iizuka 2009). Following Scott Morton (1999), we also constructed a measure of the *difference in revenue* defined as the value of the difference between the revenue potential from the entry opportunity relative to that of the manufacturers' existing mean generic NDC portfolio from all drugs enumerated in the NSP (monthly average = 381,600, standard deviation = 538,000, min. = −816, max. = 1,599). To the extent firms' existing portfolios consist of old vintages of off-patent drugs having declining sales and the entry being considered is that for a widely utilized newer molecule having large sales volume, we expect this difference measure will positively affect probability of current entry. We transform by using the difference log form of this measure (monthly average = 5.9, standard deviation = 1.5, min. = −2.5, max. = 7.4) in the estimated model and its square.

While previous literature has focused on using pre-LOE revenues (and its square, both typically log transformed) as measures of potential market size post-LOE, we augment these by constructing a measure reflecting the number of distinct conditions treated by the medicines. Specifically, we construct a measure of indication count, inclusive of FDA on-label approved and off-label Medicare reimbursed, measured in the year prior to LOE that is likely correlated with potential future revenues.[2] The number of indications for which an NDC was reimbursed for use in the US population in each year (average = 6, standard deviation = 9) is taken from the Micromedex DrugDex Evaluations database, one of several compendia approved by Congress to guide CMS reimbursement policy (Conti et al. 2012). This identified FDA-approved (on-label) and off-label indications that were contemporaneously reimbursed by the Centers for Medicare and Medicaid Services.

Finally, we matched all sample molforms and molform strengths with the University of Utah Drug Information Service to determine dates of any shortages, including resolved shortages, if present.[3] No sample molforms and molform strengths were reported in short supply between January 2001 and December 2007.

9.5   Results

9.5.1   Count Models for Descriptive Purposes

Bearing in mind the caveats on manufacturer counts created by the presence of considerable contract manufacturing activities, we first describe the average number of generic manufacturers per molform experiencing LOE by year of LOE (figure 9.1). We observe the average number to range between 1.66 and 4.9 manufacturers over all years, and what appears to be an upward trend in entry count in 2006 and 2007 compared to previous years, from a low of 1.66 in 2003 to a high of 4.9 in 2007.

Furthermore, average entrant counts differ by drug formulation: oral drugs exhibit an average of 6.26 (standard deviation = 2.7, max = 11) manufacturers entering after LOE, while physician-administered drugs exhibit an average of 4.5 (standard deviation = 2.7, max = 9) manufacturers entering after LOE.

To place these observations into wider industry-level context, we also calculated the average number of manufacturers of always generic cancer drugs available throughout the study period (appendix table 9A.2; figure 9.2). We

---

2. Incentives for manufacturers to seek additional indications for reimbursements diminish considerably after LOE, although the off-patent brand may pursue a "branded generic" strategy in which it markets a combination product consisting of the off-patent brand and a generic drug.

3. http://www.ashp.org/drugshortages/current/; http://www.ashp.org/menu/DrugShortages/ResolvedShortages.

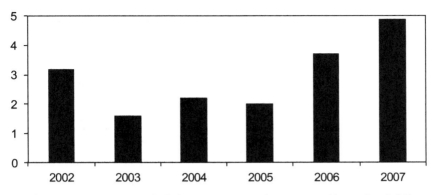

Fig. 9.1   Average number of ANDA sponsors entering a new molform after LOE, by year of LOE

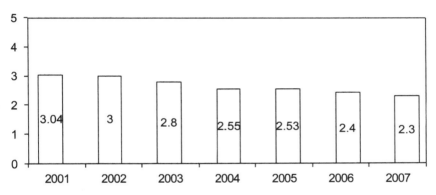

Fig. 9.2   Average number of manufacturers producing always generic molforms

observe the average number of manufacturers producing these drugs to be declining gradually but steadily from 3.04 in 2001 to 2.3 in 2007.

Interestingly, the patterns of entry and exit among specialty cancer drugs undergoing LOE during our study periods appear quite diverse, as is illustrated in the various panels of table 9.3. For example, the first column (Example 1) in table 9.3 documents a situation in which the innovator brand manufacturer (Pierre Fabre Pharma, bolded) continues to market vinorelbine IAC in injectable and intravenous formulations following LOE in 2003 and throughout the remaining study period. We also observe injectable and intravenous formulation ANDA entry in vinorelbine IAC by Baxter Pharma Division and Sicor Pharma in 2003, Bedford Labs and Teva Parenteral ME in 2004, and APP and Hospira in 2005. We observe Sicor Pharma exiting this drug market in 2004 and Baxter Pharm Division exiting in 2007. Merger and acquisition activity likely explains the apparent exit by Sicor Pharma and entry by Teva Parenteral ME in 2004 (table 9.4)—Teva acquired Sicor

Table 9.3   **Observed patterns of manufacturer entry and exit after LOE among selected sample molforms**

Year	Example 1: Innovator stays in the market after LOE — Vinorelbine IAC inject, IV	Example 2: Innovator exits the market after LOE — Carboplatin IAC inject, IV Reg.	Tamoxifen 0511 orals, sol. tab/cap RE
2001	**Pierre Fabre Pharm**	**Bristol-Myers Oncology**	**AstraZeneca**
2002	**Pierre Fabre Pharm**	**Bristol-Myers Oncology**	**AstraZeneca**
			Barr Labs
2003	Baxter Pharm Div	**Bristol-Myers Oncology**	**AstraZeneca**
	Pierre Fabre Pharm		Barr Labs
	Sicor Pharm		Mylan
			Roxane
			Teva Pharm
2004	Baxter Pharm Div	APP	**AstraZeneca**
	Bedford Labs	Baxter Pharm Div	Barr Labs
	Pierre Fabre Pharm	Bedford Labs	Mylan
	Teva Parenteral Me	**Bristol-Myers Oncology**	Roxane
		Hospira	Teva Pharm
		Teva Parenteral Me	Watson Labs
		Watson Labs	
2005	APP	APP	**AstraZeneca**
	Baxter Pharm Div	Baxter Pharm Div	McKesson Pkg Serv
	Bedford Labs	Bedford Labs	Mylan
	Hospira	**Bristol-Myers Oncology**	Ranbaxy Pharm
	Pierre Fabre Pharm	Cura Pharm	Roxane
	Teva Parenteral Me	Hospira	Teva Pharm
		OTN Pharm	Watson Labs
		Teva Parenteral Me	
		Watson Labs	
2006	APP	APP	A-S Medication
	Baxter Pharm Div	Baxter Pharm Div	**AstraZeneca**
	Bedford Labs	Bedford Labs	McKesson Pkg Serv
	Hospira	Cura Pharm	Mylan
	Pierre Fabre Pharm	Hospira	Roxane
	Teva Parenteral Me	OTN Pharm	Teva Pharm
		Teva Parenteral Me	Watson Labs
		Watson Labs	
2007	APP	APP	A-S Medication
	Bedford Labs	Baxter Pharm Div	McKesson Pkg Serv
	Hospira	Bedford Labs	Mylan
	Pierre Fabre Pharm	Cura Pharm	Roxane
	Teva Parenteral Me	Generamedix	Teva Pharm
		Hospira	Watson Labs
		OTN Pharm	
		Teva Parenteral Me	
		Watson Labs	

Table 9.4   Consolidation activity among firms in our sample

	Merging firm	Acquiring firm	Completion year
1	GREENSTONE LTD.	PFIZER	2003
2	ABBOTT PHARM PRODS.	HOSPIRA	2004
3	SICOR PHARM	TEVA PHARM	2004
4	Mayne Pharm	HOSPIRA	2007
5	Abraxis Pharm	APP	2007
6[a]	King	JHP PHARM	2007
7	BARR LABS	TEVA PHARM	2008
8	APP	Fresenius	2008
9	Wyeth Ayerst	PFIZER	2009
10	Medimmune Oncology	ASTRAZENECA	2013

Note: Capitalized manufacturer names indicate manufacturers producing drugs undergoing LOE in our sample.

[a] JHP was formed out of assets from King and other companies.

in 2004, and likely subsequently consolidated the two generic products into one market offering.

In other cases, the innovator brand is observed to exit the molform market after initial LOE, as is seen in Example (2) of table 9.3. Here, the manufacturer of the branded version of carboplatin IAC injectable and regular intravenous (Bristol-Myers Oncology, bolded) faced LOE in 2004 and remained in the market only through 2005. In 2004 we observe APP, Baxter Pharma Division, Bedford Labs, Cura Pharm, Hospira, Teva Parenteral ME, and Watson Labs and in 2005 OTN Pharmaceutical entering this molform market. The final column of table 9.3 documents a somewhat similar pattern of exit by the innovator brand manufacturer (AstraZeneca, bolded) for the oral anticancer drug tamoxifen, albeit in 2007, several years after LOE in 2002, and staggered ANDA entry by Barr Labs, Mylan, Roxane, Teva Pharmaceuticals, and Watson Labs in 2004, McKesson Pkg. Serv. in 2005, and A-S Medication in 2006. Here too, the observed Barr Labs exit from this molform in 2005 might be related to the formalization of its acquisition by Teva several years later (see table 9.4).

These observations suggest mergers and acquisitions among generic firms (horizontal consolidation) and branded firms (vertical consolidation) that occurred between 2000 and 2009 could alter our results of manufacturer count entry. To check, we identified mergers and acquisitions among manufacturers using the SDC Platinum, a collection of databases on companies registered in the United States and a product of Thomson Reuters Financial Securities Data available through the University of Chicago's electronic library. This categorization was double checked using a search of all manufacturers and the trade press. The presence, date, and type of consolidation are reported in table 9.4.

To analyze factors contributing to the diverse entry patterns, we estimated random effects generalized least squares count models with ln mancount (log number of manufacturers) as the dependent variable for each molform based on the 2001–2007 pooled cross-section and time-series data; in sensitivity analyses, we reestimate using molform strength as the unit of observation. Since with a Poisson model there was overdispersion (estimated variance greater than mean), estimates presented in table 9.5 are based on the negative binomial model. Consistent with the raw averages, we observe less entry into injectable formulations after LOE (all models). There is also greater entry into the cancer therapeutic class and less entry into other classes after LOE (all models). Another robust finding across models is that ln preentry revenue positively affects the number of manufacturers. Consistent with this finding, we also observe in each of the estimated models the greater the number of ln indications for which the molform is recommended, the greater the number of manufacturers of that molform (models 1–5). However, ln preentry revenue squared flips in sign across models. Models 3–5 report another modestly robust finding that when ln revenues of the candidate molform is much greater than the mean revenue per product of the incumbent portfolio of molform products (a positive ln revenue difference), the number of manufacturers for a molform increases, although the negative estimated coefficient on the squared ln revenue difference variable indicates this positive impact declines as the ln revenue difference increases. This suggests that all else equal, firms may face a trade-off as they contemplate additional generic entry between incremental revenue gained and the greater fixed and/or sunk production costs incurred from additional entry. Finally, note that while in models 4–5 the positive estimated coefficient on the month post-MMA1 indicator variable and the negative estimate on the post-MMA1 * Part B–covered interaction variable have the expected signs suggesting MMA reimbursement policy changes affected manufacturer entry, these estimates are not statistically significant.

9.5.2 Supplier Prices following LOE

As an initial analysis of the impact of LOE on supplier prices, we examine two measures or average monthly inflation-adjusted prices—prices and ln prices—separately for oral and injectable/infusible molforms, before LOE and generic entry and after LOE and generic entry, aggregated over brand and generic versions for each molform. As is seen in table 9.6, regardless of which price measure is used, average monthly prices are lower post-LOE and generic entry than pre-LOE for all drug formulations. Interestingly, aggregate price declines appear to be larger among physician-administered infused/injected drugs (38–46.4 percent) than among orally formulated drugs (25–26 percent).

Next, to examine the relationship between supplier prices following LOE and the number of manufacturers, we first plotted average monthly ln prices

Table 9.5   Manufacturer count model negative binomial regression results

	Model 1			Model 2			Model 3			Model 4			Model 5		
	Coef.	SE	p	Coef.	SE	p	Coef.	SE	p	Coef.	SE	p	Coef.	SE	p
Injectable	−0.27	0.17	0.133	−0.59	0.24	0.04	−0.51	0.25	0.05	−0.92	0.21	0.001	−0.95	0.31	0.001
ln indications	0.9	0.42	0.001	0.9	0.1	0.001	0.9	0.1	0.001	0.9	0.11	0.001	1.03	0.12	0.001
Cancer therapeutic class	1.2	0.2	0.001	0.65	0.28	0.02	0.8	0.3	0.007	0.66	0.25	0.008	0.48	0.28	0.07
Other therapeutic class	−0.62	0.33	0.064	−0.34	0.5	0.355	−0.35	0.53	0.355	−0.73	0.44	0.03	−0.84	0.44	0.03
Time (months starting with January 2001)	0.004	0.0009	0.001	0.006	0.0007	0.001	0.006	0.0007	0.001	0.002	0.0004	0.001	0.002	0.0004	0.001
Time squared (months starting with January 2001)	0.00001	0.000002	0.001	0.00001	0.000007	0.001	0.00001	0.000007	0.001	−0.00003	0.000007	0.001	−0.00003	0.000007	0.001
ln revenue per LOE (2012 USD)	0.007	0.003	0.001	0.009	0.0003	0.001	0.01	0.0004	0.001	0.002	0.0003	0.001	0.002	0.0003	0.001
ln revenue pre-LOE squared (2012 USD)	0.000004	0.0000002	0.001	0.000003	0.0000002	0.001	0.000003	0.0000002	0.001	−0.000003	0.0000002	0.001	−0.000003	0.0000002	0.001
ln revenue pre-LOE diff (2012 USD)							−0.05	0.01	0.001	0.05	0.01	0.001	0.02	0.007	0.038
ln revenue pre-LOE diff. squared (2012 USD)							−0.02	0.002	0.001	−0.02	0.002	0.001	−0.005	0.001	0.001
MMA1 (2004)				0.12	0.07	0.07	0.09	0.05	0.09	0.004	0.04	0.93	0.01	0.05	0.83
MMA1 * Part B covered							−0.06	0.05	0.43	−0.03	0.05	0.6	−0.02	0.05	0.7
MMA2 (2006)										0.03	0.06	0.61	0.04	0.06	0.54
MMA2 * Part B covered										0.95	0.06	0.001	0.96	0.06	0.001
MMA1 bite													−0.28	0.03	0.001
_constant	1.9	0.19	0.001	1.73	0.49	0.001	1.94	0.5	0.001	0.44	0.22	0.04	1.31	0.24	0.001
Adjusted R² (overall)	0.28			0.49			0.5			0.44			0.84		
N	3,444			3,444			3,444			3,444			3,444		

Table 9.6   **Raw inflation-adjusted prices and ln prices before and after LOE**

	Before LOE		After LOE		After – before		
	Monthly average	Std. error	Monthly average	Std. error	Difference	Std. error	Percent change
Oral (*n* = 15)							
Prices (2012 USD)	1.26	0.03	0.93	0.01	**−0.33**	0.35	−26
ln prices (2012 USD)	0.57	0.016	0.43	0.037	**0.14**	0.01	−25
Physician-administered infused/injected (*n* = 26)							
Prices (2012 USD)	1,356.1	27.8	1985.5	30.3	**629.42**	41.1	−46.4
ln prices (2012 USD)	2.4	0.03	1.3	0.02	**0.9**	0.04	−38

Note: Bold = significant at the 1 percent level.

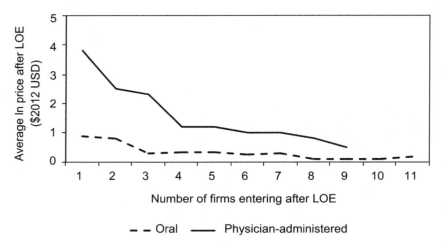

Fig. 9.3   Relationship between ln inflation-adjusted estimated supplier prices (2012 USD) and manufacturer count after LOE

(2012 USD) observed in the last quarter of 2007 against the total number of unique entrants in all years following LOE (including the innovator brand), stratified by oral versus infused/injected or otherwise physician-administered formulation. Results are displayed in figure 9.3, with ln supplier prices on the vertical axis and total number of unique manufacturers following LOE on the horizontal axis. Two sets of results are striking. First, the level of ln prices for oral formulations is much lower than that for infused/injected or otherwise physician-administered drugs, up until there are about nine unique manufacturers of the formulation. Second, for infused/injected or otherwise physician-administered drugs, when the number of manufacturers increases from one to two, average ln prices fall about 25–30 percent, there is another even larger proportional drop in ln price as the number

Table 9.7   **Relationship between inflation-adjusted supplier price (2012 USD) and manufacturer counts, by formulation and LOE status**

	Oral molforms			Injected and infused or otherwise physician-administered formulated molforms		
	Coefficient	Std. error	p-value	Coefficient	Std. error	p-value
Generic, underwent LOE						
ln mancount	−0.77	0.03	0.0001	−0.22	0.017	−12.54
ln mancount squared	−0.01	0.005	0.051	0.02	0.004	0.0001
Year	0.26	0.05	0.001	−0.29	0.03	0.0001
N	287			1,678		
Adjusted R^2	0.16			0.12		
Branded, underwent LOE						
ln mancount	0.07	0.02	0.0002	0.49	0.04	0.0001
ln mancount squared	0.07	0.05	0.0001	−0.04	0.006	0.0001
Year	−0.52	0.04	0.0001	0.26	0.04	0.0001
N	161			1,318		
Adjusted R^2	0.12			0.05		

of manufacturers increases from three to four, but in the range between four and seven manufacturers, ln prices of these drugs are relatively stable, and after that as additional manufacturers of infused/injected or otherwise physician-administered drugs enter, the average ln price continues to fall. This suggests that for infused/injected or otherwise physician-administered cancer drugs, unlike the case for oral solids, price declines accelerate as the number of manufacturers increases.

A more rigorous method for analyzing the relationship between supplier prices following LOE and the total number of manufacturers (but bearing in mind potential measurement error in manufacturer counts from unobserved and time-varying outsourcing to contract manufacturing organizations) is via regression analysis. Results of estimating a regression equation via ordinary least squares with ln inflation-adjusted supply price as the dependent variable are presented separately in table 9.7 for generic and branded formulations following LOE, and for oral and infused/injected or otherwise physician-administered formulations.

We begin with the oral molforms. As seen in the top-left panel, following LOE generic prices fall sharply as ln mancount (which now includes only ANDA holders, not the brand) increases, and this decline accelerates ever so slightly as the square of ln mancount increases. Holding ln mancount and its square constant, prices increase annually (year = 1 in 2001, 2 in 2002, etc.). For the off-patent but branded oral molforms following LOE (bottom-left panel), the relationship of supplier prices with ln mancount is very different. Specifically, ln inflation-adjusted supplier prices of branded oral molforms increase with growth in ln mancount, and this price increase accelerates with the square of ln mancount, suggesting that for oral brands, the ability to differentiate themselves from generics post-LOE enables them to continue commanding premium prices. However, this ability to increase price declines with time, other things equal, as the estimated coefficient on the year variable is negative, large, and significant.

By contrast, as seen in the top-right corner of table 9.7, for injected and infused molforms following LOE, ln inflation-adjusted supplier prices fall much less steeply as ln mancount increases than do oral molforms, and this price decline decelerates as the square of ln mancount increases; however, ln inflation-adjusted supplier prices fall as time increases. The situation is very different for branded injected and infused molforms following LOE (bottom-right panel): prices of these branded nonoral formulations increase with ln mancount, but at a decreasing rate (the estimate on the squared ln mancount variable is negative and significant). In summary, for both oral and injected/infused molforms, following LOE prices of generic molforms fall as ln mancount increases (with the price decline being much steeper for oral than injected/infused formulations), but for branded molforms following LOE, prices increase as ln mancount grows, with the price increase being steeper for injected/infused than oral formulations. These results suggest post-LOE price competition among suppliers is less intense for injected/infused than oral formulations.

9.5.3   Impact of LOE on Utilization Volume

While measures of utilization volume are relatively straightforward for oral formulations (number tablets or capsules—what IMS Health calls *standard units*, or total milligrams of active pharmaceutical ingredient), for infused, injected, or otherwise physician-administered formulations, the measure of utilization volume is more ambiguous. IMS Health defines *extended units* as the number of tablets, capsules, milliliters, ounces, and so forth of a product shipped in each unit. This number is calculated by multiplying the number of units by the product size. Another volume measure is an "each," which represents "the number of single items (such as vials, syringes, bottles, or packet of pills) contained in a unit or shipping package and purchased by providers and pharmacies in a specific time period. An each is not a single pill or dosage of medicine (unless one package consists of a single dose), but may be the same as a unit if the unit does not subdivide into packages. Eaches are usually used to examine usage of injectable products. Eaches are most meaningful at the package level, since packages and their subunits may contain different quantities of strengths and volumes."[4]

---

4. From email correspondence between Berndt and Terry McMonagle at the IMS Institute for Healthcare Informatics, September 4, 2013, 11:15 a.m.

Table 9.8   Raw use and inflation-adjusted sales trends before and after LOE by formulation

	Before LOE		After LOE		After − before		
	Monthly average	Std. error	Monthly average	Std. error	Difference	Std. error	Percent change
Oral (*n* = 15)							
Extended units	1,508.4	18.4	2,759	24.7	**1,250.3**	30.8	82.9
Eaches	121.5	1.7	158.5	1.6	**37.03**	2.29	30.5
Sales (2012 USD)	1,356.1	27.8	1,985.5	30.3	**629.42**	41.1	46.4
Physician-administered infused/injected (*n* = 26)							
Extended units	438.75	14.2	656.2	12.6	**217.5**	19.01	49.6
Eaches	271.8	11.04	47.96	0.44	**223.8**	11.05	82.3
Sales (2012 USD)	1,596.4	20.9	2,506.6	23.4	**910.2**	31.4	57.0

Note: Bold = significant at the 1 percent level.

As an initial analysis of the impact of LOE on utilization volume, in table 9.8 we examine three measures of volume—average monthly extended units, average monthly eaches, and average monthly inflation-adjusted sales (2012 USD) separately for oral and injectable/infusible molforms, before LOE and generic entry, and after LOE and generic entry but aggregated over brand and generic versions for each molform. As seen in table 9.8, regardless of which volume measure used, average aggregate brand plus generic monthly utilization is greater post-LOE and generic entry than pre-LOE and generic entry for both oral and physician-administered infused/injected drugs.

However, a closer examination focused on the share of molforms within each aggregate category experiencing an increase reveals that these aggregate trends mask heterogeneity across drug formulations. To see this, we undertake a more detailed analysis of the impact of LOE on utilization volume involving estimation of various generalized least squares models with random effects in which the dependent variable is the log of volume, where volume is measured in extended units. Here again, the unit of observation is the molform month. In the specification of model 1 in table 9.9, the omitted reference case for the various indicator variables is pre-LOE time periods, an oral formulation, and a supportive therapeutic (e.g., an antinausea drug to mitigate side effects). We find that the estimated coefficient on the generic entry year indicator variable (taking on the value of one post-LOE and initial generic entry, else zero among oral formulated drugs) is positive and significant. Also consistent with the findings in table 9.8, although the estimated coefficient on the main effect injectable variable is negative (for the pre-LOE time periods), here we find that aggregate average monthly volume increases are large for injectable/infusible drugs following LOE, that is, the parameter estimate on the injectable-entry-year interaction variable

Table 9.9   Estimated volume changes using GLS random effects

	Model 1, ln extended units			Model 2, ln extended units			Model 3, ln extended units		
	Coeff.	Std. error	$p > |t|$	Coeff.	Std. error	$p > |t|$	Coeff.	Std. error	$p > |t|$
Entry year dummy	0.24	0.05	0.004	0.51	0.02	0.001	0.51	0.024	0.228
Injectable	−2.2	0.87	0.01	−2.12	0.94	0.02	−0.72	1.14	0.527
Entry year dummy * injectable	0.39	0.03	0.001	0.63	0.03	0.001	0.63	0.03	0.001
ln indications	−0.1	0.42	0.813	−0.1	0.39	0.78	−0.08	0.37	0.83
Cancer therapeutic class	−0.12	0.96	0.89	−0.1	0.87	0.9	−0.13	0.84	0.88
Other therapeutic class	1.3	1.6	0.4	1.33	1.4	0.355	1.36	1.38	0.33
Time (months starting with January 2001)	−0.004	0.001	0.001	−0.0007	0.001	0.43	−0.0007	0.001	0.43
Time squared (months starting with January 2001)	0.00008	0.00001	0.001	0.00003	0.00001	0.01	0.00003	0.00001	0.01
Part B covered				0.59	1.02	0.56	1.26	1.03	0.22
MMA1 (2004)				0.49	0.03	0.001	0.49	0.03	0.001
MMA2 (2006)				0.26	0.03	0.001	0.26	0.03	0.001
MMA1 * part B covered				−1.3	0.03	0.001	−1.3	0.03	0.004
MMA2 * part B covered				−0.14	0.03	0.001	−0.14	0.03	0.001
MMA1 bite							−2.4	1.15	0.04
_Constant	5.01	0.86	0.001	4.5	0.92	0.001	4.75	0.9	0.001
Adjusted R^2 (overall)	0.01			0.16			0.26		
Sigma_u	2.02			2.17			2.09		
Sigma_e	0.76			0.79			0.8		
Rho	0.87			0.88			0.88		
Number of groups	41			41			41		
N	3,444			3,444			3,444		

is positive and significant. While estimates on the therapeutic class indicator variables are statistically insignificant, coefficients on the continuous time variable (1 in January 2001, 2 in February 2001, etc.) and its square are small in magnitude, and negative and positive, respectively.

In model 2, the various MMA indicator variables and interactions with Part B variables are added to model 1. The omitted reference case for these variables is pre-MMA time periods for an oral drug covered by Medicare Part D. While estimates on the oral post-LOE (entry year dummy) and physician-administered post-LOE (entry year dummy * injectable inter-action) variables in model 2 are robust in sign to their model 1 counter-parts, in model 2 the magnitude of the use change is about twice that reported in model 1. In model 2 the estimates on MMA1 and MMA2 are both positive and significant, implying utilization of oral molforms experiencing LOE increased after these policy changes. However, we find estimates on the MMA–Part B interaction variables (interpreted as differ-ences from the omitted pre-MMA–Part D variables) are both negative and significant, suggesting that the volume increases are concentrated among drugs covered under Part D, not Part B, and that post-MMA1 it is the Part B injectables whose volume decreases. Note that the absolute values of the estimated parameter on the post-MMA1 * Part B interaction value is larger than that of the post-MMA1 main effect variable, although this is not the case for the MMA2 interaction and main effect variable parameter estimates. Hence, it appears the reimbursement reduction for physician-administered Part B variables that took effect in MMA1 (between 2004:Q4 and 2005:Q1) is associated with a substantial decline in volume utilization.

Finally, in model 3, we added an additional variable "MMA1bite" to quantify the magnitude of (the absolute value of the) negative reimburse-ment shocks for some Part B–covered drugs but not others in 2004. Interest-ingly, except for the injectable and Part B main effects variables, estimated coefficients and their statistical significance for variables included in model 3 are remarkably robust to their values in model 2. Molecules that experi-enced very large drops in reimbursement between 2004 and 2005 are found to have very large and statistically significant volume declines, holding all else constant.

9.5.4   Predicting Shortage Reports as a Function of Manufacturer Counts, Preshortage Usage Trends

Although none of our forty-one molforms experiencing LOE during 2001–2007 was ever reported in short supply during that time period, by 2008 or thereafter 18/41 (44 percent) were reported in short supply, with 67 percent of these (12/18) having experienced initial LOE prior to 2005.

This raises the intriguing issue of whether preshortage manufacturer counts and revenues, as well as time-invariant molform characteristics, can be used to predict subsequent shortage occurrences. We therefore estimated a cross-sectional logit model where the dependent variable takes on the value of one if the molform was eventually ever reported in short supply by the University of Utah, and zero if not. Since none of the molforms experiencing initial LOE 2001–2007 was in short supply during that time period, but instead experienced a shortage subsequently, we have latitude in choosing what is meant by the preshortage time period. A simple way to proceed to predict eventual shortage reports involves estimating a logit model with the forty-one molecules as observations, each observed for the three months of the last quarter in our data (2007:Q4), where the explanatory variables are similar to those specified in the count models (table 9.5) and use models (table 9.9). Results of the several such logit estimations are reported in table 9.10.

A number of the results are quite striking. In model 1, the omitted reference case is an oral molecule in the cancer supportive care therapeutic class. The large, positive, and significant parameter estimate on the injectable indicator variable implies that the probability of a shortage eventually occurring is $\exp(2.4) = 11.02$ times greater for an injectable than an oral drug, and for a drug in a therapeutic class other than cancer or other therapeutic class it is only $\exp(-1.6) = 0.20$ as likely to eventually be in short supply relative to a molecule in cancer supportive care. The greater the number of ln indications (FDA approved plus Medicare reimbursed), other things equal, the more likely an eventual shortage.

In model 2 we add ln mancount in 2007:Q4 and its square as regressors. With a positive estimate on the linear term and negative estimate on its squared value, ln mancount has an inverted U-shaped impact on the shortage probability.

In model 3, ln revenue in 2007:Q4 and its square are added as regressors to the model 2 specification. The positive estimates on the linear ln revenue variable and the negative estimates on its square imply that total brand plus generic ln revenues for a given molform has a diminishingly positive impact on shortage probability.

In both models 4 and 5, a Part B indicator variable and the MMA1bite variable measuring the absolute value of the Medicare reimbursement decline to providers are added. The estimated coefficient on the injectable indicator variable remains positive, but is approximately half its magnitude in models 1–3; the model 5 estimate of 1.2 implies the probability of an injectable drug eventually experiencing a shortage is $\exp(1.2) = 3.29$ times greater than that of an oral specialty cancer drug, other things equal. An intriguing finding here is the positive, large, and statistically significant estimate on the MMA1bite variable, implying that the larger the Medicare reimbursement decline faced by providers when the MMA1 reforms were implemented between 2004:Q4 and 2005:Q1, the greater the probability that eventually in 2008 and beyond the drug would experience a shortage.

Table 9.10 Factors predicting shortages among specialty cancer drugs post-2007

	Model 1, shortage report			Model 2, shortage report			Model 3, shortage report			Model 4, shortage report			Model 5, shortage report		
	Coeff.	Std. error	$p > \lvert t \rvert$	Coeff.	Std. error	$p > \lvert t \rvert$	Coeff.	Std. error	$p > \lvert t \rvert$	Coeff.	Std. error	$p > \lvert t \rvert$	Coeff.	Std. error	$p > \lvert t \rvert$
Injectable	2.4	0.16	0.001	2.6	0.17	0.001	2.8	0.19	0.001	1.2	0.21	0.001	1.2	0.24	0.001
ln indications	0.59	0.08	0.001	0.47	0.08	0.001	0.34	0.09	0.006	0.6	0.08	0.05	0.33	0.09	0.001
Cancer therapeutic class	-0.18	0.18	0.31	-0.29	0.2	0.137	-1.4	0.26	0.001	-0.33	0.19	0.078	-0.82	0.26	0.002
Other therapeutic class	-1.6	0.22	0.001	-2.05	0.24	0.001	-2.1	0.25	0.001	-1.6	0.21	0.001	-2.1	0.25	0.001
ln mancount in Q4 2007			2.3	0.48	0.003	3.5	0.58	0.001	0.001				2.3	0.63	0.001
ln mancount squared in Q4 2007			-0.82	0.17	0.001	-1.3	0.22	0.001	0.001				-0.64	0.24	0.001
ln revenue (2012 USD) in Q4 2007							5	1.1	0.001				5.1	1.2	0.001
ln revenue squared (2012 USD) in Q4 2007							-0.34	0.06	0.001				-0.34	0.04	0.001
Part B										-1.8	0.29	0.001	-1.9	0.32	0.001
MMAbite										3.2	0.29	0.001	3.6	0.33	0.001
_Constant	-2.3	0.18	0.001	-3.3	0.31	0.001	-19.9	4.7	0.001	-2.54	0.34	0.001	-21.2	5.05	0.01
Pseudo R^2	0.25			0.26			0.33			0.36			0.4		
N	41			41			41			41			41		

9.5.5   Sensitivity Analyses

To assess the robustness of our principal findings to alternative specifications and metrics, we undertook a number of investigations. For example, we examined use of revenue variables measured as the mean over varying molforms in the twenty-four and six months preceding ANDA entry (rather than twelve months), time-varying indication counts for each molform, orphan/priority review designation as a distinct measure of clinical quality, and the presence or absence of available therapeutic substitutes as determined by the FDA. We also pursued the construction and use of several market-specific measures of firm level costs, including parent and subsidiary relationships among firms based on table 9.4, and FDA regulatory cost compliance measures. We also estimated count models for entry in the first year, and two years following patent expiration. Our main findings are robust to each of these alternative definitions and/or specifications. They are available upon request from the lead author.

Finally, we recognize our measure of generic entry may violate our assumption of "simultaneous information" for a number of reasons. This includes the fact that the timing of generic entry may be endogenous to the number of firms entering into the market due to Paragraph IV filings and notifications (Panattoni 2011). We plan to examine this issue in future research.

9.6   Discussion and Policy Implications

This research has reported a number of findings regarding entry and pricing following LOE for specialty drugs that differ from patterns reported for nonspecialty oral solid tablets and capsules. First, as expected from our institutional review highlighting large fixed costs and economies of scale and scope for injectable/infusible drug manufacturing, we find pre-LOE production of cancer drugs to concentrate in several manufacturers, including Abbott, AstraZeneca, Bayer HealthCare, Bristol-Myers Oncology, Genzyme, GSK, Novartis, Pfizer, Roche, and Watson. Among generic manufacturers, APP, Bedford Laboratories, Teva Parenteral Me, and Teva Pharmaceuticals dominate the production of drugs undergoing initial LOE in our sample. We also observe the number of entrants into specialty drug LOEs to range between 1.66 and 4.99 manufacturers over all years, and what appears to be an upward trend in entry count in 2006 and 2007 compared to previous years. The limited number of manufacturers we observe entering the production of specialty drugs post-LOE is considerably smaller in magnitude than that reported in previous studies of entry into nonspecialty drugs. Nevertheless, these findings are consistent with that of the US Department of Health and Human Services, ASPE (2011), documenting that manufacturers of generic cancer drugs experienced a general increase in the quantity and mix of drugs they were producing in 2006 and thereafter, compared to 2000. A close inspection of entry trends into selected molforms also reveals several intriguing patterns. For example, among several specialty molecules, we observe exit by the branded manufacturer after LOE, as well as delayed and sequential ANDA entry into a given molecule undergoing LOE.

We also find evidence to suggest both entry and exit to be occurring among generic cancer drugs. For example, the average number of manufacturers of always generic cancer drugs available throughout the study period declines from 3.04 in 2001 to 2.3 in 2007. This winnowing of overall manufacturer counts per generic drug is consistent with other reports suggesting that merger and acquisition activities and outsourcing and/or discontinuations of previously offered generic drugs were common business practices during this period (US Department of Health and Human Services, ASPE 2011; FDA 2011). These results suggest generic manufacturers of cancer drugs may have been exiting from producing very old generic drugs and instead entering into segments experiencing initial LOE that offered potentially more profitable opportunities.

Economic theory suggests that the number of average entrants per new LOE is likely related to molecule-specific rationales and wider industry trends. We find evidence to support this theory; in each model presented the importance of molecule formulation and pre-LOE revenues appear to affect manufacturer entry counts. These former results are similar to those reported by Scott Morton (1999, 2000) and Iizuka (2009) and are likely related to the insurer coverage and reimbursement incentives operative in this specific drug market. The latter results are similar to those reported by Scott Morton (1999, 2000), Wiggins and Maness (2004), and Reiffen and Ward (2005) who also show that among their drug samples, pre-LOE sales measures explain a significant proportion of variation in the number of sellers in the post-LOE study period. Yet, we are well aware that when performing this test another potential endogeneity issue arises when aggregating across drugs reflecting unobserved differences between drugs that might affect both the prices and the number of entrants (Reiffen and Ward 2005). Finally, we do not find evidence to suggest the presence of tighter administered pricing policies for drugs clearly targeted by 2003 Medicare Modernization Act reforms (MMA1 in 2004) negatively affected the number of manufacturers entering into generic drug markets as they became available. In fact, among new opportunities we document robust and increasing entry after MMA1 implementation. This finding is tempered when we expressly examine the impact of negative price declines due to MMA reforms implemented in 2004 on entry patterns.

We also find that physician-administered drugs have higher inflation-adjusted supplier prices compared to orally formulated drugs both before and after LOE. Furthermore, as expected, across all drug formulations we find inflation-adjusted supplier prices are negatively and statistically significantly related to the number of manufacturers producing them following LOE. Although the magnitudes of these price-number manufacturer effects are considerably larger here for physician-administered drugs, the qualitative effects reported here also mimic those found for oral generic and branded drugs following LOE (e.g., Aitken et al. 2013). Additional average price reductions continue to increase among drugs offered by five or more manufacturers (and the sign of the estimated parameter on the number of manufacturers squared is negative), particularly among physician-administered drug formulations and contrary to the literature examining nonspecialty drugs. This result is intriguing, since Gaynor and Vogt (2003), Mankiw and Whinston (2002), Berry and Reiss (2007), among others, suggest that anticipated profits in a variety of industries drops to zero after the entry of four or more firms. We also find evidence to suggest branded prices rise and generic prices fall in response to LOE and generic entry. This result is consistent with Frank and Salkever (1997), Ellison et al. (1997), Griliches and Cockburn (1994), and Aitken et al. (2013). We believe we are the first to report this finding in a specialty drug sample.

Our efforts provide contemporary estimates of volume utilization following the generic entry of specialty drugs. In all models, volume appears to increase substantially following generic entry, consistent with the usual assumptions regarding the negative relationship between prices and quantity demanded and empirical work among nonspecialty drugs undergoing LOE. However, these usage trends are much less robust among physician-administered formulations. Rather, the results of use models suggest MMA reimbursement reforms may have shifted utilization away from injectable Part B–reimbursed generic drugs after LOE, all else equal. This finding is also consistent with that reported by Jacobson et al. (2006, 2010), Jacobson, Earle, and Newhouse (2012), and Conti et al. (2012).

Regarding the welfare implications of these use results in this market, we fully acknowledge that they are complicated given the general aging of the population and increasing detection of cancer in combination with technological change supporting increased demand for combination products, all else equal (Scherer 1993; Cutler, Huckman, and Kolstad 2010). It is also unclear how to interpret these findings given the extent of simultaneous misuse, underuse, and overuse among cancer drugs (Conti et al. 2012) and the complicated agency relationship that rewards physicians and hospitals for the use of branded, highly reimbursed cancer drugs in treating cancer in the outpatient setting (Jacobson et al. 2006, 2010, 2013; Jacobson, Earle, and Newhouse 2012; Conti et al. 2012). As we discussed in the background section, this relationship among even oral specialty drugs is deepened by the lack of institutional incentives such as the tiered formularies adopted by payers to increase consumer price sensitivity regarding the use of generic drugs (Grabowski and Vernon 1992, 1996; Aitken, Berndt, and Cutler 2009).

Lastly, finding mixed effects on utilization pattern, Caves, Whinston, and Hurwitz (1991), Berndt, Kyle, and Ling (2003), and Knittel and Huckfeldt (2012) suggest simultaneous declines in advertising and product reformulation introductions may act to mitigate the relationship between presumptive price declines and utilization increases associated with drugs following LOE. Yet, one advantage of our sample choice is that these changes have limited applicability to interpreting potential volume shifts among specialty drugs, since neither advertising nor new product formulations have been widely documented among physician-administered specialty drugs (Kornfield et al. 2013). Whether this trend is consistent across oral and injected/infused drugs among many other specialty therapeutic classes is an important direction for future research.

Nevertheless, we believe we can derive "second-best" welfare consequences from our price and utilization results. Recall there is a substantial literature examining the welfare effects of a monopolist implementing third-degree price discrimination relative to requiring a uniform monopoly price. We argue here that this literature may be important in understanding plausible welfare implications of our findings. Notably, among others, Varian (1989, 619–23) has shown that in the context of two groups of consumers and under quite general conditions, a necessary condition for welfare to increase under price discrimination relative to uniform pricing is that total volume increases under price discrimination. In the current context, readers can consider uniform pricing as that occurring when the product has patent protection, that is, the brand price prior to LOE. Following LOE, however, there are two groups of customers—the cost-conscious consumers who are attracted by low generic prices and the consumers who are more brand loyal; these two groups of customers pay different prices for the same bioequivalent product (Frank and Salkever 1997). Our pricing results suggest that supplier prices of generic drugs decline quite substantially after generic entry, while supplier prices of branded drugs rise after LOE; this finding is consistent with Frank and Salkever's work. Taken together, we suggest that our finding that post-LOE aggregate volumes of the molecule (brand plus generics) are greater than pre-LOE brand volumes supports a necessary condition for economic welfare gains among consumers of at least orally formulated specialty drugs to be satisfied, holding the above concerns in mind.

We conclude with several policy implications of our study. First, we note the number of manufacturers marketing specialty injectable/infusible drugs post-LOE in 2001–2007 is considerably smaller than has been observed for oral tablet and capsule formulations in previous studies. We have argued that one likely reason for this more limited entry post-LOE is that manufacturing specialty injectable/infusible formulations likely involves greater fixed and variable costs than for oral solid capsules and tablets. In this context, it is worth noting that provisions of the 2012 Generic Drug User Fee Amendments

(GDUFA) not only assess one-time user fees for sponsors of ANDAs, but also entail annual payments by manufacturers to the FDA that vary by whether the manufacturing site is domestic or foreign, and whether the manufactured product is the active pharmaceutical ingredient or the final dosage form ("fill and finish"). This increase in manufacturing fixed costs can be expected to incentivize brand and generic drug firms to outsource their manufacturing to contract manufacturing organizations (CMOs), and since the annual user fee is site rather than product specific, it creates additional economies of scope that generate incentives for CMOs to increase the number of products manufactured at their site. To the extent that in addition CMOs are able to produce the same molform from different ANDA holders, the increased fixed costs and scale economies brought about by GDUFA may result in the further outsourcing of manufacturing to CMOs, and thereby reduce the number of distinct organizations manufacturing injectable/infusible drugs post-LOE. How these increased fixed costs in the presence of both increased economies of scope and scale will affect supplier prices is unclear, but worthy of further analysis.

Many of the injectable specialty drugs in our sample of forty-one molecules experiencing initial LOE in 2001–2007 are similar to currently patent-protected injectable biologics in the United States (Grabowski, Long, and Mortimer 2011). Thus, the patterns of entry, price, and use after LOE among specialty drugs we document may provide some insight into what might occur as patents of US biologics expire and they experience initial biosimilar entry. Yet we caution our reader: each of the drugs in our sample—branded and generic versions of specialty drugs—has been designated "fully interchangeable" by the FDA. Biosimilar entrants will likely be therapeutic substitutes to the branded innovator, but not necessarily "fully interchangeable" drugs. Thus, our estimates likely provide only an upper bound to the entry and price effects likely to occur as biologics go off patent in the United States.

Second, on drug shortages, 44 percent of our sample undergoing LOE between 2002 and July 2007 (eighteen molforms) were reported in short supply in 2008 or thereafter, and 67 percent of these molforms (twelve molforms) underwent generic entry prior to 2005. Our estimates are similar to that of IMS Institute for Healthcare Informatics' report (2011) suggesting the importance of the limited number of manufacturers of generic drugs previous to shortage reports. Among current shortages, the 2011 IMS Institute for Healthcare Informatics reported that 51 percent of the products with reported drug shortages had two or fewer suppliers, and two-thirds had three or fewer suppliers. Our results elaborate upon this finding, since the timing of our estimates suggests both the stock and flow of manufacturers into this market are constrained, that is, both the total number producing at any point in time, and the number of new entrants, are small. Our results also suggest shortage reports are concentrated among physician-administered injectable or infusible specialty drugs, having larger approved indication counts and larger revenues after LOE, holding all else equal. Intriguingly, we also find some suggestive evidence to support the contention that shortage reports concentrate among drugs particularly negatively affected by MMA reimbursement declines, holding molecule characteristics and other market features constant. This result supports Yurukoglu, Liebman, and Ridley (2012), although the effect we observe is likely via reduced physician demand, not reduced supply, given the incentives operative in "buy and bill" Medicare reimbursement policies. A thorough examination of the potential role of the MMA in inducing shortages is an important avenue for future empirical work. We also note in passing that while the probability of eventually being shorted is much greater for injectable than oral cancer specialty drugs in our sample, Stromberg (2014) reports strikingly similar temporal patterns of shortages among oral drugs, suggesting that time-varying factors common to injectable and oral drugs may be the root cause of shortages. Stromberg reports a statistically significant relationship between FDA regulatory activity (inspections and citations) and drug shortage rates over time.

Third, our review of the specialty drug market raises questions about researchers,' stakeholders,' and policymakers' definition of drug "manufacturers" in that the increasingly important presence of time-varying and unobservable contract manufacturing practices complicate and may even undermine the definition of unique "manufacturers" entering this market, well beyond the usual concerns regarding ongoing merger and acquisition activities. Under current statute, NDA and ANDA sponsors are obligated to notify the FDA of plans to discontinue drug manufacturing as well as any changes in manufacturing responsibilities, including the outsourcing of drug production after initial approval. Furthermore, FDA sources say that it is common for a sponsor to need to qualify a new facility to manufacture their drug due to either the loss of the old facility or due to changing market demand, prompting the sponsor to acquire additional capacity. In these cases, NDA and ANDA sponsors often turn to contract manufacturers. However, data on the use of CMOs and their identity upon initial filings and subsequent changes is not publicly accessible through the web portal Drugs@FDA and is exempt from being released under the Freedom of Information Act (the FDA generally treats nonpublic business relationships as confidential commercial or financial information, exempting it from public disclosure). A proprietary data source, Truven's RedBook, maintains more updated information on which NDA and/or ANDA sponsors are actively offering a drug in the US market, but even this source does not identify contract-manufacturing arrangements. The identity and nature of base ingredient manufacturing (APIs) for many drugs, also collected by FDA from ANDA sponsors, are similarly shielded from public scrutiny.

We believe these increasingly important business practices have at least two implications for measuring the extent of generic competition. First, these arrangements make it challenging for regulators charged with monitoring competition in the generic and branded drug market to predict reliably what specialty drug supply of drugs will be following mergers, acquisitions, and/ or closures of NDA or ANDA sponsors and/or contract-manufacturing facilities supplying drugs to the US market. These relationships can make economic models of such activity and their potential competitive effects on supply and/or prices by agencies such as the Department of Justice or Federal Trade Commission inaccurate, particularly if overlapping supply is present before merger and acquisition activity between the two parties. Second, under these arrangements the public and their guardians are unable to quickly identify root causes of supply disruptions when supply or quality lapses occur. Indeed, one implication of our analysis is that the number of manufacturers with adequate capacity to manufacturer generic injectable drugs for the US market, including but not limited to those affected by shortages, is likely much smaller than previously documented. How best to formulate market-level solutions to supply lapses given extreme informational asymmetry regarding which manufacturers are actually producing these drugs or their base ingredients is uncharted territory.

Appendix

Table 9A.1   **Molecules/forms in sample**

Generic always N = 50	Generic entry N = 41	Entry year
Bleomycin IAG inject, mult. adm. reg.	Arsenic IAC inject, IV reg.	2006
Carmustine IAC inject, IV reg.	Busulfan OSR orals, sol., tab./cap. RE	2003
Chlorambucil OSR orals, sol., tab./cap. RE	Carboplatin IAC inject, IV reg.	2004
Cisplatin IAC inject, IV reg.	Cladribine IAG inject, mult. adm. reg.	2004
Cladribine IAC inject, IV reg.	Cladribine IAC inject, IV reg.	2004
Cytarabine IAG inject, mult. adm. reg.	Cyclophosphamide IAC inject, IV reg.	2004
Dacarbazine IAC inject, IV reg.	Cyclophosphamide OSR orals, sol., tab./cap.	2004
Daunorubicin IAC inject, IV reg.	Dexrazoxane IAK inject, infusion reg.	2005
Dolasetron IAC inject, IV reg.	Dexrazoxane IAC inject, IV reg.	2005
Doxorubicin IAC inject, IV reg.	Dimenhydrinate IAG inject, mult. adm. reg.	2004
Estramustine OSR orals, sol., tab./cap. re	Dimenhydrinate OSC orals, sol., chewable	2002
Etoposide IAC inject, IV reg.	Dimenhydrinate OSR orals, sol., tab./cap. RE	2002
Etoposide OSR orals, sol., tab./cap. RE	Dimenhydrinate scopolamine OSR orals, sol.	2002
Floxuridine IAC inject, IV reg.	Epirubicin IAC inject, IV reg.	2006
Fluorouracil DDC derm., cream	Fludarabine IAC inject, IV reg.	2003
Fluorouracil DDL derm., liquid/lotion	Idarubicin IAC inject, IV reg.	2004
Fluorouracil IAC inject, IV reg.	Ifosfamide IAC inject, IV reg.	2004
Fluorouracil TOZ other topicals	Ifosfamide mesna SAZ other systemics	2004
Flutamide OSR orals, sol., tab./cap. RE	Leuprolide IAA inject, IM reg.	2004

Table 9A.1   (continued)

Generic always N = 50	Generic entry N = 41	Entry year
Fructose glucose phosphoric acid OLL OR	Leuprolide IAE inject, subcut. reg.	2004
Fructose glucose phosphoric acid OSC OR	Leuprolide IAF inject, subcut. L. A.	2004
Goserelin IAF inject, subcut L. A.	LeuprolidE SAZ other systemics	2004
Hydroxyurea OSR orals, sol., tab./cap. RE	Leuprolide lidocaine SAZ other systemics	2004
Leucovorin IAG inject, mult. adm. reg.	Mercaptopurine OSR orals, sol., tab./cap. RE	2004
Leucovorin OSR orals, sol., tab./cap. RE	Mitoxantrone IAC inject, IV reg.	2006
Lomustine OSR orals, sol., tab./cap. RE	Ondansetron IAC inject, IV reg.	2006
Mechlorethamine IAC inject, IV reg.	Ondansetron IVR inject, IV pigback	2007
Meclizine OSC orals, sol., chewable	Ondansetron OLL orals, liq., non-spec. L	2007
Meclizine OSR orals, sol., tab./cap. RE	Ondansetron OLR orals, liq., ready-made	2007
Megestrol OLR orals, liq., ready-made	Ondansetron OSO orals, sol., tab./cap. OT	2007
Megestrol OSR orals, sol., tab./cap. RE	Ondansetron OSR orals, sol., tab./cap. RE	2007
Mesna IAC inject, IV reg.	Pentostatin IAC inject, IV reg.	2007
Mesna OSR orals, sol., tab./cap. RE	Scopolamine JWT insert/implant, transd.	2003
Methotrexate IAG inject, mult. adm. reg.	Scopolamine OSR orals, sol., tab./cap. RE	2003
Methotrexate OSR orals, sol., tab./cap. RE	Tamoxifen OSR orals, sol., tab./cap. RE	2002
Methoxsalen IAX inject, other reg.	Tamoxifen OLL orals, liq., non-spec. L	2002
Methoxsalen YAZ all others	Tretinoin OSR orals, sol., tab./cap. RE	2007
Mitomycin IAC inject, IV reg.	Trimethobenzamide IAA inject, IM reg.	2002
Mitotane OSR orals, sol., tab./cap. RE	Trimethobenzamide OSR orals, sol., tab./cap.	2002
Paclitaxel IAC inject, IV reg.	Trimethobenzamide RRS rectals syst., supp.	2002
Pegaspargase IAG inject, mult. adm. reg.	Vinorelbine IAC inject, IV reg.	2003
Procarbazine OSR orals, sol., tab./cap. RE		
Prochlorperazine IAG inject, mult. adm. RE		
Prochlorperazine OSR orals, sol., tab./cap.		
Prochlorperazine RRS rectals syst., supp.		
Streptozocin IAC inject, IV reg.		
Testolactone OSR orals, sol., tab./cap. RE		
Thiotepa IAC inject, IV reg.		
Vinblastine IAC inject, IV reg.		
Vincristine IAC inject, IV reg.		

Table 9A.2   Number of packages associated with each molform; bold indicates experiences generic entry in study period

	Molform label	Molform * packages count			
Molform	All molform	Average 1.3503012	SD 0.60843	Min. 1	Max. 10
1	Alemtuzumab IAC inject, IV reg.	1	0		
2	Alitretinoin DDG derm., gel	1	0		
3	Altretamine OSR orals, sol., tab./cap. RE	1	0		
4	Amifostine IAC inject, IV reg.	1	0		
5	Anastrozole OSR orals, sol., tab./cap. RE	1	0		
6	Aprepitant OSR orals, sol., tab./cap. RE	1	0		

(*continued*)

Table 9A.2 (continued)

Molform	All molform	Average 1.3503012	SD 0.60843	Min. 1	Max. 10
		Molform * packages count			
7	**Arsenic IAC inject, IV reg.**	1	0		
8	Asparaginase IAG inject, mult. adm. reg.	1	0		
9	Azacitidine IAE inject, subcut. reg.	1	0		
10	Bevacizumab IAC inject, IV reg.	1	0		
11	Bexarotene DDG derm., gel	1	0		
12	Bexarotene OSR orals, sol., tab./cap. RE	1	0		
13	bicalutamide OSR orals, sol., tab./cap. RE	1	0		
14	Bleomycin IAG inject, mult. adm. reg.	4.7	2	1	7
15	Bortezomib IAC inject, IV reg.	1	0		
16	Busulfan IAC inject, IV reg.	1	0		
17	**Busulfan OSR orals, sol., tab./cap. RE**	**1**	**0**		
18	Capecitabine OSR orals, sol., tab./cap. RE	1.125	0.33	1	2
19	**Carboplatin IAC inject, IV reg.**	**4.3**	**2.81**	**1**	**10**
20	Carmustine IAC inject, IV reg.	1	0		
21	Carmustine JJS insert/implant, sub. DE	1	0		
22	Cetuximab IAC inject, IV reg.	1	0		
23	Chlorambucil OSR orals, sol., tab./cap. RE	1	0		
24	Cisplatin IAC inject, IV reg.	1.8	0.8	1	3
25	**Cladribine IAC inject, IV reg.**	**1.5**	**0.5**	**1**	**2**
26	**Cladribine IAG inject, mult. adm. reg.**	**1**	**0**		
27	Clofarabine IAC inject, IV reg.	1	0		
28	Cyclizine OSR orals, sol., tab./cap. RE	1	0		
29	**Cyclophosphamide IAC inject, IV reg.**	**1.7**	**0.8**	**1**	**3**
30	**Cyclophosphamide OSR orals, sol., tab./cap.**	**1.7**	**0.7**	**1**	**3**
31	Cytarabine IAG inject, mult. adm. reg.	1.5	0.5	1	2
32	Cytarabine IAZ inject, other L. A.	1	0		
33	Dacarbazine IAC inject, IV reg.	2.2	1	1	4
34	Dactinomycin IAC inject, IV reg.	1	0		
35	Dasatinib OSR orals, sol., tab./cap. RE	1	0		
36	Daunorubicin IAC inject, IV reg.	1.6	0.6	1	3
37	Decitabine IAC inject, IV reg.	1	0		
38	Denileukin diftitox IAK inject, infusion	1	0		
39	**Dexrazoxane IAC inject, IV reg.**	**1**	**0**		
40	**Dexrazoxane IAK inject, infusion reg.**	**1**	**0**		
41	**Dimenhydrinate IAG inject, mult. adm. reg.**	**1**	**0**		
42	**Dimenhydrinate OSC orals, sol., chewable**	**1**	**0**		
43	**Dimenhydrinate OSR orals, sol., tab./cap. RE**	**3.7**	**2**	**1**	**8**
44	**Dimenhydrinate scopolamine OSR orals, SO**	**1**	**0**		
45	Docetaxel IAC inject, IV reg.	1	0		
46	Dolasetron IAC inject, IV reg.	1	0		
47	Dolasetron OSR orals, sol., tab./cap. RE	1	0		
48	Doxorubicin IAC inject, IV reg.	2.4	1	1	4
49	Dronabinol OSR orals, sol., tab./cap. RE	1	0		
50	Electrolyte replacers OLL orals, liq., non	1	0		
51	**Epirubicin IAC inject, IV reg.**	**1.75**	**2**	**1**	**7**

Table 9A.2   (continued)

	Molform label	Molform * packages count			
		Average	SD	Min.	Max.
Molform	All molform	1.3503012	0.60843	1	10
52	Erlotinib OSR orals, sol., tab./cap. RE	1	0		
53	Estramustine OSR orals, sol., tab./cap. RE	1	0		
54	Etoposide IAC inject, IV reg.	2.2	1	1	4
55	Etoposide OSR orals, sol., tab./cap. RE	1.2	0.33	1	2
56	Exemestane OSR orals, sol., tab./cap. RE	1	0		
57	Floxuridine IAC inject, IV reg.	3	0	3	3
58	**Fludarabine IAC inject, IV reg.**	**1.9**	**1**	**1**	**5**
59	Fluorouracil DDC derm., cream	1.2	0.42	1	2
60	Fluorouracil DDL derm., liquid/lotion	1.4	0.5	1	2
61	Fluorouracil IAC inject, IV reg.	1.5	0.5	1	2
62	Fluorouracil TOZ other topicals	1	0		
63	Flutamide OSR orals, sol., tab./cap. RE	2	1	1	4
64	Fosaprepitant OSR orals, sol., tab./cap. RE	1	0		
65	Fructose glucose phosphoric acid OLL OR	1	0		
66	Fructose glucose phosphoric acid OSC OR	1	0		
67	Fulvestrant IAA inject, IM reg.	1	0		
68	Gallium IAK inject, infusion reg.	1	0		
69	Gefitinib OSR orals, sol., tab./cap. RE	1	0		
70	Gemcitabine IAC inject, IV reg.	1	0		
71	Gemtuzumab ozogamicin IAC inject, IV reg.	1	0		
72	Ginger OSZ orals, sol., other	1	0		
73	Goserelin IAF inject, subcut. L.A.	1	0		
74	Granisetron IAC inject, IV reg.	1	0		
75	Granisetron OLL orals, liq., non-spec. L	1	0		
76	Granisetron OSR orals, sol., tab./cap. RE	1	0		
77	Histrelin SAZ other systemics	1	0		
78	Hydroxyurea OSR orals, sol., tab./cap. RE	4.4	2.6	1	7
79	Ibritumomab tiuxetan SAZ other systemics	1	0		
80	**Idarubicin IAC inject, IV reg.**	**1.5**	**0.5**	**1**	**2**
81	**Ifosfamide IAC inject, IV reg.**	**2.3**	**1**	**1**	**4**
82	**Ifosfamide mesna SAZ other systemics**	**1.5**	**0.5**	**1**	**2**
83	Imatinib OSR orals, sol., tab./cap. RE	1	0		
84	Irinotecan IAC inject, IV reg.	1	0		
85	Ixabepilone SAZ other systemics	1	0		
86	Lapatinib OSR orals, sol., tab./cap. RE	1	0		
87	Lenalidomide OSR orals, sol., tab./cap. RE	1	0		
88	Letrozole OSR orals, sol., tab./cap. RE	1	0		
89	Leucovorin IAG inject, mult. adm. reg.	2.34	1	1	4
90	Leucovorin OSR orals, sol., tab./cap. RE	1.9	0.8	1	3
91	**Leuprolide IAA inject, IM reg.**	**1.4**	**0.48**	**1**	**2**
92	**Leuprolide IAE inject, subcut. reg.**	**1**	**0**		
93	**Leuprolide IAF inject, subcut. L. A.**	**1**	**0**		
94	**Leuprolide SAZ other systemics**	**2**	**0.8**	**1**	**3**
95	**Leuprolide lidocaine SAZ other systemics**	**1**	**0**		
96	Lomustine OSR orals, sol., tab./cap. RE	1	0		

(*continued*)

	Molform label	Molform * packages count			
Molform	All molform	Average 1.3503012	SD 0.60843	Min. 1	Max. 10
97	Mechlorethamine IAC inject, IV reg.	1	0		
98	meclizine OSC orals, sol., chewable	2	1	1	3
99	meclizine OSR orals, sol., tab./cap. RE	4	2	1	10
100	medroxyprogesterone IAB inject, IM L. A.	1	0		
101	Megestrol OLR orals, liq., ready-made	2.3	1.5	1	5
102	Megestrol OSR orals, sol., tab./cap. RE	3.5	2.5	1	11
103	Melphalan IAC inject, IV reg.	1	0		
104	Melphalan OSR orals, sol., tab./cap. RE	1	0		
105	**Mercaptopurine OSR orals, sol., tab./cap. RE**	**2**	**1**	**1**	**3**
106	Mesna IAC inject, IV reg.	3.5	1.8	1	6
107	Mesna OSR orals, sol., tab./cap. RE	1	0		
108	Methotrexate IAG inject, mult. adm. reg.	1.8	0.8	1	3
109	Methotrexate OSR orals, sol., tab./cap. RE	3.3	2.7	1	9
110	Methoxsalen IAX inject, other reg.	1	0		
111	Methoxsalen YAZ all others	1	0		
112	Mitomycin IAC inject, IV reg.	2.4	1	1	4
113	Mitotane OSR orals, sol., tab./cap. RE	1	0		
114	**Mitoxantrone IAC inject, IV reg.**	**2**	**2**	**1**	**6**
115	Nabilone OSR orals, sol., tab./cap. RE	1	0		
116	Nelarabine IAC inject, IV reg.	1	0		
117	Nilotinib OSR orals, sol., tab./cap. RE	1	0		
118	Nilutamide OSR orals, sol., tab./cap. RE	1	0		
119	**Ondansetron IAC inject, IV reg.**	**2.7**	**2.6**	**1**	**10**
120	**Ondansetron IVR inject, IV pigback**	**1.6**	**1**	**1**	**4**
121	**Ondansetron OLL orals, liq., non-spec. L**	**1.5**	**0.5**	**1**	**2**
122	**Ondansetron OLR orals, liq., ready-made**	**1**	**0**		
123	**Ondansetron OSO orals, sol., tab./cap. OT**	**2.3**	**1.8**	**1**	**6**
124	**Ondansetron OSR orals, sol., tab./cap. RE**	**2.25**	**2.5**	**1**	**10**
125	Oxaliplatin IAC inject, IV reg.	1	0		
126	Paclitaxel IAC inject, IV reg.	4.5	2.6	1	9
127	Palifermin IAC inject, IV reg.	1	0		
128	Palonosetron IAC inject, IV reg.	1	0		
129	Panitumumab IAK inject, infusion reg.	1	0		
130	Pegaspargase IAG inject, mult. adm. reg.	1	0		
131	Pegylated liposomal doxorubicin IAC INJ	1	0		
132	pemetrexed IAC inject, IV reg.	1	0		
133	**Pentostatin IAC inject, IV reg.**	**1**	**0.4**	**1**	**2**
134	Porfimer IAC inject, IV reg.	1	0		
135	Procarbazine OSR orals, sol., tab./cap. RE	1	0		
136	Prochlorperazine IAG inject, mult. adm. RE	1.6	0.74	1	3
137	Prochlorperazine OSR orals, sol., tab./cap.	2.8	1.5	1	6
138	Prochlorperazine RRS rectals syst., supp.	2.9	2	1	6
139	Promethazine RRS rectals syst., supp.	1	0		
140	Rituximab IAK inject, infusion reg.	1	0		
141	**Scopolamine JWT insert/implant, transd.**	**1.4**	**0.5**	**1**	**2**

Molform	All molform	Average 1.3503012	SD 0.60843	Min. 1	Max. 10
	Molform label	**Molform * packages count**			
142	**Scopolamine OSR orals, sol., tab./cap. RE**	**1**	**0**		
143	Sorafenib OSR orals, sol., tab./cap. RE	1	0		
144	Streptozocin IAC inject, IV reg.	1	0		
145	Sunitinib OSR orals, sol., tab./cap. RE	1	0		
146	**Tamoxifen OLL orals, liq., non-spec L**	**1**	**0**		
147	**Tamoxifen OSR orals, sol., tab./cap. RE**	**2.8**	**1.7**	**1**	**6**
148	Temozolomide OSR orals, sol., tab./cap. RE	1	0		
149	Temsirolimus SAZ other systemics	1	0		
150	Teniposide IAC inject, IV reg.	1	0		
151	Testolactone OSR orals, sol., tab./cap. RE	1	0		
152	Thiotepa IAC inject, IV reg.	1.3	0.5	1	2
153	Topotecan IAC inject, IV reg.	1	0		
154	Toremifene OSR orals, sol., tab./cap. RE	1	0		
155	Tositumomab SAZ other systemics	1.5	0.5	1	2
156	Trastuzumab IAC inject, IV reg.	1	0		
157	**Tretinoin OSR orals, sol., tab./cap. RE**	**1.1**	**0.4**	**1**	**2**
158	**Trimethobenzamide IAA inject, IM reg.**	**1**	**0**		
159	**Trimethobenzamide OSR orals, sol., tab./cap.**	**1.4**	**0.5**	**1**	**2**
160	**Trimethobenzamide RRS rectals syst., supp.**	**1.3**	**0.5**	**1**	**2**
161	Triptorelin IAB inject, IM L. A.	1	0		
162	Valrubicin IAX inject, other reg.	1	0		
163	Vinblastine IAC inject, IV reg.	1	0		
164	Vincristine IAC inject, IV reg.	1	0		
165	**Vinorelbine IAC inject, IV reg.**	**3.8**	**2.3**	**1**	**8**
166	Vorinostat OSR orals, sol., tab./cap. RE	1	0		

Table 9A.3   **Molecule by number of forms and clinical indications (on- and off-label)**

Molform	Molform no.	On label	Off label	Total indications
Arsenic IAC inject, IV reg.	7	1	1	2
Busulfan OSR orals, sol., tab./cap. RE	16	3	2	5
Carboplatin IAC inject, IV reg.	19	2	17	19
Cladribine IAC inject, mult. adm. reg.	25	1	8	9
Cladribine IAC inject, IV reg.	26	1	8	9
Cyclophosphamide IAC inject, IV reg.	29	18	16	34
Cyclophosphamide OSR orals, sol., tab./cap.	30	18	16	34
Dexrazoxane OAL omkct. omfisopm. reg.	39	2	1	3
Dexrazoxane IAC inject, IV reg.	40	2	1	3
Dimenhydrinate IAG inject, mult. adm. reg.	41	1	1	2
Dimenhydrinate OSC orals, sol., chewable	42	1	1	2

(continued)

Table 9A.3 (continued)

Molform	Molform no.	On label	Off label	Total indications
Dimenhydrinate OSR orals, sol., tab./cap. RE	43	1	1	2
Dimenhydrinate scopolamine OSR orals, SO	44	1	1	2
Epirubicin IAC inject, IV reg.	51	1	11	12
Fludarabine IAC inject, IV reg.	58	1	8	9
Idarubicin IAC inject, IV reg.	80	1	6	7
Ifosfamide IAC inject, IV reg.	81	1	24	25
Ifosfamide mesna SAZ other systemics	82	1	24	25
Leuprolide IAA inject, IM reg.	91	4	7	11
Leuprolide IAE inject, subcut. reg.	92	4	7	11
Leuprolide IAF inject, subcut. L. A.	93	4	7	11
Leuprolide SAZ other systemics	94	4	7	11
Mercaptopurine OSR orals, sol., tab./cap. RE	105	1	5	6
Mitoxantrone IAC inject, IV reg.	114	1	0	1
Ondansetron IAC inject, IV reg.	119	4	1	5
Ondansetron IVR inject, IV pigback	120	4	1	5
Ondansetron OLL orals, liq., no-spec. L	121	4	1	5
Ondansetron OLR orals, liq., ready-made	122	4	1	5
Ondansetron OSO orals, sol., tab./cap. OT	123	4	1	5
Ondansetron OSR orals, sol., tab./cap. RE	124	4	1	5
Pentostatin IAC inject, IV reg.	133	1	3	4
Scopolamine JWT insert/implant, transd.	141	2	1	3
Scopolamine OSR orals, sol., tab./cap. RE	142	2	1	3
Tamoxifen OSR orals, sol., tab./cap. RE	146	5	13	18
Tamoxifen OLL orals, liq. non-spec. L	147	5	13	18
Tretinoin OSR orals, sol., tab./cap. RE	157	5	8	13
Trimethobenzamide IAA inject, IM reg.	158	1	0	1
Trimethobenzamide OSR orals, sol., tab./cap.	159	1	0	1
Trimethobenzamide RRS rectals, syst., supp.	160	1	0	1
Vinorelbine IAC inject, IV reg.	165	1	11	12

Table 9A.4 **Molforms with shortages reported in years after study period**

Molform number	Molform
106	Mesna IAC inject, IV reg.
16	Busulfan IAC inject, IV reg.
111	Methoxsalen YAZ all others
152	Thiotepa IAC inject, IV reg.
24	Cisplatin IAC inject, IV reg.
54	Etoposide IAC inject, IV reg.
103	Melphalan IAC inject, IV reg.
112	Mitomycin IAC inject, IV reg.
4	Amifostine IAC inject, IV reg.
20	Carmustine IAC inject, IV reg.
80	Idarubicin IAC inject, IV reg.
84	Irinotecan IAC inject, IV reg.

Table 9A.4   (continued)

Molform number	Molform
91	Leuprolide IAA inject, IM reg.
126	Paclitaxel IAC inject, IV reg.
19	Carboplatin IAC inject, IV reg.
33	Dacarbazine IAC inject, IV reg.
39	Dexrazoxane IAC inject, IV reg.
48	Doxorubicin IAC inject, IV reg.
57	Floxuridine IAC inject, IV reg.
58	Fludarabine IAC inject, IV reg.
74	Granisetron IAC inject, IV reg.
119	Ondansetron IAC inject, IV reg.
133	Pentostatin IAC inject, IV reg.
163	Vinblastine IAC inject, IV reg.
164	Vincristine IAC inject, IV reg.
36	Daunorubicin IAC inject, IV reg.
61	Fluorouracil IAC inject, IV reg.
94	Leuprolide SAZ other systemics
144	Streptozocin IAC inject, IV reg.
32	Cytarabine IAZ inject, other L. A.
92	Leuprolide IAE inject, subcut. reg.
93	Leuprolide IAF inject, subcut. L. A.
110	Methoxsalen IAX inject, other reg.
14	Bleomycin IAG inject, mult. adm. reg.
97	Mechlorethamine IAC inject, IV reg.
120	Ondansetron IVR inject, IV pigback
29	Cyclophosphamide IAC inject, IV reg.
31	Cytarabine IAG inject, mult. adm. reg.
55	Etoposide OSR orals, sol., tab./cap. RE
89	Leucovorin IAG inject, mult. adm. reg.
96	Lomustine OSR orals, sol., tab./cap. RE
104	Melphalan OSR orals, sol., tab./cap. RE
157	Tretinoin OSR orals, sol., tab./cap. RE
40	Dexrazoxane IAK inject, infusion reg.
108	Methotrexate IAG inject, mult. adm. reg.
141	Scopolamine JWT insert/implant, transd.
142	Scopolamine OSR orals, sol., tab./cap. RE
18	Capecitabine OSR orals, sol., tab./cap. RE
109	Methotrexate OSR orals, sol., tab./cap. RE
30	Cyclophosphamide OSR orals, sol., tab./cap.
38	Denileukin diftitox IAK inject, infusion
105	Mercaptopurine OSR orals, sol., tab./cap. RE
131	Pegylated liposomal doxorubicin IAC INJ
136	Prochlorperazine IAG inject, mult. adm. RE

References

Aitken, M. L., E. R. Berndt, B. Bosworth, I. M. Cockburn, R. G. Frank, M. Klein-rock, and B. T. Shapiro. 2013. "The Regulation of Prescription Drug Competition and Market Responses: Patterns in Prices and Sales Following Loss of Exclusivity." NBER Working Paper no. 19487, Cambridge, MA.

Aitken, M. L., E. R. Berndt, and D. M. Cutler. 2009. "Prescription Drug Spending Trends in the United States: Looking beyond the Turning Point." *Health Affairs* 28 (1): w151–60.

Akscin, J., T. R. Barr, and E. L. Towle. 2007. "Key Practice Indicators in Office-Based Oncology Practices: 2007 Report on 2006 Data." *Journal of Oncology Practice* 3 (4): 200–203.

Barr, T. R., and E. L. Towle. 2011. "Oncology Practice Trends from the National Practice Benchmark, 2005 through 2010." *Journal of Oncology Practice* 7 (5): 286–90.

———. 2012. "Oncology Practice Trends from the National Practice Benchmark." *Journal of Oncology Practice* 8 (5): 292–97.

Barr, T. R., E. L. Towle, and W. M. Jordan. 2008. "The 2007 National Practice Benchmark: Results of a National Survey of Oncology Practices." *Journal of Oncology Practice* 4 (4): 178–83.

Berndt, E. R., and M. Aitken. 2011. "Brand Loyalty, Generic Entry, and Price Competition in Pharmaceuticals in the Quarter Century after the 1984 Waxman-Hatch Legislation." *International Journal of the Economics of Business* 18 (2): 177–201.

Berndt, E. R., M. Kyle, and D. Ling. 2003. "The Long Shadow of Patent Expiration: Generic Entry and Rx-to-OTC Switches." In *Scanner Data and Price Indexes*, edited by Robert C. Feenstra and Matthew D. Shapiro. Chicago: University of Chicago Press.

Berndt, E. R., and J. P. Newhouse. 2013. "Pricing and Reimbursement in US Pharmaceutical Markets." In *The Oxford Handbook of the Economics of the Biopharmaceutical Industry*, edited by P. M. Danzon and S. Nicholson, 201–65. New York: Oxford University Press.

Berry S. 1992. "Estimation of a Model of Entry in the Airline Industry." *Econometrica* 60:889–917.

Berry, S., and P. Reiss. 2007. "Empirical Models of Entry and Market Structure." In *Handbook of Industrial Organization*, vol. 3, edited by M. Armstrong and R. H. Porter, 1845–86. Amsterdam: North Holland Elsevier.

Bresnahan, T. F., and P. Reiss. 1988. "Do Entry Conditions Vary across Markets?" *Brookings Papers on Economic Activity: Microeconomics* 1987 (3): 833–81.

———. 1991. "Entry and Competition in Concentrated Markets." *Journal of Political Economy* 99:977–1009.

Caves, R., M. D. Whinston, and M. Hurwitz. 1991. "Patent Expiration, Entry and Competition in the US Pharmaceutical Industry." Working Paper, Brookings Papers on Economic Activity: Microeconomics https://www.brookings.edu/wp -content/uploads/1991/01/1991_bpeamicro_caves.pdf.

Clemens, J., and J. D. Gottlieb. 2013. "Bargaining in the Shadow of a Giant: Medicare's Influence on Private Payment Systems." NBER Working Paper no. 19503, Cambridge, MA.

Conti, R. M. 2014. "Who Makes this Drug?" *The Cancer Letter*, January 3. http:// www.cancerletter.com/articles/20140103.

Conti, R. M., A. C. Bernstein, V. M. Villaflor, R. L. Schilsky, M. B. Rosenthal, and P. B. Bach. 2013. "Prevalence of Off-Label Use and Spending in 2010 among Patent-Protected Chemotherapies in a Population-Based Cohort of Medical Oncologists." *Journal of Clinical Oncology* 31 (9): 1134–39.

Conti, R. M., M. B. Rosenthal, B. Polite, P. B. Bach, and Y-C. T. Shih. 2012. "Infused Chemotherapy Use Following Patent Expiration among Individuals Aged 65 and Older." *American Journal of Managed Care* 18 (5): e173–78.

Cutler, D. M., R. Huckman, and J. T. Kolstad. 2010. "Input Constraints and the Efficiency of Entry: Lessons from Cardiac Surgery." *American Economic Journal: Economic Policy* 2 (1): 51–76.

Drug Channels. 2014. "EXCLUSIVE: 340B is Taking over the Hospital Market—With a 25% Share." February 25. http://www.drugchannels.net/2014/02/exclusive-340b-is-taking-over-hospital.html.

Duggan, M., and F. Scott Morton. 2010. "The Effect of the Medicare Drug Benefit on Pharmaceutical Prices and Utilization." *American Economic Review* 100 (1): 590–607.

Ellison, S. F., I. M. Cockburn, Z. Griliches, and J. A. Hausman. 1997. "Characteristics of Demand for Pharmaceutical Products: An Examination of Four Cephalosporins." *Rand Journal of Economics* 28 (3): 1–36.

EMD Serono. 2013. *EMD Serono Specialty Digest™*, 9th ed. Managed Care Strategies for Specialty Pharmaceuticals. http://specialtydigest.emdserono.com/Digest.aspx.

Frank, R. G. 2001. "Prescription Drug Prices: Why Some Pay More Than Others Do." *Health Affairs* 20 (2): 325–30.

Frank, R. G., and D. S. Salkever. 1992. "Pricing, Patent Loss and the Market for Pharmaceuticals." *Southern Economic Journal* 59:165–79.

———. 1997. "Generic Entry and the Pricing of Pharmaceuticals." *Journal of Economics and Management Strategy* 6 (1): 75–90.

Gatesman, M., and T. Smith. 2011. "The Shortage of Essential Chemotherapy Drugs in the United States." *New England Journal of Medicine* 365 (18): 1653–55.

Gaynor, M. S., and W. Vogt. 2003. "Competition among Hospitals." *Rand Journal of Economics* 34 (4): 764–85.

Goldberg, P. 2013. "Drug Shortages Reach All-Time High—Ben Venue Exit Will Make Problem Worse." *The Cancer Letter*, October 11. http://www.cancerletter.com/articles/20131011.

Grabowski, H., G. Long, and R. Mortimer. 2011. "Implementation of the Biosimilar Pathway: Economic and Policy Issues." *Seton Hall Law Review* 41 (2): 511–57.

Grabowski, H., and J. Vernon. 1992. "Brand Loyalty, Entry and Price Competition in Pharmaceuticals after the 1984 Drug Act." *Journal of Law and Economics* 35:331–50.

———. 1996. "Longer Patents for Increased Generic Competition in the US: The Waxman-Hatch Act after One Decade." *PharmacoEconomics* 10 (suppl. 2): 110–23.

Griliches, Z., and I. M. Cockburn. 1994. "Generics and New Goods in Pharmaceutical Price Indexes." *American Economic Review* 84 (5): 1213–32.

Iizuka T. 2009. "Generic Entry in a Regulated Pharmaceutical Market." *Japanese Economic Review* 60 (1): 63–81.

IMS Institute for Healthcare Informatics. 2011. "Drug Shortages: A Closer Look at Products, Suppliers, and Volume Volatility." http://www.imshealth.com/deployed files/ims/Global/Content/Insights/IMS%20Institute%20for%20Healthcare%20 Informatics/Static%20Files/IIHI_Drug_Shortage_Media_ExecSumm.pdf.

Jacobson, M., A. Alpert, and F. Duarte. 2012. "Prescription Drug Shortages: Reconsidering the Role of Medicare Payment Policies." *Health Affairs* blog, May 29. http://healthaffairs.org/blog/2012/05/29/prescription-drug-shortages-reconsidering-the-role-of-medicare-payment-policies/.

Jacobson, M., C. Earle, and J. Newhouse. 2012. "Geographic Variation in Physicians' Responses to a Reimbursement Change." *New England Journal of Medicine* 365 (22): 2049–52.

Jacobson, M., C. Earle, M. Price, and J. Newhouse. 2010. "How Medicare's Payment Cuts For Cancer Chemotherapy Drugs Changed Patterns of Treatment." *Health Affairs* 29 (7): 1391–99.

Jacobson, M., T. C. Chang, J. P. Newhouse, and C. C. Earle. 2013. "Physician Agency and Competition: Evidence from a Major Change to Medicare Chemotherapy

Reimbursement Policy." NBER Working Paper no. 19247, Cambridge, MA. http:// users.nber.org/~changt/Jacobsonetal_20130624.pdf.

Jacobson, M., A. J. O'Malley, C. C. Earle, J. Pakes, P. Gaccione, and J. P. Newhouse. 2006. "Does Reimbursement Influence Chemotherapy Treatment for Cancer Patients?" *Health Affairs* 25 (2): 437–43.

Knittel, P. J., and C. R. Huckfeldt. 2012. "Pharmaceutical Use following Generic Entry: Paying Less and Buying Less." MIT Working Paper. http://web.mit.edu/ knittel/www/papers/hk_latest.pdf.

Kornfield, R., J. Donohue, E. R. Berndt, and G. C. Alexander. 2013. "Promotion of Prescription Drugs to Consumers and Providers, 2001–2010." *PLoS One* 8 (3): e55504.

Kyle, M. K. 2006. "The Role of Firm Characteristics in Pharmaceutical Product Launches." *RAND Journal of Economics* 37 (3): 602–18.

Macher, J., and J. Nickerson. 2006. "Pharmaceutical Manufacturing Research Project, Final Benchmarking Report." Report, Georgetown University and Washington University in St. Louis. http://apps.olin.wustl.edu/faculty/nickerson/results/ PMRPFinalReportSept2006.pdf.

Malin, J. L., J. C. Weeks, A. L. Potosky, M. C. Hornbrook, and N. L. Keating. 2013. "Medical Oncologists' Perceptions of Financial Incentives in Cancer Care." *Journal of Clinical Oncology* 31 (5): 530–35.

Mankiw, N. G., and M. D. Whinston. 2002. "Free Entry and Social Inefficiency." *Rand Journal of Economics* 17:48–58.

MedPAC. 2006. "Report to the Congress: Effects of Medicare Payment Changes on Oncology Services." Washington, DC, Medicare Payment Advisory Commission. http://www.medpac.gov/publications/congressional_reports/Jan06_Oncology _mandated_report.pdf.

Neumann, P. J. 2005. *Using Cost-Effectiveness Analysis to Improve Health Care.* Oxford: Oxford University Press.

Panattoni, L. 2011. "The Effect of Paragraph IV Decisions and Generic Entry before Patent Expiration on Brand Pharmaceutical Firms." *Journal of Health Economics* 30 (1): 126–45.

PAREXEL. 2013. *PAREXEL Biopharmaceutical R&D Statistical Sourcebook 2012– 2013.* http://www.barnettinternational.com/EducationalServices_Publication.aspx ?p=10145&id=115966.

Pharmacy Benefit Management Institute (PBMI). 2014. "2014 Specialty Drug Benefit." http://reports.pbmi.com/report.php?id=5.

Pindyck, R. S., and D. L. Rubinfeld. 2013. *Microeconomics,* 8th ed. New York: Prentice-Hall.

Reiffen, D., and M. R. Ward. 2005. "Generic Drug Industry Dynamics." *Review of Economics and Statistics* 87 (1): 37–49.

Scherer, F. M. 1993. "Pricing, Profits, and Technological Progress in the Pharmaceutical Industry." *Journal of Economic Perspectives* 7 (3): 97–115.

Scott Morton, F. M. 1999. "Entry Decisions in the Generic Pharmaceutical Industry." *RAND Journal of Economics* 30 (3): 421–40.

———. 2000. "Barriers to Entry, Brand Advertising, and Generic Entry in the US Pharmaceutical Industry." *International Journal of Industrial Organization* 18: 1085–104.

Stromberg, C. 2014. "Drug Shortages, Pricing, and Regulatory Authority." Unpublished Manuscript, Washington, DC:, Bates-White LLC. February.

Tirole, J. 1988. *The Theory of Industrial Organization.* Cambridge, MA: MIT Press.

Towle, E. L., and T. R. Barr. 2009. "2009 National Practice Benchmark: Report on 2008 Data." *Journal of Oncology Practice* 5 (5): 223–27.

————. 2010. "National Practice Benchmark: 2010 Report on 2009 Data." *Journal of Oncology Practice* 6 (5): 228–31. Erratum in *Journal of Oncology Practice* 2011 7 (2): 134.

Towle, E. L., T. R. Barr, and J. L. Senese. 2012. "National Oncology Practice Benchmark, 2012 Report on 2011 Data." *Journal of Oncology Practice* 8 (6): 51s–70s.

US Department of Health and Human Services, Assistant Secretary of Planning and Evaluation (ASPE). 2011. *Economic Analysis of the Causes of Drug Shortages.* Issue Brief, October. http://aspe.hhs.gov/sp/reports/2011/DrugShortages/ib.shtm.

————, Centers for Medicare and Medicaid Services (CMS). 2014. *Medicare Fee for Service Part B Drugs Reimbursement Fee Schedules 2005–2013.* http://www.cms.gov/Medicare/Medicare-Fee-for-Service-Part-B-Drugs/McrPartBDrugAvgSales Price/2013ASPFiles.html.

————. 2010. *Drug Manufacturers' Noncompliance with Average Manufacturer Price Reporting Requirements.* http://oig.hhs.gov/oei/reports/oei-03-09-00060.pdf.

————. 2011. "Medicare Payments for Newly Available Generic Drugs." Report no. OEI-03-09-00510. https://oig.hhs.gov/oei/reports/oei-03-09-00510.pdf.

US Food and Drug Administration (FDA). 2011. *Pathway for Global Drug Safety and Quality.* http://www.fda.gov/AboutFDA/CentersOffices/OfficeofGlobal RegulatoryOperationsandPolicy/GlobalProductPathway/default.htm.

————. 2013. *Strategic Plan for Preventing and Mitigating Drug Shortages.* http://www.fda.gov/downloads/Drugs/DrugSafety/DrugShortages/UCM372566.pdf.

US Government Accountability Office (GAO). 2004. "Medicare Chemotherapy Payments: New Drug and Administration Fees Are Closer to Providers' Costs." Report no. GAO-05-142R. http://www.gao.gov/new.items/d05142r.pdf.

————. 2011. "Manufacturer Discounts in the 340B Program Offer Benefits, but Federal Oversight Needs Improvement." Report no. GAO-11-836. http://www.gao.gov/new.items/d11836.pdf.

————. 2013. "Information on Highest-Expenditure Part B Drugs." Report no. GAO-13-739T. http://www.gao.gov/products/GAO-13-739T.

Varian, H. R. 1989. "Price Discrimination." In *Handbook of Industrial Organization,* vol. 1, edited by R. L. Schmalensee and R. Willig, 597–654. Amsterdam: North Holland Elsevier.

Wiggins, S. N., and R. Maness. 2004. "Price Competition in Pharmaceuticals: The Case of Anti-Infectives." *Economic Inquiry* 42 (2): 247–63.

Wilson, D. 2012. "Deepening Drug Shortages." *Health Affairs* (Millwood) 31 (2): 263–66.

Woodcock, J., and M. Wosinska. 2013. "Economic and Technological Drivers of Sterile Injectable Drug Shortages." *Clinical Pharmacology & Therapeutics* 93 (2): 170–76. http://www.nature.com/clpt/journal/v93/n2/full/clpt2012220a.html.

Yurukoglu, A., E. Liebman, and D. B. Ridley. 2012. "The Role of Government Reimbursement in Drug Shortages." NBER Working Paper no. 17987, Cambridge, MA.

10
Drug Shortages, Pricing, and Regulatory Activity

Christopher Stomberg

10.1 Introduction

Researchers and policymakers have devoted considerable attention in recent years to the increasing frequency and longevity of drug shortages in the United States. Many high-profile shortages have involved generic injectable drugs that are the frontline treatments in important areas such as cancer, where lack of availability is literally a life-or-death issue for patients. Much of the research on the causes of these shortages has reasonably focused on contributing factors specific to these high-profile shortages, such as the microstructure of the generic injectable drug industry and Medicare reimbursement (see, e.g., Conti and Berndt 2013; Yurukoglu, Liebman, and Ridley 2012; Graham 2012; Woodcock and Wosinska 2013).

As noted in Conti and Berndt, however, shortages do occur for other types of drugs. While these shortages are less frequent and have generally received less attention in the press and academic research, they have also followed a similar trend. In fact, as illustrated in figure 10.1 using data obtained from the University of Utah Drug Information Service (UUDIS), the pattern of ongoing shortages is strikingly similar for both types of

Christopher Stomberg heads the Life Sciences Practice at Bates White Economic Consulting.

I would like to thank David Kreling, Ernie Berndt, Rena Conti, Neeraj Sood, and other participants in the NBER-CRIW workshop (October 2013) for their helpful comments on an earlier draft of this chapter. I would also like to thank Erin Fox at the University of Utah Drug Information Service for kindly offering me data on shortages (and to Marta Wosinska at the FDA for making the introduction). Finally, I would like to thank Eric Barrette for his research assistance on aspects of this chapter. For acknowledgments, sources of research support, and disclosure of the author's material financial relationships, if any, please see http://www.nber.org/chapters/c13102.ack.

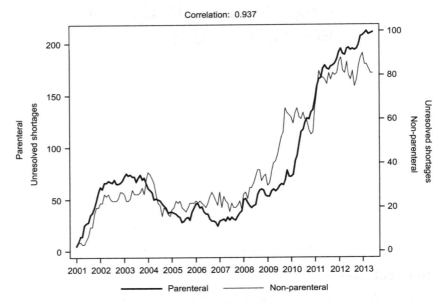

Fig. 10.1   Pattern of unresolved shortages

Source: University of Utah Drug Information Service (UUDIS).

Note: Vertical axis measures the number of drugs (typically molecule-form combinations) reported to be in ongoing shortage during that month. Note that early period data are truncated on the left, and thus do not accurately reflect the actual number of shortages in progress at the time the database was initially constructed.

drug.[1] Although a clear level difference can be read off the y-axes of this graph, the correlation between the number of ongoing injectable and noninjectable shortages is 0.94. Of concern, of course, is the nearly fourfold increase in the number of ongoing shortages between 2007 and 2013.

There are also distinctive, and again very similar, patterns in the average length of ongoing drug shortages over time for both injectable and noninjectable drugs (see figure 10.2). The correlation in these series is 0.89. Although the timing of the increase in average shortage length is more recent (beginning in 2008), this measure has nearly doubled in recent years.

The similarities demonstrated in figures 10.1 and 10.2 are not simply an artifact of tracking the stock of drugs in shortage.[2] In fact, as shown in figure 10.3, the number of new shortages reported for both injectable and noninjectable drugs on a monthly basis also follows a strikingly similar

---

1. The UUDIS data, which track reported shortages, are described in greater detail in section 10.3.1.

2. Since the previous charts measure stock variables (number of shortages in progress), there is a likelihood that high correlations could be induced by the summing process inherent in computing stocks.

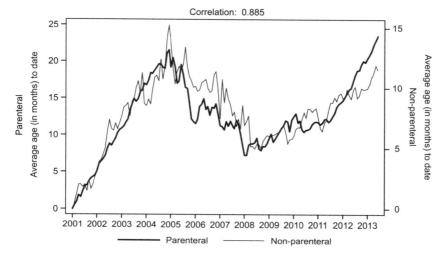

Fig. 10.2 Average age of unresolved shortages

Source: University of Utah Drug Information Service (UUDIS).

Note: Vertical axis measures the average age (in months) of drugs reported to be in ongoing shortage during that month. Note that early period data are truncated on the left, and thus do not accurately reflect the actual length of shortages in progress at the time the database was initially constructed.

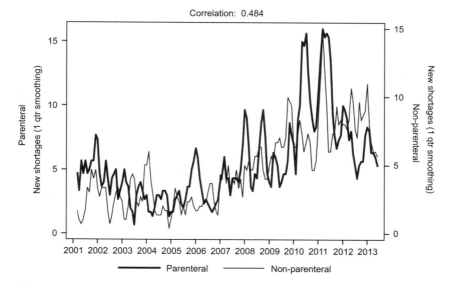

Fig. 10.3 Drug shortage starts

Source: University of Utah Drug Information Service (UUDIS).

Note: Vertical axis measures the monthly number of newly reported drugs in shortage smoothed using a quarterly moving average (current month plus previous two months). Reported correlation is based on nonsmoothed data.

Table 10.1   **Selected noninjectable drugs in shortage (UUDIS June 2013)**

Drug name	Duration (mos.)	Notified date
Carbamazepine XR tablets	0	04 Jun. 2013
Gabapentin encarbil	2	16 Apr. 2013
Cortisone tablets	3	29 Mar. 2013
Acyclovir suspension	5	29 Jan. 2013
Atorvastatin	7	26 Nov. 2012
Doxycycline oral	7	26 Nov. 2012
Pantoprazole tablets	7	29 Nov. 2012
Reserpine	9	26 Sep. 2012
Doxazosin tablets	9	12 Sep. 2012
Buspirone	9	21 Sep. 2012
Estradiol tablets	9	18 Sep. 2012
Methotrexate tablets	10	20 Aug. 2012
Buprenorphine SL tablets	18	29 Dec. 2011
Naltrexone tablets	18	15 Dec. 2011
Tetracycline capsules	27	04 Apr. 2011
Acyclovir tablets	44	23 Oct. 2009
Ciprofloxacin 500 mg tablets	45	14 Oct. 2009

pattern.[3] Although the correlation between raw new shortage starts for injectable drugs and noninjectable drugs is lower, at around 0.48, there is also considerable noise in these data. Smoothing the series using a quarterly moving average (as depicted in figure 10.3) reveals a clear coherence in the patterns of shortage.

Although the noninjectable drugs that are the subject of these shortages may not be cancer drugs, they are nevertheless important for the treatment of many serious conditions. Table 10.1 presents a selection of the noninjectable drugs that were listed by UUDIS as currently in shortage as of June 2013. A quick glance over this list reveals that several important therapies have been affected by shortages. For example, this list includes generic forms of many former blockbuster drugs—such as Buspar, Neurontin, Cardura, and Lipitor—as well as important antivirals and anti-infectives such as acyclovir, doxazosin, tetracycline, and ciprofloxacin.[4] The duration information, reported in months, gives an indication of the persistence of some of the supply issues. With limited supplies of these drugs available, patients have likely faced delays, interruptions, or substitutions in their therapies—with potentially adverse effects.

3. Also note that the rate of new shortages in early years does not exhibit the steep ramp-up over time exhibited in the two stock variables. This pattern is consistent with the way the stock variables are being calculated.

4. Anecdotes can be tied to some of these drugs. For example, atorvastatin (generic Lipitor) went into shortage when the first generic entrant (and holder of market exclusivity) experienced quality problems, issued a product recall, and shut down production in response.

These trends in noninjectable drug shortages are highly relevant to an overall understanding of the causes of shortages—not just for noninjectable drugs. Whatever factors explain these trends over time, they clearly apply equally and with the same rough timing in both markets. Theories that rely on Medicare reimbursement policies—such as ASP-based Medicare Part B reimbursement—may serve to explain level differences in shortage rates, but simply do not apply to noninjectable drugs and are not likely to explain the consistent pattern of change over time. Similarly, theories that rely on the specifics of generic injectable production do not apply to noninjectables. Although there may exist analogues to those stories in the tablet manufacturing sector, the market-wide nature of these trends seems to lend greater weight to theories suggesting broader causes such as changes in competition, market structure, and quality monitoring—effects that might be felt across both markets.

This study explores some of the alternative explanations that potentially have common influence on both markets. Section 10.2 presents a review of current literature on drug shortages, along with a heuristic framework for understanding and predicting the potential effects of alternative influences on supply, demand, and ultimately, shortage conditions. Section 10.3 explores (using econometric models) whether changes in quality monitoring by the Food and Drug Administration (FDA) (e.g., more frequent inspections and citations of manufacturers) can be connected with shortages. Although this is an explanation that could potentially apply across both markets and has been advanced by recent studies and position papers (e.g., GAO 2011; Congressional Committee Staff Report 2012), it has not been given rigorous empirical treatment in the past. Section 10.4 closes with a discussion of the empirical results of this chapter in a broader context.

Ultimately, although there may be no single "cause" of drug shortages, one thing is certain: the overwhelming majority of shortages affect generic drugs. The key difference between brand and generic drugs is the low margin available on generic drugs—particularly for those drugs that have been on the market for some time. With such low margins available, it is perhaps inevitable that shortages would result in a market where manufacturers may face weaker incentives to make investments in order to avoid supply disruptions. The United States may simply be a victim of its own success at creating an extremely competitive and price-sensitive market for generic drugs. The policy question, therefore, is whether (and how) the market could be shifted to an equilibrium that endogenously provides a desired level of quality and supply reliability without disruption.

10.2 Background

This section presents a sketch of some theoretical considerations underpinning the empirical work undertaken in this study.

10.2.1   Market Incentives for Generic Manufacturers

It is important to recognize the role that the institutional structure of the US generic market plays in creating conditions that are ripe for shortages. In particular, the notion of near-perfect substitutability of AB-rated generic drugs is built into the entire system. Many pharmacies and patients are compelled by payers to substitute the use of a generic product in lieu of the branded drug if one is available. And, by extension, generics are almost universally treated as perfect substitutes by the market. Pharmacy purchasing agents are free to select among competing manufacturers' products in order to meet their pharmacists' needs to fill prescriptions for a particular drug, so long as they are all approved AB-rated alternatives. Patients at a pharmacy generally only become aware of the manufacturer of their generic pills once they receive the bottle at the counter. They may receive the same manufacturer's product at the next refill, or they might not, depending on where the pharmacy (or its wholesaler) is sourcing its product at that time. There is very little either the patient, the doctor, or the pharmacist behind the counter can do to exert supplier preferences among generic drugs under the current market structure.[5]

This institutionalization of near-perfect substitutability is, in fact, quite a rare phenomenon in markets. Even so-called commodities like wheat, corn, or oil have grading systems. This is not the case for generic pharmaceuticals.

Both quality/purity of product and reliability of supply are costly attributes for the manufacturer to provide, and they are generally invisible to buyers. Without FDA inspections and the occasional supply disruption, these characteristics are generally obscure to the market. Nevertheless, it is reasonable to assume that these are characteristics that enter into demand, and would affect prices if they were routinely observable and could be traded upon. In many markets where these attributes are observable, a premium is paid for them. However, as Woodcock and Wosinska (2013) point out, these attributes are not readily observable for generic pharmaceuticals, so it is difficult to pay a premium for them.[6]

One of the key consequences of this institutionalized substitutability is the "near-Bertrand" price competition among manufacturers participating in these markets.[7] In a market where suppliers are often asked to meet or

---

5. Of course there are exceptions to this stylized story, for example, in the case of narrow therapeutic index drugs where slight differences in bioactivity levels in different products are known to adversely affect patients switching among products.

6. It is notable that it was not unusual at one time for generic manufacturers to agree to supply reliability terms in their supply contracts, so it is not impossible to find methods to contract for these attributes.

7. Conti and Berndt (2013).

beat the price of the competition to win a supply contract, price is set almost auction style. Wholesalers can switch suppliers and reduce prices with a few phone calls.

These markets have delivered billions of units of thousands of products at prices often in the low single-digit pennies per pill range, so much of this story is one of great success for consumers.

Surviving this sort of price competition with both contracts and any sort of profit is almost certainly a matter of relentless cost cutting. To give a rough idea of the relatively small scale of revenue earned on many generics, consider that the median average manufacturer price (AMP) for buspirone in the 2011–2013 time period was about $0.03 per tablet. In 2012 Medicaid (generally the largest single payer for retail drugs in the United States) reimbursed about 85 million buspirone tablets for all of its fee-for-service patients nationwide. At the median AMP per tablet, this amounts to a little over $2.5 million in total revenue spread across all participants in this relatively important slice of the market. Of the three manufacturers with more than 100,000 Medicaid units sold, only one would earn more than $1 million in total revenue (not profit) on its 37 million units of Medicaid volume sold.[8] Grossing this revenue up to the overall market (assuming Medicaid is roughly 15 percent of the total), would yield about $6.6 million in total US buspirone revenue for this producer. These figures are a couple orders of magnitude smaller than might be experienced by a branded drug manufacturer. Although this example is essentially synthetic, it illustrates that the revenue, and therefore total profit, generated by these products can be quite limited. Staying profitable on the margin at these levels clearly presents a challenge.

Another thing that has to be recognized is that the typical modern generic manufacturer has literally hundreds of products on the market at any one time. Unlike brand manufacturers that may have a few key products on the market that are responsible for a significant fraction of their total revenue and profit, a generic manufacturer's revenues are frequently spread across a diffuse array of products. Their greatest profits are generally earned early in the evolution of the market post–patent expiration. Once price competition has had its relentless effect on prices for more mature generic products, revenues and profits for individual products may not make a large contribution to the bottom line of the company. They may continue selling these products if marginal costs are low, or if there are economies of scope associated with producing or selling a broad array of products.

It should therefore be little surprise that when generic manufacturers are faced with supply disruptions of any magnitude on older low-margin products, they might not find it worthwhile to address them quickly, or at

---

8. Sources: CMS Medicaid State Drug Utilization Data, CMS published weighted average AMP data.

all.[9] For example, it is not hard to imagine a production situation where some manufacturers' cost-cutting efforts could lead to a reduction in maintenance or product-quality investments. Even if this ultimately results in a stoppage due to production-line failures or regulatory interventions, this behavior may be optimal from the manufacturer's standpoint. This is a classic "race to the bottom" in both price and quality. If the current costs of plant maintenance and product-quality investment exceeds the discounted expected value of lost profits due to a shutdown, then they are not worth undertaking. An option-value approach such as presented by Yurukoglu, Liebman, and Ridley (2012) would offer a refinement to this logic, but perhaps not a fundamentally different result. Once faced with the realization of a negative supply shock (such as product withdrawal or production-line failure), the manufacturer may easily find higher returns to investment in, for example, bringing a new Abbreviated New Drug Application (ANDA) product to market than attempting to resuscitate an older product for which prices may be limited.[10]

In short, there are several reasons to expect that generic supply could be inherently riskier than branded drug supply—particularly for low-priced "mature" products. As the first waves of blockbuster generics fade into the distant past, and the ranks of mature products on the production lists of manufacturers swell, it is not far-fetched to believe that the trend in observed shortages could be partly a result of this trend. These are also trends that would generally affect both markets for injectable and noninjectable drugs.

10.2.2   Regulatory Activity—Quality/Purity Concerns

Regulatory involvement may also have a role to play in drug shortages. Of particular interest are changes in policy and time-inconsistent policies. In a market where product quality is not generally observable, but the actions of the regulator are, these actions may play an important role in setting expectations of both buyers and sellers in the market.

Suppose that the regulator, in this case the FDA, advertises that only a certain level of quality is permissible, and products below that threshold will not be allowed onto the market. If monitoring is perfect, then the presence of the product on the market is a clear signal that its quality is above the advertised regulatory threshold. Differentiation of quality above that threshold may not be worthwhile because additional investments in quality by the seller would be lost on buyers that only observe market presence as opposed to quality. The profit-maximizing decision of producers in this situation may be to undertake only those expenses required to pass

9. The investment under uncertainty approach explored by Yurukoglu, Liebman, and Ridley (2012) is potentially quite relevant in this context.

10. Prescription generic drug manufacturers must receive FDA approval via an ANDA before marketing each product.

the regulator's threshold and no more—leading to a generally consistent level of quality. This highlights the important role of the regulator in setting quality levels in markets where quality is otherwise unobservable. Were product quality an observable attribute, manufacturers might find it optimal to differentiate by optimizing around different levels of observable quality.[11]

In reality, the FDA does not have perfect oversight. Instead, it might inspect facilities at a known rate of probability. The manufacturer facing this uncertainty may well pick a level of quality that is below the advertised threshold if the probability of future inspection is less than one. In the limit, if the probability of inspection is zero, then investments in quality might only rise to a level such that manufacturing does not generate observable defects (like malformed pills, broken packaging, etc.) that could lead to consumer-led actions against the company. Whatever the probability of inspection, so long as it is the same for all manufacturers, and all manufacturers believe it to be the same, then all will target roughly the same level of quality and buyers will experience a consistent level of quality, possibly somewhat below the advertised threshold. This intuition serves to explain the tendency of regulators such as the FDA and local health authorities to set relatively stringent goals.

As a hypothetical matter, manufacturers may assign different probabilities to the possibility of detection and/or may be risk averse to varying degrees, which could lead them to pick heterogeneous levels of quality. For example, risk-averse companies that believe in a high probability of inspection may feel compelled to make greater investments in quality, while those companies with less aversion to risk, or having a low assessment of the risk of inspection, might be tempted to spend less on quality. To the extent that such heterogeneity in cost structures exists—particularly if it translates to differences in marginal cost—an adverse-selection problem could arise. If competition is Bertrand-like, then the producers most likely to survive in the market are those that are most willing to take a risk with low spending on quality giving them a low marginal cost and an advantage in price competition.

Even if the relatively risk-loving low-cost firms were eventually inspected and shut down, the consequences could be substantial in this scenario if they have already edged out higher-quality competition and there is no alternative higher-quality supply available.

Setting clear expectations and time-consistent quality-monitoring policies are key ingredients in this framework. If the regulator sets expectations both about the probability of inspection and the quality threshold in one period, but then changes one or the other of these subsequently, it could potentially cause either disruption or time-inconsistency issues. Suppose, for example, that the regulator raises the probability of inspection in a period

11. In this way, manufacturers might face a downward-sloping demand for their product similar to the situation explored in Dorfman and Steiner (1954).

subsequent to the period when manufacturers set their quality-investment decisions. Caught off guard with inadequate quality more frequently than expected, manufacturing would be subject to excess disruptions—that is, shortages might occur. Now suppose the regulator in this circumstance alters its threshold downward to prevent excess disruptions. In this case, the regulator has set up a time-inconsistency problem. Manufacturers, now knowing that the regulator's threat regarding attaining the threshold quality level is not credible, will likely take that into account in their future investments.

In short, absent observable quality, the FDA has an important role to play in setting equilibrium quality. To the extent that it may seek to raise equilibrium quality by raising either standards or (possibly more likely) the probability of inspection and detection of quality lapses, then a certain level of disruption is to be expected if some manufacturers are optimized around a different expectation of quality. To the extent that the Bertrand-like competition model is right, and some manufacturers moreover feel they face weak incentives to address supply issues with older low-cost drugs, then these disruptions could well be persistent. On the other hand, manufacturers may choose to address the issues that arise and reenter the market. To the extent this raises costs, it would only be supportable under an expectation of higher future prices to support that cost structure.

Altered inspection rates, to the extent that they reflect exogenous regime changes, are thus a plausible factor that could contribute to increased shortage rates (at least in the short run), and this would be an effect likely to cut across both injectable and tablet drug markets.[12]

One example of a clearly articulated regime change is the recent implementation of the Generic Drug User Fee Act (GDUFA). This act, which set a new structure of fees for the review of generic drug ANDAs, was intended in part to provide additional resources to the FDA for inspections. In fact, according to the FDA's Generic Drug User Fee Act Program Performance Goals and Procedures, "FDA will conduct risk-adjusted biennial CGMP surveillance inspections of generic API and generic finished dosage form (FDF) manufacturers, with the goal of achieving parity of inspection frequency between foreign and domestic firms in FY 2017."[13] There are two important aspects of this program goal: (a) the apparent recognition by the FDA that inspection rates have not been at parity, and (b) the preannouncement of the new inspection goals. The former suggests a real change in

---

12. Alternatively, one can imagine that unchanging inspection rates and rules could result in an endogenous indicator of the evolving quality decisions of manufacturers if these patterns take time to play out. For example, as price competition lowers spending on quality unobservables, more firms would trip the wire when they are inspected. This might predict changes in the rate of enforcement action given an inspection, but it is less clear whether this would predict a trend in inspections.

13. See: http://www.fda.gov/downloads/ForIndustry/UserFees/GenericDrugUserFees/UCM 282505.pdf.

inspection regime for foreign manufacturers, while the latter should inform industry expectations and possibly smooth the transition.

10.2.3 Prices and Shortages

Traditional economic explanations for shortages generally rest on price inflexibility as a key element of the story. In a standard neoclassical setting, "shortage" is a very short-run disequilibrium phenomenon caused by supply or demand shocks that are quickly corrected by upward price movements that serve to reequilibrate supply and demand. Real shortages, where demand exceeds supply at going prices for extended periods of time, are generally considered to be a product of market failure: typically related to upward price inflexibility—"sticky" prices.

The ASPE's 2011 Issue Brief (Haninger, Jessup, and Koehler 2011) points to some of the basic supply and demand conditions that apply to pharmaceutical markets. In particular, both demand and supply are price inelastic (particularly in the short run). For suppliers, these inelasticities generally stem from institutionally driven requirements for approval of new manufacturing facilities and production lines, as well as technological obstacles to adding capacity. For patients the combination of medical necessity for these products, and the fact that neither they nor their doctors generally pay market prices for these products, would generally argue for low responsiveness of demand to changes in price.[14]

Taken together, these conditions would potentially be a recipe for very large price increases in response to adverse supply shocks.[15]

But, there may be some contravening institutional factors. One might, for example, look at contracts as a standard explanation for why prices might move slowly upward in the presence of a supply shock. One of the most important types of contracts on this market are those governing how pharmacies are paid (reimbursement) for drugs by third-party payers. A theory that has been expressed in popular press ties changes in Medicare reimbursement policies to increased shortage rates. Under that theory, Medicare's 2005 transition from Average Wholesale Price (AWP)-based reimbursement to Average Sales Price (ASP)-based reimbursement lowered both average margins and the upward responsiveness of Medicare reimbursements in the presence of adverse supply shocks. Yurukoglu, Liebman, and Ridley (2012)

---

14. Third-party payers generally attempt to induce some price responsiveness in patients through utilization management tools like tiered copayments or prior authorization. Although these are effective at steering patients from more expensive brands to cheaper therapeutic alternatives, they are also a blunt tool. For example, a patient's copayment for a generic drug is generally lower than for a similar brand, but is generally the same regardless of the underlying cost of the generic drug

15. Here it needs to be reinforced that we are speaking in terms of market demand and market supply. Assuming a relatively competitive market, the demand curve facing the individual manufacturer is likely to be very price elastic, with a correspondingly elastic supply faced by individual buyers (for whom alternative supply is often just a phone call away).

examine this idea using a Nash equilibrium model of investment under uncertainty to capture capacity investment dynamics. This model predicts more frequent shortages in the presence of the ASP-based reimbursement that Medicare adopted in 2005. Yurukoglu and colleague's empirical results also suggest a lower frequency of shortages in the presence of higher (i.e., AWP-based) Medicare reimbursement.

This particular explanation does not appear on the surface to offer an explanation for the increased frequency of shortages in the market for nonparenteral drugs (which are not reimbursed under Medicare Part B). However, there could be a private market analogue to the Medicare Part B–based reimbursement explanation for nonparenteral drugs. Much of the reimbursement for these types of drugs are governed by administrative rules that might not reflect market conditions. Particularly as they apply to generic drugs, these rules are not generally known publicly. For example, many generics are reimbursed on the basis of a maximum allowable cost (MAC) that is determined in a manner that is not generally transparent. To the extent that these payment methods are not flexible in the presence of supply shocks, these contracts could introduce inflexibility in prices at a point in the supply chain that would place limits on the extent of price change that pharmacies can tolerate before losing money on sales—thus possibly disconnecting price and quantity in the market. This would also presume, however, that the institutions setting reimbursement rules have weak incentives to allow flexibility in them. This might not be true if there is competitive pressure to retain plan contracts. The complaints of beneficiaries unable to obtain their prescriptions due to a payer's inflexible reimbursement rules could be a source of such pressure.

There is a certain consumer appeal to upward price inflexibility for pharmaceuticals. Especially if demand elasticity is low, shortages could cause very substantial increases in price. Anecdotal evidence suggests that some drugs in shortage have been subject to "price gouging," which is a popular pejorative that often raises public concern.[16] But, it is precisely elevated prices that are usually the equilibrating mechanism that simultaneously reduces demand (for example, causing people to identify substitutes), and creates an incentive for new supply to get on the market quickly. Absent price responsiveness in the market, endogenous incentives for manufacturers to address supply issues are likely to be attenuated.

Although it is beyond the scope of this chapter, merging aspects of the Yurukoglu, Liebman, and Ridley investment model with the regulatory framework outlined above could yield more refined insights. In particular, the regulatory framework provides a richer model for the supply-shock distribution built into the Yurukoglu, Liebman, and Ridley model.

---

16. To the extent that some of these reports reflect concerns about grey market imports that potentially circumvent FDA rules, or are outright counterfeits, this concern could be well justified.

10.3   Empirical Effects of Regulatory Activity

This section investigates the empirical linkages between FDA inspection and detection rates on shortage rates. As discussed above, change in regulatory activity is one of the variables expected to have an impact on shortage rates, at least in the short run, as manufacturers adjust to a new equilibrium. Although increased FDA vigilance is sometimes directly blamed for the increases in drug shortages, there has not been rigorous analysis behind these statements. Moreover, to the extent that these connections are being made, they have been primarily focused on injectable drug shortages. The statistical models presented in this section suggest a connection between FDA inspection and citation rates and drug shortages that cuts across both parenteral and nonparenteral drugs.

10.3.1   Shortage Data

The shortage data used in this study were provided by the University of Utah Drug Information Service (UUDIS), which also provides the information reported on the American Society of Health System Pharmacists (ASHP) website.[17] The UUDIS shortage data have become a standard resource for researchers investigating shortages due to both its comprehensiveness and to its extensive time coverage. The US Government Accountability Office (GAO) has issued two reports on shortages (GAO 2011, 2014), both of which rely primarily upon the data gathered by UUDIS.[18] As discussed in more detail below, the events tracked by UUDIS range in severity from temporary supply disruptions to full-blown shortages.

The FDA also provides online access to information on current and past drug shortages.[19] There are two main distinguishing features between the FDA data on shortages and the UUDIS database. The first is that the FDA only publishes information on a shortage when the affected drug is considered medically necessary, that is, if it is "used to treat or prevent a serious disease or medical condition, and there is no other available source of that product or alternative drug that is judged by medical staff to be an adequate substitute."[20] This definition potentially omits reports of shortages that are of economic significance or relevance to consumers, but nevertheless fall below the FDA's medical necessity threshold. The most significant limitation of the FDA data for analytical purposes, however, is the lack of

17. These data first became available in 2001: "In 2001, ASHP entered into an agreement with the University of Utah Drug Information Service (UUDIS) to use bulletins developed by UUDIS to address pharmacists' questions about shortages. Also in 2001, ASHP published guidelines on managing drug product shortages and launched a Drug Product Shortages Management Resource Center on its Web site" (ASHP 2002).

18. The data for this study is very similar to the data used by the GAO in its 2014 report.

19. See http://www.fda.gov/Drugs/DrugSafety/DrugShortages/default.htm for more information on this source. The UUDIS and FDA also share information.

20. See Fox et al. (2009) for discussion.

historical information that is made publicly available—only a few years of data on resolved shortages are available on the FDA website. Based on these considerations, the FDA shortage information was not used in this study.[21]

The supply disruptions tracked by UUDIS are voluntarily reported via several channels (e.g., the ASHP website shortage reporting feature).[22] Upon receiving a report, availability is researched among all manufacturers, along with reasons for the disruption and information about the potential for its resolution; it is then tracked. The ASHP website publishes data on shortages tracked by UUDIS, but only for drugs that meet its definition of shortage: "a supply issue that affects how the pharmacy prepares or dispenses a drug product or influences patient care when prescribers must use an alternative agent."[23] Not all supply disruptions that are reported to UUDIS meet these formal shortage criteria, but are nevertheless tracked internally by UUDIS. According to UUDIS, if the disruption becomes significant enough to meet the ASHP shortage criterion, it will be listed on ASHP's public website where extensive information on availability from all current manufacturers is provided along with other information, such as reasons for shortage.[24] As a result of this process, the data that UUDIS makes available to researchers tracks more supply disruptions than are reported on the ASHP website.[25] Among the reasons given for this dichotomy is the desire to avoid worsening disruptions by prematurely disseminating information from early reports.[26] One clear advantage of the UUDIS data beyond their time coverage, therefore, is that they also appear to be a more sensitive measure of supply disruption than the online ASHP shortage reports.[27] In subsequent discussion, the events recorded in the UUDIS data will be referred to as shortages with the understanding that many of these events could be best described as disruptions rather than full-blown shortages.

The database received from UUDIS for this study contains information on 1,686 separate shortage events reported in the United States between January

21. In its 2011 report (GAO 2011), the GAO cited similar reasons for using the UUDIS data instead of FDA data in its retrospective analysis.
22. See the ASHP website's "Frequently Asked Questions" (AHSP 2014) for more information on what the reported data consist of and how it compares to, for example, the FDA shortage reports. See also Fox's 2011 presentation (Fox 2011) for more background on the UUDIS reporting process and summary statistics generated from their data.
23. Fox et al. (2009, 1400).
24. Telephone interview, May 2014.
25. Information on the shortages tracked by the ASHP website are currently only available back to mid-2010 (earliest date observed on resolved shortage list as of 5/2014). As a result, it is not possible to comprehensively identify which of the UUDIS-tracked disruptions were, in fact, reported on the ASHP website. Anecdotally, the number of disruptions identified in the UUDIS data may exceed those listed on the ASHP website by 50 percent.
26. Fox et al. (2009) notes, for example, the potential for disruptions being exacerbated by purchasers hoarding product based on rumors of shortage.
27. It must be noted, however, that even when ASHP reports a shortage on its website, individual buyers may anecdotally be unaffected by the identified disruption. See Bhat, Roberts, and Devlin (2012) for an example of this phenomenon.

2001 and June 2013. Each record contains information for one shortage event, including: drug name, date of first reported shortage, whether the shortage remains active, the ending date of the shortage if it is no longer active, reason for shortage, type of drug (parenteral vs. nonparenteral), American Hospital Formulary Service (AHFS) drug classification, and US Department of Justice Drug Enforcement Administration (DEA) schedule if the drug is a controlled substance. Certain drugs may appear multiple times in the data if they have experienced more than one shortage event over time. The UUDIS also tracks a number of products that are beyond the scope of this study and consequently omitted from analysis, including: devices, vaccines, and vitamin therapies.[28] A small number of additional products were eliminated from the data due to being listed as resolved, but having no end date. Omitting these products removes 137 events from the data, leaving 1,549 for further analysis.

Each year, an average of about 45 percent of the new events reported in the UUDIS data relate to nonparenteral drugs. The median length of resolved shortages is relatively similar for parenteral and nonparenteral drugs (five months versus four months, respectively), but differences in average length are somewhat more pronounced (9.8 months versus 6.6 months, respectively). Focusing on events starting after 2003 reduces the average length of parenteral and nonparenteral shortages to 7.7 months and 6.0 months, respectively.[29] Taken together, the higher average length of parenteral shortages and their higher frequency both contribute to the larger number of ongoing parenteral drug shortages noted in table 10.1.

For the statistical analysis, the UUDIS data were summarized into 150 monthly counts (2001–2013) of ongoing shortages (ongoing), and new shortage reports (starts) for parenteral and nonparenteral drugs. Though the number of ongoing shortages is clearly a variable of policy interest, it is also a stock variable, which likely induces autocorrelation in this series. There are sound reasons to expect that FDA regulatory activity would affect this stock both by potentially affecting the rate at which new shortages are started and by potentially altering the length of time that it takes to clear up supply issues resulting from FDA inspection. It turns out, however, that the stock of ongoing shortages is highly autocorrelated, with first-order autocorrelation coefficients in excess of 0.97. Dickey-Fuller (DF) statistics computed for these series (ongoing parenteral and nonparenteral shortages) are small and the corresponding DF-tests cannot reject the null hypothesis that unit roots are present in the data (p-values of 0.993 and 0.807, respectively). This suggests either that these data should be differenced before performing regression analysis, or that the rate data (new shortage starts)

---

28. The following AHFS categories were eliminated from the UUDIS data: (16.) Blood Derivatives; (20.) Blood Formation, Coagulation, and Thrombosis Agents & drug_name contains "FACTOR" (blood factor products); (80.) Serums, Toxoids, and Vaccines; (88.) Vitamins; (94.) Devices; and (96.) Pharmaceutical aids.

29. The coefficient of variation on the length of shortages is quite high—on the order of 1.3.

be used instead. The shortage start data are indeed less autocorrelated with first-order autocorrelations of 0.57 and 0.49 for the parenteral and nonparenteral series, respectively. The Dickey-Fuller test soundly rejects the hypothesis of unit roots in these series (p-value < 0.0000). For modeling purposes, the count of new shortage starts will be treated as the dependent variable.

10.3.2   FDA Inspection/Citation Data

The information on FDA regulatory activity used in this study come from two separate publicly downloadable databases made available by the FDA on its website: one that focuses on the inspections performed by each of its centers and another that provides details on the citations (alleged CFR violations) that are noted during inspections. Each data set has nonoverlapping information, thus both alternatives are used separately in the regression analysis. The main limitation in these data is that they only include those events that have progressed to a point where the FDA is at liberty to disclose details.[30]

The monthly CDER drug inspection data are derived from a large database documenting all FDA inspections from October 1, 2008, to March 31, 2013.[31] These data cover inspections made by all centers within the FDA, for example, the Center for Biologics Evaluation & Research (CBER), the Center for Drug Evaluation and Research (CDER), and the Center for Devices and Radiological Health (CDRH). Each inspection record lists the name of the firm inspected, its location, the date the inspection ended, the FDA center performing the inspection, the project area (focus of inspection), and the "district decision." The district decision records in summary form the outcome of the inspection. It is broken into three possible outcomes: NAI (No Action Indicated), VAI (Voluntary Action Indicated), and OAI (Official Action Indicated).[32]

The inspections database in this study contains information on 102,160 FDA inspections across all parts of the organization. The Center for Drug Evaluation and Research (CDER) accounts for 11,410 of these inspections, and the Center for Biologics Evaluation and Research (CBER) accounts for

---

30. Particularly in months close to the end of the reporting period, the counts of included inspections and citations drop off significantly.

31. These data are updated quarterly and can be downloaded at http://www.fda.gov/iceci/ enforcementactions/ucm222557.htm. The version used in this study was downloaded in October 2013.

32. The FDA website gives further detail on the meaning of these terms: "An OAI inspection classification occurs when significant objectionable conditions or practices were found and regulatory action is warranted to address the establishment's lack of compliance with statute(s) or regulation(s). A VAI inspection classification occurs when objectionable conditions or practices were found that do not meet the threshold of regulatory significance. Inspections classified with VAI violations are typically more technical violations of the FDCA. An NAI inspection classification occurs when no objectionable conditions or practices were found during the inspection or the significance of the documented objectionable conditions found does not justify further actions." See: http://www.fda.gov/AboutFDA/Transparency/PublicDisclosure/ DraftProposalbyTopicArea/ucm211861.htm. Accessed May 2014.

another 9,353 inspections. The majority of inspections (about 55 percent) are associated with the activities of the Center for Food Safety and Applied Nutrition (CFSAN), which monitors the food supply. Since the focus of this study is primarily on pharmaceuticals, the inspections of interest are those performed by CDER. The project area variable further breaks inspections down into categories. The majority of CDER's inspections (8,348, 73 percent of the 11,410 total) are listed in the "Drug Quality Assurance" (DQA) project area. The next most prevalent project area is "Bioresearch Monitoring," which accounts for about 21 percent of CDER's inspections. The type of inspection most relevant to this study are the subset listed in the DQA project area.

Within CDER's DQA inspections it is worth noting that over 50 percent result in some kind of regulatory action. Although only 4.8 percent (401) of these inspections result in an Official Action Indicated outcome, another 48 percent (4,011) result in Voluntary Action Indicated—suggesting some kind of corrective action is needed, according to the FDA. Most of CDER's DQA inspections occur in the United States (74 percent), as one would expect. Of the remaining foreign inspections, the largest fraction occur in India (18 percent) and China (11 percent), with the remainder spread among Organisation for Economic Co-operation and Development (OECD) countries.

Ideally, one would want to connect inspections mentioned in the FDA data (via company ownership and location) to the shortage events mentioned in the UUDIS data. However, it is typically difficult or impossible to make these direct connections given just the name and address information found in the FDA data.[33] Nevertheless, FDA-inspection data do provide insight into the overall intensity of the FDA's activities, regional focus, and outcomes. For the empirical exercise in this study, these data were processed into sixty monthly counts of overall inspections by region (US/EXUS) and district decision (NAI/VAI/OAI).

In addition to the detailed inspection data, the FDA separately makes available a database of citations listed for each of its inspections. This data set covers a longer period than the inspection data (from October 2005 to September 2012). These data only list inspections for which a citation was generated, so it does not replace the inspections database as a source of information about the total number of inspections performed. Citations are recorded in the data as a specific reference to the portion of the Code

33. For example, many firms in the pharmaceutical industry own and operate a complex web of manufacturing locations, most of which are multiproduct facilities. Information about which products are produced at particular facilities is generally not made available to the public, so even knowing that a particular firm was inspected at a particular location may only allow inferential conclusions about the drugs affected. This problem is exacerbated by the fact that the UUDIS data only provide drug name information, so historical data on which manufacturers produced a particular drug at the point of time of the inspection would be needed even for an inferential analysis. Also, since many of the inspected facilities, for example, active pharmaceutical ingredient (API) plants in India and China, produce inputs for other manufacturers, the ultimate downstream impacts stemming from an inspection at one of these plants cannot be derived from public data.

of Federal Regulations (CFR) implicated, along with a text description of the specific violation. For each inspection with a citation, multiple records with different CFR references may be recorded in this database. Overall, the FDA's citation data contain 157,301 individual citation records across all of the FDA's centers; 22,791 are related specifically to CDER inspection activities. Unlike the inspection data, the citation data are not further subdividable into project area, for example, DQA activities versus Bioresearch Monitoring. However, it is possible to distinguish citations related to 21 CFR Part 211: "Current Good Manufacturing Practice for Finished Pharmaceuticals" (CGMP) from others. The CGMP citations are a dominant fraction (97.25 percent) of the total citations. The relatively small number of remaining citations are dominated (93 percent) by Part 314 references: "Applications for FDA Approval to Market a New Drug." Keeping only citations related to Part 211 leaves 22,164 total citations over the covered time period.

The 22,164 CDER CGMP citations identified in the FDA citation database are linked to 3,478 unique inspection events (month, manufacturer, country combinations), meaning that approximately 6.4 citations are given out per (citation generating) inspection.[34] Review of the particular citations involved with each of the CGMP inspections in this database reveals 236 different CFR references. The five most frequently cited are: 21 CFR 211.192 (1,401 times), 21 CFR 211.22(d) (969 times), 21 CFR 211.100(a) (909 times), 21 CFR 211.25(a) (905 times), and 21 CFR 211.110(a) (701 times). No attempt was made to classify the CFR references qualitatively.[35] For each CFR reference, a number of different text descriptions can show up. For example, for citations referencing 21 CFR 211.192 there are thirty-six different associated text descriptions, each alleging a specific form of quality-assurance lapse. A large majority of the inspections and citations in this database occur at US locations (97 percent in each case).

Both the number of citations and the number of unique inspections leading to a citation (firm/date combinations) were processed into eighty-four monthly summary counts by region (US/Ex-US). Comparing the inspection and citation data for the years where the two data sets overlap reveals that in the United States, the number of inspections with citations in the citation data set tracks the number of inspections listed with a district decision of VAI or OAI in the inspection data set reasonably well. There is less correspondence between these series for inspections occurring outside the United States.[36]

34. In a handful of instances (less than twenty) an inspection occurred at more than one location for a particular manufacturer within a country and month. Many of these occur on the same or very proximate dates in geographically close locations, so are treated here as a single event.

35. Although qualitative distinctions clearly exist, making such judgments would involve challenges.

36. In particular, there appear to be considerably fewer (often months with zero) inspections with citations compared to VAI/OAI events in the inspection data, although the correlation is still reasonably high (0.81).

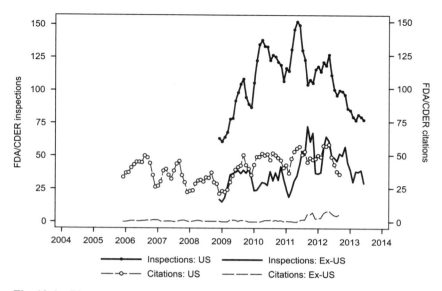

Fig. 10.4   FDA inspection and citation data
Source: FDA.

The patterns of correlation among the various measures of FDA activity suggest caution when attempting to use these measures in conjunction with one other on the right-hand side of a regression equation. For example, there is a relatively high degree of correlation between the count of inspections with citations and total inspections (0.86 and 0.82 correlation, US/Ex-US, respectively). As expected, there is also a high degree of correlation between the number of inspections with VAI/OAI district decisions and inspections with citations (0.91). Factor analysis of these data confirm that two factors can account for almost all of the variation in the six different FDA activity measures (excluding totals that are perfect linear combinations of other variables). Inspection of the factor loadings suggests a strong distinction between measures of US and Ex-US activity, whether it be overall inspections or inspections with citations.

For modeling purposes, only six measures of FDA activity were thus retained: US/Ex-US inspections (2008–2013) and US/Ex-US citations (2005–2012), along with their totals. As with the measure of new shortage starts, the FDA citation and inspection data exhibit modest autocorrelation (first-order autocorrelation generally below 0.5). Dickey-Fuller tests soundly reject a null hypothesis of unit roots in these data. Figure 10.4 illustrates the pattern over time for the FDA variables. Note that both of the US series (inspections and citations) have apparent seasonal patterns with a discernible dip near the end of each year.

Table 10.2   Summary statistics for variables used in statistical analysis

Variable	Obs.	Mean	Std. dev.	Min.	Median	Max.
Pflag	300.00	0.50	0.50	0.00	0.50	1.00
Starts	300.00	5.16	3.79	0.00	5.00	22.00
Cites	168.00	41.40	13.23	16.00	40.50	84.00
Cites_US	168.00	40.01	12.29	15.00	39.50	73.00
Cites_EXUS	168.00	1.39	2.57	0.00	0.00	15.00
Insp	114.00	143.40	35.36	66.00	144.00	239.00
Insp_US	114.00	105.05	27.50	55.00	108.00	160.00
Insp_EXUS	114.00	38.35	19.41	7.00	34.00	126.00

These data were then combined with the parenteral and nonparenteral shortage data, then pooled (stacked) into a data set with 300 total observations (fewer for the shorter FDA inspection data). Table 10.2 provides summary statistics for the variables used in the statistical analysis.

10.3.3   Modeling and Analysis

Figure 10.5 plots the total number (US/Ex-US) of monthly FDA inspections and citations against the number of newly reported shortages for noninjectable drugs.[37]

These charts suggest the potential for lagged effects and other dynamics in the relationship between FDA activity and drug shortages. Panel time-series regression models were estimated to investigate these relationships. These models are designed to be predictive in nature, and are used to determine if current and past FDA activity has an effect on new drug shortage reports. These models do not represent a reduced-form estimation of any particular underlying structural model, but can potentially be useful for identifying causation in the sense of Granger.[38] The general form of these models is the following:

$$(1) \quad y_{it} = \alpha + \beta_0 \cdot X_t + \beta_1 \cdot X_{t-1} + \ldots + \beta_l \cdot X_{t-l} + \gamma \cdot \textbf{pflag} + \varepsilon_{it},$$

where y_{it} is the number of new shortages reported for drug type i (injectable, noninjectable) in time t. The variable X_{t-1} is the measure of regulatory

---

37. The data in this figure have been smoothed with a one-quarter moving average to improve readability. These same charts appear similar for parenteral drug shortages, and have been omitted for the sake of brevity.

38. Taking a more traditional approach using IV estimation presents the typical problem of identifying an appropriate instrument, in this case for FDA regulatory activity. Fully exogenous changes, such as turnover in FDA leadership driven by political changes or (possibly) implementation of the GDUFA could serve as exogenous sources of variation. The FDA inspection and citation data provide relatively little data spanning such regimes, however.

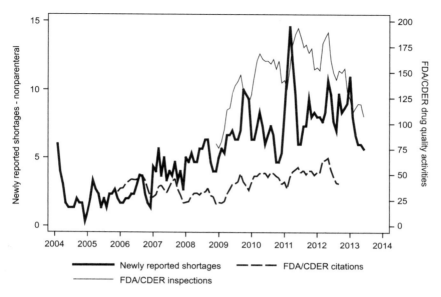

Fig. 10.5   Drug shortage rates, FDA inspections, and FDA citations
Sources: UUDIS and FDA.

activity (citations or inspections) for time t lagged by l periods. The variable
pflag is an indicator equal to one for injectable (parenteral) drugs and zero
otherwise.

Focusing first on the citation data, which provides a longer time series
for estimation, table 10.3 reports the results of six models of drug shortage where the independent variables are counts of FDA citations and the
dependent variable is the count of drug shortages reported by UUDIS as
described above. Three of the models are estimated using ordinary least
squares (OLS) and three are estimated using negative binomial regression
(NBR), a more flexible form of Poisson model that treats the dependent
variable as a count. Model (1) contains contemporaneous total citations
along with a three-month distributed lag of citations. No interaction effects
between pflag and the citation variables were included in this baseline model.
Only one of the parameters in this model is statistically significant at the
5 percent level (second lag). A Wald test for the joint significance of the
FDA citation parameters has a p-value of 0.0010, which suggests an overall
statistically significant relationship between these variables and drug shortage rates.

Model (2) adds lags of up to six months to the model. In this model,
several of the individual coefficients on the FDA citation counts are statistically significant beyond the 5 percent level. The Wald test for their joint
significance has a p-value less than 0.0001, which again suggests an overall

Table 10.3   **Regression results—FDA citations**

	(1) OLS (total)	(2) OLS (total)	(3) OLS (US)	(4) NBR (total)	(5) NBR (total)	(6) NBR (US)
Main Pflag	0.889	0.833	0.833	0.133	0.122	0.117
	(0.148)	(0.176)	(0.175)	(0.146)	(0.167)	(0.180)
Cites	0.0440	0.0409	0.0474	0.00659	0.00630	0.00726
	(0.147)	(0.205)	(0.152)	(0.146)	(0.169)	(0.119)
l_1_cites	0.00351	−0.00335	0.00102	0.000992	0.000269	0.000980
	(0.897)	(0.910)	(0.973)	(0.798)	(0.948)	(0.822)
l_2_cites	0.0751	0.0628	0.0617	0.0107	0.00866	0.00860
	(0.007)	(0.032)	(0.052)	(0.005)	(0.023)	(0.038)
l_3_cites	−0.0192	−0.0548	−0.0503	−0.00285	−0.00858	−0.00801
	(0.499)	(0.065)	(0.100)	(0.534)	(0.055)	(0.079)
l_4_cites		0.00695	0.00264		0.000761	0.000145
		(0.818)	(0.931)		(0.851)	(0.972)
l_5_cites		0.0261	0.0364		0.00467	0.00627
		(0.344)	(0.205)		(0.179)	(0.082)
l_6_cites		0.0613	0.0642		0.00921	0.00967
		(0.048)	(0.042)		(0.023)	(0.018)
_Cons	1.775	0.459	−0.294	1.145	0.927	0.808
	(0.122)	(0.681)	(0.810)	(0.000)	(0.000)	(0.000)
lnalpha				−1.738	−1.913	−1.931
				(0.000)	(0.000)	(0.000)
N	162	156	156	162	156	156
R^2	0.110	0.158	0.162			
R^2 adj.	0.082	0.112	0.116			
Wald (cites)	4.89	5.19	5.18	20.45*	41.13*	41.26*
	(0.0010)	(0.0000)	(0.0000)	(0.0004)	(0.0000)	(0.0000)
Wald (added lags)		3.54	4.15		12.11*	14.16*
		(0.0162)	(0.0074)		(0.0070)	(0.0027)

Note: The p-values are in parentheses.
* Denotes chi-square statistic.

statistically significant relationship between overall FDA inspections with citations and shortages. The Wald test for the joint significance of the added lag terms has a p-value of 0.0162, and there is a notable increase in the adjusted R^2 when these lags are added.

Noting the discrepancies between citations and inspections with actions indicated in the Ex-US data, model (3) uses only citations at US-based facilities on the right-hand side. The results of this regression are broadly similar to model (2).

Models (4)–(6) examine the same relationships using NBR estimation as an alternative to OLS. These results follow a very similar qualitative pattern compared to the OLS models, both in terms of the overall significance of the parameters associated with lagged citations, as well as the pattern of significance of some of the individual coefficients.

First-order residual autocorrelation for both the OLS and NBR models is relatively low for the nonparenteral data (0.22 or less), but is somewhat higher (up to 0.55) for the parenteral data. An alternative model including interaction effects between pflag and the citation variables was run to check whether these differences in autocorrelation were driven by the estimation of a common lag structure for both parenteral and nonparenteral citations. For these interacted models (not reported in the table), the common effects remain jointly significant at the 5 percent level for the OLS model and less than 1 percent for the NBR model. The interaction effects are jointly insignificant in both cases—suggesting both a common lag pattern and that other factors may be contributing to the higher autocorrelation in the parenteral residuals.

Table 10.4 reports the results of six additional models of drug shortage based on the shorter inspection data series. As with the citation data, model (1) is estimated via OLS and contains contemporaneous total inspections (insp.) and a three-month distributed lag of total inspections. In this case, only one of the individual coefficients on total inspections is significant at the 5 percent level (second lag). A Wald test for the joint significance of the FDA inspection parameters has a p-value of 0.0115, which suggests the presence of an overall statistically significant relationship between lagged inspection rates and drug shortage rates. Model (2) adds lags of up to six months to the model. In this model, none of the individual coefficients on the FDA inspection counts is statistically significant, and the Wald test for joint significance of the inspections is also insignificant. The Wald test for the added lags shows their parameters to be jointly insignificant. The results of model (3) (US inspection rates) are broadly similar. The NBR models (4)–(6) follow a similar qualitative pattern, but with stronger p-values attached to the tests of the joint significance for the lagged inspection variables.

Residual autocorrelations in these data are generally smaller than in the models with citations as regressors. As with the models of citations, additional models using interaction effects to allow more flexibility were also fitted. In both cases (OLS and NBR), the added interactions were jointly insignificant.

10.4   Discussion

The key insight introduced at the beginning of this chapter is that generic drug shortages are not a phenomenon isolated to parenteral drugs. Indeed, the overall similarity between the time pattern of shortages in parenteral and nonparenteral drugs is striking, and indicates that some of the causes are likely shared. Three possibilities are offered as potentially cross-cutting explanations: market structure, regulatory activity, and pricing. One of these, regulatory activity, is explored empirically.

Table 10.4   **Regression results—FDA inspections**

	(1) OLS (total)	(2) OLS (total)	(3) OLS (US)	(4) NBR (total)	(5) NBR (total)	(6) NBR (US)
Main Pflag	0.704	0.686	0.686	0.0798	0.0780	0.0653
	(0.345)	(0.387)	(0.369)	(0.371)	(0.396)	(0.458)
Insp	0.0145	0.0103	0.0305	0.00183	0.00131	0.00349
	(0.299)	(0.504)	(0.151)	(0.274)	(0.471)	(0.155)
l_1_insp	0.0107	0.00835	0.00701	0.00145	0.00106	0.000913
	(0.408)	(0.589)	(0.739)	(0.343)	(0.540)	(0.696)
l_2_insp	0.0253	0.0268	0.0380	0.00302	0.00301	0.00441
	(0.045)	(0.124)	(0.102)	(0.028)	(0.094)	(0.082)
l_3_insp	−0.0124	−0.0163	−0.0148	−0.00137	−0.00194	−0.00164
	(0.374)	(0.339)	(0.496)	(0.440)	(0.361)	(0.509)
l_4_insp		0.00447	0.0106		0.000754	0.00149
		(0.785)	(0.674)		(0.676)	(0.595)
l_5_insp		−0.00109	−0.00349		0.0000844	−0.000138
		(0.942)	(0.865)		(0.961)	(0.951)
l_6_insp		0.0113	0.00716		0.00131	0.000760
		(0.414)	(0.714)		(0.402)	(0.715)
_cons	2.112	1.290	−0.388	1.313	1.219	1.034
	(0.203)	(0.565)	(0.854)	(0.000)	(0.000)	(0.000)
lnalpha						
_cons				−2.521	−2.482	−2.689
				(0.000)	(0.000)	(0.000)
N	108	102	102	108	102	102
R^2	0.097	0.089	0.155			
R^2 adj.	0.0533	0.010	0.082			
Wald (insp.)	3.42	1.60	2.33	14.94*	11.82*	18.81*
	(0.0115)	(0.1446)	(0.0312)	(0.0048)	(0.1066)	(0.0088)
Wald (added lags)		0.37	0.18		1.39*	0.82*
		(0.7742)	(0.9072)		(0.7085)	(0.8459)

Note: The *p*-values are in parentheses.

* Denotes chi-square statistic.

The regression models presented in this chapter identified a consistent and statistically significant predictive relationship between FDA regulatory activity in the drug market (i.e., drug-quality inspections and citations) and the incidence of new drug shortages. The models tested indicate that the pattern of this relationship is generally shared across both parenteral and nonparenteral drugs. This result suggests that changes in regulatory activity may be one of the cross-cutting factors contributing to the ongoing wave of drug shortages.

It is important not to overinterpret this result, however. The OLS models, for example, exhibit relatively modest R^2 statistics. This indicates that, although these models are predictive, a substantial amount of variation in new shortage starts remains unexplained by this single factor. This should not come as a surprise given the discussion on other likely factors contributing to drug shortages; regulatory activity is only one of those factors. And, because other factors that may be important are not accounted for in these models, caution is advisable when interpreting the results presented here (particularly with respect to individual coefficient estimates).

It is also important to recognize the economic and regulatory context of this result. Apparent changes in FDA oversight activity may signal attempts to reestablish quality thresholds that may have eroded or that have been applied unevenly as the industry has evolved. The program goals of the GDUFA are potentially an example of this. Supply interruptions resulting from this activity can be viewed as a necessary step on the road to a different equilibrium. As discussed, once oversight reaches a consistent and anticipated level within the industry, a new equilibrium level of quality can be established and shortages should resolve given adequate price responsiveness. In other words, if shortages are caused by changes in regulatory oversight relative to expectations, then they should be transitory in nature—smoothing out once all participating manufacturers adjust accordingly.

Pricing and market structure are important factors to consider in future empirical work. For example, public controversy has recently arisen over a pattern of spikes in retail (i.e., nonparenteral) generic drug prices.[39] These reports may be connected with disruptions that may or may not lead to outright shortages, and appear to point toward an interesting avenue of research. Although a recent GAO study finds that the number of generic drug shortages was in decline by 2013 (GAO 2014), it is clear from the number of ongoing shortages that fragility in the supply of generic drugs remains a potential concern in the United States.

References

American Society of Health-System Pharmacists (ASHP). 2002. "Provisional Observations on Drug Product Shortages: Effects, Causes, and Potential Solutions." *American Journal of Health-System Pharmacy* 59 (22): 2173–82.
———. 2014. "Frequently Asked Questions." American Society of Health-System Pharmacists Website. http://www.ashp.org/menu/drugshortages/faqs.html. Accessed May 2014.
Bhat, Shubha, Russel Roberts, and John W. Devlin. 2012. "Posted versus Actual Drug Shortages." *American Journal of Health-System Pharmacy* 69 (16): 1363–64.
Conti, Rena M., and Ernst R. Berndt. 2013. "Anatomy of US Cancer Drug Shortages: Technology, Market Structure and Price Competition." Working Paper.

39. See, for example, Adam Fein's November 2013 blog entry (Fein 2013).

Dorfman, Robert, and Peter O. Steiner. 1954. "Optimal Advertising and Optimal Quality." *American Economic Review* 44 (5): 826–36.

Fein, Adam J. 2013. "Retail Generic Drug Costs Go Up, Up, and Away." Drug Channels. http://www.drugchannels.net/2013/11/retail-generic-drug-costs-go-up -up-and.html.

Fox, Erin R. 2011. "Drug Shortage Update Current Status and Significant Trends." US Food and Drug Administration. http://www.fda.gov/downloads/Drugs/ NewsEvents/UCM274565.pdf.

Fox, Erin R., Annette Birt, Ken B. James, Heather Kokko, Sandra Salverson, and Donna L. Soflin. 2009. "ASHP Guidelines on Managing Drug Product Shortages in Hospitals and Health Systems." *American Journal of Health-System Pharmacy* 66 (15): 1399–406.

Graham, John R. 2012. "The Shortage of Generic Sterile Injectable Drugs: Diagnosis and Solutions." Mackinac Center Policy Brief, Mackinac Center for Public Policy. http://www.mackinaw.org/archives/2012/s2012-04SterileInjectables.pdf.

Haninger, K., A. Jessup, and M. A. Koehler. 2011. "Economic Analysis of the Causes of Drug Shortages." ASPE Issue Brief, US Department of Health and Human Services, Office of the Assistant Secretary for Planning. https://aspe.hhs .gov/pdf-report/economic-analysis-causes-drug-shortages.

Staff Report. 2012. "FDA's Contribution to the Drug Shortage Crisis." US House of Representatives 112th Congress Committee on Oversight and Government Reform. https://oversight.house.gov/wp-content/uploads/2012/06/6-15-2012-Report -FDAs-Contribution-to-the-Drug-Shortage-Crisis.pdf.

US Government Accountability Office (GAO). 2011. "Drug Shortages—FDA's Ability to Respond Should be Strengthened (GAO-12-116)." United States Government Accountability Office.

———. 2014. "Drug Shortages—Public Health Threat Continues, Despite Efforts to Help Ensure Product Availability (GAO-14-194)." United States Government Accountability Office.

Woodcock, Janet, and Marta Wosinska. 2013. "Economic and Technological Drivers of Generic Sterile Injectable Drug Shortages." *Clinical Pharmacology & Therapeutics* 93 (2): 170–76.

Yurukoglu, Ali, Eli Liebman, and David B. Ridley. 2012. "The Role of Government Reimbursement in Drug Shortages." NBER Working Paper no. 17987, Cambridge, MA.

IV

Issues in Industrial Organization and Market Design

Measuring Physician Practice Competition Using Medicare Data

Laurence C. Baker, M. Kate Bundorf, and Anne Royalty

11.1 Introduction

Questions about the market structure of physician practices have grown increasingly prominent in contemporary health policy discussions. Market forces over the last couple of decades appear to have favored the growth of larger multispecialty groups, and more and more physicians seem to prefer the practice environment of larger groups to solo or smaller group practices, generating growth in the size of practices and horizontal merger activity (Liehaber and Grossman 2007). Growing vertical integration in health care delivery markets, such as through hospital purchase of physician practices (Kocher and Sahni 2011; O'Malley, Bond, and Berenson 2011), may in some cases effectively increase horizontal integration of practices as well as change vertical market dynamics.

These changes could have a number of important effects (Gaynor and Town 2012). Larger practices could lead to improvements in health care quality and outcomes by improving coordination—patients of organizations with a broader scope and more resources may benefit from things like better information systems, care organization activities, and investments in

Laurence C. Baker is professor of health research and policy, chair of the Department of Health Research and Policy, and a CHP/PCOR fellow at Stanford University and a research associate of the National Bureau of Economic Research. M. Kate Bundorf is associate professor of health research and policy at the Stanford University School of Medicine, an associate professor, by courtesy, at the Stanford Graduate School of Business and a Stanford Health Policy Fellow, and a research associate of the National Bureau of Economic Research. Anne Royalty is professor of economics at Indiana University Purdue University Indianapolis (IUPUI) and the director of the PhD program in economics.

For acknowledgments, sources of research support, and disclosure of the authors' material financial relationships, if any, please see http://www.nber.org/chapters/c13120.ack.

better infrastructure (Ketcham, Baker, and MacIsaac 2007). At the same time, larger practices may be more difficult to effectively manage and more challenging for patients to navigate and, if inefficient, could drive higher costs of care. Larger practices may also increase the amount of concentration in health care markets. If practices gain market power, they may drive prices higher and quality lower (Schneider et al. 2008; Berenson and Ginsburg 2010; Ginsburg 2010; Gaynor 2011; Berenson et al. 2012; Dunn and Shapiro 2014). Hospital acquisition of practices may independently affect prices paid for care (Cuellar and Gertler 2006; Gaynor 2011).

Understanding the impact of changes in physician market structure would help interpret changes in utilization and prices for health care services over recent years. It may also be important for developing policies going forward, with efforts to promote the integration of care delivery at the center of prominent policy efforts to grapple with rising costs (Crosson 2009). Antitrust authorities are increasingly faced with choices about the optimal response to changing practice structures, and recent policy positions promote use of the "rule of reason" in which potentially welfare-improving and welfare-decreasing effects of mergers must be assessed and weighed against each other (Federal Trade Commission [FTC] and Department of Justice [DOJ] 1996; Federal Trade Commission 2011).

While concentration has been well studied in the case of hospitals, and to an important though lesser degree, health insurers (Melnick et al. 1992; Pennsylvania Health Care Cost Containment Council 2007; Antwi, Gaynor, and Vogt 2009; Dafny 2009; Wu 2009; Melnick, Shen, and Wu 2011), there is less evidence about impacts of structural changes in physician markets. One of the primary reasons is a lack of broadly based data on practice market structure that is regularly collected. Some emerging efforts have used data on large samples of physicians to create measures of practice size and organization. Dunn and Shapiro used data that characterized the location and group affiliations of a large number of physicians to construct Herfindahl-Hirschman Indexes (HHIs) for cardiology and orthopedics practices for 2005–2008 (Dunn and Shapiro 2014). Their application creatively uses the physician data, with the drawback that it lacks information about the location of patients from which to identify the market areas of practices. McWilliams and colleagues have developed measures of physician practice structures that mimic Accountable Care Organizations (ACOs) based on American Medical Association (AMA) group practice data (McWilliams et al. 2013). Welch and colleagues have tracked the size of practices using data from the Centers for Medicare and Medicaid Services (CMS) (Welch et al. 2013).

In this chapter, we explore the creation of physician practice concentration measures using Medicare claims data. Medicare claims are available for large numbers of patients over time, and can be used to identify an important dimension of physician practices. We use claims data to construct measures of practice size and HHIs for physician practices over the period 1998–2010, and explore variations in measures of size and concentration. We explore a number of issues that arise in the construction of claims-based measures that may affect their validity and interpretation.

11.2   Some Conceptual Issues in Practice Definition

Physician practices can be organized in a number of different ways. An individual physician may organize his or her business as a solo practice. Others may work in partnership arrangements or as part of a larger organization commonly called a medical group. Medical groups may have single or multiple sites. In some cases, individual physicians or groups are further integrated into larger structures. Hospitals or health systems, for example, may own physician groups or directly hire physicians. These types of arrangements involve very different sizes of organizations, but they all tend to increase the degree of integration among providers. Physicians working in all of these arrangements are typically part of a financially integrated organization that operates as a single unified business. These organizations may be clinically integrated as well, though there is no guarantee that financial and clinical integration will always be linked.

There are also more loosely integrated organizations. In some cases, physicians with practices organized as separate businesses may agree to jointly acquire office space or practice resources with other doctors, sometimes creating links between multiple doctors who each retain a separate underlying practice. Another example is independent practice associations (IPAs), in which individual physicians or groups retain their independent status but agree to work together for some business purposes.

The types of organizations of primary interest for tracking trends and measuring concentration may depend on the issues being considered. For example, physicians in the same medical group, physicians whose practices are owned by the same hospital, and physicians whose practices are owned by the same system, are generally allowed by law to negotiate jointly over payment and other contract terms with health plans (Casalino 2006). However, under current antitrust law, physicians in separate practices with looser linkages (e.g., practices that are members of IPAs) may only bargain together for risk contracts involving capitation or other withholds that put the bargaining group (e.g., the IPA) at risk for aspects of performance (Federal Trade Commission and Department of Justice 1996; Casalino 2006).[1] Thus,

---

1. There is some ambiguity in the law. Antitrust law does allow physicians in IPAs to negotiate jointly for nonrisk contracts if they can show that they are sufficiently clinically integrated across their member practices, though IPAs using the clinical integration enforcement safety zone to jointly negotiate nonrisk contracts appear to be uncommon (see Federal Trade Commission 2011). Another source of uncertainty comes from the legality of the so-called messenger model of physician organizations and negotiations (Casalino 2006). This model is

for studies involving prices in nonrisk contracts, it may be more appropriate to focus on financially integrated organizations, while for studies involving risk contract prices, entities such as IPAs would also be relevant.

In addition, for studies focusing on quality of care or other aspects of treatment patterns, a physician's complete set of affiliations may be important, regardless of the organizational structure, while for others (e.g., studies involving the adoption of infrastructure), measures of practice organization that capture more formal organizations may be relevant (Federal Trade Commission 2011; Casalino 2006; Pelnar 2010).

We focus here on measures relevant to financially integrated organizations, which are particularly relevant to studies of fee-for-service prices. Since these organizations constitute a large and important subset of all physician organizations, they may also be more generally useful for studies of effects on quality of care and other outcomes.

11.3   Medicare Claims Data

We use data from the 1998 to 2010 Medicare carrier claims files that include bills for services provided by physicians to a 20 percent sample of traditional (fee-for-service) Medicare enrollees, and corresponding denominator files that record information about enrolled beneficiaries. These contain, among other things, the reported ZIP Code of the patient's residence, the reported ZIP Code of the physician practice, the physician specialty, the Healthcare Common Procedure Coding System (HCPCS) code of the service provided, a physician identifier (UPIN and/or NPI), and the tax identification number (TIN) of the practice.

From these files, we selected claims with positive Medicare-allowed charges, a TIN and provider NPI or UPIN with the correct format, and valid provider and patient ZIP Codes. We restricted attention to claims where the recorded provider specialty code indicated a physician in a named specialty, and we grouped physicians according to specialty for many of the analyses. We excluded claims from pediatrics and obstetrics/gynecology, which may not be well represented in Medicare claims; pain management, which was not defined as a separate specialty in all of the years we study; and preventive medicine, hand surgery, peripheral vascular disease, addiction medicine, and osteopathic manipulative therapy, which had too few claims to effectively analyze.

---

intended to allow a noninterested third party to collect and convey information from multiple physician practices to payers for the purpose of facilitating contracting, though not to engage in joint negotiations. Some have argued that some messenger model arrangements, in fact, have facilitated unlawful joint contracting. The DOJ and FTC have challenged what they believe to have been abuses of the messenger model, which may limit the degree to which this is an issue, but this remains a debated area and the actual extent of the practice is uncertain.

This left us with thirty-four specialty groupings.[2] The Medicare claims allow the specialty designation "multispecialty group." In the early years of our sample, 4–6 percent of claims used this designation, but its use declined substantially over time. After 2003, 0.5 percent of claims or fewer used this code. In the most recent years of data, the code is present on less than 0.1 percent of claims. Because many of the analyses are at the specialty level, we exclude claims with this specialty designation. In total, we analyze about 150 million claims per year from the early years of the sample, rising to about 215 million claims per year in the later years.

Some of our analyses use Medicare-allowed charges as the unit of output. This is the fee-schedule-based amount that Medicare rules allow the physician to be paid for the service. The doctor may receive some of this amount from the patient by way of applicable copayments. Other analyses use work relative value units (RVUs). We obtained these data from the annual Medicare Fee Schedule files, and attached them to the claims based on reported HCPCS and modifier codes.

11.3.1 Identifying Practices

We identify physician practices using the reported TIN. Solo practice physicians normally have a unique TIN. Financially integrated entities commonly use a single TIN for the physicians in their organization. Physicians in medical group practices, perhaps the most common and most integrated form of practice organization, appear to frequently use the same TIN. Physicians in hospitals or health systems that own practices or employ physicians also appear to commonly use the same TIN, though with some exceptions. Identifying practices using TINs thus provides a means of obtaining useful information about physician organizations. Some previous studies have used tax IDs to identify physician practices as well (Pope et al. 2002; Pham et al. 2007; Welch et al. 2013).

There is some ambiguity in the precise types of organizations that will be identified. For example, a physician group that is purchased by a hospital but retains its structure as a medical group may continue to use a group TIN or could switch to the hospital TIN. Some very large medical groups have organized themselves with subsidiaries that have their own TINs. The TINs should thus be regarded as a measure of physician organizations subject to some noise. It appears likely that to the extent there is bias, this approach would tend to understate the size of organizations and thus underestimate

---

2. The specialties are internal medicine, family practice, allergy/immunology, cardiology, critical care, dermatology, endocrinology, gastroenterology, geriatrics, hematology, infectious disease, nephrology, neurology, oncology, pulmonary disease, radiation oncology, rheumatology, cardiac surgery, colorectal surgery, general surgery, neurosurgery, ophthalmology, orthopedics, otolaryngology, plastic/maxillofacial surgery, thoracic surgery, urology, vascular surgery, anesthesiology, emergency medicine, pathology, physical medicine/rehabilitation, psychiatry, and radiology.

the concentration of physician practices (McWilliams et al. 2013; Welch et al. 2013). We present evidence below suggesting that this may have only a small effect on overall estimates of competition in physician markets. Looser forms of organizations with little financial integration across practices, such as independent practice associations (IPAs), do not use unified TINs.

One source of information about the types of organizations identified by tax IDs in the claims data is publicly available data from IRS Form 990. A 990 must be filed annually by most tax-exempt organizations in the United States, and the 990s report the name, business type, and TIN of reporting organizations. Many health care organizations file 990s. Though this is only a subset of relevant health care organizations—most small and medium and even many large physician practices, as well as some hospitals, are structured as for-profit businesses—the 990 data provide some useful insights. We find more than 1,800 hospitals among the practice entities identified by TINs in the claims, consistent with the view that a TIN-based measure will capture cases where hospitals are serving as a vehicle for physician practice consolidation. We also find nearly 400 large nonprofit physician groups among the practices we identify. Among the large organizations that we identify in both the 990 and the claims data are many large and well-known health care systems and physicians, including, among many others, the Cleveland Clinic (1,834 physicians in the claims), the Mayo Clinic (2,199 physicians), Partners Healthcare System (558), Henry Ford Health System (1,056), and the Palo Alto Medical Foundation (880). Similar patterns are evident in other years. This suggests that the claims data can identify organizations at the large end of the spectrum, not just the individual physicians or smaller groups that may be owned by larger entities.

11.3.2   Identifying Physicians

In later years of our data, individual physicians can be identified using the National Provider Identifier (NPI) included on every claim. During 2007, the CMS began requiring the inclusion of the NPI of the physician performing the service on physician bills. The NPI fields in the claims data appear reasonably complete beginning in 2008. Prior to this, claims contain the Unique Physician Identification Number (UPIN) of the physician performing the service. Though they should generally identify individual physicians, UPINs are often thought to be less precise than NPIs as a unique physician identifier. Even after the NPI phase-in, Medicare claims continued to report UPINs where they were available.

For analytic purposes, we identify physicians in two ways. Beginning in 2007, we can identify them using NPIs alone. To obtain a longer time series, we developed a UPIN-based measure as follows. We first used UPINs where available. Some claims in later years did not report a UPIN, but did report an NPI. For these, we attempted to link a UPIN based on patterns observed on previous claims and information reported on the National Plan and Provider Enumeration System (NPPES). When a match was found, we used the matched UPIN. If no matching UPIN was found, we identified the physician on the basis of the NPI.

The claims data will include information about practicing physicians who submit bills for patients in the 20 percent sample of fee-for-service Medicare beneficiaries. (This will not typically include residents and fellows, who do not file Medicare claims for their services.) We believe this will include the vast majority of physicians providing services to Medicare patients. We found 566,149 unique NPIs in the 2010 data. This is consistent with other calculations that, though done in a slightly different way, reported the number of physicians appearing in the 2010 100 percent sample of Medicare claims (Welch et al. 2013). As a further way of gaining information about the completeness of the 20 percent sample data, we computed the number of unique NPIs in the 2010 5 percent sample of Medicare claims. We found 532,375 unique NPIs, 94 percent of the 566,139 in the 20 percent sample. Because nearly all of the physicians identified in the 20 percent sample are also identified with only the 5 percent sample, we take it as unlikely that there would be a large number of additional physicians providing services to Medicare patients but not found in the 20 percent sample.

The set of physicians providing services to Medicare patients is likely to be a large subset of all physicians in the United States, though it will not contain all physicians. Based on results from the National Ambulatory Medical Care Survey, MedPAC recently reported that more than 90 percent of US physicians report that they accept new Medicare patients (Medicare Payment Advisory Commission [MedPAC] 2012). Some physicians in pediatrics and obstetrics/gynecology may not frequently see Medicare patients. Physicians who primarily serve managed care patients would not be expected to frequently appear in fee-for-service claims data. Other physicians may also have practices focused on non-Medicare patients. To get a better sense for the share of physicians represented in the claims data, we used data from NPPES to identify nonstudent physicians active in 2010, in specialties that we include in the analysis. We found 667,265 total NPIs. Our 2010 claims data identified 566,139, 85 percent of the NPPES total. This seems promising, particularly given that the NPPES may overstate the number of active physicians by retaining NPIs for a time after physicians retire, and including some physicians who are not actively practicing. The number of physicians we find is much lower than numbers derived from the AMA Physician Masterfile, though the Masterfile may substantially overstate the number of active physicians (Staiger, Auerbach, and Buerhaus 2009).

As described below, we also compare the claims data to data from SK&A, which provides another source of information consistent with the view that the claims data represent a large fraction of US physicians.

Table 11.1   Physicians per practice

	Physician ID based on UPIN			Physician ID based on NPI		
	N practices	N physicians	Mean physicians per practice	N practices	N physicians	Mean physicians per practice
1998	220,341	587,165	2.66	—	—	—
1999	211,718	581,741	2.75	—	—	—
2000	205,488	570,625	2.78	—	—	—
2001	205,179	570,667	2.78	—	—	—
2002	200,879	593,588	2.95	—	—	—
2003	204,013	605,982	2.97	—	—	—
2004	203,744	618,440	3.04	—	—	—
2005	206,139	635,734	3.08	—	—	—
2006	189,895	624,244	3.29	—	—	—
2007	184,990	634,549	3.43	171,483	601,330	3.51
2008	180,865	645,311	3.57	180,338	641,777	3.56
2009	170,683	646,879	3.79	170,682	644,901	3.78
2010	167,950	665,025	3.96	167,948	662,740	3.95

Note: Practices are defined across all specialties.

11.4   Trends in the Number and Size of Practices

For each observed practice (TIN), we counted the number of physicians billing within the practice each year. In these calculations, an individual physician can appear more than once if he or she bills with more than one practice within a year.[3] The size of practices has been increasing over time. We first computed the mean number of physicians per practice using UPINs and using NPIs (table 11.1). We observe 220,341 unique TINs in 1998, with a mean of 2.66 UPINs per practice. The number of practices declined over time to 167,950 unique TINs in 2010, and average size increased to 3.96 physicians per practice. The decline in number of practices is particularly concentrated in the 2005–2010 period. Over 2008 to 2010, estimates of the number of practices and physicians using NPIs are quite similar to the number we obtain using our approach that relies on UPINs, from which we derive some confidence that trends based on UPINs are useful to examine.

The distribution of physicians across organizations of different sizes is presented in table 11.2. The number of solo practices declined by more than 50,000 between 1998 and 2010, falling from 77 percent of practices to

3. The majority of physicians bill within one or two TINs in any given year. In 2010, for example, 80 percent of physicians billed all of their claims in a single TIN, and 96 percent billed in one or two TINs.

Table 11.2 **Distribution of practices[a] and physicians by size**

	Number of physicians per practice									
	1		2–9		10–49		50–99		≥ 100	
	N	(%)	*N*	(%)	*N*	(%)	*N*	(%)	*N*	(%)
	Practices									
1998	169,433	77	42,059	19	7,955	4	571	0.3	323	0.1
1999	161,062	76	41,753	20	7,997	4	584	0.3	322	0.2
2000	155,201	76	41,597	20	7,794	4	565	0.3	331	0.2
2001	154,533	75	41,937	20	7,811	4	565	0.3	333	0.2
2002	149,658	75	42,115	21	8,098	4	631	0.3	377	0.2
2003	151,667	74	43,062	21	8,223	4	675	0.3	386	0.2
2004	150,805	74	43,388	21	8,441	4	714	0.4	396	0.2
2005	152,855	74	43,450	21	8,642	4	744	0.4	448	0.2
2006	137,496	72	42,430	22	8,754	5	756	0.4	459	0.2
2007	132,314	72	42,450	23	8,969	5	776	0.4	482	0.3
2008	129,545	72	40,981	23	8,994	5	823	0.5	522	0.3
2009	120,334	71	39,893	23	9,046	5	852	0.5	558	0.3
2010	117,767	70	39,475	24	9,177	5	922	0.5	609	0.4
	Physicians									
1998	169,433	29	153,231	26	148,823	25	38,139	6	77,539	13
1999	161,062	28	151,882	26	149,851	26	39,051	7	79,895	14
2000	155,201	27	151,251	27	145,548	26	37,516	7	81,109	14
2001	154,533	27	151,917	27	146,421	26	37,977	7	79,819	14
2002	149,658	25	153,366	26	153,349	26	42,330	7	94,885	16
2003	151,667	25	155,917	26	154,341	25	45,220	7	98,837	16
2004	150,805	24	157,392	25	159,294	26	48,137	8	102,812	17
2005	152,855	24	158,267	25	163,143	26	50,115	8	111,354	18
2006	137,496	22	154,409	25	165,241	26	50,990	8	116,108	19
2007	132,314	21	153,855	24	170,203	27	53,030	8	125,149	20
2008	129,545	20	149,990	23	172,784	27	55,697	9	137,298	21
2009	120,334	19	146,278	23	174,642	27	58,081	9	147,544	23
2010	117,767	18	145,226	22	177,156	27	62,730	9	162,146	24

[a] Practices in this table are defined across all specialties.

70 percent. The number of practices of ten or more physicians rose. In the lower panel of table 11.2, the share of physicians in solo practice fell from 29 to 18 percent by 2010, and the share in practices of 100 or more doctors increased from 13 to 24 percent.

Much of this shift toward larger practices is driven by physicians entering and exiting practice. To explore this, we classified physicians as new entrants if they were first observed in the claims data after 1998 and still observed in 2010. We classified physicians as exiting practice if they were first observed in 1998 and last observed before 2010. Among 275,750 physicians in the entrant group, in the year in which they were first observed, about 10 percent were in a solo practice and nearly 40 percent were in practices of fifty or more. In contrast, among 139,899 exiting physicians, 33 percent were in a solo practice in the last year they were observed, compared to 21 percent in a practice of fifty or more. There was also a transition toward larger practices among physicians who neither entered nor left during our study period. In this group, the share in solo practice fell from 27 percent to 23 percent, while the share in practices of over fifty rose from 20 percent to 27 percent.

We also characterize practices on a specialty-by-specialty basis. This approach is of particular note for development of competition measures, where relevant product markets are frequently specialty specific. To compute specialty-specific practice sizes, we separated the claims by specialty of the physician, and computed the number of practices (TINs) and physicians (UPINs or NPIs) separately within each specialty. In these calculations, the same practice will appear in more than one specialty if it contains physicians in multiple specialties. Physicians can also be included multiple times if they appear in multiple specialties or multiple practices. As in the case of the aggregated measures, the number of practices calculated by specialty decreased over time, with the decrease concentrated after 2005 (table 11.3). The share of practices that were small and the share of physicians in small practices declined over time. Larger practices became more prominent. Trends in the number of practices varied across specialties. Table 11.4 shows changes in the number of practices by specialty between 2000, 2005, and 2010. A common pattern in medical subspecialties was an increase in the number of practices before 2005 and declines after. A number of surgical specialties saw smaller declines in the number of practices in the same time period, and faster declines after 2005. Figure 11.1 plots the mean number of physicians per practice for a number of individual specialties (selected to represent a range of types of medicine and sizes of practices).

By other metrics, practices were also increasing in size. For specialty-specific practices, table 11.5 reports the number of claims per practice, work RVUs per practice, and Medicare-allowed charges per practice, all of which increased markedly over time. Some of this can be attributed to changes in the number of physicians and to the amount of activity per physician, which were both increasing. Consistent with reports of changing patterns of billing, the mean work RVUs per physician across practices increased markedly over the study period.

In addition to increases in practice size, the share of practices with multiple specialties increased over time (table 11.6). The number of practices with a single specialty fell by over 50,000, while the number with three or more specialties increased. The share of physicians in multispecialty practices grew from less than half to more than 60 percent. (The number of physicians in this analysis differs from the number in table 11.3 because physicians are counted one time per specialty per practice here.)

Table 11.3   **Practices by physician-size category, practices defined separately by specialty**

	N practices	Number of physicians per practice				
		1 (%)	2–9 (%)	10–49 (%)	50–99 (%)	≥ 100 (%)
		Practices				
1998	271,804	74	22	3	0.1	0.03
1999	261,964	74	23	3	0.1	0.03
2000	253,590	73	23	4	0.2	0.03
2001	253,027	73	23	4	0.2	0.03
2002	249,540	72	24	4	0.2	0.04
2003	256,544	72	24	4	0.2	0.04
2004	257,578	72	24	4	0.2	0.05
2005	260,278	72	24	4	0.2	0.05
2006	243,292	70	25	4	0.2	0.06
2007	239,252	69	26	5	0.2	0.07
2008	236,226	69	26	5	0.3	0.08
2009	226,871	68	26	5	0.3	0.09
2010	227,179	68	27	5	0.3	0.10
		Physicians				
1998	614,710	33	35	26	4.1	1.96
1999	605,023	32	35	26	4.2	2.21
2000	592,873	31	35	27	4.3	2.14
2001	592,605	31	36	27	4.3	2.04
2002	608,661	30	35	28	4.9	2.49
2003	625,209	30	35	28	4.9	2.57
2004	638,354	29	35	28	5.2	2.74
2005	653,215	29	34	29	5.6	2.85
2006	639,751	27	34	30	5.7	3.19
2007	650,532	26	34	31	6.2	3.58
2008	662,245	25	33	32	6.5	4.29
2009	662,161	23	33	32	7.2	4.60
2010	684,301	22	32	33	7.8	5.08

Note: Physicians or practices may appear more than one time in different specialties.

11.5   Concentration Measures

To study concentration, we computed Herfindahl-Hirschman Indexes (HHIs) for physician practices. For our purposes here, we take product markets to include all services produced by physicians in one of the specialties studied in the chapter. The extent to which relevant product markets would vary within specialty, either for subgroups of services or for subgroups of patients served, is of some interest. As a practical matter, we found it difficult to compute HHIs that distinguished subgroups of patients and services for the broad range of specialties included here. Questions about more finely defined HHIs would need to be addressed in more focused analyses. It may

Table 11.4   Changes in number of specialty-specific practices, by specialty, 2000–2010

	2000	2005	2010	Percent change 2000–2005	Percent change 2005–2010
Internal medicine	45,848	48,400	41,480	5.6	−14.3
Family practice	44,789	46,529	40,341	3.9	−13.3
Allergy/immunology	2,277	2,346	2,275	3.0	−3.0
Cardiology	10,540	10,551	9,386	0.1	−11.0
Critical care	549	920	1,174	67.6	27.6
Dermatology	6,562	6,812	6,302	3.8	−7.5
Endocrinology	1,992	2,420	2,691	21.5	11.2
Gastroenterology	5,563	5,898	5,312	6.0	−9.9
Geriatrics	728	1,003	1,245	37.8	24.1
Hematology	395	518	511	31.1	−1.4
Infectious disease	1,775	2,195	2,355	23.7	7.3
Nephrology	2,440	3,034	3,094	24.3	2.0
Neurology	6,376	6,959	6,556	9.1	−5.8
Oncology	3,391	3,970	3,590	17.1	−9.6
Pulmonary disease	4,568	5,070	4,690	11.0	−7.5
Radiation oncology	2,052	2,261	2,187	10.2	−3.3
Rheumatology	2,052	2,394	2,456	16.7	2.6
Cardiac surgery	789	1,134	1,149	43.7	1.3
Colorectal surgery	591	678	773	14.7	14.0
General surgery	15,420	13,914	11,134	−9.8	−20.0
Neurosurgery	2,301	2,308	2,074	0.3	−10.1
Ophthalmology	11,039	10,588	9,255	−4.1	−12.6
Orthopedics	10,425	10,368	8,682	−0.5	−16.3
Otolaryngology	5,666	5,394	4,630	−4.8	−14.2
Plastic/maxillofacial surgery	4,891	4,815	4,601	−1.6	−4.4
Thoracic surgery	1,862	1,640	1,463	−11.9	−10.8
Urology	5,450	5,214	4,109	−4.3	−21.2
Vascular surgery	1,443	1,683	1,819	16.6	8.1
Anesthesiology	9,285	8,883	7,406	−4.3	−16.6
Emergency med	10,448	10,433	7,092	−0.1	−32.0
Pathology	3,264	3,070	2,760	−5.9	−10.1
Physical medicine/rehab	4,142	4,827	5,139	16.5	6.5
Psychiatry	16,747	16,180	13,680	−3.4	−15.5
Radiology	7,930	7,869	5,768	−0.8	−26.7

also be worth noting that in some cases the relevant product market may span specialties that are distinguished here. For example, physicians in internal medicine and family medicine may be competitors for some primary care services.

The HHIs also require defining geographic markets. We derive geographic markets for each practice empirically, based on observed patient flows in the claims data. We compute HHIs using Medicare-allowed charges as the unit of service, following the guidance issued by the DOJ and FTC for evaluation

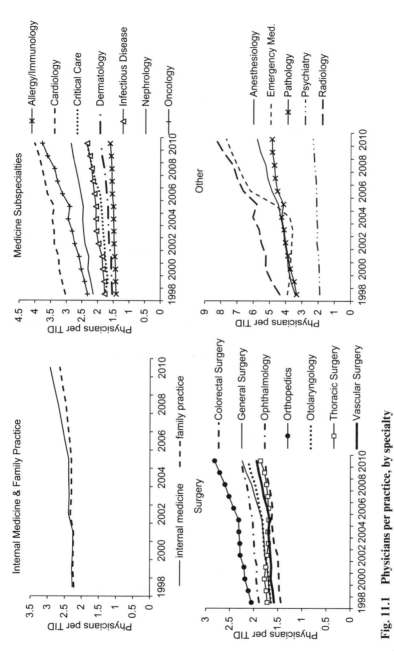

Fig. 11.1 Physicians per practice, by specialty

Table 11.5   **Measures of specialty-specific practice size**

	N practices	Claims/ practice	Work RVUs/ practice	Allowed charges/ practice	Physicians per practice	Claims/ physician	Work RVUs/ physician
1998	271,804	497	419	29,929	2.26	234	209
1999	261,964	527	444	32,717	2.31	244	218
2000	253,590	555	470	37,002	2.34	253	227
2001	253,027	581	494	41,007	2.34	262	237
2002	249,540	630	545	43,889	2.44	285	260
2003	256,544	693	599	50,190	2.44	302	276
2004	257,578	720	633	55,375	2.48	309	288
2005	260,278	749	649	57,522	2.51	318	289
2006	243,292	802	698	62,478	2.63	335	305
2007	239,252	803	798	63,313	2.72	328	343
2008	236,226	814	823	64,897	2.80	328	348
2009	226,871	840	868	69,889	2.92	334	361
2010	227,179	839	888	72,717	3.01	327	360

of market power when considering Accountable Care Organizations (Federal Trade Commission 2011). Other units of service, including individual claims and work RVUs, are also possible. Varying the choice of service unit will weight services in different ways, particularly in specialties that provide services of varying intensities, and could influence the HHIs, though we show below that the choice of service unit generally has a small impact on the final results.

Our analytic approach adapts the approach of Kessler and McClellan to the case of hospitals (Kessler and McClellan 2000). We derive HHIs for (specialty-specific) practices in two steps. We begin by constructing an HHI for each ZIP Code, by specialty, by year. Denote by $service_{i,j}$ the number of service units provided by physicians in practice i to patients who reside in ZIP Code j. Denoting the total number of service units provided to patients in ZIP j as $service_j$, the market share of practice i for ZIP j is $share_{i,j} = service_{i,j} / service_j$. The ZIP Code HHI is then the sum of squared market shares:

$$\text{ZIPHHI}_j = \sum_{\substack{\text{practices } i \\ \text{serving ZIP } j}} \text{share}_{i,j}^2.$$

This construction allows flexibility in the market size, basing the HHI on the set of practices actually providing services to patients in a given ZIP Code. We exclude from this calculation claims where the physician is more than 100 miles from the patient ZIP, to reduce the potential for bias from cases where a patient, perhaps while traveling, sees a distant physician who does not play a substantial role in competition for patients in the ZIP Code. (Distances were determined based on the centroid of the patient and provider ZIP Codes,

Table 11.6　　　　　　**Practices by number of specialties**

	N	One specialty		Two specialties		Three or more specialties	
		N	(%)	*N*	(%)	*N*	(%)
				Practices			
1998	220,341	195,726	88.8	16,893	7.7	7,722	3.5
1999	211,718	187,672	88.6	16,519	7.8	7,527	3.6
2000	205,488	182,159	88.6	16,208	7.9	7,121	3.5
2001	205,179	182,079	88.7	16,008	7.8	7,092	3.5
2002	200,879	179,011	89.1	14,415	7.2	7,453	3.7
2003	204,013	179,267	87.9	16,856	8.3	7,890	3.9
2004	203,744	178,498	87.6	17,133	8.4	8,113	4.0
2005	206,139	181,316	88.0	16,485	8.0	8,338	4.0
2006	189,895	165,935	87.4	15,754	8.3	8,206	4.3
2007	184,991	161,112	87.1	15,604	8.4	8,275	4.5
2008	180,865	157,099	86.9	15,368	8.5	8,398	4.6
2009	170,683	147,093	86.2	15,102	8.8	8,488	5.0
2010	167,950	143,325	85.3	15,779	9.4	8,846	5.3
				Physicians			
1998	587,165	307,117	52.3	70,712	12.0	209,336	35.7
1999	581,741	299,986	51.6	71,649	12.3	210,106	36.1
2000	570,625	295,891	51.9	71,609	12.5	203,125	35.6
2001	570,667	295,008	51.7	72,188	12.6	203,471	35.7
2002	593,588	289,868	48.8	73,458	12.4	230,262	38.8
2003	605,982	288,513	47.6	78,928	13.0	238,541	39.4
2004	618,440	289,963	46.9	80,704	13.0	247,773	40.1
2005	635,734	294,132	46.3	82,356	13.0	259,246	40.8
2006	624,244	277,511	44.5	83,651	13.4	263,082	42.1
2007	634,551	275,010	43.3	84,329	13.3	275,212	43.4
2008	645,314	269,994	41.8	85,053	13.2	290,267	45.0
2009	646,879	259,156	40.1	84,459	13.1	303,264	46.9
2010	665,025	254,991	38.3	86,569	13.0	323,465	48.6

using the Haversine formula. Between 90 and 95 percent of claims meet the 100-mile criteria in any given year.)

In the second step, we identify the observed market area of each practice as the set of patient ZIP Codes with nonzero service units (i.e., the set of j for which service$_{i,j}$ > 0), excluding cases where the patient ZIP is more than 100 miles from the physician ZIP. We then average the ZIPHHI values for the ZIP Codes in the market area, weighting by the number of services practice i provides in each of the patient ZIPs in its market area, to create a practice level HHI:

$$PRACHHI_i = \sum_{\substack{ZIPs\ j\ in \\ market\ area \\ of\ practice\ i}} w_{i,j} ZIPHHI_j,$$

Table 11.7   HHIs by practice, all specialties pooled

	N	Mean HHI	HHI percentiles		
			p10	p50	p90
1998	269,013	2,478	612	1,938	5,146
1999	259,543	2,477	610	1,932	5,157
2000	251,731	2,480	605	1,931	5,172
2001	250,930	2,479	599	1,919	5,197
2002	248,062	2,407	565	1,864	5,057
2003	254,826	2,377	563	1,835	5,008
2004	256,076	2,350	554	1,802	4,956
2005	258,775	2,369	556	1,836	4,983
2006	242,093	2,381	534	1,837	5,041
2007	238,253	2,405	543	1,866	5,069
2008	235,354	2,420	554	1,884	5,080
2009	226,035	2,448	561	1,904	5,130
2010	226,332	2,446	558	1,904	5,122

where $w_{i,j}$ is a weight with sum 1 derived from the service$_{i,j}$ values (i.e., service$_{i,j}$/service$_i$ where service$_i$ is the sum of all services provided by practice i).

This approach diverges somewhat from approaches that would simply define the market area of the practice as the set of ZIP Codes served and then compute the HHI from the market shares of all practices serving the area. Our approach allows us to weight more heavily the ZIPs from which the practice draws most of its patients. Since many practices draw patients from a large number of ZIP Codes in total, but have a much smaller set of areas from which the bulk of their patients come, this approach provides a more accurate representation of the market concentration in the areas in which the practice primarily operates.

Table 11.7 presents summary statistics for the resulting practice HHIs, pooling all specialty-specific practices. We compute an HHI for 269,013 practices in 1998 and for 226,332 practices in 2010. (These counts of practices are slightly lower than those reported earlier because we restrict analysis to claims where the patient and provider are within 100 miles of each other, and a few practices have no claims satisfying this criterion.) Mean HHIs exceed 2,350 in all years. Median HHIs exceed 1,802. The 90th percentile practices have HHIs exceeding 5,000. Though the approach we use to calculate HHIs differs from the specific analyses that might be used in an antitrust proceeding, it is interesting to note that the FTC and DOJ normally express concern about markets where HHIs are more than 1,500, considering markets between 1,500 and 2,500 to be moderately concentrated and markets above 2,500 to be highly concentrated (Federal Trade Commission and Department of Justice 2010). Between the beginning of the study period and 2004, HHIs were generally declining, indicating less

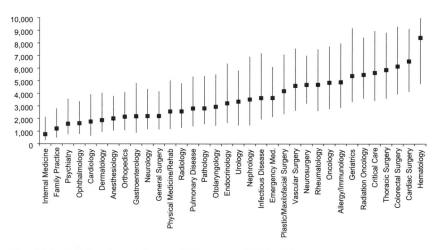

Fig. 11.2   Median (specialty-specific) practice HHI, 2010

concentration. In 2005, in contrast, HHIs began to increase, with the mean rising by about 100 points, to 2,446 in 2010. The HHIs at the 10th, 50th, and 90th percentiles also increased during the later portion of the study period. Changes of 100 points are large enough to be of interest in many antitrust contexts.

There are marked differences in HHIs across specialties. Figure 11.2 reports the median HHI by specialty in 2010, and the 10th and 90th percentiles across specialties. Internal medicine and family practice, two of the largest specialties, have the lowest median HHIs at 760 and 1,211, respectively. Cardiac surgery and hematology have the highest at 6,561 and 8,432. Twenty-three of the thirty-four specialties we studied have a median HHI of more than 2,500. Practice HHIs within each of the specialties vary considerably as well.

Changes in concentration over time vary across specialties (figure 11.3). Figure 11.4 plots 2005–2010 changes in mean HHIs by specialty against the percent change in number of practices. There are clear patterns of consolidation that vary across specialties. Thoracic surgery, emergency medicine, urology, hematology, radiation oncology, ophthalmology, and general surgery all lost significant numbers of practices and had increases of more than 200 points in the mean practice HHI. Pathology, endocrinology, critical care, and geriatrics all added practices and had declines of more than 200 in the mean practice HHI.

11.5.1   Comparisons with Alternate Approaches

To examine robustness to alternate specifications, we computed HHIs for practices in a number of different ways. Table 11.8 summarizes results. We

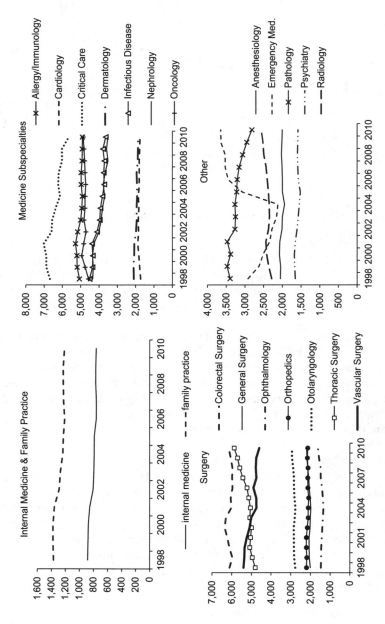

Fig. 11.3 Median practice HHIs, by specialty, by year

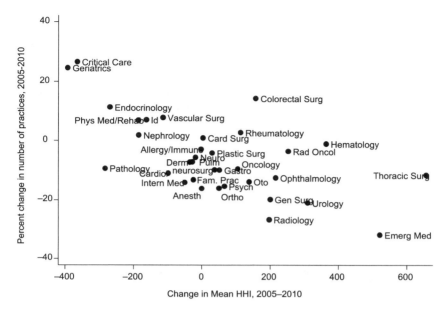

Fig. 11.4   Changes in practices and changes in mean HHI, by specialty, 2005–2010

examined the effect of using the number of claims and the number of work RVUs as the measure of output, and found results very similar to those obtained using charges. The FTC/DOJ guidance for antitrust related to Accountable Care Organizations recommends that market areas for practices be defined as the smallest number of ZIP Codes from which a practice draws 75 percent of its patients. Computing HHIs using this approach has little effect on the results, as might be expected since our approach weights ZIP HHIs by the number of claims in the practice when computing the practice HHIs, so ZIPs less important to the practice will already have less impact in the baseline approach. Finally, we examined the effect of relaxing the restriction that the physician and patient must be within 100 miles for the claim to be included, which also had little effect on the overall pattern of results. The HHIs using each alternative specification are highly correlated (≥ 0.97) with the baseline approach.

11.6   Area-Level Analyses

In many analyses, it is important to be able to summarize the degree of competition in a given geographic area. For example, one may wish to know the average HHI for providers in a given county or HRR. This can be easily computed from the practice-level measures (PRACHHI). Denoting areas by k, we take the average of PRACHHI values over the practices i with

Table 11.8   Comparison of different measurement approaches, 2010 practice-level HHIs

	N (specialty-specific) practices	Mean HHI	p10	p50	p90	Correlation with baseline approach
Baseline approach	226,332	2,446	558	1,904	5,122	—
Use claims as output measure	226,332	2,461	607	1,972	4,994	0.969
Use work RVUs as output measure	223,508	2,416	544	1,892	5,020	0.971
Impose 75% limit in practice market definition	226,332	2,395	517	1,819	5,106	0.995
Use all claims, not just those where physician-patient distance ≤ 100 miles	227,179	2,284	551	1,808	4,714	0.979

provider locations in area k, weighting by the services provided by the practice attributable to area k.

$$\text{GEOHHI}_k = \sum_{\substack{practices\ i \\ with\ provider \\ ZIPs\ in\ area\ k}} b_{i,k} \text{PRACHHI}_i,$$

where b is a weight that sums to one, capturing the distribution across practices of services attributable to area k (i.e., $b_{i,k} = \text{service}_{i,k} / \text{service}_k$). This calculation weights more heavily practices that have a prominent presence in the area, and weights less heavily practices that do not.

We have done this here for Hospital Referral Regions as defined in the Dartmouth Atlas. Paralleling the patterns seen at the practice level, there are wide variations in concentration across specialties and, within specialty, across geographic areas. Figure 11.5 shows variation across specialty and within specialty across areas for 2010. Median HHIs, calculated by specialty, at the HRR level are generally 30–60 percent higher than median practice HHIs (e.g., figure 11.2). This may reflect the fact that larger, less competitive practices naturally play a bigger role their geographic areas, and thus drive up the measure of the average HHIs by area.

Note that this calculation could also be made weighting by the location of patients, and would then give the average HHI of practices serving patients in a given geography. Results using this method are highly correlated with those weighting by the location of doctors.

11.7   Comparisons to SK&A Data

Data from the consulting firm SK&A provide an alternate way of characterizing the practice affiliations of physicians. The SK&A data is obtained by contact with physicians, and includes information about group affiliation as well as hospital or system ownership of practice. SK&A reports that the

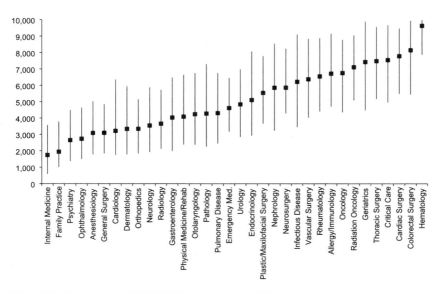

Fig. 11.5   Variation in HRR HHIs by specialty, 2010

data are updated twice per year, and contain information about nearly all physicians practicing in the United States. We used SK&A data from 2008 to 2010, selecting data for physicians in the specialties identified above. (SK&A specialty codes do not contain a code for cardiac surgery.)

Table 11.9 presents summary information. In 2010, the data contain information for 528,225 physician-specialty pairs (about 3,000 physicians appear with more than one specialty, and we include physicians in each of their indicated specialties). Of these, about 60 percent have a group, hospital, or system code indicating that the doctor is part of a larger entity. Curiously, the share of doctors with one of these codes stays approximately constant over time, despite popular reports of accelerating consolidation during this time period.

We match SK&A data to the Medicare claims data on the basis of NPI or UPIN physician identifiers. Between 83 percent and 88 percent of physicians in the SK&A data had either a UPIN or NPI with which to attempt a match (table 11.9, column [6]). Of all physician-specialty-practice (TIN) combinations in the claims data, we matched between 60 and 66 percent to information from the SK&A data. Match rates are particularly low (< 50 percent in a year) for critical care, geriatrics, anesthesiology, emergency medicine, and psychiatry. Match rates are highest for surgical specialties, near or above 80 percent for orthopedics, otolaryngology, urology, and ophthalmology. Of all doctors in the SK&A data in specialties we analyze, we find about 80 percent in the Medicare claims data, consistent with the view

Table 11.9 **Number of observations and presence of affiliations codes and NPI or UPIN, SK&A data**

	N	With group (%)	With hospital (%)	With system (%)	With group, hospital, or system (%)	With NPI or UPIN (%)
All specialties						
2008	496,339	43	18	17	58	83
2009	508,575	46	19	17	60	87
2010	528,225	46	17	18	59	88
By specialty 2010						
Internal medicine	62,915	42	16	19	52	90
Family practice	80,943	41	17	19	55	89
Allergy/immunology	4,138	42	11	12	50	85
Cardiology	21,294	61	16	18	70	89
Critical care	361	58	30	50	79	80
Dermatology	10,306	37	10	12	43	90
Endocrinology	4,300	42	23	26	59	90
Gastroenterology	11,368	53	13	14	61	91
Geriatrics	1,223	33	36	33	61	87
Hematology	364	36	40	44	71	74
Infectious disease	4,024	38	32	33	66	90
Nephrology	7,557	54	16	26	70	84
Neurology	10,137	40	20	23	57	90
Oncology	10,779	54	24	25	71	86
Pulmonary disease	4,344	46	19	18	59	85
Radiation oncology	4,186	48	34	28	74	84
Rheumatology	3,752	42	20	23	56	91
Colorectal surgery	1,064	47	12	15	57	91
General surgery	15,602	43	19	17	57	90
Neurosurgery	3,904	42	22	24	61	90
Ophthalmology	17,322	51	9	10	57	89
Orthopedics	22,567	56	13	13	65	89
Otolaryngology	8,515	46	15	15	57	91
Plastic/maxillofacial surgery	9,500	23	8	8	30	86
Thoracic surgery	2,896	44	24	25	63	90
Urology	8,835	52	14	14	62	90
Vascular surgery	2,272	43	22	23	60	86
Anesthesiology	22,423	59	14	16	70	92
Emergency med	19,865	49	22	20	67	85
Pathology	8,422	50	25	25	72	86
Physical medicine/rehab	5,358	36	15	16	49	89
Psychiatry	22,377	22	13	18	38	86
Radiology	25,005	67	12	15	75	80

Table 11.10   **Median HHIs by practice, using alternate practice measures**

	Tax ID (Medicare)		SK&A group		SK&A group or hospital		SK&A group or hospital or system	
	N	Med. HHI	N	Med. HHI	N	Med. HHI	N	Med. HHI
Internal medicine	32,996	853	40,509	750	36,942	755	34,889	786
Family practice	31,993	1,431	42,079	1,215	37,446	1,237	34,983	1,273
Allergy/immunology	2,022	5,106	2,202	4,853	2,188	4,866	2,138	4,885
Cardiology	7,953	1,914	10,085	1,577	9,165	1,576	8,694	1,587
Critical care	684	6,825	751	5,943	702	6,137	643	6,249
Dermatology	5,522	1,983	6,423	1,699	6,234	1,715	6,094	1,729
Endocrinology	2,159	3,571	2,555	3,175	2,339	3,239	2,174	3,358
Gastroenterology	4,621	2,382	6,206	1,859	5,834	1,893	5,585	1,893
Geriatrics	738	6,520	826	5,814	734	6,453	684	6,497
Hematology	388	8,862	465	8,093	424	8,520	391	8,613
Infectious disease	1,576	4,483	2,158	3,553	1,849	3,781	1,706	3,837
Nephrology	2,536	3,808	3,604	2,904	3,338	2,941	3,027	3,024
Neurology	5,204	2,473	6,295	2,162	5,602	2,224	5,231	2,280
Oncology	2,961	5,092	4,858	4,212	4,263	4,283	3,917	4,263
Pulmonary disease	3,805	3,047	4,426	2,563	4,069	2,626	3,871	2,638
Radiation oncology	1,679	6,215	2,271	5,203	1,976	5,459	1,785	5,569
Rheumatology	2,000	5,085	2,355	4,639	2,199	4,733	2,114	4,771
Cardiac surgery	877	7,143	975	6,649	929	6,812	893	6,842
Colorectal surgery	617	6,558	679	6,012	662	6,053	647	6,077
General surgery	8,579	2,516	10,376	2,216	9,555	2,291	8,938	2,310
Neurosurgery	1,682	5,112	2,280	4,740	2,049	4,829	1,890	4,901
Ophthalmology	8,280	1,703	9,692	1,554	9,331	1,564	9,109	1,567
Orthopedics	7,266	2,298	9,884	1,929	9,257	1,962	8,888	1,972
Otolaryngology	4,009	3,131	4,999	2,587	4,782	2,634	4,589	2,663
Plastic/maxillofacial surgery	3,604	4,702	3,826	4,630	3,731	4,651	3,663	4,674
Thoracic surgery	1,076	6,431	1,290	5,877	1,164	6,089	1,108	6,121
Urology	3,496	3,580	4,711	2,745	4,473	2,755	4,335	2,757
Vascular surgery	1,429	5,162	1,534	4,580	1,456	4,700	1,385	4,719
Anesthesiology	4,340	2,674	9,184	1,828	8,153	1,880	7,638	1,883
Emergency med	5,070	3,946	8,877	1,924	7,572	2,234	6,973	2,324
Pathology	1,757	3,821	3,485	2,485	2,764	2,768	2,543	2,824
Physical medicine/rehab	3,470	3,098	3,739	2,868	3,550	2,924	3,370	3,006
Psychiatry	9,352	2,090	11,618	1,820	10,897	1,870	10,047	1,908
Radiology	4,397	2,935	8,696	1,803	7,782	1,840	7,289	1,879

that a large share of all physicians in the United States are identified in the 20 percent Medicare claims sample.

Using the matched data, we computed HHIs for practices to examine the effects of characterizing practices in different ways. The first two columns of table 11.10 report the results using the method described above based on Medicare-reported TIN for specialty-specific practices. We first compare to results that use the group code reported on the SK&A data as the indicator of practice (columns [3] and [4]). This code is intended to identify medical groups of which a doctor is part, but not hospitals or systems that might own the practice. Using this code, we find more practices than using the TIN approach, and the median HHI across practices is a bit lower—between 10 and 20 percent lower for most of the specialties reported. The correlation between the specialty median HHI based on TIN and SK&A group code is 0.98.

We next consider the effect of incorporating hospital ownership information. We assign physicians to the hospital they indicate owning their practice first. If there is no hospital indicated, we assign them to their group. This reduces the number of practices by a modest amount, and slightly increases the measured HHIs relative to measures using just the group code (columns [5] and [6]). Finally, we considered the effects of assigning physicians to the indicated system owner first, followed by hospital, followed by group. This further reduces the number of practices and increases the measured HHIs. Overall, the effect of incorporating information about hospital and system ownership from SK&A has some effect on measures of concentration, but does not substantially change the patterns observed. The patterns observed across specialties and over time are also similar in the SK&A data and the Medicare data, with somewhat higher reported HHIs based on the Medicare data.

11.8   Conclusions

We reach several conclusions based on the analyses reported. First, it appears that TINs reported in Medicare claims can provide a useful tool for measuring the size and concentration of physician practices. Medicare data appear to contain a large sample of the physicians in the United States, across a broad range of specialties. Reported TINs appear to frequently represent practice structures that are meaningful for market structure identification, generally consistent with results obtained from an alternative data source that has been used in the literature.

Second, there is a considerable degree of concentration in many physician markets. A large number of practices have HHIs of more than 2,500, in many cases well more than 2,500. In many specialties, the median HRR is served by practices with highly concentrated markets. This suggests that attention to concentration may be warranted, as the potential for inefficient market outcomes appears to be substantial.

Third, there has been consolidation over time in some areas. Surgical specialties in particular have seen significant consolidation over the past decade or so. But not all specialties have become more concentrated. Some medical specialties in particular appear to have become more competitive over time. In addition, there are variations in trends at different points in time. Years before 2005 frequently saw declines in HHIs, while increases in HHIs are more apparent later in the sample period.

Fourth, the role of hospitals and systems is important in measuring concentration, but the overall impact is modest. When we used SK&A data to examine measures using different approaches, being able to account for hospital and system ownership raised HHIs by a nonnegligible, but overall modest amount.

It is perhaps worth noting that the Medicare data, though generally useful, will not capture market dynamics for physicians that primarily serve managed care patients and do not bill Medicare on a fee-for-service basis. They will also not capture patterns in specialties, like pediatrics, not well represented among bills from Medicare patients. As a result, these measures and conclusions may not generalize to these other settings. The analyses reported here focus on financially integrated practice arrangements, and will not capture market dynamics related to IPAs or other less integrated organizational forms.

References

Antwi, Y. A., M. S. Gaynor, and W. B. Vogt. 2009. "A Bargain at Twice the Price? California Hospital Prices in the New Millennium." *Forum for Health Economics and Policy* 12 (1). Published online. DOI: https://doi.org/10.2202/1558-9544.1144.

Berenson, R. A., and P. B. Ginsburg. 2010. "Unchecked Provider Clout in California Foreshadows Challenges to Health Reform." *Health Affairs* 29 (4): 699–705.

Berenson, R. A., P. B. Ginsburg, J. B. Christianson, and T. Yee. 2012. "The Growing Power of Some Providers to Win Steep Payment Increases from Insurers Suggests Policy Remedies may be Needed." *Health Affairs* 31 (5): 973–81.

Casalino, L. P. 2006. "The Federal Trade Commission, Clinical Integration, and the Organization of Physician Practice." *Journal of Health Politics, Policy & Law* 31 (3): 569–85.

Crosson, F. J. 2009. "21st-Century Health Care—The Case for Integrated Delivery Systems." *New England Journal of Medicine* 361 (14): 1324–25.

Cuellar, A. E., and P. J. Gertler. 2006. "Strategic Integration of Hospitals and Physicians." *Journal of Health Economics* 25 (1): 1–28.

Dafny, L. 2009. "Estimation and Identification of Merger Effects: An Application to Hospital Mergers." *Journal of Law and Economics* 52:523–50.

Dunn, A., and A. H. Shapiro. 2014. "Do Physicians Possess Market Power?" *Journal of Law and Economics* 57 (1): 159–93.

Federal Trade Commission, Antitrust Division, and Department of Justice. 2011. "Statement of Antitrust Enforcement Policy Regarding Accountable Care Organizations Participating in the Medicare Shared Savings Program." *Federal Register* 76 (209): 67026–32.

Federal Trade Commission and Department of Justice. 1996. *Statements of Antitrust Enforcement Policy in Health Care*. Washington, DC.

————. 2010. *Horizontal Merger Guidelines*. Washington, DC. https://www.ftc.gov/sites/default/files/attachments/merger-review/100819hmg.pdf.

Federal Trade Commission, Health Care Division, Bureau of Competition. 2011. Topic and Yearly Indices of Health Care Antitrust Advisory Opinions by Commission and Staff. Washington DC.

Gaynor, M. 2011. *Hearing on Health Care Industry Consolidation: Statement Before the Committee on Ways and Means Health Subcommittee*, 112th Cong., First Session. Washington, DC: US House of Representatives. https://waysandmeans.house.gov/hearing-on-health-care-industry-consolidation/.

Gaynor, M., and R. J. Town. 2012. "Competition in Health Care Markets." In *Handbook of Health Economics*, vol. 2, edited by M. V. Pauly, T. G. McGuire, and P. P. Barros, 499–627. Amsterdam: Elsevier North-Holland.

Ginsburg, P. B. 2010. *Wide Variation in Hospital and Physician Payment Rates Evidence of Provider Market Power*. Washington, DC: Center for Studying Health System Change.

Kessler, D. P., and M. B. McClellan. 2000. "Is Hospital Competition Socially Wasteful?" *Quarterly Journal of Economics* 115 (2): 577–615.

Ketcham, J. D., L. C. Baker, and D. MacIsaac. 2007. "Physician Practice Size and Variations in Treatments and Outcomes: Evidence from Medicare Patients with AMI." *Health Affairs* 26 (1): 195–205.

Kocher, R., and N. R. Sahni. 2011. "Hospitals' Race to Employ Physicians—The Logic behind a Money Losing Proposition." *New England Journal of Medicine* 364 (19): 1790–93.

Liehaber, A., and J. M. Grossman. 2007. "Physicians Moving to Mid-Sized, Single Specialty Practices." Technical Report, Tracking Report no. 18, Center for Studying Health System Change.

McWilliams, J. M., M. E. Chernew, A. M. Zaslavsky, P. Hamed, and B. E. Landon. 2013. "Delivery System Integration and Health Care Spending and Quality of Care for Medicare Beneficiaries." *JAMA Internal Medicine* 173 (15): 1447–56.

Medicare Payment Advisory Commission (MedPAC). 2012. "Report to the Congress: Medicare Payment Policy." MedPAC, Washington, DC. http://www.medpac.gov/docs/default-source/reports/march-2012-report-to-the-congress-medicare-payment-policy.pdf?sfvrsn=0.

Melnick, G. A., Y. C. Shen, and V. Y. Wu. 2011. "The Increased Concentration of Health Plan Markets Can Benefit Consumers through Lower Hospital Prices." *Health Affairs* 30 (9): 1728–33.

Melnick, G. A., J. Zwanziger, A. Bamezai, and R. Pattison. 1992. "The Effects of Market Structure and Bargaining Position on Hospital Prices." *Journal of Health Economics* 11 (3): 217–33.

O'Malley, A. S., A. M. Bond, and R. A. Berenson. 2011. *Rising Hospital Employment of Physicians: Better Quality and Costs?* Washington, DC: Center for Studying Health System Change.

Pelnar, Gregory J. 2010. "Are Clinically Integrated Physician Networks Candy-Coated Cartels?" *CPI Antitrust Chronicle* 10 (1). https://competitionpolicyinternational.com/are-clinically-integrated-physician-networks-candy-coated-cartels/.

Pennsylvania Health Care Cost Containment Council. 2007. *Cardiac Surgery in Pennsylvania 2005*. Harrisburg: Pennsylvania Health Care Cost Containment Council.

Pham, H. H., D. Schrag, A. S. O'Malley, B. Wu, and P. B. Bach. 2007. "Care Patterns in Medicare and Their Implications for Pay for Performance." *New England Journal of Medicine* 356 (11): 1130–39.

Pope, G. C., M. Trisolini, J. Kautter, and W. Adamanche. 2002. *Physician Group Practice Demonstration Design Report*. Baltimore, MD: Centers for Medicare and Medicaid Service.

Schneider, J. E., P. Li, D. G. Klepser, N. A. Peterson, T. T. Brown, and R. M. Scheffler. 2008. "The Effect of Physician and Health Plan Concentration on Prices in Commercial Health Insurance Markets." *International Journal of Health Care Finance and Economics* 8 (1): 13–26.

Staiger, D. O., D. I. Auerbach, and P. I. Buerhaus. 2009. "Comparison of Physician Workforce Estimates and Supply Projections." *Journal of the American Medical Association* 302 (15): 1674–80.

Welch, W. P., A. E. Cuellar, S. C. Stearns, and A. B. Bindman. 2013. "Proportion of Physicians in Large Group Practices Continued to Grow in 2009–2011." *Health Affairs* 32 (9): 1659–66.

Wu, V. Y. 2009. "Managed Care's Price Bargaining with Hospitals." *Journal of Health Economics* 28 (2): 350–60.

Risk Adjustment of Health Plan Payments to Correct Inefficient Plan Choice from Adverse Selection

Jacob Glazer, Thomas G. McGuire, and Julie Shi

12.1 Introduction

In the United States and a number of other countries, individuals choose health insurance from among competing health plans. The Affordable Care Act (ACA) mandates previously uninsured individuals choose a plan offered in the new state-level health insurance exchanges (now sometimes referred to as "marketplaces"). Parts C (managed care plans) and D (drug plans) in Medicare use private health insurance markets, as do the national health care systems of the Netherlands, Germany, Switzerland, and other countries. A fundamental premise of payment regulation in all of these markets is that plans' revenue should be "risk adjusted" to account for cost differences among enrollees. Risk adjustment protects plans and mitigates incentives related to adverse selection. The risk-adjustment formulas can be complicated, as they are in the ACA where they involve demographics, scores of diagnostic variables, and interactions. Weights on risk-adjusted variables, like age or diagnoses for certain conditions, are generally derived from regression-based statistical procedures on data sets with millions of people.

Jacob Glazer is professor of economics at Tel Aviv University and at the University of Warwick. Thomas G. McGuire is professor of health economics at Harvard Medical School and a research associate of the National Bureau of Economic Research. When this chapter was written, Julie Shi was a postdoctoral fellow at Harvard Medical School. She is currently assistant professor of economics at Peking University.

Research for this chapter was supported by the National Institute of Mental Health (R01 MH094290) and the National Institute of Aging (P01-AG032952). This chapter was prepared for presentation at the NBER Conference, "Measuring and Modeling Health Care Costs," October 18–19, 2013, in Washington, DC. We are grateful to Randy Ellis, Amy Finkelstein, Jonathan Kolstad, Tim Layton, Karen Stockley, Aaron Schwartz, and a referee for comments on a previous version. For acknowledgments, sources of research support, and disclosure of the authors' material financial relationships, if any, please see http://www.nber.org/chapters/c13122.ack.

A well-known limitation of risk-adjustment methods is that the weights are sometimes estimated from data not from the plans paid by risk adjustment. For example, in Medicare, private managed care plans are paid with a risk-adjustment system estimated with data from beneficiaries who elect *not to join* one of the private plans. In the new exchanges, the risk-adjustment formulas the federal government recommends are estimated from employees of large employers and their dependents, individuals generally not eligible to participate in exchanges.

The issue is partly practical and temporary in the sense that once data from exchanges accumulate or Medicare private plans report more complete data, weights can be recalculated based on the "real data." But there is a more fundamental problem access to data does not solve: statistical procedures make risk-adjustment weights a function of the data, and, economic equilibrium makes the data a function of the risk-adjustment formula. In other words, the risk distribution of individuals who choose to join a plan, and even the services a plan decides to offer to its enrollees, are a function of how plans are paid. This is more than a technical concern—equilibrium effects on enrollment and services are precisely the adverse-selection problems risk adjustment is designed to avoid.[1]

This chapter develops and implements a statistical methodology to account for the equilibrium effects (aka adverse selection) in design of a risk-adjustment formula in health insurance markets. We focus on the "Einav-Finkelstein" form[2] of adverse selection in which enrollees sort between plans with fixed benefit offerings as a function of the plans' premiums. Because these premiums do not reflect each person's marginal costs, the plan with the better coverage tends to be a bargain for the sick and too expensive for the healthy, leading some people to choose the wrong plan.[3] We show that risk adjustment affects the equilibrium sorting, and can be used to improve upon the adverse-selection outcome. We find the "second-best" allocation between plans, second best meaning the most efficient that can be achieved given the premium categories available, and then show how choice of risk adjustors can attain this second-best outcome.

Section 12.2 reviews the literature, highlighting recent papers by Einav and Finkelstein (EF) that study enrollee sorting between plans with fixed characteristics charging the same premium to all enrollees. Section 12.3

1. Another way to say this: if risk adjustment did not affect enrollment and/or services offered, there would be no need to risk adjust. The law of large numbers would deal with any plan-level risk.

2. For example, Einav and Finkelstein (2011), Einav, Finkelstein, and Levin (2010), and Einav, Finkelstein, and Cullen (2010).

3. Major precursors of the Einav-Finkelstein paper are Cutler and Reber (1998) who studied sorting in the benefit plans at one employer, and before that and more generally, Akerlof (1970). The second form of adverse selection in health insurance markets stems from Rothschild and Stiglitz (1976) in which plan offerings are not fixed and plans distort benefit offerings to attract less costly enrollees. Glazer and McGuire (2000) used the Rothschild-Stiglitz model to draw the implications for risk adjustment in health insurance.

incorporates risk adjustment into the EF framework, oriented around the working of the ACA. We retain the EF assumption that there are two plan types (which we call Silver and Gold) with fixed characteristics and build on EF in a number of ways: in addition to introducing risk adjustment, we allow for many premium categories (for example, premiums conditioned on age). We also incorporate an explicit model of selection in which individuals choosing between plan types make imperfect forecasts of their future health care costs. The nature of adverse selection is critical to efficiency interpretations of an EF model. The fundamental normative implication of the EF model is that when a more generous plan experiences adverse selection, the "Gold plan" premium should be subsidized to encourage more enrollment than would occur in competitive equilibrium. We show (a) the optimal subsidy should correct for individuals' imperfect forecasts in addition to the "marginal-average cost gap" in the EF model, (b) the resulting allocation minimizes but does not eliminate inefficiencies in sorting (i.e., is a second best), and (c) the optimal subsidy can be achieved by risk adjustment.

Section 12.4 implements the theoretical ideas with data from seven years of the Medical Expenditure Panels Survey (MEPS), drawing a population representative of those eligible for exchanges in the ACA. Operationalizing the model from section 12.3 requires simulating the payment system in exchanges, specifying costs in the Gold and Silver plans, and specifying the underlying demand (selection) behavior. Importantly, the regulator needs to know the nature of the inefficiency due to selection in order to design the right risk-adjustment system to correct the inefficiency.

Empirical results are contained in section 12.5 where we evaluate several equilibria in terms of the efficiency of plan sorting and in the degree to which the payment system associated with risk adjustment "fits" costs at the Silver and Gold plans (in equilibrium). We start with no risk adjustment where premiums for twelve age-geography categories are determined in equilibrium between competing Gold and Silver plans. The welfare loss from sorting is high and the fit of plan costs is poor. Conventional risk adjustment, of the type proposed in the ACA, improves sorting and improves the fit of play payments to cost. We then show how a modification of conventional risk-adjustment methods can set risk-adjustment weights so that in equilibrium, the incremental premium for the Gold plan leads to the efficient (second-best) sorting. The method is constrained regression, where the constraints (on the risk-adjustment weights) require that risk adjustment transfer sufficient funds to the premium group to achieve the desired subsidy in equilibrium.

12.2 Background and Literature Review

A foundation of the policy of managed competition, and of the many regulated health insurance markets based on the idea, is that consumers choose among competing health plans in the presence of prices that reflect the additional costs of more versus less generous plans. In the US Medicare program, for example, competing private health plans can add benefits over the required minimum but must finance these by higher premiums. The ACA creates an ordered set of plans designated Bronze, Silver, Gold, and Platinum with more coverage for higher prices.

Consumer utility maximization leads to efficient sorting among plans if consumers face premiums that present them with the "incremental cost" of benefits in the more generous plan (Keeler, Carter, and Newhouse 1998). The argument is the same as that for prices generally: when consumers face prices equal to costs, net utility equals social welfare and consumers make efficient choices. The problem is that managed competition does not deliver the required incremental prices (Bundorf, Levin, and Mahoney 2012; Glazer and McGuire 2011). When the product is health insurance, incremental cost is person-specific. In other words, the incremental cost across two plans differs for each person depending on their expected health care costs. Asymmetric information between plans and enrollees interferes with efficient pricing. Furthermore, managed competition policies purposely limit the degree to which plans may price discriminate based on observables related to health care costs. Higher premiums for those with previous illnesses are, for example, nearly universally prohibited. (The ACA also has age-band restrictions.)

Managed competition policies rely on risk adjustment of payment to plans in order to pay more for higher-cost enrollees. While this deals with some aspects of efficient plan service provision, it may not help at all with consumer sorting among plans. Our main objective in this chapter is to study how risk-adjustment payments schemes, set by a regulator, can affect the premiums that plans charge enrollees, which in turn will affect enrollees' choice of plans and, hence, welfare. We build on the model introduced in a series of papers by Einav and Finkelstein, primarily the well-known version in Einav, Finkelstein, and Cullen (2010). We will refer to the model as the "EF" model, and review its basics here.

The EF model shows how to measure the welfare losses due to adverse selection using demand and cost curves. Einav, Finkelstein, and Cullen (2010) outline a stylized version of their approach and discuss its application in different settings. In what they refer to as their "textbook example," consumers choose between a high-coverage contract, H, and a low-coverage contract, L. In their example the L contract refers to no insurance and, hence, it is costless to all consumers and is free. The (incremental) price of the H contract is denoted by p paid by all potential enrollees, and consumers purchase the H contract if their valuation of it, net of the price p, exceeds their valuation of the low contract, normalized to zero. As premium falls, new enrollees choose H, defining an average and marginal cost curve. For a given price p, average cost for plan H (denoted by $AC(p)$) is the expected costs of the enrollees, who (endogenously) choose to enroll in contract H,

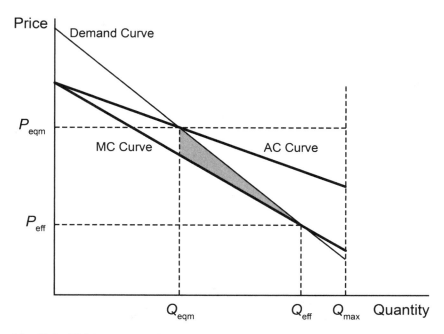

Fig. 12.1   Efficiency costs of adverse selection in Einav-Finkelstein model
Source: Einav, Finkelstein, and Cullen (2010).

divided by the number of individuals who purchase it. For a given price p, marginal cost (denoted by $MC(p)$) is the expected cost for the individual(s) whose willingness to pay is exactly p. See figure 12.1, a replica (omitting some labeling) of figure 1 in Einav, Finkelstein, and Cullen (2010).

In market equilibrium, insurers are assumed to price competitively, such that $p = AC(p)$. As in a standard welfare analysis, consumer surplus for a given individual in the high contract is measured by their willingness to pay for the H contract minus the price, and producer surplus for a given individual is measured by price minus the cost of that individual. The efficient price (premium) and quantity (enrollment in H) are given by the point where the marginal cost intersects demand, and the equilibrium price and quantity are given by the point where the average cost intersects demand. The efficiency loss, in their setting, is given by the "conventional" welfare triangle bounded by the marginal cost and demand curve, between the efficient quantity and the equilibrium one (the shaded area in figure 12.1).[4] In their

4. There are two cases, the "adverse selection" case, where individuals' willingness to pay for plan H is increasing with their cost (to the plan) and the other, the "advantageous selection" case, where individuals' willingness to pay cost is decreasing with their cost. In the adverse selection case, the one shown in figure 12.1 and the one we work with in this chapter, the welfare loss is due to the fact that "too few" individuals join the H plan, relative to social optimum.

empirical application using data on insurance choices and costs from a large employer, Einav, Finkelstein, and Cullen detect adverse selection, but they estimate the welfare costs of adverse selection to be small.[5]

We modify and extend the basic EF model in several ways to further illuminate properties of markets with insurance choice.[6] The first has to do with the relationship between willingness to pay and costs. In the "textbook case," the ordering in willingness to pay of those who join as a function of p is matched by a one-to-one ordering of falling costs. As was acknowledged by Einav, Finkelstein, and Cullen (2010), if individuals' costs are not monotonically increasing or decreasing with willingness to pay, as generally they will not be, then the point where marginal cost intersects the demand will not be first best and the welfare triangle in figure 12.1 will not describe the welfare loss.[7] The reason is that with heterogeneity in the relationship between demand and incremental cost, "marginal cost," $MC(p)$ is, in fact, an average of the marginal costs over all individuals whose willingness to pay is exactly p. Thus, even when $MC(p) = p$, there are individuals (those whose willingness to pay is higher than p but their cost is higher than their willingness to pay) who join the plan even though, from a social point of view, they should not, and there are individuals (those whose willingness to pay is less than p but their cost is lower than their willingness to pay) who will choose not to join the plan even though, from a social point of view, they should. Another way to say this is that only in the very special circumstances assumed in the textbook version of the EF model is a single premium (equal to MC) able to eliminate welfare loss from sorting.[8] In general, the situation will be as depicted in figure 12.2. Two groups (here 1 and 2) have different incremental marginal costs and demand, but must share a common incremental premium (Δp). Any Δp is associated with welfare losses. The second-best analysis we perform later essentially seeks to minimize the sum of the losses, L_1 and L_2 in the figure, as a function of the incremental premium. An example of the welfare losses that will emerge with heterogeneity is that under the ACA, plans cannot discriminate in premium across

5. The authors also discuss how the welfare losses (gains) from imperfect competition or discriminatory prices can be quantified. They also compare the estimated welfare loss to the social cost of subsidized prices or mandates.

6. Kolstad and Kowalski (2014) use a modification of the Einav, Finkelstein, and Cullen (2010) model to study the reduction in adverse selection as a result of an "individual mandate" in the recent reform in Massachusetts.

7. See their footnote 3.

8. This point is emphasized by Bundorf, Levin, and Mahoney (2012). Commenting on analyses that imply a single premium can efficiently sort a population between two plans, they observe, "These analyses, however, assume perfect correlation between enrollee risk and preferences for coverage and make strong assumptions about the relationship between preferences and plan costs. We show that if these assumptions are violated, a uniform contribution policy (i.e., a policy under which individuals face the same prices for the plans) cannot induce efficient consumer choices." (3215). Glazer and McGuire (2011) show that in general a single-premium policy cannot lead to efficiency.

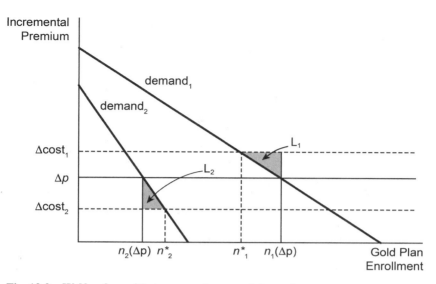

Fig. 12.2   Welfare loss with a common incremental premium

individuals with different health status or other characteristics that may affect their costs. In our analysis we allow for individual heterogeneity at the margin in our welfare analysis.[9]

Second, we consider a "real" alternative plan and take account of what is happening in equilibrium for this plan as the distribution of risks shifts in response to changes in the incremental premium for the high-coverage (Gold) plan. When the "other plan" is not a zero-cost plan, the average costs and equilibrium premium in that plan also change as demand changes for the Gold plan. This modifies the interpretation of the EF textbook diagram and is essential in any empirical application to a multiple-plan context.

Third, we allow for individuals' willingness to pay for a plan to differ from their (social) benefit from that plan.[10] If, for example, individuals are not fully informed about their health cost risk, or cannot fully understand their risks, they will not accurately anticipate the services they will receive upon joining a particular plan. They may over- or underestimate how much they have to gain from joining the H plan. This issue is tied to adverse selection, because it is just this anticipation that drives the higher-cost people to join the H plan. As long as this process is imperfect, that is, the anticipation is

9. Spinnewijn (2017) considers a different explicit model of selection in which "demand frictions" introduce heterogeneity and affect choice. He also finds that the welfare economics of the standard selection model are altered.

10. See Abaluck and Gruber (2011) for an example of an analysis of "mistakes" in buying health insurance made by the elderly in choosing their drug plans in Medicare.

only partial, then consumers will make "mistakes" in their plan choice. In such a case, demand and marginal benefit curves do not generally coincide and even if price is equal to marginal cost, equilibrium will not be socially efficient.

Fourth, we enrich the payment system studied and introduce multiple premium categories and risk adjustment. In the ACA, plans can discriminate on the basis of age (within limits), geography, and smoking status. Furthermore, risk adjustment will move funds to plans drawing a sicker population, affecting equilibrium premiums and consumer sorting. We explicitly incorporate the effect of risk adjustment within an EF model, and show that an appropriately designed risk-adjustment payment scheme may reduce welfare losses associated not only with EF adverse selection, but also with individuals' inability to perfectly evaluate the services they will receive if they join a plan.

Our chapter is also related to a number of other recent papers that have studied the welfare implications of policy changes or changes in the market conditions in the health insurance market. A comprehensive review of this emerging literature is contained in Einav, Finkelstein, and Levin (2010). Recent papers have specified more complete models of consumer preferences to enable a more thorough normative interpretation of market outcomes. These models allow authors to quantify the magnitude of welfare losses from, among other things, distortionary pricing (see Bundorf, Levin, and Mahoney 2012; Carlin and Town 2010; Geruso 2012; Handel, Hendel, and Whinston 2013), restrictions on the choice set (see Lustig 2008; Dafny, Ho, and Varela 2013; Lucarelli, Prince, and Simon 2012), and changes in the allocation of consumers to plans (see Handel 2013; Lustig 2008).

12.3   Risk Adjustment to Fix Adverse Selection

This section presents a model of a health insurance market with regulated benefits and two types of competing plans that we refer to as Silver plans and Gold plans. Enrollees face premiums and choose a plan. We allow multiple premium categories and risk adjustment. Our risk-adjustment system pays the same for an individual independent of what plan they join.[11] As in the standard EF model, we describe equilibrium and efficient sorting between plan types, and identify the efficient incremental premium for the Gold plan for each premium category.

---

11. The model captures features of the managed competition approach to individual health insurance, which serves as the intellectual basis of ACA exchanges, Medicare Parts C and D, and health policy in a number of European countries. Premium subsidies are a feature of all of these policy contexts. Incremental premiums (the difference between Gold and Silver) govern sorting and efficiency so we can be agnostic about whether there are subsidies for the basic plan type. Our approach is also consistent with "premium-support" policies awarding a risk-adjusted voucher to enrollees who can apply the voucher toward premium at any plan.

12.3.1   Costs and Demand for Health Plan Alternatives

The N people in an insurance pool vary in two observable dimensions, according to health status, the basis of risk adjustment, and according to another set of characteristics, the basis of premiums. Health status is indexed by h, $h = 1, \ldots, H$; premium characteristics are indexed by t, $t = 1, \ldots, T$. Each categorization is mutually exclusive so that a person is characterized by an (h, t) pair. There can be overlap between the factors (e.g., age might be a used in both h and t), but there is some independent information about health care costs in each of h and t. For example, geography might be used as a basis for premiums but not risk adjustment, and prior health conditions might be a basis for risk adjustment but not premiums. We will refer to a person with characteristics h and t as a person of type ht; N_{ht} is the number of people of type ht in the population and N_t is the number of people with premium type t.[12]

Plans provide services, x, according to h and t, and services a person of type ht would get are fixed in each plan. Gold is more generous so that $x_{ht}^g > x_{ht}^s$ for all ht, with x measured in dollars; x_{ht}^g and x_{ht}^s are thus also the costs of serving a person of type ht in the Gold and Silver plans, respectively. Define the incremental costs for a person of type ht as $x_{ht} \equiv x_{ht}^g - x_{ht}^s$. For simplicity in presentation, we let incremental cost x_{ht} represent both social incremental cost and plan incremental cost, implying that the out-of-pocket costs to an ht type are the same in Silver and Gold.[13]

Although every member of type ht gets the same increment in services going from Silver to Gold, individuals are heterogeneous in their valuation of Gold over Silver plans. Demand is $n_{ht}(p_t)$, the number of people among type ht who choose to enroll in the Gold plan as a function of the incremental premium for members of this premium type, where the incremental premium is the difference between the Gold and Silver plan premiums for that premium group: $p_t \equiv p_t^g - p_t^s$. Heterogeneity in demand could be due to tastes for health care services, risk aversion, or other preferences regarding cost management methods in the two plans. As in EF, our normative framework includes these preferences as a component of welfare. We assume demand is downward-sloping: $n_{ht}'(p_t) < 0$. The Gold plan's "aggregate" demand function of individuals in premium category t sums enrollment demand over the h categories:

$$(1) \qquad\qquad n_t(p_t) = \sum_h n_{ht}(p_t).$$

---

12. A similar model of plan costs is used in McGuire et al. (2013) for one plan type. That paper shows how to choose risk-adjustment weights when premiums also contribute to fit but the premiums are determined in market equilibrium.

13. Premiums, of course, will differ between plans. In exchanges, Gold plans have more coverage, so part of more services would be due to moral hazard in demand. Keeping track of out-of-pocket differences would complicate the presentation of the accounting in this chapter without adding insight.

The corresponding "inverse" demand function of each ht type is $p_{ht}(n_{ht})$, and the "inverse" aggregate demand, $p_t(n_t)$.

"Demand" can be distinct from "benefit" in the context of selection and insurance choice. Selection is driven by consumers being able to anticipate their health care costs, but they do so imperfectly. Consumers are therefore also generally imperfect in their anticipation of how much they would benefit from membership in alternative health insurance plans, introducing a distinction between what consumers *anticipate* in terms of benefits and what they *actually get* in terms of benefits of plan choice. Demand is based on what consumers anticipate ex ante, whereas welfare is naturally based on ex post benefits.

12.3.2   Efficiency

When enrollees know their type ht and face incremental premiums equal to the incremental cost, x_{ht}, their utility-maximizing choice of plan type achieves efficient sorting. However, since incremental premiums can be conditioned only on t and not on h, first-best sorting between Gold and Silver plans is generally impossible. With the first-best unattainable, we characterize the premiums that minimize the welfare loss from inefficient sorting, assuming that people know their type, and subject to the constraint that premiums must be the same for all persons with the same t.

For a premium group t, the common incremental premium that maximizes social welfare solves the following problem:

(2) $$\operatorname*{Max}_{p_t} \sum_h \left[\int_0^{n_{ht}(p_t)} p_{ht}(n_{ht}) \, dn_{ht} - n_{ht}(p_t)x_{ht} \right].$$

Recall that $n_{ht}(p_t)$ is the demand function of the ht types and $p_{ht}(n_{ht})$ is its inverse. When consumers know their type demand has the conventional interpretation as willingness to pay or consumer surplus, x_{ht} is the cost of an individual of type ht moving from Silver to Gold.

Assuming an interior solution (members from all h groups are in both the Gold and Silver plans), the solution to equation (2) is p_t^*:

(3) $$p_t^* = \frac{\sum_h n_{ht}'(p_t^*)x_{ht}}{\sum_h n_{ht}'(p_t^*)}.$$

We state this result formally:

PROPOSITION 1: *Assuming demand indicates benefit, the welfare-maximizing incremental premium for premium group t equals the Gold plan's incremental cost averaged over the h groups joining the plan.*

Proposition 1 extends the EF result by showing that the incremental premium should equate (averaged) incremental marginal cost to demand even when there is heterogeneity in the mix of persons joining Gold as a function of premium.

The EF analysis and Proposition 1 share the important assumption that individuals can accurately forecast their expected cost. When this is not true, Proposition 1 must be modified. Equating incremental marginal cost to marginal benefit is then not the same as equating marginal cost to demand. The efficient second-best premium must also correct for the gap between expected and actual benefit of joining Gold.

12.3.3 Equilibrium with Risk-Adjusted Payments and Selection

Equilibrium consists of premiums for each of the T premium categories for the Silver and Gold plans, and of an allocation of enrollees across the plan types. The equilibrium will be a function of the risk-adjustment formula. Let r_h denote the risk-adjustment payment that (Gold or Silver) plans receive for each individual of type h. Suppose, as in exchanges, the risk-adjustment system is financed by premium payments of enrollees. We can regard a plan paying into a risk-adjustment fund a constant amount for each enrollee, perhaps, as here, set equal to costs at the Silver plan averaged over the entire population, $\bar{x}^s$. The plan (either Gold or Silver) then receives r_h back from the fund for each person of type h joining the plan. The risk-adjustment system is balanced budget if $\Sigma_h N_h r_h = N\bar{x}^s$. Plans must charge premiums that cover costs (after risk adjustment) according to each t group. (The "budget constraint" for risk adjustment, $\bar{x}^s$, could be set at some other level, affecting the equilibrium premiums plans must charge.)

The premium for the Silver plan for type t is p_t^s. We can write the Gold plan premium as $p_t^s + p_t$, the Silver plan premium plus the incremental premium for group t. Risk adjustment is set the by a regulator, and premiums are determined in market equilibrium. We assume that competition drives the profit for Silver and Gold plans to zero for each premium group. Thus, for each t we have two zero-profit conditions:

$$(4) \qquad \sum_h (r_h - \bar{x}^s + p_t^s - x_{ht}^s)(N_{ht} - n_{ht}(p_t)) = 0,$$

$$(5) \qquad \sum_h (r_h - \bar{x}^s + p_t + p_t^s - x_{ht}^g)n_{ht}(p_t) = 0,$$

where $N_{ht} - n_{ht}(p_t)$ is the number of individuals of type ht in the Silver plan, and $n_{ht}(p_t)$, defined in equation (1) above, is the number in the Gold plan.

Conditions (4) and (5) incorporate utility maximization as well as competitive equilibrium among plans and thus describe a complete equilibrium in the insurance market, given a risk-adjustment system with weights, r_h.

12.3.4 Risk-Adjustment Weights That Achieve (Second-Best) Efficient Sorting

The $2T$ equations in (4) and (5) describe a relationship between the risk-adjustment weights, r_h, and the equilibrium premiums, p_t. The idea is to take this relationship into account when deciding risk-adjustment policy; specifically, to set the weights, r_h, so that the equilibrium premiums hit the desired target. When demand represents benefit, risk-adjustment weights that achieve efficient sorting in equilibrium satisfy equation (3), subject to equations (4) and (5). Each of the T premium categories generates an equation describing the condition for second-best p_t and a pair of zero-profit conditions. Substituting the equations for premiums, (4) and (5), into the efficiency condition (3) yields equation in the risk-adjustment weights, r_h. After these substitutions, there are T equations. The "unknowns" are the H risk-adjustment weights, r_h. In general there are relatively few premium categories in individual health insurance markets (e.g., age categories), and many risk-adjustment weights (age, gender, many diagnostic conditions). We refer to a set of weights that solve the T equations for efficiency as r_h^{sb}.

With $T \ll H$, as is typical (in the standard EF model, $T = 1$), there are many r_h^{sb} solutions. How should we pick among these many alternatives? The luxury of multiple solutions allows pursuit of a second criterion in the choice of weights, the fit of the payment system, which, in the case of both MA and marketplaces, consists of a risk-adjustment system and enrollee premiums. Assessing and maximizing fit in a particular institutional context requires incorporation of payment rules, and data, both of which are introduced next.

12.4   Empirical Application: Gold Plan Incremental
Premiums and Risk Adjustment

We draw an "exchange population" from the Medical Expenditure Panel Survey (MEPS) to implement the efficient (second-best) incremental premiums. Risk-adjustment weights are set by a regulator; premiums are determined in market equilibrium. Taking advantage of the multiple solutions available via risk adjustment, we use constrained regression methods to find the risk-adjustment weights that do the best job of fitting plan payments to costs subject to achieving the efficient incremental premiums. Our purpose is to develop and illustrate the application of a method for using risk adjustment to correct for selection problems. We model key features of exchanges—the population, the plans, the premium, and risk adjustment with MEPS data.

12.4.1   Data and the Exchange Population

The MEPS is a nationally representative survey of the civilian noninstitutionalized US population conducted annually since 1996. Each year MEPS collects information on approximately 33,000 individuals, enlisting a new panel of respondents followed for two years. Data are collected in five rounds of interviews covering the two-year period. The Household Component (HC) is the source for personal and household characteristics, including insurance coverage and self-reported health and health conditions. The HC is also the source of data on medical "events" (e.g., an inpatient stay or office visit) including information about diagnoses, procedures, and payments from various sources. The HC data are supplemented with information from the Medical Provider Component (MPC), based on phone surveys of hospitals, physician offices, pharmacies, and home health agencies. We use data from 2004 through 2010. The MEPS data understate health expenditures (Sing et al. 2006; Aizcorbe et al. 2012; Zuvekas and Olin 2009). We follow the correction proposed by Zuvekas and Olin (2009) to inflate total expenditures by a factor of 1.09 for individuals with an inpatient claim and by a factor of 1.546 for all other claims.[14]

We select a population of adults who would be eligible to enroll in state-level exchanges under current law based on their income, insurance, and employment status. We identify nonelderly individuals (ages nineteen to sixty-four) in households earning at least 138 percent of the federal poverty level.[15] We select those who live in a household where an adult is ever (in either year) uninsured, a holder of a nongroup insurance policy, self-employed, employed by a small employer, or paying an out-of-pocket premium for their employer-sponsored health insurance (ESI) plan that is deemed to be unaffordable (as defined in the ACA).[16] We include both years of data for a person who would qualify for exchanges in either year of the data, with the idea that these individuals are vulnerable to loss of insurance and share the same distribution of health care costs as persons who would enroll in the exchanges. In total, we have 64,667 person years.[17] Children may also be in the exchanges, but since they are paid with a separate risk-adjustment system, we confine the analysis here to adults.

Table 12.1 summarizes some statistics on this group. The population contains a relatively high proportion of Hispanics and lives disproportionately in the South. The education and income range is large because we include persons who may have health insurance, but in the individual or small-group

---

14. The MEPS surveys the "noninstitutionalized" population and underrepresents persons in nursing homes or with very long hospital stays. This also contributes to underreporting average medical expenses, but has a small effect on an exchange population.

15. Annual household income from each year is inflated to 2010 dollars using the Consumer Price Index (CPI-U) published by the Bureau of Labor Statistics, and we apply 2009 federal poverty guidelines for the forty-eight contiguous states (available online at http://aspe.hhs .gov/poverty/09poverty.shtml). We follow the methodology of the Kaiser Family Foundation that uses these income criteria to select the population eligible to purchase insurance through an exchange (Trish et al. 2011). Adults and children in households with lower incomes are deemed to qualify for Medicaid. We do not simulate employer behavior as does the CBO model (CBO 2011).

16. Small employers are either (a) those with fewer than fifty employees or (b) those with fewer than 100 employees and who report only one business location. The ACA states that individuals whose out-of-pocket premiums for employer-sponsored insurance exceed 9.5 percent of family income will be eligible to purchase health insurance through an exchange.

17. Most people contribute two years of data. If someone dies in the first year, they would contribute just one. We used no additional weighting of observations.

Table 12.1 **Sample demographic and health characteristics ($N = 64,667$)**

	%
Age	
19–30	30.0
31–50	46.1
51–64	23.7
Male	50.4
Race	
White, non-Hispanic	50.3
Black, non-Hispanic	13.7
Hispanic	27.9
Asian	5.7
Other	2.2
Education	
Less than high school	17.9
High school	34.0
Some college	17.4
College degree	29.4
Employment status	
Continuously employed	74.6
Continuously unemployed	11.7
Household income ($2010)	
Mean	$32,660
< $25,000	48.7
$25,000–50,000	32.5
$50,000–100,000	15.0
> $100,000	3.5
Geographic region	
Northeast	14.0
Mideast	19.4
South	38.2
West	28.3
Insurance status	
Uninsured	55.6
Nongroup	3.5
ESI with employee premium> 9% of income	7.7
Self-employed	0.5
Small group ESI	32.5
Health care spending (mean, $2010)	$2,648
Self-reported health status	
Excellent	28.0
Very good	32.1
Good	28.5
Fair	9.1
Poor	2.0

Source: Medical Expenditure Panel Survey (MEPS), 2004–2010.

market. By in large, this is a relatively healthy population, with 60 percent rating their health Excellent or Very Good. Average health care spending from all sources was $2,648 in 2010 dollars.

12.4.2   Silver and Gold Plan Costs

The ACA allows for four plan levels, Bronze, Silver, Gold, and Platinum (along with a high-deductible plan for young adults), distinguished by the "actuarial value" of coverage in each level.[18] All so-called Qualified Health Plans (QHPs) must cover a set of mandated benefits, but are free to contract with networks of providers and to "manage" care. We assume two plan types, and exaggerate the difference between Gold and Silver. Specifically, we assume the costs in a Gold plan are to 120 percent of costs in a Silver plan, making incremental costs equal to 20 percent of Silver plan costs for each person. In the empirical application, we use MEPS data to classify exchange participants into ht groups, and then assign the average costs within the group as Silver plan costs. We inflate the costs for each ht group by 20 percent to assign Gold plan costs.

12.4.3   Plan Revenues

The ACA specifies that premiums be based on age (with regulated rate bands), smoking status, geography, and family size, but not on preexisting conditions, gender, or other factors.[19] We set three age categories, young adult (nineteen to thirty), middle-age adult (thirty-one to fifty), and older adult (fifty-one to sixty-four), and four geographic areas, the four census regions (to mimic geographic areas within a state). We thus have twelve (3×4) premium categories for which we will study the incremental premium between Gold and Silver plans. We do not use smoking status because this variable, conditional on age, is weakly associated with health care costs in the exchange population.[20] For purposes of this analysis, we treat couples as two individuals. Rate-band regulation applies to the total premium at plans, not the incremental premiums. After risk adjustment, our equilibrium premiums satisfy ACA rate-band restrictions.[21]

---

18. Actuarial value in the ACA is the share of covered costs paid by the plan. Bronze plans have an actuarial value of .6; Silver, .7; Gold, .8; and Platinum, .9. Deductibles and copayments/coinsurance determine the actuarial value.

19. The CMS has recently recommended a particular age profile to be used in premiums, though states are free to set their own subject to the maximum 3-to-1 ratio between old and young (Department of Health and Human Services 2013).

20. We found this in our earlier paper on premiums and risk adjustment with these data (McGuire et al. 2013). Smoking status is problematic also from the standpoint of accurate reporting.

21. Our premium analyses ignore the temporary reinsurance features of exchanges. In the first three years of exchanges, plans will be forced to participate in a federally run system of reinsurance in which the "attachment point" where reinsurance kicks in is set at $60,000. Plans are responsible for only 20 percent of costs after this point. Reinsurance could be incorporated by refiguring plan net costs with this feature as we have done in other research (Zhu et al. 2013).

We risk adjust with the Hierarchical Condition Category (HCC) model recommended for exchanges by the Centers for Medicare and Medicaid Services (CMS) (Department of Health and Human Services 2013). A simpler version of this model pays private drug and managed care plans in Medicare. The exchange version maps diagnoses from ICD-9 codes from claims into one of 100 HCCs. Diseases within an HCC are similar clinically. Each individual is given a (0,1) indicator for each HCC, and these become part of a linear regression model with individual demographics and some disease interactions to predict cost. The coefficients from this model are the "weights" on age, gender, HCC, and other factors used in risk adjustment (Pope et al. 2011). We use the same age categories for risk adjustment as the CMS-HCC model. Our goal is to find the best weights on the elements going into the CMS risk-adjustment model.

Notably, CMS recommends that the HCC model for exchanges be *concurrent*, using this year's medical events to determine the risk-adjusted payment for this year. This is in contrast to its use in Medicare, and virtually all other formal risk-adjustment systems, where the model is *prospective*, using last year's medical experience to predict this year's costs. We follow CMS-recommended practice and use concurrent risk adjustment here.[22]

Our risk-adjustment model diverges from the CMS recommendation in several ways to accommodate the MEPS data. First, whereas the CMS-HCC model uses five-digit ICD-9 diagnosis codes to classify diagnoses, the MEPS public use files do not include five-digit ICD-9 codes. We use the three-digit ICD-9 codes, which are publicly available.[23] Documentation of the CMS-HCC model indicates that moving from three- to five-digit classification does little to improve model fit in MEPS.[24] In MEPS, diagnostic data come from household reports that lack the specificity and precision of physician reports (AHRQ 2011). Second, we do not include the full set of HCC indicators because of limitations of our sample size, nor do we include interaction effects for the same reason. The fifty-eight HCCs with more than twenty observations are entered in the model. The remaining nine HCCs appearing in the

---

22. Concurrent risk adjustment has two things going for it: first, it does not require data from a previous year to figure; and second, it will do a much better job of fitting plan costs than prospective risk adjustment. The main problem with concurrent risk adjustment is that it weakens incentives for plans to contain costs (Van de Ven and Ellis 2000). Medicare has a version of the same problem as exchanges of how to pay for the "new" beneficiaries without a prior year of experience. For these new beneficiaries they use a simplified age-gender risk-adjustment model. Exchanges could do the same.

23. In our model we assume that the three-digit code we observe in the data corresponds to the smallest ICD-9 code that starts with those three digits. For example, an ICD-9 code of 003 in MEPS is assumed to represent 0031, which is the smallest code within the 003 category.

24. The MEPS documentation states: "DxCG Inc. staff have examined how using 3-digit diagnoses (rather than 5-digit codes) would affect the prospective DCG/HCC model's performance. They concluded that, although using 3-digit codes would reduce the model's specificity in clinical classification and its predictive accuracy, the loss in specificity and predictive power was small" (AHRQ 2008, C-2).

data with a total of seventy-three observations are aggregated into a single category. The HCC classifications HCC108 (Chronic Obstructive Pulmonary Disease) and HCC 176 (Artificial Openings for Feeding and Elimination) are too inclusive with our three-digit classification, so we broke these into finer categories. We also added HCCs for pregnancy. The exact algorithm we used to modify the HCCs is described in table 12A.1 in the appendix. We will refer to the risk-adjustment system we use as CMS-HCCs, even though we modified it in the ways just described. Risk-adjustment regressions (conventional and constrained) are represented in table 12A.2 of the appendix.

12.4.4   Demand for Gold Plan and Efficiency of Sorting

We specify demand and efficiency in ways that can be operationalized empirically. Our assumptions respect important economic properties: first best is attained with full information and incremental premiums equal to incremental costs for all persons; no selection emerges when everyone has the same expectation about their health care costs; and, with limited premium discrimination, individuals' more accurate forecasting of their own costs increases selection.

Demand for the Gold plan depends on the benefits a person *expects to get* in Gold over Silver, and on the incremental *premium*. Efficiency depends on the added benefits a person *actually gets* in a plan, and on the incremental *cost*. We start with efficiency and assume the incremental benefit a person i of type ht gets in the Gold plan, b_{iht}, has two components, both measured in dollars:

$$b_{iht} = \beta x_{ht} + v_i, \beta > 1, v_i \sim \text{uniform}[v_{min}, v_{max}].$$

The first component of benefit is the value of incremental services type ht gets in the Gold plan, βx_{ht}, common to all members of group ht. In what follows, we assume that all individuals share the same β. When $\beta > 1$, these services are valued at more than cost (cost $= 1$). (β could also be less than one.) Second is an idiosyncratic component of benefit that differs by person, v_i, which captures idiosyncratic valuation of the incremental services, risk aversion, taste for plan management styles, and other factors. We assume for simplicity, that v_i, is uniformly distributed between a minimum and maximum value, but the range $[v_{min}, v_{max}]$ depends on t.

For efficiency, a person should be in the Gold plan if and only if the incremental benefits of Gold exceed the incremental costs. Incremental costs in Gold are x_{ht} so the rule for efficiency is that individual i should be in Gold if:

$$(6) \qquad\qquad \beta x_{ht} + v_i - x_{ht} > 0.$$

In relation to the first best, the welfare loss in any equilibrium is the lost benefits for those in the "wrong" plan. Generally, for a person in Silver when equation (6) is positive, the loss is $\beta x_{ht} + v_i - x_{ht}$; for a person in Gold when equation (6) is negative, the loss is $-(\beta x_{ht} + v_i - x_{ht})$.

Turning to demand, we specify what individuals expect in terms of incremental benefits at the Gold plan. Selection on the basis of health costs depends on individuals' ability to forecast their health care demand.[25] Better forecasting aggravates selection incentives. We assume a person of type ht expects the following incremental services in the Gold plan:

$$x_{ht}^e = \gamma x_{ht} + (1 - \gamma)\bar{x}.$$

Individuals' expectations of their added services are a weighted average of their ht-group incremental cost, x_{ht}, and the population average, $\bar{x}$. The weight, γ, on ht-group specific spending in expectations could differ by person, but for simplicity we assume all persons share the same ability to predict. The case of "no selection" corresponds to $\gamma = 0$; when $\gamma = 1$, individuals fully anticipate their incremental services in the Gold plan. We operationalize x_{ht} by the predicted values from a regression using all the h-variables from the CMS-HCC model as well as the t-variables used to define premiums. This regression is reported in table 12A.2 of the appendix.

Recalling that p_t is the incremental premium charged to a person of type t in a Gold plan, an individual i chooses Gold if:

(7) $\beta x_{ht}^e + v_i - p_t > 0.$

The equation (7) rule can be aggregated to define demand curves for Gold plan membership. Assuming an interior solution (i.e., the premium p_t is such that some individuals choose the Gold plan and some choose the Silver plan) demand for membership in Gold for one ht group is

(8) $N_{ht}^g = \dfrac{v_{\max} - [p_t - \beta x_{ht}^e]}{v_{\max} - v_{\min}} N_{ht}.$

The nature of selection and efficiency in our EF-type model can be illustrated with demand curves for two h groups of the same size with the same t and therefore facing the same premium (see figure 12.3). We let h take the values 1 and 2 and call the groups $1t$ and $2t$, with costs higher for group $1t$. Demands for Gold for each group (from equation [8]) will be linear, with a slope of $[-1/(v_{\max} - v_{\min})]N_{ht}$, (which, in this example, is identical to both types). The intersection on the vertical axis will be where $p_t = v_{\max} + \beta x_{ht}^e$, taking a value higher for the higher-demand group. Since expectations of health care use are imperfect, actual benefits will diverge from expected benefits (demand). Suppose groups $1t$ and $2t$ both underestimate their actual incremental use in the Gold plan. Benefits are also shown in figure

25. Selection could also arise based on another factor correlated with health care costs. Correlation with "other factors" is why in some settings researchers observe favorable selection. (See, e.g., Cutler, Lincoln, and Zeckhauser 2010.) For example, if risk aversion is inversely related to health care costs, more generous plans will experience favorable selection. Here we set v_i, representing "other factors," to be independent of health care costs so no such correlations are introduced.

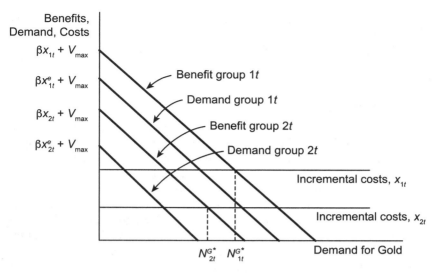

Fig. 12.3   Demand and benefit among two groups with same premium

12.3. Finally, figure 12.3 contains the incremental costs for the two groups, equal to x_{1t} and x_{2t}, respectively, and the efficient memberships in Gold, N_{1t}^{g*} and N_{2t}^{g*}.

We make several observations based on the figure. First, for any premium p_t that the two h groups have in common, more members of the more expensive group $1t$ will join Gold than the equal-sized less expensive group $2t$, that is, selection happens. Indeed, until the premium falls to $v_{max} + \beta x_{2t}^e$, only group $1t$ will join. With further premium reductions, some of both groups join Gold. Since in our model both demands have slope of $[-1/(v_{max} - v_{min})]$ N_{ht}, at the margin the mix of joiners is 50-50, reflecting the overall mix in the t category. As premium falls, the composition of the Gold joiners will move toward the mix of h groups in the t category, reducing the degree of selection. (This is consistent with the EF model.)

Second and importantly, no single premium will lead both groups to make the efficient decision about Gold membership. In other words, no premium can induce N_{1t}^{g*} to join Gold from $1t$ and N_{2t}^{g*} to join Gold from $2t$. This illustrates that the best premium for a t group is a second best—full efficiency in plan sorting is unattainable with a single premium.

Third, the "first-best" premium for each of the two groups is not incremental marginal cost, when demand diverges from benefit. Take group $1t$. We want N_{1t}^{g*} from this group to join Gold. Setting a premium for this group to be equal to x_{1t} would not do it—too few would join Gold at that premium because health care costs are anticipated imperfectly. We have to reduce the incremental premium to below this level to "correct for" the underanticipation of health care costs among members of a high-cost group.[26] Recognizing imperfect foresight implies that a Pigouvian correction for under- or overanticipation of benefits needs to be built into the second-best premium.

12.5   Results

We begin with two normative benchmarks: the (unattainable) first best in which everyone is in the best plan for them, and the (attainable) second best in which the Gold incremental premiums for each of the twelve premium categories are chosen so as to minimize welfare loss in sorting.

To implement these benchmarks, we need to make choices about the parameters describing benefits and demand. We choose parameter values for β, v and γ to lead to what we judge to be a reasonable degree of adverse selection between the two plan types (described shortly). In EF terms, that the incremental AC for the Gold plan is declining with lower premiums (selection happens), and cuts the demand curve from below (there is an equilibrium, no "death spiral"). In other words, the market demand and cost curves look something like figure 1 from the Einav, Finkelstein, and Cullen (2010) paper.

12.5.1   Benchmark: First-Best Allocation

Table 12.2 describes the first-best sorting of individuals between Silver and Gold plans for a baseline set of parameter values. We set $\beta = 1.1$. The idiosyncratic term v is uniform with three ranges, one for each of the three age groups. For the young, v is [−$1,000, $1,000], for the middle-age group [−$2,000, $2,000], and for the older group [−$4,000, $4,000], ranges roughly scaled to health care costs for the three age groups. On average, the additional services in Gold are worth their cost (since $\beta > 1$), but not for everyone because of the idiosyncratic term. For the first best, we use rule (6) to allocate membership from each ht group to the Gold plan. All persons in an ht group are the same except for their idiosyncratic v term. We can define a cutoff value of v for each ht group that defines the person whose net benefit is the same in the two plans. From equation (6):

$$v_{ht}^* = (1 - \beta)x_{ht}.$$

Persons in an ht group with $v_i \geq v_{ht}^*$ should be in Gold, and others in Silver. When $\beta > 1$, v_{ht}^* is negative, indicating that more than half of members of all ht groups will be in Gold in the first best.

---

26. If we could set premium separately for group $1t$ (which of course we cannot), it would be $p_{1t}^* = x_{1t} + \beta(x_{1t}^e - x_{1t})$. The correction for imperfect foresight is the $\beta(x_{1t}^e - x_{1t})$ term.

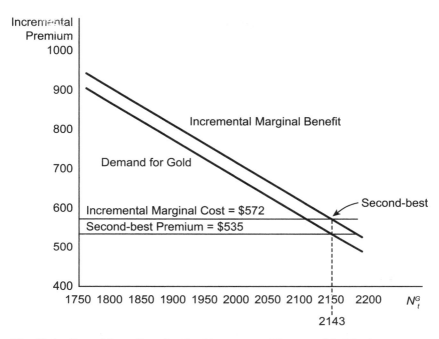

Fig. 12.4   Second-best allocation for thirty-one- to fifty-year-olds, Northeast

range of premiums.[28] (At premiums much higher or lower, this would not be true.) "Incremental average cost" refers to the difference in the average cost of the Gold and the Silver plans. This falls as premium falls. In a market equilibrium, this incremental average cost needs to be covered by the incremental premium (above a premium at the Silver plan that covers average cost) at the Gold plan.

The marginal benefit schedule is constructed as follows. As incremental premium falls, we know (by demand, which depends on x_{ht}^e) which individuals move to the Gold plan. These individuals have a benefit (that depends on x_{ht}) from the Gold plan. The marginal benefit value in table 12.3 is these benefits averaged over the people who move for a given premium difference. Figure 12.4 plots demand, marginal benefit, incremental average, and marginal cost from table 12.3. Because marginal benefit is below demand, to induce the correct enrollment, the incremental premium charged to this group must be less than incremental marginal cost.

Table 12.4 shows the second-best enrollment and premiums for all twelve premium groups. Enrollments are in all cases very close to the enrollments in the first best. Seeing 1,305 in Gold in both the first and second best does not mean the second best is identical to the first best. The 1,305 is rounded

---

28. This special feature is a consequence of our assumptions.

Table 12.4   **Second-best premiums and allocation**

Premium categories			Enrollment		Incremental marginal cost ($)	Second-best premium ($)	Welfare loss ($)
Age	Region	N	Silver	Gold			
19–30	Northeast	2,541	1,236	1,305	271	499	0.57
	Midwest	3,720	1,790	1,930	378	512	0.64
	South	7,298	3,544	3,754	288	501	0.58
	West	5,893	2,873	3,020	238	494	0.50
31–50	Northeast	4,167	2,024	2,143	572	535	0.65
	Midwest	5,703	2,773	2,930	553	533	0.82
	South	11,580	5,663	5,917	443	520	0.71
	West	8,406	4,113	4,293	424	517	0.52
51–64	Northeast	2,362	1,154	1,208	924	577	1.03
	Midwest	3,131	1,525	1,606	1,035	591	1.06
	South	5,826	2,842	2,984	972	583	0.96
	West	4,040	1,978	2,062	822	565	0.70
All		64,667	31,517	33,150	n/a	n/a	0.70

to the nearest whole person, but more importantly, there are some wrong assignments both ways in the second best, whereas everyone is in the right plan for them in the first-best scenario. Specifically, for the nineteen- to thirty-year-olds in the NE, sixteen enrollees (1.3 percent of Silver enrollment) are in Silver who should be in Gold, and sixteen in Gold who should be in Silver. For the entire population, 359 are in Gold who should be in Silver and 358 are in Silver who should be in Gold, amounting to slightly over 1 percent of the population.[29]

The last column in table 12.4 shows the average welfare loss per person for each group and overall associated with being in the "wrong" plan. In the first best, everyone in an ht group with a value of $v > v_{ht}^*$ should be in Gold. By contrast, in the second best, where individuals respond to a premium, although that premium is set at the most efficient level for the t group, it will not be efficient for each of the h groups within the premium category. In the second best, everyone with a $v > v_{ht}^{2\text{nd-best}}$ will choose Gold where this cutoff for each ht group in the second best where

$$v_{ht}^{2\text{nd-best}} = p_t^{2\text{nd-best}} - \beta x_{ht}^e.$$

Thus, within each ht group there is a range of individuals between v_{ht}^* and $v_{ht}^{2\text{nd-best}}$ who are in the "wrong" plan. For some h groups $v_{ht}^* > v_{ht}^{2\text{nd-best}}$ and for others the reverse will be true. To see how we calculate welfare loss for each h group, suppose for some groups $v_{ht}^* > v_{ht}^{2\text{nd-best}}$ implying that too few people from this group are in the Gold plan. The measure of inefficiency for

29. These numbers are not shown in the table, and are rounded to the nearest "whole person."

this *h* group is the probability that someone in the group is in the wrong plan times the average lost benefit for the person wrongly located.

$$\text{Avg Welfare Loss for } ht \text{ group in Second-Best} = \left[\frac{v_{ht}^* - v_{ht}^{\text{2nd-best}}}{v_{\max} - v_{\min}}\right]\left[\frac{v_{ht}^* - v_{ht}^{\text{2nd-best}}}{2}\right].$$

The first term of this product is the probability that a person is in the range of *v* where the person is in the wrong plan; the second term is the average of the lowest (0) and highest ($v_{ht}^* - v_{ht}^{\text{2nd-best}}$) value of the net benefit lost from being in the wrong plan.[30]

Averaged over the entire population, this comes out to only $0.70 per person, the minimum welfare loss that can be attained given these premium groups. The welfare loss in the second best also depends on the benefits in the two plan types and on the nature of individuals' expectations about their costs. The adverse selection problem would be aggravated, and the welfare loss higher, if individuals could forecast more accurately than we have assumed here in these simulations.

The second-best allocation depends only on the incremental premium charged enrollees for Gold. Silver and Gold plans must, of course, break even in an equilibrium. This consideration introduces another set of factors that will determine how much more people are charged to join Gold: the difference between the break-even premium for the Silver plan and for the Gold plan. This will not, of course, in general, be the second best. We move now to consideration of a series of market equilibria: no risk adjustment, conventional risk adjustment, and risk adjustment to hit the second-best premiums. In all equilibria considered, premium for each category for the Silver and Gold plans will be equal to average cost in that premium category.

12.5.3   Equilibrium with No Risk Adjustment

In equilibrium, premium for the Silver plan must equal Silver plan average costs, premium for the Gold plan equals Gold plan average costs, and the difference between these, the incremental premium that consumers face, must sort individuals such that the resulting plan average costs are covered by the premiums. We find the equilibrium by tracing out demand and cost curves.

The equilibrium is depicted graphically in figure 12.5 for the thirty-one-to fifty-year-olds in the Northeast. Figure 12.5 augments figure 12.4 with a lower quadrant showing the average costs for both plans.[31] The incremental average cost in the upper quadrant is seen to be the difference between the average cost curves from the lower quadrant. The lower quadrants can also

---

30. Thus, a kind of "Harberger triangle."

31. In the textbook EF model, the "other plan" has zero costs and zero premium for any enrollee. When the other plan is a real plan, its costs too will vary as enrollment changes in the Gold plan.

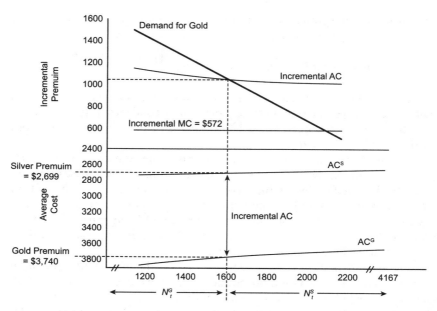

Fig. 12.5   EF equilibrium with no risk adjustment, thirty-one- to fifty-year-olds, Northeast

be used to depict the equilibrium premiums in both the Gold and Silver plans.

Results are summarized for all twelve premium categories in table 12.5. Fewer enrollees are in Gold because for all premium categories, premiums to cover average costs are "too high" in relation to either the first or second best. Instead of more than half of people in Gold in the second best, only 40 percent (26,044/64,667) are in Gold in the equilibrium without risk adjustment. Note that as in the second best, there will be enrollment mistakes in both directions, though with equilibrium premiums too high, most of the mistakes will be putting too many people in Silver. The welfare loss in this equilibrium is much greater than the second best. On average, as the last column in table 12.5 shows, the welfare loss is $32.25 per person.

Beginning with this first equilibrium, we can keep track of how well the payment system—here just premiums—fits costs for Gold and Silver plans. By "fit" we mean the degree to which variation in revenue per person tracks costs per person. To figure fit we generalize the concept of statistical fit to account for both premiums and risk adjustment of plan payments. For each individual, we construct a measure of total payments to the plan (i.e., plan revenues), including the premium and risk adjustment. This value is then

Table 12.5   **Equilibrium premiums and allocation without risk adjustment**

Premium categories			Enrollment		Premiums			Welfare loss ($)
					Silver	Gold	Incremental	
Age	Region	N	Silver	Gold	($)	($)	($)	
19–30	Northeast	2,541	1,465	1,076	1,202	1,881	679	8.69
	Midwest	3,720	2,467	1,253	1,742	2,617	876	33.81
	South	7,298	4,245	3,053	1,287	1,980	693	9.80
	West	5,893	3,165	2,728	1,046	1,639	593	2.91
31–50	Northeast	4,167	2,551	1,616	2,699	3,740	1,041	32.65
	Midwest	5,703	3,684	2,019	2,571	3,743	1,172	51.90
	South	11,580	6,899	4,681	2,030	2,978	947	23.55
	West	8,406	4,666	3,740	1,979	2,758	780	9.14
51–64	Northeast	2,362	1,479	883	4,370	6,049	1,679	76.89
	Midwest	3,131	2,010	1,121	4,923	6,753	1,830	97.06
	South	5,826	3,635	2,191	4,629	6,300	1,672	75.06
	West	4,040	2,357	1,683	3,927	5,240	1,314	35.76
All		64,667	38,623	26,044	n/a	n/a	n/a	32.25

compared with the individual's costs to construct our fit measure.[32] Specifically, let R_i be the total revenue a plan receives for person i after risk adjustment, and x_i be the total costs for person i. Total variation in Silver plan costs is $\Sigma_i(x_i^s - \overline{x^s})^2$, where $\overline{x^s}$ is the mean plan cost and the summation is over individuals in the Silver plan. Variation remaining after the payment system is $\Sigma_i(x_i^s - R_i)^2$. Thus, the R-squared or "fit" of the payment system for Silver is

$$\text{Payment system fit for Silver} = 1 - \frac{\Sigma_i(x_i^s - R_i)^2}{\Sigma_i(x_i^s - \overline{x^s})^2}.$$

A similar expression characterizes fit in the Gold plan.

Plan revenues in the current simulation are simply the premiums covering average cost for each premium group. Some "risk adjustment" is accomplished by premium categories. Values for payment system fit are 0.019 for both Silver and Gold in the no risk-adjustment case.

12.5.4   Equilibrium with Conventional Risk Adjustment

Conventional risk adjustment is based on the regression from table 12A.2. Conventional risk adjustment is estimated ex ante, before plans set premi-

---

32. There are other plausible measures of fit, such as the mean absolute difference between revenues and costs. Not squaring this difference down weights the influence of high-cost outliers in the fit measure. We chose the payment system R-squared to be easily comparable to statistics reported for risk adjustment, and on the general principle in economics that the economic value of a loss goes up approximately with the square of the difference between the actual and the optimal price.

Table 12.6   Equilibrium premiums and allocation with conventional risk adjustment

Premium categories			Enrollment		Premiums			Welfare loss ($)
Age	Region	N	Silver	Gold	Silver ($)	Gold ($)	Incremental ($)	
19–30	Northeast	2,541	981	1,560	2,572	2,870	298	10.58
	Midwest	3,720	1,602	2,118	2,944	3,355	411	3.17
	South	7,298	2,866	4,432	2,595	2,910	315	9.19
	West	5,893	2,190	3,703	2,452	2,714	262	14.01
31–50	Northeast	4,167	2,102	2,065	3,074	3,684	610	1.35
	Midwest	5,703	2,870	2,833	2,842	3,444	601	1.40
	South	11,580	5,553	6,027	2,418	2,900	482	0.89
	West	8,406	3,979	4,427	2,582	3,034	453	1.03
51–64	Northeast	2,362	1,276	1,086	2,662	3,652	990	11.67
	Midwest	3,131	1,726	1,405	2,954	4,058	1,105	17.60
	South	5,826	3,171	2,655	2,673	3,707	1,034	13.66
	West	4,040	2,130	1,910	2,617	3,482	865	6.32
All		64,667	30,446	34,221	n/a	n/a	n/a	6.32

ums and before individuals choose plans. The demand curve for Gold membership is unaffected by risk adjustment. Risk adjustment affects the costs that must be covered by premiums at the two plans because the risk-adjusted revenues now vary according to the personal characteristics of the joiners. Therefore, the incremental average cost that describes the difference in the premiums for Gold and Silver for any premium group also changes. Risk adjustment takes from each plan (either Gold or Silver) the average cost at the Silver plan, $\bar{x}^s$, and returns to each plan the risk-adjusted payment r_h estimate from a regression on Silver plan costs (from table 12A.2 in the appendix). (This risk-adjustment system is self-financing, but the amount "taken" from the plans does not affect the equilibrium so long as the amount is constant for both plan types—it only affects the level of premiums in the two plans.) We compute average cost at the Gold and Silver plans net of risk-adjustment transfers then the average incremental cost for the Gold plan. Equilibrium is, as before, where the incremental premium at the Gold plan equals this risk-adjusted average incremental cost.

Concurrent conventional risk adjustment imposes the market equilibrium compared to that with no risk adjustment, as shown in table 12.6. Equilibrium premiums are much reduced, and many more people move to Gold. This is consistent with the objective of risk adjustment: by transferring funds to more costly individuals, selection has less effect on the net average cost of the plans. (If risk adjustment were perfect and fully picked up expected costs, the mix of joiners would have no effect at all on plans' average costs.) Incremental premiums for the young groups are below the second-best premiums, and for the older groups they are above. Risk adjustment can deal with correcting premiums for selection; it cannot deal at all, at least directly, with correcting for over- or underanticipation of costs. The welfare loss per person in conventional risk adjustment falls to $6.32 per person.

Furthermore, conventional risk adjustment improves the fit of the payment system for both plans. For the Silver plans the payment system fit rises to .168 and to .164 for the Gold plans.

12.5.5   Risk Adjustment to Achieve the Second Best

In our final set of simulations, we find risk-adjustment weights incorporating constraints to ensure that the equilibrium premium is the second-best incremental premium. Consider the first premium group, the nineteen- to thirty-year-olds living in the Northeast. Call them premium group 1. With conventional risk adjustment, table 12.6 tells us that the equilibrium incremental premium is too low, $298 instead of the second-best $499, and too many from this group are in the Gold plan in the conventional risk-adjustment equilibrium. The constraint that premium for the nineteen- to thirty-year-olds in the NE is $499 in equilibrium comes from the expressions that the Silver and Gold plan premiums for this group must be zero profit. For the Silver plan, premium for group 1 is the cost for the group less the net risk-adjustment transfer:

$$(9) \qquad p_1^s = \frac{\sum_h N_{h1}^s x_{h1}^s}{\sum_h N_{h1}^s} - \frac{\sum_h r_h N_{h1}^s}{\sum_h N_{h1}^s} + \bar{x}.$$

Expressing the Gold premium as the Silver premium +$499 (the desired incremental premium), the breakeven condition for the Gold plan for group 1 is:

$$(10) \qquad p_1^s + 499 = \frac{\sum_h N_{h1}^g x_{h1}^g}{\sum_h N_{h1}^g} - \frac{\sum_h r_h N_{h1}^g}{\sum_h N_{h1}^g} + \bar{x}.$$

Substituting for the Silver premium and canceling the overall average costs, we have:

$$(11) \qquad 499 = \frac{\sum_h N_{h1}^g x_{h1}^g}{\sum_h N_{h1}^g} - \frac{\sum_h N_{h1}^s x_{h1}^s}{\sum_h N_{h1}^s} + \frac{\sum_h r_h N_{h1}^s}{\sum_h N_{h1}^s} - \frac{\sum_h r_h N_{h1}^g}{\sum_h N_{h1}^g}.$$

The $499 has to cover the difference in the average costs between the two plans (the first two terms in equation [11]), less any higher risk-adjustment transfers to Gold.

Having solved for the second best, we know average cost in the Silver and Gold plan in the second best, and the enrollments in those plans in the second best. The only "variables" in equation (11) are the risk-adjustment weights. Thus, equation (11) is linear in the r_h weights, and forms the constraint corresponding to the restriction that the incremental premium for the nineteen- to thirty-year-olds is the second best in equilibrium.

After reproducing the conventional risk-adjustment equilibrium results in the first pair of columns, table 12.7, in the second pair of columns, shows the equilibrium with a risk-adjustment system estimated by imposing the one constraint, equation (11) from above. Specifically, we estimate a conventional concurrent risk-adjustment model, identical to the one contained in table 12A.2 from the appendix and described above, but with the constraint that the risk-adjustment weights satisfy equation (11). This regression, and the regressions with more constraints are also contained in table 12A.2. With new risk-adjustment weights, there will be a new equilibrium for all premium categories. Table 12.7 shows the full set of results. Equilibrium incremental premiums generally move in the right direction (toward the second best) for all the young premium categories as the result of imposing the single constraint for the young NE group. The welfare cost per person for all four of the young groups fall as this one constraint comes into play. In aggregate, the sorting between Gold and Silver becomes more efficient, with the per-person welfare loss dropping from $6.32 to $4.75 per person.[33]

Improvement in sorting efficiency comes at a cost in terms of "fit" of the payment system to the Gold and Silver plan. With one constraint, the payment system fit in the Silver and Gold plans fall from 0.168 and 0.164 with conventional risk adjustment to 0.155 and 0.149, respectively. Fit statistics are summarized for our equilibrium cases in figure 12.6.

Table 12.7 and figure 12.6 also contain the results for risk-adjustment systems in which we include two and three constraints. Our two-constraint model imposes, in addition to equation (11) above, a constraint that the premium for the thirty-one- to fifty-year-olds in the NE must be equal to $535, the second-best incremental premium for this group. The form of the constraint is analogous to equation (11). Welfare loss from sorting falls for the middle groups and for the overall average for the population to $3.24. Fit deteriorates for both the Silver and Gold plans. Finally, we also impose a constraint on the fifty-one- to sixty-four-year-olds in the NE, making three constraints in total, bringing down welfare loss to $2.17 per person, but leading to payment-system fits for the Silver and Gold plans of 0.081 and 0.117, respectively.

In principle, we could impose more than three constraints on the second-best premium. To attain the full second best, we could impose all twelve premium constraints. In fact, we have done this in results not reported. We found that the constrained risk-adjustment regressions yielded unreasonable coefficient estimates on the HCC indicators (i.e., too large or too small), and furthermore, the plan-fit measures became very poor. We believe the instability and unreasonableness of the estimates would be relieved with a much larger sample size. In an exchange population, a relatively small share of the population has any positive HCC indicator.[34] Calibration of the

---

33. Because we are imposing just one constraint, there is no guarantee that the average welfare loss falls.
34. Only about 20 percent of the people in our exchange population have any HCC.

Table 12.7   Premium and welfare loss with risk adjustment with and without constraints

Premium categories		No constraints		One constraint		Two constraints		Three constraints	
Age	Region	Incremental premium ($)	Welfare loss ($)	Incremental premium ($)	Welfare loss ($)	Incremental premium ($)	Welfare loss ($)	Incremental premium ($)	Welfare loss ($)
19–30	Northeast	298	10.58	**499**	**0.57**	**499**	**0.57**	**499**	**0.57**
	Midwest	411	3.17	611	3.10	590	2.17	643	4.95
	South	315	9.19	475	0.75	444	1.39	452	1.17
	West	262	14.01	411	2.25	384	3.57	407	2.43
31–50	Northeast	610	1.35	670	2.92	**535**	**0.65**	**535**	**0.65**
	Midwest	601	1.40	677	3.42	556	0.89	454	1.59
	South	482	0.89	550	0.83	443	1.44	367	3.62
	West	453	1.03	515	0.52	439	1.28	410	1.96
51–64	Northeast	990	11.67	1,049	14.93	904	7.70	**577**	**1.03**
	Midwest	1,105	17.60	1,165	21.68	1,034	13.35	746	2.57
	South	1,034	13.66	1,080	16.39	953	9.51	722	2.16
	West	865	6.32	902	7.80	813	4.54	642	1.07
All		n/a	6.32	n/a	4.75	n/a	3.24	n/a	2.17

Note: "One constraint" sets incremental premium for nineteen- to thirty-year-olds in the Northeast to $499; "two constraints" adds constraint that incremental premium for thirty-one- to fifty-year-olds in the Northeast is $535; and "three constraints" adds constraint that incremental premium for fifty-one- to sixty-four-year-olds in the Northeast is $577.

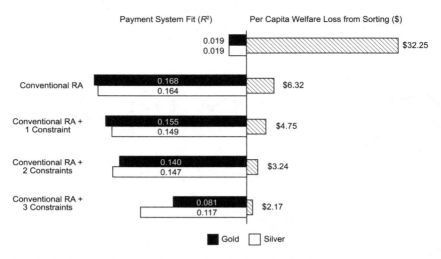

Fig. 12.6   Payment system fit and sorting efficiency trade-off

trade-off between sorting efficiency and plan fit should be next done with the much larger data sets actually used for risk adjustment.

12.6   Discussion

Our goal in this chapter is to introduce risk adjustment—a supply-side policy—into the analysis of EF-type adverse selection stemming from a pricing problem on the demand side due to consumers not facing the correct incremental price for the more generous plan. Risk adjustment can be helpful because it affects the equilibrium incremental premium. We show how this works, and how to incorporate the goal of efficient sorting between plan types into consideration of setting risk adjustment weights.

Our chapter contains theoretical extensions of the EF model and an empirical implementation. The empirical analysis involves a number of assumptions that we acknowledge here. Although we made an effort to capture important features of payment systems in exchanges, including the predominant risk-adjustment methodology, our results can only be regarded as illustrative, due to data limitations as well as many features of exchanges (such as more than two plan types, more detailed risk-adjustment categories, reinsurance and risk corridors, and others) that we could not incorporate in our simulations.

In this final section we would like to call attention to the major conceptual points in the chapter and make some comments about application of the ideas. At the most general level, we want to stress that the connection between premiums and risk adjustment is one that affects welfare outcomes. How plans are paid for various enrollees must affect equilibrium market premiums, no matter what market structure governs plan competition. Premiums are important for plan sorting and even consumer participation in exchanges, and are therefore important to consider in risk adjustment.

To anticipate the impact of risk adjustment on premiums accurately requires a conception (a model) of how premiums are set and how risk adjustment affects costs a plan must cover with the premium. Heterogeneity in a population is central to this issue. The EF-type models already incorporate some heterogeneity in demand and cost, but the textbook EF model needs elaboration for the task of incorporating risk adjustment. Principally, it is necessary to recognize payments to plans depend on the risk score of their enrollees. Groups defined on another but related dimension will pay different premiums for plans. These generalizations of the EF framework when taken to data involve many steps that we take in the chapter. The main conceptual points to take away from these generalizations are, however, straightforward:

- No single premium will sort a population efficiently between two plans. While this point has been made in the health economics literature, the textbook EF diagram makes it look like a single premium can eliminate the "welfare cost" of adverse selection.
- As a corollary, when there is more than one group in a population, the area between the demand curve in aggregate and the marginal cost curve in the EF diagram is not an accurate measure of the welfare loss at all. With multiple groups, the marginal cost curve in that picture is an average marginal cost.

There are two primary welfare frameworks for evaluating the functioning of private health insurance markets, a utility-based framework, and a demand-cost framework. Most papers in the literature use one or the other. For example, EF uses demand and cost. Our chapter uses both, starting with utility and deriving the demand and marginal benefit schedule. Doing so explicitly is a reminder of the assumptions necessary to go from utility to demand. Major assumptions have to do with what a consumer "knows" or can forecast, and the degree to which consumers are fully rational. It is very unclear the degree to which demand (willingness to pay) can serve as a welfare framework in health insurance. While ultimately utility is the gold standard for welfare in economics, demand and cost diagrams are the workhorses of applied welfare economics. An important agenda item for health economics and policy is coming up with a practical and valid method for normative analysis of health insurance markets.

It is worth recalling in this respect that the EF approach treats plan characteristics as fixed, missing an important efficiency concern, dating from some of the first research on the economics of insurance market equilibrium, about how selection influences the design of the health insurance product itself (Rothschild and Stiglitz 1976). Einav-Finkelstein, as well as the work we do here, does not incorporate equity considerations. The basic EF framework with one group and one premium is not suited to healthy-sick or other cross-group comparisons. In the current chapter, because we have age groups and risk adjustment, it would be possible to do more with equity. Interestingly, our efficiency corrections tend to level age-group differences among equilibrium premiums.

One of the practical applications of the methods developed here is to address questions around determination of population groups with respect to premium categories. A great deal of research has focused on the question of grouping people for purposes of risk adjustment. Risk-adjustment statistical models are generally populated with (0,1) variables that correspond to risk-adjustment cells. Much less work has been directed to the question of what are the right premium groups. We know one group is inefficient and two groups could improve the efficiency of sorting, but the introduction of groups implies different premiums for the different groups that may introduce fairness issues. In order to evaluate any efficiency-fairness trade-off, we need to have a sense of what the efficiency gains are for dividing a population more finely. The methods here help to address the issue.

In addition to contributions that depend on welfare or evaluation of efficiency, we have shown here how to work with the connection between premiums and risk adjustment. If a regulator is interested in premium targets (e.g., keeping premiums for young people below some level), risk adjustment can be the tool to hit the targets by adding premium constraints to the risk-adjustment formulas.

Appendix

Table 12A.1   Changes on the algorithm from ICD-9 codes to CMS-HCCs

ICD-9 codes	CCs
	Five pregnancy-related CCs are added:
650–659	200 Normal delivery
640–649	201 Complications mainly related to pregnancy
660–669	202 Complications occurring mainly in the course of labor
670–677	203 Complications of the puerperium
630–639	204 Ectopic and molar pregnancy
	HCC108 (Chronic obstructive pulmonary disease) is broken into two CCs:
	210 Chronic obstructive pulmonary disease, except asthma
	211 Asthma
	HCC 176 (Artificial openings for feeding or elimination) is broken into three CCs:
	220 Diseases of esophagus
	221 Disorders of function of stomach
	222 Other disorders of intestine

Notes: The CCs are sorted as 200, 201, 202, 203, and 204 from least to most severe conditions. Individuals are assigned to the most severe code for hierarchy adjustment if they have multiple conditions.

Table 12A.2 **Risk-adjustment regression results**

	Conventional risk adjustment	Conventional RA plus 1 constraint	Conventional RA plus 2 constraints	Conventional RA plus 3 constraints	Conventional RA plus premium categories
F18_24	1,234	979	618	739	1,189
	(120)	(120)	(121)	(125)	(192)
F25_34	1,686	1,044	516	481	1,580
	(96)	(94)	(94)	(97)	(186)
F35_44	1,504	1,756	1,741	1,195	1,275
	(96)	(97)	(98)	(101)	(223)
F45_54	1,695	1,906	1,803	630	1,358
	(95)	(96)	(96)	(98)	(228)
F55_64	2,236	2,488	1,714	1,470	1,713
	(120)	(121)	(119)	(123)	(271)
M18_24	387	1,653	2,213	2,146	349
	(111)	(104)	(103)	(107)	(184)
M25_34	582	1,064	802	1,428	463
	(90)	(90)	(90)	(93)	(183)
M35_44	853	962	149	1,112	625
	(93)	(94)	(91)	(93)	(222)
M45_54	1,490	1,632	1,496	47	1,146
	(99)	(99)	(100)	(101)	(230)
M55_64	2,106	2,303	1,626	971	1,586
	(122)	(123)	(122)	(126)	(272)
HCC1	3,235	1,525	1,553	987	3,228
	(445)	(445)	(449)	(464)	(445)
HCC2	2,161	−396	−1,650	−2,058	2,165
	(495)	(492)	(495)	(512)	(495)
HCC5	1,859	1,056	1,491	−219	1,833
	(311)	(312)	(314)	(324)	(311)
HCC7	13,565	14,010	17,368	32,757	13,559
	(885)	(892)	(894)	(893)	(885)
HCC8	13,666	14,094	18,132	30,940	13,653
	(1,186)	(1,195)	(1,199)	(1,225)	(1,186)
HCC9	17,992	13,660	15,212	16,436	17,972
	(870)	(865)	(871)	(901)	(869)
HCC10	5,526	5,171	6,846	7,592	5,510
	(242)	(243)	(240)	(248)	(242)
HCC19	3,423	3,423	4,226	5,701	3,422
	(146)	(147)	(146)	(149)	(146)
HCC26	1,724	1,728	−17	3,768	1,738
	(1,226)	(1,235)	(1,244)	(1,285)	(1,225)
HCC27	6,104	6,665	11,523	13,455	6,092
	(856)	(862)	(857)	(886)	(856)
HCC31	4,399	4,280	4,477	2,706	4,415
	(610)	(615)	(620)	(641)	(610)
HCC32	10,740	6,514	5,654	9,902	10,746
	(874)	(870)	(877)	(904)	(874)
HCC33	5,085	4,394	7,602	1,892	5,053
	(752)	(757)	(758)	(779)	(752)

(*continued*)

	Conventional risk adjustment	Conventional RA plus 1 constraint	Conventional RA plus 2 constraints	Conventional RA plus 3 constraints	Conventional RA plus premium categories
HCC37	3,188	3,064	4,221	3,237	3,181
	(353)	(356)	(357)	(369)	(353)
HCC38	2,521	2,426	3,182	3,510	2,498
	(309)	(312)	(314)	(324)	(309)
HCC44	4,382	1,836	1,445	8,343	4,384
	(772)	(773)	(780)	(799)	(772)
HCC45	13,615	10,627	18,130	18,234	13,596
	(1,157)	(1,162)	(1,150)	(1,189)	(1,157)
HCC52	4,125	1,814	1,552	−285	4,101
	(845)	(848)	(856)	(884)	(845)
HCC54	9,373	7,504	9,759	10,135	9,408
	(1,039)	(1,045)	(1,052)	(1,088)	(1,039)
HCC55	4,691	1,619	2,839	−2,409	4,666
	(423)	(414)	(416)	(422)	(423)
HCC69	2,610	867	−591	−34	2,629
	(1,160)	(1,167)	(1,177)	(1,217)	(1,160)
HCC71	5,693	6,608	8,959	7,238	5,628
	(1,242)	(1,251)	(1,260)	(1,303)	(1,242)
HCC72	17,470	11,637	17,896	23,631	17,483
	(1,005)	(995)	(986)	(1,016)	(1,005)
HCC73	2,308	2,912	3,039	6,759	2,268
	(600)	(604)	(609)	(627)	(600)
HCC74	3,811	2,021	2,206	2,137	3,783
	(762)	(765)	(772)	(798)	(762)
HCC75	4,761	4,211	3,744	12,631	4,665
	(1,283)	(1,292)	(1,304)	(1,341)	(1,283)
HCC77	3,309	3,359	4,212	5,694	3,302
	(618)	(623)	(628)	(649)	(618)
HCC79	4,219	4,457	6,112	3,250	4,193
	(840)	(846)	(852)	(880)	(840)
HCC80	5,689	5,132	5,239	9,801	5,689
	(362)	(364)	(367)	(373)	(362)
HCC82	12,477	12,748	13,539	21,898	12,459
	(463)	(467)	(470)	(469)	(463)
HCC83	3,175	3,575	3,935	10,243	3,169
	(640)	(645)	(650)	(665)	(640)
HCC92	3,943	3,638	4,446	6,567	3,921
	(418)	(421)	(424)	(437)	(418)
HCC96	10,126	9,283	10,383	18,664	10,141
	(601)	(605)	(609)	(617)	(601)
HCC104	5,493	5,401	7,983	6,390	5,486
	(315)	(317)	(310)	(320)	(315)
HCC105	12,741	10,681	16,124	16,048	12,727
	(639)	(640)	(625)	(646)	(639)
HCC119	3,332	2,721	3,132	2,878	3,323
	(404)	(407)	(410)	(424)	(404)

Table 12A.2 (continued)

	Conventional risk adjustment	Conventional RA plus 1 constraint	Conventional RA plus 2 constraints	Conventional RA plus 3 constraints	Conventional RA plus premium categories
HCC130	11,775	8,768	6,748	28,180	11,752
	(1,059)	(1,062)	(1,069)	(1,055)	(1,058)
HCC131	19,239	17,584	20,490	25,724	19,213
	(870)	(875)	(878)	(905)	(870)
HCC148	5,553	5,115	6,969	3,552	5,542
	(677)	(682)	(686)	(707)	(677)
HCC155	3,652	610	−90	−377	3,638
	(581)	(576)	(581)	(601)	(581)
HCC157	2,426	2,648	3,360	4,350	2,403
	(291)	(293)	(294)	(304)	(291)
HCC158	10,164	8,106	10,103	9,323	10,171
	(1,133)	(1,140)	(1,148)	(1,187)	(1,133)
HCC164	9,777	7,578	10,176	17,833	9,767
	(647)	(647)	(648)	(660)	(646)
HCC174	7,067	7,526	9,599	26,982	7,045
	(1,482)	(1,493)	(1,504)	(1,532)	(1,482)
HCC177	3,154	3,404	3,877	12,066	3,145
	(975)	(982)	(990)	(1,016)	(974)
HCC200	6,328	−368	−2,848	−4,376	6,354
	(754)	(728)	(730)	(755)	(754)
HCC201	5,686	3,693	4,600	991	5,671
	(689)	(691)	(696)	(718)	(689)
HCC202	11,055	−1,929	−6,509	−9,379	11,038
	(901)	(804)	(799)	(825)	(901)
HCC203	4,815	6,179	12,491	2,168	4,808
	(1,588)	(1,600)	(1,602)	(1,649)	(1,588)
HCC204	1,658	−839	−2,059	−1,987	1,680
	(674)	(674)	(679)	(702)	(674)
HCC210	4,423	4,772	5,789	11,528	4,407
	(347)	(350)	(351)	(352)	(347)
HCC211	1,742	1,121	2,025	221	1,705
	(204)	(205)	(205)	(210)	(204)
HCC220	3,442	3,251	4,612	4,261	3,429
	(177)	(178)	(175)	(181)	(177)
HCC221	2,729	1,766	1,854	2,571	2,733
	(300)	(301)	(303)	(314)	(300)
HCC222	5,297	4,662	6,597	8,292	5,275
	(665)	(669)	(673)	(695)	(664)
small_hcc	5,968	6,565	19,033	−1,637	5,939
	(951)	(958)	(891)	(864)	(951)
Restriction (Young_Northeast)		−3E+08	−5E+08	−5E+08	
		(1E+07)	(1E+07)	(1E+07)	
Restriction (Mid_Northeast)			6E+08	−4E+08	
			(2E+07)	(2E+07)	
Restriction (Old_Northeast)				9.4E+08	
				(1E+07)	

(continued)

Table 12A.2   (continued)

	Conventional risk adjustment	Conventional RA plus 1 constraint	Conventional RA plus 2 constraints	Conventional RA plus 3 constraints	Conventional RA plus premium categories
Young_Midwest					375
					(208)
Young_South					24
					(186)
Young_West					−119
					(192)
Mid_Northeast					673
					(234)
Mid_Midwest					439
					(223)
Mid_South					12
					(210)
Mid_West					173
					(214)
Old_Northeast					479
					(289)
Old_Midwest					770
					(259)
Old_South					489
					(259)
Old_West					430
					(267)
R^2	0.236	0.224	0.211	0.156	0.236

Source: MEPS, 2004–2010.

Note: All dollar estimates reported in 2010 USD, and standard errors are shown in parentheses. $N = 64,667$.

References

Abaluck, J., and J. Gruber. 2011. "Choice Inconsistencies among the Elderly: Evidence from Plan Choice in the Medicare Part D Program." *American Economic Review* 101 (4): 1180–210.

Agency for Healthcare Research and Quality (AHRQ). 2008. *MEPS HC-092 1996–2004 Risk Adjustment Scores, Public Use File.* Rockville, MD: AHRQ.

———. 2011. *MEPS HC-128: Medical Conditions File.* Rockville, MD: AHRQ.

Aizcorbe, A., E. Liebman, S. Pack, D. M. Cutler, M. E. Chernew, and A. B. Rosen. 2012. "Measuring Health Care Costs of Individuals with Employer-Sponsored Health Insurance in the US: A Comparison of Survey and Claims Data." *Bureau of Economic Analysis* 28:43–51. http://www.bea.gov/papers/pdf/Measuring%20health%20care%20costs%20of%20individuals%20with%20employer-sponsored%20health%20insurance.pdf.

Akerlof, G. A. 1970. "The Market for 'Lemons': Quality Uncertainty and the Market Mechanism." *Quarterly Journal of Economics* 84 (3): 488–500.

Bundorf, M. K., J. D. Levin, and N. Mahoney. 2012. "Pricing and Welfare in Health Plan Choice." *American Economic Review* 102 (7): 3214–48.

Carlin, C., and R. Town. 2010. "Adverse Selection, Welfare and Optimal Pricing of Employer Sponsored Health Plans." Unpublished Manuscript.

Congressional Budget Office (CBO). 2011. *CBO's Analysis of the Major Health Care Legislation Enacted in March 2010.* Testimony by Douglas W. Elmendorf before the Subcommittee on Health, Committee on Energy and Commerce, US House of Representatives, March 30, 2011.

Cutler, D., G. Lincoln, and R. Zeckhauser. 2010. "Selection Stories: Understanding Movement across Health Plans." *Journal of Health Economics* 29 (6): 821–38.

Cutler, D., and S. Reber. 1998. "Paying for Health Insurance: The Trade-off between Competition and Adverse Selection." *Quarterly Journal of Economics* 113 (2): 433–66.

Dafny, L., K. Ho, and M. Varela. 2013. "Let them Have Choice: Gains from Shifting away from Employer-Sponsored Health Insurance and Toward an Individual Exchange." *American Economic Journal: Economic Policy* 5 (1): 32–58.

Department of Health and Human Services, Patient Protection and Affordable Care Act. 2013. "HHS Notice of Benefit and Payment Parameters for 2014." *Federal Register* 2013:15410–541.

Einav, L., and A. Finkelstein. 2011. "Selection in Insurance Markets: Theory and Empirics in Pictures." *Journal of Economic Perspectives* 25 (1): 115–38.

Einav, L., A. Finkelstein, and M. Cullen. 2010. "Estimating Welfare in Insurance Markets Using Variation in Prices." *Quarterly Journal of Economics* 125 (3): 877–921.

Einav, L., A. Finkelstein, and Levin. 2010. "Beyond Testing: Empirical Models of Insurance Markets." *Annual Review of Economics* 2:311–36.

Geruso, M. 2012. "Selection in Employer Health Plans: Homogeneous Prices and Heterogeneous Preferences." Unpublished Manuscript.

Glazer, J., and T. G. McGuire. 2000. "Optimal Risk Adjustment of Health Insurance Premiums: An Application to Managed Care." *American Economic Review* 90 (4): 1055–71.

———. 2011. "Gold and Silver Plans: Accommodating Demand Heterogeneity in Managed Competition." *Journal of Health Economics* 30 (5): 1011–19.

Handel, B. 2013. "Adverse Selection and Inertia in Health Insurance Markets: When Nudging Hurts." *American Economic Review* 103 (7): 2643–82.

Handel, B., I. Hendel, and M. D. Whinston. 2013. "Equilibria in Health Exchanges: Adverse Selection vs. Reclassification Risk." NBER Working Paper no. 19399, Cambridge, MA.

Keeler, E., G. Carter, and J. Newhouse. 1998. "A Model of the Impact of Reimbursement Schemes on Health Plan Choice." *Journal of Health Economics* 17 (3): 297–320.

Kolstad, J., and A. Kowalski. 2014. "Mandate-Based Health Reform and Evidence from the Labor Market: Evidence from the Massachusetts Reform." NBER Working Paper no. 17933, Cambridge, MA.

Lucarelli, C., J. Prince, and K. Simon. 2012. "The Welfare Impact of Reducing Choice in Medicare Part D: A Comparison of Two Regulation Strategies." *International Economic Review* 53 (4): 1155–77.

Lustig, J. 2008. "The Welfare Effects of Adverse Selection in Privatized Medicare." Unpublished Manuscript.

McGuire, T. G., J. Glazer, J. P. Newhouse, S.-L. Normand, J. Shi, A. D. Sinaiko, and S. Zuvekas. 2013. "Integrating Risk Adjustment and Enrollee Premiums in Health Plan Payment." *Journal of Health Economics* 32 (6): 1263–77.

Newhouse, J. P., W. G. Manning, E. B. Keeler, and E. M. Sloss. 1989. "Adjusting Capitation Rates Using Objective Health Measures and Prior Utilization." *Health Care Financing Review* 10 (3): 41–54.

Pope, G. C., J. Kautter, M. J. Ingber, S. Freeman, R. Sekar, and C. Newhart. 2011. "Evaluation of the CMS-HCC Risk Adjustment Model." Final Report, RTI Project no. 0209853.006, RTI International. March.

Rothschild, M., and J. Stiglitz. 1976. "Equilibrium in Competitive Insurance Markets: An Essay on the Economics of Imperfect Information." *Quarterly Journal of Economics* 90 (4): 629–49.

Sing, M., J. S. Banthin, T. M. Selden, C. A. Cowan, and S. P. Keehan. 2006. "Reconciling Medical Expenditure Estimates from the MEPS and NHEA, 2002." *Health Care Finance Review* 28 (1): 25–40.

Spinnewijn, J. 2017. "Heterogeneity, Demand for Insurance and Adverse Selection." *American Economic Journal: Economic Policy* 9 (1): 308–43.

Trish, E., A. Damico, G. Claxton, L. Levitt, and R. Garfield. 2011. *A Profile of Health Insurance Exchange Enrollees.* Kaiser Family Foundation. March. http://kff.org/health-reform/report/a-profile-of-health-insurance-exchange-enrollees/.

Van de Ven, W. P. M. M., and R. P. Ellis. 2000. "Risk Adjustment in Competitive Health Plan Markets." In *Handbook of Health Economics*, vol. 1, edited by A. Culyer and J. Newhouse, 755–846. Amsterdam: Elsevier.

Zhu, J. M., T. J. Layton, A. D. Sinaiko, and T. G. McGuire. 2013. "The Power of Reinsurance in Health Insurance Exchanges to Improve the Fit of the Payment System and Reduce Incentives for Adverse Selection." *Inquiry* 50 (4): 255–74.

Zuvekas, S. H., and G. Olin. 2009. "An Examination of the Accuracy of Medicare Expenditures in the Medical Expenditure Panel Survey." *Inquiry* 46 (1): 92–108.

13
Going into the Affordable Care Act
Measuring the Size, Structure, and Performance of the Individual and Small Group Markets for Health Insurance

Pinar Karaca-Mandic, Jean M. Abraham, Kosali Simon, and Roger Feldman

13.1 Introduction

The Affordable Care Act (ACA) will dramatically alter health insurance markets and the sources through which individuals obtain coverage. All low-income Americans above the poverty line who lack access to affordable employer-sponsored insurance will be eligible for subsidies to purchase individual insurance in state-based exchanges (or "marketplaces"). This provision of the ACA will greatly expand the size and importance of the individual market. The Congressional Budget Office (CBO) projects that approximately 17 percent of the nonelderly population will obtain coverage in the individual market by 2016 (CBO 2012); today that number stands at only 5 percent.

Only 35.2 percent of private-sector establishments with fewer than fifty employees offered health insurance to their employees in 2012. In contrast, 95.9 percent of those with fifty or more employees did so.[1] Establishment of Small Business Health Options Program (SHOP) exchanges in 2014 will

Pinar Karaca-Mandic is an associate professor at the University of Minnesota's Carlson School of Management and a research associate of the National Bureau of Economic Research. Jean M. Abraham is a professor at the University of Minnesota's School of Public Health. Kosali Simon is the Class of 1948 Herman B. Wells Endowed Professor at the School of Public and Environmental Affairs, Indiana University, and a research associate of the National Bureau of Economic Research. Roger Feldman is professor emeritus at the University of Minnesota's School of Public Health.

This work was supported by the Robert Wood Johnson Foundation's State Health Reform Assistance Network (State Network) grant to the State Health Access Data Assistance Center (SHADAC). For acknowledgments, sources of research support, and disclosure of the authors' material financial relationships, if any, please see http://www.nber.org/chapters/c13108.ack.

1. http://meps.ahrq.gov/mepsweb/data_stats/summ_tables/insr/national/series_1/2012/tia1a .htm (accessed September 23, 2013).

simplify the health insurance shopping experience for small employers (fifty or fewer full-time equivalent employees), as well as allow their employees to choose from among options in an "exchange-like" setting, although without access to exchange tax credits.[2]

The ACA also increases regulation of health insurers and health insurance markets, for example, by controlling premium increases through rate-review regulation and by regulating insurers' medical loss ratios (MLRs), which broadly represents the proportion of health insurance premium revenues that is paid out in medical claims. Additional ACA provisions require policies to include essential benefits and limit price variance through modified community rating.

The MLR regulations were among the first ACA provisions to be implemented. Beginning in January 2011, insurers in the individual and small group markets must spend at least 80 percent of their premium revenue on medical care and quality improvement activities, while insurers in the large group market must have MLRs of at least 85 percent. Insurers must provide annual information on their MLRs to the US Department of Health and Human Services. Those that fail to meet the 80 percent and 85 percent minimum MLR thresholds for the individual/small group and large group segments must provide equivalent rebates to their policyholders beginning in 2012.

While the MLR regulation monitors the ratio of spending on medical benefits to premiums, another ACA provision, rate-review regulation, complements it by controlling premium increases. Under rate-review regulation, insurers must document and publicly justify "unreasonable premium increases" when they file advance notice of rates starting with the 2011 plan year. Before the ACA, states had substantial variation in their authority to review rates (Kaiser Family Foundation 2010). Almost half of the states had "prior approval" rate regulation in which regulators could review the rates[3] and approve or disapprove proposed changes. In contrast, other states had "file and use" regulations in which insurers had to provide actuarial justification for rate increases, but could proceed with rate increases without state approval. However, the state reserved the right to intervene if the rates were later found to be "unreasonable." Only a few states lacked any regulatory authority over rates. States also had different criteria for deeming rates to

2. The SHOP exchanges will administer the small business health care tax credits, but these are much more limited than the individual subsidies provided through the exchange. More details on the small business tax credits can be found at http://www.irs.gov/uac/Small-Business -Health-Care-Tax-Credit-for-Small-Employers and http://www.taxpayeradvocate.irs.gov/ calculator/SBHCTC.htm.

3. The "rate" is distinct from the "premium." While the premium is the total cost of the policy paid by an individual or group (i.e., family), rate is the "unit cost" of the policy. Rates may vary by number of dependents in a policy, benefit design of the policy, age, gender, previous claims experience, and geographic location.

be reasonable.[4] States differed in levels of enforcement of their regulations, as well as in the strength of their regulatory oversight. While the ACA does not require any changes to the states' existing rate-review regulation authority, various states have amended their laws to align them better with the federal law.

As the ACA is implemented, it is essential to monitor the intended and the unintended consequences of these regulations. To evaluate the changes in health insurance markets linked to the ACA, it is critical to consistently measure the size and structure of health insurance markets, as well as the performance of participating health insurers, prior to and post-ACA.

In this chapter we discuss challenges of describing the size, structure, and performance of the individual and small group markets. Next, we discuss improvements in data availability starting in 2010 to address some of these concerns. Finally, using data from the National Association of Insurance Commissioners (NAIC), we evaluate insurance market structure and performance during 2010–2012, focusing on enrollment, the number of participating insurers, premiums, claims spending, MLR, and administrative expenses.

13.2   The Size of the Individual and Small Group Markets for Health Insurance

13.2.1   Individual Market

Estimates based on the Current Population Survey (CPS) suggest that approximately 5 percent of the US population has individually purchased coverage.[5] However, estimates vary widely across different federal surveys. Abraham, Karaca-Mandic, and Boudreaux (2013) estimated the size of the individual market for health insurance during the period just before passage of the ACA. The authors also documented strengths and limitations of particular federal surveys and administrative data sources for addressing questions about the individual market. They considered four prominent federal surveys: the National Health Interview Survey (NHIS), the Medical Expenditure Panel Survey Household Component (MEPS-HC), the Annual Social and Economic Supplement to the Current Population Survey (CPS), and the American Community Survey (ACS). They also considered an administrative data source from the National Association of Insurance Commissioners (NAIC).

Abraham, Karaca-Mandic, and Boudreaux (2013) found that federal survey estimates of the individual market vary widely—from 9.5 million

---

4. While most states used medical trends, rate history, and MLR in determining whether the rates were "unreasonable," they used different thresholds.

5. See Kaiser Family Foundation (2011) at http://kff.org/other/state-indicator/total -population/.

nonelderly in MEPS to 25 million in the ACS (table 1). Their study suggests three important measurement issues outlined in table 13.1. First, surveys differ in how they elicit coverage in the individual market. Rather than asking respondents directly if they are covered by individual health insurance, they ask about "directly purchased" coverage with different purchasing arrangements (e.g., from an insurance company or a group such as a school). Second, surveys vary in differentiating the types of individual policies (e.g., comprehensive coverage, limited benefit, disease specific, or short term). In fact, none of the surveys ask whether the health plan includes comprehensive medical and hospital coverage. Even if the surveys asked such questions, individuals may not be aware of the comprehensiveness of their plans unless they are frequent health care users. This is important because some ACA regulations, such as the MLR regulation and the expansion of the individual market under exchanges, apply only to comprehensive coverage.[6]

Abraham, Karaca-Mandic, and Boudreaux (2013) highlighted a third point: surveys differ in the reference period of the insurance questions (e.g., coverage at the interview date versus coverage any time during the previous calendar year). While "point-in-time" surveys that ask about coverage at the interview date avoid recall bias, they miss individuals who held coverage during the year but dropped it prior to the interview date. For example, the CPS asks if a respondent had individual coverage at *any time* during the previous calendar year. This framing has the greatest potential for recall bias (Klerman et al. 2009). Moreover, it is not possible to know whether a respondent held individual coverage at the time of the interview, part of the year, or throughout the entire year. These are important measurement issues, especially because enrollment patterns in the individual market are typically dynamic throughout the year. Many who buy individual policies use it to bridge short-term coverage gaps (e.g., transitions from job-to-job or school-to-job and retirement-to-Medicare eligibility).

To partially reconcile large differences across the surveys, Cantor et al. (2007) and Mach and O'Hara (2011) defined a coverage hierarchy whereby individuals who report multiple coverage types are assigned to only one category. The hierarchy prioritizes coverage types in the following order: public, employer-sponsored coverage, direct purchase, and uninsured. Their basic premise is that a substantial portion of people who report both individual market and another coverage type on these surveys really have one comprehensive policy. For example, an individual could be covered primarily through an employer-sponsored policy, but also have a single-service dental plan and thus report both employer-sponsored insurance and the direct-purchase option. This adjustment (also presented in table 13.1) to redefine coverage types into just one main type by using a hierarchy results

6. https://www.federalregister.gov/articles/2012/05/16/2012-11753/medical-loss-ratio -requirements-under-the-patient-protection-and-affordable-care-act. Also see Congressional Research Service (September 18, 2012) http://www.fas.org/sgp/crs/misc/R42735.pdf.

Table 13.1   Individual market coverage information and estimates by survey, 2009

	MEPS	NHIS	CPS	ACS
Survey question(s)	Was anyone in the family covered by health insurance from any source listed on the card?	Which kind of health insurance or health care coverage do you have? Include those that pay for only one type of service (nursing home care, accidents, or dental care). Exclude private plans that provide extra cash while hospitalized. Which one of these categories best describes how this plan was obtained?	At any time during 2009, (was/ were) (you/ anyone in this household) covered by a health insurance plan that (you/they) PURCHASED DIRECTLY FROM AN INSURANCE COMPANY, that is, not related to current or past employment?	Is this person currently covered by any of the following types of health insurance or coverage plans?
Response option indicating directly purchased or individual market coverage	(1) Directly from an insurance agent; (2) directly from a company; (3) directly from an HMO	(1) Through workplace (self-employed or professional association); (2) Purchased directly; (3) Through school	(1) Yes	"Insurance purchased directly from an insurance company."
Reference period	Point-in-time and monthly / Any time during year	Point-in-time	Any time during year	Point-in-time
Recall period of item	None–6 months	None	4–16 months	None
Estimate of the nonelderly population US reporting directly purchased insurance	Point-in-time 9,550,414 / Any time during year 11,240,406	Point-in-time 14,030,479	Any time during year 18,454,383	Point-in-time 25,319,985
Estimate of the nonelderly population US reporting directly purchased insurance adjusted for coverage hierarchy[a]	8,215,358	13,379,765	10,812,180	16,635,033

Source: Abraham, Karaca-Mandic, and Boudreaux (2013, tables 1, 2, and 3; reproduced with authors' permission).

[a] Hierarchical assigns a maximum of one type of coverage to a respondent. Prioritization of coverage types is public, employer sponsored, and directly purchased.

in a smaller estimate of the size of individual market and a tighter alignment across different federal surveys (8,215,358 in MEPS and 16,635,033 in ACS).

13.2.2   Small Group Market

In contrast to the individual market, not all household surveys discussed above can measure coverage obtained through the small employer group market because most household surveys do not ask working individuals about the size of their employer. Several studies have used the size of the worker's establishment in conjunction with whether the establishment has more than one location as a proxy for firm size (Abraham, DeLeire, and Royalty 2009; Monheit and Schone 2004). However, this approach would classify a large-firm employee working in an establishment with few employees as a small-firm employee. Even if the survey asks respondents for firm size, it is unclear whether workers can accurately assess this, especially when the firm has multiple locations. Nationally representative employer surveys such as the MEPS-Insurance Component (MEPS-IC), in contrast, can estimate the size of the small group market more accurately than household surveys.

The MEPS-IC samples public- and private-sector establishments, collecting information on their health insurance offerings and characteristics of the workers and workplace. A firm could have one or more establishments, but each surveyed establishment provides information on the total number of employees across all establishments, which allows an inference of firm size; firm size is also checked against administrative sources. National and state-level estimates of insurance coverage by year are publicly available from the MEPS-IC.[7]

Using several statistics reported in these tables, we estimated the number of employees with health insurance in firms with fewer than fifty employees (table 13.2). In 2009, approximately 10,587,185 small-firm employees had employer-sponsored health insurance (9,359,072 through fully insured plans and 1,228,113 through self-insured plans). These numbers do not include dependents of the primary insurance holders. Previous research estimated an average of one dependent per employee in small firms (Karaca-Mandic, Abraham, and Phelps 2011), which suggests a total of 21,174,370 enrollees in the small group market and 18,718,144 in fully insured plans. Estimates of small group insurance also come from Kaiser HRET/surveys, although their sample size of small employers is typically limited and the microdata are not easily accessed by researchers.

Thus, prior estimates of the size of the individual market have relied on household surveys and provide a range of sizes due to the inherently difficult

---

7. Summary statistics at http://meps.ahrq.gov/mepsweb/data_stats/quick_tables.jsp#insurance contain publicly released data. Researchers wishing to use the MEPS-IC must obtain approval from the Census Bureau and the Internal Revenue Service and must access the data at a Census Research Data Center.

Table 13.2   Estimates of employees with health insurance coverage in firms with less than fifty employees

		2009	2010	2011	2012
(1)	Total number of employees[a]	29,804,923	29,792,468	29,717,915	30,615,432
(2)	Percent of employees in firms that offer health insurance[b]	59.6	57.8	54.7	52.9
(3)	Percent of employees enrolled in health insurance in firms that offer health insurance[c]	59.6	59.2	58.6	57.7
(4)	Percent of enrollees that are enrolled in self-insured plans in firms that offer insurance[d]	11.6	12.5	10.8	12.5
(5)	Total estimated number of employees with health insurance coverage (1) * (2) * (3) / 10,000	10,587,185	10,194,268	9,525,840	9,344,840
(6)	Covered under self-insured plans	1,228,113	1,274,284	1,028,791	1,168,105
(7)	Covered under non-self-insured plans	9,359,072	8,919,984	8,497,049	8,176,735

[a] Table I.B.1 (2009) Number of private-sector employees by firm size and selected characteristics: United States, 2009. http://meps.ahrq.gov/mepsweb/data_stats/summ_tables/insr/national/series_1/2009/tib1.htm.
[b] Table I.B.2 (2009) Percent of private-sector employees in establishments that offer health insurance by firm size and selected characteristics: United States, 2009. http://meps.ahrq.gov/mepsweb/data_stats/summ_tables/insr/national/series_1/2009/tib2.htm.
[c] Table I.B.2.b (2009) Percent of private-sector employees that are enrolled in health insurance at establishments that offer health insurance by firm size and selected characteristics: United States, 2009 establishments that offer health insurance by firm size and selected characteristics: United States, 2009. http://meps.ahrq.gov/mepsweb/data_stats/summ_tables/insr/national/series_1/2009/tib2b.htm.
[d] Table I.B.2.b.(1)(2009) Percent of private-sector enrollees that are enrolled in self-insured plans at establishments that offer health insurance by firm size and selected characteristics: United States, 2009. http://meps.ahrq.gov/mepsweb/data_stats/summ_tables/insr/national/series_1/2009/tib2b1.htm.

nature of discerning individual-level coverage. In contrast, estimates of the small group market come from employer surveys linked to administrative data and are more reliable. The challenges in estimating the size of these markets spill over to difficulties in defining the target populations of ACA insurance market policies. Having discussed these challenges, we turn our attention to measures of the structure of these markets, including the number of participating insurers, market shares, and concentration.

13.3   The Structure of the Individual and Small Group Markets for Health Insurance

Assessing the structure of the individual and small group markets has been hampered by lack of data on these insurers. Until 2011, the National Association of Insurance Commissioners (NAIC) was the only national administrative data source available to identify insurers operating in the individual and group markets. The NAIC is the organization of insurance regulators from the fifty states, the District of Columbia, and the five US territories. The NAIC data represent a compilation of health insurer filings of Annual Statements to the Insurance Department of each state in which they sell their products. Prior to 2010, NAIC data on detailed state-level insurer-level/aggregated information on premiums earned and written, amounts paid and incurred for provision of health care services, and member months of coverage by "line of business" came from the *Exhibit of Premiums, Enrollment, and Utilization*, also known as the "State Page." Lines of business include comprehensive individual coverage, comprehensive group coverage, Medicare supplements, vision, dental, FEHBP, Medicare, and Medicaid. However, the NAIC data have several major limitations. First, the vast majority of insurers operating in California are regulated by the California Department of Managed Health Care and do not file with the NAIC.

Second, as already alluded to, one cannot easily use pre-2010 NAIC data to study health insurance industry structure. One difficulty in using the NAIC data prior to 2010 relates to the classification of insurers into categories based on their primary business. Insurers with more than 95 percent of their business in health insurance were required to file as health insurers, and they filled out "exhibits" (essentially questionnaires) in the Health Blanks (including the "State Page"). However, life, fraternal, and property/casualty insurers that also write health insurance policies (but for whom health insurance is 95 percent or less of their business) did not file the same Health Blanks. As a result, until 2010, such organizations were not required to file information on enrollment, premiums, or claims specific to comprehensive (hospital and medical) coverage in individual and group market segments under the State Page.[8] Lack of such information made it impossible to assess the number of insurers selling comprehensive medical insurance in the individual market and the group market using the NAIC data. Major life insurers could potentially have a large market share in these market segments, yet it was not possible to gauge the extent of their presence and their share of total premiums in any state and year. While each insurance regulator's website typically lists the insurers operating in that state, one cannot easily obtain detailed information about their market shares.

Another problem with the NAIC data prior to 2010 is that insurer filings did not distinguish whether the insurer operated in the small group versus the large group market. Similarly, enrollment, premiums, claims, and other financial information was filed under the "group market" business line segment rather than distinguishing between the small and large group markets.

Following passage of the ACA, NAIC has actively collaborated with the US Department of Health and Human Services (HHS) to design standard

---

8. See Abraham and Karaca-Mandic (2011), Karaca-Mandic and Abraham (2013), and Karaca-Mandic, Abraham, and Simon (2013) for more detail on the comprehensiveness of the NAIC data. Dafny et al. (2011) also discuss the NAIC data.

measures, definitions, and methodologies related to the regulatory targets such as the MLR.[9] Starting in the 2010 filing year, insurers file new supplementary information with the NAIC. Karaca-Mandic and Abraham (2013) summarized the features of NAIC's new reporting exhibit titled the *Supplemental Health Care Exhibit* (*SHCE*). This exhibit is similar to the earlier State Pages, but it is also filed by life, fraternal, and property/casualty insurers (starting with filing year of 2010) that sell health insurance policies in the individual, small, and large group (fully insured) markets. The SHCE includes detailed information on the number of covered lives, number of policies, member months, health premiums earned, federal taxes, state insurance, premium and other taxes, incurred claims, incurred expenses for improving health care quality, as well as detailed information on claims-adjustment expenses, and general and administrative expenses. In the SHCE, insurers separately report on comprehensive medical coverage in the individual, small group, and large group markets, as well as on mini-med plans (with annual limits of $250,000 per person per year), for each state in which they operate.

A new independent source of data on insurers is the MLR regulatory filings collected by the US Department of Health and Human Services' Center for Consumer Information and Oversight (CCIIO) starting in 2011. There is some uncertainty regarding what fraction of insurers report data. A recent Kaiser study (see below) used the 2011 CCIIO regulatory filings and found estimates of individual and small group market size very similar to the NAIC. Since these data start in 2011, it is not possible to use them for pre-post comparisons.

13.3.1   Insurance Market Structure Prior to 2010

Although it is not possible to distinguish small and large group insurers prior to 2010, the NAIC State Pages can be used to study individual market insurers (subject to the caveat that the State Pages do not include data on life insurers that also sold health insurance). Using these data, Abraham and Karaca-Mandic (2011) presented snapshots of the number of active health insurers and estimated enrollment in the individual market from 2002 to 2009 by state. In 2009, five states (Florida, New York, Michigan, Pennsylvania, and Ohio) each had at least fifteen insurers. Ten states (Alabama, Mississippi, Vermont, Alaska, Delaware, Hawaii, North Dakota, New Hampshire, Rhode Island, and Wyoming) had three or fewer health insurers. Most states experienced an increase in the number of health insurers and modest enrollment growth from 2002 to 2009. However, the authors acknowledged their estimates do not include life insurers also selling health insurance, nor do they include insurers in California.

9. For example, see the list of NAIC responsibilities as of April 2010 at: http://www.naic.org/documents/index_health_reform_naic_tasks.pdf.

Karaca-Mandic, Abraham, and Simon (2013) also used the NAIC data to evaluate health insurance market structure and its relation to medical loss ratios in the individual market from to 2001 to 2009. In the 2011 US Department of Health and Human Services' interim final rule, insurers with less than 1,000 member years in a state are deemed to have "noncredible" MLRs for regulatory enforcement and are exempt from the minimum MLR requirements. The authors identified eleven states in 2009 with only one credible health insurer serving the individual market. Because "life insurers" do not file data with the NAIC, additional work is necessary to confirm that this really indicates these states had monopoly-like markets. In additional analysis of these eleven states, using data from the state commissioners' web pages as well as the NAIC data from SHCE in 2010 and 2011, they confirmed that the credible health insurer identified was in fact the dominant insurer in the state (in terms of market share). However, the authors found that life insurers in all these states also sold health insurance to individuals. The largest life insurer had only 4 to 8 percent of the total premium revenue in most of these markets, but there were a few states in which the largest life insurer accounted for 10 to 16 percent of individual health insurance premiums.

13.3.2   Insurance Market Structure in 2010 and After

Starting with the 2010 filing year, the SHCE provides a unique opportunity to construct a complete picture of both the individual and the small group health insurance markets. Because the exhibit is filed by life, fraternal, and property/casualty insurers in addition to health insurers, it is now possible to construct counts of all insurance carriers selling comprehensive health insurance. The reported number of policies, covered lives, member months and premiums earned can be used to conduct a more complete market share analysis because it is now possible to include the market shares of the nonhealth insurers. Similarly, given that information is now available on all market participants, one can construct measures of market structure (e.g., the Herfindahl Index) by states. In addition, the fully insured small and large group markets can be separately identified, and thus the SHCE presents the first opportunity to examine the small group market.

In this chapter, we used the 2010–2012 SHCE to examine the numbers of insurers in the individual and small group markets by state, lines of business (health insurance or life insurance),[10] and whether they are credible or not. In 2010 and 2011, credible firms were defined as those having at least 1,000 member years. Credible firms with fewer than 75,000 member years were considered "partially credible" by DHSS, while those with at least 75,000

---

10. Property/casualty and fraternal insurers are extremely small players in health insurance markets. For example, they account for less than 1 percent of premium revenues for individual market comprehensive major medical policies (Abraham and Karaca-Mandic 2011).

member years were considered "fully credible." Starting in 2012, "credible experience" is defined in a cumulative manner. If an insurer has fewer than 75,000 member years in 2012 in a given state and segment (e.g., individual, small group), its MLR is calculated using data reported for both the 2011 and 2012 MLR reporting years (US Department of Health and Human Services 2010). Therefore, even though an insurer may be "noncredible" (fewer than 1,000 member years) for the 2012 reporting year alone, it is not necessarily exempt from MLR regulation if it has at least 1,000 combined member years for 2011 and 2012. For 2012, we thus define credible insurers as those with at least 1,000 member years combined for 2011 and 2012.

Table 13.3 presents the numbers of credible and noncredible insurers in 2010 and 2012 by state in the individual market, distinguishing health and life insurers. Table 13.4 presents the breakdown of enrollment by credible versus noncredible and by health and life insurers in the state in 2010 and 2012. Tables 13.5 and 13.6 repeat the same exercises for the small group market.

Table 13.3 shows that life insurers participate actively in the individual market. In 2010, states had, on average, four credible health insurers, three noncredible health insurers, seven credible life insurers, and thirty-one noncredible life insurers. The 2012 data reveal similar patterns, although slightly smaller numbers of credible and noncredible life insurers (eight and nineteen on average, respectively). States with only one credible health insurer in 2010 (AK, DE, MS, MD, NH, RI, WY) had at least two to four credible life insurers, except for Rhode Island and North Dakota (only one credible life insurer). The majority of states with only two credible health insurers in 2010 (AL, ID, IA, IN, KS, NC, NE, NV, OK, TN) had at least five credible life insurers. Credible life insurers were largely absent from the remaining states with only two credible health insurers in 2010 (two in KY, one in ME, and none in HI and VT). Table 13.4 shows that credible health insurers comprised 70 percent of the individual market in 2010, on average, followed by credible life insurers (26 percent), and noncredible life insurers (4 percent). Overall, noncredible health insurers had a negligible market share (average of 0.01 percent). These figures remained stable in 2012.

Relative to the individual market, the small group market had more credible health insurers in 2012 (on average, seven per state), slightly fewer noncredible health insurers (on average, two), and substantially fewer credible and noncredible life insurers (on average, four and five, respectively; table 13.5). Credible health insurers comprised about 80 percent of the small group market by market share. Credible life insurers comprised the remaining fraction of the market (about 20 percent), leaving noncredible health and life insures with a negligible market share (table 13.6).

In table 13.7 we describe entry and exit of insurers, as well as transitions from credible to noncredible status and vice versa between 2010 and 2012. Of the 534 credible life and health insurers in the individual market in 2010,

Table 13.3 Number of insurers selling comprehensive health insurance in the individual market

State	2010				2012			
	Health insurer		Life insurer		Health insurer		Life insurer	
	Credible	Noncredible	Credible	Noncredible	Credible	Noncredible	Credible	Noncredible
AK	1	1	4	9	2	0	4	8
AL	2	0	5	39	1	0	4	30
AR	3	2	4	38	2	3	4	28
AZ	4	4	14	29	3	2	18	16
CA	1	0	10	39	1	1	11	24
CO	3	7	15	33	3	6	16	18
CT	3	3	4	25	3	4	7	14
DC	3	2	1	19	3	4	2	18
DE	1	3	2	22	2	2	3	15
FL	9	6	17	48	12	3	19	22
GA	5	4	15	40	6	4	16	22
HI	2	0	0	12	2	0	0	9
IA	2	3	5	32	2	3	6	23
ID	3	0	5	23	3	2	3	15
IL	4	6	18	34	3	9	19	19
IN	2	5	14	34	3	4	16	18
KS	2	4	7	30	2	4	9	23
KY	2	4	2	31	2	3	3	23
LA	5	1	8	33	5	1	7	24
MA	6	6	1	32	7	5	2	21
MD	6	3	5	32	5	5	5	18
ME	2	3	1	21	2	2	1	13
MI	4	6	13	33	9	8	12	17
MN	4	2	4	35	5	3	3	23

MO	5	8	11	36	4	6	14	23
MS	1	1	6	35	1	2	7	27
MT	3	1	5	22	2	1	6	15
NC	2	5	14	35	2	4	16	16
ND	1	2	1	18	2	2	4	14
NE	2	1	7	31	3	0	8	24
NH	1	2	3	21	1	1	3	14
NJ	7	2	0	29	7	2	2	18
NM	3	0	3	37	2	0	5	24
NV	2	5	8	31	3	3	8	19
NY	14	4	2	34	12	3	5	16
OH	5	11	10	39	5	11	13	25
OK	2	3	8	34	1	4	10	23
OR	7	3	2	30	7	2	2	20
PA	14	4	11	36	18	7	12	20
RI	1	2	1	16	1	2	0	8
SC	3	2	9	42	4	1	10	24
SD	3	2	2	30	5	1	2	18
TN	2	4	9	39	3	4	12	26
TX	3	10	25	42	2	10	23	23
UT	3	1	7	30	3	1	5	17
VA	5	5	6	43	5	6	7	26
VT	2	1	0	10	2	1	0	12
WA	9	3	3	25	9	3	3	17
WI	9	6	10	30	9	6	13	21
WV	1	2	3	38	1	2	3	25
WY	1	2	4	24	1	2	7	17
US average	4	3	7	31	4	3	8	19

Source: National Association of Insurance Commissioners, by permission.

Note: The NAIC does not endorse any analysis or conclusions based upon the use of its data. Data from California is incomplete. Credible firms have at least 1,000 member years. In 2012, "credible" status is defined by the aggregated member years over 2011 and 2012 for insurers with < 75,000 member years.

Table 13.4 Enrollment and market share by type of insurer in the individual market

State	Total member years, 2010	2010 Health insurer Credible	2010 Health insurer Noncredible	2010 Life insurer Credible	2010 Life insurer Noncredible	Total member years, 2012	2012 Health insurer Credible	2012 Health insurer Noncredible	2012 Life insurer Credible	2012 Life insurer Noncredible
AK	16,072	0.59	0.04	0.32	0.06	15,004	0.67	0	0.27	0.05
AL	176,526	0.87	0	0.1	0.02	167,361	0.91	0	0.08	0.01
AR	118,450	0.84	0	0.12	0.04	113,218	0.85	0	0.12	0.02
AZ	255,356	0.51	0	0.47	0.01	261,828	0.51	0	0.48	0
CA	986,547	0.52	0	0.48	0	1,095,684	0.59	0	0.41	0
CO	299,793	0.46	0	0.53	0.01	268,419	0.49	0	0.5	0.01
CT	107,938	0.6	0	0.37	0.03	111,942	0.55	0.01	0.44	0.01
DC	19,524	0.8	0	0.09	0.11	18,274	0.79	0	0.16	0.05
DE	18,496	0.5	0.01	0.33	0.16	17,209	0.56	0	0.37	0.07
FL	847,542	0.71	0	0.28	0	835,051	0.69	0	0.31	0
GA	353,740	0.69	0	0.29	0.01	382,239	0.67	0	0.32	0
HI	30,913	0.99	0	0	0.01	28,359	1	0	0	0
IA	177,363	0.86	0	0.11	0.03	177,532	0.89	0.01	0.09	0.01
ID	127,000	0.77	0	0.22	0.01	99,469	0.95	0	0.05	0
IL	457,366	0.7	0	0.29	0	145,949	0.18	0	0.82	0
IN	179,663	0.62	0	0.35	0.03	174,907	0.65	0	0.34	0
KS	126,792	0.28	0	0.69	0.04	120,897	0.37	0	0.61	0.02
KY	148,638	0.94	0	0.04	0.02	133,826	0.96	0	0.03	0.01
LA	179,178	0.86	0	0.12	0.02	170,759	0.91	0	0.08	0.01
MA	105,980	0.95	0	0.02	0.03	81,084	0.98	0	0	0.01
MD	188,040	0.78	0	0.22	0.01	179,917	0.72	0	0.27	0.01
ME	37,236	0.63	0	0.34	0.02	33,239	0.62	0	0.37	0.01
MI	332,637	0.6	0	0.37	0.02	323,341	0.62	0	0.37	0
MN	245,068	0.87	0	0.12	0.01	247,707	0.92	0	0.07	0.01
MO	239,103	0.62	0	0.35	0.02	245,707	0.65	0	0.34	0.01

MS	79,547	0.54	0	0.38	0.08	79,251	0.59	0	0.36	0.04
MT	52,903	0.58	0	0.4	0.02	50,626	0.68	0	0.3	0.03
NC	417,102	0.85	0	0.14	0.01	430,755	0.9	0	0.1	0
ND	42,441	0.81	0.03	0.12	0.05	43,590	0.84	0.02	0.13	0.02
NE	108,392	0.67	0	0.29	0.04	121,894	0.73	0	0.25	0.02
NH	34,484	0.67	0	0.27	0.06	35,450	0.81	0	0.16	0.02
NJ	122,853	0.99	0	0	0.01	147,306	0.98	0	0.01	0
NM	61,800	0.9	0	0.06	0.04	29,822	0.84	0	0.11	0.05
NV	87,327	0.44	0.02	0.51	0.03	90,886	0.46	0	0.53	0.01
NY	129,440	0.92	0.01	0.04	0.03	139,101	0.93	0.01	0.05	0.01
OH	202,135	0.53	0.01	0.44	0.03	323,139	0.75	0	0.24	0
OK	120,415	0.63	0	0.31	0.06	43,093	0.11	0.02	0.83	0.04
OR	185,768	0.89	0.01	0.09	0.01	169,248	0.92	0	0.07	0.01
PA	471,105	0.77	0	0.22	0.01	444,163	0.79	0	0.2	0
RI	30,949	0.47	0.01	0.52	0	16,495	0.95	0.01	0	0.04
SC	133,799	0.58	0.01	0.35	0.06	126,116	0.66	0	0.32	0.02
SD	59,021	0.89	0.01	0.07	0.03	62,808	0.96	0	0.02	0.02
TN	235,107	0.68	0	0.28	0.03	238,119	0.74	0	0.25	0.01
TX	734,307	0.57	0	0.42	0.01	290,110	0.02	0	0.97	0
UT	141,189	0.68	0	0.31	0.01	136,231	0.65	0	0.35	0.01
VA	317,279	0.84	0	0.14	0.02	315,664	0.87	0	0.12	0.01
VT	17,516	0.99	0	0	0.01	18,470	0.99	0	0	0.01
WA	315,470	0.93	0	0.07	0	284,273	0.98	0	0.02	0
WI	176,491	0.55	0	0.42	0.03	172,402	0.63	0	0.36	0
WV	22,109	0.41	0.01	0.38	0.2	24,017	0.62	0.01	0.29	0.08
WY	24,423	0.42	0.01	0.37	0.2	22,177	0.39	0.03	0.51	0.07
US total	10,098,333					9,304,128				
US average		0.7	0	0.26	0.04		0.72	0	0.26	0.02

Source: National Association of Insurance Commissioners, by permission.

Note: The NAIC does not endorse any analysis or conclusions based upon the use of its data. Data from California is incomplete. Credible firms have at least 1,000 member years. In 2012, "credible" status is defined by the aggregated member years over 2011 and 2012 for insurers with < 75,000 member years.

Table 13.5 Number of insurers selling comprehensive health insurance in the small group market

| State | 2010 | | | | 2012 | | | |
| | Health insurer | | Life insurer | | Health insurer | | Life insurer | |
	Credible	Noncredible	Credible	Noncredible	Credible	Noncredible	Credible	Noncredible
AK	2	0	2	5	2	0	4	1
AL	2	1	1	8	2	1	1	7
AR	5	2	2	11	7	0	1	9
AZ	8	3	9	12	6	1	8	9
CA	2	0	7	9	2	0	6	7
CO	8	3	3	9	7	1	3	6
CT	8	0	4	6	6	0	2	6
DC	6	4	3	5	6	5	3	2
DE	4	5	1	6	4	5	1	5
FL	13	1	3	8	13	4	4	3
GA	12	0	11	10	13	1	11	7
HI	5	0	0	1	5	0	0	1
IA	7	4	2	9	8	2	1	7
ID	4	1	0	7	4	1	1	5
IL	12	6	12	13	10	4	9	11
IN	6	5	12	12	7	4	14	7
KS	4	3	7	9	4	4	7	6
KY	4	4	1	9	6	1	1	7
LA	5	2	2	7	6	1	3	6
MA	12	2	3	6	12	2	3	7
MD	11	2	2	2	12	1	2	4
ME	4	0	2	4	4	0	2	2
MI	8	2	13	11	17	0	11	4
MN	7	1	0	5	8	1	0	4
MO	10	5	7	12	7	5	7	7

MS	1	2	4	7	3	0	4	5
MT	3	0	2	7	3	0	3	5
NC	6	1	4	11	6	1	5	7
ND	3	2	1	3	3	2	1	2
NE	3	0	6	10	3	1	4	9
NH	5	2	2	4	5	0	0	4
NJ	9	1	3	3	8	1	3	2
NM	5	1	3	8	4	1	1	3
NV	10	2	6	11	8	2	6	7
NY	22	2	2	5	19	1	4	2
OH	17	4	6	18	16	2	9	13
OK	6	1	8	8	4	2	6	7
OR	7	3	1	1	7	2	1	0
PA	20	4	5	10	20	2	5	7
RI	2	2	1	2	2	2	1	2
SC	5	1	5	11	4	3	3	8
SD	5	0	0	6	6	0	0	5
TN	7	4	5	12	5	2	6	6
TX	10	3	14	15	10	3	13	8
UT	4	1	4	8	3	1	8	4
VA	15	5	4	11	17	1	4	6
VT	4	0	1	1	3	1	1	0
WA	8	4	2	5	11	1	4	3
WI	20	2	8	7	21	0	8	5
WV	5	2	3	10	5	1	3	9
WY	2	1	3	4	2	1	4	1
US average	7	2	4	8	7	2	4	5

Source: National Association of Insurance Commissioners, by permission.

Note: The NAIC does not endorse any analysis or conclusions based upon the use of its data. Data from California is incomplete. Credible firms have at least 1,000 member years. In 2012, "credible" status is defined by the aggregated member years over 2011 and 2012 for insurers with < 75,000 member years.

Table 13.6   Enrollment and market share by type of insurer in the small group market

| | 2010 | | | | | 2012 | | | | |
| | Total member years, 2010 | Health insurer | | Life insurer | | Total member years, 2012 | Health insurer | | Life insurer | |
State		Credible	Noncredible	Credible	Noncredible		Credible	Noncredible	Credible	Noncredible
AK	27,193	0.81	0	0.13	0.06	32,982	0.75	0	0.25	0
AL	333,464	0.96	0	0.03	0.01	300,824	0.98	0	0.02	0
AR	128,104	0.73	0	0.25	0.02	135,260	0.83	0	0.16	0.01
AZ	310,048	0.41	0	0.58	0.01	224,005	0.35	0	0.64	0.01
CA	737,370	0.39	0	0.61	0	714,052	0.38	0	0.62	0
CO	296,943	0.59	0	0.4	0	234,853	0.6	0	0.39	0.01
CT	303,407	0.96	0	0.04	0.01	246,543	0.98	0	0.01	0
DC	125,154	0.89	0.01	0.09	0	97,986	0.88	0	0.1	0
DE	55,031	0.91	0.03	0.04	0.02	54,266	0.97	0.01	0.01	0
FL	873,558	0.66	0	0.34	0	823,504	0.74	0	0.25	0.01
GA	529,174	0.77	0	0.23	0	610,714	0.78	0	0.22	0
HI	191,901	1	0	0	0	168,746	1	0	0	0
IA	204,892	0.88	0.01	0.11	0.01	164,182	0.9	0	0.08	0.01
ID	99,273	0.97	0	0	0.02	85,064	0.98	0	0.01	0.01
IL	733,237	0.75	0	0.24	0	260,338	0.53	0	0.47	0.01
IN	293,311	0.66	0	0.32	0.01	334,529	0.74	0	0.26	0.01
KS	240,971	0.19	0	0.8	0.01	194,569	0.25	0	0.74	0.01
KY	184,178	0.96	0.01	0.02	0.01	183,265	1	0	0	0
LA	327,749	0.89	0	0.1	0.01	287,175	0.92	0	0.08	0
MA	679,117	0.96	0	0.04	0	581,971	0.98	0	0.02	0
MD	426,090	0.92	0	0.08	0	353,976	0.93	0	0.07	0
ME	93,656	0.61	0	0.39	0	81,686	0.72	0	0.28	0
MI	499,867	0.7	0	0.29	0.01	654,179	0.9	0	0.1	0
MN	272,651	1	0	0	0	316,387	1	0	0	0
MO	399,047	0.7	0	0.29	0.01	322,929	0.78	0	0.22	0
MS	128,627	0.8	0.01	0.18	0.01	117,300	0.9	0	0.09	0.01

MT	0.01	0.11	0	0.88	51,845	0.04	0.12	0	0.84	57,293
NC	0	0.18	0	0.81	350,545	0.01	0.22	0	0.77	440,594
ND	0.01	0.01	0	0.98	67,569	0	0.01	0	0.98	82,930
NE	0.01	0.19	0	0.8	88,153	0.03	0.31	0	0.66	96,726
NH	0.01	0	0	0.99	87,754	0.01	0.02	0	0.97	107,310
NJ	0	0.01	0	0.98	711,940	0	0.02	0	0.98	873,581
NM	0	0.15	0	0.85	40,989	0	0.17	0	0.82	81,586
NV	0.01	0.34	0.01	0.65	105,508	0.01	0.3	0.01	0.68	128,670
NY	0	0.06	0	0.94	1,444,820	0	0.02	0	0.97	1,785,384
OH	0.01	0.13	0	0.86	955,972	0	0.1	0	0.9	842,523
OK	0.01	0.61	0	0.38	80,669	0.01	0.38	0	0.61	202,981
OR	0	0.06	0	0.94	228,449	0	0.07	0	0.93	234,594
PA	0	0.02	0	0.98	1,062,836	0	0.06	0	0.94	1,110,624
RI	0	0.22	0.01	0.77	85,611	0.01	0.23	0.01	0.75	101,552
SC	0.01	0.09	0	0.9	158,375	0.01	0.14	0	0.85	195,703
SD	0.01	0	0	0.99	52,654	0.01	0	0	0.99	57,999
TN	0	0.18	0	0.82	353,371	0.01	0.17	0.01	0.82	427,090
TX	0	0.75	0	0.25	757,686	0	0.47	0	0.53	1,197,943
UT	0	0.23	0	0.77	244,766	0.01	0.24	0	0.75	213,549
VA	0	0.09	0	0.91	465,807	0.01	0.08	0	0.91	536,232
VT	0	0	0	1	60,698	0	0.38	0	0.62	66,264
WA	0	0.16	0	0.84	275,131	0	0.2	0.01	0.8	236,052
WI	0	0.42	0	0.58	407,307	0	0.49	0	0.5	368,754
WV	0.01	0.03	0	0.96	70,902	0.03	0.09	0	0.87	72,228
WY	0.02	0.34	0.01	0.62	24,148	0.03	0.32	0.02	0.64	25,910
US total					15,814,790					18,038,085
US average	0	0.19	0	0.81		0.01	0.2	0	0.79	

Source: National Association of Insurance Commissioners, by permission.

Note: The NAIC does not endorse any analysis or conclusions based upon the use of its data. Data from California is incomplete. Cred. = Credible. Credible firms have at least 1,000 member years. In 2012, "credible" status is defined by the aggregated member years over 2011 and 2012 for insurers with < 75,000 member years.

Table 13.7   Entry and exit of insurers, 2010–2012

	Comprehensive individual market				Small group market			
	Credible 2012	Not credible 2012	Not present 2012	Total	Credible 2012	Not credible 2012	Not present 2012	Total
Present in 2010, credible								
Credible in 2011	437	0	18	455	470	0	35	505
Not credible in 2011	37	11	9	57	21	12	12	45
Not present in 2011	1	2	19	22	0	0	35	35
Total	475	13	46	534	491	12	82	585
Present in 2010, not credible								
Credible in 2011	32	0	2	34	24	0	0	24
Not credible in 2011	51	815	291	1,157	40	274	62	376
Not present in 2011	0	41	495	536	0	7	93	100
Total	83	856	788	1,727	64	281	155	500
Entered in 2011, credible	11	8	19	38	12	0	1	13
Entered in 2011, not credible	13	160	104	277	12	27	16	55
Entered in 2012	3	129	0	132	9	27	0	36

Note: Credible firms have at least 1,000 member years. In 2012, "credible" status is defined by the aggregated member years over 2011 and 2012 for insurers with < 75,000 member years.

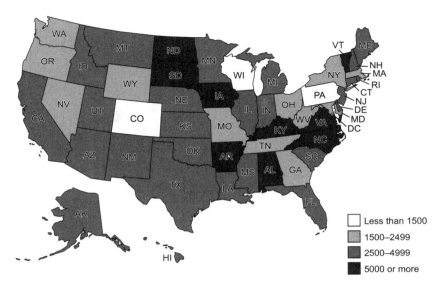

Fig. 13.1   Herfindahl-Hirschman Index (HHI) for the individual market, 2010

455 remained credible in 2011, of which 437 remained credible also in 2012. Fifty-seven were not credible in 2011, and twenty-two exited the market in 2011.

Transition from noncredible to credible status was uncommon. Among 1,727 noncredible insurers in 2010, 34 became credible and 1,157 remained noncredible in 2011. Of these 1,157 noncredible insurers, 51 became credible, 815 remained noncredible, and 219 exited the market in 2012. The exit rate of these noncredible insurers was high, with 536 of the 1,727 noncredible insurers from 2010 exiting in 2011.

In the small group market, most credible insurers in 2010 were credible also in 2011 and 2012 (470 of 585). Many noncredible insurers in 2010 remained noncredible in 2011 and 2012 (274 out of 500). As in the individual market, a large fraction of the noncredible insurers from 2010 exited in 2011 (100 of 500).

To investigate market structure further, we computed the Herfindahl-Hirschman Index (HHI) for the individual market (figure 13.1 for 2010 and figure 13.2 for 2012) and the small group market (figure 13.3 for 2010 and figure 13.4 for 2012). We present a four-category breakdown of HHI by state using the US Department of Justice and Federal Trade Commission (DOJ/FTC) *Horizontal Merger Guidelines*: < 1,500 (unconcentrated); 1,500–2,499 (moderately concentrated); 2,500–4,999 (highly concentrated); and 5,000 and above (highly concentrated). Fourteen states had an individual market HHI less than 2,500 in both years. Similarly, in the small group market, the number of states with HHI less than 2,500 remained stable (eighteen in 2010,

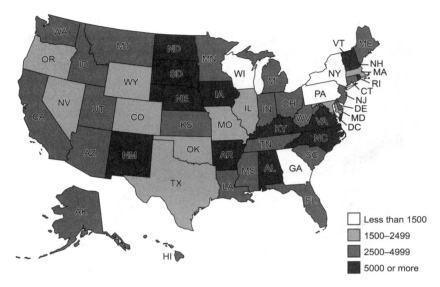

Fig. 13.2 Herfindahl-Hirschman Index (HHI) for the individual market, 2012

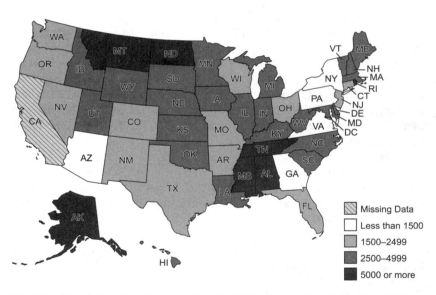

Fig. 13.3 Herfindahl-Hirschman Index (HHI) for the small group market, 2010

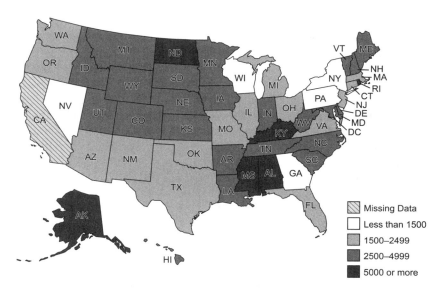

Fig. 13.4   Herfindahl-Hirschman Index (HHI) for the small group market, 2012

and twenty in 2012). Several states had HHIs exceeding 5,000 in 2012 (individual market: AL, AR, IA, KY, NC, ND, NE, NH, NM, RI, SD, VA, and VT; small group market: AK, AL, KY, MS, ND, and RI) suggesting that the individual market is highly concentrated in many states. The average HHI in the individual market across all states increased from 2010 to 2012 (3,680 and 3,920, respectively). The corresponding median and the 90th percentiles of the HHI also increased during this time period (median: from 3,300 to 3,266; 90th percentile: from 6,368 to 6,958).

These NAIC data describing market structure are consistent with findings from the CCIIO Medical Loss Ratio Annual Reporting Data (available only after 2011) prepared by the Centers for Medicare and Medicaid Services (CMS). In an analysis of the 2011 data, researchers from the Kaiser Family Foundation reported market shares of the dominant, second-largest, and third-largest insurers by state (Kaiser State Health Facts, available online).[11] For example, in our analysis of the NAIC data, Alabama is one of the most concentrated individual markets (HHI of 8,313 in 2012). Kaiser's analysis shows that the dominant insurer in the individual market of Alabama (Blue Cross and Blue Shield of Alabama) had 90 percent market share. In another high HHI state in our analysis, North Carolina (HHI of 7,312 in 2012), Blue

11. http://kff.org/other/state-indicator/individual-insurance-market-competition/ (accessed 9/23/2013) and http://kff.org/other/state-indicator/small-group-insurance-market-competition/ (accessed 9/23/2013).

Cross and Blue Shield of North Carolina was the dominant insurer with 83 percent market share in Kaiser's analysis. Similarly, in Rhode Island (HHI of 9,072 in 2012), Blue Cross & Blue Shield of Rhode Island had 95 percent market share. Kaiser's analysis of the small group market is also comparable with our analysis based on NAIC data. In our analysis, the states with highest small group market HHI were Alabama (9,429 in 2012) and Mississippi (7,639 in 2012). Kaiser's analysis shows that the largest insurer in Alabama (Blue Cross and Blue Shield of Alabama) had 97 percent market share. In Mississippi, Mississippi Insurance Group was the dominant carrier with 73 percent market share. Overall, the small group market was less concentrated relative to the individual market. Average HHI across all states were 3,252 in 2010 and 3,353 in 2012.

13.4   The Performance of Insurers in the Individual and Small Group Markets for Health Insurance

Many empirical studies have investigated factors—primarily market structure and regulations—that explain variation in health insurance premiums. A smaller body of recent research has focused on estimating the size of insurers' loading fees and/or medical loss ratios. The ACA medical loss ratio regulations implemented in 2011 have created heightened awareness of the latter. Other measures of insurer performance less commonly examined include insurer administrative expenses and operating margins.

13.4.1   Evaluating Insurer Performance Prior to 2010

Abraham and Karaca-Mandic (2011) analyzed the potential impact of the ACA's regulation of insurers' medical loss ratios (MLR, the percentage of premium that goes to clinical services). Using the NAIC State Pages data from 2002, 2005, and 2009, they documented large variation in individual market MLRs by state, with enrollment-weighted average MLRs ranging from 0.629 in New Hampshire to more than 1.0 in Alabama, Massachusetts, Michigan, and North Dakota in 2009. Additionally, they estimated that 29 percent of insurer-state observations with 32 percent of individual market enrollment would have MLRs (based on the historical definition) below the 80 percent minimum threshold imposed by the ACA regulations.

Karaca-Mandic, Abraham, and Simon (2013) also used NAIC data from 2001 through 2009 to compare the MLR and the percentage of premiums spent on administrative expenses in more and less competitive markets, measured by the number of insurers. They found that markets with only one credible insurer (at least 1,000 member years of enrollment) have lower MLRs, controlling for insurer characteristics, health care provider market structure and other market attributes, and population-level demographics and health status.

A concern with viewing MLR regulations as limiting insurer market power is that the MLR is only one component of the price-cost margin; the other component is the share of premiums spent on administrative costs. Therefore, insurers could respond to the MLR regulation by altering administrative costs in ways that leave the price-cost margin unchanged. For example, insurers could reduce their efforts to manage utilization, leading to lower administrative expenses, higher claims payments, and higher MLRs. While some reduction in utilization management may be desirable for improving access to efficient health care (e.g., through lower levels of denials or preapprovals), this reduction could also lead to increased claims for low-value medical care. Karaca-Mandic, Abraham, and Simon (2013) found no evidence that insurers' administrative expenses as a percentage of premiums are related to insurance market structure. Thus, their results are largely consistent with the suggestion that health insurance regulators can use MLRs to measure market power in the individual health insurance market, but with notable caveats relating to measurement issues, limited ability to capture product and firm heterogeneity that can influence differences in price-cost margins, and other potential unintended consequences of the regulation.

Most studies of the small group market focus on state regulations in the 1990s and their effect on premiums (Buchmueller and DiNardo 2002; Marquis and Long 2002; Monheit and Schone 2004; Davidoff, Blumberg, and Nichols 2005; Simon 2005). Karaca-Mandic, Feldman, and Graven (2013) recently investigated the effects of competition in the market for insurance agents and brokers on premiums for small employers (fifty or fewer employees). Using the Medical Expenditure Panel Survey—Insurance Component and data from the National Association of Health Underwriters, they found that premiums of policies offered by small employers are lower in markets with stronger competition among insurance agents and brokers.

A less examined performance measure is the health insurance loading fee (L) that represents the portion of a premium not related to medical care—largely administrative costs. The loading fee typically is modeled as a multiplier to expected claims:

$$prem = (1 + L)claims.$$

For example, if premium is \$125, and expected claims are \$100, the loading fee is 0.25 or 25 percent. The loading fee is closely rated to the MLR. Prior to passage of federal health reform, the MLR was defined as the ratio of expected claims paid by the insurer to the premium. Expressing the loading fee as a multiplier of expected claims, the MLR can be written as:

$$MLR = 1 / (1 + L).$$

In this framework, the loading fee captures an insurer's costs for general administration, underwriting, marketing, broker commissions, medical management and claims adjudication, as well as any profits or net income for a nonprofit insurer.

The most commonly reported loading fee estimates by firm size date back more than two decades, when the Hay/Huggins Company prepared an actuarial study for the US Congress House Committee on Education and Labor in 1988. These estimates reflected the underwriting practices of major insurers and suggested loading fees of about 40 percent for the smallest firms (one to four employees), 25 percent for those slightly larger (twenty to forty-nine employees), and 18 percent for those with fifty to ninety-nine employees. Hay/Huggins also reported that loading fees decline to 16 percent for employers with 100–499 employees, and 12 percent for those with up to 2,500 employees. These estimates from the 1980s are still cited frequently in the literature, including current health economics and health insurance texts (Phelps 2010).

Using data from the confidential MEPS Household Component–Insurance Component Linked File, Karaca-Mandic, Abraham, and Phelps (2011) recently generated new estimates of loading fees and how they differ across the firm-size distribution. They found that firms of up to 100 employees face similar loading fees of approximately 34 percent. Loads decline with firm size and are estimated to be 15 percent for firms with between 101 and 10,000 employees, and 4 percent for firms with more than 10,000 workers.

13.4.2   Insurer Performance in 2010 and After

Starting in the 2010 filing year, the SHCE includes line items for insurers to compute each component of the MLR as defined by the regulation. The SHCE also has a line item for the MLR. In comparison with the period before 2010, the ACA regulations made several changes to the historical definition of the MLR (the ratio of claims to premiums). First, the ACA classifies insurers' expenses for certain quality improvement activities as "clinical benefits" that can be counted similarly as medical claims. Certain activities for fraud and abuse detection and recovery can be included in the numerator of the MLR. Second, federal and state taxes and licensing and regulatory fees are deducted from premiums earned in the denominator.

Using data from the SHCE, several studies have examined insurer filings for reporting years of 2010 (considered as a pre-MLR regulation year) and 2011. The Government Accountability Office (GAO 2011) analyzed insurers' MLRs in the individual and group markets. Using 2010 data and the new ACA standards described above, the GAO found wide variation in MLRs in the individual market, with only 43 percent of credible insurers and 48 percent of covered lives at or above the 2011 standard. These percentages were notably higher for the small and large group markets. Hall and McCue (2012), examining the NAIC's 2010 data, estimated that rebates paid to consumers would have reached almost $2 billion ($1 billion in the individual market, $0.5 billion in the small group, and $0.5 billion in the large group market) if the MLR regulation had been implemented in 2010.

However, it is important to note that measurement of MLR in the SHCE does not exactly match the MLR used by the HHS to determine rebates. In fact, the MLR reported in the SHCE is labeled as the "preliminary MLR." Several adjustments are needed to properly calculate MLR rebates. The first is a "credibility" adjustment to reflect that insurers with smaller enrollment face more variable claims and premiums, and thus should be given additional room to meet the MLR threshold. Under formulae published in the Interim Final Rule of the regulation, insurers with more than 1,000 but fewer than 75,000 member years (known as partially credible insurers) receive a credibility adjustment of up to 8.3 percent to their preliminary MLR on a sliding scale. Insurers with 75,000 or more member years (fully credible) do not receive any credibility adjustment. Using the member years reported in the SHCE, it is possible to calculate the credibility adjustment.

A second adjustment allows insurers that sell high-deductible policies to increase the MLR. The rationale for this adjustment is that administrative cost is generally a disproportionately higher share of the premiums in high-deductible policies because the deductible reduces claims costs and premiums but not administrative costs. Because the SHCE does not include benefit design information, it is not possible to calculate this adjustment with only the SHCE data.

Third, HHS's rebate calculations allow claims paid through March of the following year to be included in the numerator of the MLR. Because the SHCE is for the reporting year only, it is not possible to make this adjustment.[12]

Finally, starting with the 2012 filing year, the SHCE calculation of the MLR becomes more complex because the rebate calculation requires the MLR experience of partially credible insurers to be aggregated across several years. For the 2012 reporting year, MLR for these insurers has to be calculated combining 2011 and 2012 data (which we detail below).[13] Similarly, the credibility adjustment for 2012 is calculated by aggregating member years over 2011 and 2012.

Several recent studies have used 2010 and 2011 SHCE filings to evaluate the early impact of the medical loss ratio regulation. McCue and Hall (December 2012) examined changes in administrative costs and profit margins. They found reductions of about $209 million in administrative costs in the individual market and $190 million in the small group market. The authors also documented reductions in profits in the individual market of

---

12. http://www.naic.org/documents/committees_e_health_reform_solvency_impact_exposure
_related_doc_shce_preliminary_mlr_cautionary_statement.pdf.

13. Beginning in the 2013 reporting year, information from two years prior to the MLR reporting year will be used.

about $351 million, but increases in profits in the small group market of about $226 million. While the average MLR increased from 80.8 percent to 84.1 percent in the individual market, it stayed about the same (83.6 percent) in the small group market.

In a follow-up study, McCue, Hall, and Liu (2013) distinguished between for-profit and nonprofit insurers and found that reductions in administrative costs and operating margins were primarily driven by for-profit insurers in the individual market. Nonprofit insurers already had high MLRs in 2010 relative to for-profit insurers (88.1 percent vs. 71.8 percent). In the small group market, the percentage of premiums spent on administrative costs declined more among for-profit firms (from 19.4 percent in 2010 to 18.7 percent among for-profits, from 12 to 11.9 percent among nonprofits). Surprisingly, however, operating margins (defined as the percentage of premiums not spent on clinical services or administrative costs) increased slightly from 1.6 percent to 2.8 percent among nonprofits with no significant change among for-profits.

Abraham, Karaca-Mandic, and Simon (2013) also examined the 2010 and 2011 SHCE filings to analyze the early responses of individual and small group market insurers to the MLR regulation. Controlling for various factors—insurers' ownership type and HMO status, insurance market competition, and existing state laws—they expected to find heterogeneous responses by insurers' baseline characteristics. They found that several factors were significantly related to insurers' MLRs. Individual market insurers with more enrollments in other market segments have lower MLRs, on average, as do for-profit organizations (2.25 percentage points lower). In contrast, HMOs have MLRs that are 4.58 percentage points higher on average, which may reflect higher actuarial value plans. In the small group market, an insurer's overall enrollment across all states and segments is inversely related to its MLR, but the magnitude is small. Additionally, small group insurers that operate in more concentrated markets, measured by the Herfindahl-Hirschman Index, have significantly lower MLRs. In contrast, insurers that operate in states with existing MLR regulations have higher MLRs.

In terms of early responses to the MLR regulation, the authors found that individual market insurers with 2010 MLRs that are more than 10 percentage points under the 80 percent threshold experienced a 10.94 percentage point increase in MLR from 2010 to 2011 (controlling for the influence of other factors), while those within five points under the threshold experienced only a 2.91 percentage point increase in MLR. Individual market insurers with MLRs more than ten points above the threshold in 2010 reported a decrease, on average, relative to insurers that were only slightly above the 80 percent threshold. A similar pattern of changes in insurers' MLRs occurred in the small group market.

The Kaiser Family Foundation (April 2012) used data from SHCE filings for 2011 to project rebates of $426 million, $377 million, and $541 million in

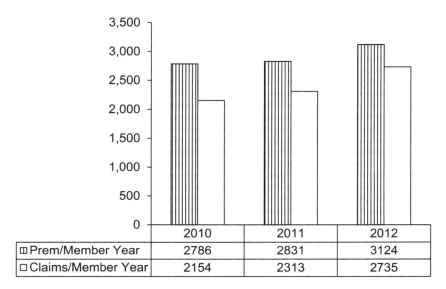

	2010	2011	2012
⊞ Prem/Member Year	2786	2831	3124
☐ Claims/Member Year	2154	2313	2735

Fig. 13.5   Premiums and claims in the individual market
Note: All dollar amounts are inflated to 2012 dollars.

the individual, small group, and large group markets, respectively. In 2012 consumers actually received about $1.1 billion in rebates for the 2011 reporting year ($394 million in the individual market, $321 million in the small group market, and $386 million in the large group market).[14] The similarity in projected rebates using the 2011 SHCE filings and actual rebates reported by the CMS is encouraging in terms of the ability to use NAIC data to study insurance market performance.

Cox, Claxton, and Levitt (2013) used the SHCE data for 2010–2012 filings of "preliminary MLRs" and projected that rebates for the 2012 reporting year would be about half the $1.1 billion received for the previous year. The CMS reported in August 2013 that rebates for the 2012 reporting year were $193 million in the individual market, $203 million in the small group market, and $109 million in the large group market, again verifying the credibility of MLRs reported in the SHCE.[15]

In this chapter, we present the first estimates in key insurer performance measures from the 2012 SCHE filings. In figures 13.5 and 13.6, we estimate changes in premiums earned and claims incurred per member year in the individual and small group markets in 2010 and 2012. These amounts

14. http://www.hhs.gov/news/press/2012pres/09/20120911a.html (accessed October 1, 2013). McCue and Hall (December 2012) also report the rebates that CMS announced.

15. http://www.cms.gov/CCIIO/Resources/Data-Resources/Downloads/2012-mlr-rebates -by-state-and-market.pdf (accessed October 1, 2013).

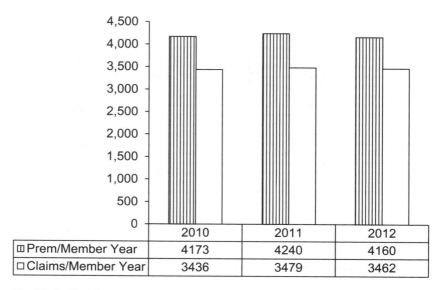

	2010	2011	2012
⊞ Prem/Member Year	4173	4240	4160
☐ Claims/Member Year	3436	3479	3462

Fig. 13.6   Premiums and claims in the small group market
Note: All dollar amounts are inflated to 2012 dollars.

are inflated to reflect 2012 dollars. On average, premiums per member year increased from $2,786 in 2010 to $3,124 in 2012, and claims per member year increased from $2,154 in 2010 to $2,735 in 2012 in the individual market. Both premiums are claims per member year and were remarkably stable in the small group market.

In figures 13.7 and 13.8, we decompose the premiums spent for clinical services (i.e., the preliminary MLR), administrative costs, and the operating margin (residual from clinical services and administrative costs) in the individual and small group markets. While the operating margin declined steadily over the time period in the individual market (from 6 percent in 2010 to 1 percent in 2012), it was stable in the small group market (around 5–6 percent). Administrative costs as a percentage of the premiums also declined steadily in the individual market (19 percent in 2010, 16 percent in 2011, and 14 percent in 2012), and declined slightly in the small group market (13 percent in 2010, 12 percent in 2011, and 11 percent in 2012).

Next, we present estimates of MLRs in the two markets from 2010 through 2012. As discussed above, calculation of rebates using the preliminary MLR reported in SCHE is complicated. To calculate rebates, HHS adjusts the MLRs based on credibility, plan design (i.e., deductibles), and claims paid through March of the following year. Moreover, for the 2012 reporting year, insurer experience was aggregated over 2011 and 2012 reporting years if the insurer had fewer than 75,000 member years (partially credible) in the state and the segment (individual, small group, or large group market) in

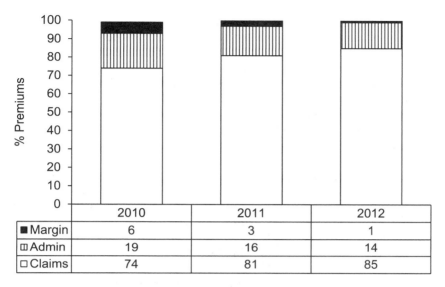

	2010	2011	2012
■ Margin	6	3	1
▥ Admin	19	16	14
▢ Claims	74	81	85

Fig. 13.7   Distribution of premiums, individual market

Note: Claims include spending for other clinical services, quality improvement activities, and spending for detection of fraud.

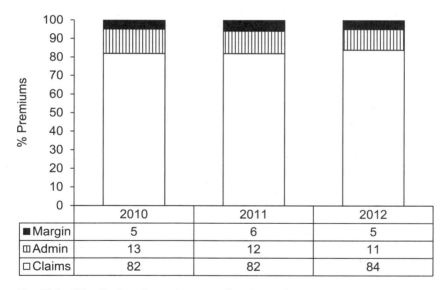

	2010	2011	2012
■ Margin	5	6	5
▥ Admin	13	12	11
▢ Claims	82	82	84

Fig. 13.8   Distribution of premiums, small group market

Note: Claims include spending for other clinical services, quality improvement activities, and spending for detection of fraud.

2012.[16] This means that both the numerator and the denominator of the MLR formula must be aggregated over the two years before taking their ratio. Moreover, insurers can include rebates paid in the previous year in the numerator to avoid double counting (MLR Interim Final Rule). An insurer's credibility and the subsequent credibility adjustment to MLR are also based on its aggregated member years in 2011 and 2012.

We were able to conduct the aggregation exercise for the 2012 reporting year. We also made the credibility adjustment for the size of the insurer from member years reported in the SCHE. However, we could not adjust for benefit design or claims payments up to the first quarter of the following year.

Table 13.8 presents our estimates of MLR for fully credible insurers with at least 75,000 member years in the state segment. The unique number of such insurers and the number of insurer-state observations are very similar, suggesting that such insurers are typically local, operating in just one state. The average MLR increased from 80.39 percent (95 percent CI 76.76 percent–84.03 percent) in 2010 to 85.38 percent (95 percent CI 83.21 percent–87.54 percent) in 2012 in the individual market, with 89 percent of the insurers meeting the MLR threshold of 80 percent. Changes in MLRs in the small group market are smaller (83.56 percent in 2010, and 84.88 percent in 2012). Median MLRs in 2012 are 83.55 percent and 83.7 percent in the individual and small group markets, respectively.

Table 13.9 reports summary statistics based on preliminary MLRs (with no adjustment), as well as MLRs adjusted for aggregation and credibility for the partially credible insurers. The number of partially credible insurers in either the individual or the small group market is noticeably higher than the number of fully credible insurers reported in table 13.8. In 2012, 169 unique insurers represented 409 insurer-state observations in the individual market, and 244 unique insurers represented 437 insurer-state observations in the small group market. Not surprisingly, the percentage of insurers meeting the 80 percent MLR threshold increased over time in both markets. Based on preliminary MLRs reported in SHCE (with no adjustment) for 2012, 60 percent of the insurers in the individual market and 68 percent of those in the small group meet the MLR threshold. However, when adjusted for the aggregation of 2012 reporting year with the 2011 reporting year, these numbers decline to 51 percent and 67 percent, respectively, suggesting that aggregation rule penalizes insurers if they have low MLRs in 2011. After incorporating the credibility adjustment to the aggregation adjustment, the percentage of insurers meeting the MLR threshold in 2012 increases (61 percent in the individual market and 76 percent in the small group market). In terms of the average MLR in 2012, the aggregation adjustment moved the average MLR from 85.39 percent (preliminary) to 83.82 percent, but

16. Starting in 2013, the experience for partially credible insurers is aggregated over three years (for example, over 2011, 2012, and 2013 for the reporting year of 2013).

Table 13.8   Medical loss ratios, 2010–2012, fully credible insurers (at least 75,000 member years)

	Individual market			Small group market		
	2010	2011	2012	2010	2011	2012
Unique number of insurers	27	30	28	56	57	53
Number of insurer-state obs.	28	31	28	64	64	57
Percent met MLR threshold (%)	46	77	89	73	80	88
			MLR			
Mean	80.39	83.64	85.38	83.56	83.34	84.88
(95% CI)	(76.76–84.03)	(81.59–85.69)	(83.21–87.54)	(82.06–85.05)	(82.22–84.47)	(83.70–86.06)
Median	79.3	81.8	83.55	82.7	83.25	83.7

Table 13.9   Medical loss ratios, 2010–2012, partially credible insurers (at least 1,000 member years, but less than 75,000 member years)

		Individual market			Small group market		
		2010	2011	2012	2010	2011	2012
Unique number of insurers		184	178	169	274	256	244
Number of insurer-state obs.		506	492	409	520	477	437
Percent met MLR threshold							
No adjustment		34	46	60	58	61	68
2012 adjusted for aggregation		34	46	51	58	61	67
Adjusted for size credibility + 2012 adjusted for aggregation		41	55	61	70	75	76
				MLR			
No adjustment	Mean	74.06	79.91	85.39	81.49	82.48	84.14
	95% CI	(72.17–75.96)	(78.06–81.77)	(83.55–87.24)	(80.28–82.69)	(80.99–83.97)	(83.02–85.26)
	Median	71.5	78	82.6	81.9	82	83.3
2012 adjusted for aggregation	Mean	74.06	79.91	83.82	81.49	82.48	83.24
	95% CI	(72.17–75.96)	(78.06–81.77)	(82.09–85.54)	(80.28–82.69)	(80.99–83.97)	(82.34–84.15)
	Median	71.5	78	80.32	81.9	82	82.55
Adjusted for size credibility and 2012 adjusted for aggregation	Mean	78.43	84.35	86.68	85.18	86.06	85.58
	95% CI	(76.54–80.33)	(82.50–86.20)	(84.93–88.43)	(83.98–86.38)	(84.58–87.55)	(84.66–86.49)
	Median	75.39	81.68	82.58	84.76	85.23	84.69

the additional credibility adjustment moved it up about 3 percentage points to 87 percent in the individual market. The adjustments moved the average MLR similarly in the small group market in 2012 from 84.14 percent (preliminary) to 83.24 percent (aggregation adjustment) and to 85.58 percent (aggregation and credibility adjustments).

13.5   Other Measurement Issues

The SHCE was developed with the primary purpose of measuring relevant components of insurers' MLRs (claims, premiums, quality improvement, and expenses for detection of fraud and abuse) as well as tracking their administrative expenses (e.g., claims adjudication, total general and administrative expenses including sales and brokers fees), and other financial aspects of the health insurers. Because the MLR regulation currently applies to individual and group markets only, the SCHE lacks information on other business segments represented in the State Pages (Medicare supplement, Dental, Vision, Federal Employees Health Benefit Plan, Title XVIII Medicare, and Title XIX Medicaid).

Another limitation of the SHCE is that it lacks information on health services utilization encounters such as physician and nonphysician ambulatory encounters and hospital inpatient days incurred, which is included in the Health State Pages. While one could use the SHCE together with the Health State Pages to obtain a more complete picture, life insurers and other nonhealth insurers selling health insurance still do not file the Health State Pages.

Finally, the figures reported in the SHCE do not allow for calculating exact rebates as discussed above. While it is possible to make credibility adjustments for partially credible insurers, neither the SHCE nor the State Pages includes information on the share of high-deductible plans or premiums. As another adjustment we did not discuss earlier, an insurer with 50 percent or more of earned premiums attributed to newly issued policies can be excluded from the MLR reports because they are likely to have lower claims. The SCHE and the State Pages do not include information on the share of newly issued policies.

As the ACA changes of 2014 begin to be implemented, it would of course be valuable for researchers to track consumers' and insurers' participation in health insurance exchanges. For example, federal household surveys could include questions on the scope of the insurance policy (e.g., comprehensive or limited benefit), premiums and subsidies for the policy, as well as whether the policy was purchased in the exchange. Similarly, employer-based surveys such as MEPS-IC could incorporate additional questions to measure small employers' participation in SHOP exchanges (for example, whether they participated, the metal levels, and the premiums of the policies). The NAIC could also request information that separates each insurer's business separately in and out of the exchange in each state both for the individual and small group markets.

13.6   Conclusion

We provided a synthesis of the research available to measure and evaluate the size, structure, and performance of the individual and small group markets. We discussed the availability and use of different data sets in measuring these concepts and we highlighted important measurement problems and possible solutions to consider when assessing the performance of health insurance markets as the ACA is fully implemented. Finally, we presented new estimates from 2012 using the NAIC SCHE filings.

Even after coverage hierarchies are imposed, federal household surveys give widely different estimates of how many individuals were covered in the individual market prior to the ACA. While it is premature to know precisely how the individual market will evolve given the introduction of exchanges and additional regulatory structures created by ACA, we will presumably have better information on enrollment starting in 2014. Nevertheless, it may be difficult to track changes in enrollment and to conduct studies based on a pre/post-ACA design using the federal household surveys because of the limitations in properly estimating the size of the individual market at the baseline. Unlike in the individual market, we have better estimates of the small group market enrollment from the MEPS-IC.

The NAIC was the only source available to identify insurers operating in the individual and group markets until 2011. However, the NAIC data were quite limited until 2010, when major improvements occurred through the introduction of the SHCE. This new exhibit filed by all insurers allows for estimating participation of nonhealth insurers (e.g., life insurers) in health insurance markets and provides a breakdown of the group market into small and large groups. We used the NAIC data from 2010 to 2012 to estimate the share of life insurers as well as changes in market structure (counts of insurers and HHI) during this period.

The SHCE provides a unique opportunity to construct a complete picture of both the individual and small group health insurance markets starting with the 2010 filing year. Although we only have one "pre-ACA" year (2010) for early implemented ACA provisions such as the MLR regulation, we can make some assessments of ACA effects. Despite the fact that MLR measurement from the SHCE does not exactly match CMS's measurement of MLR for rebates, the SHCE seems to perform well in predicting rebates.

References

Abraham, J. M., T. DeLeire, and A. B. Royalty. 2009. "Access to Health Insurance at Small Establishments: What Can We Learn from Analyzing Other Fringe Benefits?" *Inquiry* 46 (3): 253–73.

Abraham, J. M., and P. Karaca-Mandic. 2011. "Regulating the Medical Loss Ratio: Implications for the Individual Market." *American Journal of Managed Care* 17 (3): 211–24.

Abraham, J. M., P. Karaca-Mandic, and M. Boudreaux. 2013. "Sizing Up the Individual Market for Health Insurance: A Comparison of Survey and Administrative Data Sources." *Medical Care Research and Review* 70 (4): 418–33.

Abraham, J. M., P. Karaca-Mandic, and K. Simon. 2013. "How Has the Affordable Care Act's Medical Loss Ratio Regulation Affected Insurer Behavior?" Working Paper, University of Minnesota.

Buchmueller, T., and J. DiNardo. 2002. "Did Community Rating Induce an Adverse Selection Death Spiral? Evidence from New York, Pennsylvania, and Connecticut." *American Economic Review* 92 (1): 280–94.

Cantor, J. C., A. C. Monheit, S. Brownlee, and C. Schneider. 2007. "The Adequacy of Household Survey Data for Evaluating the Nongroup Health Insurance Market." *Health Services Research* 42 (4): 1739–57.

Congressional Budget Office (CBO). 2012. "Updated Estimates for the Insurance Coverage Provisions of the Affordable Care Act." Washington, DC, CBO. March.

Cox, C., G. Claxton, and L. Levitt. 2013. "Beyond Rebates: How Much are Consumers Saving from the ACA's Medical Loss Ratio Provision?" Kaiser Family Foundation, June 6. http://kff.org/health-reform/perspective/beyond-rebates-how-much-are-consumers-saving-from-the-acas-medical-loss-ratio-provision/.

Dafny, L., D. Dranove, F. Limbrock, and F. Scott Morton. "Data Impediments to Empirical Work on Health Insurance Markets." *B.E. Journal of Economic Analysis & Policy* 11 (2). Published online. https://www.degruyter.com/view/j/bejeap.2011.11.2/bejeap.2011.11.2.2822/bejeap.2011.11.2.2822.xml.

Davidoff, A., L. Blumberg, and L. Nichols. 2005. "State Health Insurance Market Reforms and Access to Insurance for High-Risk Employees." *Journal of Health Economics* 24:725–50.

Government Accountability Office (GAO). 2011. "Private Health Insurance: Early Indicators Show That Most Insurers Would Have Met or Exceeded New Medical Loss Ratio Standards." GAO-12-90R, October 31. Accessed September 30, 2013. http://www.gao.gov/products/GAO-12-90R.

Hall, M. A., and M. J. McCue. 2012. "Estimating the Impact of the Medical Loss Ratio Rule: A State-by-State Analysis." Issue Brief, The Commonwealth Fund, New York. April. Accessed September 30, 2013. http://www.commonwealthfund.org/publications/issue-briefs/2012/apr/estimating-rebates.

Kaiser Family Foundation. 2010. "Rate Review: Spotlight on State Efforts to Make Health Insurance More Affordable." Executive Summary, December. Accessed October 1, 2013. http://kaiserfamilyfoundation.files.wordpress.com/2013/01/8122.pdf.

Karaca-Mandic, P., and J. Abraham. 2013. "Using Data from the National Association of Insurance Commissioners for Health Reform Evaluation." State Health Reform Assistance Issue Brief, Princeton, NJ, The Robert Wood Johnson Foundation. July.

Karaca-Mandic, P., J. Abraham, and C. Phelps. 2011. "How Do Health Insurance Loading Fees Vary by Group Size? Implications for Healthcare Reform." *International Journal of Health Care Finance and Economics* 11 (3): 181–207.

Karaca-Mandic, P., J. Abraham, and K. Simon. 2013. "Is the Medical Loss Ratio a Good Target Measure for Regulation in the Individual Market for Health Insurance?" *Health Economics* 24 (1): 55–74.

Karaca-Mandic, P., R. Feldman, and P. Graven. 2013. "The Role of Agents and Brokers in the Market for Health Insurance." NBER Working Paper no. 19342, Cambridge, MA.

Klerman, J. A., M. Davern, K. T. Call, V. Lynch, and J. Ringel. 2009. "Understanding the Current Population Survey's Insurance Estimates and the Medicaid 'Undercount.'" *Health Affairs* 28 (6): w991–1001.

Mach, A., and B. O'Hara. 2011. "Do People Really Have Multiple Health Insurance Plans? Estimates of Nongroup Health Insurance in the American Community Survey." SEHSD Working Paper no. 2011-28, US Census Bureau's Social, Economic, and Housing Statistics Division. https://www.census.gov/content/dam/Census/library/working-papers/2011/demo/SEHSD-WP2011-28.pdf.

Marquis, M. S., and S. Long. 2002. "Effects of 'Second Generation' Small Group Health Insurance Market Reforms, 1993 to 1997." *Inquiry* 38:365–80.

McCue, M. J., and M. A. Hall. 2012. "Insurers' Responses to Regulation of Medical Loss Ratios." Issue Brief, The Commonwealth Fund, New York. December. http://www.commonwealthfund.org/~/media/files/publications/issue-brief/2012/dec/1634_mccue_insurers_responses_mlr_regulation_ib.pdf.

McCue, M. J., M. Hall, and X. Liu. 2013. "Impact of Medical Loss Regulation on the Financial Performance of Health Insurers." *Health Affairs* 32 (9): 1546–51.

Monheit, A., and B. S. Schone. 2004. "How Has Small Group Market Reform Affected Employee Health Insurance Coverage?" *Journal of Public Economics* 88 (1–2): 237–54.

Phelps, C. 2010. *Health Economics.* Reading, MA: Addison-Wesley.

Simon, K. 2005. "Adverse Selection in Health Insurance Markets? Evidence From State Small-Group Health Insurance Reforms." *Journal of Public Economics* 89:1865–77.

US Department of Health and Human Services. 2010. "Health Insurance Issuers Implementing Medical Loss Ratio (MLR) Requirements under the Patient Protection and Affordable Care Act." *Federal Register* 75 (230): 74864–934. http://www.gpo.gov/fdsys/pkg/FR-2010-12-01/pdf/2010-29596.pdf.

Potpourri

The Distribution of Public Spending for Health Care in the United States on the Eve of Health Reform

Didem Bernard, Thomas Selden, and Yuriy Pylypchuk

14.1 Introduction

US health care spending in 2012 was $2.8 trillion or 17.2 percent of US gross domestic product (GDP) (Martin et al. 2014). Spending of this magnitude can place significant pressures on families striving to afford premiums and out-of-pocket payments for care, on employers providing insurance to current and retired employees, and on governments concerned with the fiscal implications of public spending on health care. Despite the recent slowdown in health care expenditure growth, these pressures are likely to increase, with growth in health care spending predicted to outpace growth in GDP over the next decade (Cuckler et al. 2013). As a result, the role of government in the financing of health care is likely to remain at the forefront of public policy debate for the foreseeable future.

In this chapter we examine several basic questions: What is the overall percentage of health care paid for by the public sector? How has the public share changed over time? And what is the incidence of public spending across key subgroups of the population? These questions may be basic, but the complexity of health care finance in the United States makes it difficult to provide answers

Didem Bernard is senior economist in the Division of Modeling and Simulation, Center for Financing, Access and Cost Trends, Agency for Healthcare Research and Quality. Thomas Selden is the director of the Division of Modeling and Simulation, Center for Financing, Access and Cost Trends, Agency for Healthcare Research and Quality. Yuriy Pylypchuk is a health economist at Social and Scientific Systems, Inc. and a visiting professor at Georgetown University, McCourt School of Public Policy.

The views expressed in this chapter are those of the authors, and no official endorsement by the US Department of Health and Human Services or the AHRQ is intended or should be inferred. For acknowledgments, sources of research support, and disclosure of the authors' material financial relationships, if any, please see http://www.nber.org/chapters/c13098.ack.

with commonly available statistics. Measuring public spending entails tracking not only outlays from public insurance coverage (such as Medicaid and Medicare), but also implicit tax subsidies (such as those for employer-sponsored insurance), public grants to providers (such as Medicaid Disproportionate Share payments), and private premium payments for public coverage (such as Part B Medicare premiums). Because no single data source provides all of this information, in this chapter we combine aggregate measures from the National Health Expenditure Accounts (NHEA) with microdata from the Medical Expenditure Panel Survey (MEPS). The second section of the chapter adjusts NHEA estimates to provide a historical look at the public-private spending mix since 1960. The third section presents a "benefit incidence analysis" of public spending in 2010 by age, poverty level, insurance coverage, and health status, and across ACA-relevant subgroups on the eve of reform.

14.2   Aggregate Public Spending on Health Care

The NHEA, produced by the Centers for Medicare and Medicaid Services (CMS), combine data on provider revenues and administrative claims to produce aggregate estimates of US health spending by service type and payment source (CMS 2014a). We modify the NHEA estimates in two ways. First, we reclassify as private the portion of Medicare paid for by private premiums (these payments are voluntary, and thus more akin to a "user fee" than to a tax).[1] Second, we shift to public spending the portion of private spending that is defrayed by tax expenditures.

Unfortunately, we are aware of no consistent and comprehensive time series for tax expenditures, and published tax expenditure estimates can be only imperfectly reconciled. For 1987, 1996, 2002, 2007, and 2010 the tax subsidy estimates are from calculations performed by one or more of this chapter's authors, providing a reasonably consistent and comprehensive set of adjustments.[2] We describe the 2010 estimates in greater detail below, but our basic objective is to include: (a) federal income, state income, and payroll tax expenditures for employer-sponsored insurance ([ESI]; subsidies for employer contributions and for tax-exempt employee contributions);

1. Medicare premiums paid by households for 1987 to 2010 are from NHEA "sponsor" estimates (CMS 2014b), supplemented with pre-1987 data on Medicare financing from Trustee Reports. Although we use NHEA sponsor estimates for Medicare premiums, note that our public/private estimates differ from NHEA sponsor estimates in several key respects. First, we exclude nonpatient revenue. Second, we count Medicare as public, whether it is funded by payroll taxes or general revenues (excluding only the portion paid by premiums). Third, we treat all employer-sponsored insurance as private, including that for government employees. Lastly, we account for tax expenditures. As a result, our estimates of the public share are substantially larger than those in the NHEA sponsor estimates.

2. Estimates for 1996 are from Selden and Moeller (2000), which is also our source for unpublished 1987 estimates. For 2002, estimates are from Selden and Sing (2008) (see also Sheils and Haught 2004). Note that tax expenditures that reduce health care spending (such as property tax exemptions or exemptions from ad valorem sales taxes) effectively increase the total amount of health care spending by a small percentage.

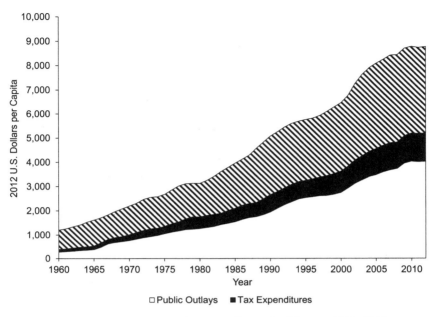

Fig. 14.1   **Per capita public and private spending on health care, 1960–2012**

(b) the excess medical care itemized deduction; (c) the tax preference for self-employment health insurance; (d) tax preferences for (health care) flexible spending accounts and health savings accounts; (e) the exemption of medical care from sales taxation; and (f) a range of smaller tax expenditures, such as those available to nonprofit providers. Tax expenditure estimates were constructed assuming that all preferences were removed simultaneously (rather than, say, allowing the excess medical care deduction to grow in response to removal of the ESI and self-employment preferences).

We fill gaps between 1987 and 2012 by interpolation and extrapolation, building on estimates of the ESI subsidy for current workers from Miller and Selden (2013), Selden and Gray (2006), and the Joint Committee on Taxation (JCT, various years, available for 1967–present, but only covering the federal income tax portion of the ESI subsidy), as well as estimates in Sheils and Hogan (1999) and Sheils and Haught (2004). For earlier years, we construct estimates that are as consistent as possible from Feldstein and Allison (1970) and Helms (2008), filling any remaining gaps back to 1960 using Barro and Redlick's historical average tax rates (National Bureau of Economic Research 2012) and NHEA estimates of private insurance premiums. Due to the variety of data sources used to construct our time series for tax expenditures, our results should be viewed as an approximation of how public spending has evolved over time.

Figure 14.1 clearly shows both the remarkable rise in real per capita spending and the rising public share. Combining public outlays with implicit public spending through tax expenditures, the public share of total health spending increased from 31.2 percent in 1960 to 46.8 percent in 1970 (following the implementation of Medicare and Medicaid). Subsequent changes were more gradual, but tended to increase the public share, which reached 53.6 percent in 1990, 57.2 percent in 2000, 58.7 percent in 2007, and 59.2 percent in 2012. Tax expenditures as a percentage of health care spending peaked in the 1979–1981 period at an average of 15.5 percent of total health care spending, declining thereafter to approximately 13 percent at present. This decline is due primarily to lower marginal tax rates. Together with the fact that private spending itself is a declining share of total spending, declines in marginal rates more than offset the shift toward the use of Section 125 plans to exempt employee premium contributions from taxation. In contrast, public outlays have quite steadily increased as a share of US health care spending, even after the initial introduction of Medicare and Medicaid.

14.3   Benefit Incidence of Public Spending on Health Care

Given that the public sector accounts for well over half of all US spending on health care, a natural next question concerns the incidence of benefits from this spending across key socioeconomic groups. To answer this, we move beyond aggregate NHEA estimates, updating and extending the "benefit incidence analysis" for 2002 in Selden and Sing (2008). Benefit incidence analysis is a "statutory" method of accounting in a simplified manner for the distribution of benefits from public spending (Selden and Wasylenko 1992). Public programs are assumed to confer benefits in proportion to services or payments received. We do not attempt to measure the risk-reducing benefits associated with public insurance or the cash-equivalent valuation by recipients for benefits received, and we ignore shifting across generations and throughout the economy—our rationale being that we seek to provide a complete overview of a very complex sector.[3]

Our starting point is the MEPS household survey sponsored by the Agency for Healthcare Research and Quality (AHRQ) and the National Center for Health Statistics (NCHS). The MEPS contains individual and household-level data on health expenditures and use, health insurance coverage, health status, and a wide range of demographic and socioeconomic characteristics for a nationally representative sample of households in the civilian, noninstitutionalized population (Cohen 1997).

Although MEPS is an ideal starting point for analyzing the distribution of public spending, no household survey, by itself, can support a complete

---

3. For an analysis of how alternative assumptions regarding wage formation might affect the tax subsidy incidence, see Selden and Bernard (2004). For incidence analyses of Medicare's benefits net of payments, see McClellan and Skinner (2006) and Bhattacharya and Lakdawalla (2006). With respect to valuing in-kind benefits, see Wolfe and Moffitt (1991).

distributional analysis. First, household data suffer from underreporting, and high-cost cases may be underrepresented. Second, household respondents cannot be expected to report certain types of spending, such as administrative costs or some hospital payments not tied to patient events. Third, although MEPS provides much of the data to compute tax expenditures, such subsidies are implicit by nature and thus not readily reportable by household respondents.

To remedy the first gap, we begin with 2007 NHEA benchmarks that have been aligned with the type of service and source of payment definitions in MEPS and adjusted to exclude spending for the institutionalized, active-duty military and foreigners visiting the United States—groups not included in MEPS (Bernard et al. 2012). We age these benchmarks forward to our analysis year, 2010, and then align MEPS by type of service and source of payment. Gaps are closed in part by upweighting high-cost cases and, in part, by scaling reported amounts (Bernard, Selden, and Pylypchuk 2014).

Next we allocate amounts in NHEA that were outside the scope of MEPS. Personal care services are allocated in proportion to home health care spending. Administrative costs are allocated in proportion to benefits received, with any premiums paid by households for public coverage netted out of public benefits received. Medicaid and Medicare Disproportionate Share payments and state and local funding for public hospitals are allocated using MEPS data on uncompensated care.[4] For completeness, we also allocate: research spending in proportion to prescription drug spending, investment in structures and equipment in proportion to hospital use, and public health spending evenly across the population. Throughout the analysis, health insurance provided by public employers to their employees is considered private spending (a noncash form of compensation in lieu of higher cash wages), rather than public insurance.

Finally, we estimate a comprehensive array of tax expenditures. To simulate the tax subsidy from exclusion of employer-sponsored insurance premiums from federal income, state income, and Social Security and Medicare payroll taxation, we combine marginal tax rates (simulated using the National Bureau of Economic Research TAXSIM model)[5] with MEPS HC data on employee premium contributions and employer premium contributions (imputed using regressions estimated with the MEPS Insurance Component survey of employers).[6] We also simulate the medical expense deduction and the exemption of health care spending from most, but not all, state

---

4. The MEPS uncompensated care was constructed by comparing event payments with charges that were adjusted for reasonable discounts.

5. Feenberg and Coutts (1993). TAXSIM version 8 was used (accessed September 1, 2013, at http://www.nber.org/taxsim).

6. Each family's ESI tax subsidies were allocated across policyholders and their covered dependents in proportion to spending paid for by private insurance (or pro rata across covered persons in families that had no care paid for by private insurance).

and local sales taxation. Finally, we allocate to MEPS individuals national estimates of a variety of smaller tax subsidies, such as the tax exemption of nonprofit hospitals (Bernard, Selden, and Pylypchuk 2015). All differences discussed in the text are statistically significant at the 5 percent level, and all standard errors and statistical tests reflect the complex design of MEPS.

14.3.1   Aggregate Results

The top row of table 14.1 presents the incidence of benefits from public spending on health care in aggregate. Overall, public spending accounted for 57.6 percent of total spending on health care (a slightly lower percentage than in figure 14.1, due to the exclusion of active-duty military and persons residing in institutions). We report expenditures in five subcategories: "Medicaid and CHIP" includes payments for patient care and administration costs, net of premiums paid by households, for Medicaid, the Children's Health Insurance Program (CHIP), and a small number of similar state-funded programs. "Medicare" is defined similarly. These two categories comprise 67.6 percent of all public outlays. "Other public general" includes the NHEA categories of public health, public investment in structures and equipment, Medicare Graduate Medical Education, and public research—amounts that tend to benefit broad groups of the population and may have public goods attributes. All remaining public outlays are grouped in "other public targeted." This includes other public third-party programs such as the Veterans Administration, workers' compensation, and the MEPS expenditure categories of Other Federal and Other State and Local, all of which entail payments linked to specific beneficiaries (i.e., payments that can be measured in MEPS). The "targeted" category also includes Medicaid and Medicare Disproportionate Share payments, which are payments to hospitals based on their caseloads of lower-income populations.[7] Finally, the "tax expenditures" category includes all of the tax preferences mentioned above, accounting for just over one-quarter (26.6 percent) of all public expenditures on health care (within the civilian noninstitutionalized population).

14.3.2   Age Groups

Public spending in 2010 was strongly related to age, with children from birth to age eighteen receiving $1,809 on average, versus $3,539 for adults age nineteen to sixty-four and $9,678 for seniors (all amounts in 2010 dollars). In part, these differences mirror the overall age gradient in health care spending. Despite the large differences in average public spending between children and seniors, the public share of total spending for seniors (65.2 percent)

---

7. For instance, Medicare DSH is tied to hospital caseloads of persons receiving Supplemental Security Income (SSI). Medicaid DSH payments are targeted at hospitals treating indigent populations.

Table 14.1   Benefit incidence of public spending on health care by age and poverty level, civilian noninstitutionalized population, 2010

	Population (millions)	Public outlays				Tax expenditures	Total public expenditures	Public as percentage of total expenditures
		Medicaid/SCHIP	Medicare	Other public targeted[a]	Other public general[b]			
All	308.6	852 (57)	1,045 (65)	435 (34)	474 (5)	1,039 (16)	3,913 (112)	57.6 (0.9)
Age groups								
0–18	79.3	831 (73)	24 (18)	133 (29)	318 (6)	491 (13)	1,809 (94)	63.9 (1.8)
19–64	188.1	828 (74)	371 (50)	406 (37)	475 (7)	1,374 (20)	3,539 (105)	52.8 (1.1)
65+	41.2	1,008 (144)	6,094 (374)	1,153 (192)	770 (15)	566 (22)	9,678 (504)	65.2 (1.6)
Poverty level								
< 100% FPL	46.8	3,239 (280)	1,148 (160)	1,010 (165)	470 (16)	120 (14)	6,070 (437)	79.9 (1.9)
100–199% FPL	57.1	1,033 (86)	1,542 (164)	544 (91)	486 (12)	492 (21)	4,196 (230)	67 (1.7)
200–399% FPL	93.0	441 (69)	964 (96)	331 (52)	455 (8)	1,003 (18)	3,262 (136)	53.2 (1.4)
400%+ FPL	111.7	102 (23)	814 (102)	226 (36)	484 (8)	1,734 (24)	3,406 (129)	46.8 (1.2)

Source: Authors' calculations using 2010 Medical Expenditure Panel Survey (MEPS) data aligned with 2010 National Health Expenditure Accounts (NHEA) data and other national benchmarks.

Note: Sample contains 32,846 positively weighted observations. Standard errors (in parentheses) are adjusted for the complex design of the MEPS sample, but do not reflect the uncertainties regarding the adjustments to align the MEPS with national benchmarks.

[a] Includes Medicaid and Medicare Disproportionate Share, Department of Veterans Affairs, workers' compensation, Medicare retroactive and capital pass-through payments, and administrative costs of public coverage.

[b] Includes Medicare General Medical Education, other federal, state, and local, public health, public research, investment in structures, and equipment.

is very similar to that of children (63.9 percent). On a percentage basis, adults age nineteen to sixty-four receive less than children or seniors (public spending is 52.8 percent of total spending for this group).

The lower public shares for adults age nineteen to sixty-four is not surprising given that Medicare provides nearly universal coverage for seniors and given that public coverage expansions in recent years, prior to the ACA, have been disproportionately targeted at children (Medicaid and CHIP). Medicare and Medicaid/CHIP together comprise only 17.9 percent of total spending for adults under age sixty-five (calculated from table as [$828 + $371]/$6,703) versus 30.2 percent for children and 47.8 percent for seniors.

14.3.3   Poverty Level

Table 14.1 also shows the incidence of public benefits by family income as a percentage of the Federal Poverty Line (FPL). Not surprisingly, Medicaid/CHIP spending was targeted at lower-income groups. In contrast, the remaining categories of public health care outlays were somewhat more evenly distributed, and tax subsidies strongly favored high-income families. Overall, public spending accounted for 79.9 percent of total health care among those under 100 percent of FPL. Perhaps more surprisingly, even among those at or above four times the poverty line the public share was 46.8 percent.

14.3.4   Health Status

The top panel of table 14.2 shows the incidence of public benefits by self (or proxy) reported health status.[8] Our results highlight the extent to which the public sector targets those with the greatest health care needs. This is particularly true for public outlays on third-party reimbursement for care (i.e., Medicaid, CHIP, Medicare, and other public targeted). It is not surprising that public outlays would be highest for those in fair or poor health; these groups also have the highest private expenditures. More noteworthy is that the public share rises as health status deteriorates, so that the public sector in the United States disproportionately cares for those with greatest health risks.[9]

---

8. Persons with missing health status were excluded from the analysis.

9. Our methodology generally follows that of Selden and Sing quite closely; however, one difference concerns the treatment of private spending in public share calculations. Selden and Sing measure the benefit of private insurance using premiums paid by households (or employers). In this chapter, the benefit of private insurance is based on paid claims (plus an implied load). This is more symmetric with our use of claims paid by public insurers (plus net administrative costs) to value the benefit of public spending on coverage. This refinement has negligible effect on our public share computations based on age, income, insurance, or ACA-relevant groups. It does, however, improve our public share estimates across health risk, lowering the public share estimates for those with high health risks.

Table 14.2 Benefit incidence of public spending on health care by health and insurance status, civilian noninstitutionalized population, 2010

	Population (millions)	Public outlays				Tax expenditures	Total public expenditures	Public as percentage of total expenditures
		Medicaid/ SCHIP	Medicare	Other public targeted[a]	Other public general[b]			
Health status								
Excellent	105.6	287 (26)	152 (37)	87 (13)	330 (4)	938 (19)	1,819 (52)	55.5 (1.8)
Very good	92.5	410 (59)	532 (74)	233 (35)	417 (8)	1,182 (20)	2,814 (115)	52.9 (1.4)
Good	73.9	980 (127)	1,273 (9,157)	491 (61)	534 (12)	1,077 (28)	4,428 (249)	55.6 (1.7)
Fair	26.9	2,092 (235)	3,308 (318)	1,496 (279)	787 (23)	923 (37)	8,865 (510)	62.1 (2.0)
Poor	9.0	7,301 (873)	7,825 (967)	2,752 (589)	1,305 (66)	845 (80)	20,265 (1,432)	66.0 (2.9)
Insurance status								
Private	173.5	80 (16)	39 (7)	204 (26)	436 (6)	1,678 (18)	2,490 (40)	42.6 (0.8)
Medicaid	47.5	3,802 (281)	140 (42)	379 (64)	395 (12)	25 (4)	4,740 (315)	91.6 (0.9)
Medicaid & Medicare	8.6	7,951 (794)	8,612 (789)	1,705 (264)	878 (51)	145 (15)	19,291 (1,453)	89.6 (1.2)
Medicare	38.5	0	6,091 (409)	1,147 (206)	806 (17)	631 (24)	8,783 (487)	60.1 (1.7)
Uninsured	40.4	0	0	546 (121)	326 (7)	68 (9)	1,124 (136)	51.6 (3.7)

Source: Authors' calculations using 2010 Medical Expenditure Panel Survey (MEPS) data aligned with 2010 National Health Expenditure Accounts (NHEA) data and other national benchmarks.

Note: Sample contains 32,846 positively weighted observations. Standard errors (in parentheses) are adjusted for the complex design of the MEPS sample, but do not reflect the uncertainties regarding the adjustments to align the MEPS with national benchmarks.

[a] Includes Medicaid and Medicare Disproportionate Share, Department of Veterans Affairs, workers' compensation, Medicare retroactive and capital pass-through payments, and administrative costs of public coverage.

[b] Includes Medicare General Medical Education, other federal, state, and local, public health, public research, and investment in structures and equipment.

14.3.5   Insurance Coverage

The bottom panel of table 14.2 shows the incidence of public benefits by insurance coverage. Not surprisingly, public expenditures are largest on average ($19,291) for dual eligibles (persons ever covered by Medicare and Medicaid). Also not surprising is that the public share for persons ever covered by Medicaid/CHIP (but not Medicare or private) is very high (91.6 percent). More noteworthy is that the public share is just over 50 percent for the full-year uninsured (though the absolute amount, $1,124, is small relative to other insurance groups). Even for persons with private coverage during the year the public share is 42.6 percent, due to $1,678 in tax expenditures and $436 in other public general (both per covered person).

14.3.6   ACA-Relevant Subgroups

Table 14.3 shows the incidence of public benefits for adults age nineteen to sixty-four by ACA-relevant subgroups.[10] For simplicity, we focus on US citizens who are never enrolled in Medicare and who do not receive Supplemental Security Income (SSI).[11] We identify six groups. The first consists of persons enrolled at any point during the year in Medicaid (or, in a few cases, CHIP). Even after excluding "dual" Medicaid/Medicare enrollees and persons receiving SSI, this group currently benefits from extensive public expenditures ($4,780 on average), with a public share of 83.3 percent.

The second and third groups consist of persons with modified adjusted gross income (MAGI) under 138 percent of FPL. In group 2 are adults in expansion states who would be eligible for Medicaid as of January 1, 2014 (if not earlier).[12] Group 3 consists of adults in nonexpansion states who will not in general be eligible for Medicaid.[13] Neither group receives a particularly high benefit from public spending on health care; average amounts for groups 2 and 3 are $1,536 and $1,566, respectively.

10. Because income (and thus eligibility) can fluctuate during the year, this portion of our analysis focuses on income measured as of the first interview during 2010 (and we subset the full-year MEPS sample to those in MEPS as of that interview).

11. The ACA main coverage provisions do not apply to persons with Medicare or who receive SSI-related Medicaid coverage for disability. While some ACA coverage provisions apply to some noncitizens (those who are documented and who meet residency tests), immigration status is not measured in MEPS and must be inferred probabilistically based on a number of observed characteristics. Including noncitizens would have very little effect on the estimates in table 14.3.

12. Some adults in these states were eligible for, but not enrolled in Medicaid under pre-ACA rules, and some lived in states that implemented ACA-related expansions prior to the start of 2014.

13. Included in this group are some adults who were eligible for, but not enrolled in Medicaid under prereform rules. Note that in nonexpansion states, persons with MAGI between 100 percent FPL and 138 percent FPL are eligible for subsidized exchange coverage (if they lack access to affordable ESI), so that this group is excluded from group 3. Note also that in nonexpansion states the change from pre-ACA Medicaid income counting rules to MAGI and the elimination of asset tests may make some current enrollees ineligible, while conferring eligibility on some adults who would previously have been ineligible.

Table 14.3 Benefit incidence of public spending on health care by Affordable Care Act subgroups, among adults age nineteen to sixty-four in the civilian noninstitutionalized population, 2010 ($ amounts are per capita)

ACA eligibility	Population (millions)	Public outlays ($)					Total public expenditures ($)	Total expenditures ($)	Public as percentage of total expenditures
		Medicaid/ CHIP	Medicare	Other public targeted[a]	Other public general[b]	Tax expenditures ($)			
Enrolled in Medicaid	12.0	3,887 (461)	0	336 (68)	394 (13)	163 (20)	4,780 (497)	5,741 (504)	83.3 (2.7)
Income < 138% FPL & ineligible for subsidized marketplace coverage									
Living in expansion states	11.8	0	0	717 (205)	368 (11)	452 (35)	1,536 (211)	3,462 (341)	44.4 (4.2)
Living in nonexpansion states	9.2	0	0	638 (139)	426 (33)	502 (55)	1,566 (161)	4,581 (873)	34.2 (5.3)
Eligible for subsidized marketplace coverage	19.0	0	0	613 (164)	378 (12)	398 (22)	1,389 (173)	3,485 (306)	39.9 (3.1)
Income > 138% FPL & offered ESI (own or spouse)	91.8	0	0	268 (33)	461 (9)	2,177 (20)	2,905 (41)	6,457 (198)	45.0 (1.1)
Income > 400% FPL & no offer	9.6	0	0	508 (265)	414 (19)	894 (53)	1,816 (275)	4,784 (452)	38.0 (4.3)

Source: Authors' calculations using 2010 Medical Expenditure Panel Survey (MEPS) data aligned with 2010 National Health Expenditure Accounts (NHEA) data and other national benchmarks.

Note: Sample contains 32,846 positively weighted observations. Standard errors (in parentheses) are adjusted for the complex design of the MEPS sample, but do not reflect uncertainties regarding the adjustments to align the MEPS with national benchmarks. These results are for persons age nineteen to sixty-four who are citizens due to the cross-state variation in eligibility rules for noncitizens.

[a] Includes Medicaid and Medicare Disproportionate Share, Department of Veterans Affairs, workers' compensation, Medicare retroactive and capital pass-through payments, and administrative costs of public coverage.

[b] Includes Medicare General Medical Education, other federal, state, and local, public health, public research, and investment in structures and equipment.

The fourth group consists of those gaining eligibility for subsidized marketplace coverage. We define this group as adults who (a) would be ineligible for Medicaid using 2014 rules, (b) have MAGI between 100 and 400 percent of FPL, and (c) lack access to affordable ESI coverage (neither the person nor their spouse is offered ESI through current jobs).[14] From a benefit incidence perspective, this group looks quite similar to lower-income groups 2 and 3.

Group 5 consists of persons with MAGI over 138 percent of FPL who are offered coverage through their own job (or whose spouse is offered coverage)—the offers making them (in most cases) ineligible for subsidized marketplace coverage even if their MAGIs are under 400 percent of FPL. As has been well-documented in prior studies regarding the regressive incidence of the ESI tax subsidy, this group has access to affordable coverage (at least for single coverage), and it receives approximately double the public benefit on average ($2,905) compared to adults in groups 2, 3, 4—who generally have lower incomes and whose public benefit ranges from $1,389 to $1,566.

Looking at these first five groups, benefit incidence analysis clarifies the extent to which the ACA, as designed, targeted Medicaid expansions and private coverage subsidies at groups in-between Medicaid enrollees and those with access to ESI. As designed, the ACA would help to level what was, pre-ACA, a U-shaped pattern of benefits across these groups (see, for instance, Rennane and Steuerle 2011). The actual effects of the ACA on this distribution of public benefits will depend, for groups 2 and 4, on their take up of coverage and their resulting use of medical care. For group 3 the question is whether their states decide to adopt the ACA Medicaid expansions.

The final group consists of persons with MAGI over 400 percent of FPL who lack their own or spousal ESI offers. Compared to groups 2–4, this group currently receives approximately the same level of public outlays and nearly twice as much in tax expenditure (reflecting in part tax preferences for self-employment and retiree coverage). Because of this group's higher income, it was not targeted by the ACA—though members of this group may be affected by ACA provisions regarding guaranteed issue, community rating, and other reforms in the nongroup market.

14.4   Limitations

There are several noteworthy limitations of our study. First, figure 14.1 presents published NHEA estimates that we have modified using tax expen-

14. The ACA also specifies that such coverage must have an actuarial value of at least 60 percent and a single coverage premium under 9.5 percent of MAGI. Also, a spouse's offer would not affect a person's subsidy eligibility unless the person can be covered through the spouse's plan. The MEPS does not provide data on actuarial value and only observes employee contributions and coverage of other family members for plans actually chosen. Given that most ESI plans meet these tests for most employees, we focus solely on own and spousal offers in defining group 4 for table 14.3.

diture estimates drawn from a variety of published and unpublished sources. These tax expenditure estimates can be only imperfectly reconciled and interpolated, raising caveats regarding the consistency of the resulting time series. Second, our incidence analysis focuses on average spending by subgroups, and we do not measure the risk-reducing benefits associated with public insurance or the cash-equivalent valuation by recipients for benefits received. Third, the ultimate beneficiaries of public spending may be different in some cases from those we identify. For instance, public spending on behalf of seniors may offset private transfers from (or increase bequests to) their children (Sloan, Zhang, and Wang 2002). Fourth, tax expenditure estimates were constructed under the assumption that employers shift the burden of employer premium contributions to workers based on the plans they take up (rather than based on their ability to pay or their underlying health risks), and, while this likely has little effect on aggregate estimates (Miller and Selden 2013), alternative assumptions might affect the measured incidence of ESI tax subsidies across workers (Selden and Bernard 2004). Finally, persons in institutions (and active-duty military) are outside the scope of MEPS and thus were not included in our incidence analysis.

14.5 Discussion

The estimates presented in this chapter provide basic background information on the overall public share of health care spending, its growth over time, and the distribution of public benefits across key population subgroups. Overall, the public share of US spending on health care in 2012 totaled 59.2 percent when we include tax expenditures as a form of public spending (and when we treat household-paid premiums for public coverage as being akin to a user fee). Our historical analysis documents a long-term trend toward higher public shares in total spending, with growth in public outlays representing the primary driver over time (versus tax expenditures, which peaked as a percentage of health care spending in the years 1979–1981).

Our incidence results for 2010 show that the distribution of public spending across age, poverty, insurance, and health status have not changed since 2002 (Selden and Sing 2008). Publicly financed health care, both in magnitude and as a percentage of total spending, is largest for seniors, while benefits as a percentage of total spending are lowest for adults age nineteen to sixty-four. Moreover, even though it was public outlays, more than tax expenditures, that drove the rising public share of total health care spending from 1960 to present, our incidence estimates for 2010 show that all income groups (classified by poverty level) share in the benefits of public spending. Even among families with incomes above 400 percent of the poverty line, public spending accounted for nearly half of total spending.

This chapter also presents benefit incidence estimates for ACA-relevant groups of nonsenior adults. Our results highlight the relatively low level of pre-ACA public benefits flowing to adults under 400 percent of FPL who neither were enrolled in Medicaid nor had access to ESI—precisely those adults the ACA targets for expanded access to government-subsidized, affordable coverage.

In future work, "benefit incidence analysis" can provide a valuable tool to evaluate ACA-related changes in public spending. The Congressional Budget Office (CBO 2013) shows that ACA provisions to expand health insurance will increase the public share of total spending,[15] and an important question for public policy will be the extent to which the ACA evens the distribution of public benefits across adults. Furthermore, tracking the benefit incidence of public spending can provide a useful backdrop for the ongoing debate over further steps the country might take on entitlements and tax policy to ensure long-term fiscal stability.

References

Bernard, Didem M., Cathy Cowan, Thomas M. Selden, Liming Cai, Aaron Catlin, and Steven Heffler. 2012. "Reconciling Medical Expenditure Estimates from the MEPS and NHEA, 2007." *Medicare & Medicaid Research Review* 2 (4): E1–19. Accessed January 25, 2014. http://www.cms.gov/mmrr/Downloads/MMRR2012 _002_04_a09.pdf.
Bernard, Didem M., Thomas M. Selden, and Yuriy Pylypchuk. 2015. "Aligning the Medical Expenditure Panel Survey to Aggregate US Benchmarks." MEPS Working Paper no. 15002, Rockville, MD, Agency for Healthcare Research and Quality.
Bhattacharya, Jay, and Darius Lakdawalla. 2006. "Does Medicare Benefit the Poor?" *Journal of Public Economics* 90 (1–2): 277–92.
Centers for Medicare and Medicaid Services. 2013. *Analysis of Factors Leading to Changes in Projected 2019 National Health Expenditure Estimates: A Comparison of April 2010 Projections and September 2013 Projections.* Accessed January 25, 2014. http://www.cms.gov/Research-Statistics-Data-and-Systems/Statistics-Trends-and -Reports/NationalHealthExpendData/Downloads/ProjectionsRevisionAnalysis.pdf.
———. 2014a. *National Health Expenditure by Service and Source of Funds, CY 1960–2012.* Accessed January 25, 2014. http://www.cms.gov/Research-Statistics -Data-and-Systems/Statistics-Trends-and-Reports/NationalHealthExpendData/ NationalHealthAccountsHistorical.html.
———. 2014b. *National Health Expenditures by Type of Sponsor: Business, Households, and Governments, 2012.* Accessed January 25, 2014. http://www.cms.gov/Research -Statistics-Data-and-Systems/Statistics-Trends-and-Reports/NationalHealth ExpendData/Downloads/sponsors.pdf.
Cohen, Steven B. 1997. "Sample Design of the 1996 Medical Expenditure Panel Survey Household Component." MEPS Methodology Report no. 2, Pub. no. 97-0027. Accessed December 1, 2012. http://www.meps.ahrq.gov/mepsweb/data_files/ publications/mr2/mr2.pdf.

---

15. See also CMS (2013) and Cuckler et al. (2013).

Congressional Budget Office (CBO). 2013. "CBO's Estimate of the Net Budgetary Impact of the Affordable Care Act's Health Insurance Coverage Provisions Has Not Changed Much over Time." May 14. http://www.cbo.gov/publication/44176.

Cuckler, Gigi A., Andrea M. Sisko, Sean P. Keehan, Sheila D. Smith, Andrew J. Madison, John A. Poisal, Christian J. Wolfe, Joseph M. Lizonitz, and Devin A. Stone. 2013. "National Health Expenditure Projections, 2012–22: Slow Growth until Coverage Expands and Economy Improves." *Health Affairs* 32 (10): 1820–31. Accessed October 8, 2013. http://content.healthaffairs.org/content/32/10/1820.full.pdf.

Feenberg, Daniel, and Elisabeth Coutts. 1993. "An Introduction to the TAXSIM Model." *Journal of Policy Analysis and Management* 12 (1): 189–94. Accessed January 25, 2014. http://users.nber.org/~taxsim/feenberg-coutts.pdf.

Feldstein, Martin, and Elisabeth Allison. 1970. "Tax Subsidies of Private Health Insurance." In *Hospital Costs and Health Insurance*, edited by Martin Feldstein. Cambridge, MA: Harvard University Press.

Helms, Robert B. 2008. *Tax Policy and the History of the Health Insurance Industry.* Washington, DC: American Enterprise Institute. Accessed December 30, 2012. http://www.aei.org/files/2008/02/29/healthconference-helms.pdf.

Joint Committee on Taxation (JCT). Various years. *Estimates of Tax Expenditures.* Accessed January 26, 2014. https://www.jct.gov/publications.html?func=select&id=5.

Martin, Anne B., Micah Hartman, Lekha Whittle, and Aaron Catlin. 2014. "National Health Spending in 2012: Rate of Health Spending Growth Remained Low for the Fourth Consecutive Year." *Health Affairs* 33 (1): 67–77. Accessed January 15, 2014. http://content.healthaffairs.org/content/33/1/67.abstract.

McClellan, Mark, and Jonathan Skinner. 2006. "The Incidence of Medicare." *Journal of Public Economics* 90 (1–2): 257–76.

Miller, G. Edward, and Thomas M. Selden. 2013. "Tax Subsidies for Employer-Sponsored Health Insurance: Updated Microsimulation Estimates and Sensitivity to Alternative Incidence Assumptions." *Health Services Research* 48 (2, part 2): 866–83.

National Bureau of Economic Research. 2012. "TAXSIM Model Output for Barro and Redlick, Macroeconomic Effects from Government Purchases and Taxes." NBER Working Paper no. 15369. Cambridge, MA. Retrieved December 30, 2012. http://users.nber.org/~taxsim/barro-redlick/.

Rennane, Stephanie, and C. Eugene Steuerle. 2011. *Health Reform: A Four-Tranche System: Updated and Revised.* Washington, DC: The Urban Institute. Accessed January 28, 2014. http://www.urban.org/publications/901408.html.

Selden, Thomas M., and Didem M. Bernard. 2004. "Tax Incidence and Net Benefits in the Market for Employment-Related Insurance: Sensitivity of Estimates to the Incidence of Employer Costs." *International Journal of Health Care Finance and Economics* 4:167–92.

Selden, Thomas M., and Bradley M. Gray. 2006. "Tax Subsidies for Employment-Related Health Insurance: Estimates for 2006." *Health Affairs* 25 (6): 1568–79.

Selden, Thomas M., and John F. Moeller. 2000. "Estimates of the Tax Subsidy for Employment-Related Health Insurance." *National Tax Journal* 53 (4, part 1): 877–88. Accessed January 25, 2014. http://ntj.tax.org/wwtax%5Cntjrec.nsf/616D54664E20170485256AFC007F32E6/$FILE/v53n4p1877.pdf.

Selden, Thomas M., and Merrile Sing. 2008. "The Distribution of Public Spending for Health Care in the United States, 2002." *Health Affairs* 27 (5): w349–59. Accessed January 25, 2014. http://content.healthaffairs.org/content/27/5/w349.abstract?sid=8f4a881f-2e57-4834-a16f-439e44e72f8c.

Selden, Thomas M., and Michael J. Wasylenko. 1992. "Benefit Incidence Analysis in Developing Countries." Working Paper no. WPS 1015, Policy Research Public Economics, Washington, DC, World Bank.

Sheils, John, and Randall Haught. 2004. "The Cost of Tax-Exempt Health Benefits in 2004." *Health Affairs* 23:w106–12. Accessed January 25, 2014. http://content.healthaffairs.org/content/early/2004/02/25/hlthaff.w4.106.short.

Sheils, John, and Paul Hogan. 1999. "The Cost of Tax-Exempt Health Benefits in 1998." *Health Affairs* Mar/Apr:176–81. Accessed on January 25, 2014. http://content.healthaffairs.org/content/suppl/2004/02/25/hlthaff.w4.106v1.DC1.

Sloan, Frank A., Harold H. Zhang, and Jingshu Wang. 2002. "Upstream Intergenerational Transfers." *Southern Economic Journal* 69 (2): 363–80.

Wolfe, Barbara, and Robert Moffitt. 1991. "A New Index to Value In-Kind Benefits." *Review of Income and Wealth* 37 (4): 387–408.

15

The Impact of Biomedical Research on US Cancer Mortality
A Bibliometric Analysis

Frank R. Lichtenberg

15.1 Introduction

Many people and organizations have expressed the view that biomedical research has yielded substantial improvements in longevity and health. Nabel (2009) said that "biomedical research provides the basis for progress in health and health care." Moses and Martin (2011) said that "since 1945, biomedical research has been viewed as the essential contributor to improving the health of individuals and populations, in both the developed and developing world." Cutler, Deaton, and Lleras-Muney (2006) "tentatively identif[ied] the application of scientific advance and technical progress (some of which is induced by income and facilitated by education) as the ultimate determinant of health." The Federation of American Societies for Experimental Biology (2013) said that "research in the biomedical sciences has generated a wealth of new discoveries that are improving our health, extending our lives and raising our standard of living." The National Institutes of Health (NIH) said that "in the last twenty-five years, NIH-supported biomedical research has directly led to human health benefits that both extend lifespan and reduce illnesses" (NIH 2013a). The Australian Government (2013) said that "the purpose of health and medical research (HMR) is to achieve better health for all Australians. Better health encompasses increased life expectancy, as well as social goals such as equity, affordability and quality of life."

Frank R. Lichtenberg is the Courtney C. Brown Professor of Business at Columbia University and a research associate of the National Bureau of Economic Research.

For acknowledgments, sources of research support, and disclosure of the author's material financial relationships, if any, please see http://www.nber.org/chapters/c13114.ack.

The hypothesis that biomedical research has yielded substantial improvements in longevity and health has been examined using two kinds of evidence. The first type of evidence consists of qualitative "case studies" of specific diseases. The NIH (2013b, 2013c) describes the impacts of its long-term efforts to understand, treat, and prevent chronic diseases (including cardiovascular disease, cancer, diabetes, and depression), and how it has worked to combat infectious diseases such as HIV/AIDS and influenza by helping to develop new therapies, vaccines, diagnostic tests, and other technologies.

The second kind of evidence is indirect, (partially) econometric evidence. This evidence is indirect because it is based on evidence about two links in the following causal chain:

biomedical research → new drugs, devices, and procedures → longevity and health.

Regarding the first link: the National Cancer Institute (NCI) says that "approximately one half of the chemotherapeutic drugs currently used by oncologists for cancer treatment were discovered and/or developed at NCI" (NCI 2013a), and Sampat and Lichtenberg (2011) demonstrated that new drugs often build on upstream government research. Regarding the second link: a number of studies have examined the impact of the introduction and use of new drugs, devices, and procedures on longevity and health.[1] For example, Lichtenberg (2011) analyzed the impact of new drugs and imaging procedures on longevity in the United States using longitudinal state-level data, Lichtenberg (2014) analyzed the impact of new drugs on longevity in France using longitudinal disease-level data, and Lichtenberg (2013) analyzed the impact of therapeutic procedure innovation on hospital patient longevity in Western Australia using patient-level data.

In this chapter, I will use a different econometric approach to assess the impact that biomedical research has had on longevity: a direct examination of the relationship across diseases between the long-run growth in the number of research publications and the change in the mortality rate (in most cases controlling for the disease incidence rate). I hypothesize that the growth in the number of research publications about a disease is a useful indicator of the growth in knowledge about the disease. As the National Science Foundation (NSF) says, "Research produces new knowledge, products, or processes. Research publications reflect contributions to knowledge" (NSF 2013). In his model of endogenous technological change, Romer (1990) hypothesized an aggregate production function such that an economy's output depends on the "stock of ideas" that have previously been developed, as well as on the economy's endowments of labor and capital. The mortality model that I will estimate may be considered a health production function, in which the

---

1. Fuchs (2010) stated that "since World War II . . . biomedical innovations (new drugs, devices, and procedures) have been the primary source of increases in longevity."

mortality rate is an (inverse) indicator of health output or outcomes, and the cumulative number of publications is analogous to the stock of ideas.

Previous research on the agricultural and manufacturing sectors of the economy has found that counts of publications are useful indicators of the stock of knowledge. Evenson and Kislev (1973) used the publication of crop-specific scientific papers as a measure of agricultural research output in seventy-five wheat- and maize-growing countries to explain increases in yield per unit land in these crops over the period 1948–1968. They observed a strong and persistent relationship between agricultural research and biological productivity yield in wheat and maize. This relationship existed both "between" countries and "within" countries over time. Adams (1990) utilized article count data in each science as measures of knowledge in his analysis of productivity growth in two-digit manufacturing industries during the period 1949–1983.

The diseases we will analyze are almost all the different forms of cancer, that is, cancer at different sites in the body (lung, colon, breast, etc.). About one-fourth of US deaths during the period 1999–2010 were due to cancer. The main reason we focus on cancer is that the NCI publishes annual data on cancer incidence[2] as well as on cancer mortality, by cancer site. Incidence data are not available for most other diseases. A less important reason is that the NCI uses a uniform cancer-site classification scheme for data covering the entire period 1975–present. There were significant changes in the disease-classification scheme for other diseases between 1998 and 1999, when the system used to classify underlying cause of death was changed from the International Classification of Diseases (ICD) Ninth Revision to the ICD Tenth Revision. As the Centers for Disease Control (2013) notes, the two classification schemes are different enough to make direct comparisons of cause of death difficult.

In the next section, I will briefly describe the biomedical publications data I will use. In section 15.3, I develop the econometric model I will use to investigate the impact of contributions to knowledge (as measured by publication counts) on cancer mortality rates. Descriptive statistics will be presented in section 15.4. Estimates of the econometric model will be presented in section 15.5. Section 15.6 provides a summary and conclusions.

15.2   Biomedical Publications Data

Time-series data on the number of publications pertaining to each cancer site were obtained from PubMed, a database developed by the National Center for Biotechnology Information (NCBI) at the National Library of

---

2. A **cancer incidence rate** is the number of new cancers of a specific site/type occurring in a specified population during a year, usually expressed as the number of cancers per 100,000 population at risk.

Medicine (NLM), one of the institutes of the National Institutes of Health (NIH). The database was designed to provide access to citations (with abstracts) from biomedical journals. PubMed's primary data resource is Medline, the NLM's premier bibliographic database covering the fields of medicine, nursing, dentistry, veterinary medicine, the health care system, and the preclinical sciences, such as molecular biology. Medline contains bibliographic citations and author abstracts from about 4,600 biomedical journals published in the United States and seventy other countries. The database contains about 12 million citations dating back to the mid-1960s. Coverage is worldwide, but most records are from English-language sources or have English abstracts. In addition to Medline citations, PubMed provides access to non-Medline resources, such as out-of-scope citations, citations that precede Medline selection, and PubMed Central (PMC) citations.[3]

A controlled vocabulary of biomedical terms, the NLM Medical Subject Headings (MeSH), is used to describe the subject of each journal article in Medline. MeSH contains approximately 26,000 terms and is updated annually to reflect changes in medicine and medical terminology. MeSH terms are arranged hierarchically by subject categories with more specific terms arranged beneath broader terms.[4] PubMed allows one to view this hierarchy and select terms for searching in the MeSH Database. Skilled subject analysts examine journal articles and assign to each the most specific MeSH terms applicable—typically ten to twelve. Applying the MeSH vocabulary ensures that articles are uniformly indexed by subject, whatever the author's words (NCBI 2013). Table 15.1 shows an abridged sample of a PubMed bibliographic citation. I use three attributes (search fields) in the citation: the date of publication (line 8), the MeSH headings (lines 27–36), and the publication type (lines 18–20).

For articles published since 1975, the publication types identify US government and non-US government[5] financial support of the research that resulted in the published papers when that support is mentioned in the articles (NLM 2013b). Figure 15.1 shows data on the number of PubMed publications pertaining to cancer that were published during the period 1975–2009, by extent and source of research support. Cancer was one of the main topics discussed (i.e., cancer was a "MeSH Major Topic") in about

3. Together, these are often referred to as "PubMed-only citations." Out-of-scope citations are primarily from general science and chemistry journals that contain life sciences articles indexed for Medline, for example, the plate tectonics or astrophysics articles from *Science* magazine. Publishers can also submit citations with publication dates that precede the journal's selection for Medline indexing, usually because they want to create links to older content. The PMC citations are taken from life sciences journals (Medline or non-Medline) that submit full-text articles to PMC.

4. The MeSH Tree Structure can be browsed online (see NLM 2013a).

5. Non-US government financial support includes support by American societies, institutes, state governments, universities, and private organizations, and by foreign sources (national, departmental, provincial, academic, and private organizations).

Table 15.1   Abridged sample of a PubMed bibliographic citation

Line	
1	PMID—20425429
2	OWN—NLM
3	STAT—Medline
4	DA—20100428
5	DCOM—20100810
6	VI—4
7	IP—3
8	**DP—2009 Jul**
9	TI—Application of immunotherapy in pediatric leukemia.
10	PG—159-66
11	LID—10.1007/s11899-009-0022-5 [doi]
12	AD—Center for Cancer Research, National Cancer Institute, National Institutes of
13	Health, Building 10, Room 1W-3750, 9000 Rockville Pike, MSC-1104, Bethesda, MD
14	20892, USA. waynea@mail.nih.gov
15	FAU—Wayne, Alan S
16	AU—Wayne AS
17	LA—eng
18	PT—Journal Article
19	**PT—Research Support, N.I.H., Intramural**
20	PT—Review
21	PL—United States
22	TA—Curr Hematol Malig Rep
23	JT—Current hematologic malignancy reports
24	JID—101262565
25	RN—0 (Immunotoxins)
26	SB—IM
27	MH—Child
28	MH—Graft vs Leukemia Effect/immunology
29	MH—Hematopoietic Stem Cell Transplantation/methods
30	MH—Humans
31	MH—Immunotherapy/*methods
32	MH—Immunotherapy, Adoptive/methods
33	MH—Immunotoxins/immunology/therapeutic use
34	**MH—Leukemia/immunology/pathology/*therapy**
35	MH—Models, Immunological
36	MH—Transplantation, Homologous
37	RF—50
38	EDAT—2010/04/29 06:00
39	MHDA—2010/08/11 06:00
40	CRDT—2010/04/29 06:00
41	AID—10.1007/s11899-009-0022-5 [doi]
42	PST—ppublish
43	SO—Curr Hematol Malig Rep. 2009 Jul;4(3):159-66. doi: 10.1007/s11899-009-0022-5.

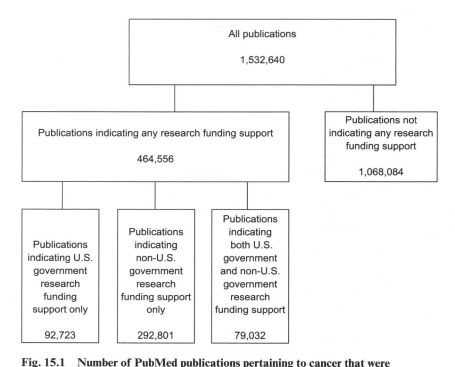

Fig. 15.1   Number of PubMed publications pertaining to cancer that were published during the period 1975–2009, by extent and source of research support
Note: PubMed publications pertaining to cancer are those identified by the search "neoplasms [MeSH Major Topic]."

1.5 million articles published during this period. About 30 percent of these articles mentioned either US government support, non-US government support, or both.[6] Twenty percent of the articles indicating any research funding support mentioned only US government support, 63 percent of the articles indicating any research funding support mentioned only non-US government support, and 17 percent of the articles indicating any research funding support mentioned both US government and non-US government support. This distribution of funding support by source is quite consistent with data compiled by Research!America (shown in figure 15.2) on the distribution of 2011 US biomedical and health research and development (R&D) spending, by source of funding. The Research!America data indicate that the federal government accounted for 29 percent of 2011 US biomedical and health R&D spending. If we assume that the US government deserves "half the credit" for articles that mentioned both US government and non-US gov-

6. Although reporting of financial support may be incomplete, I am not aware of any evidence that the extent of reporting varies across cancer sites.

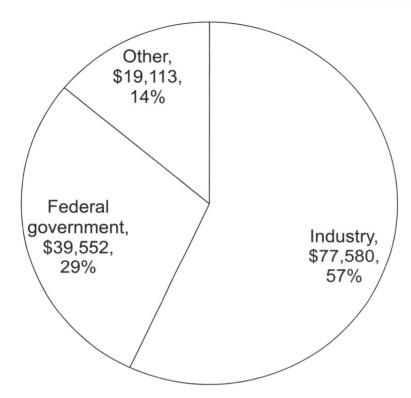

Fig. 15.2   2011 US biomedical and health R&D spending (millions of dollars)
Source: http://www.researchamerica.org/uploads/healthdollar11.pdf.

ernment support, we can say that the US government support accounted for 28.5 percent (= 20% + (17% / 2)) of the funding support for articles that received any funding support.

By combining data on government-funded publication counts derived from PubMed with data on government-funded research expenditure[7] obtained from NIH's Research, Condition, and Disease Categorization system (NIH 2014),[8] we can see whether publication counts and research

---

7. Data on non-government-funded research expenditure by cancer site are not available.

8. The NIH does not expressly budget by category, but at the request of Congress, in 2008 the NIH embarked on a process to provide better consistency and transparency in the reporting of its funded research. This new process, implemented through the Research, Condition, and Disease Categorization (RCDC) system, uses sophisticated text data mining (categorizing and clustering using words and multiword phrases) in conjunction with NIH-wide definitions used to match projects to categories. The RCDC use of data mining improves consistency and eliminates the wide variability in defining the research categories reported. The definitions are a list of terms and concepts selected by NIH scientific experts to define a research category. The research category levels represent the NIH's best estimates based on the category definitions.

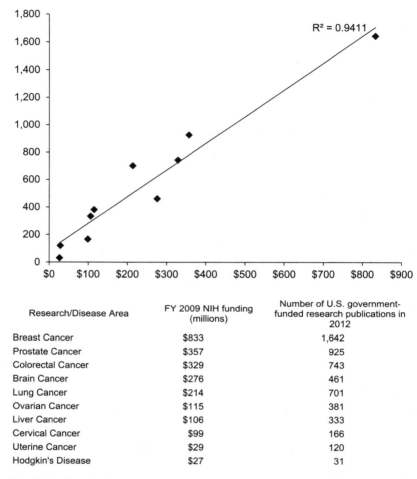

Research/Disease Area	FY 2009 NIH funding (millions)	Number of U.S. government-funded research publications in 2012
Breast Cancer	$833	1,642
Prostate Cancer	$357	925
Colorectal Cancer	$329	743
Brain Cancer	$276	461
Lung Cancer	$214	701
Ovarian Cancer	$115	381
Liver Cancer	$106	333
Cervical Cancer	$99	166
Uterine Cancer	$29	120
Hodgkin's Disease	$27	31

Fig. 15.3   Correlation across ten major cancer sites between FY 2009 NIH funding and number of US government-funded research publications in 2012

Sources: FY 2009 NIH funding: NIH Research, Condition, and Disease Categorization system (NIH 2014). Number of US government-funded research publications in 2012: author's calculations based on PubMed database.

expenditure are strongly correlated across cancer sites. As shown in figure 15.3, there is a very strong positive correlation ($r = 0.97$) across ten major cancer sites between FY 2009 NIH funding and the number of US government-funded research publications in 2012.

Our ability to distinguish between publications indicating and not indicating any research funding support will allow us to test the hypothesis that an increase in the number of publications indicating any research funding support has a larger (more negative) effect on mortality than an increase in

Table 15.2 Mortality and incidence rates in 1995 and 2009 and PubMed publication counts ten years earlier (in 1985 and 1999), top eighteen cancer sites (ranked by mean mortality rate)

Site	mean mort_rate	mean inc_rate	Year	mort_rate	inc_rate	cum_pubs	cum_research_pubs	cum_non_research_pubs	cum_US_gov_research_pubs	cum_other_research_pubs
Lung	52.8	62.9	1995	58.4	66.8	53,044	8,171	44,873	3,515	5,781
			2009	48.5	58.8	102,847	24,704	78,143	8,623	19,825
Colonic	19.9	41.2	1995	19.4	39.7	23,420	5,757	17,663	2,771	4,030
			2009	12.9	30.5	41,498	13,776	27,722	5,414	10,770
Breast	16.8	67.7	1995	17.4	72.8	56,987	11,766	45,221	4,941	8,554
			2009	12.4	69.8	138,938	46,391	92,547	18,331	36,643
Prostatic	11.9	61.6	1995	13.5	72.2	18,053	3,677	14,376	1,826	2,381
			2009	8.6	69.4	58,195	21,043	37,152	10,400	15,453
Pancreatic	10.7	11.7	1995	10.4	11.1	15,068	2,764	12,304	1,274	1,948
			2009	10.8	12.8	33,384	8,582	24,802	3,199	7,081
Lymphoma non-Hodgkin's	7.2	17.0	1995	8.7	19.9	24,535	4,979	19,556	2,165	3,789
			2009	6.3	20.2	53,953	14,397	39,556	4,830	12,061
Stomach	5.9	9.6	1995	5.3	8.3	28,427	2,309	26,118	498	1,957
			2009	3.4	7.3	50,347	9,076	41,271	1,205	8,380
Ovarian	5.2	8.2	1995	5.2	8.0	19,902	3,398	16,504	1,337	2,629
			2009	4.4	6.8	41,689	11,493	30,196	4,220	9,473
Urinary bladder	4.7	20.8	1995	4.4	20.6	17,011	2,866	14,145	1,313	1,966
			2009	4.3	20.4	30,209	6,773	23,436	2,356	5,292
Brain	4.5	6.5	1995	4.7	6.5	43,989	6,557	37,432	3,147	4,651
			2009	4.4	6.6	78,921	17,739	61,182	6,821	14,331
Esophageal	4.1	4.5	1995	4.3	4.4	12,573	953	11,620	314	742
			2009	4.2	4.5	25,312	4,464	20,848	1,071	3,860
Kidney	4.0	10.7	1995	4.3	11.1	20,046	2,597	17,449	1,184	1,869
			2009	3.9	14.9	37,923	6,775	31,148	2,332	5,456
Rectal	3.6	16.1	1995	3.1	14.4	16,615	2,037	14,578	752	1,493
			2009	2.8	12.2	26,336	3,769	22,567	1,056	3,052
Multiple myeloma	3.5	5.5	1995	4.0	5.7	10,753	1,727	9,026	681	1,247
			2009	3.3	6.1	19,888	5,449	14,439	1,801	4,569

(continued)

Table 15.2 (continued)

Site	mean mort_rate	mean inc_rate	Year	mort_rate	inc_rate	cum_pubs	cum_research_pubs	cum_non_research_pubs	cum_US_gov_research_pubs	cum_other_research_pubs
Skin	3.4	16.2	1995	3.5	18.1	34,051	5,061	28,990	2,330	3,581
			2009	3.7	24.6	67,141	13,234	53,907	4,930	10,464
Liver	3.2	3.9	1995	3.5	3.7	36,499	8,241	28,258	3,824	5,678
			2009	4.5	7.1	73,272	20,603	52,669	5,951	16,988
Leukemia myeloid acute	2.5	3.4	1995	2.4	3.7	14,685	5,363	9,322	2,299	4,167
			2009	2.9	3.6	25,170	10,049	15,121	3,507	8,492
Leukemia lymphoid	2.3	6.4	1995	2.4	6.5	22,164	6,512	15,652	2,733	5,112
			2009	2.0	6.3	39,587	14,531	25,056	4,848	12,447

In order for the parameter β in equation (6) to be an estimate of the impact of biomedical research on cancer mortality, $\text{cum\_pubs}_{s,t-k}$ must be exogenous with respect to mort_rate_{st}. Lichtenberg (2001) developed a simple theoretical model of the allocation of biomedical research expenditure that suggests that this is not an unreasonable assumption. That model indicated that research expenditure should be an increasing function of technological opportunity (the "supply of innovations")—the ease of achievement of innovations and technical improvements—as well as of disease burden (the "demand for innovations").[15] Therefore, diseases with greater technological opportunities and heavier disease burdens should experience more rapid medical innovation. Equation (6) controls (albeit imperfectly) for disease burden by holding constant the number of people diagnosed with a medical condition. Therefore, much of the residual variation across diseases in the rate of innovation may be attributed to heterogeneous technological opportunity, which I assume to be exogenous.

I will estimate models based on equation (6) using three alternative values of k: 0, 5, and 10.[16] For concreteness, suppose that $k = 10$. Now, let's write specific versions of equation (6) for the first and last years of the sample period ($t = 1995$ and $t = 2009$):

$$(7) \quad \ln(\text{mort\_rate}_{s,1995}) = \beta \ln(\text{cum\_pubs}_{s,1985}) + \gamma \ln(\text{inc\_rate}_{s,1995}) \\ + \alpha_s + \delta_{1995} + \varepsilon_{s,1995}$$

$$(8) \quad \ln(\text{mort\_rate}_{s,2009}) = \beta \ln(\text{cum\_pubs}_{s,1999}) + \gamma \ln(\text{inc\_rate}_{s,2009}) \\ + \alpha_s + \delta_{2009} + \varepsilon_{s,2009}.$$

Subtracting equation (7) from equation (8),

$$(9) \quad \ln(\text{mort\_rate}_{s,2009} / \text{mort\_rate}_{s,1995}) \\ = \beta \ln(\text{cum\_pubs}_{s,1999} / \text{cum\_pubs}_{s,1985}) \\ + \gamma \ln(\text{inc\_rate}_{s,2009} / \text{inc\_rate}_{s,1995}) \\ + (\delta_{2009} - \delta_{1995}) + (\varepsilon_{s,2009} - \varepsilon_{s,1995})$$

or

$$(10) \quad \Delta\ln(\text{mort\_rate}_s) = \beta \, \Delta\ln(\text{cum\_pubs}_s) + \gamma \, \Delta\ln(\text{inc\_rate}_s) + \delta' + \varepsilon_s'$$

where

- $\Delta\ln(\text{mort\_rate}_s) = \ln(\text{mort\_rate}_{s,2009} / \text{mort\_rate}_{s,1995})$
- $\Delta\ln(\text{cum\_pubs}_s) = \ln(\text{cum\_pubs}_{s,1999} / \text{cum\_pubs}_{s,1985})$
- $\Delta\ln(\text{inc\_rate}_s) = \ln(\text{inc\_rate}_{s,2009} / \text{inc\_rate}_{s,1995})$
- $\delta' = (\delta_{2009} - \delta_{1995})$.

The cancer-site fixed effects that were included in the "within" model (equation [6]) are no longer present in the "long-difference" model (equation [10]);

---

15. Growlec and Schumacher (2013) derive an R&D-based growth model where the rate of technological progress depends, *inter alia*, on the amount of technological opportunity.

16. Since data on financial support of research that resulted in published papers begin in 1975, it is not practical to specify longer lags ($k > 10$).

the intercept of equation (10) is the difference between the initial- and end-year year fixed effects. In this simple model, the long-run growth of the age-adjusted cancer mortality rate depends on the long-run growth of the (lagged) cumulative number of publications, the long-run growth of the age-adjusted cancer incidence rate, and a constant.

Equation (10) can easily be generalized to allow for two or three different stocks of publications:

$$(11)\quad \Delta\ln(\text{mort\_rate}_s) = \beta_{\text{RESEARCH}}\,\Delta\ln(\text{cum\_research\_pubs}_s)$$
$$+\ \beta_{\text{NON-RESEARCH}}\,\Delta\ln(\text{cum\_non\_research\_pubs}_s)$$
$$+\ \gamma\,\Delta\ln(\text{inc\_rate}_s) + \delta' + \varepsilon_s'$$

$$(12)\quad \Delta\ln(\text{mort\_rate}_s) = \beta_{\text{RESEARCH\_US\_GOV}}\,\Delta\ln(\text{cum\_US\_gov\_research\_pubs}_s)$$
$$+\ \beta_{\text{RESEARCH\_OTHER}}\,\Delta\ln(\text{cum\_other\_research\_pubs}_s)$$
$$+\ \beta_{\text{NON-RESEARCH}}\,\Delta\ln(\text{cum\_non\_research\_pubs}_s)$$
$$+\ \gamma\,\Delta\ln(\text{inc\_rate}_s) + \delta' + \varepsilon_s',$$

where

- $\text{cum\_research\_pubs}_{s,t-k}$ = the number of PubMed articles indicating any research funding support published by the end of year $t - k$ that were about cancer at site s,
- $\text{cum\_non\_research\_pubs}_{s,t-k}$ = the number of PubMed articles not indicating any research funding support published by the end of year $t - k$ that were about cancer at site s,
- $\text{cum\_US\_gov\_research\_pubs}_{s,t-k}$ = the number of PubMed articles indicating US government research funding support published by the end of year $t - k$ that were about cancer at site s,
- $\text{cum\_other\_research\_pubs}_{s,t-k}$ = the number of PubMed articles indicating non-US government research funding support published by the end of year $t - k$ that were about cancer at site s.

I will estimate equations (10)–(12) for three different values of k (0, 5, and 10). These equations will be estimated via weighted least squares, weighting by the mean mortality rate of cancer at site s during the period 1985–2009. Since the dependent variable is the log of the mortality rate, I am analyzing percentage changes in the mortality rate. As shown in figure 15.5, the data exhibit heteroscedasticity: cancer sites with low average mortality rates exhibit much larger positive and negative percentage changes in mortality rates than cancer sites with high average mortality rates. Weighted least squares is appropriate in the presence of heteroscedasticity.

15.4 Descriptive Statistics

Data on age-adjusted incidence and mortality rates were obtained from SEER Cancer Query Systems (NCI 2013b). Incidence and mortality rates of given the high correlation across cancer sites between the growth of government and other research publications.

Models 6–10 are identical to models 1–5, except the assumed lag from cumulative publications to the mortality rate is five years rather than zero years. The estimates of models 6–8 are similar to the estimates of models 1–3, but the contrast between models 9 and 4 (which include both cum_research_pubs and cum_non_research_pubs) is interesting. Although $\beta_{RESEARCH}$ is only marginally significant (p-value = 0.092) in model 4, it is highly significant (p-value = 0.012) in model 9. This means that although the mortality rate is only weakly inversely related to the contemporaneous stock of publications that had received research funding (controlling for the contemporaneous stock of publications that had not received research funding), it is strongly inversely related to the stock of publications that had received research funding five years earlier. Moreover, the magnitude of the point estimate of $\beta_{RESEARCH}$ is 46 percent larger in model 9 than it is in model 4.

In models 11–15, the assumed lag from cumulative publications to the mortality rate is ten years. As shown in figure 15.7, the magnitude of the point estimate of $\beta_{RESEARCH}$ in model 14 is 14 percent larger than it is in model 9, and 66 percent larger than it is in model 4. Since previous research has shown that innovations tend to diffuse gradually,[20] this lag structure is not surprising.

Figure 15.8 shows the partial correlation across cancer sites between the 1985–1999 log change in the number of research publications and the 1995–2009 log change in the mortality rate, controlling for the 1995–2009 log change in the incidence rate. The figure is a plot of the residuals from the weighted simple regression of $\Delta ln(mort\_rate_s)$ on $\Delta ln(inc\_rate_s)$ against the residuals from the weighted simple regression of $\Delta ln(cum\_research\_pubs_s)$ on $\Delta ln(inc\_rate_s)$, where we assume a ten-year lag from cumulative publications to the mortality rate.[21] The figure suggests that the strong inverse correlation between mortality growth and growth in the lagged number of publications that were supported by research funding is not being driven by a small number of outliers. If we exclude lung cancer, which receives the greatest weight by far, from the sample, the estimate of $\beta_{RESEARCH}$ in model 13 hardly changes: $\beta_{RESEARCH}$ = −0.285 (T = −3.22; p-value = 0.003).

The magnitude of $\beta_{RESEARCH}$ in model 13 is quite large. As shown in table 15.3, the weighted mean value of $\Delta ln(cum\_research\_pubs_s)$ is 1.538. The average annual rate of increase in lagged cum_research_pubs during 1995–2009 was 11.0 percent (= 1.538 / 14). Model 13 implies that, during the period 1995–2009, the growth in the lagged number of publications

---

20. Lichtenberg (2009) showed that utilization of a cancer drug tends to increase steadily for about seven years after launch ("year zero"). In years seven to ten, annual utilization is about twenty times as high as it was in year zero, and about twice as high as it was in year four.

21. Figure 15.8 is a partial regression plot of model 13 in table 15.4.

Table 15.4   Weighted least-squares estimates of models of 1995–2009 growth of the age-adjusted cancer mortality rate (equations [10]–[12])

Model	Publication lag (years)	Statistic	$\Delta\ln(\text{inc\_rate}_s)$	$\Delta\ln(\text{cum\_pubs}_s)$	$\Delta\ln(\text{cum\_research\_pubs}_s)$	$\Delta\ln(\text{cum\_non\_research\_pubs}_s)$	$\Delta\ln(\text{cum\_US\_gov\_research\_pubs}_s)$	$\Delta\ln(\text{cum\_other\_research\_pubs}_s)$	Intercept (δ')
1	0	Estimate	.	−0.249	.	.	.	.	−0.034
		T	.	−1.588	.	.	.	.	−0.295
		P-value	.	0.120	.	.	.	.	0.769
2	0	Estimate	**0.732**	**−0.426**	.	.	.	.	0.130
		T	**6.772**	**−3.801**	.	.	.	.	1.573
		P-value	**0.000**	**0.000**	.	.	.	.	0.124
3	0	Estimate	**0.653**	.	**−0.262**	.	.	.	0.120
		T	**6.102**	.	**−3.555**	.	.	.	1.404
		P-value	**0.000**	.	**0.001**	.	.	.	0.168
4	0	Estimate	0.698	.	−0.195	−0.172	.	.	0.149
		T	5.745	.	−1.726	−0.792	.	.	1.596
		P-value	0.000	.	0.092	0.433	.	.	0.118
5	0	Estimate	**0.721**	.	.	−0.217	0.024	−0.202	0.186
		T	**5.148**	.	.	−0.819	0.117	−0.937	1.110
		P-value	**0.000**	.	.	0.418	0.907	0.355	0.274
6	5	Estimate	.	−0.245	.	.	.	.	−0.029
		T	.	−1.619	.	.	.	.	−0.254
		P-value	.	0.113	.	.	.	.	0.801
7	5	Estimate	**0.738**	**−0.422**	.	.	.	.	0.140
		T	**6.869**	**−3.928**	.	.	.	.	1.697
		P-value	**0.000**	**0.000**	.	.	.	.	0.097
8	5	Estimate	**0.664**	.	**−0.300**	.	.	.	0.202
		T	**6.555**	.	**−4.366**	.	.	.	2.281
		P-value	**0.000**	.	**0.000**	.	.	.	0.028

9	5	Estimate	**0.673**		**-0.284**	-0.037	.	.	0.206
		T	**5.928**		**-2.641**	-0.191	.	.	2.239
		P-value	**0.000**		**0.012**	0.850	.	.	0.031
10	5	Estimate	**0.632**	.	.	0.074	-0.156	-0.157	0.156
		T	**4.781**	.	.	0.317	-0.823	-0.831	0.953
		P-value	**0.000**	.	.	0.753	0.416	0.411	0.346
11	10	Estimate	.	-0.092	.	.	.	.	-0.134
		T	.	-0.587	.	.	.	.	-1.027
		P-value	.	0.561	.	.	.	.	0.310
12	10	Estimate	**0.718**	**-0.299**	.	.	.	.	0.071
		T	**5.967**	**-2.476**	.	.	.	.	0.701
		P-value	**0.000**	**0.018**	.	.	.	.	0.488
13	10	Estimate	**0.663**	.	**-0.319**	.	.	.	0.316
		T	**6.132**	.	**-3.578**	.	.	.	2.278
		P-value	**0.000**	.	**0.001**	.	.	.	0.028
14	10	Estimate	**0.660**	.	**-0.324**	0.011	.	.	0.316
		T	**5.551**	.	**-2.807**	0.067	.	.	2.248
		P-value	**0.000**	.	**0.008**	0.947	.	.	0.030
15	10	Estimate	**0.608**	.	.	0.189	-0.302	-0.162	0.336
		T	**5.090**	.	.	1.092	-1.546	-1.089	2.031
		P-value	**0.000**	.	.	0.282	0.130	0.283	0.049

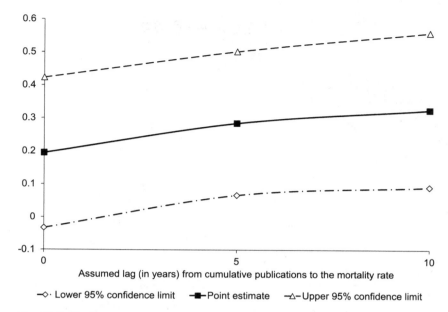

Fig. 15.7 Estimates of $-\beta_{RESEARCH}$ in equation (11) based on three alternative assumed values of the lag (k) from cumulative publications to the mortality rate

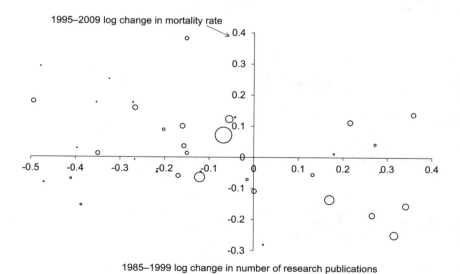

Fig. 15.8 Partial correlation across cancer sites between 1985–1999 log change in number of research publications and 1995–2009 log change in mortality rate, controlling for 1995–2009 log change in incidence rate

Note: Bubble sizes are proportional to mean age-adjusted mortality rate during 1973–2009.

that were supported by research funding reduced the age-adjusted cancer mortality rate by 3.5 percent ($= -0.319 * 11.0$ percent) per year. During that period, the age-adjusted cancer mortality rate declined at an average annual rate of 1.5 percent.[22] This means that, in the absence of *any* growth in the lagged number of publications that were supported by research funding, the age-adjusted cancer mortality rate would have *increased* at an average annual rate of 2.0 percent. However, since there was such rapid growth in the number of publications, estimating what would have happened in the absence of any growth requires substantial out-of-sample prediction, which is certainly subject to great uncertainty.

15.6   Summary and Conclusions

Previous research on the agricultural and manufacturing sectors of the economy has found that counts of publications are useful indicators of the stock of knowledge: they are strongly positively correlated with productivity. In this chapter, I have examined the relationship across diseases between the long-run growth in the number of publications about a disease and the change in the mortality rate from the disease.

The diseases I analyzed are almost all the different forms of cancer, that is, cancer at different sites in the body (lung, colon, breast, etc.). About one-fourth of US deaths during the period 1999–2010 were due to cancer. The main reason I focused on cancer is that the National Cancer Institute publishes annual data on cancer incidence as well as on cancer mortality, by cancer site. Failure to control for the growth in incidence (which it is not feasible to do for noncancer diseases) may bias estimates of the effect of publication growth toward zero, because growth in the number of publications is positively correlated across diseases with growth in incidence.

Time-series data on the number of publications pertaining to each cancer site were obtained from PubMed. For articles published since 1975, it is possible to distinguish between publications indicating and not indicating any research funding support.

My estimates indicated that mortality rates: (a) are unrelated to the (current or lagged) stock of publications that had not received research funding, (b) are only weakly inversely related to the contemporaneous stock of published articles that received research funding, and (c) are strongly inversely related to the stock of articles that had received research funding and been published five and ten years earlier. The effect after ten years is 66 percent larger than the contemporaneous effect. The strong inverse correlation between mortality growth and growth in the lagged number of

---

22. Equation (13) implies that declining incidence accounted for about 1/6 of the decline in mortality.

publications that were supported by research funding is not driven by a small number of outliers.

Research!America (2013) estimates that US biomedical and health R&D spending (from all sources) declined by more than 3 percent in fiscal year 2011, and that this is the first drop in overall spending since 2002. While most of that decrease reflects the end of American Recovery and Reinvestment Act (ARRA) funding, which allocated $10.4 billion to the National Institutes of Health over two fiscal years (2009–2010), federal funding declined beyond the drop attributable to ARRA. In subsequent years, across-the-board cuts could cut billions more out of the federal research budget. The White House Office of Management and Budget estimated that the NIH alone could lose $2.53 billion in funding in fiscal year 2013. The evidence in this chapter strongly suggests that reductions in biomedical and health R&D spending will ultimately have an adverse effect on US longevity growth.

Appendix

Table 15A.1 Mortality and incidence rates in 1995 and 2009 and PubMed publication counts ten years earlier (in 1985 and 1999), twenty-nine cancer sites not included in table 15.2 (ranked by mean mortality rate)

Site	mean mort_rate	mean inc_rate	Year	mort_rate	inc_rate	cum_pubs	cum_ research_pubs	cum_non_ research_pubs	cum_US_gov_ research_pubs	cum_other_ research_pubs
Uterine cervical	2.0	5.3	1995	1.8	4.6	22,427	2,696	19,731	951	2,033
			2009	1.2	3.5	40,186	8,743	31,443	2,440	7,209
Laryngeal	1.5	4.5	1995	1.5	4.4	10,896	712	10,184	272	513
			2009	1.1	3.1	16,687	1,780	14,907	404	1,511
Soft tissue	1.3	2.6	1995	1.5	2.8	5,568	851	4,717	365	581
			2009	1.3	3.3	14,062	1,967	12,095	626	1,552
Gallbladder	1.0	1.4	1995	0.8	1.4	2,682	126	2,556	35	102
			2009	0.6	1.1	4,829	437	4,392	67	392
Tongue	0.8	2.6	1995	0.7	2.5	3,066	172	2,894	60	124
			2009	0.6	3.3	4,998	641	4,357	120	563
Hodgkin's disease	0.7	2.9	1995	0.5	2.8	16,042	2,100	13,942	959	1,379
			2009	0.4	2.9	21,495	3,772	17,723	1,311	2,894
Bile duct	0.7	0.5	1995	0.8	0.8	3,768	258	3,510	69	210
			2009	1.3	0.8	8,299	962	7,337	232	845
Bone	0.5	0.9	1995	0.5	1.0	39,473	2,573	36,900	1,041	1,809
			2009	0.4	1.0	67,454	6,968	60,486	2,125	5,714
Thyroid	0.5	6.8	1995	0.4	6.2	5,946	1,235	4,711	302	1,076
			2009	0.5	14.3	18,907	4,484	14,423	950	4,040
Intestinal	0.4	1.5	1995	0.4	1.7	48,426	8,720	39,706	3,588	6,525
			2009	0.4	2.2	107,614	30,022	77,592	9,530	24,852
Vulvar	0.3	1.3	1995	0.3	1.3	3,028	239	2,789	99	177
			2009	0.3	1.4	4,935	493	4,442	142	406
Salivary	0.3	1.2	1995	0.3	1.2	5,633	467	5,166	121	370
			2009	0.2	1.3	9,873	1,155	8,718	217	1,014
Nasopharyngeal	0.3	0.7	1995	0.3	0.8	4,381	628	3,753	232	461
			2009	0.2	0.6	8,289	2,167	6,122	348	1,946
Tonsillar	0.3	1.3	1995	0.2	1.2	933	52	881	21	35
			2009	0.2	1.8	1,396	130	1,266	35	104

(*continued*)

Table 15A.1 (continued)

Site	mean mort_rate	mean inc_rate	Year	mort_rate	inc_rate	cum_pubs	cum_research_pubs	cum_non_research_pubs	cum_US_gov_research_pubs	cum_other_research_pubs
Nose	0.2	0.7	1995	0.2	0.7	6,017	309	5,708	117	214
			2009	0.2	0.7	10,094	692	9,402	166	562
Hypopharyngeal	0.2	1.0	1995	0.2	0.9	453	53	400	11	49
			2009	0.1	0.6	1,374	213	1,161	24	203
Oropharyngeal	0.2	0.3	1995	0.2	0.3	1,488	141	1,347	43	113
			2009	0.2	0.3	3,254	540	2,714	132	459
Pleural	0.2	0.0	1995	0.2	.	3,160	310	2,850	86	251
			2009	0.1	0.0	7,062	1,058	6,004	246	947
Testicular	0.2	2.4	1995	0.1	2.3	10,173	1,471	8,702	598	1,050
			2009	0.1	2.9	16,191	2,707	13,484	852	2,158
Vaginal	0.2	0.4	1995	0.2	0.4	2,221	153	2,068	90	79
			2009	0.1	0.4	3,119	233	2,886	113	148
Tracheal mediastinal	0.2	0.2	1995	0.1	0.2	7,340	371	6,969	215	213
			2009	0.1	0.2	10,607	604	10,003	261	420
Peritoneal	0.2	0.4	1995	0.1	0.4	3,250	267	2,983	94	215
			2009	0.2	0.6	7,395	931	6,464	258	781
Anus	0.1	1.2	1995	0.2	1.2	1,822	138	1,684	53	102
			2009	0.2	1.7	3,175	372	2,803	132	289
Retroperitoneal	0.1	0.5	1995	0.1	0.4	3,436	128	3,308	55	89
			2009	0.1	0.4	5,445	255	5,190	85	198
Eye orbital	0.1	0.8	1995	0.1	0.9	14,335	2,241	12,094	1,059	1,705
			2009	0.1	0.8	23,738	4,771	18,967	1,638	4,047
Ureteral	0.1	0.6	1995	0.1	0.6	1,765	47	1,718	13	36
			2009	0.1	0.5	2,738	125	2,613	20	111
Penile	0.1	0.4	1995	0.1	0.3	1,947	107	1,840	44	73
			2009	0.1	0.4	3,211	193	3,018	59	150
Leukemia monocytic acute	0.1	0.2	1995	0.1	0.3	978	258	720	96	205
			2009	0.0	0.2	1,416	423	993	115	364
Lip	0.0	1.5	1995	0.0	1.3	1,469	48	1,421	12	42
			2009	0.0	0.6	2,064	103	1,961	17	95

Contributors

Jean M. Abraham
Division of Health Policy and
  Management
University of Minnesota
420 Delaware Street SE, MMC 729
Minneapolis, MN 55455

Murray L. Aitken
IMS Institute for Healthcare
  Informatics
901 Main Avenue, Suite 612
Norwalk, CT 06851

Ana Aizcorbe
Bureau of Economic Analysis
4600 Silver Hill Road
Suitland, MD 20746

Colin Baker
US Department of Health and Human
  Services
200 Independence Avenue SW
Washington, DC 20201

Laurence C. Baker
Department of Health Research &
  Policy
HRP Redwood Building
Stanford University
Stanford, CA 94305-5405

Didem Bernard
Agency for Healthcare Research and
  Quality
Center for Financing, Access, and Cost
  Trends
540 Gaither Road
Rockville, MD 20850

Ernst R. Berndt
MIT Sloan School of Management
100 Main Street, E62-518
Cambridge, MA 02142

Barry Bosworth
The Brookings Institution
1775 Massachusetts Avenue
Washington, DC 20036

Ralph Bradley
Division of Price and Index Number
  Research
Bureau of Labor Statistics
2 Massachusetts Avenue, NE
Washington, DC 20212

M. Kate Bundorf
Health Research and Policy
Stanford University
HRP T108
Stanford, CA 94305-5405

Brian Chansky
Bureau of Labor Statistics
Division of Industry Productivity
    Studies
2 Massachusetts Avenue, NE
Washington, DC 20212

Michael E. Chernew
Harvard Medical School
Department of Health Care Policy
180 Longwood Avenue
Boston, MA 02115

Iain M. Cockburn
School of Management
Boston University
595 Commonwealth Avenue
Boston, MA 02215

Rena M. Conti
University of Chicago
Department of Pediatrics
Section of Hematology/Oncology
5812 S. Ellis Street
Chicago, IL 60637

David M. Cutler
Department of Economics
Harvard University
1875 Cambridge Street
Cambridge, MA 02138

Abe Dunn
Bureau of Economic Analysis
4600 Silver Hill Road
Suitland, MD 20746

Roger Feldman
Division of Health Policy and
    Management
University of Minnesota
420 Delaware Street SE, MMC 729
Minneapolis, MN 55455

Armando Franco
Department of Economics
University of California, Berkeley
Berkeley, CA 94720

Richard Frank
Department of Health Care Policy
Harvard Medical School
180 Longwood Avenue
Boston, MA 02115

Corby Garner
Bureau of Labor Statistics
2 Massachusetts Avenue, NE
Washington, DC 20212

Kaushik Ghosh
National Bureau of Economic
    Research
1050 Massachusetts Avenue
Cambridge, MA 02138

Jacob Glazer
Department of Economics
Warwick University
Coventry CV4 7AL United Kingdom
and Coller School of Management
Tel Aviv University
Ramat Aviv, Tel Aviv, Israel

Dana P. Goldman
Schaeffer Center for Health Policy and
    Economics
University of Southern California
635 Downey Way
Los Angeles, CA 90089-3333

Anne E. Hall
Office of Microeconomic Analysis
US Treasury Department
1500 Pennsylvania Avenue, NW
Washington, DC 20220

Tina Highfill
Bureau of Economic Analysis
4600 Silver Hill Road
Suitland, MD 20746

Pinar Karaca-Mandic
Division of Health Policy and
    Management
University of Minnesota
420 Delaware Street SE, MMC 729
Minneapolis, MN 55455

Michael Kleinrock
QuintilesIMS Institute
QuintilesIMS
One IMS Drive
Plymouth Meeting, PA 19462

J. Steven Landefeld
Economics Department
US Naval Academy
589 McNair Road
Annapolis, MD 21402-5030

Adam Leive
Frank Batten School of Leadership
    and Public Policy
University of Virginia
235 McCormick Road
Charlottesville, VA 22904

Frank R. Lichtenberg
Graduate School of Business
Columbia University
3022 Broadway
New York, NY 10027

Eli Liebman
Bureau of Economic Analysis
4600 Silver Hill Road
Suitland, MD 20746

Matilde Mas
Faculty of Economics
Universitat de València
Edificio Departamental Oriental
Avda. Tarongers, s/n.
46022 Valencia, Spain

Daniel McFadden
University of California, Berkeley
Department of Economics
508-1 Evans Hall #3880
Berkeley, CA 94720-3880

Thomas G. McGuire
Department of Health Care Policy
Harvard Medical School
180 Longwood Avenue
Boston, MA 02115

Yuriy Pylypchuk
Office of the National Coordinator for
    Health Information Technology
330 C Street, SW
Washington, DC 20024

Ronjoy Raichoudhary
Bureau of Labor Statistics
2 Massachusetts Avenue, NE
Washington, DC 20212

Allison B. Rosen
Department of Quantitative Health
    Sciences
University of Massachusetts Medical
    School
368 Plantation Street, AS9-1083
Worcester, MA 01605

Anne Royalty
Department of Economics
Indiana University Purdue University
    Indianapolis
425 University Boulevard
Indianapolis, IN 46202

Paul Schreyer
Organisation for Economic Co-
    Operation and Development
2, rue André Pascal
75775 Paris Cedex 16 France

Thomas Selden
Agency for Healthcare Research and
    Quality
Center for Financing, Access, and Cost
    Trends
540 Gaither Road
Rockville, MD 20850

Bradley T. Shapiro
University of Chicago Booth School of
    Business
5807 South Woodlawn Avenue
Chicago, IL 60637

Adam Hale Shapiro
Economic Research Department
Federal Reserve Bank of San Francisco
101 Market Street
San Francisco, CA 94105

Julie Shi
School of Economics
Peking University
5 Yiheyuan Road
Haidian District
Beijing 100871 China

Kosali Simon
School of Public and Environmental
  Affairs
Indiana University
1315 East Tenth Street
Bloomington, IN 47405-1701

Christopher Stomberg
Bates White Economic Consulting
1300 Eye Street NW
Suite 600
Washington, DC 20005

Author Index

Subject Index